POLITICAL SCIENCE

PRENTICE-HALL INTERNATIONAL, INC., *London*
PRENTICE-HALL OF AUSTRALIA, PTY. LTD., *Sydney*
PRENTICE-HALL OF CANADA, LTD., *Toronto*
PRENTICE-HALL OF INDIA PRIVATE LIMITED, *New Delhi*
PRENTICE-HALL OF JAPAN, INC., *Tokyo*

POLITICAL SCIENCE
AN INTRODUCTION

Robert L. Cord

James A. Medeiros

Walter S. Jones

All of Northeastern University

PRENTICE-HALL, INC., ENGLEWOOD CLIFFS, NEW JERSEY

Library of Congress Cataloging in Publication Data

Cord, Robert L
  Political science: An introduction.

  Includes bibliographical references.
   1. Comparative government.   2. Political science.
I. Medeiros, James A., 1938–   joint author.
II. Jones, Walter S., 1942–   joint author.
III. Title.
JF51.C63   320   73-13577
ISBN 0-13-687889-X

Designer: Jack George Tauss
Illustrator: Danmark & Michaels, Inc.
Picture Editor: Ann Novotny
Text set in Bodoni Book

©1974
by PRENTICE-HALL, Inc.,
Englewood Cliffs, New Jersey

10 9 8 7 6

Acknowledgments

Photographs

Part One, pp. x–1   Black Man with Department of Agriculture Food (Photograph by Ken Heyman); Indian Painting Sign on Alcatraz Wall (United Press International Photo); Montreal's St. Jean Baptiste Day Parade (United Press International Photo); Fidel Castro Cheerers (Magnum Photos, Inc.).

Part Two, pp. 72–73   Housewife with Pistol (United Press International Photo); Hitler (Culver Pictures, Inc.); Washington Embassy Party, Admiral King (Photograph by Elliott Erwitt, Magnum Photos, Inc.); Abbie Hoffman Saluting (Photograph by Charles Gatewood, Magnum Photos, Inc.).

Part Three, pp. 178–79   Counting Votes, U. K. (United Press International Photo); Demonstrators and Riot Police, Japan (World Wide Photos); National Political Convention, U.S.A. (United Press International Photo); Red Square Rally, USSR (Photographed by B. Glinn, Magnum Photos, Inc.).

(Acknowledgments continued on page 645)

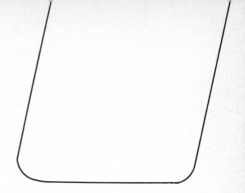

Contents

Part FOUR   The Institutions of Government

Part FIVE   The Policies of Government

Preface

This book appears at a time when political systems throughout the world are experiencing major difficulties, both internally and in their relations with their neighbors. On any given day in the 1970s, we may be confronted with a report of violence in Belfast, with news of industrial pollution or inadequate housing in Tokyo, with complaints about apathy among U.S. voters, with an analysis of the shift in the traditional cold-war alignment of nations, or with a debate about the suitability of Western-style democracy for the world's developing nations. How are we to understand such diverse and complicated situations? And how are we to know what action we should take, when action is called for? The first step, we feel, is to understand the basic concepts and processes of political science.

Political Science: An Introduction is designed for use in introductory courses on the college level. Our aims are twofold. First, we hope to acquaint our readers with the complex and vitally important subject of contemporary government and politics. We have tried to provide all our readers with the background of information and analytical skills they will need to understand today's difficult political issues and to deal with the pressing problems they face as citizens. For those who will go on to major in political science or government, we have tried to supply a grasp of the scope and content of the field, a working knowledge of its vocabulary, and an understanding of its research methods. Our second aim is both more difficult and more subjective. We have tried to communicate some of the excitement and vitality of political science as a field of study by illustrating the kinds of contemporary issues political scientists deal with, the diversity of approaches they take, and the significant results they hope to achieve. In short, we have tried to show our readers what it is about political science that fascinates those of us who have chosen to specialize in the field.

The Plan of the Book

Because this is an introductory book, it encompasses a wide range of theoretical viewpoints. We have tried to bring theoretical discussions "down to earth" for our readers by using a wide variety of practical and contemporary examples. Many of our chapters concentrate on the institutions common to most political systems, but we have tried, wherever possible, to emphasize the functions and processes of government and the ongoing interactions among various segments of society that affect the political decision-making process.

The book is divided into five parts. Part One defines political science, describes its development and its present-day divisions, introduces the research methods used in modern political science, and ends with a discussion of government's goals and the influences on public policy making.

The subject of Part Two is political power. This part of the book includes a discussion of the nature, purposes, and adaptability of constitutions, a description of the democracy–totalitarianism spectrum of political systems, an analysis of how the U.S. democratic system measures up to its ideals, and a survey of contemporary political ideologies.

Building on this theoretical foundation, Part Three analyzes the many ways the people of a society can make their needs and wishes known. The section includes discussions of political socialization, the role of the media in modern societies, the impact of interest groups, the organization and functions of political parties in different political systems, voting behavior, and the theory and practice of representative government.

Part Four surveys the institutions of government, starting with legislative and executive processes, then moving on to discussions of the bureaucracy and the judiciary, and ending with a comparison of federal and unitary systems of government.

Part Five focuses on government policy in a variety of critical areas— international relations, minority rights, political violence, and the problems of the cities.

The chapters in the book are designed to stand on their own so that the instructor can deal with the topics in whatever order suits his plan. Terms are defined in context, so no chapter depends on the preceding ones. There is also an extensive glossary at the end of the book. Its emphasis is on words that have a special meaning in political science, and it is meant to serve as a review tool for the student.

No textbook is useful unless it can be read and understood by students. A poorly written and unnecessarily difficult textbook is a hindrance to the instructor as well as to the student. Every effort has been made to insure that this textbook will be both readable and interesting for students. Wherever possible we have tried to avoid the use of specialized terminology and to include examples and illustrations that will make the book stimulating and "real" to the reader.

Each chapter is followed by an annotated list of suggested readings. Care has been taken to select books and articles that will be of interest to the student and will add to his understanding of the topics discussed in the chapter. In addition, a study guide and ACCESS® workbook is available to help the student understand and integrate the material presented in the text. Our hope is that these supplements will make the book easy to study—as well as enjoyable and thought-provoking.

Acknowledgments

We have been assisted by many people in the preparation of this book. This volume profited immensely from the careful reading of Professors Steven Spiegel and Mark Stern, who read the chapters in various drafts and made many valuable comments and suggestions. In addition, the painstaking care of the editors at Appleton-Century-Crofts contributed immensely to the preparation of the manuscript and to the production of the finished book. A large part of what is worthwhile in this book is due to their patience, dedication, and high standards.

R.L.C.
J.A.M.
W.S.J.

POLITICAL SCIENCE

ONE
Politics and Political Science

What is politics?

CHAPTER 1

In the December 1970 elections, the Bengali Awami League gained a majority in Pakistan's National Assembly, and Sheikh Mujibur Rahman was expected to become Pakistan's next prime minister. A sectional party representing the interests of the poor East Pakistani people, the Awami League had long charged that the West Pakistan regime was exploiting them. As the new national leader, Sheikh Mujib was expected to institute changes which would balance the scales. It appeared that the two-decades-old political struggle of the Bengali people for autonomy within a federal Pakistani state was about to come to a successful close.

But the solution was not that simple. Zulfikar Ali Bhutto, leader of the most powerful political party in West Pakistan, promised a boycott of any arrangement that increased the Bengali voice in government. The Bengalis, in turn, flatly denounced Ali Bhutto's stand. Caught in the middle, President Yahya Kahn indefinitely postponed the opening of the National Assembly and outlawed the Awami League, then sent troops into East Pakistan. In reaction, Rahman's followers proclaimed the independence of Bangla Desh on March 26, 1971. The Pakistani civil war was on, and before it ended in independence for Bangla Desh, some twelve million people lost their homes, and several million were killed.

A year later, and halfway around the world, Alabama's Governor George C. Wallace entered the Florida Democratic presidential primary. Softening his early segregationist image, Wallace sought to broaden his appeal by playing down the race issue and addressing himself to the fears of the white middle class. He stressed the need for tax reforms to ease the financial burdens of the middle-class homeowners and asked for a mandate against school busing to achieve desegregation. The governor struck a responsive chord, and walked off with more than 40 percent of the Florida vote in a ten-candidate field which included such national figures as Hubert Humphrey, George McGovern, and Edmund Muskie. The impact of Wallace's "populist" victory reached far. President Nixon pledged to seek legislation to override compulsory busing ordered by the federal courts.[1] Congress was soon pondering a host of anti-busing bills and amendments. And almost every major Democratic contender softened his support of busing, and strengthened his stand on popular issues such as tax reform and law enforcement.

In August of 1971, President Nixon announced a sweeping economic program to end inflation. Acting under emergency authority granted by Congress, he began "Phase One" by freezing prices of consumer goods, halting all wage raises for ninety days, and adjusting tax credits and surcharges to boost American business. In November, "Phase Two" went into effect. A Wage and Price Commission was established to enforce long-term federal economic guidelines. Retail stores were ordered to post "base price lists" so that customers could be sure that prices weren't quietly raised above the guidelines. And to make the United States more competitive in foreign markets, long-term tariff arrangements were made, and the dollar was devalued. President Nixon's policy met with grumbling from all sides: consumers complained that food prices still soared; labor unions wanted raises; and businesses, especially the auto and steel industries, charged that they couldn't make a profit under the new plan. But Phase Two remained in effect for over a year before being succeeded by "Phase Three," a period of voluntary wage and price controls, and later by "Phase Four," a return to stricter regulation.

What do a civil war in a far-off land, an American presidential primary election, and an economic clampdown all have in common? On the surface, very little. Yet they do share one very important feature: all are political

---

[1] While the announcement was made after the Florida primary, President Nixon noted that he had prepared his statement *before* the election.

events. They involve groups of people with conflicting interests competing for government power. Each group seeks to exert influence to insure that its vital interests will be officially protected. The Bengalis wanted autonomy within a federal state to protect themselves from exploitation by West Pakistan. The ruling groups of West Pakistan, in turn, were determined to protect their own dominant position. When neither side was able to compromise, only the most extreme course of action seemed to remain—civil war. In the Florida primary, white voters felt that perhaps government had gone too far, that nobody had the right to ask them to send their children on hour-long bus rides to attend distant schools. Instead of resorting to secession, as did the Bengalis, they chose the legitimate channel of a presidential primary election to register their feelings. As a result, they were able to influence the mainstream political leaders of the nation. Finally, President Nixon's economic program was designed to stop the inflationary spiral of labor wage raises, business price increases, and consumers' complaints that they needed more raises to be able to afford expensive goods. Labor's strikes, industry's lobbies, and consumers' complaints are all designed to get government to bend an ear toward each group's own interests—not the other guy's. Mr. Nixon's executive order, however, was designed to carry impartial authority.

Issues like these are the meat of politics. Conflicting groups try to influence or control society or government, and the administration either responds to their demands or judges that they are not in the "public interest." The way in which government policy affects society, and how this effect gives rise to fresh demands, will be our concerns in this book. We shall see how individuals, groups, and organizations—from Rhodesian blacks, to the IRA in Ulster, to the American Medical Association—attempt to influence laws and programs to their advantage; how the decision makers in government react to their pressures; and how other groups respond to resulting government programs.

Politics and Power

The word *politics* often carries an unfortunate connotation in modern American usage—implying something a little off the straight-and-narrow. We may rationalize the fact that the other guy got the promotion by blaming it on "office politics"—implying that merit was no factor in the decision. A baseball manager who is fired by his team explains to reporters that the clubowner's decision was politically motivated. All of us have a tendency to stigmatize public officials we don't like as "politicians"—reserving the honored title of "statesman" for those we admire. Government policies we object to are attributed to "political deals" or "political pressures," but those we like are "disinterested acts of statesmanship" carried out for the good of the nation.

"Keep calm, folks. Nothing to worry about. Just a little struggle for power."

What Is Politics?

Political scientists are not concerned with these subjective definitions of the political. As we define it, *politics* is a morally neutral term which carries connotations of neither good nor evil. Politics is the human interactions involved in the authoritative allocations of values for society.[2] It involves people deciding, or having decided for them, how to distribute material goods and services, or even symbolic values, and it includes the procedures and "power plays" involved in reaching those decisions.

How does politics differ from economics, or from the activities that go on when new fraternity members are chosen? Economics, too, deals with the allocation of goods and services for a society. But economics is not authoritative, except as it is enforced by a political system: no one will be arrested for breaking the law of supply and demand. Fraternity rush week at many universities is termed "political." It involves decisions about who will gain the status of membership in a fraternity, and many young men compete for this prize. But while the decision of who can become a pledge and who cannot is certainly authoritative within the limited scope of one branch of one fraternity, it is of little importance to society as a whole.

What separates the politics of the state from the politics of all other organizations is its society-wide scope, and the government's ability to back its decisions with the use, or implied threat, of legitimate, legally sanctioned force. A fraternity can't imprison anyone; the government can. In the politics of the state, the government, through its institutions and processes, is the final decision maker within the territorial limits of a society.[3] It is the final arbiter of "who gets what, when, and how." [4]

Political Authority

One of the most striking attributes of government is the pervasiveness of its authority. An employer cannot pay his workers less than the legally established minimum wage, even though there may be jobless persons eager to work for almost nothing. A driver cannot speed through a twenty-five-mile-per-hour zone at fifty miles per hour, although there may be no traffic. A bar cannot serve liquor to people under eighteen (or, in some states, under twenty-one) years of age, even though they may have a better capacity for alcohol than some people over the age limit.

[2] David Easton, *A Framework for Political Analysis* (Englewood Cliffs, N.J.: Prentice-Hall, 1965), p. 51.
[3] A good discussion of "What is politics?" may be found in Robert A. Dahl, *Modern Political Analysis* (Englewood Cliffs, N.J.: Prentice-Hall, 1963), pp. 4–7.
[4] As Harold D. Lasswell so aptly put it in the title of his book, *Politics: Who Gets What, When, and How* (New York: McGraw-Hill, 1936).

What, then, is political authority? And what gives the state, local, or federal governments the right to exercise it? [5]

Power and Authority. As diagrammed in Figure 1-1, authority is the ability of A to get B to do what he wants, whether B wants to or not.[6] It is a relationship of obedience in which one man acknowledges another man's right to regulate his actions. Authority is a means of exercising power, but there are many other types of power. A parent can use "child psychology" to get his son to act as he wishes, without the child even being aware that he is being influenced. This type of power is known as manipulation: B doesn't realize that A is controlling his actions.

Another form of power is persuasion, in which A uses rational appeals to influence B's behavior. President Nixon goes before Congress to ask for a new revenue-sharing program and gives as his reason the desperate financial plight of state and local governments throughout the nation. But appeals to reason through persuasion do not always work, and no matter how much time the president spends talking to congressmen en masse or individually, they will never pass every bill he wishes to enact. Thus, in order to rule effectively, government must exert a stronger form of power, in the form of authority.

While the exercise of power involves strategies of persuasion, manipulation, or force, authority need not employ any of these tactics. Here, an order is met with unquestioned acceptance, without need for force or persuasion (although there may be an implied threat). In acknowledgment of government's authority, we normally drive without exceeding the speed limit and stop at red lights, even though there may be no policeman in sight. When April 15 comes around, many of us find ourselves writing out a check to Uncle Sam, even though we don't want to. We purchase licenses for pet dogs, pay for the items we pick up in stores, and refrain from physically attacking even our worst enemies. Of course, the implied threat of punishment may be at the back of our minds: fines, arrests, and revocation of drivers' licenses are things that we all try to avoid. But, in general, government's authority is well enough established so that it does not need to rely on the overt use of force.[7]

Legitimacy. What would happen if everyone decided to disobey the law? If we all ran through red lights, and hijacked planes when we wanted to take

[5] See Harold D. Lasswell and Abraham Kaplan, *Power and Society: A Framework for Political Inquiry* (New Haven, Conn.: Yale University Press, 1950); and Harold D. Lasswell, *Power and Personality* (New York: W. W. Norton, 1948).

[6] Our discussion follows David Easton, "The Perception of Authority and Political Change," in *Authority*, ed. Carl J. Friedrich (Cambridge, Mass.: Harvard University Press, 1958), pp. 178–81.

[7] In his landmark work, *The Theory of Social and Economic Organization* (New York: The Free Press, 1947), pp. 324–26, Max Weber distinguishes between "three pure types of political authority" by the reasons for their legitimacy. Authority may rest on (a) *rational grounds*, where legitimacy rests with the office, such as the Presidency in the United States, (b) *traditional grounds*, where power comes naturally to the *person* who holds office, as a hereditary king, or (c) *charismatic grounds*, where the person creates the office and gives legitimacy to that office, as in the case of Mao Tse-tung.

Figure 1-1
Influence, Power,
and Authority

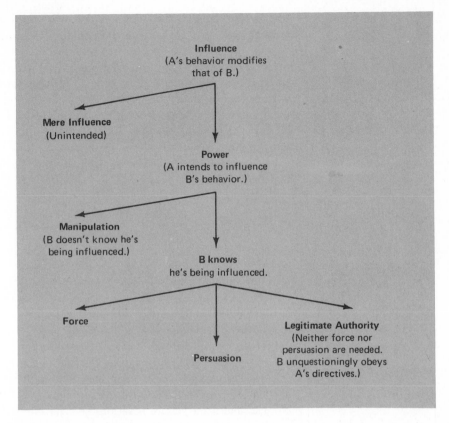

Source: Adapted from David Easton, "The Perception of Authority and Political Change,"
in Authority, ed. Carl V. Friedrich (Cambridge, Mass.: Harvard University Press, 1958),
178–81.

a long-distance trip; or if everyone decided that stealing was easier than purchasing and wantonly broke into stores and took whatever seemed attractive, the government would be in serious trouble. Although the government's authority relies partly on its implied ability to punish lawbreakers, this would count for nothing if everyone decided to call its bluff at the same time. The massive riots in the Los Angeles district of Watts in 1965, where stores were looted and thirty-four people were killed, and the guerilla warfare which raged in Ulster in the early 1970s showed that there is little that government can do, at least in a limited period of time, to control large numbers of people who don't want to be controlled. The unsuccessful era of Prohibition, when otherwise lawful American citizens purchased liquor in speakeasies en masse, had proved this point earlier. Authority in the form of the threat of punishment alone is not sufficient to keep a government in power.

Most people obey laws because they recognize and respect the legitimacy of their government. Whether or not we consciously realize it, most of us recognize that the laws of society, imperfect as they may be, are far better than the laws of "fang and claw," where the strong are always right and the weak have no rights.[8] If a large enough number of people feel strongly enough that the government is misusing its authority, there is little that a president, a king, or even an army can do to control them. The American and French Revolutions of the eighteenth century and the Russian Revolution of the twentieth century are but three of the many cases where this has proved to be true.

Legitimacy is integral to a government's authority. In order to maintain it, all governments must in some way be able to satisfy the basic needs of their citizens. The conversion of the people's needs into national policies is basic to all forms of government, even primitive tribes who must feed and shelter their members. One useful tool for studying this common pattern is the systems approach.

Political Systems

In the study of politics, a handy perspective is provided by the systems approach, a method borrowed from the biological sciences.[9] A system is a collection of individual parts which work together toward a common end. In the human circulatory system, the heart pumps blood; the lungs bring in oxygen and expel carbon dioxide; the arteries spread oxygen throughout the body; and the veins carry carbon dioxide to the lungs for expulsion. Each organ performs its own function, but all work together, and depend on one another, to keep the body alive. If one part fails, the entire system will be affected, and if the failure is serious enough, the organism will die. An automobile is also a collection of parts which form a system. But a parking lot full of cars is not: the cars in the lot are all systems themselves, but together they serve no integrated function. The removal of one or more cars from the lot would have no effect on those which remained behind, nor would the addition of several new vehicles. In a system, the separate parts work together to accomplish a collective end.

How does a systems approach apply to politics? It is true that if any one of us—or even an entire university—decided to pack our bags and leave the United States for France, Italy, or Russia, the political system would keep on

---

[8] The classic formulation of man's fear of a society without government is Thomas Hobbes's *Leviathan*, which was written during a period of great turmoil in England: the civil war of the seventeenth century. Erich Fromm updates the idea in *Escape from Freedom* (New York: Holt, Rinehart and Winston, 1941).

[9] See David Easton, *A Systems Analysis of Political Life* (New York: John Wiley & Sons, 1965); and Anatol Rapoport, "Some System Approaches to Political Theory," in *Varieties of Political Theory*, ed. David Easton (Englewood Cliffs, N.J.: Prentice-Hall, 1966), pp. 129–41. Also, Morton R. Davies and Vaughan A. Lewis, *Models of Political Systems* (New York: Praeger Publishers, 1971), Part Two, "Structural-Functional Analysis, General Systems Theory, Communications Theory"; and Gabriel A. Almond and G. Bingham Powell, Jr., *Comparative Politics: A Developmental Approach* (Boston: Little, Brown, 1966); and Gabriel A. Almond and James S. Coleman, *Politics of the Developing Areas* (Princeton, N.J.: Princeton University Press, 1960), Chapter 1.

going as if little or nothing had happened. In this sense, the political scene seems to be no more a system than the parking lot we just mentioned. But what would happen if the Republican party dissolved, leaving only one major party? Or if a group supporting environmental controls decided that the forces opposing them were just too strong, and decided to quit fighting? In each of these cases, the balance of American politics *would* be noticeably affected. And in this sense, the systems model does have relevance in helping us understand how government and its environment interact.

The Parts of the Political System

The political system of Papa Doc Duvalier's Haiti depended on terror and superstition for its existence. That of Louis XIV of France depended on a rigid social-class structure, severe economic distinctions between the small elite and the people, and a monopoly of power in the hands of a monarch. And the governments of England and the United States are dependent upon a good deal of individual and group participation. While the political systems of Haiti, England and the United States, and sixteenth-century France vary greatly in their specific modes of operation, they do share a common purpose: the function of all political systems is authoritative decision making for the entire society.

All political systems operate in a similar manner (see Figure 1-2). Decision

Figure 1-2
A Model of the Political System

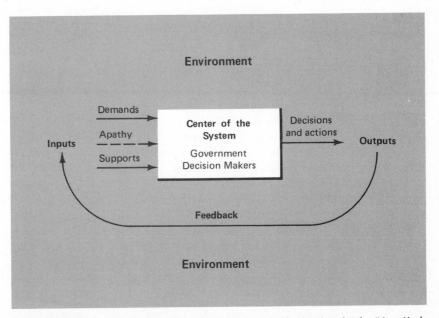

Source: Adapted from David Easton, A Systems Analysis of Political Life (New York: John Wiley & Sons, 1965), diagram 2, p. 32.

makers in government respond to inputs in the form of demands of interest groups and the support of citizens who believe in their legitimacy. They formulate outputs such as specific laws, general policies, and decisions about conflicting interests. They work within a social environment and must make policies in keeping with the people's culture. And all political systems make use of feedback in order to survive. If the people are dissatisfied with a government, but that government makes no move to adjust policy accordingly, it is likely that the system may break down through revolution or civil war.

The political system can be compared to a factory. Raw materials are put into the factory, power or energy supports the system, and finished products are the factory's output. If the consuming public buys its products, the factory will flourish. If consumers are unhappy and the factory fails to adjust its product or its price, the system will probably fail. An interesting analogy, but how does it work in real life? [10]

Inputs. There are two basic kinds of inputs in a political system: the demands and the supports which government receives from domestic and foreign interests. Supports consist primarily of the people's passive recognition of the government's legitimacy, allowing it to function without major interferences at normal times, and their more active participation in its processes. We don't impeach every president who comes into office; we do pay taxes, obey laws, and—at least ideally—go to the polls on election day. Involvement in politics by voting, supporting candidates, and working for causes serves as a more positive support. Public opinion—the views people hold on political or social issues—can also act as a support. Government organizes our armies, cares for our aged, and supervises highway construction—measures which are all supported by public opinion. Governments watch carefully to see that their policies satisfy the public's expectations.

But not all of the inputs into a political system are supportive. Most of the public opinion surveys in 1968 showed that the public was dissatisfied with Lyndon Johnson's Vietnam policies. This undoubtedly had some effect on his decision that year not to run for a second full term as president. When a group of American Indians took over Wounded Knee, South Dakota, in 1973, they were hardly registering support for the government's policies toward the Indian population. Demands are signs that the people, or interested parties, want action. They can be expressed in all manner of ways—through public opinion polls, political parties, organized interest groups, riots and demonstrations, and letters written to government officials. They can also come from within the governmental system. When a president asks Congress to pass a law or okay a budget, he is requesting that the legislature take action. And when the Supreme Court strikes down an act of Congress as unconstitutional, it is making a demand for change.

---

[10] An excellent introduction to the workings of the American political system is William C. Mitchell, *The American Polity* (New York: The Free Press, 1962).

A third kind of influence on the political system is more of a *lack* of input than an input. Apathy is all too characteristic of many areas of political life, and it can have a profound effect on what government does. Perhaps the most extreme example is that of Germany and her conquests during World War II. Millions of Jews and political prisoners were carted off to concentration camps "behind the backs" of citizens who took no action to find out what was happening. But apathy is also a factor in less striking ways. As we shall see in Chapter 13, less than two-thirds of American voters usually go to the polls in presidential election years, and far fewer during off-years. The fewer that bother to participate in politics, the less representative the government.

Government Outputs: What Government Does. In modern America, the hand of government reaches almost everywhere. Aside from making laws and deciding Supreme Court cases, government activity includes the actions of regulatory agencies, government-run utilities, bureaus such as the FBI and the Internal Revenue Service, scientific researchers in aerospace industries, and policemen. It also includes services such as subways and highways, and interstate roads and waterways. The list continues ad infinitum, and all of its activities can be grouped under the broad heading of the outputs of government. What government does is to allocate values for society, and in doing this, it works in response to the demands and supports of the people and of special interests.

Essential to the effectiveness of political decisions are the actions taken by government to ensure that its will is enforced. After the legislature passes a new program to control air pollution, and the executive signs it into law, some sort of environmental protection agency must enforce the new statute. Technicians set standards and devise plans to eliminate the causes of pollution; inspectors run tests to see who is disobeying the new law; lawyers prepare legal action against polluters. Enforcement activities are naturally most easily recognized on the one-to-one level of the cop on the beat, who serves as an arm of the executive branch of government. But these activities play an important role in every area of politics.

In the act of enforcing, the "spirit of the law" is sometimes twisted or misinterpreted. The policeman is human: he may be more inclined to ticket a long-haired young man for speeding than a pretty, smiling girl. An unusual amount of publicity may embarrass government officials into closing one housing project, while others with similar building-code violations are given at least temporary reprieve. But mistakes and different shadings of interpretation are bound to accompany any human action. In general, workable legislation is enforced by the executive and administrative branches.

Feedback: Reactions from the People. Every government action is bound to stimulate some reaction from at least some of the people. This feedback often acts as a new demand on government decision makers, as when students rioted in 1970 against President Nixon's decision to escalate American troop action in Vietnam and to invade the neighboring country of Cambodia. Feedback is seen in many ways. Most visible is the protest, which includes pickets, rallies, and riots, and which has inundated our television screens and newspaper front pages in recent years. Other forms include the many public opinion surveys which register people's reaction to everything from commercial TV shows to new legislation; editorials in newspapers; official statements from foreign governments; actions of interest groups and lobbyists; and mail sent to congressmen and the White House.

Government is acted upon and reacts in order to maintain a stable system. But how are decisions made, so that one policy is chosen over another? Who are the decision makers, and how do they act on all the information, demands, and supports which they receive from the system?

Government Decisions and Decision Makers

Every government, from the most primitive tribe to the most complex modern system, performs certain functions. It protects lives and property as best it can, it enforces contractual obligations, and it defends its citizens against possible foreign invasion. Most modern governments also render certain services in order to maintain reasonable standards of health, education, and economic comfort for their citizens.

Political Values: The Choices of Government. In every society, there are groups of people—orphans, the elderly poor, the chronically ill—who have a real need for assistance. In this modern age, we expect our government to assist such persons. But we seldom stop to think that any government program undertaken to aid the orphans, the elderly, or the ill is money out of the pockets of the rest of us. Values—be they property, money, or services—are finite. In helping one group, government must take from other groups, most noticeably in terms of tax revenues. Government decisions regarding who should give and who should receive, or public choice, involve the distribution of costs and the allocation of services.[11] Just as important as the question of whom to help is the question of whom to take from, and in each case there are always interested persons and groups—lobbyists, protesters, individual letter-writers—who try to influence government policy in their favor. What are the costs and services which government regulates? All can be lumped into the single word *values*, a catch-all which includes both tangibles, like money, services, taxes, and property, and also abstract or symbolic goods, such as

[11] In modern political theory, only the Marxist conception of the perfect society relieves government from the task of deciding who should give and who should get. This theory says that government ultimately isn't needed because each person gives according to his abilities, and each will get according to his needs. In non-Communist theory, however, there is no such golden era envisioned, and government will continue to decide who gets what, when, and how.

ideals, ethics, respect, and freedom to live one's own life without interference.
Money. Government does two things with money. It collects it through
taxes, bonds, and fines; and it dispenses it through subsidies, low-interest
loans, actual services such as police protection and food stamps, and many
other means, both simple and complicated. Whether it collects or spends
money, government must decide among conflicting interests. In collecting
taxes, for example, there are many decisions: should taxation be progressive,
regressive, or proportional? A proportional tax is one that takes the same
proportion of each taxpayer's income; those with higher incomes pay more in
absolute dollars, but the taxation rate is the same for all taxpayers. In the
United States, most sales taxes are regressive. That is, they tax the poor just
as heavily as they tax the rich—and thus effectively take a larger bite out of
the poor person's smaller paycheck. Income taxes are more progressive, since
the rate of taxation increases as income rises. But the presence of tax loopholes, which allow extra deductions designed to encourage private investment,
also tend to work against some of those who can't afford to pay. And many
from the large middle-income section of American society can be heard grumbling loudly about the "unfair tax structure" around the eve of April 15
each year.

There is room for improvement in American taxes, but the decision of who
should pay is hardly a simple one. It involves both keeping the entire economy
healthy by stimulating big business investment, and keeping the middle and
lower classes solvent enough to be able to consume at a good pace. Should
taxes be progressive, regressive, or proportional? The federal, state, and local
governments must decide which, where, and on what.

The allocation of money presents another decision-making problem. Indians
on reservations in the Southwest may be long overdue for an increase in educational aid and welfare benefits, while the handicapped in the suburbs of
Chicago may need a new training center to learn saleable skills. But the amount
of money that government can dispense is limited. When the chief executive
announces his budget near the start of each fiscal year, he must juggle a host
of different causes and functions, from national defense to controlling a corn
blight in Iowa, and end up with a reasonable balance of all of them.

Deciding who gets what is no small task. National defense spending may
take too large a portion of the budget according to the average American, but
what does cutting defense spending mean? In the Seattle, Washington, area,
close to 80 percent of the residents were in some way dependent upon the
aerospace industry before defense-spending cuts forced Boeing to let many
employees go. The result of the cuts was massive unemployment in the area:
Seattle became the first American city to receive aid from a foreign country
(Japan) and for some time had the highest unemployment figure in the nation.
But on the whole, defense cuts were designed to bring long-term benefits to
the country, allowing more funds to be available for other pressing needs.
Property. Americans like to think of their homes as their castles—that they
may do whatever they please with their own property. But it is not that simple.

Government's role in deciding who does what with property is indeed pervasive. Local community governments enact zoning codes which are designed to protect the "character" of those communities. Thus, if a suburban homeowner who also happens to be an excellent cook decides to convert her dining room into a restaurant and her lawn into a parking lot, it is most improbable that she will be permitted to do so. In order to keep the streets from becoming overcrowded with the cars of hungry clients, the neighborhood lawns from being trampled by families taking after-dinner constitutionals, and the noise levels from growing loud enough to bother other homeowners on the street, the government enacts zoning laws which limit the area in which, among other things, commercial establishments can be operated.

Government's control of property goes farther than drawing zoning maps to define what areas can be used for what purposes. In many communities, it prevents merchants from opening their stores on Sundays. It tells barbers, plumbers, and pharmacists that they may not practice their trade without state licenses. It requires suburban homeowners to repair sidewalks and use city sewage facilities. It even interferes with a person's right to dispose of his own property: dumping of refuse is limited to certain well-defined areas in most communities, or garbage trucks have regular pick-up schedules with which people must comply. And finally, government has the power of "eminent domain": if it is deemed necessary for the public good—as in the case of building a new highway—the government may acquire a given piece of property, with or without the owner's consent, after reimbursing the owner at fair market value.

The "public interest" governs all official decisions about property and other political values, and it is a term which eludes easy definition.[12] Will a new highway through a residential area harm or help a community? What is the best location for a housing project or a new school? When questions like these are asked, the answers are usually a difficult balance between individual or group opinions and the objective "good," and the public interest can often be reached only at the cost of a lot of private pain. The recent policy of the Federal Housing Authority (FHA) to build low-income projects in middle-class residential areas, for example, was designed to break up the concentrations of poor people in stagnant inner cities. But residents of many such areas —most notably Forest Hills, Queens, in New York City—complained bitterly that the proposed housing projects would destroy the quiet, safe character of their neighborhoods. Many had moved to the area to find a crime-free refuge from the hurly-burly of the central city. When authorities decided to bring the city to them, they felt that if the government was looking out for the public, it was looking out for the *wrong* public. In all areas where public interest is involved, it is always a partial public—and sometimes a minority— whose needs are met. Only rarely does everyone benefit from a government policy decision.

[12] For an excellent discussion of "public interest," see Charles E. Jacob, *Policy and Bureaucracy* (Princeton, N.J.: Van Nostrand, 1966), Chapter 8, "Public Policy and the Public Interest."

Government Services. Closely related to the question of taxation and property control is the question of what services government should provide its citizens, and to whom these services should be given. For example, most Americans feel that the government should educate their children in public schools. But is the government also obligated to subsidize the cost of educating children in religiously affiliated schools? While the Constitution has been interpreted to mean that church and state should remain separate entities, the fact is that without government aid, many parochial schools all over the country are finding themselves close to bankruptcy. If such schools close, their children will have no place to go but the public schools. The public education system would find itself short of teachers, desks, books, and classrooms to accommodate the new load of pupils. Another question involving who gets services is the question of the elderly and the poor, who both receive government-subsidized medical care. Should health insurance be made universal and compulsory for all citizens? Where should the line be drawn between healthy and ill, poor and lower-middle class, elderly and middle-aged? (Or should it be drawn at all?)

These questions deal not only with how public funds should be spent, but also with the fundamental issue of the proper role of government. If government supports the poor on public welfare, does it also have a right to demand that the poor work for this service? Many people feel that government is never justified in using public funds to support able-bodied men or women.[13] Questions such as these, which concern the rightful limits of government, are often central to political conflict, as men and women differ in their conceptions of what government should and should not do for citizens.

Symbolic Values. As soon as a new president says the last words of the oath of office and takes his hand off the Bible, even his closest friends stop calling him by his first name and begin addressing him as "Mr. President." He has become both the actual head of government and the symbol of the nation, and is accordingly treated with respect.

While government cannot completely regulate the balance of symbolic status, respect, or ethics within a society, its handling of these symbolic values is a very important part of its role. Havoc would result if any nation tried to change its national symbol, the flag, without first making sure that the new flag was generally acceptable to most groups of the population. Canada found that the problems of replacing a modified Union Jack with a plain maple-leaf flag were almost serious enough to prevent any change at all. (Various groups protested this new symbol, and the removal of the Union Jack, for many reasons.) And the Americans, the Vietnamese, and the Viet Cong argued for months about the shape of the discussion table for the Paris peace talks before

---

[13] But others argue that government already provides more services for the rich than for the poor. Government subsidizes "private" enterprise and the middle and upper classes through aid to airports, passenger ships, mail service for businesses, train services through Amtrack, and land grants to railroads. For this point of view see William C. Mitchell, ed., *Public Choice in America* (Chicago: Markham, 1971), Chapter 4, "Socialism for the Rich and Free Enterprise for the Poor."

settling on an agreement that could allow them to begin actual talks. The problem centered around the symbolic difference between being on the odd end of a rectangular table or being seated equally around a round table, which was crucial to establishing the status of each party.

An important function of government is to regulate symbols.[14] A nation like America must make all of its policies appear to be in accordance with a national code of ethics. For example, equality, liberty, and freedom of expression are all bywords of American political ideals, and government regulations and services must seem to align, as closely as possible, with these ideals. Maintenance of national monuments, statues, and Fourth of July parades; adherence to a national morality (which can become very complicated in issues such as legalized abortion or deciding who is entitled to welfare assistance and who isn't); and balancing a clubowner's freedom to do what he wants with his own property against the right of minority groups to receive equal treatment at clubs or restaurants, are all important issues in spreading and maintaining symbolic values. Who are the officials who make these decisions about our money, our property, and our liberties?

Government Decision Makers: Who They Are and What They Do.

In primitive tribes, and even in many underdeveloped countries, the government isn't divided into functional categories. Instead of a legislature, an executive, and a judicial system, there may be one tribal chief who is also the judge and the military leader, or there may be one dictator who oversees all of the roles of government himself.[15] This is in sharp contrast to most modern nations. Most governments in Europe, the Americas, and Asia are in some way divided according to three main functions. Although there is considerable variation in the relative strength of each branch and in the actual duties each performs, the lawmaking, law-enforcing, and law-interpreting institutions are common to most modern governments.

The Legislature. In the United States, the Congress and the legislatures of the fifty states, along with numerous councils of more than thirty-five thousand incorporated municipalities, towns, and townships, constitute the legislative branch of government. Legislatures have two primary functions: the representation of interests, and the making of laws.

The legislature is a representative body; it gives voice to the interests of the people or of special groups.[16] A congressman may introduce a bill drafted by a consumer action group calling for tough auto safety standards to be

---

[14] Political scientist Murray Edelman sees politics as the interaction of symbolic phenomena, where the creation and change of a people's understanding of symbols provides the only adequate explanation of political behavior. See his *Symbolic Uses of Politics* (Urbana, Ill.: University of Illinois Press, 1967); also *Politics as Symbolic Action: Mass Arousal and Quiescence* (Chicago: Markham, 1971).

[15] See Almond and Coleman, *Politics of the Developing Areas.*

[16] See the discussion of representation in Chapter 14. Legislatures are also discussed in considerable detail in Chapter 15; and the executive, judicial, and administrative branches are covered in Chapters 15 through 17.

enforced by the government; but the auto industry may find the stand. too rigid. In this case, Ford, General Motors, and Chrysler would probab look for other congressmen (probably from a district where the auto industry is a major part of the economy) to represent the industry's interests. In this way, both sides are represented in Congress, and, ideally, an objective decision will be made by the House as a whole. Congressmen also represent regions, sex or race groups, and liberal or conservative ideologies.

The legislature's second main function, making laws, is naturally of major importance in keeping a government running. Civil rights acts, tax reform measures, air and water pollution bills, foreign aid appropriations, and draft reform legislation are just a few of the many areas which depend heavily upon legislative bodies for enactment.

The legislature is usually a bicameral system divided into two houses, often with very unequal powers.[17] The Senate, the House of Lords, and the German Bundesrat are all upper houses, while the House of Representatives, House of Commons, and the Bundestag are all lower houses. The upper house is almost always less directly responsible to the electorate, and in many countries has evolved from a hereditary body. In the United States, for example, senators are elected every six years; congressmen every two. The original reasoning was that senators, being held less accountable to the masses (senators were originally elected by state legislatures), would be freer to formulate policy without popular interference.

The Executive and the Bureaucracy. The role of the executive and the administrative bureaucracy is primarily to apply laws, to handle the mechanics of seeing that programs are put into action, and to enforce new statutes. Of course, the executive also initiates programs, as when the president announces a new tax reform or a major break in foreign policy, such as Mr. Nixon's visit to China. But in most cases, the executive must depend upon legislative approval to put his policy into law.

The Internal Revenue Service, the Federal Communications Commission, the National Security Council, and the National Aeronautics and Space Administration are but a few of the agencies and offices in the bureaucratic structure of our nation. Much of the bureaucracy (most notably, the cabinet) is under the direct supervision of the president or his staff. Other agencies are more independent: the regulatory agencies, such as the Federal Communications Commission, while appointed by the chief executive (with the advice and consent of the Senate), are meant to act as impartial moderators rather than executors. Finally, some of the bureaucracy is not appointed by the executive at all. The attorneys general of many states are elected directly by the people.

The Courts. The interpretation of laws is the primary concern of the judicial system. This task is, of course, shared with the executive and the bureau-

---

[17] The American legislature is more truly bicameral than most. The Senate in the United States has far more power than do most upper houses, such as the British House of Lords or the German Bundesrat.

cracy: a meter maid judges whether a car is parked too close to a fire hydrant; the Federal Communications Commission judges whether a radio station is allowing too many commercials on the air. In most cases executive judgment is accepted without contest. But if the car's owner feels that he was parked legally, or if the radio station feels that it has not exceeded the rightful limits for commercial messages per broadcast hour, then the case is removed from executive hands. In some political systems (the American system is a prime example), the courts are the final arbiters of the meaning, intent, applicability, and constitutionality of the law. The system of judicial review means that any citizen who feels that a law is invalid has the right to seek redress in the courts, and that both the legislative and the executive branches are expected to abide by the decisions of the judiciary.

Interaction of the Decision Makers. While each branch of government performs a distinct role, none exists or works in a vacuum, and a decision made by one branch invariably affects the others. Indeed, the responsibilities of the three systems frequently overlap, and it is often difficult to fix the exact boundaries of each branch's authority. While the president appoints the members of the Federal Trade Commission (with the advice and consent of the Senate), both Congress and the courts determine the extent of its jurisdiction. The courts can strike down an act of Congress, and the Senate can reject Supreme Court appointees nominated by the chief executive. A breakdown in any one branch will have a profound effect upon the others, as the government functions efficiently only when all of its parts are working properly.

The executive, legislature, and courts, the interest groups of society, and the subsidies, services, and values which government distributes all work together to keep the political system operating. But this system of inputs and outputs does not work in a vacuum. It operates within the culture of a society, and it is greatly affected by this environment. The diversity of ethnic, religious, and language groups within the nation; the history of the country; its geography; its literature; its social and military traditions—all of these are bound to influence the structure and the workings of a nation's political life.

The Environment of Government: Political Culture

The politics of a nation is influenced by many aspects of society: its economy, its religion, its traditions. As Karl Marx pointed out a century ago, the way people earn their living has a lot to do with the type of government they choose. Industrial societies require far more services—welfare, transportation, urban housing, sanitation facilities—than do agricultural nations, as a glance at the America of the Civil War era and the nation we know now will reveal. When a nation develops a complex industrial system, its culture and political needs will change accordingly. Indeed, Marx argued that the economy of a nation was *the* determinant of its political system, and a basic tenet of Communist ideology today is that the economy is the foundation for the social and political superstructures of every nation.

A people's religious beliefs also are reflected in politics. The current controversy over abortion law reform is a case in point. In contrast to the noble American groundrule of separation of church and state, the state is here involved in the sanctity of human life—an issue which can hardly be separated from religion and morality. In Roman Catholic Italy, religion is recognized as a concern of the state. Until recently, Italy did not permit divorce because of the church's opposition, and many politicians who advocated divorce reform did so at the risk of their political careers.

The social structure of a country is also reflected in the political system. The strict class divisions of medieval society found their political expression in a hereditary government where kings, barons, and lords were born into leadership roles. Despite the Wilsonian tradition of "keeping the world safe for democracy," the dragging conflict in Vietnam caused many political scientists to argue that perhaps not all societies are able to sustain a democratic government for various reasons including physical size, economic level, educational levels of the people, and traditions of class divisions and authoritarian forms of government.[18] A nation's culture influences its political order in numerous ways, far more than can be mentioned here. Indeed, the political system is just one part, although an integral one, of the general culture of a people.

What Is Political Culture? [19]

As defined by political scientist Sidney Verba, political culture is "the system of empirical beliefs, expressive symbols, and values, which defines the situation in which political action takes place." [20] What are these beliefs, symbols, and values which determine how a people interpret the proper role of government, and how that government itself is organized?

A people's perception of the role of government—the proper relationship between ruler and ruled—has a great deal of influence on the political system. In Japan, where the vestiges of a traditional feudal class system still pervade social structure and social relationships, it is often possible to tell who is

[18] See our Chapter 5 for a summary of these arguments. See also M. Rejai, *Democracy: The Contemporary Theories* (New York: Atherton, 1967), Part Two. See also Charles F. Cnudde and Deane E. Neubauer, eds., *Empirical Democratic Theory* (Chicago: Markham, 1969), Part Three.

[19] For excellent discussions of political culture, see Gabriel A. Almond, "Comparative Political Systems," *Journal of Politics* 18 (1956) : 391–409; Gabriel A. Almond and Sidney Verba, *The Civic Culture: Political Attitudes and Democracy in Five Nations* (Princeton, N.J.: Princeton University Press, 1963); Lucian W. Pye and Sidney Verba, eds., *Political Culture and Political Development* (Princeton, N.J.: Princeton University Press, 1965); and Samuel C. Patterson, "The Political Cultures of the American States," *Journal of Politics* 30 (1968) : 187–209.

[20] Pye and Verba, *Political Culture and Political Development*, p. 513.

whose social superior by watching the way acquaintances greet each other when they meet in the street: the person who bows lower is of "inferior" status.[21] The Japanese have also been traditionally submissive to the authority of those in office, preferring to leave fundamental policy decisions in the hands of their leaders. Americans, who are not influenced by a tradition of strict class divisions, take a far different view of the people's right to participate in government. Although the American man in the street may not be particularly well informed about the issues of the day (and most of us aren't),[22] he considers it his democratic birthright to have a say in the way his country is governed. Clearly, the way a people think of themselves, their leaders, and the relationship between the two has a vital bearing upon the nature of a political system.

In America, even people who are hostile to the president will, in most cases, respect his office and his authority. But Latin Americans do not share the same tradition of respect for their head of government. They have instead been historically more loyal to *caudillos* (charismatic military leaders), with less attachment to the executive office, and have been plagued with coup and countercoup. Nations that stress the importance of institutions are generally more stable than those that depend upon charismatic figures for leadership.

The Civic Culture. The pioneering study of cross-national differences in political beliefs, symbols, and values was made by Gabriel Almond and Sidney Verba.[23] Interviewing some five thousand people in five different nations, the authors sought to measure national political attitudes by testing three important variables: what impact the people felt government had on their lives; what obligation they felt they had toward government; and what they expected from government. What emerged was a picture of five strikingly different political cultures.

Reflecting a traditional respect for equality and individualism, the United States was found to have a highly "participant" political culture. On the whole, American citizens are actively and emotionally involved in political events and issues, and have a high degree of respect for civic participation. The average American thought it was natural that he should help to determine gov-

---

[21] When questioned in 1958, 60 percent of the Japanese people who were questioned preferred using status-connoting pronouns to neutral ones such as "I" or "you." When asked who should control policy making for national reconstruction, over one-third thought that the job should be in the hands of the preeminent politicians, *not* elected representatives. Warren Tsuneishi, *Japanese Political Style* (New York: Harper & Row, 1966), pp. 16ff.

[22] Indeed, when Gabriel Almond and Sidney Verba asked Americans how well they understood national and international issues, only 7 percent said they understood them very well; 38 percent answered "moderately well"; 37 percent "not so well"; 14 percent "not at all"; and 4 percent answered that it depended on the issue. In Robert A. Dahl, *Democracy in the United States*, 2nd ed. (Chicago: Rand McNally, 1972), p. 237.

[23] Almond and Verba, *The Civic Culture*. The nations which Almond and Verba studied were Great Britain, the United States, Germany, Italy, and Mexico.

ernment policy, and many went so far as to state that all problems could be solved if the politicians would only follow the instructions of the electorate.

Britons also feel a strong sense of personal involvement in government, but are more likely than Americans to defer to the judgment of those with superior knowledge and expertise. In Italy, where the people have lived under a long series of unstable and short-lived governments since that nation's humiliation in World War II, political attitudes are characterized by a high degree of alienation, little national pride, and little obligation to participate in government decision-making processes.

The Mexican political culture is a combination of alienation and aspiration. Government traditionally had an uncomplimentary reputation because of its history of oppression, but the revolution of 1910 helped erase this image. There is a feeling of national pride in the progress which has been made since 1910 and a sense of potential for the future, but most people still shy away from politics.

Finally, the tradition of Prussian discipline symbolized by the goose-stepping soldiers in German parades has had a powerful influence on the German civic culture. Highly informed and confident of the fairness of government, the West German people have not yet developed a sense of participation in its processes. They tend to regard themselves as subjects rather than involved participants in a democracy, and still bow to authority with little hesitation. Social discipline is still prized above individual independence, and this relationship is mirrored in the German people's attitude toward government.

It is evident, as Almond and Verba have shown, that national cultures vary considerably in their views toward government and politics, and that governments in turn vary according to their cultural environments. No stable political structure can be grafted upon a national culture which is completely alien to it, any more than a cactus can thrive in a swamp. The political system is a part of a nation's culture, and as such it reflects the total experience of that society.

Political Subcultures. While Americans as a group have been shown to place a high value on their right to participate in the decisions of government, this orientation is only dominant—not all-inclusive. There are numerous groups within American society who do not share the general pattern of beliefs, attitudes, and values. Since before the Civil War, the South has traditionally placed less faith in federal government and more in states' rights.[24] Governor Wallace speaks for many when he castigates the "intellectual morons in Washington" who, he says, have the effrontery to tell the people of Alabama how to run local affairs. American blacks, who for many years were excluded

[24] The best study of southern politics remains V. O. Key, Jr., *Southern Politics* (New York: Random House, 1950).

from the political processes, have been found to have far less faith in "participatory democracy" than have white Americans. This lack of faith, and the apathy it causes, also characterize other minority groups. Mexican-Americans, American Indians, and the poor whites of Appalachia are in effect separate subcultures which, through years of being the minority groups in our society, see the ruler-ruled relationship in a very different light than do the majority of Americans.[25]

Subcultures do not result only from economic differences. Ethnic groups, religious denominations (the Mormons in Utah and the Mennonites in Pennsylvania and Maryland being more extreme examples), occupation, age, and regional differences may all affect the way a person views both particular issues and the overall role of his government.[26]

The existence of subcultures within a political community affects the dominant political culture and can act as a disrupting force when group ties are stronger than the larger community loyalty. In Northern Ireland, where the Roman Catholics have long been isolated from the mainstream of Ulster politics and society, the sense of dissent is far more pervasive than any feeling of national unity. The United States of the 1860s, Nigeria in 1968, and Pakistan in 1971 were also breeding grounds for large-scale civil conflict. How does a political culture become overpowered by smaller group loyalties to the point of disintegration? How do people learn to think of themselves as a part of a political culture—as an American instead of a Roman Catholic or a Washingtonian?

Political Socialization

When we think of the socializing process, we remember how we "picked up" behavior patterns like table manners, correct terms of address, and the do's and don'ts of personal hygiene. Such behavior is not formally taught; it is mostly absorbed by watching other people who know what they're doing, and imitating their actions. Political socialization operates in much the same manner: we watch, listen, and imitate the political attitudes and values of family, friends, and others whom we respect. Political socialization is the induction into the political culture and is the developmental process through which we learn the accepted attitudes and values of our political culture and

---

[25] For an excellent study of how political views are formed in the Appalachian subculture, see Dean Jaros, Herbert Hirsch, and Frederic J. Fleron, Jr., "The Malevolent Leader: Political Socialization in an American Sub-Culture," *American Political Science Review* 62 (1968) : 565–75. For the middle-class contrast see Fred I. Greenstein, "The Benevolent Leader: Children's Images of Political Authority," *American Political Science Review* 54 (1960) : 937–39.

[26] A few of these variables are examined in Duane Lockard, *New England State Politics* (Princeton, N.J.: Princeton University Press, 1959) ; and John H. Fenton, *Midwest Politics* (New York: Holt, Rinehart and Winston, 1966). Chapter 8 of our text describes political subcultures and political socialization at greater length than we could spare here.

subcultures.[27] Learning to pledge allegiance to the flag, to stand up when the national anthem is sung at ball parks, and to acknowledge the authority of political figures, from presidents to policemen, are all part of the political learning process. And families, friends, schoolteachers, and even television are all important teachers. If Catholic children in Northern Ireland or poor children in the urban ghettoes of America are raised to see only the problems and ways of life of their isolated neighbors, with no perspective as to how their small group fits into the national whole, then their political views will most likely be very provincial and off the mainstream. If the process of political socialization disintegrates so much that membership in a small group becomes more relevant than membership in a nation, then the entire political culture will likely break down. Political socialization—the learning of political attitudes and social preferences—is crucial to stable government.

A Look Ahead

In the modern world of poverty and luxury, violent protest in the name of peace, democracy confronted by apathy, and televised crisis after televised crisis, an understanding of the processes and institutions of government is vital to everyone who hopes for improvements. While the systems model of politics provides at best an imperfect and abstract framework for viewing the political world we live in, it does give us a useful perspective for understanding how the parts of the political system fit into a larger scheme of things. It provides a basic model into which all governments may be fit. It helps us to see both the way in which government reacts to what people think, and the way people are affected by government's actions.

After an introduction in Parts I and II to the basic concepts, theories, and controversies of modern politics and political science, our text will be organized roughly in the input-institutions-output structure of David Easton's political system. Part III discusses the people's indirect and direct influences on government through public opinion, interest groups, political parties, communications, voting, electoral systems, and theories of representation. Part IV describes federal and unitary systems of government and the decision-making institutions: the legislature, the executive, the courts, and the administrative bureaucracy, and the common themes and national variations of each. And Part V takes a look at the decisions themselves, through governmental policy and current issues. International affairs, the urban crisis, civil rights, developing nations, and the world environment itself are all crucial to the political world, and each directly affects our personal lives. By learning about the

[27] Herbert Hyman, *Political Socialization* (Glencoe, Ill.: The Free Press, 1959); Roberta Sigel, ed., "Political Socialization: Its Role in the Political Process," *Annals of the American Academy of Political and Social Science* 361 (1965); and Fred I. Greenstein, *Children and Politics* (New Haven, Conn.: Yale University Press, 1965).

institutions and the environment of government, we hope to be better able to understand its policies—and, perhaps, to improve them.

Suggested Readings

Almond, Gabriel A., and Verba, Sidney. *The Civic Culture*. Princeton, N.J.: Princeton University Press, 1963. A major study of the political culture in five nations, with a comparative study of the socialization process.

Aristotle, *Politics*. Translated by Ernest Barker. New York: Oxford University Press, 1962. An invaluable work for beginning students of politics.

De Grazia, Alfred. *Politics for Better or Worse*. Glenview, Ill.: Scott, Foresman, 1973. A new view of the concerns of politics.

Easton, David. *The Political System: An Inquiry into the State of Political Science*. 2nd ed. New York: Alfred A. Knopf, 1971. A modern classic in political science that is considered to be the most important contemporary statement of the new view of politics as a process and as a system.

Lasswell, Harold. *Politics: Who Gets What, When, How*. New York: Meridian, 1958. A statement of the concerns and questions asked by American political scientists.

Mitchell, William C. *The American Polity*. New York: The Free Press, 1962. A comprehensive look at the American political system, employing a systems approach throughout.

————. *Public Choice in America*. Chicago: Markham, 1971. A perspective that brings together decision making, economic questions, and an economic approach to political questions.

Plato. *The Republic*. Translated by Francis MacDonald Cornford. New York: Oxford University Press, 1945. The basic discussion of politics, justice, and the philosopher king.

Ranney, Austin, ed. *Political Science and Public Policy*. Chicago: Markham, 1968. A series of essays giving an overview of the public-policy approach to political science.

Rosenau, James N. *The Dramas of Politics: An Introduction to the Joys of Inquiry*. Boston: Little, Brown, 1973. An introduction to politics as theater, with the student as dramatist, director, and actor.

Sigel, Roberta S., ed. *Learning about Politics: A Reader in Political Socialization*. New York: Random House, 1970. A comprehensive collection of readings that embraces each of the major areas in political socialization.

Science and the study of politics
CHAPTER 2

Like other social sciences, political science examines patterns of human behavior. Political inquiries have explored a wide variety of areas, some of which can be clearly recognized as political and others of which cannot. While we might expect to find a political scientist in the United States Senate office building, or perhaps in the halls of the Pentagon, we might not so readily expect to find him studying an aborigine tribe in the Australian desert. While we would expect a sociologist to have an interest in the TV fare of children or the effect of family life on children's values; an economist to study trade laws and unemployment rates; and psychologists to examine identification, repression, and sublimation, these areas of study are also within the domain of the modern political scientist. A primitive tribe such as the aborigines, though it has no formal legislature or courts, does have a system for allocating

values in its society, and political scientists would be concerned with the
decision-making process of tribal councils and chieftains in such a primitive
society. Television and the family transfer political values as well as more
general social values to children. Thus, they are within the realm of political
science as well as sociology. Trade laws have important effects on international
politics, and unemployment rates have important effects on national politics.
And concepts of psychology have been used often in political studies of great
leaders, mass political movements, and many other phenomena of government.

Political Science: What It Is

Political science studies the political system, and all of the processes and
activities that result in authoritative decisions for the allocation of values in
the society. The range of political science extends from the awareness and
interests of the individual citizen to the institutions and processes of nations
and international communities. Its primary concern is with the purpose of
government, the institutions of government, the policy-making processes of
government, and all of the individual and group interactions and motivations
associated with those processes.[1]

[1] For a further definition of political science, see Francis J. Sorauf, *Political Science: An
Informal Overview* (Columbus, Ohio: Charles E. Merrill Books, 1965), p. 5. The basic
work from which contemporary political science has drawn the definition of its field
of study is David Easton, *The Political System*, 2nd ed. (New York: Alfred A. Knopf,
1971).

Political Science as a Discipline

If the legitimate concern of political science is so broad-based, how is it possible to distinguish it as a separate discipline? The problem is not limited to the field of political science alone. It has been said that any division of the social sciences, and even the natural sciences, is necessarily artificial.[2] No field of study can be clearly separated from all other disciplines, for inquiries constantly cut across dividing lines. For example, the study of the DNA molecule is the concern of both chemistry and biology. A character analysis of Adolf Hitler may be classified as history, political science, or psychology. Any attempt to divide the study of all human experience into neat academic disciplines will always be confronted with the difficulty of overlapping boundaries. But does this mean that we should abandon any attempts to make distinctions between disciplines? While boundaries may overlap, few would deny that scholarship and scholars do fall into natural clusters of interests and perspectives, such as history, philosophy, and politics. An academic field or discipline is recognized as a distinct category of knowledge and inquiry; and though it may be a bit fuzzy around the edges, it has, nonetheless, an identifiable perspective and core of concern for the collection and study of facts about the universe.[3] Thus, political science—along with sociology, history, economics, and philosophy—is a discipline. And like the other social sciences, it contains many areas of specialization.

The Academic Field.   The academic field of political science covers a great deal of ground. Its subject matter can be organized into three major areas of specialization: the study of politics within a particular society; the study of politics and political systems outside a society; and the field of political theory.[4]

Politics within a society concerns the study of the governmental institutions and processes of one political system. American government and politics, for example, includes the study of public law; the study of the federal system and institutions, including the presidency and Congress and their relationship to one another; the study of political participation and the contest for political power through political parties, voting behavior, public opinion, and interest groups; and the study of public administration, the analysis of public policy as carried out by bureaucracies and large organizations. New fields of specialization are emerging: they include the fields of urban politics and ethnic and minority politics.

---

[2] Maurice Duverger, *Introduction to the Social Sciences*, trans. Malcolm Anderson (New York: Praeger Publishers, 1964), p. 38.

[3] Cyril Roseman, Charles G. Mayo, and F. B. Collinge have developed eight criteria, or "ideal ingredients," for determining whether a body of scholarship is a discipline. See *Dimensions of Political Analysis* (Englewood Cliffs, N.J.: Prentice-Hall, 1966), pp. 4–6.

[4] This three-part classification of political science is based on that of Joe Allman. See *Creative Politics* (Pacific Palisades, Calif.: Goodyear, 1972), p. 40.

MIDDLE EAST · VIETNAM · POLITICS · SPORTS · INFLATION · SILENCE

Kaufman in The Christian
Science Monitor © 1968
TCSPS.

The second major area of the political science discipline is not confined to one particular society. This field encompasses the areas of comparative government and international relations. Comparative government studies the political experiences, institutions, behavior, and processes of several governments, identifying the similarities and differences of several national systems. For example, the British Parliament and the United States Congress can be compared to the legislatures of other nations to learn whether legislative committees are as likely to use seniority to choose leaders in nations with strong political party centralization as they are in nations with little party discipline. The field of international relations concerns the struggle for power and influence in the international community, the operations of international law and international organizations, and the foreign policy processes of nations.

Political theory, the third area of study, defines and establishes basic terms and concepts, and examines the underlying nature, functions, and purposes of political processes, communities, and institutions. Traditionally, political theory had a normative orientation: Plato and Aristotle were concerned with the value judgments involved in determining what *should* be the proper role of government. Today, political theory is more empirical in nature. Rather than asking "What is good government?" many political theorists avoid subjective judgments by concerning themselves with questions such as "How does government function?" [5]

The Development of Political Science as a Discipline. Political science is one of the newest of the social sciences, having emerged as an independent academic discipline in the latter part of the last century. Yet, even though its existence as a separate discipline is very recent, its origins are very old.

The first Western thinker to make a systematic study of government and politics was Aristotle, who wrote in the fourth century, B.C.[6] Less concerned with utopias than previous philosophers had been, Aristotle combined his philosophy of what the relationship between citizens and state should be with direct observations of what they actually were. The primarily theological considerations of the Middle Ages replaced the political philosophy of the classical Greeks, and it was not until Machiavelli, a statesman of the Renaissance, that politics was again separated from religion. Machiavelli believed in the study of men and governments as they are, not as they should be. His successors— Hobbes, Locke, and Rousseau—largely retained Machiavelli's secular approach to the subject, but they combined this with more idealistic considerations of what governments should be.[7]

Politics remained fused with other branches of knowledge until the nineteenth century, when the spirit of scientific inquiry, which began with the Renaissance and had swept through the natural sciences two centuries before, finally caught up with the social sciences and the study of politics as well. The constitutional issues underlying the events leading up to the American Civil War provoked a host of works examining and describing the role of the American Constitution and government. The works composed the first large-scale empirical examination of existing political institutions. They could be classified neither as philosophy, history, economics, nor law, and scholars began to think of the study of government as a separate branch of knowledge.

Political Science: Its American Origins. Partly because of the influence of the Civil War on American scholars, it was in the United States that political

---

[5] However, there is still considerable concern among traditional political scientists about the proper end of government. See the discussion later in this chapter.

[6] Karl Deutsch maintains that every science passes through three stages of development: the philosophical, the empirical, and then a necessary revision of the empirical stage. In political science, Deutsch identifies the first stage as the period from Aristotle to the American Civil War; the second as the century following the Civil War; and the third as the current post-World War II age of controversy, when many political scientists are arguing that their discipline must be concerned with the proper ends of government. See *The Nerves of Government: Models of Political Communication and Control* (New York: The Free Press, 1969), pp. 3-4.

[7] We have provided only the barest thumbnail sketch here. For more detail, see George H. Sabine's *History of Political Theory*, 3rd ed. (New York: Holt, Rinehart and Winston, 1961), considered by many to be the standard history of the great political philosophers. An excellent comparison of traditional and modern theorists may be found in William T. Bluhm, *Theories of the Political System*, rev. ed. (Englewood Cliffs, N.J.: Prentice-Hall, 1972).

science first became recognized as a discipline separate from the other social sciences. In 1857, Francis Lieber created the first chair of "History and Political Science" at Columbia College (now Columbia University), and John Burgess headed the first school of political science, which was founded in 1880, also at Columbia College. By 1890, many American colleges and universities had formed departments of government and political science that were separate from history, social studies, and philosophy departments. Such major American works of political science as Woodrow Wilson's *Congressional Government and the State* and John Burgess's *Political Science and Comparative Constitutional Law* were published during the later years of the nineteenth century, as was *The American Commonwealth,* by the British writer, Lord Bryce. A third major development was the founding of the American Political Science Association in 1903 "to assemble on common ground those persons whose main interests are connected with the scientific study of the organization and function of the state." [8] While in 1904 the American Political Science Association had only 214 individual and institutional members, the discipline has grown rapidly.[9] Today the American Political Science Association has a membership of well over 16,000, and American universities graduate nearly 500 Ph.D.'s in political science every year.

Political Science in Other Nations. Political science began as a separate discipline in the United States, and it developed here at a much more rapid pace than anywhere else in the world. Not only is most political science research being done in the United States, but the United States has more political scientists than all other countries combined. This is not to say, however, that political science is an American discipline.

The International Political Science Association (IPSA), established in 1948 under the auspices of the United Nations Educational, Scientific and Cultural Organization (UNESCO), has been very influential in promoting the development of political science around the world. The Association conducts meetings every three years for the purpose of bringing scholars together to discuss the conditions and problems of the discipline. As of 1970, thirty-three nations listed their political science associations as collective members of IPSA.

Political science has developed differently in every nation. Each nation's unique history, traditions, ideologies, and political culture are reflected in the way in which the discipline of political science has developed in that country. **Political Science in the Communist World.** In the Communist nations, the development of political science as a distinct discipline has been slow.[10] In Russia, the government of Stalin was openly hostile to the social sciences,

---

8 From Jesse S. Reeves, "Perspectives in Political Science, 1903–1928," *American Political Science Review* 22 (1929): 2.

9 See Albert Somit and Joseph Tanenhaus, *The Development of American Political Science* (Boston: Allyn and Bacon, 1967), p. 55.

10 An excellent description of Communist political science development is David E. Powell and Paul Shoup, "The Emergence of Political Science in Communist Countries," *American Political Science Review* 64 (July 1970): 572–88.

and so it was not until after Stalin's death in 1953 that the hard-line Marxist-Leninist dogma of the Stalin period began to be replaced by objective social science research. The Political Science Association of the USSR was established in 1960, and Russian political scientists conduct research on political subjects and institutions. However, political science has still not gained recognition as a totally independent discipline. Russian political science reflects the Communist ideology. It has been heavily influenced by the ideas of Marx, and, as a result, has given primary emphasis to the effects of economic factors on political events.

Poland and Yugoslavia have more advanced political science disciplines than the USSR. Poland has broken successfully with the Marxist-Leninist approach: under the leadership of Jerzy J. Wiatr of the University of Warsaw, Polish political scientists have employed Western techniques and concepts in their analysis of their own national political behavior. The Yugoslavs began a school of political science at the University of Zagreb in 1962, where their primary concern has been Titoist political philosophy, which emphasizes nationalistic communism, free from central Soviet influences.

Political Science in Western Nations. Political science in the West bears the stamp of a wide variety of national political cultures.[11] Italian political science since World War II has been dominated by the effort to understand the factors that influenced their nation to embrace Fascist leadership during that war. Swedish political science, reflecting the traditional insularity of the Swedish nation, is primarily concerned with the descriptive process of tracing the origin and development of its political institutions from the Middle Ages. The discipline in West Germany, on the other hand, is most concerned with constitutional and administrative law and the science of the state. Political science in America includes countless different fields of specialization. One of the most popular in recent years has been the field of political psychology (see Table 2-1). The discipline of political science, and all its fields of specialization, can be divided into two major categories. These two approaches are institutionalism, or traditionalism, and behavioralism.[12]

The Major Approaches to Political Science: Institutionalism and Behavioralism

Most of the Greek, medieval, and Renaissance political thinkers took a normative approach to the study of government and politics. As political philosophers, they were primarily interested in discovering what man's relationship with the universe, society, and government should be. Using the

[11] See UNESCO publication no. 426, *Contemporary Political Science* (Paris: UNESCO, 1950).
[12] On the historical development of these two approaches, see Charles F. Andrain's *Political Life and Social Change* (Belmont, Calif.: Wadsworth, 1970), Chapter 2. For discussions about the approaches themselves, see Joe Allman's *Creative Politics*, Chapter 2.

Table 2-1
First-Choice Fields of Specialization for Political Scientists Born in 1930 and Later

Rank	Specialization
1	Political Psychology
2	Political Socialization
3	Methodology
4	Judiciary: Organizations, Processes, Behavior
5	Voting Behavior
6	Empirical Political Theory
7	Revolutions and Political Violence
8	Legislature: Organization, Processes, Behavior
9	International Politics
10	Normative Political Theory
11	Metropolitan and Urban Government and Politics
12	Political Parties and Elections
13	Public Opinion
14	Foreign Policy
15	National Security Policy
16	Historical Political Theory
17	State and Local Government and Politics
18	Executive: Organization, Processes, Behavior
19	Administration: Organization, Processes, Behavior
20	Constitutional Law
21	International Organization and Administration
22	International Law
23	Political and Constitutional History
24	Budget and Fiscal Management
25	Government Regulation of Business
26	Administrative Law
27	Personnel Administration

Source: Heinz Eulau, "Quo Vadimus?" American Political Science Review 2 (Winter 1969): 13.

methods of philosophical speculation and analysis, they imposed a system of values on their investigations, seeking to discover the best mode of human existence. To this end, they tried to ascertain which system of government would bring man closest to the good life.

Institutionalism. Political science as an independent branch of thought developed in the late nineteenth century in the United States. Apparently, most post-Civil War scholars felt that earlier philosophical speculations about the best type of government could be laid to rest: with the establishment and success of the United States of America, they felt the best form of government had been realized. Political scientists thus turned their attention to examining and describing existing political institutions.

Early institutionalists focused on formal institutions of the government of the United States. They studied the executive branch, the two houses of Congress, and the operation of the courts in the judicial branch. Constitutional law was a major concern, and concepts that had guided the Constitution —such as federalism, the doctrine of implied powers, and the system of checks and balances—were examined in detail. Early in the twentieth century, the focus of political scholars broadened to include less formal political institutions, like political parties, pressure groups, and the dynamic interactions among the several branches of American government as well. The methodology of observation and description, which relied heavily on the case study, remained dominant until World War II.

But while institutionalist scholars emphasize the importance of direct observation in keeping close to the facts, their approach contains some normative elements as well, for the traditionalist approach is also concerned with reform and good government. Political scientists observe the institutions of government, but they also look for ways to improve their operation. The effort to use their specialized knowledge to improve government is just as much the concern of political scientists as the amassing of that knowledge. This traditionalist approach dominated the political science discipline from the mid-nineteenth century to the middle of the twentieth century.

Then events occurred both during and after World War II which presented the institutionalist approach with information and questions which it was not equipped to deal with. The institutionalist emphasis on existing political institutions could not explain why, in spite of their apparent democratic institutions, both Germany and Italy were swept by fascism. Furthermore, it could not explain why, when familiar Western institutions were transplanted to new non-Western cultures, they operated in a manner very different than originally intended. Such questions shook the Western institutionalist's belief in the operation of democratic political institutions.

Political scientists began to look for a different way to make sense of the myriad of events that confronted them.

Behavioralism. As early in the discipline's beginnings as the writings of Woodrow Wilson in the 1880s, another approach to the study of political science existed. It deemphasized the importance of institutions and focused instead on political behavior. It developed into what is now known as the behavioralist approach, and it rapidly gained popularity in the years following World War II.

The behavioralist approach covers such a variety of different concepts, methods, and areas of study that it is extremely difficult to characterize. It is earmarked, however, by two broad characteristics.[13] First, behavioralism is

---

[13] Two excellent references on the behavioralist approach are Howard Ball and Thomas P. Lauth, Jr., eds., *Changing Perspectives in Contemporary Political Analysis* (Englewood Cliffs, N.J.: Prentice-Hall, 1971); and David Easton, "The New Revolution in Political Science," *American Political Science Review* 63 (December 1969): 1051–61.

concerned with human behavior, and with the application of science to the study of human actions. It assumes that people will exhibit similar patterns of behavior in a variety of different situations. Thus, information obtained in one discipline of the social sciences can be applied to the problems of another. For example, a sociologist's examination of the hierarchical organization of a large corporation can be just as pertinent to a political scientist as his study of government bureaucracies. Behavioralists accordingly have borrowed liberally from the theories and findings of the other social sciences to add to their body of knowledge about political behavior.

Second, and most important, behavioralists place a great deal of emphasis upon scientific methodology. They apply the standards of pure science and the scientific method to the study of politics. Behavioralists formulate theories to explain political events; they construct research designs to guide them in their collection of data; and they prove or disprove their hypotheses by rigorous empirical methodology. A high value is placed on the ability of research to explain and predict political occurrences without the interference of value judgments, and there is a constant concern for precision in research techniques.

What are the reasons for the popularity of the behavioralist approach in the years following World War II? Robert Dahl has given several explanations.[14] First, during the 1930s, several groups of European scholars who had received training in applying science to political studies immigrated to the United States, and their ideas influenced American approaches to the discipline. Second, World War II had an effect on the way political scientists looked at their world: many felt that the traditional academic viewpoint could no longer answer the questions that confronted the discipline. And third, the technological advances of the mid-twentieth century, including refinements in survey techniques, statistical devices, and communications, gave political scientists— and other social scientists—tools whose precision enabled them to bring their discipline closer than ever to a science. The behavioralist approach has dominated the political science discipline since World War II, and today practically all students of political science are exposed to the behavioralist methodologies.

Major Developments in Behavioralism.   *Structural-Functional Analysis.*   Structural functionalism is one of the major theoretical outgrowths of the behavioralist approach to political science.[15] The need for a new approach to looking at political institutions arose when non-Western nations

[14] Robert A. Dahl, "The Behavioral Approach," *American Political Science Review* 55 (December 1961) : 763–65.
[15] This and policy impact studies are part of what has been called the "postbehavioral" period. Easton's "The New Revolution in Political Science" outlines the tenets of the postbehavioral movement. For description of other postbehavioral developments see Morton R. Davies and Vaughn A. Lewis, *Models of Political Systems* (New York: Praeger Publishers, 1971).

confronted political science with many new and different structures serving political purposes. While kinship groups, clans, and extended families may not have been important political units in the West, they served a definite political role in many other societies. Political scientists needed some way to classify and deal with political structures in developing states. To do this, they borrowed a sociological concept that originally came from biology, and structural functionalism was the result.[16]

Societies are similar in many ways to living organisms: just as the heart performs a vital function for the body, so a large corporation employing thousands of people and supplying a large quantity of goods is a vital part of society. In addition, a society, like an organism, becomes more structurally organized and centrally controlled as it develops.

In political science, this concept—known as the systems approach—became a framework for assessing the actions of any one part on the rest of the political system and on the whole of the society, and for drawing distinctions between political systems in various stages of development. Building on the systems approach, structural functionalism was able to compare similar parts in different political systems and so make generalizations about their political roles. Thus, a structural functionalist might compare the function of political parties in the United States (to represent electoral interests) with the function of political parties in the USSR (to legitimatize the Soviet concept of democracy). The structural-functional approach has also been widely used to help classify both fully developed and developing political systems. The first major statement of structural functionalism appeared in 1960 in Gabriel A. Almond and James S. Coleman's *Politics of the Developing Areas*.[17] Since this first work, the theory has been a major influence on the field of comparative politics, giving this one area of political science a considerable degree of order and coherence.

Policy Impact Studies. Policy impact studies are a behavioralist offshoot of structural functionalism. Unlike large segments of political science which treat policy-making processes, policy impact focuses on the content of policy and its actual impact on society as a whole. A policy impact study might focus, for example, on the Supreme Court's unanimous decision in *Brown* v. *Board of Education of Topeka* (1954) that public education facilities may not be racially segregated. The researcher might attempt to assess the effectiveness of this decision (and others that have followed) in eliminating racial segregation in public universities and in nullifying the specific legal barriers to public school integration. The approach is especially useful to decision makers because of its analysis of the impact of proposed and existing policies on society.

[16] See Martin Landau's *Political Theory and Political Science* (New York: Macmillan, 1972), Chapter 4.
[17] Gabriel A. Almond and James S. Coleman, eds., *Politics of the Developing Areas* (Princeton, N.J.: Princeton University Press, 1960).

Political Science Methodology

The behavioralist approach is the most "scientific" of all the approaches to political science. The discipline has, since its founding, aspired to be as scientific as possible. John Burgess, head of the first school of political science, maintained that those methods of inquiry, "which [had] been found so productive in the domain of Natural Science. . . ,"[18] could be applied to politics. What is the scientific spirit and method which from the time of Burgess to the present day has influenced the study of politics? Science strives to be objective, with the unique requirement of verifiability. It requires that other researchers be able to go through the same procedures as any scientist and obtain the same result. Science is cumulative: it builds upon a previous body of knowledge, and seeks to generalize specific findings to laws of a universal nature.[19]

Science and the Scientific Method

The word *science* has two meanings. First, it is an accumulated body of knowledge; and second, it is a process: "a sequence . . . of interrelated thoughts and actions which are carried out in order to solve a problem,"[20] that is, the application of demonstrated data to systematic hypotheses.

Scientific statements are objective: they must be testable. All terms in a scientific statement must have empirical referents that can easily be shown to be true or false. Thus, empirical falsifiability is at the heart of any science. The difference between an objective statement, which is scientifically testable, and a normative statement is evident in comparing the following three assertions:

1. Richard Nixon received more votes in 1972 than George McGovern.

2. Richard Nixon won a majority of the traditionally Democratic labor vote in 1972.

3. Elections are the best way of choosing a nation's leaders.

The first two statements can easily be proved true or false: they are objective statements. The last statement, however, is impossible to prove. It is a normative statement, and a normative statement ultimately rests on the subjective

---

[18] Somit and Tanenhaus, *The Development of American Political Science*, p. 28.
[19] See Thomas S. Kuhn, *The Structure of Scientific Revolutions*, 2nd rev. ed. (Chicago: University of Chicago Press, 1970); Abraham Kaplan, *The Conduct of Inquiry* (San Francisco: Chandler, 1964).
[20] Allman, *Creative Politics*, p. 25.

assessment that something is good or bad in and of itself. Many Americans may believe that elections are the best way of choosing leaders, but people who live in a theocratic state may be just as convinced that divine guidance is the best method. In Tibet, the Dali Lama was "found" by monks after an intensive search throughout the land for the one individual who showed the characteristics of holiness which would mark him as the Dali Lama. In Western history, kings ruled by "divine right," and it was not popular election, but "election" by birth that created a nation's leaders. Thus, one's preference for a way of choosing leaders depends on subjective criteria involving a judgment of what is "best"; but science deals only with things that can be confirmed by directly observable facts. Normative statements are therefore outside the realm of science.

The Scientific Method. The scientific method is an objective way of acquiring information about the universe.[21] Developed in the natural sciences in the seventeenth century, it can most simply be described as a three-step sequence of interrelated thoughts and actions for solving problems. The first step involves the identification of a problem; the second, the development of a theory to explain the problem; the third, the observation of events to test the hypothesis. In the first step, the scientist forms a question about the relationship between the events or objects he wishes to understand. In the second, he theorizes about what the relationship between them might be; his theory is his unconfirmed explanation. In the third step, he constructs hypotheses for testing his explanation, and then through systematic and controlled observation, he either confirms or disproves his theory. This "ideal" of the scientific method approximates the framework for research which political science strives to meet.

Techniques of Political Science

Four methods have been widely and fruitfully used to collect and analyze political data. They are (and our list is by no means exhaustive): experimental research, comparative studies, case studies, and historical analysis. Experimental research and comparative studies are two of the most rigorously scientific methods in use in political science today. Both rely heavily on sophisticated techniques for gathering data, such as surveys, questionnaires, and public opinion polls, and both are making more and more use of quantitative methods to analyze data. The case study and historical approaches were widely used in the earlier years of this century.

[21] Allman, in Chapter 2 of *Creative Politics*, gives a good, brief discussion of science and the scientific method. See also Thelma F. Batten, *Reasoning and Research: A Guide for Social Science Methods* (Boston: Little, Brown, 1971).

Experimental Research. Experimental research may be done in laboratory settings and in real-life community settings.[22] In both cases, research design is extremely important. The laboratory research method uses artificially created, temporary, small-scale social situations, established in a laboratory under simulated conditions closely controlled by the researcher. As a result, it is able to adhere quite closely to the standards of the scientific method. However, this method of research has been criticized for the artificiality of the lab situation and the effect this may have on the "reality" of the participants' behavior and consequently on the reliability of the findings.

Field research attempts to examine a problem in the real world and still meet scientific standards of inquiry. For example, the political scientist may want to determine the influence of the League of Women Voters on voter turnout. The researcher would choose two or more communities, attempting to "match" communities on all important variables that he expects to have an impact on voter turnout, except the variable under study. Thus, ideally, he would have two communities of similar population, income, and racial background, except that one would have an active League of Women Voters chapter and the other would not. Then, if it is found that voter turnout is higher in the first community than the second, the conclusion would be that the women's organization was probably influential in this community.

Field research is more realistic than the lab, but it is very difficult to carry out. To the extent that a researcher can match communities, he will be able to obtain accurate results. Yet even with matched communities the researcher cannot be sure that unknown factors have not influenced the outcome. Social science research is always limited by the uncontrollable variables of the real world. No two communities are ever identical: they have different histories, and they exist in different environments. The political scientist can only assume that all relevant variables are being controlled, and to do this he must abstract from reality to try to pinpoint the variables which he considers crucial—an action that involves a human judgment.

Comparative Studies. The difficulty of studying human behavior through field research and the artificiality of lab research means that political scientists often find that other methods are better suited to their research needs. The comparative study is conducted in real-world situations, and though it does not match the scientific precision and control of experimental research, it has the advantage of allowing the political scientist to draw comparisons.

A comparative study compares several similar institutions, events, or oc-

[22] This discussion draws from Joe Allman's discussion of experimental research in *Creative Politics*, Chapter 2. A good example of a political science experiment is James D. Barber's *Power in Committees: An Experiment in Governmental Process* (Chicago: Rand McNally, 1966).

currences. It might, for example, examine four city councils and generalize from this information about the characteristics of all such councils. This comparative study would require a theoretical concept of city councils which would guide the political scientist in the selection of information to be collected. For example, if the political scientist was trying to find out what factors make for a city council that accurately represents its constituents' views, he would be guided by his own definition of representativeness. If he hypothesized that representativeness is related to the intensity of competition for council seats, then he would set out to collect information on election rules in each community, the number of candidates who normally run for a single seat, the margin of victory achieved by council members in past elections, and the frequency with which council members are unseated. Thus, while the comparative study has an advantage over experimental research in that it does not require a "matched pair" of situations which may actually not exist in real life, it, too, has the drawback of requiring the scholar to make a selective judgment to guide his research.

The comparative study's main advantage lies in the fact that the comparison of a large number of similar situations allows for detection of important influences and the relationships between them.[23] The case study method lacks this advantage.

The Case Study. The case study is similar to the comparative study in that it involves the examination of a real institution or occurrence in order to draw generalizations from specifics. However, where a comparative study deals with several events or institutions, a case study examines just one. One of the major advantages of the case study is its adaptability: it does not require several comparable quantities, and so it can be applied to almost any case a scholar wishes to research. Through the use of such data-collection methods as direct personal observation of events and survey research, it gathers information from situations where more systematic and controlled methods of data collection are either not possible, or not available.

Case studies are valuable as an exploratory approach, and they have been used by many political scientists, especially in the traditionalist school. But case-study results are limited by the fact that they are an attempt to draw broad conclusions from the close examination of only one example—which may or may not be representative. The researcher can only compare his data with other case studies whose subjects, methods, or data sources may have been quite different. Thus, case studies may not be reliable as a source of generalization about the broader category the case is meant to represent. The

---

[23] See John C. Wahlke and Alex N. Dragnich, eds., *Government and Politics: An Introduction to Political Science* (New York: Random House, 1971), pp. 706–08; and Arend J. Lijphart, "Comparative Politics and the Comparative Method," *American Political Science Review* 65 (September 1971): 682–93.

case study has been very widely used in the past, but with more precise and controlled methods now available, it will probably be used less in the future.[24]

Historical Analysis. Historical analysis is one of the oldest methods of political research: it flourished in the nineteenth century when political science was first developing. This method consists of collecting data about a particular political event in the past, using primary sources such as newspapers, public records, and personal accounts. Its advantages lie in its ability to direct attention to the time sequence of events and the importance of unique conditions to shaping particular events; but its drawbacks are many. The researcher is limited by the availability (or lack) of data, and often there is little information in existence, particularly in cases where the event being studied occurred long ago. Also, it is impossible to verify all of the data. A researcher who must rely on the accounts of eyewitnesses to the great Chicago fire is placed at the disadvantage of not being able to verify the information they present.

The political scientist whose primary research tool is historical analysis is put at a definite disadvantage, and may well be criticized for not being a "scientist" at all. Indeed, many political scientists, particularly those of the traditionalist school, argue that political science is not a "science" at all— nor should it even attempt to be one.

The Study of Politics: Can It Be a Science?

The argument that the study of politics is not a science takes place on two fronts: a practical one and a moral one. While behavioralists argue that political science is a science, their critics take one of two stands: first, that political science cannot be a science; and second, that it should not even attempt to be one.[25]

The Case against Political "Science": It Cannot Be

The nature of man and human societies, it is argued, is such that neither can be studied scientifically. No social science should therefore pretend to the precision of the pure sciences. Man is not like a star or an atom which

---

[24] This is not to say that the case study is no longer widely used. Most notably, it has recently been applied to the study of community power structures. Robert Dahl employed this method in his famous study of New Haven, Connecticut, and Edward Banfield used it to study Chicago, Illinois. See Robert A. Dahl, *Who Governs? Democracy and Power in an American City* (New Haven, Conn.: Yale University Press, 1961); and Edward C. Banfield, *Political Influence: A Contribution to the Theoretical Understanding of Patterns of Political Pressure in Various Settings* (New York: The Free Press, 1961).

[25] See Landau's *Political Theory and Political Science*, Chapter 1.

"Did you make any interesting 'value judgments' today, dear?"

© 1972 by NEA, Inc.

is relatively unaffected by the scientist's observations. Instead, man reacts: he talks back; he objects to some definitions applied to him; and he gives his own meanings to his behavior.

Second, men are capable of reacting to scientific predictions so as to destroy their usefulness—a capability known as prophecy. When a scientist makes a prediction about human behavior, the prediction itself can enter into the situation in a way that the prediction does not account for. For example, when an economist predicts a fall in the stock market, people trading in the stock market may be influenced by the prediction and act in such a way as to make it come true. During an election year, a pollster will usually predict that one candidate is going to win and another is going to lose. The effect of this prediction may be to help a groundswell of electoral sympathy for the underdog, or it may be to create a "bandwagon effect," causing voters and financial contributors to give up hope and support the leading candidate.[26]

Third, critics argue that it is impossible for a political scientist to be truly scientific, because he cannot escape the effects of his own personal values and his cultural viewpoint. His work, therefore, is inescapably biased. Another

[26] See the discussion in Chapter 8 on "The Reliability of the Polls."

criticism is that it is impossible to discover general laws of human behavior by studying a particular culture, for the generalizations derived will be true only under the particular cultural conditions of one specific time and place.

Finally, critics charge that the new methodological techniques of behavioralism can bring the study of human behavior no closer to a science than it has ever come. The traditionalist criticism of the scientific methods of behavioralism is well put by Professor Hans J. Morgenthau:

> *. . . As far as those new approaches to politics are concerned, I should also say that I have no prejudice against them. . . . But I simply cannot see that here is a new opening which shows us new vistas of political life and the possibility of the solution of political problems, which has not been available to us before. . . . If somebody can show me that he has found a way to solve a problem [by applying a new method to an old problem] I shall be convinced. If he can show me a way to predict the decision of the Hanoi government with regard to peace negotiations which is more reliable than those upon which nonmethodologically inclined scholars must rely, I shall embrace him and congratulate him. But this has not happened yet, and as long as it has not happened, I would say that the traditional methods have at least one argument in their favor, and that is tradition itself.*[27]

These arguments all illustrate the contention that human society cannot be studied scientifically, as can an atom, a paramecium, or a fern. Each points out a difficult or previously unencountered area for science to handle, but in no case, the behavioralist would counter, do they present an insurmountable difficulty. Behavioralists hold that even though people, unlike atoms, think about their behavior, this has not proved to be too confusing a problem for research to handle. What people say about their own behavior and that of others is considered valuable new information for scientific analysis.

The problem of the self-fulfilling prophecy, too, has been confronted and solved in studies of election outcomes, argue those who feel that political science can be a science. The effect of a prediction on an eventual outcome can be accounted for, just like any influence. Successful predictions can include any bandwagon or underdog effects the prediction itself brings about.[28]

The charge that values influence a researcher's work in spite of his best efforts is acknowledged by behavioralist political scientists as a possibility— just as any scientific researcher may show subjective influence in his selection of problems for data-gathering techniques. To try to counteract this possibility, political scientists attempt to state their values at the outset and make their research findings public, so that others may judge the impact of these values on the work and can check the validity of the political scientists' findings through duplication.

[27] Taken from James C. Charlesworth, ed., *A Design for Political Science: Scope, Objectives, and Methods* (Philadelphia: The American Academy of Political and Social Science, 1966), pp. 138–39.
[28] See Herbert Simon's "Bandwagon and Underdog Effects of Election Prediction," *Public Opinion Quarterly* 18 (Fall 1954) : 245–53.

The criticism that investigation of particular societies will not yield general laws of human society points up an area that needs careful handling. The culture or subculture that is being scrutinized needs to be clearly defined, and the generalizations derived from any research need to be examined carefully to see how widely applicable they are. Some conclusions drawn from a particular culture may be true only for limited circumstances; however, many can have universal application.

The Case against Political "Science": It Should Not Be

The second kind of argument against political science rests on the belief that the scientific study of politics is morally wrong. This charge is levelled by individuals from three very different perspectives.

The first of these is a theological viewpoint. Many people believe that science is a threat to man's humanity. Man, they feel, is a very special creature, unlike anything else on earth; so special, in fact, that his soul is beyond nature and should be beyond science. To subject man to scientific inquiry is to treat him as though he were no different from any other natural entity. The scientific study of man is thus seen as a violation of his essential humanity. Political scientists had to deal with theological arguments when they first began their studies. Their reply was then, and is now, that the theological assessment of man's nature can no longer be taken at face value. Beliefs about man's place in the universe must be tested by the independent check of experience.

The second moral argument also holds that science is dangerous to human beings, but for a very different reason. If human behavior can in fact be predicted, the argument goes, this knowledge can be used to control society. Thus, the pursuit of any information that can be used to manipulate human beings is considered morally wrong. It is a mistake, however, to think that the possible applications of a science of human behavior are all bad or that a sophisticated understanding of methods of control would necessarily lead to a world like that of Orwell's *1984*. We are controlled right now, the political scientist maintains, by a host of conditions that we know nothing about. If they are understood, there is a risk that they will be used to manipulate society. But there is also the possibility that by understanding these conditions, we can gain greater control over our own lives.[29]

A third body of opinion that accuses political science of being immoral comes from within the discipline itself. The argument is that political science has a moral responsibility to apply its knowledge about human political behavior to help solve current critical problems in the world. This point of view runs head on into established political opinion, which maintains that in

[29] This debate is by no means limited to political science. The controversy aroused by psychologist B. F. Skinner's recent book, *Beyond Freedom and Dignity* (New York: Alfred A. Knopf, 1971), focuses on the role of the social sciences in investigating methods of controlling human behavior.

order to keep his scientific objectivity, a scientist must not become involved in the situation he is studying. This clash of views can be illustrated by an example. Suppose two researchers, one an advocate of involvement and the other a nonsupporter, are studying an election district. They notice that the percentage of blacks registered to vote in the district is much lower than the percentage of whites. The activist would argue that he has moral responsibility to apply his expertise to correcting this imbalance; the nonactivist would argue that becoming involved in an aspect of some area he is studying would destroy his ability to be objective and thus ruin the scientific validity of his work.

In 1967 the activist movement crystallized into the Caucus for a New Political Science, a group of predominantly young political scientists within the American Political Science Association. Members of the Caucus maintain that it is no longer sufficient for political scientists to merely observe, describe, and analyze the political process. They accuse the political science establishment of "invest[ing] its energies primarily in celebrating and supporting the economic, social, and political status quo, both here and abroad," and are trying to change the direction of the discipline as a whole. The Caucus's 1969 statement of principles declared, "The resources of the APSA must be used to redirect some of the energies and expertise of the discipline to encourage the development of a new political science devoted to radical social criticism and fundamental social change." [30] The clash between social action and scientific detachment is doubly fierce because political science's claim to being a science is seriously questioned by many people.

Is Political Science a Science?

Unlike the natural sciences, political science cannot defend itself by pointing to a large body of proven scientific generalizations. It does not even have the kind of widely accepted frameworks for analysis that characterize a field like economics. Today, political science's claim to being a science is based, as it was in the beginning, on its aspirations. And those aspirations have probably never been better phrased than by Lord Bryce in an address to the American Political Science Association in the early part of this century:

[I]n calling Politics a Science we mean no more than this: that there is a constancy and uniformity in the tendencies of human nature which enable us to regard the acts of men at one time as due to the same causes which have governed their acts at previous times. Acts can be grouped and connected, can be arranged and studied as being the results of the same generally operative tendencies.

[30] *P.S.: Newsletter of American Political Science Association* 1 (Winter 1968) : 38–40; and 2 (Winter 1969) : 47–49.

The data of politics are the acts of men. The laws of political science are the tendencies of human nature and are embodied in the institutions men have created. These tendencies are so far uniform and permanent that we can lay down general propositions about human nature and can form these propositions into a connected system of knowledge.[31]

This statement is the foundation upon which political scientists are attempting to build a science and the one upon which this text is based.

[31] Quoted from Reeves, "Perspectives in Political Science," p. 2.

Suggested Readings

Bluhm, William T. *Theories of the Political System.* Rev. ed. Englewood Cliffs, N.J.: Prentice-Hall, 1972. An intriguing comparison of contemporary political theorists with their forerunners.

Deutsch, Karl. *The Nerves of Government: Models of Political Communication and Control.* New York: The Free Press, 1969. A review of some of the more interesting attempts at developing a science of politics and models of politics. Deutsch's cybernetic model is given a fascinating presentation in this work.

Kuhn, Thomas S. *The Structure of Scientific Revolutions.* Chicago: University of Chicago Press, 1970. Rev. ed. A controversial and readable work that presents a model for the development of a body of science.

Landau, Martin. *Political Theory and Political Science.* New York: Macmillan, 1972. A collection of essays written by a persuasive advocate of the science of politics.

Marx, Karl, and Engels, Friedrich. *The Communist Manifesto.* Edited by Samuel H. Beer. New York: Appleton-Century-Crofts, 1955. A basic statement of the Communist platform.

Meehan, Eugene J. *Contemporary Political Thought: A Critical Study.* Homewood, Ill.: The Dorsey Press, 1967. The philosophy of science as applied to political science.

Mill, John Stuart. *On Liberty.* Edited by Alburey Castell. New York: Appleton-Century-Crofts, 1947. A basic statement of democracy by a great nineteenth-century democrat.

Somit, Albert, and Tannenhaus, Joseph. *The Development of American Political Science.* Boston: Allyn and Bacon, 1967. The history of political science from its humble beginnings to its competitive present.

Storing, Herbert J., ed. *Essays on the Scientific Study of Politics.* New York: Holt, Rinehart and Winston, 1962. A blistering critique of the behavioral revolution. The essay by Leo Strauss gives the beginning student an idea of the tone of the traditional-versus-behavioral debate.

Wolfe, Alan, and Surkin, Marvin, eds. *End to Political Science: The Caucus Papers.* New York: Basic Books, 1970. A collection of essays by the advocates of more moral stance and less pure analysis in political science.

Government and public policy making

CHAPTER 3

During most of man's history, any organized human society was considered a nation. A nation was a people with its own history, culture, and language; it did not always have a formal government or a clearly defined homeland. Many nations were actually tribes, such as the Zulus of South Africa and the Cherokees of Oklahoma. But in the seventeenth century, the definition of a nation changed, as the ideal of the "nation-state" became the world's most powerful political force.[1] With the emergence of the modern concept of na-

---

[1] The most correct label for an autonomously governed territory is "nation-state," but for purposes of simplicity, we will use the term "nation" throughout this text. The standard history of the rise of the modern nation is Hans Kohn, *Nationalism: Its Meaning and History* (New York: Crowell-Collier and Macmillan, 1955). Also useful are Karl Deutsch, *Nationalism and Social Communication: An Inquiry into the Foundations of Nationality*

tionalism—a sense of cultural, historical, and territorial identity—peoples saw themselves as having the right to govern themselves in their own nation-states. Today, we define a nation, or nation-state, as any sizable population with a distinct cultural identity that rules itself within formal territorial boundaries by an autonomous national government.

The dramatic rise of the modern nation has changed the face of the globe in a few centuries. Citizens transferred their loyalties from monarchs, churches, or feudal lords to the nation.[2] The twentieth century has continued to produce radical changes in the political structure of the world, as the development of modern communication and transportation has helped to make nationalism an even more powerful political force. Vast empires, such as those of Austria-Hungary and Great Britain, fell apart as subjected peoples around the world asked for the right to govern themselves. As a result, many new states were created, especially in the Americas, Asia, and Africa.[3] There are today at least 143 separate nations, and the emergence of new nations continues, although not at the same rapid pace.

What Is a Nation?

Characteristics of Modern Nations

The many nations of the world community represent a spectrum of stages of social, economic, and cultural development. Some, like the United States and Great Britain, are technological societies with high standards of living. Others, like Zaire (the Congo) and India, are struggling desperately to overcome centuries of poverty. But, despite their differences, all nations share a set of common characteristics that marks them as nation-states.[4]

(New York: John Wiley & Sons, 1953); and Louis Snyder, *The Meaning of Nationalism* (New Brunswick, N.J.: Rutgers University Press, 1954). A more recent work of interest is Seymour Martin Lipset, *The First New Nation: The United States in Historical and Comparative Perspective* (Garden City, N.Y.: Doubleday, 1967).

[2] Kohn, *Nationalism: Its Meaning and History*, p. 9.

[3] For treatments of non-Western nationalism and newly independent states, see Rupert Emerson, *From Empire to Nation: The Rise to Self-Assertion of Asian and African Peoples* (Cambridge, Mass.: Harvard University Press, 1960); David E. Apter, *The Politics of Modernization* (Chicago: University of Chicago Press, 1965); Fred R. von Der Mehden, *Politics of the Developing Nations* (Englewood Cliffs, N.J.: Prentice-Hall, 1964); Gabriel A. Almond and James S. Coleman, *Politics of the Developing Areas* (Princeton, N.J.: Princeton University Press, 1960); and John H. Kautsky, *Political Change in Underdeveloped Countries* (New York: John Wiley & Sons, 1962).

[4] For discussion of what comprises a nation, see Karl Deutsch and William Foltz, *Nation Building* (New York: Atherton, 1963); and Bruce M. Russett, J. David Singer, and Melvin Small, "National Political Units in the Twentieth Century: A Standardized List," *American Political Science Review* 62 (September 1968): 932–51.

Territory and Independence. Every nation occupies and independently controls a specific geographical area with the acknowledgment (if not approval) of most of the world community. For example, the world concedes that Wales is part of Great Britain and that the Ukraine is part of the Soviet Union: thus, neither Wales nor the Ukraine is a nation. Occasionally, one nation will refuse to grant diplomatic status to another for political or ideological reasons. For almost twenty-five years, the United States has denied the People's Republic of China as the true and lawful regime of mainland China. But the People's Republic of China has been accepted as a sovereign state by the majority of the world community.

The territorial claims of nations sometimes lead to boundary disputes when two states feel that they should rightfully control a certain area. The United States and Mexico went to war over Texas in 1846, and India and Pakistan have clashed in the last decade over Kashmir and Bangla Desh. Such controversies are often not resolved until a war brings the victorious nation recognition of its claim.

A Cohesive Population: Nationalism. Nationalism is a mainstay of nationhood. In times of change, upheaval, and turmoil, a sense of national community serves as a unifying force, enabling a people to maintain a feeling of cohesiveness which makes the task of government easier. Nationalism helps to justify the authority of the state, as a people who share a sense of national community are less likely to view their government as a foreign political organization superimposed upon them. Nationalism thus helps legitimatize the state's use of force against its own people and other nations.[5]

A crucial element of nationalism is an emotional identification with a specific geographical area.[6] Every people attach a special psychological meaning to their homeland. English colonists tried to bring a bit of the homeland with them to America when they gave settlements names like Georgia, Virginia, and New York. Today, Russians speak of "Mother Russia," and the Japanese see Mount Fuji as a symbol of their nation.

But a territorial attachment is not enough to build a united national feeling. Nationalism also depends on the existence of a common history and culture.[7] The sharing of a historic past seems to bind people together, as it has the citizens of the Republic of Ireland, who remember centuries of struggling against England. Similarly, a common cultural heritage, such as a shared religion, a national literature, or an artistic or musical tradition, can promote a sense of national identity. Italy's Roman Catholicism and Renaissance heritage of art and architecture, and Russia's literary traditions of such writers as Tolstoy and Dostoevsky all contribute to the sense of national identity felt by Italians and Russians. Indeed, the absence of shared traditions is a part of

[5] Kohn, *Nationalism: Its Meaning and History*, p. 11.
[6] Our discussion follows those of Kohn, *Nationalism*; and Snyder, *The Meaning of Nationalism*.
[7] See Lipset, *The First New Nation*, pp. 26–30.

the instability of many new Asian and African nations. These countries have had to depend upon reinforcement from the mass media, "indoctrination" in schools, and the charisma of new national heroes (often military men) to develop a national spirit and sense of community in what often approximates a historical and cultural vacuum.[8]

Like a common history or cultural heritage, national language is also an element of nationalism. Language is the carrier of a nation's history, culture, traditions, and social customs, and it is the sharpest way to distinguish ethnic groups. Some nations, like India and Switzerland, survive with two or more languages. But often the existence of many tongues will fragment a society, while a national language will unify it. The division of Canada into French- and English-speaking populations has been a particularly disruptive force in that nation's history. Ironically, in some new states of Asia and Africa, which include many tribes, the closest thing to a national language is the English or French that was imposed on these nations while they were British or French colonies.

What holds a nation together when it lacks a common tradition and contains people from many ethnic groups, each with its own distinct customs, religion, and history? The United States seems to lack many criteria of nationhood: it has no national religion, and its culture is a "melting pot" of many foreign traditions. Dennis W. Brogan, a British observer, finds that American nationalism is sustained primarily by a symbolic force: the country's ideals, as embodied in the Constitution and the Bill of Rights, act as a strong unifying force.[9] Indeed, the Mormon church, one of the few religious groups to spring from American soil, teaches that the Constitution is a divinely inspired document drafted by the hand of God.

Autonomy and Legitimacy. A large part of nationalism is a historical and cultural heritage, but another part of nationalism is desire for autonomy. Nations are independent, governing their own affairs without outside interference.[10] The Canal Zone is not a nation, nor is Guam: both are non-self-governing territories of the United States. Bangla Desh was not a nation until it won independence in 1971, even though it had for years retained a terri-

---

[8] An excellent new study on the possibilities of political integration in societies with serious ethnic or religious differences is Alvin Rabushka and Kenneth A. Shepsle, *Politics in Plural Societies: A Theory of Democratic Instability* (Columbus, Ohio: Charles E. Merrill Books, 1972).

[9] See Dennis W. Brogan, *Politics in America* (New York: Harper & Row, 1954); also Karl Deutsch, *Politics and Government* (Boston: Houghton Mifflin, 1970), Chapter 6.

[10] Does a nation cease to be a nation if it is occupied by a neighboring power? This question is debated in Russett, et al., "National Political Units in the Twentieth Century," and in a rejoinder in the *American Political Science Review* 62 (September 1968): 952–55. Russett and his colleagues categorize nations as "independent," "dependent," or "part of a larger entity" from 1900 to the present. They assert that a country occupied by hostile foreign troops (such as Belgium from 1940–1944) is not an independent and contributing member of the international system.

torial identity, a sense of community, and a cultural heritage distinct from that of West Pakistan.

A bulwark of national independence is legitimacy, which can be defined as the ability of the government system to sustain the faith and trust of the people.[11] The citizens of a nation will feel that their government is legitimate if they have a general sense that it is responsive to their needs, and that their well-being will be served best by continuing the existing method of running the country. If the people see their government as illegitimate and not serving their needs, they may attempt to overthrow it, as the American colonists did in the late eighteenth century.[12]

Political Organization. When the Americans ended British colonial rule in 1783, they created a new nation, and one of the first steps they took was to draw up the blueprint for a new political organization, or government. Every society has certain institutions that are responsible for making rules or policies and for allocating resources. A nation needs a government, just as the human body needs a brain, to direct and guide the process of carrying decisions into action. Without such a central force, society would become lawless and chaotic.

Government converts the needs of the nation—including territorial independence, economic well-being, and political stability—into public policies, and enforces these policies throughout the society. It may take many forms, from the chieftaincies of African tribes to the complex bureaucracies of Western nations. But regardless of the particular form, no nation has been able to exist without a government for any length of time. A stable society requires some organizing force, and governments are created to perform that function.

Government: What It Is and What It Does

All but the most primitive societies have had well-defined governmental structures. Mankind seems to need a way of organizing and making rules for communities, and various theories have been offered to explain this tendency. Psychologist Erich Fromm argues that men fear social isolation and the responsibilities of independence, and form larger groups (whether national, religious, or ideological) in order to escape from the tensions and demands of individual freedom and autonomy.[13] On the other hand, political theorists like John Locke have viewed governments as devices to protect the rights and

[11] See Seymour Martin Lipset, *Political Man: The Social Bases of Politics* (Garden City, N.Y.: Doubleday, 1963), p. 63. Chapter 3 is especially useful in analyzing legitimacy.
[12] Of course, many oppressive governments have remained in power for centuries. A large part of the success of the feudal system for centuries in medieval Western Europe, and of the Roman Empire, lay in the perspective of the era. What we may think of as oppressive in modern America was viewed as acceptable and legitimate in medieval and ancient cultures.
[13] Erich Fromm, *Escape from Freedom* (New York: Holt, Rinehart and Winston, 1941).

property of the people. "The great and chief end," wrote Locke in *Two Treatises of Civil Government*, "of men uniting . . . under government, is the preservation of their property [and so, their natural rights]."[14] To Locke, government represented an agreement between the rulers and the ruled, who would support those in power as long as the government served in their interests.

A society without a government might be like a baseball game without umpires. The players would argue forever about whether the pitch was a ball or a strike, or whether the runner was safe or out. Each contest would turn into a raucous brawl. Government performs the same tasks as the umpires: it sets down the basic groundrules that everyone must abide by.[15]

In part, a government is able to enforce its rules (or laws) because it controls the supreme penalty of death and has a monopoly on the legal use of force.[16] Yet, to stay in power, a government must enjoy the support of its people. One way of maintaining legitimacy is to successfully fulfill the goals of nationhood.

Common Goals of Governments

The task of every government is to provide for the independence, stability, and economic and social well-being of all its citizens.[17] These are the ultimate goals of every nation in the modern world.

Each nation must preserve itself as a state and insure its national survival, so that the world community recognizes that nation's autonomy and the integrity of its boundaries. Recognition by other nations depends in part on a country's stability. A politically stable nation has an established system providing for the orderly transfer of power from one party or leader to another. It preserves domestic peace by maintaining law and order and by protecting property. A government can also enlist popular support by promoting an acceptable standard of living for all of its citizens: people who are receiving what they believe to be their due are less likely to rebel. Promoting the general welfare can include attempts to eliminate poverty, maximization of educational opportunities for all areas of society, and technological advances.

How can government best advance the economic and social well-being of its citizens? There is wide disagreement, which generally can be divided into

[14] John Locke, *Two Treatises of Civil Government* (London: J. M. Dent & Sons, 1924), p. 180.

[15] Of course, there are those who argue that there is no need for government. A good basic work which provides a background on anarchism and its advocates is Daniel Guerin's *Anarchism: From Theory to Practice* (New York: Monthly Review Press, 1970). Many of the classic statements of anarchists are provided in Robert Hoffman, ed., *Anarchism* (New York: Atherton, 1970).

[16] Richard A. Watson, *Promise and Performance of American Democracy* (New York: John Wiley, 1972).

[17] See the discussion in Marian D. Irish and Elke Frank, *An Introduction to Comparative Politics: Twelve Nation States* (New York: Appleton-Century-Crofts, 1972), p. 83.

three basic governmental approaches to promoting the general welfare: the laissez-faire approach, the socialist society, and the welfare state. Under the philosophy of laissez-faire ("let alone") of Adam Smith, government is the greatest enemy of human liberty, and therefore should under no circumstances be allowed to intervene in the economy. Thomas Jefferson voiced his support of a laissez-faire approach in his statement that "that government is best which governs least." Proponents of the laissez-faire approach believe that people will prosper or fail on the basis of their own intelligence, ambition, and hard work, and that government has no right to intervene in this natural order.

In a socialist society, almost the opposite is true. Government, rather than private individuals, owns the means of economic production and distribution, such as factories, mines, and transportation and communications networks. Government runs these industries in the interests of the society as a whole— something which private interests are not likely to do in a laissez-faire system.

Finally, the welfare-state approach is an attempt to preserve part of the laissez-faire philosophy while answering some of the socialist critiques of capitalism. The government establishes basic rules for the economic order and can act to eliminate industrial abuses. To protect the needy and under-privileged, it runs programs such as Social Security, aid to dependent children, and workmen's compensation. At the same time, the economy remains in private hands, and private funds finance most industrial development. The welfare state is not without fault, though, and many have argued that its application in the United States has acted to aid industrial giants at the expense of the "little guy." [18]

Classifying Governments

We could arrange all of the world's governments into a typology according to whether they follow the laissez-faire model, the socialist model, or the welfare-state model. Of course, any model represents only an ideal situation, and not its application in the real world. Despite the fact that they represent an unreachable situation, models are very useful to social scientists in classifying and comparing different political systems, and they aid in the understanding of a nation's political culture and development. But categorizing according to the economic strategies of governments is only one of many schemes for understanding governments.[19] The earliest and most famous sys-

[18] For a discussion of welfare statism in the United States, see William C. Mitchell, *Public Choice in America: An Introduction to American Government* (Chicago: Markham, 1971), Chapter 4.

[19] In this section, we will discuss four major schemes for classifying "all" of the world's governments. There are of course many more—like those presented by Arthur S. Banks and Robert B. Textor in *A Cross-Polity Survey* (Cambridge, Mass.: The M.I.T. Press, 1963), which uses as its criteria the form of the executive branch and the power given it. Douglas Verney divides systems of government into presidential and parliamentary types. See "Analysis of Political Systems," in *Comparative Politics: A Reader*, ed. Harry Eckstein and David E. Apter (New York: The Free Press, 1965), pp. 175–91.

tem of classification was developed by the Greek philosopher Aristotle in the fourth century B.C.

Aristotle's Six Types of Government. Aristotle distinguished between three benevolent kinds of government—where the ruling authority acts only according to legal guidelines, ruling in the interests of the entire society—and three corrupt types—where government acts only in its own selfish interests (see Figure 3-1).

A monarchy, or kingship, is a benevolent dictatorship. Governmental power is vested in a man of preeminent virture and wisdom who is considered godlike in his moral and intellectual qualities. The ideal monarch rules in behalf of all and will not benefit any one person or group at the expense of another. But monarchy can degenerate into tyranny, under which one man exercises all power for the benefit of himself and his allies and ignores the good of the people.

Aristocracy can be thought of as a collective monarchy, ruled by the most virtuous, intelligent, and morally enlightened men in the state. But this benevolent rule by an elite class can decay into oligarchy. Instead of governing in the best interests of the society, the oligarchs only wish to defend their privileged positions.

Aristotle saw a polity (or constitutional democracy) as the most practical form of government because of the limitations of man. All citizens have a voice in the selection of leaders and the framing of the law, but at the same time, formal constitutional procedures protect minority rights. In Aristotle's classification, democracy (the rule of the many) was a corruption of the polity. Deluded into thinking that one man is as good as another, the masses in a democracy blindly follow the lead of corrupt and selfish demagogues and plunder the property of the hard-working and the capable.

The Autonomy of Subsystems. Aristotle's classification system was used by scholars for nearly twenty-five centuries, but it is no longer satisfactory. Modern political scientists have had to create new models in order to understand a rapidly changing world. One of the most respected contemporary efforts identifies the extent of subsystem autonomy as a key feature that distinguishes one type of government from another.[20]

Every modern society contains many institutions and organizations that can be thought of as subsystems of society. Religious denominations, colleges, labor unions, industrial corporations, civic associations, political parties, and the mass media are all subsystems of a modern industrial society such as the United States or Great Britain. We can classify governments according to how

[20] Robert A. Dahl, *Modern Political Analysis* (Englewood Cliffs, N.J.: Prentice-Hall, 1963), pp. 35–37. See also Gabriel A. Almond and G. Bingham Powell, Jr., *Comparative Politics: A Developmental Approach* (Boston: Little, Brown, 1966), pp. 257–71; and S. V. Monsma, *American Politics: A Systems Approach*, 2nd ed. (Hinsdale, Ill.: Dryden Press, 1973).

Figure 3-1
Aristotle's System
for Classifying
Governments

WHO GOVERNS	LEGITIMATE FORMS In the Interest of All	PERVERSIONS In the Interest of the Rulers
One man	Kingship	Tyranny
A few men	Aristocracy	Oligarchy
The majority	Polity	Democracy

much autonomy they allow these subsystems. In other words, are churches, unions, and colleges free to run their own internal affairs without interference from government?

Totalitarian governments, such as Nazi Germany, permit little or no subsystem autonomy. As Carl J. Friedrich and Zbigniew Brzezinski have pointed out, such societies have official and dogmatic ideologies that all social institutions must adhere to.[21] Thus, in the late 1930s, German churches had to reflect Nazi racial theories by trying to prove that Jesus Christ was a blondhaired, blue-eyed Aryan instead of a dark-haired, dark-eyed Jew.

Democratic or constitutional governments, on the other hand, give a relatively high degree of independence to subsystems. While there are limits established for the conduct of any private association, a constitutional state will allow as much autonomy as is consistent with the general well-being of the society. Thus, labor unions can strike without fear of government reprisal in the United States, except when the nation's security is affected. No subsystem has absolute freedom, but most are allowed to run their own affairs unless they threaten the public interest.

Centralization of Political Power within the State. Governments differ not only in the degree of initiative they allow subsystems but also in the way political power is distributed among its different levels. Nations can be classified as unitary states, federal states, or confederations, depending on the way they distribute governmental authority.[22]

Great Britain, France, Italy, Israel, and the vast majority of the world's 143 nations are unitary states. A single national or central government exercises supreme power over all areas of society and can override the decisions of local governments. Thus, the ministries in London or Paris can order Lincolnshire or Bordeaux to impose laws or programs in their localities. Such actions are unlikely in the world's twenty-one federal states. In federal nations such as the United States, West Germany, Australia, and Canada, power is

[21] Carl J. Friedrich and Zbigniew Brzezinski, *Totalitarian Dictatorship and Autocracy* (Cambridge, Mass.: Harvard University Press, 1965), p. 9. See also our discussion in Chapter 5.
[22] See Chapter 17 for a more complete treatment of federal and unitary systems of government.

divided between the national governments and the state or provincial governments. Usually, national governments control foreign affairs, military defense,
and currency, while local authorities handle education, welfare, and policing.
This division of authority is also generally found in confederations. But the
central governments in these nations have much less authority than in federal
states, and the state governments often can veto actions of the national legislatures. Switzerland is one of the few confederations in existence today.

Primitive, Traditional, and Modern Systems.   While the classification
of governments according to the division of central and local powers may be
useful in understanding the differences between the political systems of the
United States and Great Britain, such a typology gives us little insight in
comparing highly industrialized South Africa with Togo, an agricultural
African nation which gained independence in 1960. Political scientists Gabriel
Almond and G. Bingham Powell developed a classification scheme that types
nations according to their degree of economic and political development (see
Table 3-1).[23] According to their model, primitive governments would include
preindustrial societies such as the Nambikuara Indians of Brazil or the
Eskimos of the Arctic. Both groups are led by chiefs or headmen who possess
no special political authority, but are chosen as a result of their skill at hunting or food gathering.

All governments in existence prior to the seventeenth century were traditional. They clearly separated political from nonpolitical institutions, but
lacked political parties and interest groups. The machinery of government
revolved around the head of state, and there was little formal distinction
between the state (or the nation) and the government. Some African countries still follow the traditional form of government.[24]

Modern systems of government are present in all developed nations today,
and in many developing nations. They are characterized by well-defined political institutions, such as political parties, civic associations, and trade union
and business lobbying groups. Modern systems also have highly elaborate
bureaucracies which do not depend on current political leadership for their
effectiveness. For example, during the tumultuous Fourth Republic in France
(1945–1958), many coalitions gained and then lost control of the government.
While this was happening, the bureaucracy in effect ran the state.[25]

It is often the responsibility of administrative agencies to develop government programs that reflect public-policy choices. Occasionally, this can bring
the bureaucracy into conflict with the elected political leadership. In the

---

[23] Almond and Powell, *Comparative Politics*. We are presenting only a very simplified
sketch of their major criteria. An examination of Table 3-1 will reveal that modern systems
are further subdivided according to the criterion of subsystem autonomy discussed above,
and that each major category of primitive, traditional, and modern systems contains several gradations.
[24] See Daniel Lerner, *The Passing of Traditional Societies: Modernizing the Middle East*
(New York: The Free Press, 1958).
[25] See Philip M. Williams, *Crisis and Compromise: Politics in the Fourth Republic*
(Garden City, N.Y.: Doubleday, 1966).

Table 3-1
**Classifying
Political Systems
According to
Degree of
Modernization**

I. Primitive Systems: Intermittent Political Structures
    A. Primitive Bands (*Bergdama*)
    B. Segmentary Systems (*Nuer*)
    C. Pyramidal Systems (*Ashanti*)

II. Traditional Systems: Differentiated Governmental Political Structures
    A. Patrimonial Systems (*Ouagadougou*)
    B. Centralized Bureaucratic (*Inca, Tudor England, Ethiopia*)
    C. Feudal Political Systems (*Twelfth-century France*)

III. Modern Systems: Differentiated Political Infrastructures
    A. Secularized City-States: Limited Differentiation (*Athens*)
    B. Mobilized Modern Systems: High Differentiation and Secularization
        1. Democratic Systems: Subsystem Autonomy and Participant Culture
            a. High Subsystem Autonomy (*Britain*)
            b. Limited Subsystem Autonomy (*Fourth Republic France*)
            c. Low Subsystem Autonomy (*Mexico*)
        2. Authoritarian Systems: Subsystem Control and Subject-Participant Culture
            a. Radical Totalitarian (*USSR*)
            b. Conservative Totalitarian (*Nazi Germany*)
            c. Conservative Authoritarian (*Spain*)
            d. Modernizing Authoritarian (*Brazil*)
    C. Premobilized Modern Systems: Limited Differentiation and Secularization
        1. Premobilized Authoritarian (*Ghana*)
        2. Premobilized Democratic (*Nigeria prior to January 1966*)

Source: Gabriel A. Almond and G. Bingham Powell, Jr. Comparative Politics: A Developmental Approach (Boston: Little, Brown, 1966), p. 217.

winter of 1970–1971, for example, there was an exodus of young lawyers from the Civil Rights Division of the Justice Department. Those who resigned were protesting what they felt to be a change in policy to provide less legal support to minority groups seeking to establish themselves as first-class citizens by working through the courts. Such tensions between politicians and bureaucrats occur in most modern governments.

Modern Government: Making Public Policy

All modern governments are involved in the complex business of making public policy. Public policies, the authoritative actions (not proposals or debates) of government officials and agencies, are created in order to meet perceived national needs. Policies include legislation, judicial edicts, executive decrees, and administrative decisions.[26] Thus, when the United States was suffering from serious inflation in 1972, President Nixon adopted a government freeze on wages and prices as one part of an economic policy to restore stability. Policies are implemented through programs, which are specific measures aimed at influencing the direction of government activity and public life. The creation of the Peace Corps under President Kennedy was one program in a policy effort to improve living conditions in underdeveloped countries.

Government adopts policies and programs consistent with the broad goals of the nation.[27] Since resources are always limited, a priority of values must be established. For example, is it more important for the United States to send a man to the moon or to rebuild the ghettos of our cities? [28] Should we use public funds to clean up polluted rivers or to put additional police officers on our streets? Decision makers must face this kind of choice in formulating public policy.

The determination of national priorities is a complex decision which is a crucial part of the political process.[29] In societies such as the United States, many groups lobby for policies that suit their own economic or ideological interests. The automobile industry works for increased spending for highways, and "Right-to-Life" groups pressure legislators into a strong stand against legalized abortions. Ultimately, the legislature and the executive must decide in the name of the people which policies the nation will pursue. If they bankroll the space program rather than public housing, they have in effect made a statement of national priorities. In this sense, the creation of public policies usually involves a public choice between competing values and needs.[30] In the early years of the Johnson Administration, the president faced a choice between spending government funds on "guns" (for the Vietnam War) or "butter" (the "Great Society" social welfare efforts, including the antipoverty program and Model Cities). Costs of the war had escalated so rapidly that he could no longer finance both "guns" and "butter," as he had previously hoped; "guns" received priority.[31]

When public policies involve a choice, they are often controversial, and

[26] Donald Allensworth, *The U.S. Government in Action: Essentials* (Pacific Palisades, California: Goodyear, 1972).

[27] At least in theory; Theodore Lowi, however, argues that the policies and programs of government in practice more often than not have little to do with any long-term visions of national goals. Instead, they tend to be rather short-sighted, stop-gap measures. See *The End of Liberalism: Ideology, Policy and the Crisis of Public Authority* (New York: W. W. Norton, 1969).

[28] For a discussion of America's national goals and priorities, see David Broder, *The Party's Over* (New York: Harper & Row, 1972), pp. 128–32.

[29] See the discussion in Joyce M. Mitchell and William C. Mitchell, *Political Analysis and Public Policy: An Introduction to Political Science* (Chicago: Rand McNally, 1969), Chapter 1. Also, Charles L. Schultz, et al., *Setting National Priorities* (Washington, D.C.: Brookings Institution, 1971).

[30] Mitchell and Mitchell, *Political Analysis and Public Policy*, Chapter 9.

[31] For an analysis of public choice and the costs of war, see Bruce Russett, "Who Pays for Defense?" *American Political Science Review* 63 (June 1969), 412–26.

must be defended as being in the "public interest." In theory, the public interest is defined as the benefit of everyone as opposed to one specific group of people. But in practice, this term is impossible to define, and usually ends up being loosely invoked in public-policy debates by all sides in an attempt to gain support for rather one-sided interpretations of the "public interest." [32]

Public Policies: Material and Symbolic

Modern governments adopt and pursue many kinds of public policies to protect what they define as the public interest. These policies can range from extensive preparations for national defense to efforts to end racial, ethnic, and sexual discrimination in public and private agencies. All policies, however, fall into two major categories: those that are material in nature, and those that are symbolic.

Material public-policy decisions require the expenditure of public funds— a scarce national resource in every country.[33] No government can spend much more money that its tax revenues yield without risking popular discontent and economic problems. Thus, the national budget can be seen as a pie that must be divided among many hungry guests: there is only a limited amount to be distributed.

Once a national policy has been decided upon, and a concrete legislative program has been enacted, machinery must be created to see that resources are properly distributed. For example, if Congress adopts a measure to defray hospital costs for the indigent, a government agency must determine who is eligible for such benefits. For a policy to be effective, adequate resources (both money and personnel) must be allocated to deal with the problem. If they are not, the program may disappoint the intended beneficiaries and accomplish little.

Unlike material policies, symbolic public policies usually do not involve the allocation of money or personnel, and often are not a part of the legislative process. By symbolic or nonmaterial public policies is meant those acts of government that create sentimental attachments (patriotism, loyalty, deference, or national pride) or that confer social status on key segments of society. The proclamation of a new public holiday, for example, is a symbolic policy.

As Murray Edelman points out in *The Symbolic Uses of Politics*, symbolic policies can be more important than actual government performance and results, for what often matters is what people think, more than what the government really does.[34] Because of this, all governments are careful to sup-

---

[32] See Charles E. Jacob, *Policy and Bureaucracy* (Princeton, N.J.: Van Nostrand, 1966), Chapter 4.
[33] See Mitchell and Mitchell, *Political Analysis and Public Policy*, Chapter 3.
[34] Murray Edelman, *The Symbolic Uses of Politics* (Urbana, Ill.: University of Illinois Press, 1964), Chapter 1.

port and foster outward symbols of national unity. Institutional symbols are created and popularized to give people something they can identify with. Thus, when an American thinks of the United States, he may get an image of the Statue of Liberty, "Old Glory," or the Liberty Bell. Occasionally, such symbols can become a source of controversy: in Canada a bitter debate over a proposal for a new national flag contributed to the defeat of John Diefenbaker's Conservative Party in 1963.

Moral symbols are often invoked by public officials to build a climate supportive of the institutions in which they serve. Thus, in America, all candidates for public office are careful to be photographed in church often, regardless of their true religious feelings. This is because religious worship has become a powerful moral symbol linked with national pride and stability. Few high public officials are seen smoking cigarettes in public, or relaxing with a glass of scotch; and for many years it was taboo for any elected officer to obtain a divorce. In some cases, legislation does play a role in symbolic politics by suggesting the onset of a different moral climate. Much of the civil rights legislation of the early 1960s had little immediate impact on the lives of American blacks, but it did signal a national commitment to equal justice that was felt throughout the country.[35]

Strategies for Influencing Public Policy

In the 1960s, American blacks were successful in persuading the government to pass legislation that would prohibit racial discrimination and help poor people to receive training for decent jobs. During the same decade, British lobbyists succeeded in persuading Parliament to support a liberal abortion law.[36] How do groups influence government decision makers to adopt material and symbolic policies in their own interests? If public employees want a shorter work week, or oil companies wish to protect the oil depletion allowance, what methods will they use to try to gain their ends? There are at least five distinct strategies for influencing government action: they include bargaining, cooperation, coalition formation, political conflict, and command.[37]

Bargaining. Often individuals or groups that wish to influence public policy find that they cannot do so without the support of others. In such a situation, one group may try to bargain with other political groups in an attempt to create a mutually profitable exchange of favors or support. For example,

[35] See Thomas R. Dye and L. Harmon Ziegler, *The Irony of Democracy: An Uncommon Introduction to American Politics* (Belmont, Calif.: Wadsworth, 1972), Chapter 12. See also our Chapter 19.
[36] See the account in Chapter 10.
[37] We have relied on the discussion in Mitchell and Mitchell, *Political Analysis and Public Policy*, Chapter 10.

lobbyists for the Roman Catholic church might endorse the sale of arms to Israel in exchange for Jewish support for federal aid to parochial schools. Or a congressman from Montana who wants a new federal highway project in his district might make a deal with a congressman from South Carolina who is fighting to keep a defense installation in Charleston from being closed.[38]

Any *quid pro quo* arrangement in politics is arrived at through the bargaining process. The essence of a good bargaining position is to have something (perhaps votes, or connections to key political leaders) that is desired by another group or individual; this can then be traded for something that one's group or oneself needs. Bargaining can be an uneasy process, because the partners often do not trust each other. Some secrecy is usually implicit in the bargaining process, since each dealer may worry that his supporters will learn of the deal and decide that too much was "given away," or else that outsiders will learn of the bargain, and both parties will be discredited.

Cooperation. In the relatively rare situation in which all participants can gain by pursuing a common policy or agreeing to a particular decision, cooperation is the most likely strategy. Thus, if a bill comes up that proposes to increase the staff of all ministers of Parliament, and the public is either supportive of the idea or indifferent, then all MPs will profit by cooperating to pass the legislation.

As a rule, cooperation is a practical strategy only in issues of importance when the public is universally favorable, such as increases in Social Security benefits or pensions for servicemen. There must be no threat to the position of any of the political factions, or else cooperation will be unlikely. Nevertheless, cooperation is not always motivated by altruism. By joining in well-publicized gestures for the public good, an interest group may be able to win popular support and more easily achieve its goals later on. The American Medical Association (AMA) might campaign with other other groups for higher benefits for the aged under Medicare programs, and then use the good will that it builds up in order to work against community control of city hospitals.

Coalition Formation. Groups cannot always advance their long-term interests through strategies of cooperation or bargaining on individual issues. Indeed, in most cases, a coalition is the most effective tactic for influencing public policy.[39] In a coalition, two or more persons or organizations share

---

[38] When officials bargain in this way over public projects, it is usually known as *logrolling*. Each has an issue of particular concern and will bargain for support on that issue by offering to back the other's pet project.

[39] We have relied upon Mitchell, *Public Choice in America*, pp. 223–30, 383. The "landmark work" on political coalitions is William H. Riker's *The Theory of Political Coalitions* (New Haven, Conn.: Yale University Press, 1962).

a complementary goal (although they may be at odds on most other issues) and join forces to achieve this goal. Coalitions can involve either interest groups or government officials or departments: any political official or group can be part of a coalition. Republicans and southern Democrats in Congress formed a famous and successful conservative coalition in the early 1960s to block much of the social welfare legislation of the Kennedy Administration. Presidents and prime ministers attempt to build coalitions when they ask for support for administration programs. In order to gain Parliament's approval for Britain's entry into the European Common Market in 1972, Conservative Prime Minister Edward Heath enlisted the support of an effective coalition of several interests in Parliament—some of whom came from the Labourite camp.

Partners in coalitions must be willing to share their gains with their allies and to pay out high bargaining costs. The process is more difficult than trading support on one particular issue, because constant compromises must be made to maintain trust between the partners. In 1972, conservatives within the Republican Party were hesitant to support President Nixon's trip to China and his use of government wage and price controls. They hinted that if he expected them to remain in his "winning coalition" in the 1972 presidential election, he would do well to keep conservative Vice President Spiro Agnew on the Republican ticket.

Coalitions are often formed of "strange bedfellows." Groups that may in other ways be antagonistic may unite on a common and specific goal. In 1967 conservative economist Milton Friedman and pacifist spokesman Sanford Gottlieb worked together to create a Council for a Volunteer Military. At a press conference, Gottlieb observed: "I've never appeared on the same platform with a Goldwater man. . . . This is a unique issue with us. It's the one thing we agree on." [40]

At one point during the years of Johnson's Administration, the issue of when and how to join coalitions became explosive due to an incident involving the black civil rights movement of the sixties. Young blacks became furious when the 1964 Democratic National Convention failed to oust the regular, predominantly white, Mississippi delegation and seat in its place the black-dominated Freedom Democratic Party. Stokely Carmichael and Charles V. Hamilton became convinced that blacks could no longer depend on the coalition of white liberals, union leaders, and established black groups like the NAACP which had carried the civil rights movement since the fifties. In their book, *Black Power: The Politics of Liberation*, they argued that blacks had to organize a secure power base of their own, through direct control of the economic, social, and political institutions in the black community.[41] Only when the civil rights coalition depended on black power instead of the

[40] Neil Sheehan, "Draft Is Uniting Right with Left," *The New York Times*, May 21, 1967, p. 1; quoted in Mitchell, *Public Choice*, p. 225.
[41] Stokely Carmichael and Charles V. Hamilton, *Black Power: The Politics of Liberation* (New York: Vintage Books, 1967).

temporary "good will" of white liberals would the coalition be effective, since the white liberals did not have the same basic goals at heart as did the black partners in the movement.

Political Conflict. Bargaining, cooperation, and coalition building may be effective tactics for influencing public-policy outcomes in some cases, but they will not be successful if the goals of political individuals or groups are at odds. Conflict involves political activities where two or more groups seek the same object, and the success of one group excludes the success of the other. It may be nonviolent or violent, institutionalized or noninstitutionalized, depending on the degree of force brought into play and the extent to which the political system provides regular channels for conflict.[42]

Any political system provides institutionalized channels for some political conflict. In the United States Congress, the committee system is an accepted arena for conflict. Its system of hearings, investigations, and decision making allows Defense Department groups to compete for increased funds within an organized system rather than confronting each other in the streets; it allows industrial interests and antipollution groups to confront one another without sabotaging factories or picketing offices.

Another institutionalized channel for conflict is the competition for political office through elections and the party system. Candidates of the same party will run against one another for the right to represent the party in public office, and will try to shape the party's attitude on the issues of the day. Thus, in 1972, Senator Henry Jackson sought the Democratic presidential nomination on a platform of extensive defense spending, while George McGovern built his quest for the nomination, in part, on a pledge to decrease defense spending. Since they stood for different policies while competing for the same goal, they were in direct conflict; yet the Democratic party primary system allowed for a peaceful resolution of this conflict.

Political coalitions often compete against each other just as candidates do. Throughout the 1960s, a coalition of unions, minority groups, and liberal politicians attempted to pass civil rights and social welfare legislation in Congress, including programs to establish medical care for the aged, to further guarantee voting rights for southern blacks, and to combat urban and rural poverty. They were opposed by a coalition of congressional Republicans, southern Democrats, and conservative interest groups such as the American Medical Association and the Americans for Constitutional Action.

Groups cannot always achieve vital goals through bargaining, cooperation, or institutionalized channels of conflict. The political system does not provide a regular framework for conflicts on the level of armed rebellion, or even

---

[42] Gabriel A. Almond and James S. Coleman distinguish between two types of political conflict: patterned and nonpatterned. Patterned conflict follows regular institutionalized channels; nonpatterned conflict involves regularly apolitical anomic groups, such as lynch mobs and ghetto rioters, who sporadically disrupt the political system. See *Politics of the Developing Areas*, Chapter 1.

for labor disputes where the demands of employees and management are in direct opposition. In these cases, political conflict must follow irregular patterns. Noninstitutionalized conflict includes labor strikes, wars, and rebellions, but it does not have to involve violence.

The most extreme conflict situation is war.[43] In 1860 and 1861 the southern states seceded from the Union, and President Lincoln chose to go to war in order to keep the nation intact. The Algerians rebelled against the French in 1958 after realizing that France would never grant them independence without a military struggle, and similarly, Bangla Desh rebelled against West Pakistan in 1971. Usually, the appeal to arms is a last resort when all else has failed. Another type of noninstitutionalized conflict, which may not involve violence at all, is the strategy of "confrontation politics."

Confrontation Politics. [44] In certain conflict situations, a nonviolent but forceful tactic known as confrontation is used. Confrontation politics was largely formulated by Mahatma Gandhi in India, and was popularized in America by Martin Luther King. Confrontation politics in the last decade in the United States has included nonviolent occupation of territory, such as "sit-ins" at segregated lunch counters in the South in the early 1960s, and takeovers of college buildings by radical students later in the decade.

Part of the theory behind confrontation politics is that the orderly conduct of demonstrators is likely to gain support for their well-publicized activities. In addition, the fact that the enemies of the protesters often react to the demonstration with violence helps to gain publicity and sympathy for the demonstrators. Thus, when Columbia University students took over a few college buildings in the spring of 1968 to protest an unpopular construction project and defense research on the campus, the University's administration called on the police to expel the students. This led to a brutal scene with many injuries which turned campus sentiment strongly against the administrators.

The symbolic element is a strong part of confrontation politics. At the height of the Vietnam War, some Catholic radicals, including priests and nuns, invaded draft board offices and poured blood over Selective Service records as a vivid protest against the violence of American bombings. Their expectation was not to paralyze the draft system, but rather to awaken the conscience of the nation. Similarly, American Indians took over the town of Wounded Knee, South Dakota, in early 1973 to remind Americans of the slaughter of Indians that had taken place there in 1890—an event which they saw as symbolic of Indian mistreatment at the hands of the federal government. Often such protests have the aim of shocking the public into thinking about the moral issues raised; sometimes they backfire and lead to increased antagonism toward protesters.

[43] See also Chapter 20 of this book for a discussion of the causes and symptoms of political violence.
[44] See also Chapter 10's discussion of interest group tactics.

Command. Confrontation politics is often used by groups with little or no control over governmental institutions. It is a useful tactic for gaining publicity and sympathy without having an established financial or power base. More powerful individuals and groups can sometimes command certain policy results.[45] In a command situation, one person makes a decision and others must obey. Thus, the president could unilaterally order increased bombing of Vietnam. And the Politburo of the Communist party of the USSR, headed by General Secretary Leonid Brezhnev, could order a change in the activities of any local Communist party organization.

The command model is derived from the military and depends on a strict hierarchy of authority, where one person has the power to order another to do something. Occasionally, it is used in civilian institutions in the same way. Under J. Edgar Hoover, the Federal Bureau of Investigation (FBI) was run as a command organization. Men in the field had little control over agency policy, which was decided by Hoover. Thus, when he chose to concentrate the bureau's energy on surveillance of political activists rather than protecting the rights of black voters in the South, he had commanded a national priority.

Most groups that wish to influence public policy have no chance of directly commanding a particular result. They may be able to bargain or cooperate with those in power, or even enter a coalition that wins governmental authority (perhaps through a political party). But generally, it is the very powerful who command, while the majority of political actors must follow strategies of bargaining, cooperation, coalition building, and institutionalized or noninstitutionalized conflict.

Summary

The modern concept of the nation-state has evolved over the last four centuries. Each nation consists of a people, headed by an organized political structure, which maintains autonomous control over a specific geographic territory. The nation preserves itself by promoting the faith and trust of the people in its system of government. Feelings of nationalism include a sense of national identity and pride, which stems from a feeling for the homeland, or a common history, language, and culture. Government organizes society politically and preserves order within the modern nation-state.

Government creates rules, known as laws, which all citizens must obey. It is the highest authority within a society, yet in order to maintain its legitimacy it must have the support of the people. The goals of independence, stability, and the economic and social well-being of the majority of the citizens are common ends of all governments—although these ends may be

[45] See Robert A. Dahl and Charles E. Lindblom, *Politics, Economics, and Welfare* (New York: Harper & Brothers, 1953), Chapters 8–9.

approached in a myriad of different methods. Because there are many different kinds of government, social scientists have devised numerous classification
systems in order to better understand how man directs his society. The most
famous method of classification was created by the Greek philosopher Aristotle. Other schemes created since then include classifications according to
the degree of autonomy given to subsystems or groups such as churches or
political clubs, the degree of centralization of political power in government,
and the degree of modernization of the social and political system.

The authoritative actions of modern governments are public policies and
programs. Public policies may be either material or symbolic in nature. They
can involve the collection and allocation of resources or of services, or the
allocation of symbolic values (as when the mayor of a small town indicates
his respect for "public decency" by advocating the censure of an X-rated
film). Government decision making involves a choice between competing
priorities. Political actors or interest groups all try to influence the choices
of government decision makers. The most common strategies for influencing
public policy are bargaining, cooperation, coalition formation, political conflict and confrontation, and command.

Suggested Readings

Almond, Gabriel A., and Coleman, James S. *Politics of the Developing Areas.*
Princeton, N.J.: Princeton University Press, 1960. A systematic, comparative treatment of the developing nations that uses the structural-functional approach. The
first section provides an especially interesting discussion of the development of a
structural-functional framework.

Banks, Arthur S., and Textor, Robert B. *A Cross-Polity Survey.* Cambridge, Mass.:
M.I.T. Press, 1963. A compendium of data and analysis for cross-national survey
work.

Dahl, Robert A., and Lindblom, Charles E. *Politics, Economics, and Welfare.*
New York: Harper & Row, 1953. A classic look at incrementalism and policy
making.

Easton, David. *A Systems Analysis of Political Life.* New York: John Wiley &
Sons, 1965. The systems approach comprehensively applied to the study of nations.

Kohn, Hans. *Nationalism: Its Meaning and History.* New York: Crowell-Collier
and Macmillan, 1955. A thorough examination of the historical development of
the modern nation-state.

Lerner, Daniel. *The Passing of Traditional Societies: Modernizing the Middle
East.* New York: The Free Press, 1958. A classic study of change and its impact
in modernizing nations.

Lipset, Seymour Martin. *The First New Nation: The United States in Historical
and Comparative Perspective.* Garden City, N.Y.: Doubleday, 1967. An examination
of the United States as the first new nation with a revolutionary birth, and the

problems, both similar and dissimilar, of the emerging nation-states of the twentieth century.

Mitchell, Joyce M. and William C. *Political Analysis and Public Policy: An Introduction to Political Science.* Chicago, Ill.: Rand McNally, 1969. A political economy approach to comparative analysis.

Pye, Lucian W. *Aspects of Political Development.* Boston: Little, Brown, 1966. The developmental approach used in the study of non-Western nations.

Rabushka, Alvin, and Shepsle, Kenneth A. *Politics in Plural Societies: A Theory of Democratic Instability.* Columbus, Ohio: Charles E. Merrill, 1972. A pessimistic but, perhaps, realistic view of the possibility of democratic government surviving in pluralistic societies.

TWO

Political Power: Who Holds It?

The individual
and the constitution
CHAPTER 4

The problem of establishing and limiting power exists in every political system. Government and the people both must have certain powers and rights, but their activities must also be limited in order to keep them from encroaching on the rights of others. The choices involved in determining a "fair" balance between government powers and civil liberties, between the welfare of the majority and the rights of the minority, are not easy ones. For example, if bus drivers in Rome want higher wages, do they have the right to call a work stoppage and inconvenience millions of people until their employer offers them a satisfactory raise? If the president of the United States finds that he hasn't been able to complete all the programs he had hoped to initiate during his second term of office, should he be given the power to postpone elections until he has done all he wanted? If a religious sect such as the Amish believe that their children should stop attending school after the eighth grade, do they have the right to take their children out of school even though most state laws require that all children attend school through the twelfth grade?

Each of these questions raises problems of rights and political power— and some of these problems are admittedly more difficult than others. Few of us would agree that the president of the United States should have the power to extend his term of office beyond the constitutionally fixed end of his second term, no matter how praiseworthy the programs he wants to initiate are. There is probably more disagreement, though, on the right of Roman bus drivers to strike. It can be argued that the drivers should not be denied the right to ask for decent wages simply because they perform a public service. Yet, a case can also be made that no one, including under-paid bus drivers, has the right to deny the people such an important public service. Many individuals depend on the buses for their livelihood, and the stoppage of bus service would inconvenience millions. The question of whether the Amish have the right as a minority to bypass the law of the

Drawing by D. Fradon;
© 1971 The New Yorker
Magazine, Inc.

majority is also a difficult one.[1] On the one hand, the Amish have religious reasons for keeping their children out of high school; to deny them this would be to deny them the right to practice their religion. Some might argue that such a denial would be the "tyranny of the majority" which de Tocqueville expressed fear of in his *Democracy in America*, written in the 1830s. But, on the other hand, most state laws require that all children attend school through the completion of the twelfth grade. Are the Amish denying their children a fundamental right to equal education by keeping them out of school? Are they setting a dangerous precedent for neglect of the needs of minors?

How does society determine how to limit political power and how to balance in the most equitable fashion the needs of the majority with the rights of individuals and minorities? While decisions about who is right and who is wrong in specific cases such as those mentioned above must always be made by the decision makers in office at a particular time, it is evident that governments need some guidelines in determining where this balance should fall. These guidelines are provided by traditions, by statutes, and by national constitutions which lay down the basic groundrules for governing society.[2]

Constitutions in the Modern World

In common usage, we think of a constitution as a written document which sets forth the fundamental rules by which a society is governed. Political scientists, though, define the word more broadly: a constitution is that set of rules and customs, either written or unwritten, legally established or extralegal, by which a government conducts its affairs.[3] By this definition, all nations have constitutions, since each nation operates according to some set of rules. England has no written constitution, but custom, law, precedent, and tradition are so strong that the British government considers itself bound by practices which have developed over the centuries. Thus, England is governed by a constitution.

In the modern world, nearly every nation has a written constitution which establishes the forms, institutions, and limits of government and sets guidelines for balancing minority and majority interests. The Constitution of the

---

[1] The Wisconsin State Supreme Court acted on this question in 1971, deciding that the Amish did have the right to bypass mandatory attendance laws, and the United States Supreme Court upheld the Wisconsin Supreme Court's decision in *Wisconsin* v. *Yoder*, decided in 1972.

[2] See Charles H. McIlwain, *Constitutionalism Ancient and Modern* (Ithaca, N.Y.: Cornell University Press, 1940); William G. Andrews, *Constitutions and Constitutionalism* (Princeton, N.J.: Van Nostrand, 1961); and Herbert J. Spiro, *Government by Constitution* (New York: Random House, 1959).

[3] See Francis D. Wormuth, *The Origins of Modern Constitutionalism* (New York: Harper & Brothers, 1949), p. 3.

United States is very short: it is limited to seven articles, most of which have to do with establishing the powers of each branch of government, and twenty-six amendments. In contrast, most of the nations that have won independence since World War II have adopted constitutions of remarkable detail.[4] The postwar Japanese Constitution, for instance, contains no less than forty separate articles outlining the rights and duties of the people alone. Among the individual rights enumerated in the Japanese Constitution are the rights to productive employment, a decent standard of living, and social welfare benefits—a sharp contrast to the general values of "justice, domestic tranquility, common defense, general welfare, and liberty" outlined in the American preamble. Article 1 of the German Constitution (the Basic Law) also enumerates a long list of rights. These include not only fundamental rights, like legal and political freedoms, but also a number of social and economic safeguards, including state supervision of the educational system and public control of the economy.

If an established nation such as England is able to get by with no written constitution per se, and another like the United States manages to function with a very general constitution, why has almost every recently established nation (with the exception of Israel) found it necessary to commit itself to not only a written constitution, but a very detailed constitution at that?

The Highest Law of the Land

Most modern nations adopt written constitutions for the same reason that the ancient Mesopotamian lawgiver, Hammurabi, codified the laws of Babylon: to establish a supreme law of the land. Constitutions are the fundamental laws of society, and are not meant to be easily revised. They stand as the yardstick by which any activities of the government or the people are to be measured.[5] A legislature can pass a law one year and repeal it the next, but basic constitutional provisions cannot be amended so easily.[6] In Sweden, constitutional amendments must be passed by two successive legislatures, with a general election in between. In the United States, amending the Constitution is even more difficult. The most common procedure is to secure the approval of two-thirds of both the Senate and the House of Representatives, then obtain ratification by three-fourths of the state legislatures. The fact that our Constitution has been amended only sixteen times since the adoption of the Bill of Rights in 1791 illustrates how difficult the amendment procedure is.

[4] The best compilation of world constitutions is Amos J. Peaslee, ed., *Constitutions of Nations*, 3 vols. (The Hague: Martinus Nijhoff, 1956).
[5] K. C. Wheare, *Modern Constitutions*, 4th ed. (New York: Oxford University Press, 1964), Chapter 6.
[6] England is a notable exception. Parliamentary procedures can be changed by a simple legislative majority and the monarch's approval. The fact that they never have been changed without prolonged debate can be used to argue the point that truly constitutional rules need not be committed to writing. See Spiro, *Government by Constitution*, p. 390.

The General Nature of Constitutional Law. Since constitutions, no matter how detailed, cannot provide specifically for every legal or administrative problem that may arise, they must be fairly general in nature. The United States Constitution says that "Congress shall make no law respecting an establishment of religion, or prohibiting the free exercise thereof" in Amendment I of the Bill of Rights. This is a very general statement. The way it will be interpreted in a specific case (such as the Amish who wanted to withdraw their children from high school, or perhaps a Satan cult that believes that animal sacrifice or illegal drugs are necessary for the practice of their religion) must depend on the decision makers in power at the time the case arises.

Constitutional law must be interpreted in order to be applied to specific incidents. Who is given the immense authority to decide what the general wording of a constitution means? In some thirty nations, including the United States, this responsibility belongs to the highest national court. The procedure by which the court rules on the constitutionality of a governmental act and declares null and void those acts it considers unconstitutional, is known as judicial review.[7] The power of judicial review is a controversial one. Many critics have accused the United States Supreme Court (most notably when Earl Warren was chief justice from 1953 to 1969) of imposing a personal philosophy as the law of the land. To a large extent, the constitution is indeed what its interpreters say it is, but the possibility of too subjective an interpretation seems to be a necessary risk taken by any nation that has a constitution.[8]

The courts do not always interpret the constitution in a consistent fashion. In the United States, the Warren Court best exemplified the type of judicial philosophy generally known as "loose constructionist" or "judicial activist." It broadly interpreted constitutional guarantees in favor of citizens' rights and nullified many laws and governmental practices which infringed even slightly upon those safeguards. The opposite of loose constructionist is "strict constructionist" or "judicial quietist"—a generalization which describes a Supreme Court that sees its job not as legislating but as following the lead

---

[7] Actually, the United States Constitution does not specifically give the Supreme Court the authority to rule acts of Congress unconstitutional. The precedent was set in 1803, when the Supreme Court under Chief Justice John Marshall declared a section of the 1789 Judiciary Act to be unconstitutional in the case of *Marbury* v. *Madison.* Thomas Jefferson, Andrew Jackson, and Abraham Lincoln all expressed the view that the Supreme Court was not the sole or final arbiter of constitutionality. However, it has been commonly recognized as such since the Civil War. See David Deener, "Judicial Review in Modern Constitutional Systems," *American Political Science Review* 46 (December 1952): 1079–99; also William H. Riker, *Democracy in the United States* (New York: Macmillan, 1965).

[8] Robert A. Dahl, "Decision Making in a Democracy: The Role of the Supreme Court as a National Policy Maker," *Journal of Public Law* 6 (1957): 279–95. For other discussions, see Martin Shapiro, ed., *The Supreme Court and Constitutional Rights* (Glenview, Ill.: Scott Foresman, 1967); and George W. Spicer, *The Supreme Court and Fundamental Freedoms,* 2nd ed. (New York: Appleton-Century-Crofts, 1967).

of Congress.[9] The late Justice Felix Frankfurter, who counselled the Court on judicial restraint, was regarded by many as a "strict constructionist."

Not all nations give their highest court the power to rule on the constitutionality of laws. In nations that do not have a clearly established procedure of judicial review, this responsibility is often given to the legislature. In Great Britain, it is Parliament itself which makes the final determination of what is constitutional.

Constitutions and Constitutional Government. The meaning of a constitution depends largely on the way in which it is interpreted. Indeed, two separate nations could conceivably adopt the same constitution (with a few variations in wording or language), but have entirely different forms of government and allow their citizens very different rights. What is written in the constitution does not necessarily represent what occurs in practice. The Constitution of the Soviet Union sets a framework for that nation's government—a federal system with a bicameral legislature, with executive and administrative powers given to the cabinetlike Council of Ministers—and accords to its citizens a long list of democratic rights. Yet in actuality, the government is controlled by the Communist party, with little authority given to the states or to the legislature, and the rights of people are totally dependent on the interpretation of the leaders in power.

The governments of Canada, Great Britain, and the United States are constitutional governments; the government of the Soviet Union is not. Constitutionalism refers to the degree to which the power of government is limited and individual rights are respected. In a constitutionally governed nation (whether it has a written constitution or not), government is limited by internal institutions in such a way that the fundamental rights of citizens—such as freedom of speech, the right to practice one's religion, and freedom from arbitrary imprisonment—are safeguarded from violation by either government or hostile minorities. In contrast, a totalitarian government is not limited by the guidelines of the constitution. In a totalitarian government, the individual citizen and minority groups are assured no protection against arbitrary acts of government, in spite of what the constitution may say.[10]

The Purpose of a Constitution

If many nations seem to pay no heed to what is written in their constitutions, why do some nations bother to write a constitution at all? Constitutions fulfill a variety of roles: they provide the symbolic function of

---

[9] The terms *strict* and *loose constructionist* or *judicial activist* and *quietist* are only generalizations, to which there are many exceptions. See the article by Anthony Lewis, "The Same Judge Can Be Both a 'Strict' and a 'Loose' Constructionist," *New York Times Magazine*, May 24, 1970.

[10] See Andrews, *Constitutions and Constitutionalism.*

putting in writing a statement of national ideals; they formalize the structure of government; and they attempt to justify the government's right to govern.

A Statement of National Ideals. According to the Preamble of the United States Constitution, our nation is dedicated to six goals: to form a more perfect union; to establish justice; to insure domestic tranquility; to provide for the common defense; to promote the general welfare; and to secure the blessing of liberty. The Soviet Constitution proclaims the Soviet Union to be a "dictatorship of the proletariat," dedicated to eliminating capitalism and establishing a classless society. The Constitution of the Federal Republic of Germany, seeking to divest the nation of any traces of Nazi rule, states its determination to "serve the peace of the world," [11] and expressly proclaims that no group of people can be denied the right to German citizenship—a reaction to Hitler's Nuremburg Laws which stripped hundreds of thousands of citizens of their rights.

Preambles and lists of rights are symbolic statements: they indicate the values, ideals, and goals which seem to best express the spirit of the national political culture. But the value statements in preambles are by nature very general and have no legal force. How are they interpreted? What does the U. S. Constitution mean by a "more perfect union," for example? There is considerable disagreement over this question; in fact, debate over the meaning of this term led to the Civil War a century ago. What does the Constitution mean by "establishing justice"? What is justice, and is it the same for all citizens? If American blacks have been denied equal rights for two centuries, does this mean that it is just for them to be given an advantage now in admission to colleges, in hiring practices, or in securing low-rent housing? Or again, what does the Preamble mean by "promoting general welfare"? The question of what the general welfare is, and how it is to be balanced against the rights of the individual or of a minority group, are questions which are almost certain to produce different answers from everyone. Were the Amish people who wished to withdraw their children from high school setting a precedent disruptive to the general welfare? Do laws allowing private citizens to purchase handguns like the "Saturday-night special," which are not accurate enough to have any legitimate use for hunting or target practice, harm the general welfare, even though the Bill of Rights specifically gives citizens the right to bear arms?

Although constitutions provide a statement of national ideals, the interpretation of these goals and values necessitates an active choice by the decision makers of government.

Formalizes the Structure of Government. In addition to acting as a symbolic statement of national values, a constitution is also a blueprint. It

[11] Most modern constitutions include an acknowledgment of their membership in the larger world community—an acknowledgment which is lacking in our two-century-old document and which reflects the broader perspective of a twentieth century which has seen many international conflicts and agreements.

is a written description of who does what in government, defining the authority and limiting the powers of each branch, and providing for regularized channels through which conflict may be resolved. Articles I through III of the United States Constitution outline the duties of Congress, the president, and the judiciary. Congress may collect taxes and customs duties, but is prohibited from taxing exports. The president is named commander in chief of the armed forces, but he must have the "advice and consent" of the Senate in order to conclude treaties. In a system where there is a separation of powers the constitution divides authority and responsibilities among the various branches of government; it also limits the power of each branch.

A constitution also outlines the division of power between central and regional governments in a federal state. In a federal system of government, powers and responsibilities are divided between one national government and several regional or state governments.[12] West Germany and Australia, like the United States, are federal states. Their constitutions give their central governments control over certain areas of responsibility—such as foreign policy, foreign commerce, and coinage. Thus, the state of Bavaria in the Federal Republic of Germany may not sign a treaty with Austria; neither may the state of Texas mint its own currency. While certain powers are delegated to the central government, the constitution leaves others to the states. In the United States Constitution, this division is a general one; any powers not accorded to the central government are reserved for the states and for the people. Thus, the states traditionally control education, police protection, health and welfare services, and local commerce. Of course, this division of power has become less clear-cut, especially in recent years, as the federal government has taken on a greater share of financing operations of education, health, welfare, housing, and scores of other services. But in spite of federal control of many of the purse strings, the states still retain predominant control of these powers.

Establishes the Legitimacy of Government. A third role of a constitution is to give a government the stamp of legitimacy. Although this function is undeniably a symbolic role, its practical utility cannot be denied. Many nations in the world community will not even recognize a new state until it has adopted a written constitution; it is a sign of permanence and responsibility.

Most constitutions were written shortly after revolutionary upheavals, and their purpose was to help establish the new regime's right to rule. The Articles of Confederation and subsequently the United States Constitution symbolized American independence by replacing British authority with tangible evidence of a new government. The French Constitution of 1791 (which never went

---

[12] See Chapter 17 for a discussion of federal systems. Also, Duane Lockhard, *American Federalism* (New York: McGraw-Hill, 1969); William H. Riker, *Federalism: Origin, Operation, Significance* (Boston: Little, Brown, 1964); A. W. MacMahon, ed., *Federalism: Mature and Emergent* (New York: Columbia University Press, 1955); and K. C. Wheare, *Federal Government*, 4th ed. (New York: Oxford University Press, 1964).

into effect) tried to replace the divine right of Louis XVI with the sovereign right of the people. And the first Soviet Constitution of 1918 established a "dictatorship of the people" to replace Tsarist rule. Constitutions proclaim the values of a new regime, while they also establish in writing a permanent outline for the organization of government. As a symbolic statement of intentions, with a practical outline of structure, a constitution helps to set the stamp of legitimacy on a new regime. This is the primary reason why almost every nation, and especially new nations established since World War II, have adopted constitutions almost as soon as they have gained independence.

Of course, a written constitution is not absolutely necessary for a legitimate, stable regime. Both Great Britain and Israel are established members of the international community, yet neither has found it necessary to commit all its fundamental precepts and laws to writing in one document. England's "constitution" consists of many documents such as the Magna Carta, the Petition of Right, and the Bill of Rights; judicial decisions which have established precedents of common law; major acts of Parliament; and customs and traditions which have grown over the centuries. Israel's "constitution" is also an accumulated body of documents and precedents—some of which date back to biblical times—and Israel gained acceptance by many nations in the world community soon after proclaiming nationhood after World War II.

Even in nations that have written constitutions, there are countless traditions, customs, and laws which are also a part of the constitutional order.[13] For instance, no mention is made of political parties anywhere in the United States Constitution. Yet our party system is an established part of the American political process; indeed, a change in the party system would very likely change the entire American political structure.[14] Judicial precedents and government traditions, too, make up the fundamental laws of a society. Thus, the body of constitutional law encompass a wide variety of documents and traditions in all nations whether they have "written" or "unwritten" constitutions.

The Adaptability of the Constitution

The United States Constitution

In 1789, when the American Constitution was adopted, the world was far different from what we know now. The United States was primarily agrarian, needing little in the way of technological services. The communications net-

---

[13] See Wormuth, *The Origins of Modern Constitutionalism*, Chapter 1.
[14] See the discussion in Seymour Martin Lipset, *The First New Nation: The United States in Historical and Comparative Perspective* (Garden City, N.Y.: Doubleday, 1967).

work was limited to little-read newspapers and pamphlets, and mostly to word-of-mouth. There were no skyscrapers, automobiles, pollution, or anti-ballistic missile systems. How can a constitution which was written to fill the needs of such a primitive world be adapted to the highly industrialized, urbanized, crime-ridden society of modern America? A look at the way in which the Constitution has adapted in two major areas of change—the "right to bear arms" in a violent society and the growth of "big government" in the twentieth century—might give some insight into the flexibility of this document.

The Right to Bear Arms. In 1789, the United States was a sparsely settled frontier nation where men often literally had to fight for their lives. Guns were necessary to the settlers' very survival, and the Constitution reflected this. Amendment II of the Bill of Rights (adopted in 1791) guarantees the right of the citizens to "keep and bear arms."

In the 1970s, the United States is no longer sparsely settled: it is highly urbanized. Guns are no longer necessary to the average citizen's survival; instead, they add fuel to the fire in an already tense and violent society. In the last decade we have witnessed the assassinations of President John F. Kennedy, Dr. Martin Luther King, and Senator Robert F. Kennedy. Governor George Wallace was seriously wounded by a would-be assassin, and Senator John C. Stennis of Mississippi was critically wounded by muggers who merely wanted his money. Instances of armed robbery, sniper attacks on police and civilians, and killings by firearms have risen at an alarming rate. As a result, many concerned citizens argue that the age of the frontier has long since passed, and that it is time to drastically restrict the sale of lethal weapons. Yet opponents of gun-control legislation argue that the Constitution insures the right of every citizen to purchase and own firearms. Sportsmen, shop-keepers who find themselves constant victims of armed robberies, and those who may feel their persons or property are in danger but cannot secure full-time protection from the police all argue that their constitutional right to pursue a hobby or to protect their very lives will be jeopardized by gun-control legislation.

The "right to bear arms" case illustrates that a two-century-old constitution—at least in its traditional interpretation—may not provide the right answer for all of the needs of modern society. If gun controls are necessary to limit violence in America (and there is by no means a consensus on the issue), can the Constitution be interpreted to allow such legislation to be passed? The Constitution is written in very general terms; it lends itself to the interpretations dictated by the times. Amendment II reads: " A well regulated Militia, being necessary to the security of a free State, the right of the people to keep and bear Arms, shall not be infringed." Does this mean that the citizens can own guns privately, or that they can own guns for the purpose of maintaining a militia or army? The traditional interpretation has been that individual persons can purchase and own firearms for private use. In the future, it may be necessary to reinterpret Amendment II to mean that the right to bear arms only applies to members of an organized militia.

Besides the specific Amendment in the Bill of Rights which applies to the citizens' right to bear arms, the Constitution has other clauses which make it flexible enough to keep up with changing times. The so-called elastic clause gives Congress the power to enact all legislation necessary and proper to carry out its enumerated powers. Under this clause too, the Constitution might be interpreted to mean that Congress can impose restrictions on the people's right to bear arms.[15] So, the general nature of the eighteenth-century Constitution does allow it to adapt to an age of violence even where it gives citizens the right to bear arms. How has the Constitution adapted to the more general shift from the sharp division between federal and state powers envisioned by the founding fathers to the highly centralized "big government" of the late twentieth century?

The Shift in the Federal Balance of Power. The role of the central government has grown markedly in relation to the powers of the state governments since the era of the New Deal in the 1930s. This shift in balance stems partly from the changing needs caused by the Great Depression, which left around twelve million people out of work. They needed assistance in finding housing and in feeding their families, and the states could not afford to provide all of these services. In response, the federal government took on a broader range of education, welfare, health, and housing services than ever before, and this responsibility has grown since then. With the recent fiscal crises which have hit all areas of American society from the cities to the farms, and with the great increase in the need for highways, public transportation, and an endless list of other services, the role of the central government has continued to expand.[16]

The writers of the American Constitution never envisioned that the federal government would some day take on the tasks of feeding welfare clients, licensing communications networks, financing chemical and atomic research, or building highways. They assumed that the basic balance of power between state and central government would remain relatively stable, and that this balance would be quite even (or weighted more heavily toward the states). How has the document they wrote been able to adapt to the highly centralized system of modern American federalism?

As it has been able to adapt to the growing undesirability of making the right to own firearms a basic right, so too, the Constitution has been able to adapt to the increased role of the central government. While the powers of the federal government have expanded into areas which the founding fathers couldn't possibly have foreseen, the writers of the Constitution did have the

[15] See the discussion of the elastic clause in Edward S. Corwin and Jack W. Peltason, *Understanding the Constitution*, 4th ed. (New York: Holt, Rinehart and Winston, 1967).
[16] See Chapter 17 on federalism and the balance of regional central powers.

foresight to realize that the nation would experience many changes and would develop many needs which they couldn't specifically provide for in the document.[17] So the Constitution was written in a deliberately flexible form, and the result is that it can still be interpreted to fit the needs of modern society and government. Feeding welfare clients, financing scientific research, and building highways can all be seen as promoting the general welfare (atomic and scientific research also help to provide for the common defense), and licensing communications networks falls under the powers granted to Congress to lay and collect taxes and to regulate commerce.

The United States Constitution is considerably more general than are most of the constitutions written in the twentieth century. Are the more detailed laws of states founded since World War II equally adaptable? The Turkish Constitution, for example (adopted in 1961), contains elaborately detailed lists of individual, economic, and political rights and duties of both the people and the government. These lists specifically enumerate the confidential nature of the postal service, the secret ballot, the liberty of science and art, and the necessity of a multiparty system. Yet, in any constitution, the specific wording will be interpreted by whoever is in power. Even the multiparty system described in Turkey's Constitution was modified when, ten years after its adoption, a military coalition forced the government to agree to a system of no party competition. Necessity dictates that no matter how detailed a constitution, it must be flexible enough to adapt to the needs of the government.

The Adaptability of Constitutions: Can They Insure Rights?

The case of the right to bear arms illustrates that it is not always practical for the government to follow the original intent of the constitution. Changing times mean that people's needs change, and so a constitution written for one age may not always provide the best solutions for another age. If this is the case, and if constitutions must constantly be reinterpreted to keep up with the times, how can they insure the rights of citizens?

Civil Liberties and Civil Rights.   In the 1930s, Joseph Stalin imprisoned nearly twenty million Soviet citizens in labor camps. Another ten to fifteen million were killed for resisting his agricultural collectivization program. At about the same time, Adolf Hitler began organizing scientifically designed concentration camps which would systematically exterminate thousands of lives every hour of the day. And halfway around the world, the Japanese

---

[17] For discussions of the expansion of federal power into state and local functions, see Wheare, *Federal Government;* Lockard, *American Federalism;* and, Frederick Mosher and Orville F. Poland, *The Costs of American Government: Facts, Trends, Myths* (New York: Dodd, Mead, 1964).

armies of Hideki Tojo were raping and pillaging their way through China.

In reaction to the outrages of World War II, the world community has taken steps to prevent any future tragedies of such great magnitude. In 1948, the General Assembly of the United Nations adopted the Universal Declaration on Human Rights to guarantee basic rights to all the citizens of the world.[18] As a symbolic statement of world opinion (with no real power of sanction), the Universal Declaration establishes fundamental precepts and ideals which most nations are reluctant to violate. Of course, if a nation does choose to violate the "universal rights" named in the declaration, there is little anyone can do, short of war, to stop them. The Universal Declaration's value is symbolic.

The Universal Rights of Man. The Universal Declaration, patterned on the French Declaration of the Rights of Man and Citizen and on the American Declaration of Independence and the Bill of Rights, affirms the basic civil rights and civil liberties which are thought by most Western political thinkers to be fundamental.[19] It declares that all people have certain rights which government may not arbitrarily take away. These include the rights to life, free assembly, freedom of expression, freedom of movement, freedom of religion, and freedom to participate in the political process by voting or holding office. In addition to this list of civil and political rights, the Universal Declaration provides for many of the economic and cultural needs of citizens of every land. It specifies that the rights to work and to receive equal pay for equal work; the right to an education; the right to marry, raise a family, and provide that family with a decent standard of living; and the right to live according to one's culture are the heritage of every citizen. The Universal Declaration is not the only international list of fundamental rights and liberties: the Organization of American States and the Council of Europe have also published similar documents.

The overwhelming sentiment of the civilized world favors equal rights for all. Yet in spite of the lofty declarations that have been published, the fact is that rights and liberties are difficult to define, and all nations restrict civil liberties in some way. The problem of minority groups is almost universally applicable as a case in point.

---

[18] On the subject of international protection of human rights see: Ian Brownlie, ed., *Basic Documents on Human Rights* (Oxford: Clarendon Press, 1971); John Carey, *International Protection of Human Rights* (Dobbs Ferry, N.Y.: Oceana, 1968); and *UN Protection of Civil and Political Rights* (Syracuse, N.Y.: Syracuse University Press, 1970); Maurice Cranston, *What Are Human Rights?* (New York: Basic Books, 1962); Hersh Lauterpacht, *International Law and Human Rights* (New York: Praeger Publishers, 1950); Evan Luard, ed., *The International Protection of Human Rights* (New York: Praeger Publishers, 1967); Moses Moskowitz, *Human Rights and World Order* (Dobbs Ferry, N.Y.: Oceana, 1958); and Egon Schwelb, *Human Rights and the International Community* (Chicago: Quadrangle, 1964).

[19] The terms *liberties* and *rights* are frequently used synonymously. Technically, however, rights refer to natural rights such as freedom of speech, assembly, religion, and equality before the law, while liberties are the formal manifestations of these rights as defined in constitutions. Liberties are the finite vehicles of natural rights.

Minority Groups and Civil Liberties.[20] Of the more than 143 nations that comprise the world community, none is homogeneous. Most have citizens with a variety of racial, ethnic, religious, cultural, or linguistic backgrounds, and as a result, nearly every nation has at least one minority group whose civil or cultural liberties are compromised to some extent. French-Canadians living in Maine, or Chicanos living in New Mexico, are put at a disadvantage unless they speak a language foreign to their culture; Indians and Pakistanis in Great Britain must conform to a way of life far different from what they are accustomed to. It is the minority group which must adjust itself to the ways of the majority.

The Universal Declaration states that minorities have the right to preserve their cultural uniqueness. But to make a statement such as this and to carry it through are two different things. Most difficult is defining exactly who or what a minority group is (Can black separatists speak for black America? Can the radical Jewish Defense League speak for American Jews?) and what its rights should be in a state controlled by a dominant group with different interests. It may be easy to condemn South Africa, because its discrimination against blacks is open and blatant. But nations that grant all citizens a theoretical equality before the law may discriminate against minorities in other, more subtle ways. If Tyrolian Germans are forced to use the Italian language, is their cultural heritage being stifled? Is the inclusion of Croatia-Slavonia in the state of Yugoslavia an infringement of the cultural rights of Croatians, who are accustomed to a different language and different traditions from the dominant Serbs? Should Russian Jews be permitted to set up their own school systems to teach their youngsters about their heritage? If so, should American blacks be permitted to do the same, with state funding? What of Spanish-speaking Puerto Ricans in New York, or Chicanos in the Southwest, or Italian-Americans? Assimilation of minority groups involves a compromise of traditions and culture, and, therefore, sometimes one of equal rights. But it is also true that a state that does not assimilate its minorities stands little chance of remaining stable. Thus, despite the Universal Declaration's denunciation of discrimination against minorities, some discrimination is inevitable in every society.

In the Soviet Union, Joseph Stalin's rule proved that the rights guaranteed in the Soviet Constitution are totally subject to the interpretation given them by the government in power. In the United States, we are accustomed to thinking that the rights guaranteed in our Bill of Rights are indeed inalienable, but we also realize that these rights are subject to the interpretation of those in power. Are our rights guaranteed any more than those of citizens of a totalitarian nation? Let us look at a case history—the history of freedom of expression in the United States—to see a sample of our government's record in protecting the constitutional guarantees of the Bill of Rights.

[20] Chapter 19 gives a detailed discussion of the problem of defining and insuring minority rights.

Freedom of Expression in the United States

"Congress shall make no law . . . abridging the freedom of speech, or of the press; or the right of the people peaceably to assemble, and to petition the government for a redress of grievances." So says Amendment I of the United States Bill of Rights. We think of freedom of expression as one of the hallmarks of any nation calling itself democratic. If a person thinks his president or prime minister is ruining a nation's economy, he has every right to say so, to whomever he wishes. Or if a college student interested in cinematography decides to make a surrealist antigovernment film, his activity should draw no interference or investigation from any agencies of government.

But while freedom of expression seems at first glance to be a straightforward guarantee, it is not all that simple. Does freedom of speech give a charismatic young radical the right to incite masses of people to commit political murders? Does a newspaper have a right to publish information which might damage the security of the nation? [21] Did the now-defunct *Fact* magazine have the right to suggest that some psychiatrists considered then-candidate Barry Goldwater unfit to be president—or should columnist Jack Anderson have been permitted to publish the erroneous information that Senator Thomas Eagleton (George McGovern's running mate for a few short weeks at the start of the 1972 presidential contest) had an arrest record for drunken driving? While we may all believe in the right of free expression, most of us would agree that this does not mean that anyone can say or write whatever they want, whenever they want, regardless of the consequences. In the example used by Justice Oliver Wendell Holmes, nobody should be permitted to yell "fire" in a crowded theatre unless there really is a fire. Free speech does not necessarily include the right to spread dangerous or malicious falsehoods. Thus, *Fact* magazine was found to have maliciously libeled Senator Goldwater: it published informal opinions of psychiatrists who had never actually examined the senator as if they were considered professional opinions. And so it was judged that the story that he was unfit for the presidency was designed solely to discredit him with the electorate. (While several newspapers subsequently published apologies for the Jack Anderson column about Thomas Eagleton's "drunken driving," no suit has been brought.) Likewise, free speech does not include the right to make a crank phone call to the local police advising them that there is a bomb in one of the city hall washrooms when, in fact, there is not.

According to Justice Holmes, freedom of expression must also be restricted in cases where statements or publications present a "clear and present danger" of bringing about "substantive evils" which Congress has a right to prevent.[22]

[21] See the discussion of the Pentagon Papers controversy in Chapter 9, "Political Communication and the Media."

[22] See Zechariah Chafee, *Free Speech in the United States* (New York: Atheneum, reprinted 1969). Also useful is Robert E. Cushman, *Civil Liberties in the United States* (New York: Johnson Reprint, 1969).

Under this reasoning, the Supreme Court in its 1925 *Gitlow* v. *New York* decisions upheld the conviction of a radical who had called for the violent overthrow of the government on the grounds that his words had represented a "bad tendency" which could "corrupt morals, incite crime, and disturb the public peace."

The questions of what presents a "clear and present danger" and what is a "substantive evil" are, of course, open to very subjective interpretation. Many people today would see no danger in publicly advocating the violent overthrow of government; indeed, to some, such dissent is the sign of a "healthy intellectual climate." And so, the interpretation of the meaning of the constitutional guarantee of freedom of expression has varied considerably over the years since the Bill of Rights was adopted.[23]

A History of Freedom of Expression

Free Speech and Sedition.   Sedition is defined in the Common Law as any criticism of the government or government officials designed to produce discontent or rebellion among the populace. The charge of sedition has been used by the American government to suppress some forms of radical expression during several periods of our history since the adoption of the Bill of Rights.

Congress enacted the first Sedition Act in 1798, after the infamous XYZ affair. The law (which followed the Common Law definition) was aimed against the "Jacobins," as American defenders of the French Revolution were called, at a time when the United States was involved in an undeclared naval war with France. The Sedition Act was supposed to expire the day that President John Adams left office (a curious coincidence which indicates that its raison-d'être may have also had something to do with the election contest). The act aroused controversy, but it lapsed without any test of constitutionality in the Supreme Court. The next Sedition Act went into effect during the Civil War, when President Lincoln acted under the war powers vested in his office to suppress northern opponents of the Union effort. The president's action was brought to the Supreme Court, which declined to judge on the legality of his actions. While the action went untested, all "political prisoners" were pardoned at the end of the war. It was not until the twentieth century that another Sedition Act was passed in an attempt to tighten national security during World War I.

23 For accounts of the Supreme Court and First Amendment rights, see Henry J. Abraham, *Freedom and the Court: Civil Rights and Liberties in the United States* (New York: Oxford University Press, 1967) ; Thomas I. Emerson, *Toward a General Theory of the First Amendment* (New York: Random House, 1966) : Milton R. Konvitz, *Fundamental Liberties of a Free People* (Ithaca, N.Y.: Cornell University Press, 1957) ; Martin Shapiro, *Freedom of Speech* (Englewood Cliffs, N.J.: Prentice-Hall, 1966) ; and Robert L. Cord, *Protest, Dissent and the Supreme Court* (Cambridge, Mass.: Winthrop Publishers, 1971).

Twentieth-Century Sedition Acts. It was the Espionage Act of 1917 that gave rise to Justice Holmes's "clear and present danger" doctrine. At a time when socialists and pacifists were urging people to protest U.S. involvement in World War I by refusing to serve in the army and to disrupt the war effort in other ways, this act prohibited any attempts to interfere with the military recruitment policies of the United States government. The Espionage Act resulted in several court cases in 1919. In one case, the Supreme Court upheld the law on the grounds that free speech could be restricted if it created a "clear and present danger" to national security. And so several hundred people, including Socialist party leader Eugene Debs, were imprisoned under the act, but most were pardoned as soon as the war ended.

More recent Sedition Acts have been directed primarily against Communists. The Smith Act of 1940, the most comprehensive Sedition Act ever passed by Congress, made it a crime to advocate the violent action of overthrow of government, to distribute literature urging such an overthrow, or to knowingly join any organization or group that advocated such actions. The Smith Act aroused much controversy, but was not put to a constitutional test until 1951, when the Supreme Court upheld the convictions of the leaders of the American Communist party even though they had not been charged with any overt acts of force against the government. "It is the existence of the conspiracy which constitutes the danger," ruled Chief Justice Vinson, "not the presence or absence of overt action." Since then, there have been other court rulings on the constitutionality of the Smith Act, and they have fluctuated. In *Yates* v. *the United States* in 1957, the Warren Court reversed the conviction of American Communist party leaders on the grounds that there was no overt action, only abstract advocacy of rebellion.[24] And four years later, in *Scales* v. *the United States*, the court upheld the section of the Smith Act which makes membership in the Communist party illegal—but this ruling also specified that it is active membership, involving the direct intent to bring about the violent overthrow of government, which is criminal. The Court was careful to point out that membership per se was not made illegal by the Smith Act.

Probably the most stringent legislation ever enacted in our history to counter the threat of Communist subversion was passed during the "McCarthy era" following World War II. The McCarran Act of 1950 (the Internal Security Act) barred Communists from working for the federal government or in defense-related industries, established a Subversive Activities Control Board (SACB) to enforce the act, and required organizations declared by the SACB to be Communist-influenced to register with the Attorney General. The McCarran Act aroused a great deal of controversy. Its critics charged that the law not only encroached on the rights of free speech and free assembly, but also violated the self-incrimination clause of the Fifth Amendment. While the

[24] For accounts of the Warren Court and the First Amendment, see Milton R. Konvitz, *Expanding Liberties* (New York: Viking, 1966); and Philip B. Kurland, *Politics, the Constitution and the Warren Court* (Chicago: University of Chicago Press, 1970).

Internal Security Act in its entirety has never been declared unconstitutional, every action by the SACB demanding specific organizational or individual registration with the Attorney General's office has been declared unconstitutional.[25]

The history of legislative action against sedition in the United States indicates that the guarantees of the First Amendment have been interpreted to mean different things at different periods, varying according to both the general aura of national security and the president, Congress, and Supreme Court justices in power at the time. The Supreme Court recognizes the danger of subversion, and it acknowledges that government must have some powers to restrict the freedoms of expression and assembly for the preservation of society as a whole. But its interpretation of what is subversive has fluctuated. While recent decisions have leaned toward free exercise of liberties wherever possible, many of the decisions of earlier periods have been more protective of the state's security. It is almost impossible to find a balance between the exercise of free expression and free assembly, and the state's need to safeguard its own security. And so the courts have never been able to produce a definitive statement on the extent to which government may restrict freedom of speech.

The Sedition Acts and Communist activities controls cover only one aspect of freedom of expression in America's history. How has this liberty fared in the "age of protest" of the sixties and early seventies?

Freedom of Expression in the Sixties and Seventies

With the decline of cold war tensions in the period since the fifties, sedition and subversion have received less attention from the courts, the press, and the government. But the guarantees of the First Amendment still remain major issues as the emergence of the age of protest has raised new questions about the limits of citizens' rights to assemble, protest, and practice passive resistance. Beginning in the early 1960s, black civil rights protesters followed the lead of Mahatma Gandhi and Martin Luther King as they joined mass marches and protest demonstrations to fight discrimination.[26] In the mid-sixties, the tactics of mass protest marches and passive resistance were picked up by college students from Berkeley to Columbia, and many campus administration offices were "captured" and occupied for days and even weeks. Later, anti-Vietnam War protesters brought their teach-ins, sit-ins, peace marches, and public meetings from the campus to the centers of America's major cities.

[25] Including the 1961 *Communist Party* v. *the Subversive Activities Control Board* case, *United States* v. *the Communist Party* (1964), *Albertson* v. *the Subversive Activities Control Board* (1965), *Cole* v. *Young* (1956), and *United States* v. *Robel* (1967).
[26] For an excellent analysis of the impact of civil disobedience on political thinking, see Paul F. Power, "On Civil Disobedience in Recent American Democratic Thought," *American Political Science Review* 64 (1970): 35–47.

The waves of demonstrations and protests which began in the sixties raised new questions concerning the limits of democratic dissent and peaceful protest. What are the acceptable bounds of peaceful protest? Sit-ins that block traffic at a construction site, and demonstrations that block doorways and corridors of selective service offices may not constitute a clear and present danger to anyone, yet they do cause expensive slowdowns.

If the age of passive resistance means that new criteria must be sought to judge what forms of protest are acceptable, where is the line to be drawn between an annoying nuisance (such as a noisy picket line in front of a store or restaurant and a protest which harms the public interest (such as a lie-in on a major city artery)? And is the latter really more hazardous than a strike by subway workers, bus drivers, or railroad signalmen—a common event in this day and age? As more and more people resorted to both violent and peaceful protest tactics in the sixties and seventies, the question of what demonstrators' rights should be took on a new urgency. As a result, many cases concerning the limits of dissent were brought to the Supreme Court.[27]

The Right of Peaceful Assembly. The right of citizens to assemble peaceably received somewhat inconsistent treatment from the courts during the sixties. In 1963, the Supreme Court upheld the right of protesters to stage sit-ins on private and public property. *Lombard* v. *Louisiana* and *Edwards* v. *South Carolina* paved the way for future demonstrations and made the sit-in a legitimate mode of protest. But by the mid-sixties, pressure was growing from all sides in reaction to the increase in demonstrations, and the Supreme Court began to modify its earlier broad stand. In *Adderly* v. *Florida* (1966) a previous conviction of several blacks for demonstrating outside a jailhouse was upheld on the grounds that they had violated the trespass laws of the state. The Court majority held that a jailhouse, unlike a statehouse, was not an appropriate place to demonstrate for a change in governmental policy.

By restricting the right of peaceful assembly, in *Adderly* v. *Florida*, the Supreme Court was trying to strike a balance between the right of the people to protest in demonstrations and the right of the state and the public to carry out their functions without interference from protestors. This conflict between two rights was graphically demonstrated on May 3, 1971, when Washington, D.C., authorities arrested seventy-two hundred antiwar demonstrators (most of whom were not convicted of any wrongdoing). Their right to protest wasn't questioned, but their right to block traffic, obstruct government buildings, and prevent people from going to work was. Such massive arrests caused many observers to denounce the government's actions as "police-state

---

[27] Alexander M. Bickel, *The Supreme Court and the Idea of Progress* (New York: Harper & Row, 1970) discusses the Warren Court's decisions on freedom of expression. In this section, we will discuss the limits of peaceful dissent; violent dissent is not protected by the Constitution, and is the subject of Chapter 20.

"My, what a beautiful day. I think I'll restore partial freedom of assembly."

Drawing by Donald Reilly; © 1971 The New Yorker Magazine, Inc.

tactics." But the question of when peaceful assembly becomes destructive to the rights of others has not been resolved.

Freedom of Individual Expression. Another phenomenon of the sixties was the growth of individual expressions which indicated in some cases outright protest, and in other cases, at least a certain disrespect for both the authority and symbols of government. Many pacifists who objected to American involvement in Vietnam expressed their discontent through the illegal action of burning their draft cards. What was the court's reaction? The Supreme court took the view that the First Amendment guarantees did not include the right to express oneself by burning draft cards. The *United States*

v. *O'Brien* decision (1968) rejected the argument that burning a draft card was a symbolic act of free speech; instead, it was seen as a gratuitous gesture of defiance of the law. Nevertheless, in *Tinker* v. *Des Moines* (1969) the Court held that armbands worn by public school students to protest the war in Vietnam were protected, symbolic acts of free speech.

Another genre of personal expression that gained popularity in the sixties included the phenomena of "flag art" and the exploitation of the flag for a wide range of unintended purposes, from shirts to shower curtains to toilet seat decorations. Most states have for many years carried flag desecration laws on their books, and in 1968, Congress passed a federal flag desecration law. This act makes it a crime to "knowingly cast contempt upon any flag of the United States by publicly mutilating, defacing, defiling, burning, or trampling upon it," and the penalty is up to one thousand dollars and a year in jail.[28] During the late sixties and early seventies, there were as many cases of "flag desecration" brought to the courts as there had been in the entire previous history of the United States, and in 1971, a case of "flag art" was brought before the Supreme Court. In this case, the defendant had been arrested for exhibiting about a dozen constructions in which the American flag was used to represent a cannon barrel, a sex organ, a hanging figure, and other objects designed to show their creator's opposition to the Vietnam War. The Supreme Court was divided four to four on the case, and so let the artist's conviction stand.

Convictions on issues such as flag art have aroused much controversy, as many people feel that because this genre of free expression causes no harm or threat to the security of the nation, the operations of government, or the public welfare, it should draw no interference from the state. But the issue illustrates the importance of symbolism in politics: convictions reflect the court's interpretation that the exploitation of the flag has been contemptuous in intent. If the flag is exploited for patriotic or "innocuous" reasons—glittery Uncle Sam uniforms made of starred-and-striped material which drum majors wear in parades; toilet seats or coffee mugs with the flag design printed on them—neither court cases nor convictions are likely to result. But if the misuse of the flag seems to be an act of disrespect—as when Yippie leader Abbie Hoffman appeared in a flag shirt—the act is more likely to draw interference from government.[29] It is evident that the interpretation of the proper limits of personal freedom of expression in the case of the exploitation of the national flag is one which must depend on a very subjective decision by the courts.

[28] For a discussion of the unevenness with which flag desecration laws are applied, see the article by Robert W. Dietsch, "Raising the Flag," in *The New Republic*, June 12, 1971, pp. 18–19. An interesting contrast on the "state of the art" in the Soviet Union is provided in Paul Sjeklocha, "Modern Art and the Shackles of Dogma," *Problems of Communism*, November–December 1965, pp. 83–89.

[29] See the discussion in Dietsch, "Raising the Flag." Also, the "Flag Burning Case," *Street* v. *New York*, 394, U.S. 576 (1969).

Government by Constitution: Does It Guarantee Anything?

In the quick look we have taken at constitutions, two observations are strik
ing. First, almost every nation in the world has adopted a written constitution.
The two most prominent exceptions, Great Britain and Israel, are in a very
small minority in a world which seems to be placing more and more emphasis
on not only having a formal constitution, but on enumerating as many details
as possible in that one document.

The second observation is that, in spite of the almost universal use of
written constitutions, the documents must depend to a very great extent on the
interpretation given them by whoever is in power. After the Soviet Union
adopted its 1936 Constitution which enumerates a long list of democratic
rights for its citizens, Joseph Stalin proceeded to strip those rights from
broad segments of the population. And even in the United States, it is strik
ingly apparent that the freedoms of speech and free assembly have meant very
different things at different times in our history, depending on the president,
Congress, courts, the climate of American public attitude, and general air of
national security (or lack of it) which reign at the moment.

The primary purpose of constitutions is not to provide inflexible guarantees
of human rights. Indeed, there is sound reasoning behind the argument that
a citizen's wartime rights should be different from his peacetime liberties, for
during periods of war the national security may be threatened and may re
quire extra measures of protection. Nor is the primary purpose of constitu
tions to outline a structure for the organization of the government. The gov
ernment of the Soviet Union could hardly be recognized from its description
in that nation's constitution; and the federal system of the United States is a
far cry from that envisioned by the writers of our constitution.

While in some countries like the United States the constitution is the
supreme law of the land, in almost all societies, written constitutions are more
appropriately viewed as expressions of intention and ideals; they are embodi
ments of the highest goals of a people. A developing nation often feels that
it must impose restrictions on its citizens' right to publish criticisms of gov
ernment, even though its constitution gives them the right of freedom of the
press. It is assumed that freedom of the press is a national goal, even though
it may not be attainable during the first few years of nationhood, and so this
liberty is listed in the document. The United States may have placed restric
tions on free speech during World War I, but this action reflected the prevail
ing opinion that there was a need for tightened national security rather than
an all-out abandonment of the ideal of free expression. Because the needs of
a nation vary so sharply between periods of war and peace, and depression
and prosperity, the function of a constitution must be symbolically rather
than literally binding. And as a symbolic statement, its utility seems unques
tionably to be borne out by its popularity. It is an accepted (if not quite
universal) document of a nation's legitimacy in the modern world.

Suggested Readings

Bagehot, Walter. *The English Constitution.* New York: Oxford University Press, 1936. A study of the written, and unwritten, constitution of Great Britain.

Bickel, Alexander M. *The Supreme Court and the Idea of Progress.* New York: Harper & Row, 1970. A contemporary analysis of the United States Supreme Court under Earl Warren's leadership, with attention to basic decisions on the limits of expression.

Corwin, Edward S. *The Constitution and What It Means Today.* New York: Atheneum, 1963. A useful guide for the beginning student, with case references.

Holcombe, Arthur H. *Human Rights in the Modern World.* New York: New York University Press, 1947. A survey of civil liberties in theory and as practiced within contemporary nation-states.

Kelly, Alfred H., and Harbison, Winifred A. *The American Constitution: Its Origins and Development.* 3rd ed. New York: W. W. Norton, 1963. A history of American constitutional law.

MacMahon, Arthur W., ed. *Federalism: Mature and Emergent.* New York: Columbia University Press, 1955. An excellent collection of essays, with Mac-Mahon's analysis of federalism as the capstone.

McIlwain, Charles H. *Constitutionalism, Ancient and Modern.* Ithaca, N.Y.: Cornell University Press, 1940. A classic study of constitutional evolution.

Peaslee, Amos J., ed. *Constitutions of Nations.* 2nd ed., 3 vols. The Hague, Netherlands: Martinus Nijhoff, 1956. A summary of the constitutions of modern nations and their institutions.

Riker, William H. *Federalism: Origin, Operation, Significance.* Boston: Little, Brown, 1964. A provocative and original study of the origins and impact that federal systems have on their citizens.

Wheare, Kenneth C. *Modern Constitutions.* New York: Oxford University Press, 1951. A comparison of modern constitutions, with emphasis on their differences and similarities.

Democracy and totalitarianism: The distribution of governing power

CHAPTER 5

In 1943, when the Soviet Union was one of the allies in the war against the Axis Powers, George Orwell startled the public with his publication of *1984*, a thinly disguised satire of his view of life in the Soviet Union in particular, and in totalitarian societies in general. In this nightmare utopia, the individual has no rights, only obligations. The government may spy upon him, arrest him, and interrogate him at will; television cameras monitor the streets, scan public places, and peer into homes. The purpose of this unrelenting surveillance is to insure that everyone is under the state's control—even in his private thoughts. The media are controlled carefully, and the people are told only what the government wants them to know. Every citizen needs the state's permission to marry, to bear children, and to change his job or place of residence. He is a creature of the state.

Perhaps the most extreme opposite we can find in the annals of history is the traditional image of life in Athens during the fifth century B.C. Here, all adult male citizens had the right to attend the General Assembly that met ten times a year. Regardless of his wealth or social standing, each man's vote carried the same weight. The Assembly enacted all laws, elected the state's officers, and could compel the state's leaders to appear before it to justify their actions. Decisions of the Assembly were reached by a simple majority vote. In general, the individual had a role in the decision-making processes of state and was thereby accorded an important, if intangible, sense of dignity and human worth.

George Orwell's picture of totalitarianism and the Athenian ideal of democracy are at opposite ends of the spectrum of governmental power, and in between are many variations. (Actually, anarchism [1] is the true opposite of totalitarianism, but since its essence is a rejection of government, it need not concern us here.) Table 5-1 shows the principal gradations from perfect democracy to perfect totalitarianism and lists some characteristics typical of each of the governmental power systems. The table follows the custom in countries adhering to the Western political tradition (specifically the United States) of classifying nations generally as either "democratic" or "nondemocratic"—the democratic nations having governments with limited powers and the nondemocratic nations having governments with more or less unlimited power.[2]

As with all attempts at generalization, the effort to list general characteristics for governmental systems in Table 5-1 cannot be wholly successful. There is no "average" democratic state or "average" nondemocratic state. Even Athens' democracy fell far short of being a perfect democracy, for women, resident aliens, and slaves were excluded from participation in the political process, and effective control actually belonged to an elite. The various characteristics listed for each governmental system may vary in different nations. For example, the Soviet Union, which is a totalitarian state, claims to offer a broad voting franchise to its adult citizens and reports that more than 90 percent of eligible voters turn out for elections. However, Soviet voters have little freedom of choice on the ballot, and therefore the franchise has limited value. Similarly, while the democracies claim to protect civil liberties carefully, some persons would argue that these liberties are accorded unevenly—in high degree to middle-class whites and grudgingly or not at all to impoverished nonwhites. Still, within its limitations, Table 5-1 does provide

---

[1] Anarchism is more a philosophical than a governmental system, and has never been put into practice on a large scale. See Chapter 7 for a fuller discussion.

[2] This simple classification arises from the American assumption that our form of government is currently the most successful one, and any political system that wishes to lay claim to being democratic must measure up to American standards. More recently, Americans have realized that their governmental system is not the only one which contains elements of democracy. A basically nondemocratic government can have some democratic characteristics, and what seems democratic to one nation may seem despotic to another. In politics, as in any area of life, one man's meat can be another man's poison.

Table 5-1
The Spectrum of Governmental Power

	Democratic Government		Nondemocratic Government		
Perfect Democracy (Power in hands of the people)	Democracy (USA, Great Britain, France)	Limited Democracy (Mexico, India, Chile)	Authoritarianism (Spain, Egypt, Latin American dictatorships)	Totalitarianism (Communist China, USSR, Fascist Italy, and Nazi Germany)	Perfect Totalitarianism (All power held by government)
Nonpartisan politics	Two-party or multi-party politics	Two-party or multi-party politics	Single-party politics	Single-party politics	Single-party politics
Full individual participation in government	Popular elections with progress toward universal franchise	Popular elections with limited franchise	Self-determined or party-determined leadership	Self-determined or party-determined leadership	Absence of voting franchise
Virtually unlimited individual liberties	Carefully protected individual liberties	Limited individual liberties	Narrow voting right if franchise exists	Voting franchise varies in scope, limited to approval of party candidates	Absence of individual liberties
Absolute social and economic equality	Vertical mobility with progress toward social and economic equality	Approximate freedom of the press	Irregular tolerance of individual liberties	Absence of constitutionalism	Direct military participation in government
Free access to administrative office	Detailed constitutional restraints on government	Limited social and economic equality	Little or no constitutional restraint on government	Extremely narrow political liberties	Governmental control of press
Absolute freedom of the press	Freedom of the press	Limited constitutional restraint upon government	Intermittent martial law	Enforced social stratification	Enforced economic and social stratification
	Broad access to public office	Relatively broad access to public office	Direct military influence on government	Total economic control by government	Intermittent to consistent martial law
	Unrestricted formation of political groups	Free formation of political groups	Social structure determined by state	Intermittent martial law	Thought control and obliteration of individual conscience
			Governmental determination of economic system and structure	Direct military participation in government	
			Government control of press	Government control of press	

general guidelines for differentiating between various types of governmental systems.

Modern Democracy

Within the entire vocabulary of political science, there is probably no single word which has been given more meanings than *democracy*. At the present time, the word has a rather magical connotation and a somewhat tranquilizing effect. Any citizenry which is persuaded that its own governmental system is a democratic one is likely to accept the political power exercised by that system. Hence the Soviet Union under Stalin claimed that it was democratic; the government of mainland China calls itself the "People's Republic"; and governments the world over advertise their democratic attributes. However, the word *democracy* (from the Greek *dēmokratía: dēmos* = people and *kratia* = government) was not always held in such esteem and carried an unfavorable meaning until the nineteenth century. The Athenian example of direct democracy was for many years interpreted to mean unrestrained mob rule,[3] for a "true" democracy had to be a system in which all citizens who so desired met periodically to elect state officials and personally enact laws. This kind of government has been extremely rare throughout history (the few examples are Athens' General Assembly, the New England town meeting, the Israeli kibbutz, and the Swiss Langesdemain) because the classic model of democracy is extremely difficult to execute. While it may have been possible to have everyone's direct participation in a small town where the citizens were well known to each other and matters to be voted upon were comparatively simple, it is far different to attempt direct democracy in a nation such as the United States, which has over 200 million citizens and which must deal with extremely complex issues.[4] A government that had to submit each issue requiring a decision to so many voters would be too unwieldy to function efficiently in a modern technological society. Therefore, representative democracy has evolved as the only workable alternative.

Representative Democracy

In the modern world, democracy is no longer the direct determination of all government policy by the people. Instead the people play a more general role. Democracy today is "a political system which supplies regular constitu-

---

[3] Mostafa Rejai, ed., *Democracy: The Contemporary Theories* (New York: Atherton, 1967), pp. 1–20.

[4] In Chapter 2 of his *In Defense of Anarchism* (New York: Harper & Row, 1970), Robert P. Wolfe discusses the possibility of a modern nation having mass participation in public decisions.

tional opportunities for changing the governing officials, and a social mechanism which permits the largest possible part of the population to influence major decisions by choosing among contenders for political office." [5] "Constitutional" means that the government is a limited one. Restrictions of the legal exercise of power apply not only to the people, who must usually wait for election time to change their leadership, but also to the government, which can wield its authority only in specific ways. Representative democracy has several essential ingredients.[6]

Popular Support of Government. Popular support is the crucial test of modern democratic government, for in a democracy the policy makers' legitimacy usually depends upon the support that they receive in the form of a majority or a plurality of votes cast. The preservation of such support for the leaders by their followers is a key underpinning of democracy, for in a democratic state no one has an inherent right to occupy a position of political power: he must be constitutionally elected by his fellow citizens. To prevent legitimacy from becoming identified with only certain individuals, democratic systems provide for elections either at regular intervals (as in the United States) or at certain maximum time spans (as in Britain). Most such systems do permit and encourage reelection for the purpose of continuity. However, the twenty-second amendment of the United States Constitution, which limits each president to two full terms plus a maximum of two years of a predecesssor's unexpired term, all in sucecssion, is an exception.

The institutions of democratic government also hold lesser officials accountable for their actions, and provide for their dismissal if their leadership is found to be wanting. Senators, representatives, local justices of the peace, as well as prime ministers and presidents, who perform their roles to most voters' satisfaction will usually be returned to office; if they fail to do what the majority of the voters want, they are not likely to be reelected. Thus reelection is the people's means both of expressing support and of controlling the general direction of government policy.[7]

Political Competition. The people's right to reject unsatisfactory officials at the polls is bolstered when a wide range of policies (usually represented by competing political parties) is offered on the ballot. In the United States, for example, the leadership of the Democratic party has stood, generally, for extensive social programs to correct economic and social problems (e.g., Social Security, unemployment insurance, Medicare, job training programs)

[5] Seymour M. Lipset, *Political Man* (Garden City, N.Y.: Doubleday, 1963), p. 27. This definition parallels and is drawn from the definition of democracy given in Joseph Schumpeter, *Capitalism, Socialism, Democracy*, 3rd ed. (New York: Harper & Row, 1950).
[6] Our discussion follows in part Alexander D. Lindsay, *Modern Democratic State* (New York: Oxford University Press, 1962) ; and Seymour M. Lipset, *Political Man*.
[7] The most important statement of this position, and of the logical consequences which follow from it, is in Anthony Downs, *An Economic Theory of Democracy* (New York: Harper & Row, 1957).

and has deemphasized a balanced budget. The leaders of the Republican party, on the other hand, have been more inclined to let the forces of the marketplace determine economic direction, and have stressed fiscal responsibility.[8] While the lines between the two parties are usually not very clear-cut, in most elections there are discernible differences in both philosophy and approach between the two parties, which may aid in voter selection.[9] But the party system is not the sole means (and often it is not the most important means) by which the people may choose alternatives. In addition, voters may always choose among individual candidates, regardless of party backing. One representative or prime minister may be personally identified with an issue such as peace, or with corrupt government or clean government. For example, Harold Macmillan's ouster from 10 Downing Street in 1963 was largely due to the Profumo scandal in his cabinet; Frank Rizzo's election as mayor of Philadelphia in 1970 stemmed from his record as a hard-line law-and-order police commissioner.

Popular Representation.   In representative democracies, the voters elect representatives to act as legislators and, as such, to voice and protect their general interests. Each legislator usually acts for a given district or group of people. The question of just how he should act has concerned political theorists for centuries.[10] Some theorists claim that a system is not democratic unless the legislator treats his election as a mandate to carry out his constituents' wishes. In this case, the legislator informs his constituents about the alternatives in forthcoming decisions, lets them decide what course of action they prefer, and then casts his vote in accordance with their preference. Other theorists disagree, on the grounds that the constituents don't always have an opinion on issues, and claim that a representative must act as a trustee, carrying out the wishes of his constituents when feasible but acting for what he feels are the best interests of the community as a whole. Joseph Schumpeter puts the argument against the mandate theory as follows:

> *. . . Our chief problems about the classical [democratic] theory centered in the proposition that "the people" hold a definite and rational opinion about every individual question and that they give effect to this opinion—in a democracy—by choosing "representatives" who will see to it that that opinion is carried out.*[11]

Of course, the people as a whole do not hold definite opinions on each subject. If they were asked to vote on every question of international shipping

[8] See Herbert J. McClosky, Paul J. Hoffman, and Rosemary O'Hara, "Issue Conflict and Consensus among Party Leaders and Followers," *American Political Science Review* 54 (June 1960) : 406–29.

[9] In a recent article, Gerald Pomper describes the extent to which the American public has come to see the issue difference between the major political parties. See his article, "From Confusion to Clarity: Issues and American Voters," *American Political Science Review* 66 (September 1972) : 415–428.

[10] This question is discussed at far greater length in Chapter 13.

[11] Schumpeter, *Capitalism, Socialism and Democracy*, p. 269.

tonnage restrictions, fine points of parliamentary rules of order, or changes in the staff organization of the Weather Bureau, it is unlikely that voter turnout would be very great. Representative democracy, therefore, does not mean that the representative must become a cipher for his constituents; rather, it means that the people as a body must be able to control the *general* direction of government policy. For example, if the people have made the general policy decision that equal economic opportunity belongs to everyone, they will leave the administrative details of achieving this goal to their legislators. It is this partnership between the people and the lawmakers that is the essence of modern democracy. E. E. Schattschneider summarizes the case succinctly:

The beginning of wisdom in democratic theory is to distinguish between the things that the people can do and the things the people cannot do. The worst possible disservice that can be done to the democratic cause is to attribute to the people a mystical, magical omnipotence which takes no cognizance of what very large numbers of people cannot do by the sheer weight of numbers. At this point the common definition of democracy has invited us to make fools of ourselves.[12]

Majority Rule. In any government decision involving important policy making, there is rarely complete agreement among all parties on all points. Usually one group of citizens will be strongly in favor of an issue, and another group will be just as strongly against it. If the government is to be the instrument of the popular will, but disagreement on issues is customary in society, then how shall the popular will be determined? The simple answer is that the majority shall rule: in any controversy, the policy that has the support of the greatest number of citizens will become the policy of the government. This is the procedure that was used in the democracies of ancient Greece. However, our more modern and practical concept of democracy is "majority rule with minority rights."

A look at any political controversy reveals that, as a fact of political and social life, political minorities do exist. Their members can be seen picketing outside Parliament in London, or hiding behind barricades in Paris, or making their presence known in some way in most of the other major capitals of the world. And the influence of these minorities upon governments is very important. It is safe to say that every view that is now widely held was once a minority view. Virtually everything that is now public policy—except for laws prohibiting crimes such as murder and embezzlement—became public policy as a result of social conflict between majority and minority groups. Furthermore, just as it is true that a minority view may grow to be almost universally accepted over a period of time, so, too, a majority decision may eventually prove to be unwise, unworkable, or unwanted. Just as minorities may be "right," so, too, may majorities be "wrong."

---

[12] E. E. Schattschneider, *The Semisovereign People: A Realist's View of Democracy in America* (New York: Holt, Rinehart and Winston, 1960), p. 139.

Modern liberal democratic tradition tends to place limits on the concept of majority rule. It should not, for example, be used to oppress minorities, and minority rights should only be overruled within certain "accepted standards." If minorities are oppressed by it, the will of the majority then becomes the "tyranny of the majority," which is just as foreboding as executive tyranny. In representative democracies, the burden is upon the majority to persuade minorities rather than to coerce them, and the right of all citizens to dissent is protected. If the majority in power does *not* act in accordance with democratic practice, then citizens may refuse to accept as legitimate the decisions of the governing party since, in their judgment, it is not governing legitimately. (Of course, whether or not a government's actions are in accordance with democratic practice can be a point of great debate. When citizens refuse to accept government decisions as legitimate, they are often subject to the penalties which go along with that disobedience.)

Ideally, in a democracy there should be a high level of social integration so that society will be tolerant of the differences among its members, and political conflict will be interest-oriented—that is, directed to issues and policies—rather than based upon differences of color, race, religion, nationality, or sex. In large industrialized states and in nations now striving to modernize, where society is composed of groups having very different political interests, the prospects for democracy may depend in large measure upon the ability of social organizations to resolve conflicts. If members of different groups do not have adequate contact with one another in order to realize the pettiness of their prejudices, their intolerances, and other differences and to thereby develop a sense of community, then the fundamental conflicts of society may be irreconcilable by democratic and peaceful methods. The result is likely to be a tyranny of more powerful groups over less powerful ones, even though democratic institutions may exist, and members of the dominant groups may feel quite secure in their convictions of democracy. It is worth considering whether this is what has befallen the American blacks, the Roman Catholics of Northern Ireland, and the Pakistani Bengalis prior to the declaration of the state of Bangla Desh in 1971.

One more point deserves mention in our discussion of majority rule. In a democracy, the reins of power will occasionally change hands, both in terms of actual officeholders and in terms of prevailing ideals. The party that was in the majority then becomes a minority. A vivid illustration was the change in the presidency from Herbert Hoover to Franklin Roosevelt in 1933, from an almost complete laissez-faire ("hands off") economic approach toward government to the more controlled policies of the New Deal. The Republican party, which had been in the majority, had to assume a minority role. In a democratic system it is assumed that such changes will be accepted by those who identify themselves with the current minority party and that their opposition will be respectful, civil, legal, and tolerant. The British aptly label their out-parties as "The Loyal Opposition," which remains ready to take the reins of government by lawful means but which meanwhile engages vigorously in the political process in anticipation of the next election. These political tolerances are crucial to the maintenance of a stable democracy and for peaceful successions of power.

Right of Dissent and Disobedience. If government exists to serve the people, then the people must have the right to resist the commands of government if those commands no longer serve the public will. This right was invoked in 1776 by Thomas Jefferson in the Declaration of Independence, and Henry Thoreau made probably the most profound American defense of civil disobedience when he declared, "All men recognize the right of revolution; that is, the right to refuse allegiance to, and to resist, the government, when its tyranny or its inefficiency are great and unendurable."[13] But the most celebrated advocate of civil disobedience was the Indian philosopher Mahatma Gandhi. Gandhi considered his method of resistance to be "civil" because it was legal; that is, while it was disobedience, it did not exceed the general legal structure of the state and did not breach moral codes by doing personal harm to others through violence.

While for the most part Thoreau and Gandhi looked upon civil disobedience as an individual act of conscience, others have sought to organize it and mobilize it. The most prominent American organizer was the late Reverend Martin Luther King, Jr., whose nonviolent resistance campaigns of the 1960s in the name of civil rights brought him into controversy. The many sit-ins and marches which he planned, directed, and often led, kept him face to face with the law for nearly a decade; and he and other members of his Southern Christian Leadership Conference were often imprisoned. The long-range consequence of their actions, however, was a minor revolution in judicial decisions concerning peaceful protest.[14]

Political Equality. In a democracy, at least in theory, everyone is equally able to participate in government and to compete freely for public office. Critics of democracy point out that the reality is often different. They say it takes a great deal of money—and often specific racial and religious ties— to be able to enter public life, and so large numbers of people are barred from seeking public office. A less cynical observer will note, though, that our democratic system of government allows for a change in this situation. Opportunities to serve in public office, at least at the lower levels, are gradually broadening, and minority groups are becoming more adept at political organization.

But there is a second side to political equality, and that is responsibility. If, in a democratic political system, each individual has equal opportunity to express his talents and to achieve personal advancement, then each indi-

---

[13] Henry David Thoreau, *Civil Disobedience* (Brookline, Mass.: David R. Godine, 1971).
[14] For an essay on this subject and a brief anthology of pertinent judicial decisions, see Robert L. Cord, *Protest, Dissent, and the Supreme Court* (Cambridge, Mass.: Winthrop Publishers, 1971), Chapters 4 and 5.

"Look, friend, in a democracy a man has the right to claim he can lick any man in the house but then to change his mind when confronted with overwhelming evidence that he *can't* lick any man in the house."

Drawing by J. Mirachi; © 1971 The New Yorker Magazine, Inc.

vidual is also honor-bound to resist the temptation to exploit society to achieve such personal advancement. In other words, democracy demands individual self-restraint. For example, a person who holds public office should not use that office for individual profit or for preferential treatment of a small group. Although citizens in a democracy are cynically (and perhaps rightly) prepared to assume that politicians are in politics for their own benefit, or that many selected officials are "on the take," they are still appalled by revelations of corruption in government and approve public censure of officials who misuse public funds or use their office for private gain. A case in point is the public's reaction to the involvement of White House aides and presidential advisers in the 1972 attempts to place electronic surveillance equipment inside the Democratic National Headquarters in the Watergate. Some commentators, however, pointed to the success of the grand jury investigation and the Senate inquiry as an example of the effectiveness of the built-in checks and balances in our political system. When both individual self-restraint and some form of checks and balances are lacking, the government may have to impose restraints. A familiar example of government-imposed restraint is antitrust legislation. Monopolistic business practices may provide an opportunity for a few businessmen to become wealthy. But a business having a monopoly on a product is able to exploit its advantage by charging its customers very high prices. Since the businessmen, anxious to make as large profits as they can, may not regulate their own practices adequately, the government may introduce legislation to regulate their activities.

Popular Consultation. Most government leaders realize that to govern effectively they must know what the people want and must be responsive to these needs and demands. Are citizens disturbed—and, if so, *how* disturbed —about foreign policy, taxes, unemployment, the cost of living? Intelligent leaders realize that they must not get too far ahead of—or fall too far behind —public opinion. Therefore, a range of techniques has evolved to test opinion.[15] Public opinion polls are taken on specific issues. The media, by thoughtful probing, can create a dialogue between the people and their leaders. At press conferences and news interviews with elected officials, reporters will ask those questions that they believe the people want answers to. Editorials and letters to the editor are also indicators of citizens' moods and feelings.

In recent years, several critics have noted that U.S. officials often rely heavily on the opinions of small segments of their constituencies, simply because they are well organized and highly vocal. On the issue of gun control, for example, several polls have shown the public at large to be in favor of stronger regulation of the manufacture and sale of firearms. But the National Rifle Association, a tightly knit and outspoken lobbying organization, has managed to effectively block efforts to strengthen legislation in this area.

While public opinion on issues is not nearly so important in nondemocratic states, these leaders also want to know the mood of their people to determine their own limitations of power.

How Democratic Are Democracies?

The New Left is critical of the United States because it believes that the nation is ruled by a small power elite which the voters do not control, and that the national wealth is distributed inequitably. Critics from the Right say that democracy allows mass passions rather than the rule of law to hold sway. Still others point to the excesses of the McCarthy era, or the current drive for a constitutional amendment to forbid school busing, as examples of popular emotion gaining too much control.

Other democracies may also be criticized for various reasons: Great Britain has a hereditary aristocracy; until very recently Switzerland did not grant women the right to vote; Mexico is essentially a one-party state; Venezuela's government has been overthrown frequently by coups d'état. Yet all of these countries consider themselves democracies and, in many respects, legitimately

[15] See Chapter 8, "Socialization and Public Opinion," for more on this.

so. Thus we are left with a question of degree—or the question of *how* demo-cratic is a democratic nation. To cope with this problem, political scientists have attempted to develop an empirical, objective rating system.

Rating Systems of Democracy. While rating systems are useful tools of analysis, it should be stated at the outset that they are imperfect. While the criteria used may be objective in themselves, the choice of *which* criteria to use is necessarily subjective because it reveals what the rater himself believes to be most important in a democracy. However, a system such as the one devised by Deane E. Neubauer, taken together with others, does enable us to make reasonably fair judgments about the various democratic countries.

Professor Neubauer believes that four elements are crucial in judging a democracy. The questions he asks are: What percentage of the adult popula-tion is eligible to vote? Is representation equal? How free are the press and the information media? How great is party competition? For his study, he selected a sample of twenty-three democratic countries and developed an index score for each one. The higher the index score, the greater the degree of democracy within that nation. The results of his rating are shown in Table 5-2.[16]

The United States ranks sixteenth on the list of twenty-three nations, mostly because representation in Congress has been unequal and because there has been a traditional absence of a vigorous two-party system in the South. However, it is evident that these situations are now changing, especially when we remember that President Nixon carried every normally Democratic southern state in 1972, and an updated version of Professor Neubauer's 1967 rating might give the United States a higher index score. The Supreme Court's one-man, one-vote decisions, too, are resulting in a legislative reapportion-ment throughout the country, and this would also have quite an effect on Professor Neubauer's rating. And, as any rating system is inherently subjec-tive, it is more than possible that Northern Irishmen and Commonwealth blacks, and Asians living in England, do not share Professor Neubauer's evaluation of Great Britain as *the* most democratic nation. Similarly, the Walloons might look askance at Belgium's high rating, and Palestinian Arabs might question Israel's rating.

Other rating systems have been devised by Italian political scientist Gio-vanni Sartori, who is concerned with the diffusion of power within the state and popular control of governmental institutions,[17] and by Phillips Cutright, a British sociologist whose rating system considers the frequency of legislative sessions, the length of executive terms, and whether the political opposition

---

[16] Deane E. Neubauer, "Some Conditions of Democracy," *American Political Science Review* 61 (December 1967) : 1005. See Phillips Cutright's rejoinder and Neubauer's reply in *American Political Science Review* 62 (June 1968) : 578–81.

[17] Giovanni Sartori, *Democratic Theory* (New York: Praeger Publishers, 1965), pp. 151–52. A useful collection of articles dealing with this subject is Charles F. Cnudde and Deane E. Neubauer, eds., *Empirical Democratic Theory* (Chicago: Markham, 1969).

Table 5-2
A Rating of Twenty-three Selected Democracies

1.	Great Britain	236.3
2.	France	231.4
3.	Finland	229.4
4.	Sweden	225.8
5.	Netherlands	220.9
6.	Belgium	214.9
7.	Japan	212.7
8.	Luxembourg	210.1
9.	Norway	209.7
10.	New Zealand	209.4
11.	Denmark	205.7
12.	Israel	203.2
13.	West Germany	199.4
14.	Italy	198.6
15.	Canada	196.8
16.	United States	190.9
17.	Venezuela	188.3
18.	Austria	186.9
19.	Chile	184.6
20.	Ireland	181.4
21.	India	172.7
22.	Switzerland	169.3
23.	Mexico	121.9

Source: Deane E. Neubauer, "Some Conditions of Democracy," American Political Science Review 61 (December 1967): 1005.

controls 30 percent or more of the legislature.[18] Anthony Downs holds the following criteria to be essential for a state to be judged democratic: (1) one party (or coalition) must be able to govern effectively; (2) elections must be held at stated intervals, not subject to the wishes of the party in power alone; (3) the rights of citizenship must not be withheld, arbitrarily, from any minority group; (4) every vote must be equal to every other vote; (5) there must be an orderly transfer of power following elections; (6) the losing party must yield to the winner; (7) the party in power must not attempt to restrict the opposition; and finally, (8) two or more powers must contest each election freely.[19]

While none of these systems is perfect (as is evidenced by their variety), they *can* serve as useful guides. Democracy is a fluid, evolving concept that means different things to different people, and will continue to change in

[18] Phillips Cutright, "National Political Development: Measurement and Analysis," *American Sociological Review* 38 (April 1963): 256.
[19] Downs, *An Economic Theory of Democracy*, pp. 23–24. See also Robert A. Dahl, *A Preface to Democratic Theory* (Chicago: University of Chicago Press, 1956), p. 84.

meaning and direction. While totalitarian systems of government adhere to perhaps more specific guidelines, they, too, are not all the same, and variations exist among them just as among the democracies.

Totalitarian Government

It is natural for Americans to think of their system of government as democratic, and of governments of the Communist and Fascist states as totalitarian. But not all countries would agree with this judgment. Some nations which Americans regard as totalitarian consider themselves to be "people's democracies" and claim that *their* form of democracy, not ours, is the authentic democratic system. The problem lies in basic perspectives: all of us evaluate what we see against the background of our own preconceived, culturally ingrained notions. Thus, the Western democracies see democracy as a means of achieving their end, which is the greatest freedom and happiness of men consistent with the general good; the Communist states see democracy as an end in itself, to be achieved by unpleasant means if necessary. For the Communists, a truly democratic society is one in which social classes and the organized state

"If political ferment bugs you, you might be happier with our All-Dictatorship Cruise Itinerary."

Drawing by Donald Reilly; © 1970 The New Yorker Magazine, Inc.

have ceased to exist. To make this goal a reality, there must be a temporary dictatorship with the power to destroy all vestiges of bourgeois capitalist society. In practice, then, totalitarian communism has stressed the role of the state in bringing society close to the ideal. In common with fascism, it holds that the individual cannot develop in isolation, but only within the framework of service to the state.

What Is Totalitarianism?

The twentieth-century phenomenon of totalitarianism is far removed from the autocracies of the past. While rulers such as Peter the Great and Louis XIV were powerful despots, the scope and extent of their power and authority were severely limited by the relatively primitive means of communication and transportation and by the weaponry of the time. Until the twentieth century, communications were so slow and often so difficult that it was impossible for the most autocratic ruler to control effectively or completely all of the territory in his domain. He could demand and receive outward submission to his rule and acknowledgment of his authority, but even Louis XIV—who perhaps came closest to the figure of a modern totalitarian dictator—was not able to bend powerful feudal aristocrats to his will. The average citizen retained control of his private life. In contrast, totalitarian states of the twentieth century now have the potential to remold and transform the people under their control and to regulate every aspect of human life and activity.

Totalitarianism, then, is a unique development dating only from World War I and made possible by modern technology. It is essentially a system of government in which one party holds all political, economic, military, and judicial power. This party attempts to restructure society, to determine the values of society, and to interfere in the personal lives of individual citizens in such a way as to control their preferences, to monitor their movements, and to restrain their freedoms. Where the autocratic ruler was largely indifferent to his subjects' wishes, the totalitarian state insists upon mass participation in activities and makes a deliberate effort to generate enthusiasm for the success of the system. With modern electronic devices, the state is able to control communications and thereby regulate political life and thought; through electronic data control it is able to coordinate and centralize the utilization of resources and thereby regulate economic life.

Basic Features of Totalitarianism.   Carl J. Friedrich and Zbigniew Brzezinski identify six basic features that are common to all totalitarian states.[20] Four of them would have been impossible to achieve in preindustrial societies and are central to the system.

[20] Carl J. Friedrich and Zbigniew Brzezinski, *Totalitarian Dictatorship and Autocracy* (Cambridge, Mass.: Harvard University Press, 1965). Another important study in this area is Hannah Arendt's *The Origins of Totalitarianism* (New York: Harcourt Brace Jovanovich, 1951).

An All-Encompassing Ideology. Totalitarian ideology is an official body of doctrine that applies to all areas of human life. It includes theories of history, economics, and future political and social development, and provides the philosophical framework according to which all decisions are made. Any failures that occur in carrying out the doctrines are presumed to result from human error, because the ideology cannot be wrong. The ideology portrays the world in terms of black and white, with very little gray in between. Thus a citizen is judged to be either whole-heartedly for the state or totally against it—there is no middle ground. And the ideology usually points toward a perfect society which mankind will attain at some distant point in the future (such as Marx's prediction that the classless society would lead to an eventual withering away of the state).

All citizens must give tacit adherence to the official ideology, and they usually devote a good portion of their time to its study. Courses on Marxist-Leninist thought are required in the schools of all Communist states, and in China, the sayings of Chairman Mao are added to the curriculum. The modifications of Stalin, Mao, and Che Guevara to the *Communist Manifesto* are studied in the same way as literary essays that interpret and explain the works of the great masters.

A Single Party. Only one party may exist legally, and that party is usually led by one man who is so strongly identified with the doctrine and with the destiny of the state that he establishes a cult of personality while dictator. Throughout its history, Fascist Italy was ruled by Mussolini; no one but Hitler ruled Nazi Germany; and Mao Tse-Tung has been the sole formal leader of the People's Republic of China from its inception. Stalin was the undisputed leader of the Soviet Union while he lived, though the USSR has had collective leadership in most years since his death.

Entrance into the party is controlled (official membership never exceeds 10 percent of the population) and is considered a great honor. Certain privileges usually accompany membership and, in return, the members give their unquestioning dedication and support to the party. Hierarchically organized and oligarchically controlled, the party is either superior to or completely tied in with the formal institutions of government. The party leader wields considerable power in the government, and party functionaries hold important posts in the bureaucracy. The party's cadres are responsible for imposing at least outward conformity at all levels of society. Some are responsible for their streets or towns; some for their assembly lines at factories; and still others for their fellow students.

Organized Terror. A secret-police apparatus, using both physical and psychological methods, is an essential prop of totalitarian regimes to ensure mass allegiance to the party ideology. The Nazi Gestapo, the Soviet secret police under Stalin, and Mussolini's OVRA were immune from judicial restraints. Constitutional guarantees either did not exist or were ignored in these societies, thus making possible secret arrests, holding people in jail without bringing charges, and torture. The secret-police system may be directed not only against specific individuals, but against whole classes of people as well. Depending on the particular society, these "enemies of the people" may be Jews, landlords, capitalists, socialists, or clergymen. The threat of the "knock at the door" serves two purposes: it terrorizes large segments of the population into acquiescence; and it convinces the more gullible citizens that a conspiracy against the security of the state does, in fact, exist. The mass extermination of entire groups of people under Hitler and Stalin demonstrates the state's enormous power and the individual's corresponding helplessness. Systematic terror rarely enforces loyalty to the regime, however, and the Russians long ago abandoned the more extreme tactics of Stalin's era. But the purges and mass executions have been replaced by the political trial, which dramatizes the value of conformity and also provides a forum for publicizing political doctrine. The trials of dissident literary figures in Russia, for example, emphasize the limits of freedom there to write and to publish.

Monopoly of Communications Control. The primary function of the mass media in totalitarian states is to indoctrinate the people with the official ideology. Enlightenment and entertainment are subordinated to the supposed needs of the state. However, while the communications media are basically organs of propaganda, they are also used to present entertainment, especially as the totalitarian states of the World War II era have become less extreme. The Russians have made films of their prerevolutionary classics, and the Chinese perform traditional Chinese operas and ballets. The rulers of totalitarian states also believe in the unifying effect of cultural pride.

Monopoly of Weapons Control. Governments of totalitarian nations have a complete monopoly on the use of weapons within their borders, thus effectively discouraging any possible armed resistance by dissatisfied minorities. Of course, this statement does not imply that the opposite extreme of popular ownership of weapons is an approved feature of democracy, even though the gun laws in some countries such as the United States are weak. Laws restricting gun ownership in European democracies are quite severe.

Controlled Economy. Rigid, centralized control is imposed on the economy of every totalitarian state. This control serves a twofold purpose. First, it helps make the state powerful, for all natural resources can be allocated to heavy industrialization, to the production of weapons, or to other requirements of the state. Second, a centralized economy serves as an instrument of political management. For example, people can be forcibly moved wherever they are needed to increase productivity in underpopulated areas, and incentive programs can be initiated to stimulate productivity. In all totalitarian states, the needs or wants of the consumer are secondary to those of the government. This is demonstrated by comparing the technological development of two differently controlled national economies: Russia was the first to send men to outer space, for example, but the United States has always had superior consumer products such as automobiles, clothing, and household appliances.

The Russian Five-Year Plans and the Chinese agrarian reforms are examples of major, all-encompassing economic efforts, and their results cannot be denied. For the first time in Chinese history, the spectre of famine no longer exists. And even the totalitarian systems can bend when necessary: while agriculture in Russia is collectivized, farmers are permitted to grow vegetables on small private plots and these vegetable gardens are, ironically, one of the most productive sectors of Russian agriculture. Highly controlled economies are also possible in democracies (such as Sweden and Israel), but in these states the goals are determined by democratically elected governments. In times of crisis, however, Western democracies are also capable of executing major, centralized economic plans that subordinate individual desires to the general good. During World War II, for example, both England and the United States imposed systems of rationing to insure that available supplies of food and other necessities would be distributed equitably among their citizens.

Two Totalitarian Outlooks

While all totalitarian states employ the six techniques described above, not all totalitarian systems are the same. Just as we speak of the Right-wing Conservatives and of the New Left radicals in democracies, so there are more conservative and more radical totalitarian ideologies, depending upon the political and economic conditions out of which the various systems developed.[21]

Right-wing Totalitarianism. Right-wing totalitarianism, as exemplified in Italian Fascism and German National Socialism, developed in industrialized nations that were plagued by economic depression, social upheaval, and political confusion and weakness, and in which democratic roots and traditions were shallow and weak. Germany in the late 1920s and early 1930s was in turmoil. The nation was saddled with an enormous reparations debt following World War I; unemployment was widespread; labor disputes were frequent and violent; and a runaway inflation was wiping out the savings of the lower-middle and middle classes—the shopkeepers, the petty bureaucrats, and the skilled workers. In his rise to power, Hitler promised to crush the labor unions, to restore order, to revoke the humiliating Versailles Treaty, and to protect private property from the Communist menace to the East. His program appealed to the industrialists, the militarists, and the middle-class workers, who typically constitute the backbone of a Fascist state's support.[22]

Right-wing totalitarianism does not seek to revolutionize society completely; rather it aims to strengthen the existing social order and to glorify

[21] See Chapter 7 for a more detailed discussion of ideologies.
[22] Arendt, *The Origins of Totalitarianism.*

the state. It attempts to get rid of those elements of society or those institutions that are believed to prevent the state from achieving greatness—as Hitler strove to annihilate the Jewish and gypsy populations who interfered with his concept of the master Aryan race. Economic policies are also directed toward the national glory, so Fascist states are not wedded to one type of economic organization. Usually the state will direct economic development and production through cartels and national trade associations. However, these organizations normally permit industry to exercise some advisory and technical control over the party functionaries who formulate basic policy.

Left-wing Totalitarianism. The more radical totalitarian ideologies, as exemplified by Russian and Chinese communism, seek to revolutionize society —to overthrow existing social and political structures in order to form entirely new ones modeled on some futuristic utopia. A primary concern of the Communist system is to provide all citizens with basic economic needs by taking wealth from the "haves" and distributing it among the "have nots." [23] Communism, therefore, does not appeal to a frustrated middle class that already "has" a little and seeks to "have more." Karl Marx proved to be a poor prophet when he predicted that communism would triumph first in an industrially advanced nation. The system does not flourish either in the poorest and most backward countries, but rather in those developing societies in which only the first stages of modernization have taken place. The societies most receptive to communism are those that have a frustrated intelligentsia, an urban industrial working class (small as it may be), and a peasantry that has become sufficiently awakened to demand land distribution and a voice in politics.[24] Communism is the totalitarian method of achieving the goals of these three groups, as is illustrated by the economic reforms Marx proposed in his *Communist Manifesto:*

1. Abolition of property in land and application of all rents of land to public purposes.

2. A heavy progressive or graduated income tax.

3. Abolition of all rights of inheritance.

4. Confiscation of the property of all emigrants and rebels.

5. Centralization of credit in the hands of the state, by means of a national bank with state capital and an exclusive monopoly.[25]

---

23 Friedrich and Brzezinski, *Totalitarian Dictatorship and Autocracy.*
24 William Ebenstein et al., *American Democracy in World Perspective* (New York: Harper & Row, 1970), p. 72.
25 Karl Marx, "The Communist Manifesto," in *Essential Works of Marxism,* ed. Arthur P. Mendel (New York: Bantam, 1961), p. 32.

In Communist states, economic change comes as soon as the new leaders have consolidated their control. The change is fundamental, and reaches every area of economic activity. Agriculture is collectivized; and the factories, means of transportation, communications, and other industries are taken over by the state and run by a centrally directed bureaucracy. The system in practice today is not completely rigid, however, and some of the states that formerly followed a strict Communist line are experimenting with greater worker participation at the lower levels of decision making. Yugoslavia is a good example: after Tito made his famous break with Stalin in 1948, workers' councils, unions, commune assemblies, and economic associations were formed and given important and far-reaching powers. While the basic policy decisions are still made by the party leaders, the level of industrial democracy that does exist makes the individual worker feel that his views are wanted and needed.[26]

Economics and Politics: A Digression

Americans are in the habit of equating totalitarianism with a communistic economy, and democracy with capitalism. The fact is, of course, that no causal relationship exists between economic and political systems. History has proved that totalitarianism can coexist with capitalism (Nazi Germany, Fascist Italy) and that socialism can coexist with democracy (Sweden, Israel, and some sectors of the British economy). Just as no "pure" political system exists, neither does a "pure" economic system. Some form of public regulation must exist in modern industrial states despite the periodic lip-service given to the "free enterprise system." In all European democracies, for example, the railroads have always been state controlled. The United States government has powerful regulatory agencies that make important policy decisions concerning the direction that our economy will take. Franklin D. Roosevelt's New Deal and Richard Nixon's wage and price control program were both cases of the government taking an active role in changing the "natural course" of economic events. Moreover, specific actions such as a decision by the Food and Drug Administration to take a drug off the market because it is unsafe can be taken as well. Government intrusions into private decisions have become inevitable in our complex world. And, as we have indicated above, Communist states bend in the direction of private initiative when necessary.

The degree of private or public ownership and the ways in which the economic systems are administered will depend upon local circumstances. As economist Barbara Ward points out:

In every country the mix between public and private enterprise is likely to be different, because it will in each case reflect local political pressures, local

[26] For a more detailed description and evaluation of workers' participation in decisions in Yugoslavia, see Carole Pateman, *Participation and Democratic Theory* (Cambridge, England: Cambridge University Press, 1970), Chapter 5.

opportunities, the local scale of developed private enterprise, and the capacity of the country itself to find resources within its own borders.[27]

Thus, a nation's economic system is no indicator of its political system; the two are not so closely interrelated that one must follow the other.

Authoritarianism and the "Third World"

What Is Authoritarianism?

The terms *authoritarianism* and *totalitarianism* are often confused, but the two words have quite different meanings. Authoritarianism is a system of government in which power is exercised by some particular element. The element may be a family, in which case the authoritarian regime is an absolute monarchy. It may be a social class, as in a liberal monarchy ruled by a king with the assistance of the nobility, or in an elitist democracy where power is shared by a few prominent individuals. Or the element may be a strong political party, whose principal concern is to forge domestic solidarity at a time of national need. This type of one-party system is typical of the developing nations of Africa below the Sahara, most of Asia, and much of Latin America.

Authoritarian governments generally do not attempt to control every aspect of human activity. Economic, social, religious, cultural, and familial matters are usually left up to the individual. Shakespeare's King Henry V summed up the authoritarian philosophy when he said, "Every subject's duty is the king's; but every subject's soul is his own."

This is not to say that authoritarian regimes promote individual freedoms. Authoritarianism views society as a hierarchical organization with a specific chain of command under the leadership of one ruler or group. Command, obedience, and order are higher values than freedom, consent, and involvement. Therefore, the citizen is expected to obey laws and pay taxes that he has no voice in establishing. While the institutions of democracy may exist in an authoritarian state, they have little real function. The national legislature, for example, is usually little more than a "rubber stamp" to approve the ruling element's proposals. The theory and practice of an authoritarian ruler were best expressed by Louis XIV when he declared, "I am the state."

Authoritarian regimes have been the most common form of government throughout history and remain so today, even though we hear relatively little about them in comparison to democracies and totalitarian states. The reason

[27] Barbara Ward, *The Rich Nations and the Poor Nations* (New York: W. W. Norton, 1962), p. 10.

why we hear less about authoritarian states is a simple one: the major powers of the modern world are either democratic or totalitarian. News about the overwhelming numbers of authoritarian nations is therefore less likely to make the front pages.

Authoritarianism and the Developing Nations

Perhaps the most significant political movement since the end of World War II has been the breaking up of former colonial empires into independent nations. For the most part, the ideological struggle for national independence in these states followed the general philosophical argument of the American Declaration of Independence and the French Declaration of the Rights of Man and Citizen. Yet, once their national independence was won, democracy did not seem suitable to the conditions in these societies, and if it was adopted, it did not last long. A political culture in which self-rule and self-determination were never integral values may not adapt well to the immediate introduction of political democracy. Then, too, democracy in the Western tradition is characterized by the individualism that is, in large part, the result of a capitalist market system that stresses competition. The developing societies are preindustrial, traditional peasant economies in which family and tribal cooperation have traditionally been far more important than individual competition and self-enrichment. In fact, capitalistic enterprise, which we value so highly, has a poor reputation in many of these countries since it was often superimposed upon them by colonial powers without regard for their particular needs.

In many of these societies where the levels of education and economic prosperity are very low, the majority of the people are often completely absorbed in the struggle to survive. The leadership often feels that political and economic survival and growth are dependent on strong leaders who can act according to what they perceive is really needed, rather than what is immediately popular. Rejecting both Western-style democracy and Communist totalitarianism,[28] most of the developing countries have thus opted for a third alternative—that of single-party dominance. Some, like Kenya, experimented with a two-party system immediately after independence, but found that the parties encouraged ancient tribal animosities and were, therefore, contributing to disunity. Eventually, after a series of disruptions and assassinations, a one-party state was established officially in Kenya. The single national party has proved to be effective in reducing tribal hostilities, allocating resources efficiently, and speeding economic development. Under present economic and

[28] See Edward A. Shills, *Political Development in the New States* (The Hague: Mouton, 1962); and Daniel Lerner, *The Passing of Traditional Society* (New York: The Free Press, 1958).

social circumstances, therefore, nations such as Kenya, the Ivory Coast, Algeria, and Guinea regard authoritarianism as more relevant to their national needs than Western democracy, and far more practicable than totalitarian communism. It should also be pointed out that authoritarianism can—and does—exist in developed states as well. (Spain and Portugal are current examples.)

Democracy's Future Prospects in the World

Of the 143 nations that comprise the world community, probably not more than two dozen can be regarded as democratic in the usual way in which the term has been applied to Western democracies. Two hundred years ago, men like Thomas Jefferson and Thomas Paine had high hopes for democracy and expected that the fledgling United States would be an inspiration to the rest of the world to throw off the "shackles" of authoritarian rule. Their dream has not come to pass, and it appears unlikely that it will—at least within the foreseeable future.

Governments tend to reflect the social and political cultures of their societies. Western democracy rests, in large part, upon individualism. But family, tribe, and community are far more important than the individual in most of the world. The Chinese family was traditionally the most important segment in Chinese society. One did not act for one's own good, but for the good of the entire clan; to do otherwise would have been unthinkable because personal happiness was considered impossible outside the framework of the family. This tradition of giving up individual needs for the good of the whole made Chinese society more receptive to a totalitarian form of government.

Some scholars apply similar reasoning to the tradition of democracy and claim that since democracy is an outgrowth of Protestantism and capitalism, it cannot be transplanted successfully to societies of different religions and economic systems. Others vehemently deny this cultural argument, on the grounds that religion, economic systems, and forms of government have no necessary relationship.

As democracy is the form of government that we are accustomed to, it is quite natural that we should look upon it as the most desirable form. However, we should remember that democracy rests upon our own value system and, just as Shintoism would have a difficult time winning converts in Kentucky or Ohio, we cannot expect our values and forms of government to be easily adopted by non-Western cultures. Even if the emerging nations should achieve the levels of education and economic development that would sustain democracy, it may be difficult to persuade their rulers to relinquish power voluntarily. And it may well be that the Eastern, nonindustrial, collectivist societies are not capable of supporting Western-style industrial democracy.

Suggested Readings

Brzezinski, Zbigniew. *Between Two Ages: America's Role in the Technocratic Era.* New York: The Viking Press, 1970. In essence, an argument that technocracy will lead to the convergence of the major "isms."

Dahl, Robert A. *A Preface to Democratic Theory.* Chicago: University of Chicago Press, 1956. Original, insightful essays on democratic theory, from Madisonian democracy to polyarchy.

Downs, Anthony. *An Economic Theory of Democracy.* New York: Harper & Row, 1956. A formal model that applies the democratic formula to party politics and systematically examines the results.

Friedrich, Carl J., and Brzezinski, Zbigniew. *Totalitarian Dictatorship and Autocracy.* Cambridge, Mass.: Harvard University Press, 1965. A comprehensive and penetrating analysis of the nature of totalitarianism.

Orwell, George. *1984.* New York: The New American Library, 1971. A futuristic vision of a society in which all human activity is regulated.

Schumpeter, Joseph. *Capitalism, Socialism, Democracy.* 3rd ed. New York: Harper & Row, 1950. A comprehensive examination of these three systems and the nature of the political systems that mix parts of each.

Democracy in America: The pluralist and elitist views

CHAPTER 6

Among the many nations that claim democracy as the basis for government is there one in which the people actually make decisions? Do the people really rule in the Democratic Republic of East Germany or in the People's Republic of China? Do the citizens of the United States decide whether to build a road, subsidize farmers, or sell wheat to the Soviet Union?

In theory, the American people do make these decisions—indirectly, through elected representatives. Few people would maintain that in a country as large and complex as the United States a democracy should or could be run in the classical sense of mass participation in every political decision. It might have been possible in ancient Greece,[1] but some theorists argue that classical democracy has never been possible—and never will be. Italian

[1] See the discussion of democracy in Chapter 5 of this text.

political scientist Gaetano Mosca, for example, argues that government always falls into the hands of a few.

In all societies—from societies that are very undeveloped and have largely attained the dawnings of civilization, down to the most advanced and powerful societies—two classes of people appear—a class that rules and a class that is ruled. The first class, always the less numerous, performs all of the political functions, monopolizes power, and enjoys the advantages that power brings, whereas the second, the more numerous class, is directed and controlled by the first, in a manner that is now more or less legal, now more or less arbitrary and violent.[2]

Even those political scientists who question Mosca's generalization to "all societies" feel that participatory democracy is not possible in large modern societies. Government is too big and the issues too complex for every citizen to have a voice in decisions. In the words of Robert Dahl, "The key political, economic, and social decisions . . . are made by tiny minorities. . . . It is difficult—nay impossible—to see how it could be otherwise in large political systems."[3]

"At last! One Nation, indivisible."

Drawing by Koren; © *1970 The New Yorker Magazine, Inc.*

[2] Gaetano Mosca, *The Ruling Class* (New York: McGraw-Hill, 1939), p. 50.
[3] Robert A. Dahl, "Power, Pluralism, and Democracy: A Modest Proposal" (Paper delivered at the 1964 annual meeting of the American Political Science Association), p. 3.

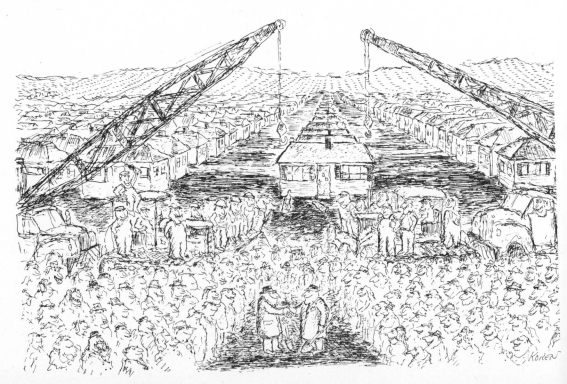

Given the impracticality—and impossibility—of classical, participatory democracy in modern societies, and given the variety of governments "by the few" which claim to be democratic, the problem is to find answers to two questions: How can we determine whether or not a government is democratic? And, who actually governs in a democracy?

In Chapter 5, democracy was defined as a political system which provides opportunities for changing public officials and which allows the people to influence decision making through voting.[4] In that chapter, a set of criteria was proposed for evaluating the democratic nature of a governmental system:

1. Officials must have popular support in the form of votes and elected officials must be held accountable.
2. There must be choice in voting and competition in the political system.
3. Legislation must be made through representation.
4. There must be majority rule with tolerance for the minority voice.
5. There must be right of dissent and civil disobedience.
6. There must be equal opportunity to try for public office.
7. Officials must strive to know public opinion.

Using these criteria as a basis for judgment, we can begin to determine whether or not a system of government is democratic, thereby answering the first question posed before. But what about the second question? Who actually governs in a democracy? Are the wishes and desires of the majority reflected in the decisions of elected officials? In the United States, do the people govern, or is this country, too, a government "by the few"? In an attempt to answer these questions, this chapter examines two theories of democracy —elitism and pluralism.

Two Theories: Elitism and Pluralism

To discuss elitism and pluralism is really to discuss two elitist theories: single elitism and plural elitism. Pluralism in the sense of direct government by the citizenry is not at issue. Because this country's political culture is predominantly democratic, the concept of elites is offensive to many Americans. We associate the term with the feudal aristocracies of medieval Europe, the warlords of China and Japan, and the political and military dictatorships of modern times (Hitler's and Stalin's inner circles).[5] But an elite is not necessarily hereditary, tyrannical, or self-seeking.

---

[4] See Chapter 5, pp. 102–12.
[5] This chapter focuses on the United States. For a discussion of traditional and contemporary elites in other nations, see Marian D. Irish and Elke Frank, *An Introduction to Comparative Politics: Twelve Nation States* (New York: Appleton-Century-Crofts, 1970), pp. 98–119.

Broadly defined, an elite is a small group of people who rule in the sense of directly initiating (or vetoing) decisions about "who gets what, when, and how." For example, in a hospital doctors constitute an elite. They decide who gets what treatment, when, and how. No one is born a doctor; their elite status derives from expertise that is available to anyone who can complete medical training. Nor are doctors "tyrannical"; they do not deprive people of their freedom to move about or eat certain foods out of caprice or out of desire for power.

A political elite may, like the medical profession, be open to anyone who seeks a position in government and is capable of filling that position, or it may be closed to all but those who were born to the "right" family or those with large sums of money or those of a certain religion. It may be responsive to the needs and desires of the many, or it may be aloof and self-seeking.[6] A political elite may be temporary (lasting for a single administration or until a specific problem is solved) or long-lasting. It may hold a monopoly over power within a society, or it may share power with other, competing elites.[7]

Elitism

Political scientists are divided over the question of what kind of elite or elites govern America. Some—for example, C. Wright Mills—take a "single elitist" position.[8] According to this view, America is ruled by a single, relatively closed, upper-class elite that responds to public pressure only when its position is threatened. This group holds a power monopoly in America because it controls essential resources—including wealth, education, executive and legal experience, and "connections" (with political, military, business, and educational leaders). Membership in the ruling elite depends on socioeconomic status, not on elections or expertise. The elite is stable over time and through changing issues.

This elitist view holds that America's power elite does admit new members—partly to rejuvenate its own ranks, partly to prevent potential leaders from building counterelites. Once admitted, however, new members tend to become conservative. A common interest in preserving the system and their position in it holds the elite together. When members differ over specific issues they accommodate one another, rather than disturb the existing power structure. The elite does take the "masses" into account, but only when it chooses to do so. Elections are felt to be largely symbolic: a candi-

[6] Thomas R. Dye and L. Harmon Zeigler, *The Irony of Democracy: An Uncommon Introduction to American Politics* (Belmont, Calif.: Wadsworth, 1970), pp. 1–2.

[7] By *power*, we mean the ability to carry out decisions. In Robert Dahl's words, "A has power over B to the extent that he can get B to do something that B would not otherwise do." See "The Concept of Power," *Behavior Science* 2 (July 1957): 202; and Chapter 2 of this textbook.

[8] C. Wright Mills, *The Power Elite* (New York: Oxford University Press, 1956).

date can seldom be elected to public office without elite support (specifically, money and "connections"). In short, the people must choose between two candidates who basically share a common orientation and background; thus, they have little chance of making a dramatic change in public policy.

A number of advocates of this elitist theory argue that in the United States and other Western democracies this power elite actually protects the basic democratic values of individual liberty, due process of law, limited government, and free enterprise. In general, they feel members of the elite are far more tolerant than the average man, who is typically ill-informed, intolerant, and antidemocratic.[9] The single elitist position thus suggests that government by the elite, which seems inimical to the nature of democracy, is actually the means by which we preserve the basic tenets of our system.

Pluralism

A second school of political scientists, the pluralists, contends that America is governed not by a single elite, but by a number or plurality of specialized, competing elites.[10] Membership in these influential groups varies with the times and with the issues. Business lobbyists and union leaders, for example, may unite to support high tariffs on foreign goods but oppose one another on the issue of wage controls, while neither takes an active role in the controversy over school busing. Competition among several elites prevents any one person or group from gaining control of the political system.

Pluralists do not argue with the view that elites are bound together by common interests and that they take a public-minded stance when it serves those interests. But while elitists feel that this posture unites influential individuals and groups "for the good of the system," pluralists hold that the elite unites for the purpose of inhibiting competition—and competition is the key to the pluralist position. Pluralists maintain that political decisions are the result of bargaining and competition among elites. The government, according to this view, plays the role of arbitrator, making sure that elites with differing interests adhere to the "rules of the game."

Robert Dahl, among others, believes that this pluralist system is essentially democratic, in the sense that individuals and minorities *can* influence decision makers through elections and interest groups. No public official can afford to ignore his electorate. If a group of people with a stake in a particular decision organize and speak out, and if their viewpoint is considered legitimate by the majority of the electorate, their representatives will respond.[11] In the American political system, Dahl writes, "all active and

[9] Dye and Zeigler, *The Irony of Democracy*, Chapter 5.
[10] Note that pluralists do not believe America is a populist democracy, ruled by the people. For this reason pluralists are sometimes called "plural-elitists." See Robert A. Dahl, *A Preface to Democratic Theory* (Chicago: University of Chicago Press, 1956).
[11] Organization is a key point here. Pluralists do not argue that private individuals can influence decision makers, but that "active and legitimate" interest groups can.

legitimate groups in the population can make themselves heard at some crucial stage in the process of decision." [12] Thus, pluralists suggest that America is governed by a plurality of elites and interest groups that check one another in open competition—what Dahl calls "minorities rule."

Who Rules America?

Neither elitists nor pluralists accept the traditional image of America as a populist democracy governed by the common man. Both recognize that policy decisions are made by a small number of people who tend to be wealthier, better educated, and "better connected" than the average American. However, elitists and pluralists differ sharply over the question of elite solidarity and the meaning of public participation in elections and interest groups. Elitists hold that the "men at the top" work together and that elections and interest groups are largely symbolic; pluralists contend that those in power are highly competitive and that elections and interest groups give the common man access to the system.

The Elitist View

America's Founding Fathers, according to elitists, were "bond holders, investors, merchants, real-estate owners, and planters"—not average citizens.[13] To these men, the primary function of government was to protect individuals from political tyranny (a king) and mass movements. They designed the Constitution to limit government and thus preserve economic individualism.

Between the Revolution and the Civil War, the government was dominated by three different elites. In 1800 Thomas Jefferson, a Virginia planter, unseated the mercantile aristocracy and and its Federalist party; in 1828 Andrew Jackson, a member of the Western nouveau riche, replaced the Jeffersonians. But basic policy changed only slightly when Jefferson and Jackson each took office. This peaceful transfer, say elitists, is evidence that the elite considered stability more important than political ideology.

Only once in American history did elite consensus break down—in the years leading up to the Civil War. Both northern and southern aristocrats

[12] Robert A. Dahl, *A Preface to Democratic Theory*, p. 137. Dahl suggests that to be effective, a group must be *both* active and legitimate. Blacks prior to the 1960s had a legitimate claim to a role in politics, but they were not active; Communists have long been organized and active, but the majority of the electorate does not consider their viewpoint legitimate.

[13] See Charles Beard, *An Economic Interpretation of the Constitution* (New York: The Free Press, 1935); and Forrest McDonald, *We the People: The Economic Origins of the Constitution* (Chicago: University of Chicago Press, 1958).

saw the West as the key to power. This rivalry, not ideological differences, led to war. When the South was defeated, control of the economy and, indirectly, of government passed to the rising class of industrial capitalists, who ruled unchecked for the next fifty to sixty years.

Plural elitists often cite the New Deal as evidence that the people do influence the government. Single elitists disagree. Roosevelt himself was a member of the upper class. He saw that the "rugged individualism" of the early capitalists had failed (in the Great Depression) and realized that the elite would have to become more public-minded if it was to maintain its position. The New Deal was based on a growing sense of noblesse oblige, and this new attitude led directly to America's involvement in international affairs as the guardian of democracy, and indirectly to the growth of the military.[14]

Since World War II, the military has been industry's biggest consumer, and industry government's biggest supporter. "Corporate chieftains" and "professional warlords" rule America, according to C. Wright Mills.[15] President Eisenhower warned of this when he left office in 1961:

The total influence [of an immense military establishment and a large arms industry]—economic, political, even spiritual, is felt in every city, every statehouse, every office of the federal government. We recognize the imperative need for this development. Yet we must not fail to comprehend its grave implications. Our toil, resources, and livelihood are involved; so is the very structure of our society.

In the councils of government, we must guard against the acquisition of unwarranted influence, whether sought or unsought, by the military industrial complex. . . .

Most elitists see this trend as continuing.[16]

Of course, the past is always open to a degree of interpretation. How do elitists document the existence of a power elite in America today?

The Power Elite. A quick reading of *Who's Who in America*, elitists argue, shows that a relatively small group of men dominate executive positions in government, finance, industry, and education. These men move back and forth, working now in government, now in business. For example, the Secretaries of Defense from 1953 to 1972 all had held key positions in industry and finance (see Table 6–1). Elitists feel this overlap in personnel disproves the pluralist concept of independent, competing elites. Although

---

[14] See Dye and Zeigler, *The Irony of Democracy*, Chapters 2, 3, and 13, for a detailed presentation of the elitist view of history.

[15] C. Wright Mills's *The Power Elite* is the classic statement of this position.

[16] At least one observer argues that the radical left of the sixties—whose membership was largely white, upper class, and highly educated—was still another branch of the elite. See Aaron Wildavsky, *The Revolt Against the Masses, and Other Essays on Politics and Public Policy* (New York: Basic Books, 1971), pp. 29–55.

Table 6-1
Background of Recent Secretaries of Defense

Secretary of Defense	Background
Charles E. Wilson (1953–57)	Electrical engineer, Westinghouse; chief executive officer, General Motors.
Neil H. McElroy (1957–59)	President, Procter and Gamble; member, board of directors, General Electric, Chrysler Corporation, Equitable Life; trustee, Harvard University, National Safety Council, National Industrial Conference.
Thomas S. Gates, Jr. (1959–61)	Law partner, Drexel and Company; president, Morgan Guaranty Trust; Undersecretary of the Navy; Secretary of the Navy.
Robert S. McNamara (1961–67)	President, Ford Motor Company; member, board of directors, Scott Paper; assistant professor of Business Administration, Harvard University.
Clark Clifford (1967–69)	Senior partner, Clifford and Miller law firm; member, board of directors, National Bank of Washington, Sheridan Hotel Corporation; trustee, Washington University, St. Louis.
Melvin Laird (1969–72)	State senator, U.S. congressman, Wisconsin.
Elliot L. Richardson (Jan.–April 1973)	Partner, Ropes and Gray law firm; director, New England Trust; member, board of governors, Harvard University; member, Advisory Council, Trustees of the Reservation; trustee, Massachusetts General Hospital; director, Massachusetts Bay and United Bay; member, board of directors, World Affairs Council, Boston United Community Services; Clerk to Judge Learned Hand, U.S. Court of Appeals, and to Justice Felix Frankfurter, U.S. Supreme Court; Assistant Secretary for Legislation, HEW; U.S. Attorney for Massachusetts; Lieutenant Governor of Massachusetts; Attorney General of Massachusetts; Under Secretary of State; Secretary of HEW.
James R. Schlesinger (April 1973–)	Director, CIA; chairman, Atomic Energy Commission; strategic analyst, Rand Corporation; assistant director, Bureau of the Budget, Atomic Energy Commission.

Sources: Compiled from the following material: Christopher Lydon, "Richardson and Justice," The New York Times Magazine (May 20, 1973); The World Almanac, 1973 (New York: Newspaper Enterprise Association, 1973); Congressional Quarterly Almanac, 1972, vol. 28; Who's Who in Government, 1972–73, first edition (Chicago; Marquis Who's Who, 1973); Who Was Who in America, 1961–1968 (Chicago: Marquis Who's Who, 1968); Who's Who in America, 1972 (Chicago: Marquis Who's Who, 1972); John W. Finney, "Senate Confirms Schlesinger as Pentagon Chief," Boston Herald American (June 29, 1973).

formally separated, American business and American government are run by the same people.

The effect of personnel overlap is most obvious in the government's thirty-three regulatory agencies. According to G. William Domhoff's analysis, these agencies often become a covert lobby for the interests they are supposed to regulate.[17] Logically, the president appoints executives who have experience in the field. Most of these appointees consider their position in government temporary and are reluctant to make decisions that might jeopardize future jobs in the private sector. Because of budget limitations, regulatory agencies sometimes depend on private research for information. For example, a decision about whether to permit an oil company to drill offshore may depend on that company's study of the ocean floor.[18] In addition, agency officials and industry lobbyists spend a good deal of time together. Familiarity—not necessarily corruption—may gradually cause them to think alike.[19]

To these arguments, elitists add the fact that most government officials are wealthy, upper class, and well-educated [20]—for several reasons. Only people who can afford to temporarily abandon their careers for a campaign or to take relatively low-paying government jobs are able to seek public office, appointed or elected. Moreover, a person who does not have executive experience and connections may fail as an administrator. C. Wright Mills wrote,

To be celebrated, to be wealthy, to have power, requires access to major institutions, for the institutional positions men occupy determine in large part their chances to have and to hold valued experience.[21]

In *America, Inc.*, elitist theorists Morton Mintz and Jerry Cohen suggest that the executives of the country's biggest corporations have as much or more to say about "who gets what, when, and how" as do government officials.[22] Despite antitrust laws, a handful of giant corporations dominates the economy. Like the government, they have the power to levy taxes (by raising prices), to affect the quality of life (with products and wages), and to change the environment (with chemical wastes, strip mining, smoke stacks). Corporations may influence legislators with campaign donations, with personal favors such as the loan of an airplane, and through their

17 G. William Domhoff, *Who Rules America?* (Englewood Cliffs, N.J.: Prentice-Hall, 1967), pp. 97–114.
18 See Malcolm F. Baldwin, "The Santa Barbara Oil Spill," *Law and the Environment*, Malcolm F. Baldwin and James K. Page, eds. (New York: Walker, 1970), pp. 5–47.
19 Richard Harris, *The Real Voice* (New York: Macmillan, 1964), p. 145.
20 Five of eight Secretaries of State and eight of thirteen Secretaries of Defense between 1932 and 1967 were listed in the Social Register (Domhoff, *Who Rules America*). For a description of elected officials, see Donald Matthews, *Social Background of Political Decision Makers* (New York: Doubleday, 1954).
21 C. Wright Mills, *The Power Elite*, pp. 10–11.
22 Morton Mintz and Jerry S. Cohen, *America, Inc.: Who Owns and Operates the United States* (New York: Dell, 1971). Introduction by Ralph Nader.

power to close a plant which a congressman's constituents depend on for jobs.

In recent years, regulation of corporations has been complicated by the growth of holding companies (whose only "product" is stock certificates) and institutional investors (banks, mutual funds, insurance companies) who have taken over the role once played by men like Henry Ford.[23] If the government suspects "foul play," it prosecutes General Motors or the Dreyfus Fund—not individuals; corporate officials are not held accountable for their decisions. In addition, a single man may be on the board of directors of several companies. Antitrust laws are, according to elitists, ineffective against these interlocking directorates.

Pluralists argue that the people—groups of people—*can* influence and regulate government and corporation policy. If a president or mayor appoints corrupt officials to regulatory agencies, the people can vote against him. They can refuse to buy unsafe automobiles or give time and money to citizen's lobbies. Elitists do not feel that public pressure—through elections or interest groups—influences those in power.

Elections. For elections to be a truly effective democratic institution, say elitist theorists Dye and Zeigler, they would have to meet four conditions:

1. Competing candidates would offer clear policy alternatives.
2. Voters would be concerned with policy questions.
3. Majority preference on these questions would be ascertained in election results.
4. Elected officials would be bound by the positions they assumed during the campaign.[24]

Only rarely, these authors conclude, do the two major parties offer voters a true choice of "policy alternatives"—partly because Republicans and Democrats agree on goals, if not on methods; partly because both recognize that voters do not respond to ideological debate. Despite strong party loyalties, few Americans can identify their own political position (liberal, middle-of-the road, conservative), and few see clear differences between the two major parties. Apparently voters choose candidates on the basis of their personalities and presentation, not for their policies. In 1964, for example, Lyndon Johnson strongly opposed Barry Goldwater's "hawkish" stand on Vietnam. Polls indicated, however, that 52 percent of those who favored a stronger stand—even if it meant invading North Vietnam—voted not for Goldwater, but for Johnson.

Since so many eligible voters fail to exercise their franchise, no presi-

[23] See Adolf Berle, *The Modern Corporation and Private Property*, rev. ed. (New York: Harcourt Brace Jovanovich, 1969).
[24] Dye and Zeigler, *The Irony of Democracy*, pp. 149 ff., forms the basis for this section.

dent in modern times has won the votes of a majority of the American people. In fact, in 1968 a majority of eligible voters either stayed away from the polls or voted for a third-party candidate. In 1972 only 55 percent of the eligible population voted. In an average presidential election, only 60 to 65 percent of the eligible population votes. Elections thus do not represent majority opinion.

But even if a majority did express its opinion on the issues at the polls, there is no guarantee that elected officials would abide by their campaign platforms. Once elected, President Johnson followed a policy in Vietnam that came close to Goldwater's platform. Between 1968 and 1972, President Nixon imposed wage and price controls, took steps toward a wide-ranging détente with the USSR, and improved relations with the People's Republic of China—policies and actions the Republicans had traditionally opposed.

For these reasons, elitists consider elections a mere "symbolic exercise," designed to give the people the feeling that they participate. According to Murray Edelman, elections allow the people to express "quiet resentments and doubts about particular political acts [and] reaffirm belief in the fundamental rationality and democratic nature of the system. . . ." [25]

Interest Groups. According to elitist theorists, labor unions, professional associations, mass political movements, PTAs, and so on tend to become oligarchical. Few people have time to work actively in interest groups; control falls into the hands of the active few. As long as these leaders act within broad limits of propriety, the inactive majority accepts their authority as spokesmen. Gradually the leaders begin to personify the group; rank-and-file opinions are considered "unofficial." [26] For example, in the early 1960s, AFL-CIO officials backed Johnson's civil rights legislation, although the rank and file generally preferred *not* to compete with black workers.[27] Like government and corporation officials, interest group leaders develop a vested interest in maintaining the system and their position in it. In a sense, they join the elite.

To these criticisms of the pluralist idea that interest groups are a medium for public opinion, Robert Presthus adds that private organizations sometimes "achieve their ends at the expense of a broader, unorganized public. . . ." [28] For example, despite the number of dramatic assassinations and attempted assassinations involving guns, the National Rifle Association has successfully blocked congressional attempts to pass gun control legislation. The people who do not own guns and who favor controls on their sale might be in the majority, but unorganized, these people cannot make their

[25] Murray Edelman, *The Symbolic Uses of Power* (Urbana: University of Illinois Press, 1964), p. 17.
[26] Robert Presthus, *Men at the Top* (New York: Oxford University Press, 1964), pp. 20–21.
[27] Edelman, *The Symbolic Uses of Power*, p. 124.
[28] Presthus, *Men at the Top*, p. 18.

voices heard. Consumer advocate Ralph Nader has campaigned actively for safer cars, but perhaps the majority of car buyers would prefer taking risks with cars as they are built now to paying higher prices for safer cars. The point elitists make is that although Mr. Nader may be working for the public good, he is not necessarily expressing public will.

The Pluralist View

The pluralist view of America is basically an extension of Madisonian democracy. Like other early American political thinkers, Madison believed that power corrupts—that public officials tend to become tyrannical if left unchecked. "Ambition must be made to counteract ambition," he wrote.[29] The constitutional system of separated legislative, executive, and judicial functions he and others designed was intended to check the power of individuals and the interests they represented.

Madison also believed that class conflict was inevitable and potentially disruptive: "Those who hold and those who are without property have ever formed distinct interests in society."[30] At any time, the unpropertied majority might rise up, threatening the propertied minority. In a rather sophisticated argument, Madison suggested that the way to protect minorities (such as the wealthy Founding Fathers) was to extend the vote to the entire population. The diversity of the American population, he reasoned, would prevent majority tyranny.

Extend the sphere, and you take in a greater variety of parties and interests; you make it less probable that a majority of the whole will have a common motive to invade the rights of other citizens; or if such a common motive exists, it will be more difficult for all who feel it to discover their own strength, and to act in unison with each other.[31]

In *A Preface to Democratic Theory*, pluralist Robert Dahl maintains that America *does* operate on a checks-and-balances system—although not exactly the one Madison foresaw. The writers of the Constitution assumed that the House would become the instrument of the people—a hotbed of radical, populist thinking—and that the president would check the House with his veto. In practice today, according to Dahl, these roles are reversed.

---

[29] *The Federalist*, No. 51.
[30] *The Federalist*, No. 10.
[31] *Ibid.* The writers of the Constitution, for example, might have stipulated that only landowners could vote; small farmers might then have banded together to force their will on large landowners. (In fact, this happened in states that instituted property qualifications for the vote.) With everyone—that is, every white male—voting, clerks, merchants, shopkeepers, and so on would check the small farmers.

It is the president who is the policy maker, the creator of legislation, and the self-appointed spokesman for the national majority, whereas the power of Congress is more and more that of a veto—a veto exercised, as often as not, on behalf of groups whose privileges are threatened by presidential policy.[32]

To carry out his policies, the president depends heavily on his party's organization. Madison did not foresee the role political parties would play in the American political system.

How do pluralists rebut the evidence that a power elite rules America? They reject, first, the notion of elite consensus.

Decentralized Power. Pluralists feel that there is abundant evidence of disagreement and competition between powerful individuals and groups, both in government and in the private sector. During President Nixon's first term, for example, Congress rejected two of his nominees for the Supreme Court and voted to discontinue the antiballistic missile (ABM) project. In 1972, the Justice Department ordered IBM to disband or face antitrust suits. During the same period, Congress voted to subsidize passenger railroads but did nothing for passenger ships. If government, industry, and military leaders were working together, as elitists suggest, these disagreements and inconsistencies would not occur.

What about personnel overlap? Pluralists argue that C. Wright Mills and other elitists overemphasis positions in government and business, confusing potential and actual power. The fact that a man is a chairman or a department secretary or a general does not necessarily mean that he controls his local school board, interferes with plans for a state highway, or influences foreign policy. The man may not be interested in anything but his business; his company or agency may be organized in a way that limits his influence. For example, in most cases, members of a board of directors limit participation in a company to selecting managers. These managers, not the directors, form company policy. Pluralists feel that Mills and others have failed to demonstrate that people in powerful positions actually use their potential influence.

In addition, elitists are criticized for having failed to show evidence of a significant level of interaction between individuals in key positions. Does America's elite meet regularly to decide how to proceed on new issues? Does the automobile industry consult with the president of IBM before announcing that it will not be able to meet a deadline for antipollution devices in a bill before Congress? Pluralists see little proof of continuing accommodation and cooperation among members of the elite.

---

[32] Dahl, *A Preface to Democratic Theory*, p. 142. Dahl also notes that whereas the Founding Fathers saw government as a potential threat to individual liberty, the public today tends to see government as the guardian of civil liberty.

In a study of New Haven, Connecticut, Dahl found that the upper class tended to be aloof toward politics and community affairs. Decisions were the result of bargaining among interested groups. Some business leaders supported the mayor's efforts in urban renewal, primarily because they had a stake in the inner-city. They did not become involved in education (most of their children attended private or suburban schools) or in local party politics. Power in American communities, Dahl concludes, is highly decentralized.[33]

Electoral Accountability. Pluralists categorically reject the idea that elections are merely a "symbolic exercise." All elected officials must go to the voters periodically, and this eventually influences both their policy decisions and their personal conduct in office. "Elected officials," writes Dahl, "keep the real or imagined preferences of constituents constantly in mind in deciding what policies to adopt or reject." [34]

How do officials judge what their constituents want? They read their mail, the newspapers, and the polls.[35] They meet with businessmen who are bidding for a contract, backing a job training program or a new arts center, or contributing to their campaign fund. They also meet with senior citizens, black activists, and mothers demanding day-care centers—if these people are insistent. Their exposure to public opinion is thus biased in favor of those with a stake in a particular decision and those who express their views publicly. The so-called silent majority does not directly influence decisions, but active interest groups do. The people an elected official has either helped or offended are the people most likely to vote; he cannot afford to ignore them.

However, the silent majority does influence officials indirectly. If an official does not successfully reconcile competing or conflicting activists within his jurisdiction, he is likely to create new interest groups that oppose him. For example, if the schools close because the school board can neither find the funds to pay teachers what they demand nor convince the teacher's union to accept a compromise, parents who voted for a particular school board member or did not vote in the previous election are likely to oppose him the next time he is up for reelection, if they feel that he was responsible for the problem. Thus, elected officials must keep both the active and the potentially active "constantly in mind."

Why are so many Americans apathetic? Nonvoting, according to pluralists, is primarily an expression of "passive consent"—not just disillusionment

---

[33] Robert A. Dahl, *Who Governs?* (New Haven, Conn.: Yale University Press, 1961). This study is discussed further in the next section.

[34] *Ibid.*, p. 164.

[35] A recent study of the factors that influence a congressman's vote showed that it is the official's *perception* of his constituency's opinion rather than his constituency's actual attitude that influences his position. See Warren E. Miller and Donald E. Stokes, "Constituency Influence in Congress," *American Political Science Review* 57 (March 1963): 45–56.

with the political system. Although many members of minority groups have been discouraged or prevented from voting, most nonvoters are simply more concerned about their homes, families, and jobs than about politics. It is only when these elements are threatened (for example, with forced school busing), that the politically passive form interest groups and vote; otherwise they often leave decisions to the experts. Elections thus tend to be a combination of interested minority will and tacit majority consent. Voters and nonvoters influence political decision makers, even though they do not control them directly.

But do interested voters have a choice in elections? Pluralists reject the idea that the elite consensus within and between the two major parties goes so deep as to deny conflict over issues. Both parties are composed of people from different locales with different interests. The divisions within the Democratic party, which includes southern conservatives and northern ultra-liberals, are legendary; the ideological spectrum is nearly as broad in the Republican party. Because parties lack even internal consensus, party power is decentralized to state and local organizations.[36] Party politics is a process of endless bargaining among interested minorities.

If party programs are ambiguous, says V. O. Key, it is because mass opinion is "uncertain or nonexistent"—not because an elite controls the parties. For example, most Americans feel the government should "do something" about unemployment, "but they are unlikely to have views about whether a boost in the interest rate or an adjustment of the tax rate at a given time will achieve the desired end." [37] As a result, decisions fall to experts and to active interest groups.

Interest Groups. Pluralists see interest groups as the key to American democracy. A single man may not be able to make his views heard, but organized groups can—in one of two ways. They can help candidates who are sympathetic to their cause by providing manpower, special skills, equipment, money, and publicity. A printer's union may donate handbills and posters; a PTA may invite a candidate to address its meeting; a student group may raise money with a street fair.

The degree of positive support a group can offer depends on its membership and resources, and on whether it finds a sympathetic elected official. If it does not, it can nevertheless influence decision makers by threatening the stability of their district. The ability to influence public opinion extends power to the powerless—to average citizens.

[36] Decentralization is related to several variables, including (1) federalism, (2) separation of powers, (3) locally controlled nominations, and (4) locally oriented financing and organization of campaigns. See William J. Keefe, *Parties, Politics, and Public Policy in America* (New York: Holt, Rinehart and Winston, 1972), pp. 26–29.

[37] V. O. Key, "Linkage and Political Parties," in *Political Parties and Political Behavior*, William F. Crotty, Donald M. Freeman, and Douglas Gottin, eds. (Boston: Allyn and Bacon, 1971), p. 530.

A group excluded from the normal political arena by prohibitions against normal activity may nevertheless often gain entry. It may do so (1) by engaging or threatening to engage in "abnormal" political activity—violence, for example; (2) by threatening to deprive groups already within the arena of their legitimacy; (3) by acquiring legitimacy, and hence motivating the in-groups to incorporate the out-group.[38]

In order to restore stability and public confidence, an official must respond to organized pressure, whatever its source.

Similarly, interest groups can influence corporate policy by pressuring elected officials to intervene on their behalf or by generating adverse publicity. Civil rights groups pressured the government to insist on integration in construction companies working on federal contracts; the grape boycott in the late sixties resulted in industry and government recognition of the farmers' union; Ralph Nader and his supporters made car safety a public issue.

Pluralists thus argue that organized minorities and social movements play an integral role in the American system. As Dahl wrote, "the making of governmental decisions is not a majestic march of great majorities united upon certain matters of basic policy. It is the steady appeasement of relatively small groups."[39]

But what of the unorganized minorities? What role can be played by those easily identifiable and easily oppressed groups who, until recently, were joined only on the basis of common skin color and common misery? How do the pluralists and elitists view the sociopolitical struggle of the American black? How can Dahl's "steady appeasement of relatively small groups" work with the black liberation movement?

The Black Liberation Movement: Elitist and Pluralist Interpretations

The Elitist Interpretation

According to elitist theory, the survival of the American system depends on the ruling elite's ability to quiet tensions that arise within the society.[40] Mass movements threaten both stability and democracy; they appeal to the

---

[38] Dahl, *A Preface to Democratic Theory*, p. 138. While Dahl assumes that people will organize in groups for their own self-interest, Mancur Olson, Jr. indicates that this will not happen unless very special conditions prevail. See Olson, *The Logic of Collective Action: Public Goods and the Theory of Groups* (New York: Schocken Books, 1965), discussed in Chapter 10 of this book.

[39] Dahl, *A Preface to Democratic Theory*, p. 140.

[40] Dye and Zeigler, *The Irony of Democracy*, p. 289.

insecure, uneducated, and unsuccessful who occupy the fringes of society. These people, elitists believe, would destroy democracy if they gained power. The elite must prevent the masses from mobilizing to protect the basic democratic values of individual liberty, due process of law, limited government, and free enterprise.

There are two ways in which an elite can control a mass movement: it can destroy the movement by jailing or discrediting its leaders and threatening followers with reprisals; or it can co-opt leaders by admitting them to the elite, offering them privileges, and granting some of their demands.[41] In the elitist view, the American elite has tried both methods with the black liberation movement.

The elite was caught off guard when blacks began to mobilize and demonstrate behind such leaders as Martin Luther King, Jr. in the late 1950s. Eisenhower sent troops into Little Rock, Arkansas, but resisted pressure for strong civil rights legislation. Gradually, however, the elite began to bend. President Kennedy befriended Dr. King; northern legislators allied themselves with black leaders; and Congress passed the Civil Rights Act of 1964 and the Voting Rights Act of 1965.

This attempt to co-opt the black movement by granting some of its programs and awarding black leaders prestige was only partially successful. Middle-class blacks benefited; lower-class blacks did not. To them, civil rights legislation was largely symbolic: it did not provide food or jobs or even job training. The elite was willing to make some room for blacks who shared their values, but it could not accept the black masses. When the liberation movement opened a new front in the ghettos, it was violently suppressed: rioters were shot; revolutionary leaders such as Huey P. Newton and Angela Davis were jailed. Today the elite is pursuing a policy of mixed control and co-option. In effect, increased opportunities for middle-class blacks have skimmed the leadership off the top; the ghettos are without strong leaders and are, for the moment, relatively quiet.

The Pluralist Interpretation

Pluralists view social movements as part of, not a threat to, the American political system. Social movements give previously unrepresented groups a voice in decisions. They also rejuvenate the system by forcing groups already in the political arena to reevaluate policies and seek new allies. To pluralists, the success of the civil rights movement, however limited, is evidence of the flexibility of the American system.

Before the mid-fifties, blacks were not politically active. The largest integrationist organization, the NAACP, confined its efforts to the courts. By

[41] Jack L. Walker, "A Critique of the Elitist Theory of Democracy," *American Political Science Review* 60 (June 1966): 285–95.

1960, however, a black counterelite (Dr. King and others) had shown its capacity to mobilize black communities in the South and to influence public opinion throughout the country. At this point blacks found an ally: northern liberals. In the fifties a coalition of conservative southern Democrats and Republicans dominated Congress through their numbers and their control of committees. By linking this power bloc to the moral issue of civil rights in the public mind, liberals were able to "expose" and disarm conservatives.[42] In return, blacks won two strong civil rights bills—and a place in the system.

In the meantime, a new group of black leaders and a new movement were developing in the ghettos of major cities across the country. The riots of the late sixties—an expression of political frustration directly from the people— challenged the authority of traditional leadership in the cities; caused a major reevaluation of federal policy toward housing, education, and welfare; and fed the campaigns of "backlash" candidates such as Governor George Wallace. Most recently, urban black leaders have begun to fight for local control of community affairs—a position that paradoxically allies blacks with many white conservatives.

According to pluralists, then, blacks have had a significant impact on the American political system, both directly and indirectly. Although they have not yet won economic equality, they have begun to gain a more substantial voice in government bargaining. In December 1970, 1,769 blacks held elective office in the country, 684 of them in the eleven states that once formed the Confederacy (see Table 6-2). Southern governors no longer campaign on segregationist platforms—a historic change.[43]

The Study of Power Distribution

Perhaps the most important consequence of the pluralist-elitist debate is the interest it has generated in research methods. How can a political scientist measure power? How can he determine who is in charge of a political party or a corporation? How can he determine whether an interest group has had an impact on a particular decision? In the last ten to twenty years, political scientists have developed several distinct approaches to the study of power distribution.

C. Wright Mills has focused on positions. He assumed that a person who was president of General Motors or Secretary of State was able to grant favors and thus accumulate debts owed to them. For example, if a corporation decides to build a new plant in a town where unemployment is high,

[42] See Stephen K. Bailey, *Congress in the Seventies* (New York: St. Martin's Press, 1970).
[43] See Earl Black, "Southern Governors and Political Change: Campaign Stances on Racial Segregation and Economic Development, 1950–69," *Journal of Politics* 33 (1971): 703–34.

it will expect a degree of cooperation and perhaps privileges from local officials. People who are in a position to make such decisions, according to Mills, have power. The fact that a small group of men tends to rotate between top positions in government and business, he felt, indicates that America is ruled by a power elite.

Floyd Hunter drew similar conclusions from a study of the power structure in Atlanta, Georgia. Hunter, focusing on "reputed power," chose names that appeared frequently in news and society columns, and then asked a panel of average citizens to indicate which were the ten most powerful individuals on the list. After a number of interviews, Hunter concluded that power in Atlanta rested in the hands of a few business leaders. Public officials, he found, were "loathe to act before consulting and 'clearing' with these interests." [44]

Pluralists reject both Hunter's conclusions and his methods. Raymond Wolfinger points out that his data were based on hearsay. Hunter did not determine whether his informants had direct knowledge of manipulation on the part of the men they listed. He had no way of knowing whether they perceived the situation correctly. Wolfinger also points out that people tend to accept a researcher's hypothesis (that Atlanta is run by ten powerful men) and try to supply the information, rather than ask why the researcher thinks anyone is particularly powerful in their community.[45] Asking a person "Who runs your town?," says Nelson Polsby, "is like asking 'Have you stopped beating your wife?' in that virtually any response short of total unwillingness to answer will supply the researcher with a 'power elite' along the lines presupposed. . . ." [46] Moreover, Hunter—like Mills—failed to consider the possibility that the "ten most powerful men" disagreed with each other some or all of the time. Perhaps five had a special interest in schools, three were involved in construction and road building, and two had good connections with union leaders. Hunter overlooked the possibility that these individuals' power was limited and specialized.

In studying community power, pluralists focus not on positions, reputations, or resources (wealth, education), but on key issues. For example, Dahl, Wolfinger, and Polsby studied party nominations, an urban redevelopment program, and public education in New Haven, Connecticut.[47] In contrast to Hunter, Dahl and his colleagues found that New Haven's "notables" (the top families, socioeconomically) had little direct influence in any of these areas. Political nominations were decided within the parties, without reference to the socioeconomic elite. The mayor and a committee of busi-

[44] Floyd Hunter, *Community Power Structure* (Chapel Hill: University of North Carolina Press, 1935), pp. 100–101.
[45] Raymond E. Wolfinger, "Nondecisions and the Study of Local Politics," *American Political Science Review* 65 (December 1971): 1063–79.
[46] Nelson W. Polsby, *Community Power and Political Theory* (New Haven, Conn.: Yale University Press, 1963), p. 113.
[47] See Dahl, *Who Governs?*

Table 6-2
Black Elected Officials by Office, 1970 to 1972, and by Region and States, 1972

Year, Region, and State	Total	U.S. and State Legislatures	City and County Offices	Law Enforcement	Education
1970 [1]	1,472	182	715	213	362
1971	1,860	216	905	274	465
1972	2,264	224	1,108	263	669
Northeast	423	42	124	48	209
North Central	589	79	287	58	165
South	1,073	80	642	133	218
West	179	23	55	24	77
Alabama	83	2	58	12	11
Alaska	3	2	–	–	1
Arizona	10	4	–	1	5
Arkansas	97	–	44	5	48
California	134	[2] 9	44	15	66
Colorado	7	3	3	1	–
Connecticut	51	6	28	5	12
Delaware	11	3	7	–	1
District of Columbia	8	[3] 1	–	–	7
Florida	51	2	46	1	2
Georgia	65	15	39	1	10
Hawaii	1	–	1	–	–
Illinois	123	[2] 21	50	13	39
Indiana	52	2	32	7	11
Iowa	10	1	3	1	5
Kansas	18	3	8	–	7
Kentucky	57	3	36	9	9
Louisiana	119	8	59	29	23
Maryland	54	[3] 19	23	7	5
Massachusetts	16	[4] 4	7	–	5
Michigan	179	[2] 20	92	13	52
Minnesota	8	–	3	1	4
Mississippi	129	1	67	41	20
Missouri	77	[3] 16	31	9	21
Nebraska	3	1	1	–	1
Nevada	4	1	1	2	–
New Hampshire	1	–	–	–	1
New Jersey	121	5	48	–	68
New Mexico	4	1	3	–	–
New York	163	[2] 14	22	24	103
North Carolina	103	2	71	1	29
Ohio	110	[3] 14	60	14	22

Table 6-2
(continued)

Year, Region and State	Total	U.S. and State Legislatures	City and County Offices	Law Enforcement	Education
Oklahoma	62	6	35	1	20
Oregon	5	–	1	1	3
Pennsylvania	63	³ 12	16	19	16
Rhode Island	7	1	2	–	4
South Carolina	66	3	48	9	6
Tennessee	48	8	21	13	6
Texas	61	3	37	–	21
Vermont	1	–	1	–	–
Virginia	54	3	47	4	–
Washington	9	3	1	4	1
West Virginia	5	1	4	–	–
Wisconsin	9	1	7	–	1
Wyoming	2	–	1	–	1

As of March, except as indicated. Six states had no Negro elected officials in 1972: Idaho, Maine, Montana, North Dakota, South Dakota, and Utah.

[1] As of February.
[2] Includes 2 members of U.S. House of Representatives.
[3] Includes 1 member of U.S. House of Representatives.
[4] Includes 1 U.S. Senator.

Source: Metropolitan Applied Research Center, Inc. (Washington, D.C., National Roster of Black Elected Officials, February 1970 and March 1971 and 1972).
From: Statiscal Abstract of the United States, 93rd annual ed. (Washington, D.C.: U.S. Department of Commerce, 1972), no. 596, p. 372.

nessmen he persuaded to join him were responsible for launching and carrying through a massive urban redevelopment program. School policies were the result of bargaining between the mayor, the school board, and interest groups—and of day-by-day decisions made in the school bureaucracy.[48] In addition, Dahl found that only a few people were active in more than one area. In short, power in New Haven was decentralized; there was no evidence of a single, upper-class elite.[49]

Both the study of Atlanta and the study of New Haven have been criticized in recent years. Wolfinger suggests that Hunter and Dahl ignored the more

[48] Wolfinger notes that the notables' lack of interest in schools and city elections may be explained by the fact that they live in the suburbs of New Haven and send their children to private schools. See "Nondecisions and the Study of Local Politics," p. 1064.

[49] After a similar study, Wallace Sayre and Herbert Kaufman characterized New York City's political system as "vigorously and incessantly competitive." Power is divided between party leaders, elected and appointed officials, bureaucracies, unions and interest groups, and state and federal officials. Elections in New York, they found, are extremely important; all of these groups pay close attention to public opinion. Wallace S. Sayre and Herbert Kaufman, *Governing New York City* (New York: W. W. Norton, 1965).

subtle aspects of power relationships.[50] In some cases officials or private citizens refrain from participating in a decision or from advocating a particular position because they fear retribution. For example, a mayor may refuse to support plans for a low-income housing project because he fears middle-class voters in the neighborhood will vote against him in the next election. In other cases, people do not participate in a decision because they do not know about it. The middle-class citizens in the example above may not learn about public hearings until after they've been held. Similarly, lack of information may prevent people from taking advantage of a law or program designed specifically for their benefit. When the first voting rights act was passed in the fifties, few blacks in the South knew how to file complaints. Local officials did little to enlighten them. All of these "nondecisions," as Peter Bachrach and Morton Baratz called them, must be taken into account in any study of decisions and decision makers.[51]

Jack Walker takes a somewhat different perspective. "In their quest for realism," he writes, pluralists and elitists "have fundamentally changed the normative aspect of democracy." [52] Theorists in both schools tend to glorify the "professional" political leader at the expense of the masses, and to consider democratic procedures (such as due process of law) a substitute for direct participation in the decisions that affect people's lives. To suggest that the common man is passive and apolitical, says Walker, is to ignore the prevailing mood in America today. Speculating on the relationship between the political stability and social unrest that characterized the early seventies, he writes: "High crime (or suicide) rates and low rates of voting may very well be related; the former may represent 'leakage' from the political system." [53] By implication, Walker suggests that democracy without participation is not democracy at all.

Conclusion

If we accept the definition of democracy given in Chapter 5 and the criteria for judging the democratic nature of a government, then it is possible to discover which nations among the many that claim to be democracies are actually governed democratically. The question to be answered, then, is who

---

[50] Wolfinger, "Nondecisions and the Study of Local Politics."

[51] Peter Bachrach and Morton S. Baratz, "Two Faces of Power," *American Political Science Review* 56 (December 1962): 947–52. See also Frederick W. Frey, "Comment: On Issues and Nonissues in the Study of Power," *American Political Science Review* 65 (December 1971): 1081–1101—a comment on Wolfinger, "Nondecisions and the Study of Local Politics."

[52] Walker, "A Critique of the Elitist Theory of Democracy," p. 63.

[53] *Ibid.*, p. 69. Walker points out that crime rates dropped sharply during civil rights protests in Atlanta, Georgia, and Cambridge, Maryland.

actually governs in a democracy? More specifically, for the purposes of this chapter, who makes decisions in the United States?

The single elitist view holds that America is governed by a single power monopoly whose members are similar in background, wealth, and interests. Although this group is self-serving, bowing to public opinion only when that opinion serves the interests of the elite, it maintains that its function is that of a trustee of democracy. Because they are better educated and more tolerant than the average citizen, the elitists' control of decision making and politics is ultimately in the best interests of the people.

The pluralist (or plural elitist) maintains that the United States is governed by a plurality of competing elites. These groups can bargain, agree, disagree, and compete, thereby providing a system in which a variety of voices can be heard. While elitists hold that their approach protects democratic values, pluralists contend that it suppresses the individual and denies him meaningful choice.

The single elitist believes in the existence of the power elite, in the catharsis of symbolic election, and in the eventual oligarchical nature of any interest group. The pluralist, on the other hand, maintains that people in key positions do interact, that elected officials can be held accountable by the public, and that interest groups can influence public policy.

These conflicting positions have been tested by the apathy at the polls and by the advent of the black liberation movement. Do people fail to vote because they are discouraged by what they perceive as a lack of choice or because they are content with the way things are? Have blacks gained rights and freedoms because they are now an organized minority whose voice has been heard or because they have been co-opted and controlled by the power elite?

As political scientists develop new methods to determine whether a political system is dominated by plural or single elites, citizens will be better able to assess for themselves whether or not they live in a system where political decision making is contemporary society's best possible approximation of democracy.

Suggested Readings

Backrach, Peter. *The Theory of Democratic Elitism.* Boston: Little, Brown, 1967. A critique of pluralism and a discussion of the need for equal opportunity.

Chomsky, Noam. *American Power and the New Mandarins.* New York: Pantheon, 1969. A discussion of the emergence of a new "intellectual elite" and their role as advocates of American expansionism.

Dahl, Robert A. *Who Governs: Democracy and Power in an American City.* New Haven, Conn.: Yale University Press, 1961. A classic study of pluralism.

Dye, Thomas R., and Ziegler, L. Harmon. *The Irony of Democracy: An Uncommon Introduction to American Politics.* 2nd ed. Belmont, Calif.: Wadsworth, 1972. A systematic presentation of the elitist argument, with supportive evidence for the plural- and single-elite model.

Edelman, Murray. *The Symbolic Uses of Power.* Urbana: University of Illinois Press, 1964. A study of the power, operation, and use and abuse of symbols in politics.

Hunter, Floyd. *Community Power Structure.* Chapel Hill: University of North Carolina Press, 1953. A classic study of elitism.

Kolko, Gabriel. *Wealth and Power in America.* New York: Praeger, 1962. A discussion of the distribution of wealth in America, with the claim that it has become more concentrated, as has power, in twentieth-century America.

Mills, C. Wright. *The Power Elite.* New York: Oxford University Press, 1956. A forceful, original, persuasive, if not sophisticated, argument regarding the power elite in America.

Mintz, Morton, and Cohen, Jerry S. *America, Inc.: Who Owns and Operates the United States?* New York: Dell, 1971. A tour de force in exposing the public-be-damned and full-speed-ahead attitudes of corporate America in its pursuit of the dollar.

Mosca, Gaetano. *The Ruling Class.* New York: McGraw-Hill, 1939. An early statement that the few will rule.

Contemporary
political ideologies
CHAPTER 7

The first steps toward America's involvement in the war in Vietnam
show how political ideology influences government policy. Although Joseph
McCarthy had been silenced years before, the cold war was very much alive
when John Kennedy took office. At that time, political camps were clearly
defined: Americans were "good guys," Communists "bad guys," and rap-
prochement seemed impossible. As a new, young president, Kennedy felt
compelled to prove that he was not "soft on communism." His meeting with
Khrushchev in Vienna and the confrontation in the Cuban missile crisis
heightened the pressure. The Communists had to be shown that America
meant business. When Khrushchev spoke out in support of wars of national

liberation, Kennedy took his speech as a challenge and shortly after, sent advisory troops to Saigon.[1]

In the early sixties, most Americans were predisposed to seeing events in a certain way: few in government questioned the idea that the Communists were our enemies. Most saw the struggle in Vietnam as a new front in the continuing international tug-of-war between a totalitarian monolith—the Communist bloc—and freedom. Given these ideological assumptions, it was quite logical for the United States to support South Vietnam's President Diem.

It was just as logical for the North Vietnamese and Viet Cong to fight back, but their logic was based on an entirely different ideology. While the Americans saw themselves as the defenders of freedom, the North Vietnamese saw them as a colonial power—as imperialists: the United States was picking up where the French had left off. While Americans saw the Viet Cong as an arm of the international Communist conspiracy, the Viet Cong saw themselves as nationalists defending their homeland: they had defeated the French and were willing to take on the Americans.

Ideology played an important role throughout the entire Vietnam War for all the parties involved. But this is not the only case where ideology has strongly influenced the course of national and international events. Since political ideologies form the basic belief systems around which governments are built and through which people view the world, they are basic to the study of politics and political systems.

What Is Ideology?

The word *ideology* has a long and complicated history. It was originated by an eighteenth-century French philosopher, Antoine Destutt de Tracy, to describe the "science of ideas," but its meaning has changed with the times. Napoleon, for example, threw the word at dissenting liberals who questioned his right to absolute rule. Karl Marx considered ideology a tool of the ruling class—a set of ideas designed to justify capitalism and the suppression of the worker. At the height of the cold war, Americans tended to think of ideologies as mistaken beliefs—as tools of propaganda that had no place in a free society. They supported this idea by viewing democracy not as an ideology, but as a friendly political system devoid of the sinister connotations that characterized absolutism, Marxism, socialism, and fascism.[2]

[1] As it turned out, Khrushchev was making a threat—but to China, not to the United States. For a behind-the-scenes account of how the United States became involved in Vietnam, see David Halberstam's *The Best and the Brightest* (New York: Random House, 1972).

[2] Reo M. Christenson et al., *Ideologies and Modern Politics* (New York: Dodd, Mead, 1971), pp. 3–5.

In its most general sense, ideology can be defined as a set of attitudes about political behavior on both international and domestic levels. In contrast to political philosophy, which studies how men should behave in politics but prescribes no course of action, and political theory, which studies the political behavior of man without making any value judgments, ideology is both an interrelated collection of beliefs about the nature and purposes of man and society and a guide to attaining these beliefs. It deals with such questions as who should rule, how rulers should be chosen, and by what principles they should govern. According to Anthony Downs, ideology is "a verbal image of the good society, and of the chief means of constructing such a society." [3]

Every political ideology has its own concept of how the various institutions and processes of society should operate and suggests methods for putting them into practice. In addition, all ideologies provide a framework for interpreting the complex events of the world by offering a means for making situations and circumstances—from a revolution halfway around the world to the taxes we all must pay—more understandable. Americans tend to believe that all people have a desire for and a right to self-government, and they tend to interpret all wars as struggles for or against freedom. During the Nigerian civil war of the late sixties, many Americans were sympathetic towards the Biafrans, whom they saw as an oppressed minority. But much of African ideology is derived from the needs of struggling new nations. Most African officials believe unity is essential to modernization and economic independence, and so they saw the rebellious Biafrans as unthinking and irresponsible.

The contrast between the way most Americans saw the Nigerian civil war and the view taken by most African officials helps to point out the effect that ideology has on a person's interpretation of a political event. The traditional "American ideology" is a world view from the perspective of a highly developed nation who won her independence by revolution against an oppressive power: Americans tend to identify with the underdog. But the ideology of most Africans is derived from a different perspective. Their experience pointed out the need for strong government in nation building, and so they took the view that minorities must make concessions for the good of the whole. So most Africans sided with the ruling Nigerians rather than the Biafrans.

Political ideologies not only define attitudes about what is happening in the rest of the world; they also shape attitudes towards domestic affairs— what forms of taxation are acceptable, if and how the poor should be provided for, what rights a citizen has, how people may express their dissatisfactions with the social or political structure, how to deal with riots in the cities, crime in the streets, economic crises. National ideologies help to pro-

[3] Anthony Downs, *An Economic System of Democracy* (New York: Harper & Row, 1957), p. 96.

vide a justification of the existing political system by giving support to the manner in which power is organized, distributed, used, and limited and by defining an individual's role in the society. Ideology thus provides a basis for a government's legitimacy.[4]

Ideology as a Dynamic Force

Ideologies are abstractions. They always propose ideals, such as "equality of opportunity," "law and order," and "a classless society." By setting up goals to be pursued, ideology provides a sense of mission and purpose and is a moving force in the life of a nation. It can motivate people to become involved in politics, to fight for their country, to settle a wilderness, or to battle for changes in the social or political structure. "Ideologies are action-related systems of ideas. They typically contain a program and a strategy for its realization, and their essential function is to unite organizations which are built around them. . . . [They] unite a party or other group for effective participation in political life."[5]

Ideologies not only affect the actions of people and the policies of nations; they are also acted upon. Ideologies constantly undergo change to "keep up with the times." President Nixon presided over the United States' first official contacts with the People's Republic of China in 1971, after it had become apparent that the official American policy of ignoring the existence of a nation of 787 million people could not go on indefinitely. The ideological stance of the United States had to change with the times.

The dynamics involved in both the constant adjusting of ideology to meet reality and in the influence which ideology has on a person's—or a nation's—actions, is reflected in the fact that ideologies include certain contradictions.[6] Americans, for example, believe in freedom of the press, but they also believe that the government has a right to keep some information secret if it is for the national interest. In part, this incongruity exists because no ideology is a single monolithic unit; instead, an ideology is composed of many different factions. Disagreements often arise over which aspect of an ideology is most important. Dissatisfaction with certain ideological goals or the tactics used to achieve these goals may lead to the development of new ideologies as can be seen in the emergence of the "new politics" in the United States in the last decade (discussed later in this chapter).

Despite the fact that ideologies are abstract ideals and attitudes, they have

[4] For further definitions of political ideology, see Samuel P. Huntington, "Conservatism as an Ideology," *American Political Science Review* 51 (June 1957): 454; and Robert E. Lane, *Political Ideology: Why the American Common Man Believes What He Does* (New York: The Free Press, 1962), pp. 14–15.

[5] Carl J. Friedrich, *Man and His Government: An Empirical Theory of Politics* (New York: McGraw-Hill, 1963), p. 90.

[6] See Everett Carll Ladd, Jr., *Ideology in America* (Ithaca: Cornell University Press, 1969).

a significant influence on the behavior of governments and people. They provide people with a common way of looking at themselves, at their society, and at others. They have strong moral overtones, often setting up simple dichotomies of good and evil: for example, "all Communists (or all Capitalists) are bad." They describe boundaries for political life and set standards for political behavior. They motivate people either to work in support of the existing system or to develop new ideologies to replace a system that they are unhappy with. A wide variety of specific ideologies exists in the world today. Each one plays an important part in shaping both the political cultures and the policies of the nations that ascribe to them.

Ideologies in the Modern World

Since the eighteenth century, the popular way of classifying political ideologies has been to place them along a spectrum, with anarchy and revolution on the left, reactionary conservatism on the right, and all the others somewhere in the middle. This left-right continuum dates back to the First French Republic when the National Assembly, made up of three political groupings, met in Paris in the summer of 1789. The meeting hall was a horseshoe-shaped amphitheater where the conservatives (who favored the continuation of the monarchy) sat to the right of the speaker; the radicals (who advocated liberty and equality, a constitution, a free press, trial by jury, and fairer taxation) sat to the left of the speaker; and the liberals (who favored limited representation) sat in the center. The 1789 Assembly was short-lived, but the ideas of a left, right, and center in politics have persisted (see Figure 7-1). We continue to think of political ideologies according to this scale, with the left representing groups that support greater popular participation in government, and the right including movements that are more skeptical of popular government. Political ideologies of the twentieth century range

Figure 7-1
The Spectrum of Political Ideologies

LEFT		CENTER			RIGHT
Revolutionary Radicalism	Radicalism	Liberalism	Conservatism	Reactionism	Revolutionary Reactionism
Communists (Russia)	Socialists (England)	Democrats (USA)	Republicans (USA)	Nationalists (Taiwan)	Fascists (Germany)

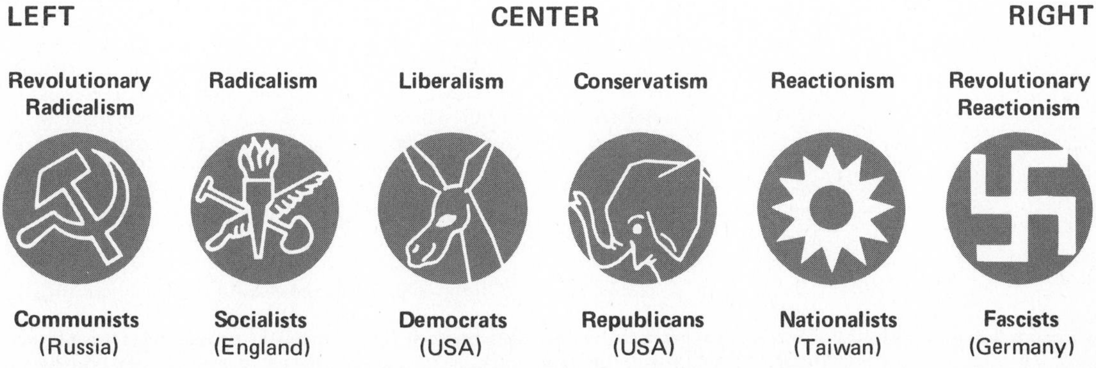

Source: Adapted from Kenneth K. Krogh, "Needed: New Political Labels" in Saturday Review 43 (December 3, 1960): 17.

from the complete popular rule with no formal government, which anarchists support, to the rigid government control of fascism.

Anarchism. Anarchism lies at the extreme left of the political spectrum, because it is an ideology that advocates the abolition of *all* government.[7] Anarchists believe man is innately good, but that the state, which maintains itself through coercion and force, pushes him into unnatural competition and hostility. Anarchists oppose constraints of any kind, from government to sexual proscriptions, marriage laws, and compulsory education. They reject the concepts of rule by law and obedience to authority, and they argue that if men were totally free, they would voluntarily perform whatever work is necessary for a satisfactory and comfortable life. Without government, they propose, men would live together in harmony.

Anarchism as an ideology has appeared and disappeared sporadically throughout the nineteenth and twentieth centuries. It was very much in the news at the turn of the century, when the United States refused anarchists passports after several bombing incidents involving the early labor movement, and again in the twenties, when journalists and demagogues conjured up pictures of foreign men with black beards and explosives in their briefcases.[8] Such an image was largely responsible for the robbery and murder conviction in 1921 and execution in 1927 of anarchists Nicola Sacco and Bartolomeo Vanzetti. Little was heard about anarchism again until the late 1960s, when European students began carrying anarchist banners in demonstrations and protests. Since then, there have been other indications of a revival of anarchist thought around the world.

Communism. Communism falls next to anarchism on the political spectrum.[9] It represents the most active of the extreme left ideological orientations, and several present-day governments adhere to its beliefs. The

[7] For a recent anthology of anarchist writing, see Leonard I. Krimerman and Lewis Perry, eds., *Patterns of Anarchy: A Collection of Writings on the Anarchist Tradition* (Garden City, N.Y.: Doubleday, 1966). Two of the major figures in the anarchist movement were Prince Peter Kropotkin and Pierre-Joseph Proudhon. Their writings are considered classics in anarchist thought. See Peter Kropotkin, *Conquest of Bread*, reprint of 1906 edition (New York: Kraus Reprint); and also by the same author, *Memoirs of a Revolutionist* (New York: Dover Publications, 1970). For a collection of Kropotkin's important writings see Martin A. Miller, ed., *Selected Readings on Anarchism & Revolution* (Cambridge, Mass.: The M.I.T. Press, 1970). Of additional interest is Pierre-Joseph Proudhon, *General Idea of the Revolution in the 19th Century* (1923; reprint ed., New York: Haskell House Publishers, 1970). For a collection of Proudhon's major works see L. S. Edwards, ed., and Elizabeth Fraser, trans., *Selected Writings of Pierre-Joseph Proudhon* (Garden City, N.Y.: Doubleday, 1969).

[8] Actually, most anarchists are pacifists; only a few advocate the violent destruction of society.

[9] We are making a distinction here between the political theory and the form of government. As we will discuss later in this chapter, the amount of control exercised by Communist governments makes them, in some regards, resemble fascist states more closely than the anarchist's ideal "nongovernment."

foundations of communism are found in the writings of Karl Marx. Marx believed that nineteenth-century capitalism contained the seeds of its own destruction. He claimed that the bourgeoisie, who owned the means of production and reaped most of its rewards, could not exploit the working class indefinitely. Eventually the capitalist system would collapse from its own internally imposed problems, and at that time, Marx believed, the workers would see their chains and rebel. Marx thought proletariat revolution was inevitable, but he did not specifically advocate violence. After a brief dictatorship of the proletariat, or working class, the state would wither away, leaving a free and just, classless society.

For all his impact on modern political thinking, Marx was never directly involved in government. In fact, he spent much of his life in the library of the British Museum. It was Vladimir I. Lenin who first translated Marx's ideas into action, modifying them in the process.[10] Early in his political career, Lenin made two observations which suggested revolution was not as imminent as Marx believed. First, the major industrial nations had saved themselves by acquiring colonies, which provided them with raw materials and a new market for industrial goods. Second, Lenin felt that the proletariat was too absorbed in the struggle of keeping alive to think about revolution.[11] The potential was there, but neither the leadership nor the spark. Lenin conceived the idea of the professional revolutionary class, which would act as the vanguard of the revolution, stir class consciousness with propaganda, and create local party organizations to serve as the foundation for a new state. In so doing, Lenin departed from the Marxist model in several ways. First, Marx had predicted revolution in a heavily industrialized nation with problems of overproduction. In Russia, it was the shortage of goods and the limited capacity to produce needed supplies that brought about the revolution. Also, Lenin's proletariat was a distinct minority which was far from being solidified in support of the revolution, in contrast to Marx's vision of a closely united majority of working people.

It was Lenin's party that took control of Russia during the October Revolution of 1917, and it is essentially Lenin's party that retains control today. This is not what Marx had described. He had foreseen the dictatorship of the proletariat as the rule of the many over the few, not vice versa. In theory, Lenin's Communist party is the embodiment of the people and acts on their behalf, but it is still one political party with only one small group of leaders. (Lenin believed this was a necessary interim step given the problems facing revolutionary Russia; in time, a true dictatorship of the proletariat would develop.) In addition to deciding matters of foreign policy, the party exer-

[10] The transformation of Marxism into what is known as Marxism-Leninism is discussed in an article by George Lichtheim, "The Transmutations of a Doctrine," in *Problems of Communism* 15 (July–August 1966) : 14–25.

[11] For Lenin's views on how capitalism would develop and eventually collapse, see Vladimir I. Lenin, *Imperialism: The Highest Stage of Capitalism; A Popular Outline* (New York: International Publishers, 1969).

cises strict control over the economy—deciding what the country needs, where and how it will be produced, and so on. In practice, the party is not the impregnable monolith it seems to many Westerners. Although little dissension is allowed once a decision has been made, there is relatively free discussion preceding the making of this decision. Lenin called this "democratic centralism." The party acts as a channel between the diverse peoples and competing interests of the country and its central leadership, gathering information and seeing that policies are carried out.

Like Lenin, Mao Tse-tung adapted Marx's ideas to suit the needs of his country and his people.[12] At the turn of the century, China was an extremely poor and underdeveloped nation, run largely by outsiders. But Mao saw in the colonial relationship the seeds of revolution. For the capitalist he substituted the imperialist; for the oppressed proletariat, the colonized people. Instead of a class struggle, Mao envisioned a nationalistic struggle with the peasants, not the workers, in the vanguard. He went on to develop a People's Army in the outlying provinces of China and what proved to be successful strategies for guerilla warfare.[13]

As in the USSR, the Communist party is the political center of China today, with Mao still at its head. The Chinese have gone somewhat farther than the Russians in the development of communes as semi-autonomous, self-governing, and self-sufficient units. They have also tried to eliminate class distinctions by requiring intellectuals and professionals to work in the fields or factories for part of each year. But neither country has completely eliminated either class divisions or the need for government control.

In recent years a number of young Communists, particularly in Eastern Europe, have become disillusioned with the continuing dictatorship of the proletariat in their countries. Drawing on the existentialist concept of alienation (which party bureaucracies have not eliminated), writers such as Adam Schaff and Lezek Kolakowski [14] urge a return to Marx's humanism—to his concern for the individual and his vision of a stateless, classless society.

Democratic Socialism. The next step to the right on the traditional left-right spectrum is democratic socialism. Democratic socialism refers to an ideology based on both economic and political concerns, while the term socialism refers only to an economic system entailing collective or government ownership and administration of the means of production and distribution

---

[12] Each nation interprets an ideology to fit its own background. For a discussion of the ideology behind the Communist movements in Cuba and North Vietnam, see Christenson et al., *Ideologies and Modern Politics*, pp. 157–72.

[13] Briefly, his plan was as follows: "The enemy advances, we retreat; the enemy camps, we harass; the enemy tires, we attack; the enemy retreats, we pursue." Mao Tse-tung, "A Single Spark Can Start a Prairie Fire," in *Selected Works of Mao Tse-tung*, Vol. I (Peking: Foreign Languages Press, 1961), p. 124.

[14] See Adam Schaff, *Marxism and the Human Individual*, ed. Robert S. Cohen, trans. Olgierd Wojtasiewisc (New York: McGraw-Hill, 1970); and Lezek Kolakowski, *Toward a Marxist Humanism: Essays on the Left Today*, trans. Jane Zielonko Peel (New York: Grove Press, 1968).

of goods. Democratic socialism is an effort to introduce democratic control into the economic as well as the political life of a nation. It is achieved by elected governments and stops far short of totalitarian economic control. It introduces the operation of socialism, in terms of equality of distribution of goods and services, into the institutional mechanisms of democratic principles. Democratic socialism has proven to be the most successful non-Marxist-Leninist form of socialism and is being used in many Western European nations, including England and the Scandinavian countries.

Like communism, democratic socialism is dedicated to the elimination of mass poverty and suffering. Along with other Marxists, democratic socialists view economic exploitation as a dehumanizing form of slavery that ruins lives and harms society. But unlike Communists, democratic socialists reject the idea that revolution is necessary or inevitable. They oppose the dictatorship of the proletariat and the belief that civil liberties are bourgeois and therefore evil. They are moderates; but this is not to say that democratic socialism is merely "watered down" communism. It is based on the belief that popular participation in political and economic decisions makes better citizens, and better citizens make better societies. To democratic socialists, civil and spiritual freedom are just as important as economic justice.

As practiced in England and Scandinavia, democratic socialism depends on three programs: the nationalization of major industries, government regulation of the economy, and extensive provision of social services. The emphasis in all of these programs is on social priorities. The government controls those aspects of the economy that affect public welfare, and ensures that no person goes sick or homeless. In England, the government owns and operates most of the coal and oil industry, utilities, transportation, banks, and television. The directors of industry are appointed by elected officials, and all profits are returned to the government. The government controls other areas of the economy through tax incentives, negative taxes, licensing, and so on. A national health insurance program provides free medical care and some sick-pay to all citizens. The government of Sweden provides, in addition, free college tuition and some expense money, maternity-leave pay, housing subsidies for low-income families, and even interest-free furniture loans to newlyweds. All of these benefits are provided by a government that adheres to the political principles of democracy.

Democracy. The difference between democratic socialism as practiced in Britain and democracy as practiced in the United States is one of degree rather than kind, stemming from different attitudes about how the economy should function. In theory, Americans believe in the separation of the state and the economy, with an open market where every person has an equal opportunity to succeed or fail. In practice, however, the government exercises considerable control over the U.S. economy, but the ideological reasons behind this control differ from those in Britain. In general, Americans believe people should be free to do anything that does not harm another individual or society, and that the government exists to protect this individual freedom. Democratic socialists, on the other hand, believe the main function of the government is to protect the "public good"—at the expense of individuals, when necessary. This contrast is clearest in the area of social services: Americans have Social Security but no large-scale national health insurance; unemployment insurance but no national sick-leave pay. Aside from these differences, both systems are grounded in democratic political ideals.

Democracy is based on the belief that, because "all men are created equal," they have a right to govern themselves. Under democracy, the people exercise their authority directly, in town meetings and referendums, and indirectly, through elected representatives. These representatives act as agents for their constituents, as a two-way channel between the government and the people, and in some cases (particularly in matters of foreign policy) as "concerned citizens" exercising their own judgment.[15]

In practice, democracies vary widely from this model. The American system of government and the government of Great Britain are both democracies, but one is a presidential-congressional system and the other a parliamentary democracy. In America, the executive, legislative, and judicial branches are largely separate. In Britain, the prime minister is exactly what his name implies: he is the first minister of Parliament. Both he and his cabinet are drawn from the legislative branch. But despite the variety of methods through which democracy can be put into practice, all democracies are based on the idea that the people should have some say in who governs them and how.

Nationalism in Developing Nations. Nationalism forms a part of all political ideologies. All states, whatever their particular ideology, consider themselves sovereign; and nearly all people identify themselves by nationality, whether or not they accept their current government's policies. This kind of identification with one's country is similar to what we think of as patriotism.[16]

But nationalism has a special meaning for the countries of Africa, Asia, and the Middle East that have only won their independence in the last ten to twenty years. The Americans, British, and French take their countries for granted; the Guineans, Indonesians, and Israelis do not. To them, nationalism means freedom from foreign domination and the right to self-government according to their own traditions and needs. The dominant political ideology of states that have recently won independence, which developed as a result of their unique experiences, goes under the various labels of modernizing nationalism, anticolonial nationalism, or simply nationalism.

Many of the countries in Africa and Asia were created by colonial ad-

[15] See the definition of democracy provided in Chapter 5.
[16] See the definition given in Chapter 3.

ministrations that paid little attention to indigenous political and social organization. Colonial boundaries cut across tribal territories, dividing peoples and combining traditionally hostile groups into single states. When the colonial empires began to crumble, the movements for independence that developed in Asia and Africa temporarily united the diverse peoples who had been artificially brought together under foreign rule. But their primary loyalty still belonged to their tribes. Thus, the new nations created by the movements for colonial independence in the twentieth century were faced with the task of creating a sense of community among several cultural groups—otherwise, it would be difficult to maintain a stable society. The ideology of nationalism for these countries represents, in part, an attempt to create a national identity where none had previously existed.

The new governments of developing nations also face the problem of modernization. Anticolonial wars or movements raised the people's economic hopes: many believed independence would bring immediate prosperity. They wanted the material goods of the modern world now. But few of these countries had the industry or skills to satisfy these hopes. Nationalist leaders, therefore, asked their people to make temporary sacrifices for the sake of national development and future generations, arguing that advancing a society two centuries in a few decades requires more planning and more concentration of power than is necessary in already industrialized nations. The leaders felt that the need for fast development and mobilization of resources also meant that political dissension, individual freedom, and, in some cases, economic individualism were luxuries the people could not yet afford.

This form of nationalism led to the creation of a number of one-party states—some dominated by popular leaders such as Sukarno in Indonesia, Sekou Toure in Guinea, and Kenyatta in Kenya, and some by military dictatorships, like those in Nigeria and Uganda. For these countries, nationalism is a pragmatic ideology. It is based on the belief that entry into the modern world depends on the economic and political strength of the nation and on the development of a strong sense of national unity and purpose, and that both of these tasks may call for individual sacrifice for the good of the whole.

Fascism and National Socialism. The nationalist ideology of developing states falls on the "right" of the political spectrum, because it acknowledges a need for strong government at the expense of popular rule. Even more extreme are the rightist ideologies of fascist and national-socialist states, such as Mussolini's Italy and Hitler's Germany. Under both of these ideologies, the nation—which embodies the culture and spirit of the people— is supreme. The individual is a small and insignificant part of the whole; he exists for the nation, to which he owes his complete, unquestioning devotion. Nothing matters but that the nation survive and prevail over its enemies.

Fascists (whether the fascists of Mussolini's Italy or the national socialists, or Nazis, of Hitler's Germany from 1933 to 1945) see life as a continuing struggle for national dominance. It is a primal struggle for blood (or race) and soil—man's most basic instincts. In this battle, as in nature, only the strongest survive. Political competition, debate, and freedom as interpreted by democracies are signs of weakness. The nation must dominate the hearts and minds of the people, inspiring their absolute obedience. Only in this way can the will of the nation be realized.

From these rather mystical ideas about man and nations, Hitler in national-socialist Germany and Mussolini in fascist Italy derived very concrete principles of government. Both believed in a totalitarian state—a government that exercises authority over all areas of public and private life, from the education of children to control of the economy.[17] The achievement of this state, they believed, depends on a rigid hierarchy of authority, where every person owes absolute obedience to his immediate superior, and ultimately to the Fuehrer or Il Duce. The Fuehrer's word is law: he alone can interpret the will of the nation. The main function of the state is to educate the people in the arts of self-discipline, self-sacrifice, and obedience—to make them fit and ready for their glorious destiny.

The national-socialist ideology of Hitler was even more extreme than Mussolini's fascism. Although Mussolini believed fascists were superior men in every way, he never carried racism as far as Hitler did. While Mussolini spoke of the Italian people, Hitler's national socialism idealized the Aryan race:

All human culture, all the results of art, science, and technology that we see before us today, are almost exclusively the creative product of the Aryan . . . [who represents] the prototype of all that we understand by the word "man." [18]

There was no Auschwitz, Dachau, or Buchenwald in Italy. Moreover, Mussolini's empire never compared to Hitler's Third Reich at the height of its expansion. Nevertheless, the two men and their ideologies were remarkably similar. Both rose to power during periods of economic hardship and political uncertainty; both were extremely adept at manipulating crowd psychology and using terrorism to intimidate and mold the people; and both succeeded in mobilizing their countries to quite remarkable achievements.

Although Nazi Germany and Fascist Italy were buried with their leaders at the end of World War II, fascism as an ideology was not destroyed. There are small, active fascist groups in Germany, Italy, Japan, the United States, and elsewhere. Frequently, swastikas are painted on Jewish temples in South America. Such widely separated politicians as former Vice President Ky of South Vietnam and President Amin of Uganda have publicly praised

[17] See the definition of totalitarianism in Chapter 5.
[18] Adolf Hitler, *Mein Kampf* (Boston: Houghton Mifflin, 1962), p. 290. (First published in Berlin, 1925.)

Hitler. One recent survey concluded, "Fascism and Nazism are still with us. Regimes and organizations inspired by them, or using the methods they have made all too famous, are still operating in all the five continents." [19]

Current political ideologies extend from the extreme left of anarchism to the extreme right of fascism, but it is important to consider the similarities of many of these ideologies as well as their differences.

Is the Left-Right Political Spectrum Valid? Today the left-right spectrum is used throughout the world to identify and compare the political ideologies of nations, parties, and individuals. The term *left-wing* is applied to all groups associated with mass participation in government and with sympathy for the poor; the term *right-wing* to those who are more distrustful of popular government. But is this traditional model valid? In many ways, it doesn't accurately reflect the similarities and differences between contemporary governments and their ideologies.[20] While the placement of communism at the extreme left and fascism at the extreme right of the political spectrum suggests that they are worlds apart, in reality, their similarities often outweigh their differences. Both communism and fascism view politics as a struggle between forces of good and evil; both see war as a tool for national development; both demand unquestioning loyalty from their citizens; and both resulted in one-party, totalitarian states with strong leaders and secret police. This similarity extends even to economics: as did the Communist governments, the Nazi and fascist governments strictly controlled the means of production and distribution in their countries. All these facts indicate that the left-right concept is not always the most useful model for viewing political ideologies and forms of government. Since totalitarianism exists at either end of the political spectrum while the more limited forms of government exist in the center, perhaps contemporary ideologies should be viewed according to this criterion instead of according to their left-wing or right-wing leanings. We recognize that there are many different dimensions along which we can classify political systems and that an ideological perspective does tend to blur some of these distinctions. However, for explanatory purposes, we use this shorthand approach because there does appear to be some consistency within an ideological framework which is utilized within a given system.

Of course, another problem with any type of categorization of national ideologies is that they are based on the assumption that people view all aspects of life from the same ideological viewpoint. In spite of the fact that most Americans espouse the democratic ideology we've just discussed, this hardly means that all Americans have a consistent set of beliefs that apply to all issues. A Roman Catholic may favor liberalizing aid to private edu-

[19] Angelo Del Boca and Mario Giovana, *Fascism Today: A World Survey*, trans. R. H. Boothroyd (New York: Pantheon Books, 1969), p. 428.
[20] For a further discussion of the problems of this type of labeling, see Kenneth K. Krogh, "Needed: New Political Labels," *Saturday Review* 43 (December 3, 1960): 17–19; 63–64.

cation, but be against abortion. Or, a Republican black may support federal government intervention on civil rights, but not on medical care. There are few, if any, pure ideological types, and such labels as democratic, fascist, and Communist can only apply to the broadest aspects of an ideology.

Ideology in American Politics

In the preceding section we placed American democracy at the center of the political spectrum, between democratic socialism and nationalism. But any simple, monolithic characterization of American political ideology is incomplete. Anarchists, Communists, socialists, nationalists, fascists, and even monarchists have all contributed to political thinking in this country, and all have followings in the heterogeneous mixture of America's population. American political ideology is a complex hybrid of many political beliefs.

The Conservative and Liberal Traditions

In everyday politics, we tend to identify liberals and conservatives according to their positions on specific issues. Liberals want to expand social services to a national health insurance plan; conservatives want to cut back the welfare rolls. Liberals supported the desegregation decisions made by the Supreme Court under Chief Justice Earl Warren; many conservatives criticized them. Most liberals protested America's involvement in Vietnam in the sixties and early seventies; conservatives generally supported our national policy of intervention. But such specific examples can only give the most general indication of what a liberal and a conservative each believe in. What exactly do the liberal and conservative traditions in American thought encompass?

Conservatism. Conservatives tend to believe in tradition and in preserving the tried-and-true institutions of the past, tending to resist social experimentation. Conservatives oppose the use of government to improve the human condition, taking the view that governmental power should be reduced in this area and that individuals should make their own way in the world. They accept as fact that men are born unequal and some people will fail, but see this as a "natural order."

Conservatives object to extensive social services on the grounds that they encourage mediocrity. Welfare, they argue, breeds dependency.[21] Free, rela-

---

[21] Many liberals would agree, but for different reasons.

tively unregulated competition is best for society, because competition is the primary source of creativity and progress. If there are limits to how much a person can win or lose in life, he will not work as hard as he might otherwise. This position, which approaches the social Darwinist doctrine of laissez-faire, is what one-time presidential candidate Barry Goldwater referred to as "rugged individualism." [22] Although conservatives tend to see broad economic and social controls as interfering with the natural course of events, they are more likely to support governmental power when it is used to uphold traditional moral standards. They believe this type of limitation on individual freedom is necessary. Conservative columnists Walter Lippmann and William F. Buckley maintain that political freedom depends on widespread respect for tradition and authority.[23] (It is worth noting that much of the conservative criticism of the Watergate incident focused on the belief that the involvement of top White House officials helped to undermine the American people's respect for traditions and authority.) Consistent, purposeful social restraints, conservatives argue, make freedom possible and tolerable. "Without the chaos-chaining, the id-chaining heritage of rooted values, what is to keep man from becoming Eichmann or Nechayev —what is to save freedom from 'freedom?' " [24]

Economics plays an important role in the American conservative tradition. Conservatives see economic freedom as a prerequisite for political freedom. Economist Milton Friedman explains this as follows:

On the one hand, freedom in economic arrangements is itself a component of freedom broadly understood, so economic freedom is an end in itself. In the second place, economic freedom is also an indispensable means toward the achievement of political freedom. . . . I know of no example in time or place of a society that has been marked by a large measure of political freedom, that has not also used something comparable to a free market to organize the bulk of economic activity.[25]

Laissez-faire captalism is expected to ensure a wide distribution of goods and property, thereby preventing the concentration of economic or political power in the hands of a few.[26]

In general, then, conservatives prefer to see events follow their own natural course with little if any interference from government or other outside sources. They tend to resist changes in social arrangements, believing

---

[22] See *The Conscience of a Conservative* (Shepardsville, Ky.: Victor, 1960).

[23] See Lippmann's *The Public Philosophy* (Boston: Little, Brown, 1955); and Buckley's *Up From Liberalism* (New York: Honor Books, 1959).

[24] Peter Viereck, "The Philosophical 'New Conservatism'," in *The Radical Right,* ed. Daniel Bell (Garden City, N.Y.: Doubleday, 1964), p. 207.

[25] Milton Friedman, *Capitalism and Freedom* (Chicago: University of Chicago Press, 1962), pp. 8–9.

[26] See Kenneth M. Dolbeare and Patricia Dolbeare, *American Ideologies: The Competing Political Beliefs of the 1970s* (Chicago: Markham, 1971), pp. 209–15.

that the human condition will only improve slowly and naturally and that this process should be allowed to follow its own course.

Liberalism. In contrast to conservatives, liberals emphasize the people's need for many kinds of government assistance, believing that a primary role of government is to guard freedom. The liberal concept of freedom rests on the tradition of natural rights—that all people are born with the inalienable rights to govern themselves, to speak freely and assemble peacefully, to hold property, and to pursue their own interests. Liberals consider civil liberties all-important; therefore, the government must protect them.[27]

Liberals also contend that government must and can help man to live a better life and fulfill his potential as an individual. As opposed to conservatives, who believe that man should fend for himself and that government intervention will prevent him from realizing his potential, liberals feel that the government should provide assistance to those people who cannot help themselves. Some liberals support government aid on purely humanitarian grounds; others defend it as a means to building a more stable society.

Liberal thought holds that some degree of economic security is a prerequisite for freedom. A black man in the deep South who does not vote for fear of losing his job is not free; nor is any man or woman who cannot get a good education or a decent place to live. Liberals argue that it is government's responsibility to see that all people are able to obtain the basic necessities of life, and that this ultimately benefits society. They reason that a person who is struggling to survive has neither time nor energy to improve himself or his world. Finally, liberals believe that social problems can only be solved through the government's application of social and economic programs, since only the government has adequate resources. In this they differ from conservatives.

Liberals are more convinced of the positive aspects of change than are conservatives. They see change as a crucial element in societal growth and progress. This does not mean that liberals want revolution, but that they advocate constant modifications within the framework of current political, legal, and economic systems. In the words of Hubert H. Humphrey, "Liberals fully recognize that *change* is inevitable in the patterns of society and in the challenges which confront man." [28] To a liberal, flexibility is the strength of democracy.

---

[27] In emphasizing civil liberties, liberals differ from populists, who believe that the majority rules and should have its way even though the rights of minorities are overlooked in the process. The populist values the needs of the majorities above the importance of defending minorities and considers civil liberties a weapon used by elitists to protect their status and property. Populists advocate the common man and attempt to use government authority to bring about economic equality by breaking up big corporations and strictly controlling big business. They totally oppose concentration of wealth and power in private hands.

[28] Introduction in Milton Viorst, *Liberalism: A Guide to Its Past, Present and Future in American Politics* (New York: Avon Books, 1963), p. vii.

Despite small, vocal enclaves of conservatism (most notably in Senate and House committees), liberals have dominated American politics for some forty years. Liberals engineered the great social reforms of the thirties and the civil rights legislation of the sixties—as well as the cold war.[29] Yet today, liberals seem to be losing their foothold. Suddenly men who considered themselves the vanguard of social change are under attack from the right *and* the left. What has brought about these changes in attitude?

The Decline-of-Ideology Thesis

In the late fifties and early sixties, a number of Western intellectuals predicted an end to ideology. They felt that modern societies had reached a point where the traditional categories of belief systems were no longer relevant. Many concluded that, since it had been proven that differing demands could be reconciled, ideological controversy was dying down. The idea that ideology was on the decline was given further publicity at a conference on "The Future of Freedom" sponsored by the Congress of Cultural Freedom in September, 1955, in Milan. The representatives of the Western nations arrived at the general conclusion that extremist ideologies were on the wane due to increasing affluence in Western countries: people were comfortable, so there was no need to call for radical change. They saw evidence of this in the fact that traditionally conflicting ideologies were moving closer together.

In the nineteenth century, the gap between factory owners and factory workers had been enormous, but the gap was closing in the twentieth century. Workers in all major industrial nations had a relatively high standard of living. Mass affluence and mass education in these countries had all but eliminated class differences and deep hostilities.[30] Underdeveloped countries focused their energies on modernization and economic development. Everywhere, debate about methods was replacing debate about ideological principles.[31] Political decisions were increasingly being delegated to experts and bureaucrats. The emotional fervor for utopian visions and moral absolutes had faded, and the cold war seemed to be thawing.[32]

Writing in 1960, Daniel Bell attributed the decline in ideology to "a rough consensus among intellectuals on political issues: the acceptance of a welfare state; the desirability of decentralized power; a system of mixed

---

[29] For the liberal position on foreign policy, see Arthur Schlesinger, Jr., *The Crisis of Confidence: Ideas, Power and Violence in America* (Boston: Houghton Mifflin, 1969).

[30] Seymour Martin Lipset, "The Changing Class Structure and Contemporary European Politics," *Daedalus* 93 (Winter 1964): 271–72.

[31] See H. Stuart Highes, "The End of Political Ideology," *Measure* 2 (Spring 1951): 146–58.

[32] A more complete discussion of the decline-of-ideology debate is found in Mostafa Rejai, ed., *Decline of Ideology?* (New York: Atherton, 1971).

economy and of political pluralism." [33] Seymour Martin Lipset was more concrete:

The change in political life reflects the fact that the fundamental political problems of industrial revolution have been solved; the workers have achieved industrial and political citizenship; the conservatives have accepted the welfare state; and the democratic left has recognized that an increase in overall state power carries with it more dangers to freedom than solutions to economic problems.[34]

The last ten years have proven both of these authors wrong. The ideological truce of the late fifties did not result in an end of ideology but saw the emergence of new ideas. It was not ideology that had disappeared, but a particular ideology of a particular period that had changed under modern conditions.[35] Economic development and the growth of "the politics of collective bargaining" (to use Lipset's phrase) did give many people a greater political voice, but it left many others behind. Poverty and race were anything but dead issues. During the sixties, groups that had spent generations on the outskirts of the American system—blacks, Chicanos, Puerto Ricans, Indians, women—"found" politics. Young people loudly rejected the social and material victories of their parents' generation. James Perry's description of America in 1969 differs markedly from what Bell and Lipset had seen ten years earlier:

The New Deal is dead. The Great Society is prostrate. The cities are in desolate decay, the suburbs are in turmoil. . . . There is a race gap in America. There is a generation gap too.

The decade of the '60s, to repeat an altogether inadequate cliche, has been a time of change. Searing, disabling, destructive change, on the face of it. The change that began in the '60s will lead to a new order in the '70s—or to no order at all.[36]

The "new politics" that emerged in the sixties was based partly on the search for a new order, partly on the fear of disorder, and partly on the shared conviction that "politics as usual" would no longer do.

The "New Politics"

During the sixties, a number of isolated groups—civil rights workers, peace activists, students, professionals, women—began to rebel against a sense

---

[33] Daniel Bell, *The End of Ideology; on the Exhaustion of Political Ideas in the Fifties,* rev. ed. (New York: Collier Books, 1962), p. 397.
[34] Lipset, *Political Man: The Social Bases of Politics* (New York: Doubleday, 1963), pp. 442–43.
[35] For a more detailed discussion of this idea see Ladd, *Ideology in America,* pp. 1–14.
[36] "A New Order—Or no Order at all," *The National Observer,* Sept. 8, 1969, p. 1.

of powerlessness they felt toward government. The "new politics," a perspective more than an organized movement, was born. The term *new politics* describes a wide range of formal and informal political groups that advocate change—change in foreign policy and in welfare, in party structure, city planning, education, highway construction, and above all in government procedures.

The new politics is primarily a reaction against the old political system which failed to cope adequately with new issues and forces in American life, especially the problems of a technological society. Its aim is to bring about a closer relationship between the people and the government—a quicker response to popular demands.

"One thing about youngsters' participating in politics—the smoke-filled rooms sure smell different."

Reproduced by special permission of PLAYBOY Magazine; copyright © 1972.

The new politics rejects the old political styles and issues, going so far as to say that they often obscure unresolved and critical problems. Spokesmen for the new politics believe that as long as the old-line politicians, who do not have the sense of urgency, will, or drive to deal with today's situations, remain in charge, the political system will not meet and solve the new and pressing problems.

According to many sociologists, rapid technological advance has disrupted the traditional values of society and contributed to the alienation of the individual and the destruction of the environment, without eradicating social ills. The new politicians believe something can and should be done to alleviate these problems, and the reject the "politics of compromise" as the means for achieving their goals. They argue that many groups are left out of this bargaining process. Also, compromise encourages parties and candidates to avoid issues. A politician who takes a strong stand on either side of a controversial subject—for example, forced school busing to achieve racial balance or reform of abortion laws—risks alienating voters. Therefore, he avoids committing himself, and so avoids solving the problem. Compromise may not lead to the best decisions. The urgent problems of the seventies— race relations, poverty, urban decay, pollution—require strong action, not compromise.

The new politics is issue-oriented. Rebelling against personality and party politics, it seeks candidates who will take stands in campaigns and provide strong action if they are elected. It seeks decentralization of government and a return to participatory democracy, with citizens making the decisions that directly affect their lives. Finally, it seeks to reestablish morality in technology: computers may be able to design a game plan for war, but they cannot decide whether that war is right or wrong. The new politics argues that politics cannot be separated from morality.[37]

The new politics is perhaps best exemplified by the McCarthy campaign in 1968 and the McGovern campaign in 1971–72, each of which had a large number of nonprofessionals—students, housewives, and other volunteers—rather than "party regulars" working on their staffs. An outgrowth of the new politics, yet more radical in the actions it advocates, is the "New Left."

The New Left. The New Left, which includes such groups as Students for a Democratic Society (SDS), the Peace and Freedom Party, the Yippees, and Youth against War and Fascism, is a product of the sixties. Unlike older leftist organizations in this country, many New Left organizations oppose all political establishments—including the parties and bureaucracies of Communist nations. They seek the economic, political, and social liberation of the middle class as well as of the workers. One of the most vocal

---

[37] See Carey McWilliams, "Time for a New Politics," *The Nation*, 194, no. 21 (May 26, 1962) : 466.

elements of the New Left has been the student movement, which views youth as a separate constituency and as the chief source of social and political change.

New Left ideology is based on a sweeping condemnation of American society—its values as well as its institutions. Writers such as Tom Hayden have characterized the American system as an immense, dehumanizing machine run by a small military-industrial elite for its own profit.[38] The materialist ethic permeates all levels of society, encouraging competition, exploitation, racism, and violence—even distorting human relationships. With assembly-line production and advanced technology that few people can understand, even work has become meaningless. Americans are alienated, "trivialized," one-dimensional.[39] The government has separated itself from the people; its bureaucracies are stagnant and unresponsive. Wartime production and "superconsumption" exemplified by bigger and flashier cars each year are the basis of the economy, while human problems are neglected. "The potentiality for abundance" in America, said SDS leaders, has become "a curse and a cruel irony." [40]

Rejecting the status quo entirely, the New Left seeks social and political revolution; it envisions a new order based on individual freedom, brotherhood, and community. Economic equality is seen as a prerequisite for freedom: all people should have the basic necessities of life. However, New Left spokesmen do not consider these necessities very many, and in some instances advocate "voluntary poverty" as well as communal ownership of property. The New Left rejects the democratic-socialist idea of a welfare state (which it sees as still another bureaucracy) in favor of decentralized, participatory democracy on the town-meeting model. In its emphasis on community, brotherhood, and the natural cooperativeness of man, and its distrust of all government, the New Left is closer to anarchism than to socialism or communism.

Abbie Hoffman, who describes himself as a cultural revolutionary, explained his interpretation of the New Left during his trial for conspiracy to incite riot in Chicago:

Q. Where do you reside?
A. I live in Woodstock Nation.
Q. Will you tell the Court and Jury where it is?
A. Yes. It is a nation of alienated young people. We carry it around with us as a state of mind in the same way the Sioux Indians carried the Sioux nation around with them. It is a nation dedicated to the coopera-

38 This idea comes from C. Wright Mills, an elitist theorist who strongly influenced New Left thinking. See his "On the New Left" in *The New Radicals: A Report with Documents*, ed. P. Jacobs and S. Landau (New York: Random House, 1966), pp. 101–14.
39 This phrase comes from Herbert Marcuse, another thinker who strongly influenced New Left ideology. See his *One Dimensional Man* (Boston: Beacon Press, 1969); and *An Essay on Liberation* (Boston: Beacon Press, 1968).
40 See "The Port Huron Statement" (Chicago: SDS, 1966).

tion versus competition, to the idea that people should have better means of exchange than property or money, that there should be some other basis for human interaction. . . . It is in the state of mind, in the mind of myself and my brothers and sisters. It is a conspiracy.[41]

The activities of the New Left were focused on the university and the war in Vietnam in the late sixties. The university was pictured as an arm of the establishment, designed to promote and perpetuate capitalist values. But most of the New Left's activity in the late sixties was directed against the war in Vietnam, which it saw as an unjust war caused by American intervention to support a corrupt regime against the wishes of the Vietnamese people. On both the university and the war issues, the New Left practiced the politics of confrontation: demonstrations, sit-ins, marches intended to disrupt the system and to educate ("radicalize") those who had not yet realized how bad the situation was.

The leaders of the New Left who began their activities in the civil rights movement in the deep South, first confronted "the establishment" in the Free Speech Movement at Berkeley in 1964.[42] The New Left movement grew as opposition to the war in Vietnam mounted, reaching its peak in 1968–69 with demonstrations at the Democratic National Convention in Chicago and with the marches on the Pentagon. Just after that, the largest New Left organization, SDS, broke apart.[43] Although there were massive demonstrations on college campuses across the country in the spring of 1970, when the United States invaded Cambodia and student demonstrators were shot at Kent State and Jackson State, the New Left seems to have lost some of its momentum. According to recent reports, membership in New Left organizations is falling. Only 11 percent of college students in one survey identified themselves as New Left in 1971,[44] and the number and size of campus demonstrations has declined. But at the same time, more and more students from a variety of backgrounds are willing to criticize the American system, and the theoretical branch of the New Left—Herbert Marcuse, Noam Chomsky, and others—has a much wider audience than it did in the past. It may be that, although the New Left failed to mobilize the poor and the

---

[41] *The Tales of Hoffman,* ed. from the official transcript by Mark L. Levine, George C. McNamee, and Daniel Greenberg (New York: Bantam Books, 1970), p. 140.

[42] The Free Speech Movement, led by Mario Savio, was a clash between students who "wanted the right to meet freely on campus, to raise funds, to recruit supporters, and to discuss the whole range of issues that concerned them" and the administration, which outlawed all activities not directly related to university life. See Nathan Glazer, "Student Power in Berkeley," *Public Interest* 13 (Fall 1968) : 7.

[43] Once a loose federation of leftist youth groups, SDS broke away from older, more dogmatic leftists at its convention in Port Huron, Michigan, in 1962, when it issued the first "New Left Manifesto." By the late sixties, its leadership was split and SDS divided into small autonomous groups, including the Weathermen faction.

[44] "Pessimism Voiced in Student Study," *The New York Times,* April 11, 1972, p. 11.

workers as it once hoped to do, it succeeded in "raising the consciousness" of young Americans.

The Radical Right. The counterpart of the New Left in radical American ideology is the Radical Right—an outgrowth more of the conservative tradition than of the "new politics." When we hear of the Radical Right, we usually think of the John Birch Society, the Liberty Lobby, the Christian Anti-Communist Crusade, and the more radical Minutemen. Most of these groups came into existence in the late 1950s. In their belief in individual initiative, minimal government, and traditionalism, Radical Right spokesmen Robert Welch, Reverend Carl McIntyre, Billy James Hargis, and others, closely resemble the traditional conservative position.[45] But the new right is concerned with general issues such as bureaucratic growth, big government, and big labor as well as hostile foreign ideologies and revolutionary movements.[46] "The greatest enemy of man is, and always has been government; and the larger, the more extensive that government, the greater the enemy," wrote Welch, the founder of the John Birch Society.[47]

Although the various Radical Right groups express a wide range of policy proposals, they share an obsessive concern with communism which dates back to the early fifties and the anti-Communist hysteria symbolized by Senator Joseph McCarthy. There is still a tendency to attribute the undesirable—including federal income tax, Warren Court rulings, the civil rights movement and civil rights laws, student radicalism, and ghetto riots—to Communist influence. This emphasis on the danger of communism has come to be the most pronounced aspect of Radical Right thought.[48] "The ideological conflict is between the East and the West—slavery versus freedom. Communism versus capitalism, socialism versus Christianity, Satan versus God!" [49]

Some members of the Radical Right also protest moral trends in America. They see America as being in the throes of a moral breakdown, with the Communists behind it all. Such factions tend to be religiously fundamental and moralistic as well as old-fashionedly individualistic. The members of Edgar Bundy's Church League of America, Hargis's Christian Crusade, McIntyre's Twentieth Century Reformation Hour, and Schwartz's Crusade demonstrate these characteristics.

---

[45] For a history of right-wing political thought in America, see Seymour Martin Lipset and E. Raab, eds., *The Politics of Unreason*, vol. 5, *Right-wing Extremism in America 1790–1970* (New York: Harper & Row, 1970).

[46] See Robert Schoenberger, ed., *The American Right Wing* (New York: Holt, Rinehart and Winston, 1969).

[47] *The Blue Book* (Belmont, Calif.: Robert Welch, 1961), p. 108.

[48] Raymond Wolfinger et al., "America's Radical Right; Politics and Ideology," in *Ideology and Discontent*, ed. David Apter (New York: The Free Press, 1964), pp. 10–11.

[49] Dr. Frederick C. Schwartz of the Christian Anti-Communist Crusade, quoted in Arnold Foster and Benjamin R. Epstein, *Danger on the Right* (New York: Random House, 1964), p. 56.

Who belongs to the Radical Right? The supporters of this movement tend to come from the West and South and from the following general groups, in varying numbers:

1. The new rich who feel excluded from established citadels of power.
2. Southern elite groups trying to maintain their power against the pressure of rising black and working class groups.
3. Military elite groups in whom the authoritarian tradition is very strong and who are strongly indoctrinated with distrust of the democratic process.
4. Small businessmen who feel frustrated, threatened, and particularly vulnerable to the changing socioeconomic currents around them.
5. Working-class and lower-middle-class people who feel alienated, isolated, threatened, and frustrated, and who are seeking scapegoats for their feelings.
6. Elderly people, who feel threatened by change and yearn for the security of the good old days.
7. Members of certain religious groups whose ideological patterns make them more susceptible to authoritarian ways of thinking.[50]

Today's Radical Right can be traced back to widespread distrust of foreigners in the years following World War I and to the talk of the Red Menace in the twenties and thirties. These fears were voiced through a revitalized Ku Klux Klan and somewhat later through William Dudley Pelley's Silver Shirts and Fuehrer Fritz Kuhn's Bund.[51] While these organizations became less prominent in the forties, the conspiracy theory surfaced again in the fifties with Senator Joseph R. McCarthy's investigations of communism in the federal government and the intellectual community. McCarthy's "witch hunts" gave the Radical Right a new respectability. It was in this period that Robert Welch founded the John Birch Society, the largest and best organized of the Radical Right groups. The Right grew during the sixties and early seventies, its membership fed by reactions against the constitutionally liberal Warren Court, the civil rights and peace movements, and the emerging New Left. By 1967, the John Birch Society boasted four thousand local chapters, seventy-five full-time professional coordinators, and over eighty thousand dues-paying members, and was running about three hundred and fifty American Opinion Bookstores that sold five million dollars worth of books, films, and other materials a year. In addition, the Radical Right supports over five thousand radio shows and periodicals with a circulation that exceeds fifty thousand a month.[52] Estimates of the total expenditure for

[50] Judd Marmor, "The Psychodynamics of Political Extremism," *American Journal of Psychotherapy* 22 (October 1968) : 566.
[51] Christenson et al., *Ideologies and Modern Politics*, pp. 284–85.
[52] Fred Grupp, "The Political Perspectives of Birch Society Members," in *The American Right Wing*, ed. Robert Schoenberger (New York: Holt, Rinehart and Winston, 1969), p. 83.

publications, activities, lobbying and so on come to fourteen million dollars a year.[53]

Governor George Wallace's American Independent Party, which joins the Radical Right in opposition to bureaucratic government but stops short of attributing contemporary social problems to a Communist conspiracy, played a significant role in the presidential election of 1968 and the primaries of 1972, drawing votes from both the Democrats and the Republicans. But like new politics candidate George McGovern, Barry Goldwater, the right-wing presidential candidate in 1964, lost by a landslide at the polls. Apparently the average American voter rejects positions he perceives to be extreme.

In this section we have focused on emerging political ideologies of the last few decades. The new politics is an attempt to rejuvenate "the system" by introducing new blood, new ideas, new commitments. The New Left opposes the system (indeed, all systems), advocating revolutionary changes in the American way of life. The Radical Right, in contrast, feels America has lost its way and seeks to restore the attitudes and values that they believe made this country what it is. At the same time, however, these movements have much in common. All three oppose big government and advocate decentralization. For different reasons, all three movements feel the domestic policies of the New Deal and the Great Society have failed, and that American foreign policy is ineffective at best. To what degree they will influence the government or the voters remains to be seen.

Ideologies and Government

The maintenance of a political system depends greatly on the people's support of government. Ideologies are part of the belief systems which confer legitimacy on presidents and parliaments, courts and police, space programs and health insurance, mass education and the draft, elections and revolutions.

The political ideologies discussed in this chapter represent the major belief systems operating in the world today. When considering the workings of these ideologies, it is important to keep in mind that in reality, there are very few pure types. Ideologies overlap: a person who believes in America's democratic system can also advocate many aspects of democratic socialism. A fascist and a Communist have in common their belief in a totalitarian form of government, and an American New Leftist and Radical Right-winger share a distaste for "big government." Ideologies are not monolithic. They influence the actions of people and governments, and they adjust to keep up with the times. Ideologies thus serve as a dynamic force in the political structure of a nation.

Ideologies form the building blocks of political systems. They determine

[53] Christenson et al., *Ideologies and Modern Politics*, p. 285.

how the people will participate in their government, and they provide the framework for the development and functioning of the institutions of government. The importance of political ideologies to political participants and institutions will be demonstrated in the next two sections of this text.

Suggested Readings

Barber, Benjamin. *Superman and Common Men: Freedom, Anarchy and the Revolution.* New York: Praeger, 1971. An argument for a revolutionist democracy.

Christenson, Reo M. *Heresies Right and Left: Some Political Assumptions Re-examined.* New York: Harper & Row, 1973. An analysis of contemporary issues in which the opinions of prominent political spokesmen are evaluated.

Dahrendorf, Ralf. *Society and Democracy in Germany.* Garden City, N.Y.: Doubleday, 1965. A sociological-philosophical inquiry into why democracy did not take root in post World War I Germany.

Hitler, Adolf. *Mein Kampf.* Translated by Ralph Manheim. Boston: Houghton Mifflin, 1962. The blueprint and rationale for the rise of the national socialist movement as written by its most important leader.

Hoffman, Robert, ed. *Anarchism.* New York: Aldine-Atherton, 1970. A collection of essays by such well-known writers on anarchism as Proudhon, Tolstoy, Shaw, Russell, and Goodman.

Ladd, Carll Everett. *Ideology in America.* Ithaca, N.Y.: Cornell University Press, 1969. An argument concerning the changing nature of ideology in America.

Lane, Robert. *Political Ideology: Why the American Common Man Believes What He does.* New York: Free Press, 1962. An insightful analysis based on in-depth interviews conducted by a leading political psychologist.

Lipset, Seymour Martin. *Political Man: The Social Bases of Politics.* Garden City, N.Y.: Doubleday, 1960. Part I should be studied by all students of democracy, as it is a brilliant analysis of the conditions for democracy and for the rise of authoritarianism in societies.

Sargent, Lyman Tower. *Contemporary Political Ideologies.* Homewood, Ill.: The Dorsey Press, 1972. A succinct, easy-to-read summary of the basic tenets of major contemporary ideologies.

_____. *New Left Thought: An Introduction.* Homewood, Ill.: The Dorsey Press, 1972. A discussion of the basic ideas of the New Left and those groups that support them.

Schoenberger, Robert A., ed. *The American Right Wing: Readings in Political Behavior.* New York: Holt, Rinehart and Winston, 1969. Empirical examinations of the organizational, social, and psychological perspectives of the right wing in America.

THREE

The Voices of the People

Socialization and public opinion

CHAPTER 8

A citizen of the People's Republic of China expects his government to house, educate, and feed him. But he also expects it to tell him what books he may read and what films he may see. He does not own his own property; the government does. The citizen of twentieth-century America wouldn't stand for Uncle Sam's telling him what to do (or not to do) in his spare time. Government attempts to censor films, books, and news publications have always met with protests that free speech is being impaired. The modern American expects to own property, and when the government taxes him, he complains.

The modern American and Chinese ideas of the proper role of government are, in many ways, poles apart. But so are American conceptions of the twentieth century and the eighteenth century. If Thomas Jefferson suddenly found himself in the twentieth century, he would probably be aghast. Instead of a government limited to protecting our frontiers and our Bill of Rights, he would be confronted with a monstrous organization that collects our garbage, keeps tabs on our earnings, tells us not to eat swordfish or cyclamates, and makes us obtain licenses to sell liquor or own a dog.

The modern Chinese, the modern American, and the American of two hundred years ago have very different perceptions of what government is and should be. What are the forces that work to make their opinions and ideals so strikingly different?

Political Culture and Socialization

We are familiar with the idea that every nation has its own distinctive political and social system. Each society imparts its own characteristic set of norms and values to its people, and the people in turn have distinct sets of ideas about how the political system is supposed to work, about what the government may do to them and for them, and about their own claims on the system and their obligations to it. This set of beliefs, symbols, and values about the political system forms the political culture of a nation—and it varies considerably from one nation to another.[1]

Political Culture and Subculture

There are many more dimensions in the difference between one political culture and another than are suggested by such traditional categories as democracy and communism, or primitive and modern. Does the individual perceive government as something near or remote? Does he respect it or regard it with distrust? Is government something which touches virtually every part of his life, or does he view it as a distant official who sends a tax bill once a year and leaves him alone the rest of the time? Does he regard himself as a participant in government or merely a subject? Does he feel he can affect government as a citizen, or that it is solely under the control of others? These questions suggest some of the different dimensions of political culture.[2]

Measured by these dimensions, each political culture has a distinctive configuration. Just as there is a great difference between the political atti-

---

[1] See the discussion of political culture in Chapter 1.

[2] The major work in the field, and the most comprehensive collection of data, is Gabriel Almond and Sidney Verba's *The Civic Culture* (Princeton, N.J.: Princeton University Press, 1963), which studied five modern democracies—the United States, United Kingdom, West Germany, Italy, and Mexico—and showed strikingly different patterns of attitudes regarding interest and participation, feelings of "civic competence," and many other dimensions. See the discussion in Chapter 1.

tudes of a Frenchman and those of a Ubangi, there is also a great deal of diversity within each nation's own political culture. People of higher incomes and higher education identify much more positively with the government, and feel more able to affect it, than do people of lower economic or educational levels. Deprived or disadvantaged groups, such as the American Indian or Chicano minorities, may feel less certain about the legitimacy of their government and about their own ability to change it than will a member of the local chapter of the DAR (Daughters of the American Revolution). The suburban homeowner is likely to view the police patrol car as a trusted arm of a protecting government; but the ghetto resident may have a more ambivalent view of the "fuzz." [3] Indeed, the American college student is a member of a minority "subculture" which differs sharply from most of American society: he has more information and more sophisticated views on how (and why) government should function than do almost all of his noncollege compatriots.

An urban ghetto, a hippie commune, and the "country-club set"—each comprises a separate political subculture, a smaller group of citizens who may hold divergent views on some issues from those held by the national culture. In many cases, the reason people in these different subcultures view the government in different ways is because it *is* different for one group than it is for another. The Almond and Verba study shows that the "have" groups are more confident than the "have-not" groups that their demands can affect the political system. And, indeed, a corporation magnate is able more often to affect policy than a migrant farmer: he can hire a lawyer or a lobbyist to press his demands, and there is a good chance that the government will be willing to listen.

But many aspects of a nation's political culture and subcultures cannot easily be explained by labels such as "haves" and "have-nots," because they reflect more complicated attitudes deeply embedded in the traditions, customs, style, and "personality" of a people or group. An examination of the political socialization process shows us a more complex interaction is at work.

Political Socialization

Carry an American flag and whistle the "Stars and Stripes" at a Columbus, Ohio, parade, and crowds will cheer. But don't try the same thing in Peking or Hanoi. Why is the same action considered a proper show of emotion in one setting, but a gross faux pas in another? What patterns of training lie behind the fact that most members of the American political culture respect

---

[3] Angus Campbell and Howard Schumann make this comparison in *Racial Attitudes in Fifteen American Cities* (Washington, D.C.: Superintendent of Documents, 1968), p. 44. For a study of political attitudes among poor Appalachian white "losers," see Dean Jaros, Herbert Hirsch, and Frederic Fleron, Jr., "The Malevolent Leader: Political Socialization in an American Subculture," *American Political Science Review* 62 (June 1968): 564–75.

this piece of cloth, while another nationality holds it in contempt? The reason that the two political cultures hold such different symbolic value systems is because each society trains its citizens—if only indirectly—to feel a certain way toward particular political symbols and institutions.

Political socialization is the process by which the individuals in a given social system learn their values, norms, concepts, and attitudes about both politics and the individual's relationship to the political system. Just as an American child is trained to expect families to be made up of fathers and mothers in his social system, so is he trained to expect his political system to be made up of governors, presidents, and senators. The first process is called socialization because it relates to society as a whole. The second—political socialization—relates only to the political aspect of society.

In the broadest sense, political socialization is the way in which a society perpetuates its political culture.[4] It is a continuous, lifelong process which is part of each individual's conditioning and education as a member of the culture he is born into. It is a phenomenon of all political systems,[5] and it does not necessarily involve deliberate indoctrination by agencies of the government.

The Roles of Political Socialization

Political socialization performs several functions, for both the individual and the political system as a whole.

Training the Individual. Political socialization instills in each person the prevailing values of the political system. It enables him to relate to the system: to expect certain treatment from government, and to know what it expects of him. It teaches the high school or college graduate to expect to be able to find a decent job and to become a respected member of his community. In turn, he also learns that certain actions are expected of him: obeying the laws, keeping involved in local affairs, and voting at election time. Whether the picture he acquires through political socialization is accurate or not is beside the point for our immediate purposes. The point is that

[4] Kenneth P. Langton, *Political Socialization* (New York: Oxford University Press, 1969), p. 4. For other definitions and a wealth of ideas on the subject, see Lucien W. Pye's *Politics, Personality, and Nation-Building* (New Haven, Conn.: Yale University Press, 1962), pp. 44–56 especially; and his "Political Modernization and Research on the Process of Political Socialization," *Items* 13 (1959): 25–28. See also Richard E. Dawson and Kenneth Prewitt's definition in *Political Socialization* (Boston: Little, Brown, 1969), p. 17. An excellent new reader which covers all of the basic literature on political socialization is Jack Dennis, ed., *Socialization to Politics: A Reader* (New York: John Wiley & Sons, 1973).

[5] One of the early works on political socialization which explicitly attempted to place it in a framework for comparative analysis is Gabriel A. Almond, "A Functional Approach to Comparative Politics," in Gabriel Almond and James S. Coleman, eds., *The Politics of Developing Areas* (Princeton, N.J.: Princeton University Press, 1960), pp. 26–33.

political socialization transmits to the individual an idea of how the world beyond his own immediate experience is governed. And a person generally bases his political actions and attitudes on this picture.

Supporting the Political System. Political socialization helps to maintain and legitimize the political system and the government in office. It maintains the system by conditioning and educating its members to obey its rules and to fulfill its roles. The system works as it does, and succeeds in governing to the extent that it does, because most people obey the laws and accept different roles—such as judge, policeman, party activist, candidate, and voter—which interact to keep the system going.

Political socialization also plays the important role of training people to recognize those who have the right to exercise official authority, and to accept this right. The mother who brings her son to school on his first day and tells him, "Do as the teacher says," is legitimizing the teacher's authority by training her child to respect the teacher. In a more complex sense, we are all socialized to such an extent that even though we may be adversely affected by a law we disagree with, enacted by legislators we voted against, and carried out by order of a president we dislike, we will nevertheless feel obliged to obey the law. Forty years ago, thousands of Americans who would have otherwise freely taken an "occasional nip" refused to let liquor touch their lips solely because it was against the government's prohibition policy (although thousands also broke the law and indulged). To some extent, of couse, we obey the law because we fear punishment, but in perhaps many more cases, this obedience is due to our training to accept government's authority over us.

The Agents of Socialization

We all grow up to think of ourselves as Americans or Belgians, whites or blacks, members of a neighborhood community or "outsiders," and Republicans, Democrats, or Independents. What are the influences that make one person a Democrat first and a housewife last, and another person a welder first and a member of a community last?

The Family. Psychologists tell us that long after we've left home, our parents continue to exert a profound influence on every aspect of our behavior. Social science researchers have documented this continuing parental influence in the area of political behavior. An obvious example is that most people vote as their parents did. But the formative influence of the family on control of others? These questions suggest some of the different dimensions political behavior also works in a much more basic way: it forms the psychological makeup of the individual, which in turn determines many of his political attitudes. It imparts a set of norms and values that become the individual's "map" of what to expect of himself and others in all areas of life, including its political aspects; and it transmits beliefs and attitudes that are specifically political, such as party loyalty, and trust or cynicism about government.

The family is the dominant influence in a person's political behavior because it controls his early years, and the effect of the conditioning and training he receives in these years is the strongest. A study of the shaping of political attitudes found that the most decisive of these attitudes are shaped in the years from ages three to thirteen.[6] The family has almost exclusive control of the child's training in the first three of these years, and continues to have the dominant influence during school years as well.[7] It is natural that the child's mother and father are his important models because they are the main source for the satisfaction of all his basic needs—such needs as food and warmth, physical protection, love, and identity.[8] Parents are figures of great power and authority in the child's world, and from them he accepts many norms, values, and attitudes unconsciously and uncritically.

The psychological set a child acquires as a result of family relationships affects his political behavior in adult life in many different ways.[9] In general, people give back to the world as adults what they got from it as children. One extensive study found that American college students with authoritarian personalities had almost invariably been treated roughly as children.[10] But, on the other hand, parental overprotection may be just as harmful, causing children to fear leaving the shelter of the family. This sense of fear may later be expressed politically as distrust and dislike of public figures.

As adults, people differ widely in the degree to which they participate in political affairs. Underlying this difference in behavior is a strong difference in beliefs about the effectiveness of their political activity. Those who feel they can influence government policy are, naturally, much more likely to be active. But where does the difference in beliefs originate? The five-nation study by Almond and Verba found an important clue in the style of family

[6] David Easton and Stephen Hess, "The Child's Political World," *Journal of Political Science* 6 (August 1961): 229–46.

[7] Although the parents' role in socializing is not necessarily recognized by the children themselves, especially during adolescence. A 1969 survey of eight thousand high school students in Phoenix found that less than one-fourth of juniors and seniors gave their parents primary credit for the development of their political opinions. See Leo Bogart, *Silent Politics: Polls and the Awareness of Public Opinion* (New York: John Wiley & Sons, 1972), p. 77.

[8] See James C. Davies, "The Family's Role in Political Socialization," *The Annals of the American Academy of Political Science* 361 (September 1965): 10–19.

[9] For example, political scientist Robert Lane found that tense father-son relationships can result in the grown son's inability to criticize any figure of political authority. See "Fathers and Sons: Foundations of Political Belief" in *American Sociological Review* 24 (August 1959): 502–11.

[10] T. W. Adorno, Else Frenkel-Brunswick, D. J. Levinson, and R. N. Sanford, *The Authoritarian Personality* (New York: Harper & Row, 1950).

decision making.[11] Adults interviewed in the study were asked whether they remembered having had a voice in family decisions when they were children, and whether they felt that their actions as adults could influence the government. The answers showed a clear relation between the remembered family participation and the adult sense of "political competence": those who took part in family decisions were, on the average, more inclined to feel the expression of their political beliefs could influence the government.

Most of the political socialization that takes place in the family is informal—and sometimes it is unconscious. Neither the parent nor the child is actively aware that future political behavior is being shaped when, for example, the father "lays down the law" and refuses to hear any argument, or when the mother thinks aloud that there's no use complaining about the unfair amount of work she has to do around the house without any help because her husband won't pay any attention.[12] And parental attitudes and actions about political matters—for instance, their level of interest in election campaigns, or their readiness to accept special favors when they have a slight legal problem (getting a traffic ticket "fixed")—probably are more important in shaping the child's future political behavior than any of the specific ideas about government and politics that the parents consciously try to impart. In contrast is the more deliberate type of socialization that occurs in the schools.

The School. When a new nation is created, be it by revolution, civil war, or peaceful independence from a colonial power, one of the most important steps that the government must take is to teach its citizens that they are a national community. Schools are among the most important agents of socialization in turning scattered groups of people into a nation, since they are able to reach large numbers of individuals simultaneously and teach them that they belong to a community—a job which the family is ill equipped for. The developing nations of Africa are currently trying to unify a number of tribes who speak different dialects and who often have histories of conflict with each other. Clearly, the role of the schools has been profound, as they have been called upon in some instances to turn out graduates who have a different set of political values, norms, and loyalties than their own parents. The Communist nations have also relied heavily on the schools for systematic inculcation of new political loyalties and concepts.

In nations where the government is already well established, the content of the school's political socialization is generally more in harmony with what the family teaches. Yet there is no doubt that even here, primary schools have a strong effect: they are able to reinforce the students' identification with the community and the nation. In classrooms around the globe, chil-

---

[11] Almond and Verba, *The Civic Culture*, pp. 330–74.
[12] See, for example, the discussion in M. Kent Jennings and Richard G. Niemi, "The Transmission of Political Values from Parent to Child," *American Political Science Review* 62 (March 1968): 169–84.

dren salute different flags and are taught to feel a surge of positive emotion toward their own national symbols. The advocates of broad public schooling have usually stressed its value for teaching the meaning of citizenship and inculcating convictions about one's obligation to the national community. In the history of the United States, the need to "Americanize" the children of immigrant families has been a vital concern (especially during the heavy migrations of the last century), and this task has fallen primarily on the schools.

The amount of schooling a person receives affects political attitudes at a more sophisticated level than the programmed loyalty to the Stars and Stripes or the Union Jack. For example, people with several years of education have a stronger sense of responsibility to their community and feel more able to influence public policy than do less educated citizens. As Table 8–1 shows, even though there may be differences between the political cultures of separate nations, there is a striking correlation between a person's formal education and his attitudes toward the political system. Persons with more schooling show a greater awareness of political questions, pay more attention to politics, are more likely to engage in political discussion, and are more inclined to participate in politics.

How much of this is the direct result of what a person learns in class about his rights and responsibilities, and how much is explained by the fact that longer schooling is associated with higher socioeconomic status? Though this poses an analytical riddle, there is general recognition that education is a force in its own right, aside from economic considerations, and consequently, intense battles are often fought over what and how the schools should teach. In recent years, black leaders have rebelled against the use of textbooks which ignore or slight the accomplishments of black people, especially those that appear to do so deliberately. They see the formal teaching of racial identity to be a vital element of what is needed for black people to progress toward the effective exercise of their political and civil rights. The school's power of political indoctrination is also the underlying issue in the objections to compulsory saluting of the flag which have been

Table 8-1
Percent Who Say the Ordinary Man Should Be Active in His Local Community, by Nation and Education

Nation	Total	Primary Schooling	Some Secondary	Some University
United States	51	35	56	66
Great Britain	39	37	42	42
Germany	22	21	32	38
Italy	10	7	17	22
Mexico	26	24	37	38

Source: Gabriel A. Almond and Sidney Verba, The Civic Culture (Princeton, N.J.: Princeton University Press, 1963), p. 176.

raised by religious groups such as Jehovah's Witnesses and by individual parents and students on grounds related to war protest.

According to one study,[13] civics and government courses may impart very specific ideas, and may even lay the basis for significantly greater political participation and sophistication. This study analyzed the political attitudes of high school students in three communities of varied economic background, before and after taking a civics course. It found that after taking the course, students were somewhat more likely to believe political participation was worthwhile, were more likely to support the rights of citizens and minorities to voice demands and dissent, and were less likely to have chauvinistic feelings that their nation was the only right nation.

Peer Groups. While school lessons are a powerful socializing force, there is also some evidence that they may not have a very lasting effect unless other influences are pushing the individual in the same direction. For example, working-class children in Jamaica who went to school with children of higher social classes tended to take on the political attitudes of those classes, but when they attended school with only working-class peers, their attitudes did not change.[14]

The relative strength of peer-group influence compared to that of school and family appears to be growing. In 1961, social scientist James S. Coleman observed that "our adolescents today are cut off, probably more than ever before, from the adult society. They are still oriented toward fulfilling their parents' desires, but they look very much to their peers for approval as well." [15] As a result of rapid change and economic specialization in modern society, parents cannot give their children a lot of the knowledge, skills, and perceptions they need to "make it" in the outside world. Children consequently spend more time in school and out with their peers, and less with their families. The results are that both schools and peer groups are growing more influential than the family, and peer groups seem to have increasingly more to do with the individual's assimilation of what the school presents. Hippies, long hair, student dissent, and the rise of a youth counterculture may all reflect the growing importance of peer groups as socializers.

The Mass Media. The media of mass communications constitute a fourth important socializing force. These media are part and parcel of modern industrial civilization.[16] They have no counterpart in primitive societies, nor in classic civilizations of the past, and this is no accident. Modern tech-

[13] Edgar Litt, "Civic Education, Community Norms, and Political Indoctrination," *American Sociological Review* 28 (February 1963): 69–75.
[14] Kenneth P. Langston, *Political Socialization* (New York: Oxford University Press, 1969), pp. 126–31.
[15] James S. Coleman, *The Adolescent Society* (New York: The Free Press, 1961), p. 9.
[16] As the following chapter, "Communications and the Media," covers the political role of the media in much more detail, the reader is referred to that discussion.

"I'm afraid my views are those put out by mass media, based on opinion polls."

nology created them, but more to the point, modern society, and particularly its government, depends heavily on them to perform even simple functions. Mass communications constitute a revolution in the way people get information about the world beyond their own daily experience and the way they form their perceptions about it.

The importance of the mass media in the process of governing is apparent when we look at traditional societies that are trying to "modernize." Here, the formal education of children in schools is aided by newspapers, radio programs, and any medium that can possibly be used to spread a feeling of community goals through standardized messages which encourage the people to develop a new identity.[17] While the influence of these media is profound in developing nations, in some respects it is even greater in advanced societies, where they are practically ubiquitous. The task of informing people about what's happening politically, and what their government is doing for them and in their name, is completely beyond the capability of the word-of-mouth grapevine which primitive societies rely on: the modern world relies on the mass media.

Another way in which the media act as a socializer is illustrated by a

[17] Richard E. Dawson and Kenneth Prewitt, *Political Socialization* (Boston: Little, Brown, 1969), pp. 194–95.

survey of children in several nations in different stages of development.[18] It found that in the more modernized nations, TV and films are among the leading sources of children's information about foreign people. How else would millions of people in foreign lands learn to picture the typical American as either a cowboy, a millionaire, or a gangster? But while the mass media act as an important socializing force, their effect, like that of the schools, is to reinforce existing orientations, or to "support existing arrangements and to convey interpretations considered appropriate by [the holders of] social power." [19]

The Government. Government itself is, inevitably, an agent of political socialization. Virtually everything it does takes into account its citizens' reactions, and many government activities are intended explicitly to explain or display the government to the public.

All the actions of governing affect the people, and consequently, their attitudes; and the information, education, and propaganda supplied by the government is never designed to weaken public support and loyalty. Great spectacles of state, such as the crowning of an English king or queen, have a strengthening effect; so do parades with flags flying and impressive displays of military power. But many other activities, of a less formal character and implemented through other agents of socialization, such as the media and the schools, have similar effects. Schools, hospitals, and many office buildings fly flags; and proclamations of kings, presidents, prime ministers, and other dignitaries are announced in tones of respectful awe to young schoolchildren of all nations.

The power of government to control political attitudes is limited, however, because virtually all messages and experiences eventually reach the individual through conversations with primary groups of kin or peers, who interpret the original messages in terms of their own interests and established attitudes. Where alienated groups exist in a society, it is the family and the community that have "socialized" their children to dislike the government, in spite of the government's efforts to the contrary. What are the patterns by which families and friends, schools, and governments indoctrinate citizens into the political culture? [20]

The Dynamics of Socialization

None of us is born a Republican, a liberal, or a states'-rights advocate. People "grow into" their adult political values and attitudes, and for most of us, this development usually follows well-defined patterns.

---

[18] *Ibid.*
[19] *Ibid.*, pp. 198–99.
[20] See Chapter 9 for a discussion of the "two-step flow" of mass communications. Also see the discussion of alienated groups in Jaros et al., "The Malevolent Leader."

The "Idealization Syndrome." Young children tend to idealize the role of government in everyday life, attributing only positive characteristics to their nation and the people who run it.[21] Basic political attitudes are formed in the period between the ages of three and thirteen. By the age of seven, children have well-established feelings of trust and attachment for the larger community—extending from school to nation—which they express as belief in "the beauty of their country" and "the goodness and cleanliness of its people." They also hold an intense, almost religious attachment for their flag.

Young children see political authorities as benevolent, investing them with many of the feelings of respect they hold for their parents. Only as they mature do they gradually recognize (just as they do with their parents) that authority doesn't necessarily mean infallibility.

The Office versus the Official. Young children see government as particular people first, recognizing only at a later stage that the office is separate from the official. They tend to learn who these people are in a fixed order. A child will recognize the blue uniform of a local policeman as a symbol of authority before he sees the more distant and less visible officials like governors and senators in the same terms. When asked to give examples of who public officers are, children in early years respond by naming the president and their local policeman—the highest and the nearest. Only as they advance in age do they become aware that there are officials in between —the mayor, the governor, and their senators and congressmen.[22]

The two clearest patterns in the development of political attitudes as a child matures are the gradual shift from idealistic to realistic conceptions of authority, and a change from seeing authority as people (such as policemen or mayors) to understanding power in more abstract terms of law, institutions, and offices (such as the presidency, the Congress, elections, and majority rule).

Different Dynamics in Political Cultures and Subcultures. While these patterns and tendencies may be seen in children of all cultures, there are pronounced variations between different nations, and among the subcultures within each nation. In the Netherlands, young children have been found to idealize the queen more than their own fathers. But French children trust their fathers first, and the heads of government second.[23] Per-

---

[21] Fred Greenstein's *Children in Politics* (New Haven, Conn.: Yale University Press, 1965) analyzes education and social differences in schoolchildren on a year-by-year basis and shows how the "idealization syndrome" develops. David Easton and Stephen Hess study the formation of political attitudes in children in "The Child's Political World."

[22] See David Easton and Jack Dennis, *Children in the Political System* (New York: McGraw-Hill, 1969). Also by the same authors, "The Child's Image of Government," *The Annals of the American Academy of Political Science* 361 (September 1965): 40–57.

[23] Paul R. Abramson and Ronald Inglehart, "The Development of Systemic Support in Four Western Democracies," *Comparative Political Studies* 2 and 4 (January 1970): 419–42.

Figure 8-1
The Decline in
Idealization of
Government:
Black versus
White Children

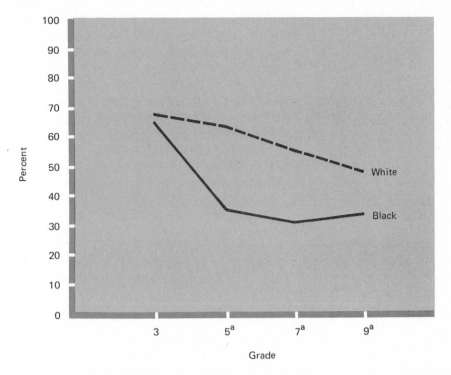

Source: Edward S. Greenberg, "Black Children and the Political System," Public Opinion Quarterly 34 (Fall 1970): 339.

haps even more significant are the differences which have been observed in the poverty-ridden subculture of America.

Political scientist Edward S. Greenberg surveyed children in American public schools, and found a striking difference in the development of black and white children's attitudes toward government [24] (see Figure 8–1). From an almost equal starting point of the third-grade "idealization syndrome," the idea of the political system's benevolence declined much faster among black children than among whites. Is this the result of the children's race, or was their cynicism caused by something else? A study of primary school-children in Appalachia showed that poverty, rather than race, is probably the key factor in socializing cynicism.[25] When urban middle-class children and poor Appalachian children of the same age were compared, the latter showed much less trust in the government. One quarter of the Appalachian children were openly hostile toward the president, as compared with less than 5 percent of the white urban children of the same age.

In summary, the three most significant aspects of the dynamics of political

[24] Edward S. Greenberg, "Black Children and the Political System," *Public Opinion Quarterly* 34 (Fall 1970): 333–45.
[25] Jaros et al., "The Malevolent Leader."

socialization appear to be, first, that family influence completely dominates the early years, but in later years the family shares its influential position with a widening array of other influences—principally, the school, mass media, and peers. Second, the child's initial view of authority is highly idealized, but it gradually becomes more realistic. Finally, the young child sees authority as a particular person such as a policeman or a president; only as he grows older does he begin to think in more abstract terms of offices and institutions. By the time he reaches adulthood, most of the ideas and attitudes toward government and its policies that he learned through the process of political socialization have become jelled into a framework of public opinion.

Public Opinion

What is public opinion? James Bryce, the English scholar whose *American Commonwealth* of 1888 is now a classic, wrote that "public opinion is a congeries of all sorts of discrepant notions, beliefs, fancies, prejudices, aspirations. . . . It is confused, incoherent, amorphous, varying from day to day and week to week." Certain contemporary examples seem to support Lord Bryce's observation. When asked who they favored as the Democratic presidential candidate during the early months of 1972, a surprisingly large number of Americans startled pollsters by answering, "Either George Wallace or George McGovern—I haven't made up my mind yet." But underneath the seeming incongruity of public opinion, there are often logical forces at play. The voters who hadn't yet decided between the liberal McGovern and the conservative Wallace weren't thinking about American Vietnam policy or civil rights programs. They wanted to register their dissatisfaction with the "establishment," and both McGovern and Wallace were populist, grass-roots candidates. A vote for either may have been one way for the electorate to voice a desire for change.

Public Opinion: What Is It?

Political socialization and public opinion are closely linked. They are formed, generally, through the same influences, and they merge together in a way that makes it hard to judge where one leaves off and the other begins. There is a clear connection between the process that shaped the general attitude of Americans toward communism during the late forties and early fifties, and the process that shaped American opinion about the right of China's claim to Taiwan in 1972. Yet, they are not the same thing. Political socialization focuses on more-or-less permanent values, attitudes, and ideas which people learn from their culture and apply to political questions. In the fifties, most Americans were indoctrinated with the idea that communism in all its forms was evil: this feeling was built into the permanent value structure of American political culture just as clearly as was the conviction that democracy is the only just form of government. Public opinion, while it is based on long-term convictions and ideals, relates to people's reactions to specific policies and problems rather than long-term value systems.

Just as public opinion is not synonymous with socialization, it is not to be confused with individual opinion, either. A woman's opinion of her neighbor's hairdo would not be part of public opinion; but her feeling that adolescents with long hair should be barred from school would. Public opinion refers to political and social issues, not private matters of taste.

Finally, public opinion does not necessarily imply a strong, clear, united conviction of the masses. To be sure, there are subjects on which the majority of people are thus united in their opinions; and when that is the case, public opinion has mighty force indeed. But most often, public opinion is composed of several small groups of people whose views are in conflict with each of the others, plus a large number who are undecided, plus an even larger number with no interest or opinion at all on the matter. On most subjects, public opinion is an array of diverse ideas and attitudes concerning political and social issues.

The Role of Public Opinion

As a primary input by the people into the political system, does public opinion direct public policy? *Should* it? Both these questions are controversial, and difficult to unravel.[26] In a democracy, the man on the street's offhand answer would probably be, "Maybe it doesn't, but it certainly should." But the practical difficulties of realizing control by public opinion are profound. How could pollsters possibly keep tally of what the people think about every issue that comes before legislators and executives? The public doesn't even have an opinion on most issues, and the willingess of its members to make up answers when they don't feel competent to rely on their own knowledge further complicates matters. In 1948 a poll asked respondents what they thought of the "Metallic Metals Act." Fifty-nine percent supported the act, provided that discretion be left to individual states. Sixteen percent thought the act should not be imposed upon the American people, and only 30 percent admitted they had no opinion on the matter. Needless to say, no such act existed, nor had any such bill been proposed.[27]

Aside from the problem of the public's ignorance of many issues of government policy is the problem of morality: does might make right? Most

[26] An excellent discussion may be found in Leo Bogart's *Silent Politics*, Chapter 1.
[27] *Ibid.*, p. 19.

Americans are opposed to raising tolls on highways: does that mean that government should bar this means of taxation at all costs? In spite of its inadequacies as a guide for policy making, however, it cannot be denied that public opinion plays an important role in governing. Even in totalitarian states, the government knows that public support is vital for a stable rule, and keeps an ear open for murmurs of dissent.

The role of public opinion in the political system is difficult to define. In a democracy, elections provide a formal means of popular control of government. But they provide only a very crude expression of public opinion. An election can only register the verdict of the voters on an official's overall performance; rarely is one issue so important that an election rides on it alone.[28] Of course, if opinion is running strong in one direction, few candidates or legislators will defy it, so in this sense public opinion does provide some control. No election hopeful would run on a platform which advocated heavy tax increases or a severe cut in Social Security benefits. But, for the most part, candidates, especially in two-party systems such as the British and the American, manage to ride through elections with as little commitment to issues as possible.

In many cases, public opinion is created, not followed, by the executive.[29] Why else would some of our government leaders spend as much time as they do addressing the nation in front of TV cameras? When Richard Nixon announced in late 1971 that he would be the first American president to visit the People's Republic of China, he opened many avenues of previously "unthinkable" thought about relations with this mysterious land. In many ways, Mr. Nixon revolutionized public opinion about China.

If elections provide only a foggy outlet for public opinion, and executives often lead rather than follow the will of the people, the more direct participation of interest groups, be they concerned citizens or lobbyists, often allows opinions to be expressed in crystal-clear terms.[30] In democracies which provide freedom to express dissent in bold and dramatic form, strategies for bringing grievances to public attention can be very effective in exciting widespread sympathy. The confrontation between sheriff's deputies in Selma, Alabama, and blacks who were protesting denial of their right to vote, was witnessed by television viewers across the nation, and the public reaction was a decisive force in passing the Voting Rights Act of 1965.

The Role of Public Opinion in Nondemocratic States. Any government is vulnerable to public opinion powerfully mobilized against it. Mahatma Gandhi, by a simple drama of nonviolent protest, used the weapon of public opinion to win independence for India. A gaunt, bespectacled old man in a loincloth, he threatened to starve himself to death if the British government did not pull out of India. So powerful was the support he

---

[28] See Chapter 12 for a much more detailed discussion.
[29] See Seymour M. Lipset, "The President, The Polls, and Vietnam," *Transaction*, September–October 1966, p. 220.
[30] See the discussion in Chapter 10.

generated, that the British decided they could not risk the consequences of defying him.

Government by sheer violence and coercion cannot last for any length of time. Even Nazi Germany, with all its brutal apparatus for suppressing dissent, depended on the dream of Germany's world supremacy—not night raids by the gestapo—to rouse patriotic fervor. The importance of public support to the Hitler regime is attested to by the fact that the government kept careful tabs on how the German public felt about its policies. Documents found after World War II showed that the top Nazi leaders created a monumental network to test the people's reaction to each new policy and propaganda piece, and to gather reliable data on the people's morale.[31] Ironically, the regime's enormous power of coercion so intimidated expression that officials were afraid to send in negative reports. The result was that the Nazi government received rose-colored accounts rather than an accurate feedback, so that "public opinion" was never really fathomed.

Determinants of Public Opinion

When asked what they think of legalized abortion, the people of Italy and the people of England will give very different answers. Catholic Italy has a national policy against artificial birth control based on religious principles, and the public opinion is overwhelmingly against abortion. But England has, since 1967, taken a far more liberal view. Abortion is now legal, and the citizens of England for the most part accept it as a national policy.

A survey taken a few years back asked people of several countries what their views were on capital punishment, and here, too, there were striking differences from one country to the next.[32] In England and West Germany, over three-fourths favored capital punishment, in contrast to only 11 percent in Norway.

It is apparent that, at least on some issues, national political culture has an impressive effect on public opinion. But political scientists have also found that a person's political opinions are likely to be influenced by other factors, such as where he lives, how long he went to school, what he earns, and what color his skin is.

Social Class. "Those who hold and those who are without property have ever formed distinct interests in society," wrote James Madison in *The Federalist*, no. 10. These and other divisions of interest, he said, "divide [nations] into different classes, actuated by different sentiments and views."

Social class or socioeconomic status is a complex concept, but much of it boils down to, as James Madison observed, a matter of "haves" and

31 Aryeh L. Unger, "The Public Opinion Reports of the Nazi Party," *Public Opinion Quarterly* 29 (Winter 1965) : 565–82.
32 A 1958 survey by International Research Associates, cited in Hazel Erskine, "The Polls: Capital Punishment," *Public Opinion Quarterly* 33 (Winter 1969) : 298.

"have-nots." We can ordinarily expect that on any question which involves the sharing of what the "haves" have—for example, closing tax loopholes in America, or breaking up great estates among peasants in Peru—the "haves," who stand to lose, will be diametrically opposed to the "have-nots," who stand to gain.

But the issues are not always so clear. There is no single measure of social class. Income is the most important component, and probably the most serviceable for identifying differences related to the "have/have-not" dichotomy, especially in clear-cut cases like those mentioned before. But "social class" is only one part of the picture. Family, regional and ethnic background, political traditions, occupation, education, and such considerations as whether one's money is "old" or "new" (the nouveaux riches versus the "Boston Brahmins") are also part of the reckoning. A Rockefeller and a Kennedy, while they may be equally "comfortable," can certainly not be counted on to have the same opinions on all political matters.

Table 8-2
Opinions on Heckling

"During the last election many speeches by candidates were interrupted by hecklers. Do you think there should be a law against trying to disrupt a speech?"

	Yes	No	No Opinion
National total	75%	21%	4%
Whites only	75	21	4
By sex:			
Men	73	23	4
Women	76	20	4
By education			
College	59	39	2
High school	76	21	3
Grade school	85	7	8
By occupation:			
Professional and business	65	31	1
White collar	66	30	4
Farmers	85	13	2
Manual	77	17	6
By age:			
21–29 years	64	34	2
30–49 years	72	23	5
50 years and over	83	13	4
By religion:			
Protestant	78	20	2
Catholic	72	21	7

Table 8-2
(continued)

	Yes	No	No Opinion
By politics:			
Republican	80	18	2
Democrat	74	20	6
Independent	70	26	4
By region:			
East	69	24	7
Midwest	74	22	4
South	86	11	3
West	69	29	2
By annual family income:			
$10,000 and over	68	29	3
$ 7,000–9,999	70	27	3
$ 5,000–6,999	79	16	5
$ 3,000–4,999	78	15	7
$ Under 3,000	83	9	8
By size of community:			
1,000,000 and over	67	29	4
500,000 and over	66	30	4
50,000–499,999	75	20	5
2,500–49,999	79	14	7
Under 2,500, rural	81	15	4

Source: Table from Hazel Erskine, "The Polls: Freedom of Speech," in Public Opinion Quarterly 34 (Fall 1970): 495–96. Poll taken in May of 1969 by Gallup Associates.

Education. On many issues, education is an important determinant in forming public opinions. In the most direct way, we rely on facts or principles we learned at school in framing our opinions on specific issues. We saw earlier in this text that a significant number of scholars feel that America is run by a small, elite group, and that the little man doesn't really have as much of a say in a democracy as we thought when we were in high school.[33] As a result of being introduced formally to the elitist concept of American democracy, many readers may now view democracy with a slightly more critical eye.

Education also has a less direct effect on public opinion than what one learns in textbooks and classes. For example, the consistency of a person's opinions is directly related to his ability to think in abstract concepts; and development of this ability is a function of education.[34] In Table 8-2, we can see that there is a greater difference in public opinion between those of low

[33] See the discussion in Chapter 6.
[34] Roy T. Bowles and James T. Richardson, "Sources of Consistency of Political Opinion," *American Journal of Sociology* 74 (May 1969): 676–84.

and high education levels about heckling candidates than there is for any other factor (39 percent of the college-educated opposed laws against heckling candidates, while only 7 percent of adults who had completed only grade school opposed such laws). While we can be sure that most of these people believe in the American ideal of free speech, more of the college-educated were willing to apply this tenet to the case of overzealous crowds. So education seems to lead to more consistent application of ideals, including tolerating dissent.

Age. In a 1960 poll, German people were asked, "Do you think that moral standards among young people are lower than in the past?" Answers were predictable: Only 25 percent of the young people (ages sixteen to twenty-nine) said "Yes," but 63 percent of those sixty and older said "Yes." [35] The same divisions could easily be found in American public opinion on many issues. If asked their opinion on raising taxes in order to increase Social Security benefits, Americans over the age of sixty would be much more likely to favor the idea than any other group in our society.

The influence of age goes much beyond such issues as young people's morals or older people's needs, however. Advancing age has many characteristics which affect opinion on a wide range of issues. One is a tendency toward increased conservatism. This is due, of course, to a combination of factors, of which age is only one part. If the radical antiestablishment college youth of the sixties can be found ten years later mowing his own suburban lawn after a rough nine-to-five day at the office, it isn't only because he's "aged." When put into the position of having to house, clothe, feed, and educate a family, many former free spirits are likely to find that there's little leeway to be free anymore. With age there generally come possessions, earnings, and a sense of community. As perspectives change, so often do opinions.

Religion. Another characteristic which can influence public opinion is a person's religion. A poll taken in 1967 asked a cross section of the American people a series of questions dealing with the continued conflict in the Middle East between the Arab states and Israel (see Table 8-3). One of the questions asked whether the Arabs or the Israelis were right in their claims. The answers were striking, not only in the 99-percent consistency of Jewish support, but also in the number of "undecideds" among Catholics and Protestants. The poll seems to indicate that in forming public opinion, we tend to develop attitudes on those issues we feel most involved in. American Jews have an emotional stake in Israel. Protestants and Catholics don't, and, as a less attentive public, their attitudes aren't nearly as firm.

Religion has also been an important factor in presidential voting in many

[35] Elisabeth Noelle and Erich Peter Neumann, eds., *The Germans: Public Opinion Polls 1947–1966* (Bonn: Verlag für Demoskopie, 1967), p. 146.

Table 8-3
"Who Do You Think Has More Right on Their Side—The Arabs or Israel?"

	Israel	Arabs	Both, Neither	No Opinion
Religion				
Protestants	48	1	9	42
Catholics	46	6	8	40
Jews	99	—	—	1

Source: Based on a table in Hazel Erskine, "The Polls: Western Partnership in the Middle East," Public Opinion Quarterly 33 (Winter 1969): 630–31.

United States elections. Perhaps the major voter issue in Al Smith's Democratic candidacy in 1928 was his Roman Catholicism, and not until John F. Kennedy's victory in 1960 was the ice broken—at least for Roman Catholics who want to become president.[36] The day when a Jew or a Muslim will reside in the White House is still probably a long way off.

Region. In the United States, the profile of public opinion on many issues is different in the Midwest, South, and Northeast. In late 1971, one out of every four westerners favored interdistrict school busing of black and white children, but only one out of every ten southerners felt the same way.[37] The Civil War of the last century and the issues for which it was fought have generated differences which reach into states' rights, federal spending, welfare administration, and so many other areas that there have traditionally been few issues on which the balance of southern opinion is the same as that of the rest of the nation (although this division has begun to soften in the last few decades). But the South is not the only region with a distinctive opinion configuration. Differences in standard of living, crops, resources, and traditions make for regional opinion differences all over the nation.[38]

Cities and rural areas also tend to register quite different opinions on many issues. This is most easily measured by the size of community, and there is often a sharp contrast in public opinion between large cities and small towns. In late 1971, Americans were asked if they would favor a law requiring everyone to obtain a police permit before buying a gun. Ninety percent of residents of large cities answered yes, but only 57 percent were in favor in small towns, where gun ownership posed less of a threat.[39]

---

36 See Seymour Martin Lipset, "Religion and Politics in the American Past and Present," in *Religion and Social Conflict,* ed. Robert Lee and Martin Marty (New York: Oxford University Press, 1964).

37 *Gallup Opinion Index* 77 (November 1971): 24.

38 It should be noted that regional conflict often times masks underlying socioeconomic conflict. See H. S. Perloff, E. J. Dunn, Jr., E. E. Lampard, and R. F. Muth, *Regions, Resources, and Economic Growth* (Baltimore: Johns Hopkins Press, 1960).

39 *Gallup Opinion Index* 78 (December 1971): 20.

"I love every square foot of this great country of ours, except for the liberal Northeast."

Drawing by Dana Fradon; © 1970 The New Yorker Magazine, Inc.

Questions on whether tax money should be allocated to mass transportation facilities such as subways or to superhighways will also result in predictably different replies from city and country residents, reflecting the different needs of each group.

Racial and Ethnic Background. In May of 1972, the small African nation of Burundi was the scene of a slaughter of at least one hundred thousand people. The reason? The Hutu majority, long ruled by the Tutsis from the East African plateaus, tried to win back its sovereignty from this foreign group and was put down in a bloody massacre. Northern Ireland, Nigeria, and Pakistan have undergone similar conflicts between ethnic groups in recent years. Race, of course, has been the overriding ethnic issue in American politics, and still dominates domestic politics in many ways. The turmoil of the sixties has still not resulted in true equality, and racial opinion differences in many areas will be significant for many years to come.

America's "melting pot" has left us with strong ethnic ties among many immigrant groups. These people naturally want recognition and respect as full-fledged citizens and, as a group, they tend to feel the same way about many issues.[40] Politicians realize that ethnic groups are politically very im-

---

[40] See Lloyd Free and Hadley Cantril, *The Political Beliefs of Americans: A Study of Public Opinion* (New Brunswick, N.J.: Rutgers University Press, 1967), p. 152.

portant. Thus the big-city candidate wears a yarmulke, dances Irish jigs, and eats pizzas, blintzes, and borscht as part of his routine campaigning.

Party Identification. Whether a person is a Conservative or a Labourite also has much to do with his opinion on political issues. Often, public opinion and party membership both stem from another, more basic interest: an industrialist may favor both import tariffs and the Republican platform because he thinks each is good for his business. But party identification is also, as we've seen, often a loyalty acquired from one's parents without clear ideological content; and on some questions this loyalty may almost automatically determine a person's public opinion, particularly if it involves supporting or complaining about an adminstration in general. The ITT controversy of 1972, where it was charged that the Republican party had accepted donations from the industrial giant, is a case in point. The Republican party and a Republican administration were under attack. One could safely predict that most Republicans would claim that nothing irregular had occurred, while Democrats would automatically believe that something fundamentally unethical had taken place.

The Influence of Primary Group Membership

Within the broad categories of regional, religious, and social-class blocs, there are often smaller, primary groups that are much more homogeneous. Within a religion are many particular congregations, and within ethnic groups are usually small communities of neighborhoods, churches, and schools. The homogeneity, or sameness of opinion, in these groups is very high on most subjects because people who live in the same areas and are of similar backgrounds—ethnic, economic, and religious—are subjected to the same pressures, problems, and biases. It should be no surprise that the black families who live in projects on 125th Street in Harlem have relatively consistent opinions about their president, governor, mayor, and police force. Which groups are most consistent? As a class, husband/wife teams are the most likely to feel the same on political issues. Other consistent blocs are work associates, groups of friends (usually in the same age groups), and local political clubs.

How much influence do primary groups have on a person's political ideas? While membership in a university's Young Republicans Clubs may be very important to some students, it probably means very little to others. And while some blacks may be staunch black-power advocates, there are many others who care more about their own personal problems than about national reforms. The degree to which a group member sees his affiliation with that group as important is called group salience. The color of his skin is central to a black-power advocate's identity, while the same may not hold true for his parents or many of his neighbors.

Group salience is important in determining how a person's membership in a primary group will influence his attitudes. So is a primary group's degree of integration into the larger national category. In predicting how blacks will feel about a new plan for the racial integration of schools, politicians must take into account the fact that there is a very powerful black minority who feel that schools shouldn't be integrated, insisting instead upon "separate but equal" facilities. Thus, while blacks as a national group may support school integration, many black subgroups dissent loudly.

Personality and Public Opinion

While a person's attitudes about political issues can be partly predicted according to his membership in income, racial, and regional categories and the smaller groups he belongs to, there are other measures of his political attitudes. Two brothers who lived together and who received the same socialization until the age of seventeen may develop radically different views as adults. Childhood friends who grew up on the same street, went to the same school, and belonged to the same clubs should, statistically, have the same political ideas. But often they don't.

Our knowledge of the relation between psychological variables and political opinions is not fully developed. But what we do know suggests that psychological factors play a very important role, particularly in such basic areas as one's attitude toward authority and one's disposition to be satisfied or dissatisfied. Persons who feel alienated from society tend to have quite a different pattern of opinions than those who do not feel such estrangement.[41] They are more likely to want greater governmental action in foreign affairs. They are less likely to approve of racial integration, and more disposed to favor limiting free speech. (Of course, individuals who shared a sense of "alienation" but were different in other respects, such as the level of education attained, showed corresponding opinion differences.)

One recent study explored the psychological differences between people whose opinions were characteristically deviant from those in line with prevailing values and attitudes, and people of generally conformist views.[42] The deviants, they found, were more likely to show high test scores on such psychological traits as alienation, anomie, bewilderment, pessimism, anxiety, personality disorganization, hostility, paranoia, and rigidity. The character profile of the conformists was more likely to show high scores in such test areas as community identification, folksiness, life satisfaction, social re-

[41] Marvin E. Olsen, "Alienation and Political Opinions," *Public Opinion Quarterly* 29 (Summer 1965) : 200–212.
[42] Giuseppi DiPalma and Herbert McCloskey, "Personality and Conformity: The Learning of Political Attitudes," *American Political Science Review* 64 (December 1970) : 1054–73.

sponsibility, political awareness, intellectual curiosity, self-confidence, and faith in people.

Other researchers have investigated a condition known as *cognitive dissonance*. When we are faced with a fact or event that does not accord with our beliefs, we seek some way to relieve the tension of the cognitive dissonance. How a person responds to cognitive dissonance depends on a number of personality factors, including the strength of the original belief, the person's self-esteem or insecurity, and so on. Sometimes a person will simply reject the discordant new evidence; in other cases, he will alter his beliefs; in still other situations, he might search for an explanation that will reconcile the two and thereby reduce the dissonance.

Even though knowledge is far from precise on the effect of psychological factors on public opinion, it is apparent that personality affects the way in which political and social information is processed once it reaches us. It is commonplace that when a group of people receive the same information about an event, or even witness the same event, the version they will give back of what happened, and their explanations of its cause and meanings, will display a remarkable diversity. While everyone tends to interpret information in his own way, some do more "interpreting" than others.

Aggregate Public Opinion Patterns

What do the people as a whole think about a particular issue? In general, they can be for, against, or undecided. But the factors of uncertainty and changeability are so prominent in many areas that we can't always be confident that the "patterns" tell us a dependable story.

Classic Opinion Curves. The way that different people feel about a question is often summarized statistically in a curve which shows the distribution of the different opinions sampled along a range from one extreme position to the opposite extreme. A noncontroversial issue—a "home, mother, and apple pie" matter on which there are only a few doubters and dissenters—will show most opinions massed at one extreme, a much lesser number with qualified opinions, and virtually none at the opposite extreme. For example, if a cross section of America is asked whether more effective measures should be developed to prevent plane hijackings, the answers could be mapped out along a very stable, one-sided curve (see Figure 8-2).

On most issues, however, there is less consensus and little certainty. Here, public opinion takes the form of a "bell-shaped" curve, which shows a relatively few people totally committed to a position at one extreme or the other, with the vast majority in the gray area of "I don't know" in between. If the people of the average rural town are asked a noncontroversial question, such as whether the size of their police force is too small, too large,

Figure 8-2
Classic Public
Opinion Curves

Stable Curve

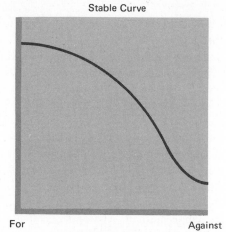

For   Against

"Should we develop more effective
defenses against hijacking?"

Bell-Shaped Curve

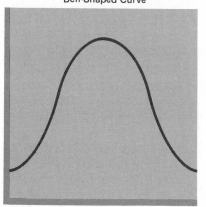

Too small   Too large

"Is the police force too small, too
large, or about right?"

Extreme Division

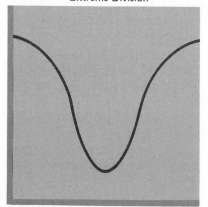

Secede   Remain in Union

Civil War: "Should the South secede
from the Union?" (1860)

or about right, it is unlikely that the majority will answer with either of the extremes. Conflicting factors such as the wish to keep taxes low, fear of crime, and personal attitudes toward police in general will cause the "too smalls" to be about equal to the "too larges"; but most people will reply with an "I don't know" or an "about right."

A third characteristic pattern which aggregate public opinion can take is that of extreme division. On a large enough scale, this kind of opinion difference can lead to civil war. For years, there has been an almost total divergence between the Protestants and Catholics of Northern Ireland on virtually every question touching majority and minority rights, relations with England, and relations with Eire. The result has been violent civil conflict, with almost no middle-of-the-roaders.

Most often, though, opinion distribution does not fall into such well-defined patterns. The most important reason for this is that most people, most of the time, pay very little attention to political and government issues. They have little sustained interest in issues that do not directly touch their lives, and therefore they acquire very little information about these issues. Most public surveys, for example, will find that nearly half those questioned don't know who their congressman is.

Thus on most issues, only a small portion of the total public is attentive enough to news reports and editorials to hold a decisive opinion. And in many situations, a general public opinion curve will be a rather dim reflection of the opinion pattern within this "attentive public." [43] With all of the uncertainties, personality quirks, and just plain ignorance involved in public opinion, how are surveys able to reflect an accurate picture of what the people are thinking?

Public Opinion Polls

Any effort to gauge the attitude of the public by means of a representative sample is called a survey or poll. Published polls, particularly in election years, are prominent in today's political landscape. Almost daily we see statistics and percentages on what America thinks of crime, of civil defense, of abortion, of one candidate as opposed to another. The ubiquity of public opinion surveys serves as testament to their usefulness to policy makers and candidates alike. But debate has developed over some of their political side effects. For example, do the polls give undue attention and influence to uncertain opinions? Do journalists create "self-fulfilling prophecies" by treating the polls as authoritative verdicts which people read about, then

[43] See Chapter 9 on "Political Communication and the Media" for a more complete discussion of how the "two-step flow" of communications allows the more-informed to influence the opinions of the less-informed.

"jump on the bandwagon"? Another area of controversy concerns the role of public opinion surveys. Should they be treated, as some propose, as a "truly democratic" method of deciding public policies? Even if one feels that all government action in a democracy should take its cue from the people's will, are public opinion polls reliable enough to determine policy? [44] Who uses polls, what purpose do they serve, and can we trust them?

The History of Public Opinion Polls

In 1824, the *Harrisburg Pennsylvanian* sent its reporters to the streets to ask passers-by whether they intended to vote for John Quincy Adams or Andrew Jackson. The tally was printed on the theory that these "straws in the wind" indicated which way the political wind was blowing. Many other papers, using a variety of both careful and haphazard methods, conducted "straw polls" in various elections thereafter. But the popular magazine *Literary Digest* was the first to develop a survey of great prestige. In the early years of this century, it earned itself quite a batting average, accurately predicting the 1916, 1920, 1924, 1928, and 1932 presidential elections. The guiding principle of the *Literary Digest* technique was to use a huge sample, on the notion that the more people questioned, the more dependable the result. It conducted its survey by mail, drawing close to ten million addresses from lists of subscribers, car owners, and phone books. All went well until 1936, when 2.4 million people replied that they wanted Franklin D. Roosevelt out of office. The *Literary Digest* predicted the Republican candidate, Alfred M. Landon, as victor with 59.1 percent of the vote. Franklin Roosevelt's landslide victory—with over 60 percent of the vote—signalled the demise of both the straw-poll method of sampling and of *Literary Digest* itself.

As it happened, 1936 was also the first year that practitioners of the newly developed techniques of "scientific polling" were on the political scene, branching out from the field of market research. Several newspapers had begun syndication of George H. Gallup's survey results, which, in contrast to *Literary Digest*, forecast Roosevelt's victory. Gallup publicly predicted that the *Digest* poll was riding for a fall, and identified the reason: its sample was drawn heavily from higher-income people, many of whom were angered by Roosevelt's social and economic policies, and who were thus likely to vote Republican. The guiding principle of the new technique used by Gallup was to select a sample as representative, rather than as large, as possible.

This scientific sampling method has dominated the field since then, with a very successful record. But even it met its match with the 1948 election, when almost every poll predicted that Thomas E. Dewey would defeat Harry S. Truman by a landslide. (It looked so certain to one leading pollster that he stopped taking samples in mid-September.) But even science can

[44] Leo Bogart gives an excellent discussion of these questions in *Silent Politics*.

prove fallible, and Truman won with 49 percent in a four-way contest.

Some of the other hazards of election forecasting are highlighted by an analysis of what went wrong with the polls in 1948. A committee of the privately financed Social Service Research Council did the analysis.[45] It found that the sampling methods used were sound, but the key error came in assuming that respondents who said they were undecided would wind up voting in the same ratio as those who had made up their minds. In fact, these voters decided much more heavily in favor of Truman—close to 75 percent. The major polls have further refined their methods since that time, and today make special efforts to detect late swings to one candidate or the other. It should be noted, however, that they do not even claim to be able to predict divisions within closer than 2 to 3 percent. The margin of victory in several presidential elections has been less than 1 percent; so it is clear that even the most accurate polls cannot furnish a confident prediction of the winner in such elections.

Polling Techniques

How can a sample of as few as three thousand people be used to predict the actions of ninety million? The answer is complex, but it revolves around a technique which can be summarized in a few basic steps.[46]

Asking the Questions. The goal of a public opinion survey is to get candid replies from a representative sample at a minimum cost. The problem of cost is yet to be overcome, as today's least expensive methods still tend to be the least accurate also. But there are fairly universal guidelines for getting the most candid replies possible and for choosing useful samples.

In finding out what the people think about an issue, the cheapest method is to mail out ballots to a sample and tally their replies, but invariably, the people who are involved enough to make the effort to reply will not be representative of the sample that was mailed to. The same factors which motivate some to respond while others don't bother, also make for opinion differences, as the *Literary Digest* experience showed. Telephone polling can avoid this, but it rarely establishes sufficient rapport to obtain really candid replies. The most dependable method is still the costly face-to-face interview. For reliable results, the interviewers should be carefully selected and trained. But even this method has drawbacks. Because it is costly, it often creates pressure on the pollster to make do with a minimum number of interviews.

The wording of questions so as to avoid leading the respondent toward

---

[45] *The Pre-Election Polls of 1948: Report to the Committee on Analysis of Pre-Election Polls and Forecasts,* Social Science Research Council Bulletin no. 60 (New York, 1949).
[46] An excellent introduction to the problems and techniques of survey sampling is Charles H. Backstrom and Gerald D. Jursh's *Survey Research* (Evanston, Ill.: Northwestern University Press, 1963).

"No prizes, no
answers!"

Cartoon by Alvin Hale.

one conclusion or the other is also an important element in sound polling technique. For example, the question, "Don't you think it's about time America sent an ambassador to China?" would be likely to bring more "yesses" than would the question "Should we establish diplomatic ties with the People's Republic of China?" The pollster must also avoid tones of voice or sympathetic looks that might encourage one response over another—an ability that is much harder than it seems. But while phrasing and asking opinion questions requires some amount of skill, a problem even more difficult is that of selecting the sample.

Selecting the Sample. In deciding who to use as the sample, the pollster must make a choice between two major schools of thought. One, the quota method, tries to include a proportionally representative cross section of the society. Though the method has an undeniable logic, it is very difficult to carry out in practice. It puts a tremendous burden on the individual interviewer, requiring him to pick and choose among respondents in order to maintain representative ratios as to income, sex, race, age, religion, and party preference. The judgments he must make in doing so can easily introduce unintentional errors, as they separate the procedure from a centralized control.

The second major approach is to try for a truly random sample, eliminating all elements of deliberate choice and judgment in deciding which individuals to include in the sample. The ideal method to obtain such a sample would be put the name of every potential voter in the country in an enormous bowl, stir them up, and have someone pluck out several thousand names at random. Paradoxically, this method seems to produce a more dependable end result than does the quota system.

However, to truly carry out the random sample procedure would impose excessive costs of interviewing time and travel. Interviewers would have to be dispatched to several thousand separate localities. So instead, the method most often used is to use one hundred to two hundred regular interviewers whom the polling company has hired from different areas around the country, each of whom interviews fifteen to twenty persons in a designated locality. The result is a total sample which is both random and highly representative. The method is called area sampling. It involves an initial decision of which geographic districts should become sample areas, the classification of these districts into groups according to population characteristics, and random selection of both which categories to use and which people to question from each category. The resulting sample is quite close to that which a completely random selection would obtain, and is considerably less expensive.

How Reliable Are the Polls?

The widespread use of public opinion surveys suggests that they have achieved a high degree of public confidence, and this is indeed true. Overall, the opinion research business sells services to the tune of more than a hundred million dollars a year in the United States alone, and the number of private polls commissioned by candidates in primary and general elections each year is now in the thousands. In 1968, then-candidate Richard Nixon paid more than $250,000 to Opinion Research Center for preelection polls.[47]

Published surveys are certainly a fact of life, and we all tend to take them at face value. But in recent years, there has been considerable questioning of the reliability of published polls, and with good reason. At the time of this writing, no federal law required the news media to disclose the polling methods used for any survey results they publish (although House committee hearings were held on the subject in September of 1972). Thus, a newspaper can give equal front-page coverage to a survey of all the users of the Empire State Building's observation-tower washroom within a twenty-four-hour period, and a national public opinion poll conducted by a major pollster such as Louis Harris or Gallup Associates. While the reader may be able to guess that the poll results bearing the national pollster's copyright may be more reliable than the "straw-poll" findings, he may easily be misled by the front-page importance accorded to the straw poll and by the lack of any clear identification of who the sample was and what method of questioning was used.[48]

[47] Bogart, *Silent Politics*, p. 38.
[48] While many feel that there should be a federal regulation making disclosure of this information mandatory, both pollsters and the media argue that such a bill would impose a dangerous precedent of government regulation of information gathering. See Louis Harris's September 19 testimony as reported in "Political Polling," in *Congressional Quarterly Weekly Report*, September 30, 1972, p. 2430.

Another limitation of polls, especially for election forecasting, is the unpredictability of voter turnout. This presents an extremely difficult problem because many respondents who say they intend to vote actually will wind up staying home on election day. These voters and the "I don't knows" are quite likely not to divide up the same way as those who are very conscientious about voting.[49] Thus, election results may be very different if there is a heavy voter turnout rather than if only a few show up at the booths. The election-year pollster must adjust his raw findings for this factor, but there is no way he can be certain how big the turnout will be, and what, if any, will be the effect of last-minute events such as rain storms and foreign-policy announcements.

A similar problem occurs with issue-opinion polls. Since public opinion is often uncertain, findings reported in the news may give more credence than is justified to the opinions of people who aren't sure what they think, and who may easily change their minds with a turn of events. Here, the problem arises of how people respond to polls when they feel there is little danger that the issue in question will touch on their lives. Public opinion of whites with no children is much more strongly in favor of long-distance school-busing as a means of integration than is the opinion of people with school-age children. As Leo Bogart points out, "surveys can . . . elicit the expression of quick responses of a kind that most people would reconsider if confronted with the consequences." [50]

Finally, a survey that is accurate in its overall results cannot assure the same degree of reliability when broken down into finer categories. In order to get an accurate reading, the sample must be large enough to average out any quirks. But a sample adequate for a national finding will probably not involve a big enough sample from any one category, such as region, income, or religion, to provide the same degree of reliability.[51]

Public Opinion and the Polls: Conclusion

In addition to the pitfalls of an inadequate sample, poorly phrased questions, and the uncertainty of public opinion itself, published surveys have also come under criticism for influencing the people's thinking. For example, the news media may give considerable attention to polls that indicate that one candidate is leading another by a 35 percent margin. The result of such publicity, underdog candidates claim, can be devastating to a campaign. Would-be supporters may give up hope and jump on the opposite camp's bandwagon, and, more importantly, campaign funds can be dried up because

[49] See the discussion in Chapter 12, "Voting Behavior."
[50] Bogart, *Silent Politics*, p. 18.
[51] The pitfalls of inadequate sample size, poor questions, and so on are all discussed thoroughly in Julian L. Simon, *Basic Research Methods in Social Science: The Art of Empirical Investigation* (New York: Random House, 1968).

the candidate looks like a bad investment. While there are few political scientists who feel the average voter is likely to change his vote because a poll shows that his candidate is losing, it does seem probable that poor poll showings, especially early in the game, can sometimes act as a self-fulfilling prophecy.[52] But this is more in terms of freezing financial donations from wealthy supporters. So in addition to measuring public opinion, it seems likely that published surveys are also capable—at least in some limited cases—of making it.

The public opinion poll has, in many respects, been able to predict the "unpredictable" with a high degree of accuracy. It has given us a fairly clear picture of what the people are thinking about all kinds of issues, from inflation to auto safety measures to the Vietnam War, and has predicted election outcomes with remarkable reliability. It is only natural that most of us have come to take them at face value. But it is important for the political scientist and the student of politics to look beyond the statistics that polls present, keeping in mind the type and size of the sample, the wording of the question, the type of issue, and who the pollster is and what his method of contacting respondents is. With this background we should be able to make the most of published public opinion surveys.

Suggested Readings

Campbell, Angus, et al. *The American Voter*. New York: John Wiley, 1964. An innovative study of American political behavior, with a concentration on public opinion and political socialization and development.

Cohen, Bernard C. *The Public's Impact on Foreign Policy*. Boston: Little, Brown, 1973. An attempt to show the linkages between public opinion and policy formation in one area of interest.

Dennis, Jack, ed. *Socialization to Politics: A Reader*. New York: John Wiley, 1973. An excellent introductory review of problems in political socialization research, as well as a comprehensive collection of articles on the subject.

Easton, David, and Dennis, Jack. *Children in the Political System*. New York: McGraw-Hill, 1969. The largest, most comprehensive survey of children's political development undertaken to date.

Greenstein, Fred I. *Children and Politics*. New Haven, Conn.: Yale University Press, 1965. A study of how and what elementary and junior high school students learn about politics.

Hyman, Herbert H. *Political Socialization: A Study in the Psychology of Political Behavior*. New York: The Free Press, 1959. An early attempt at synthesizing what is known about the socialization process.

---

[52] See Joe Napolitan's account of the 1968 Humphrey campaign, which he claims got off to a bad start partly because of discouraging public opinion surveys. *The Election Game and How to Win It* (Garden City, N.Y.: Doubleday, 1972).

Key, V. O., Jr. *Public Opinion and American Democracy*. New York: Alfred A. Knopf, 1961. An eminent authority on American politics gives the basic statement of public opinion and its properties.

Lane, Robert E. *Political Thinking and Consciousness: The Private Life of the Political Mind*. Chicago: Markham, 1969. An examination of why and how people come to think about politics as they do, based on twenty-four in-depth analyses of individuals.

Merelman, Richard M. *Political Socialization and Educational Climates: A Study of Two School Districts*. New York: Holt, Rinehart and Winston, 1971. An interesting comparison of socialization in two different socio-economic settings that exist near each other.

Rieselbach, Leroy N., and Balch, George, I., eds. *Psychology and Politics: An Introductory Reader*. New York: Holt, Rinehart and Winston, 1969. A collection of material by historical and contemporary writers on political socialization and the development of political behavior in citizens.

Political communication and the media

CHAPTER 9

The mass media have always dominated American politics. In the 1780s, the Federalist Papers were published in daily newspapers throughout the colonies in an all-out effort to win over the people to the idea of a new constitution. Andrew Jackson's victory in 1828 over John Quincy Adams marked the end of one of the most bitter "media campaigns" in America's history. In it, mudslinging reached its high point (or low point) when Jackson and his wife were accused of moral irregularities, and the press played a key role in the exchange of propaganda. In the early twentieth century, we had a media candidate in Teddy Roosevelt: he tailored his rough-and-ready image to fire the imagination of the people, with great success. And Franklin D. Roosevelt used his famous fireside chats on radio, along with hundreds of press conferences, to win support for his policies. Today, the mass media are a recognized institution of American politics, and modern campaigns depend on television so much that many critics complain that candidates no longer run for office on issues—instead, they package and sell themselves like a new brand of laundry soap.[1]

On an international level, too, mass communications have had a powerful political impact. For example: Tokyo Rose's broadcasting radio programs in order to demoralize American troops during World War II; modern satellite television which allows people all over the world to witness special events such as the crowning of a queen through the same eyes; and Adolf Hitler's rise to prominence through a campaign of mass persuasion which relied on radio, leaflets, and even films in its later stages. It is evident that the media of mass communications have become a political tool of crucial importance; it is also evident that they can be misused as effectively as they can be used. What is their proper role in politics today: to report, to inform, or to sell?

Communication in Politics

A castle whose moat is both unnavigable and too wide to shoot a cannon-ball over is not a very suitable seat for a government. Why? The reason is obvious: If the king can't communicate with his kingdom, his base of power is useless.

The analogy is oversimplified, perhaps, but political scientists have long recognized the dependence of political power upon communications—as any quick comparison of Abraham Lincoln's power and that of Richard Nixon will reveal. Karl W. Deutsch, among the first to systematically study the political uses and implications of modern communications systems,[2] has developed models that carry the science to such a degree of accuracy that the rate of modernization of developing nations and the rise and decline of metropolitan areas around the globe can be measured from patterns and flow of mail, telephone calls, and migration paths of the labor force.[3] Since communications systems are so vital to government and to politics, we shall examine them at some length, beginning with the basic building blocks of a system of communication.

[1] For interesting reading and an excellent presentation of this point of view, see Joe McGinniss, *The Selling of the President 1968* (New York: Trident Press, 1969).

[2] His basic concepts can be found in *The Nerves of Government: Models of Political Communication and Control* (New York: The Free Press, 1966), and *Nationalism and Social Communications: An Inquiry Into the Foundation of Nationality* (New York: John Wiley & Sons, 1953).

[3] Richard Savage and Karl W. Deutsch, "A Statistical Model of the Gross Analysis of Transaction Flows," *Econometrics* 28 (July 1960): 551–72; and Philip E. Jacob and James V. Toscano, eds., *The Integration of Political Communities* (Philadelphia: J. B. Lippincott, 1964), Chapters 2–3; 6–7.

The Stages of Communication

Figure 9-1
A Model of a Communications System, Indicating Opportunities for Distortion and Overload

When President Nixon appeared on television in July of 1971 to announce his impending visit to the People's Republic of China, he set in motion a series of actions and messages, reactions and responses, which bounced back and forth like a table-tennis ball. The parts of this communications system, as Figure 9-1 shows, may be simplified into a communications system like that launched by any political action.

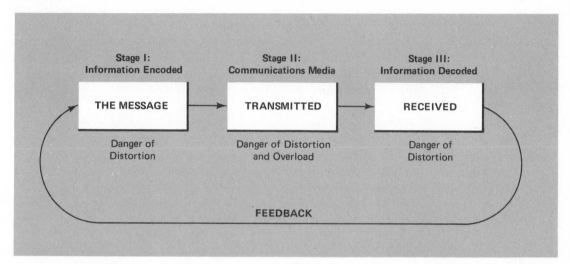

Source: From the discussion in M. Margaret Conway and Frank B. Feigert, Political Analysis: An Introduction *(Boston: Allyn and Bacon, 1972), Chapter 10.*

The Message. This basic unit is defined by Lester W. Milbrath as "any thought that is complete or stands by itself." [4] It is a body of information or set of demands which is expressed through symbols, and which tries to affect the thoughts or actions of others—political parties, elected officials, or the general public.

President Nixon's announcement of his plans to visit China, plus his avowal of world peace, formed the basic message in his announcement. But beyond the simple message, the president set in action other forces and responses.

Communications Media. In order to have some effect, a message must be carried to its audience through some medium, be it a friendly conversation, a newspaper editorial, radio or television programs, or a publicized protest march. In the modern age of mass-produced everything, the mass media have naturally emerged as the most important transmitters of political

[4] Lester W. Milbrath, *The Washington Lobbyists* (Chicago: Rand McNally, 1963), p. 187.

information. Thus, the medium President Nixon chose to transmit the China announcement to the people was television—with the understanding that newspapers, radios, magazines, and even books would soon repeat and enlarge upon the message.

The Receiver. The receiver is the audience to which a particular message is directed. Political messages may be aimed at specific groups: blacks, Italian-Americans, homeowners, farmers, students. In this case, though, the primary audience was the television (and radio) owners of America, who received the signals directly. The secondary audience, who depended upon satellite TV and other media, was the rest of the world.

Few audiences in the age of mass media are homogeneous. In our example, the message was received with many different reactions, varying from the dismay of Taiwanese officials and many American conservatives to the delight of many Washington liberals.

Feedback. The final stage of our simplified model of a communications system is feedback. Feedback is the way in which individuals and groups respond to the message they receive—the way they let government know how they react to its behavior. In a society where the government depends on popular opinion to guide many of its actions, feedback plays a very important role. For government positions will be strengthened or weakened, altered or abolished, in direct response to the reactions the public "feeds back."

Immediate feedback to the president's China message came in the form of mail to the White House, editorials and letters from newspaper readers, street demonstrations in New York's Chinatown, and protests from the Taiwanese government. Lack of response may also be interpreted as feedback: the people approve if they do not protest. How these reactions affected the president's policy toward China—and toward Taiwan—is not yet evident. But we may be sure that the effects of the message will be long-ranging.

Distortion

Complicating the communications process is the possibility of distortion, a phenomenon familiar to anyone who has played the parlor game "Telephone" and heard a message emerge from a line of whispering participants in a form completely changed from the original. A message can be distorted at any stage of communication, not just at transmission.[5]

[5] M. Margaret Conway and Frank B. Feigert present an excellent summary of the distortion process in *Political Analysis: An Introduction* (Boston: Allyn and Bacon, 1972), pp. 221–25.

Propaganda. A message may be distorted when it is formulated. One common form of distortion at this stage is propaganda—a word whose definition is as elusive as its identification in real life. In general, propaganda involves the deliberate distortion of a message. It involves more than just a slip-up on the part of a man pressing the Morse code button or a woman editing a speech (although these are also cases of distortion.).

Since propaganda is so hard to identify, it more often than not becomes a very subjective label for messages we disapprove of. The United States government dismisses the broadcasts on Radio Moscow, Radio Peking, or Radio Hanoi as Communist propaganda, while the Moscow, Peking, and Hanoi governments in turn denounce the Voice of America and Radio Free Europe as capitalist-imperialist propaganda. Messages we agree with we call education; those we disagree with we label propaganda.

As a lack of bias is, in fact, impossible, the fine line between propaganda and education will always remain fuzzy. For our purposes, therefore, we will call the two communications and avoid value judgments about truth or falseness.

Selective Perception and Selective Attention. A message may also be distorted when it is received. With the possible exception of computer banks—which are able to assimilate and store all information fed them with no change in emphasis or message—selective perception and selective attention are bound to distort all reception of political messages.

A John Bircher, a sociologist, and a California importer all watched the president's China announcement. Each was influenced by the speech, but each in a different way. Their perceptions of what Mr. Nixon said reflected the individual bent of each: the John Bircher saw the trip as a liberal sellout more than a plea for world peace; the sociologist looked forward to the cross-cultural fertilization that would result; and the importer saw the announcement as an opening of lucrative trade avenues. If the three were asked afterwards what the president had said, they would give three very different answers. Selective perception was at work in each person's understanding and interpretation of the event.

The phenomenon of selective attention is evident when a viewer automatically switches his mind off when a TV commercial comes on, or when a student daydreams during the more tedious moments of an English class. A person is aware of, and responds to, the messages that are of interest to him at the moment, and relegates all others to the back of his mind.[6] Thus, a young man facing the draft will read avidly about proposals for an all-volunteer army, but will probably not bother to keep abreast of the latest developments on Social Security benefits.

[6] Lester W. Milbrath, *Political Participation: How and Why Do People Get Involved in Politics* (Chicago: Rand McNally, 1965), p. 39.

Overload. A student who has just spent three days and nights preparing for and taking a series of exams might react to the news of an additional, last-minute assignment with a groan, a request for a beer, and an eighteen-hour nap.

The symptoms of overload appear in the communications system, affecting both the message being transmitted and its reception. Communications channels such as newspapers and television can carry only a given amount of information: if they are swamped with messages, they cannot properly digest and transmit them, and they become ineffective means of communication. Likewise, receivers such as the unfortunate student just mentioned cannot intelligently absorb more than a fixed amount of information in a given period. If political messages and demands exceed their saturation points, the receivers will be unable to respond to the information they receive. Overloading of communications channels and receivers can produce paralysis or apathy at a time when action and decisions are most needed.

Levels of Communication

All political action is a reaction to communication of one kind or another. There are, however, different levels and types of communication. Face-to-face communication is the most basic: friends talk to each other, and always will. It is also the most effective means of altering or reinforcing political opinions because it allows for a dialogue where mass media cannot. Listeners in an auditorium can question or challenge the speaker, and he can respond directly to his audience to overcome their resistance.

Until the early 1930s, face-to-face communication was the main method of political campaigning and proselytizing.[7] Nominees for office would stump their districts and address small groups of voters, appealing for their support with the help of ward bosses, precinct captains, and political organizers. However, the rise of television and the complexity of modern society have today largely destroyed the tradition of grass-roots stumping, except as a means of getting free coverage on newspaper front pages and news programs.

The Mass Media. The great advantage of the mass media over face-to-face communication is that they reach an infinitely larger audience, and therefore yield a greater voter or public-opinion return. A speech that gets on television can reach millions of people at once, but a speech given at even the largest rally may be heard by only a few thousand people. If even a small percentage of television viewers responds positively to what the speaker says, that response can become tens of thousands of votes—perhaps enough to swing an election.

[7] Leon D. Epstein, *Political Parties in Western Democracies* (New York: Praeger Publishers, 1967), pp. 238–40.

But the mass media are essentially a one-way avenue of communication. If a viewer dislikes President Nixon, she can turn the channel; if she disagrees with his message, he can't counter her objections with a custom-made response. Sociological studies of the impact of the mass media on individual thinking and behavior show that mass media can effectively reinforce existing political opinions but can't really convert anyone.[8] Radio and television do have stronger persuasive power than the printed word because they approximate interpersonal communication, but their impact on the people still depends largely upon the influence of chats with friends after the program has been switched off.

The Two-Step Flow of Mass Communications. If most messages bounce off most people without leaving much of an impression, how do the mass media penetrate to an audience? Paul Lazarsfeld and Elihu Katz[9] were among the first to perceive a two-step pattern in this process. They found that every community has respected opinion leaders—teachers, ministers, community and civic leaders, outstanding businessmen and professional leaders—who follow the media carefully. These people take political cues from the mass media, and pass them on to their less attuned friends in normal daily contact. In this way, political messages filter down to everyone. The effectiveness of mass-media appeal depends upon these opinion leaders, and it is they whom successful politicians must reach, influence, and convince.

In the past quarter-century, the mass media (especially television) have played a greater and greater role in politics. Television not only serves by transmitting direct political messages but it also serves indirectly as an instrument of social change by bringing news events into the homes of the people. Almost everyone knows something about the black civil rights movement of the late fifties and sixties. If this social movement had occurred a hundred years ago, it might have escaped the attention of many people in that pre-television era.

The Mass Media

Life in a world without mass media is hard for anyone born into Western society in the twentieth century to imagine. Virtually every European and

[8] Joseph T. Klapper, *The Effects of Mass Communication* (New York, The Free Press, 1960), p. 15; Richard E. Dawson and Kenneth Prewitt, *Political Socialization* (Boston: Little, Brown, 1969), pp. 198–99; and Paul Lazarsfeld, Bernard Berelson, and Hazel Gaudet, *The People's Choice: How the Voter Makes His Mind Up in a Presidential Campaign* (New York: Columbia University Press, 1948), Chapter 15.
[9] Paul Lazarsfeld and Elihu Katz, *Personal Influence* (New York: The Free Press, 1955); also Elihu Katz, "The Two Step Flow of Communication: An Up-to-Date Report on an Hypothesis," *Public Opinion Quarterly* 21 (1957): 61–78.

North American (as well as increasing numbers of Asians, Africans, and Latin Americans) spends part of each day reading newspapers and magazines or listening to radio and watching television. Indeed, many of us find it impossible to avoid daily exposure to radio and television, and long for the solitude and tranquility of the B.T.V. (before television) era. But if the mass media are often a nuisance and a vexation to the spirit, they are also indispensable to the functioning of modern industrial society, and their development has gone hand in hand with the growth of today's technological world.

The Development of the Press

Were it left to me to decide [between government without] newspapers and newspapers without government, I should not hesitate a moment to prefer the latter.

Thus wrote Thomas Jefferson in a letter in 1787, and his words, while proclaiming the basic principle of free expression, have been tried and stretched many times in the history of the press.

Johann Gutenberg's invention of movable type in 1454 is one of the most important technological developments in human history. Without it, the Bible might not have been widely distributed, and the sixteenth-century Protestant Reformation would not have taken hold. Europe might never have experienced its political revolutions or been modernized,[10] and the United States might not exist as a separate nation.

Newspapers, broadsides, and political pamphlets such as Thomas Paine's *Common Sense* played an important role in winning support for the patriot cause during the American Revolution of 1776–83. The mass media thus deserve some credit for the very existence of the United States. During the 1830s and 1840s, the press grew in importance, becoming a major part of the then-powerful political machine. Newspapers aligned with parties, voicing their platforms and winning new converts for their political views. During the 1850s, Horace Greeley's *New York Tribune* became the organ of the radical Republicans, urging positive action to abolish slavery. For the most part, though, nineteenth-century newspapers had small circulations, serving only a small elite[11] until the mid-1890s, when Joseph Pulitzer and William Randolph Hearst radically changed the nature of the press. Seeking a larger market for their newspapers, the two publishers deemphasized "hard" news in favor of human interest, crime, and sports stories. It was a

[10] Eugene F. Rice, Jr., *The Foundation of Early Modern Europe, 1460–1559* (New York: W. W. Norton, 1970), pp. 5–14.

[11] As late as the early 1890s, only ten American newspapers had daily circulations of one hundred thousand or more, as Frank Luther Mott points out in *American Journalism* (New York: Macmillan, 1962), pp. 403; 546–47.

huge success: circulation doubled, tripled, and doubled again. Soon the mass circulation dailies were championing social and political reforms, and politicians had to respond to the political demands of the "yellow press." [12] A result was the emergence of the politician's art of cultivating the press—an art which would expand enormously as the twentieth century progressed.

Who Uses the Media?

Not everybody watches TV, especially TV news coverage. And not everybody reads on subways or buses or listens to the radio while driving to work. The various modern media appeal to different audiences which can be distinguished by education, income, and age.[13] The better educated an individual is, the more he will use the mass media. College graduates tend to read newspapers, magazines, and books as well as listen to the radio and watch television and motion pictures. But grammar- and high-school graduates, who use the mass media more for entertainment, generally favor television, radio, and motion pictures more than the print media. Likewise, people in high-income brackets read a lot, while low-income groups rely more heavily on television and radio for information and entertainment. Ninety percent of the people in high-income brackets are regular magazine and book readers, but only half of the low-income groups are.

Age or maturity also affects the use of the mass media. In general, people between the ages of thirty and fifty pay more attention to the editorial and news content of newspapers and magazines than do teen-agers and young adults, who tend to use newspapers for entertainment. Young readers tend to study the sports pages, follow the doings of theatrical celebrities, and pay more attention to feature articles than to hard news stories. The eighteen-year-old who keeps up on news and editorial opinion is the exception, not the rule.

The All-or-None Principle. Paul Lazarsfeld and Patricia Kendall [14] have discovered what they designate the "all-or-none" principle. People who make extensive use of one communications medium tend to use all the media heavily. A regular *Washington Post* reader probably also follows magazines

[12] The reformist role of the "yellow press" is discussed in W. A. Swanberg's two biographies: *Citizen Hearst* (New York: Charles Scribner's Sons, 1961); and *Pulitzer* (New York: Charles Scribner's Sons, 1967).

[13] The discussion that follows is based on M. Kent Jennings and Richard G. Niemi, "Patterns of Political Learning," *Harvard Educational Review* 38 (Summer 1968): 443–67, and V. O. Key, Jr., *Public Opinion and American Democracy* (New York: Alfred A. Knopf, 1964), pp. 344–58.

[14] Paul Lazarsfeld and Patricia Kendall, as cited in William L. Rivers, Theodore Peterson, and Jay W. Jensen, *The Mass Media and Modern Society*, 2nd ed. (San Francisco: Rinehart Press, 1971), p. 282. This contention is sustained by the Magazine Advertising Bureau, which found that 50 percent of all magazine readers buy four or more magazines, 32 percent buy two or three, and only 18 percent read just one magazine.

Table 9-1
Private Ownership of Television and Radio Receivers in Several Nations, 1960 and 1969 [a]

	Radio		Television	
	1960	1969	1960	1969
United States [b]	941	1,431 [c]	310	399
England	289	324 [d]	211	284
Federal Republic of Germany	440	468	193	260
Japan	133	255 [d]	73	214
France	313	314	41	201
USSR	205	375	22	128

[a] By total number of receivers per thousand inhabitants.
[b] Radio statistics include Guam, Puerto Rico, and the Virgin Islands; television averages include Guam and Puerto Rico.
[c] 1967.
[d] 1968.
Source: *Information taken from 1970 Statistical Yearbook (Paris: UNESCO, 1971), pp. 731–37; 747–51.*

such as *Atlantic, Esquire,* and *Harper's,* and perhaps another paper or two; constant book readers spend a lot of time at the movies; radio fans devote considerable time to television; and television addicts are often cinema bugs. And those who do not read newspapers also spend less time at the movies or watching information programs on TV. The use of one mass medium encourages the use of the others, and there is substantial overlap in the audiences which the various media reach. In effect, the "all-or-none" principle reinforces the power of the mass media to shape an individual's social and political outlook and awareness. The man or woman who is constantly absorbing messages from the media is more likely to formulate political opinions on many issues. The person who does not use the media extensively may have fewer opinions on world events and problems.

Mass Media in the Western World. It should not be surprising that the mass media are concentrated in the highly developed nations of North America, Europe, and Japan. Mass communications are linked to high income and advanced technology, and North Americans own one-half of the world's 674 million radio receivers even though they constitute only about 7 percent of the world's total population. Like radio, television is also concentrated in North America and Europe, and has only recently begun to catch on in Latin America, Asia, and Africa.[15] In the Western world, the different media all compete for the attention of the public, and since World War II television has begun to emerge as the winner. Table 9-1 gives an indication of the relative popularity of radio and television over the past decade.

[15] "World Boom in TV and Publishing," *School and Society* 99 (Summer 1971): 265–68.

Modern Mass Media

The Conglomerate Press: Modern Newspapers and Magazines. In 1910, the United States had more than twenty-six hundred daily newspapers, and 57.1 percent of all American cities had two or more competing papers. Today, a bit over half of these newspapers remain, and they have monopolies in almost every community.[16] Does this decline in competition mean that the people are being denied access to a healthy variety of political and editorial opinion? The charge that the fabled "free press" is little more than a sham is backed up by certain facts. The newspapers that have survived tend to be parts of centrally controlled syndicates or chains, and corporation ownership of most large newspapers may give them a conservative editorial bias.[17]

But most newspapers do not present the news in an obviously partisan manner. The reasons are both practical and idealistic. Sixty-five to ninety percent of newspaper revenue comes from advertising, and fees to advertisers reflect the newspaper's circulation. Thus, keeping circulation high is the main concern, and the result is usually a middle-of-the-road policy calculated to please most people. Even papers that take strong editorial stands— William Loeb's conservative *Manchester Union-Leader*, for instance, or Dorothy Schiff's liberal *New York Post*—must satisfy enough readers to maintain circulation and hold onto advertisers. And these papers are exceptionally outspoken. Journalism itself has a long tradition of objectivity in news reporting (although the editorial page may be another story). The profession's own idealism no doubt influences newspaper people to present the news fairly and honestly.

Many magazines are able to take somewhat stronger stands because they appeal to more specialized audiences across the country. William Buckley's *National Review* caters to a conservative crowd, whereas the *New Republic* and the *Nation* reach a liberal audience. And no matter what their political stands, magazines published weekly or monthly have the time to prepare more thorough news analysis than daily papers are able to do.

Despite these advantages, magazines are not surviving much better than newspapers. They, too, have been unable to compete in the face of rising wages, falling advertising income, and the strength of television. And oddly enough, it is the general interest magazines, aimed at no particular audience, that have fared worst. First the *Saturday Evening Post*, then *Look*, and finally *Life*—the three giant weeklies of a few decades ago—have succumbed to the changing needs of the world of the seventies.

[16] Raymond B. Nixon and Jean Ward, "Trends in Newspaper Ownership and Intermedia Competition," *Journalism Quarterly* 38 (Winter 1961): 5; and, Rivers et al., *Mass Media and Modern Society*, pp. 66–67.

[17] In England, for example, most newspapers favor the Conservative over the Labour party; while in the United States, some three-fourths of the nation's press leans toward the Republican party or the conservative (southern) wing of the Democratic party.

In fact, it sometimes seems that the written word will go under, swamped by the sounds and images of television. As TV becomes the number-one medium, it tends to become the one we believe, often at the expense of newspapers and magazines. The centralizing of newspapers and magazines under large syndicates seems to contribute to this erosion of credibility; as the newspaper combines become larger, they become less believable.

The Demise of the Written Word: Its Effect on Credibility. According to a 1971 Roper poll, 32 percent of the people trusted newspapers *least* as an accurate source of information about political events. Only 20 percent said they trusted newspapers more than radio or television.[18] The influence of newspapers on political attitudes, though still formidable, has accordingly declined. Magazines have suffered roughly the same credibility loss as newspapers, and most Americans now rely on television as their major source of political information (see Table 9-2); this is also becoming true for Western Europe.

Motion Pictures and Books. In totalitarian nations, motion pictures and books are heavily censored and are made to serve the needs of the state. Dr. Joseph Goebbels, Adolf Hitler's propaganda chief, was a great master of the art of political propaganda, using movies to show the superiority of the Aryan "master race." Films shown in the USSR and the People's Republic of China today are also government regulated, and present a vastly different image of "the good guys and the bad guys" from what we're used to—but then we return to the question of where education ends and propaganda begins.

[18] The Roper Organization, Inc., "An Extended View of Public Attitudes Toward Television and Other Mass Media, 1959–1971" (New York: Television Information Office, June 1971), pp. 2–4.

Table 9-2
The Relative Credibility of Mass Media in America, 1959–1972

Question: *If you got conflicting or different reports of the same news story from radio, television, the magazines, and the newspapers, which of the four versions would you be most inclined to believe?"*

Most Believable Medium	Date and Response (by percentage)							
	12/59	11/61	11/63	11/64	1/67	11/68	1/71	11/72
Television	29	39	36	41	41	44	49	48
Newspapers	32	24	24	23	24	21	20	21
Radio	12	12	12	8	7	8	10	8
Magazines	10	10	10	10	8	11	9	10
Don't know or no answer	17	17	18	18	20	16	12	13

Source: The Roper Organization, Inc., "An Extended View of Public Attitudes Toward Television and Other Mass Media, 1959–1972" (New York: Television Information Office, June 1972), p. 3.

In democratic states, motion pictures are usually made by privately owned film companies or independent producers. Their main purpose is to entertain the public (while reaping rich profits), but sometimes their purpose is to inform or to present a moral message. Except for the openly propagandistic movies made during World War II and modern movies presenting the filmmaker's political view, the majority of motion pictures which appear on the screen today are intended to entertain and divert their audiences. Any political message is usually secondary.

The three-billion-dollar movie industry, too, has been dealt a severe blow by television. In 1947, motion pictures commanded 80 percent of the American entertainment dollar. By 1970, that figure had dropped to under 50 percent (though the United States still remains the largest moviemaker in the world). Today, over two-thirds of movie audiences are under thirty years of age, and teen-agers dominate the film market.[19]

Although the United States annually publishes some ten thousand different hardcover and paperback titles each year, books reach fewer people than any of the other mass media. Per capita book readership in the United States lags far behind that in Japan, the Soviet Union, and Great Britain. Serious books are usually read by people with above-average education and income or by students. "Opinion leaders" also tend to be avid book readers, and by the two-step flow described earlier in this chapter they spread the messages of books they read to their friends.[20]

Radio. Before television arrived on the American scene, radio was the "universal medium" in America—although it must be remembered that radio preceded TV by only a few decades. In the late 1940s, the typical American family listened to radio shows an average of four and a half hours each day. Radio programming was very similar to today's television: soap operas during the day; children's shows in the late afternoons and weekend mornings; and family entertainment during the evenings. As with television, news and public affairs programming took no more than 10 percent of total broadcasting time.[21]

With the onslaught of television, radio too seems marked for oblivion, and today Americans listen to radio less than two hours per day, most often while driving to and from work, doing household chores or homework, or sitting on the beach. Radio stations now seek out very specific audiences, with all-news formats, "soul stations," and country and western programs. Once the home-entertainment king, radio now plays second fiddle to television.

Television. Super salesman of toothpastes, underarm deodorants, and cosmetics guaranteed to help girl catch boy—and hair tonics, automobiles, and

---

[19] Rivers et al., *Mass Media and Modern Society*, pp. 280–81.
[20] As Kenneth M. Dolbeare and Murray J. Edelman point out in *American Politics: Policies, Power, and Change* (Lexington, Mass.: D. C. Heath, 1971), pp. 339–43.
[21] Rivers et al., *Mass Media and Modern Society*, pp. 279–80.

"little cigars" guaranteed to help boy catch girl—television is the chief pacifier of small children and the most pervasive single element in modern American society. Ninety-eight percent of the American people live within the broadcasting range of at least one television station, and 95 percent of all American homes have one or more television sets. The typical American family has a TV set going for a bit over seven hours each day.

Since the television set has become such an institution, it's not very surprising that it has become the chief source of political information too. As Table 9-3 shows, over half of America today derives most of its information about public affairs and political issues from television.[22] Since most Americans trust television, and since they devote such a large portion of each day to it, it is the primary force in influencing and motivating political attitudes and behavior. Who controls this giant?

Ownership and Regulation of Television

Television and radio broadcast over the public airwaves. Because this is so, government has the responsibility to make sure the media function in what it considers the public interest. Everywhere in the world, government regulates the media in some way. In the Soviet Union and the Communist nations of Eastern Europe, radio and television (like the press) are organs of the Communist Party and are used to reinforce popular support for the

Table 9-3
Primary Sources of News Information for the American Public, 1959–1972

[22] 1971 poll, The Roper Organization, Inc., "An Extended View of Public Attitudes Toward Television," pp. 2–4.

Question: "Where do you usually get most of your news about what's going on in the world today?"							
	Dates and Responses (by percentages) [a]						
Source of Most News	12/59	11/61	11/63	11/64	1/67	11/68	1/71	11/72
Television	51	52	55	58	64	59	60	64
Newspapers	57	57	53	56	55	49	48	50
Radio	34	34	29	26	28	25	23	21
Magazines	8	9	6	8	7	7	5	6
People	4	5	4	5	4	5	4	4
Don't know or no answer	1	3	3	3	2	3	1	1

[a] Percentages include multiple answers.
Source: The Roper Organization, Inc., "An Extended View of Public Attitudes Toward Television and Other Mass Media, 1959–1972" (New York: Television Information Office, June 1972), p. 2.

policies of the state. Even entertainment programs on Soviet and Eastern European television have a marked ideological bias. In the world's democracies, television regulation may be less direct, but it is nevertheless present, and each nation has developed a government-controlled agency for that purpose.

The FCC

Of all the Western nations, the United States exercises the least amount of control over radio and television programming. But even so, the government's jurisdiction is wide-ranging and sometimes controversial. The Federal Communications Commission (FCC), created in 1934, has regulatory control over all forms of intra- and interstate broadcasting systems. Radio, television, telephone, telegraph, military and police broadcasting bands, ham radio operators, teletype systems, communications satellites (Comsat), and cable television (CATV) all come under its domain. These varied forms of communication generate a wide range of duties for the FCC.

The Tasks of the FCC. The FCC must see that one form of communication or one individual broadcaster does not interefere with the operations of others. Ham radio operators, if left alone, could interfere with the broadcasting frequencies of commercial stations, and radio stations could block the signals of sister stations broadcasting on the same frequency in different localities. It is the FCC's job to prevent this kind of occurrence.

The FCC does this by assigning frequencies to all radio and television stations—more than 6,400 AM and FM radio stations, over 660 commercial and 175 educational television stations, and a growing number of cable-TV systems. It specifies the hours when each station may broadcast and the level of power it may generate—and thus the size of its audience.

A second, more complex duty of the FCC is to make sure that broadcasters work "in the public interest." Here, the commission is called upon to make decisions that are often very controversial, for who can say what the public interest is? [23] Are the violent westerns which show bloody killings during prime time in the public interest just because they present no naked bodies or nasty words? The problem of defining the "public interest" has been a sticky one for the FCC in almost every area of its control. Even so, if a broadcaster violates FCC regulations or its interpretation of the "public interest," the commission has the power to suspend or revoke the license of the offender.

---

[23] The obligation to broadcast "in the public interest" has never been adequately defined by either Congress or the courts. The 1934 Federal Communications Act specifically prohibits the FCC from censoring program content, and the courts have ruled that radio and television stations are protected by First Amendment guarantees of free speech. At the same time, the courts have also ruled that the FCC may regulate the use of the airwaves, and supervise what goes out to the public over them.

Equal Time Provisions. The 1934 Federal Communications Act requires a radio or television station that gives or sells air time to a political party or candidate for the expression of its viewpoint to give or sell an equal amount of time to all other legally qualified parties or candidates. The equal time requirement has produced results that were not foreseen back in 1934. As television time is expensive, broadcasters aren't eager to offer free time to the major parties for fear that countless minor parties might demand equal treatment. Thus, the major parties have had to buy time in order to publicize their views, and since the minor parties don't have as much money, the regulation has often served to bar them from equal TV exposure.

In 1959, Congress amended the law to exempt bona fide news events from the equal time provision. Thus, if President Nixon holds a press conference, or if a senator up for reelection appears on a news program in his role as senator, not candidate, the equal time rule does not apply. This gives incumbent politicians an enormous advantage in terms of television exposure and access to the mass media. The problem of enforcing the *spirit* of the equal time clause has been one of the thorniest difficulties facing the FCC.

The Fairness Doctrine. A radio or television station may present advertising, programming, or editorials concerning controversial public issues. Indeed, many people feel it has a duty to do so. But it must also present the opposing view, so that the public can see both sides of the issue. Enforcement of this policy has been difficult.

The problem of how to judge—let alone enforce—what is a controversial public issue was brought home in the early seventies when anti-Vietnam groups claimed the right to appear on television and radio to counter armed forces recruitment spots, and when Friends of the Earth (an antipollution group) demanded air time for public service spots [24] to protest gasoline and automobile commercials. In the first case, the FCC determined that military recruitment was a noncontroversial function of government, not directly related to the Vietnam War. The second case may well result in antiautomobile public service spots in the near future.

To Control or Not to Control? Another power of the FCC is to set the basic groundrules for all broadcasting. Here again, the problem of determining what is fair and consistent arises, for the commission is not always able to apply the law with perfect justice. Radio and television cannot advertise whisky for fear they might encourage alcoholism, but they can advertise beer and wine. New York's WNEW-TV was barred by the FCC from announcing winning numbers in the New York State Lottery on the grounds that its programming encouraged gambling, but the station is per-

---

[24] Public service announcements are advertising spots which stations offer free of charge to various charitable and civic organizations so that they can request public support in promoting their activities.

mitted to announce the winning horses for the convenience of those who patronize state-owned betting parlors.

Because the FCC has so much power to decide for the public what the interests of the people are, this agency—like the media it regulates—has a great influence on public opinion. By making and enforcing the rules, the FCC helps to shape the message conveyed by television to its audience.

But how is such power to be controlled? Having created regulatory agencies, and given them broad power, how are we going to control them? Precautions have been taken to make the FCC as nonpartisan as possible. Its seven commissioners are appointed by the president, with the advice and consent of the Senate, for seven-year terms. No more than four commissioners can come from the same political party, and the terms of the seven commissioners are set to expire at different times. Thus, the probability of seven vacancies occurring during any president's term of office is quite small.

A president can, however, tip the scales in either a liberal or a conservative direction. Dean Burch, former chairman of the Republican National Committee and a Nixon appointee to the FCC, said as much. In 1970 he asserted that the expiring terms of two commissioners would give President Nixon a chance to change the ideological orientation of the FCC in a more conservative direction.[25] Is "packing the FCC" really a threat? So far, it hasn't happened, and the requirement for Senate approval makes it fairly difficult.

Another danger is that the FCC may favor some groups over others. It has been charged that the agency has gone out of its way to cooperate with certain private interests. Can the FCC justify a recent decision that one radio station could broadcast thirty-three minutes of commercials per hour on the grounds of "protecting the public interest"?[26] As the Special Investigations Subcommittee of the House Interstate and Foreign Commerce Committee once remarked, "The Commission apparently confused its role as guardian of the public interest with that of guardian of the private interest!"[27]

But for all its faults, where would we be without the FCC? Some regulation is surely better than none. The FCC does provide us with both basic and necessary safeguards, and has managed to rule with a fairly light hand while doing so. How do other nations tackle the problem of regulating the broadcast media?

Ownership and Control in Great Britain: The BBC

The British Broadcasting Corporation (BBC), created in 1927, is a public corporation; its board of governors is appointed by the Crown upon recommendation of the prime minister. Members of the board are nonpartisan but

25 Rivers et al., *Mass Media and Modern Society*, p. 158.
26 *Ibid.*, p. 158.
27 *Ibid.*, p. 160.

serve at the pleasure of the government, so that they may be subject to some political pressure, at least indirectly. The board of governors supervises BBC programming, which is centrally produced, and establishes program policy. There is no commercial advertising on the BBC, because the agency is supported by license fees, which all "telly" and radio owners must pay, and by foreign program sales. Consequently, the BBC produces programs it believes the public should be exposed to, rather than those which appeal to the broadest market.

In 1954 the British government permitted commercial television networks to be established under the control of the Independent Television Authority (ITA), which resembles the American FCC in its operations. Independent Television Authority stations are owned by newspapers, motion picture studios, and private corporations, and they sell time to commercial advertisers between programs. Programming on ITA is designed to appeal to a mass audience, and American television shows are a staple of its presentations.[28]

Television did not become widespread in Great Britain until the late 1950s, and its political uses have grown with its popularity. During the 1959 general elections, both the BBC and the ITA made broadcast time available to each of the three major parties (Conservative, Labour, and Liberal), according to its strength in the House of Commons. The practice is now an institution. Ministerial broadcasts, similar to American presidential announcements and press conferences, are now regularly presented by the BBC as nonpolitical news events, and here, the political opposition may request equal time.

By 1964, 90 percent of British households owned television sets, and the general elections of that year saw an enormous increase in the political use of television. Candidate interviews complemented party broadcasts, and British voters were exposed to a heavy barrage of televised political programming. Harold Wilson's "media personality" is thought to have been a major factor in his victory.

Indeed, almost two-thirds of British voters rely primarily upon television to decide how they will vote—and less than 20 percent rely on newspapers.[29] Television is an important political tool in England, just as it is in America, and British politicians, like Americans, are paying increased attention to television as a campaign device.

The French ORTF

Politicians in France cannot afford to ignore the political effectiveness of the media either. Under the Fourth Republic (1945–58), television was in

28 Burton Paulu, *British Broadcasting in Transition* (Minneapolis: University of Minnesota Press, 1961), p. 17.
29 Jay G. Blumler and Dennis McQuail, *Television in Politics* (Chicago: University of Chicago Press, 1969), pp. 34–43; and, Paulu, *British Broadcasting in Transition*, pp. 102–17.

its infancy and radio was a government monopoly, and neither had much effect on the public. But Charles de Gaulle recognized the political potential of broadcasting and made every effort to put these media to use. His government continued to control radio and purchased a total monopoly over television, which now reaches 90 percent of French homes. In 1962 he established the Office de Radiodiffusion-Télévision Française (ORTF) as a bureau of the Ministry of Information, and it regulates the nation's radio and television stations. The minister and his staff, who are directly responsible to the French government, have the authority to censor, ban, or force the airing of any radio or television program.

De Gaulle gained some notoriety for his use of radio and television. In 1967 the government gave Gaullist legislative candidates half of the available broadcast time, forcing all of the opposition parties to divide the remaining time into so many small pieces that none received much of a hearing. His heavy-handedness produced a strong reaction: today only a third of the French public give credence to broadcast news. The situation seems to be improving, though: under public pressure, Georges Pompidou has taken steps to divide political broadcast time evenly among the major parties.[30]

French television has not enjoyed the political impact of British and American television, partly because the French people distrust it. A medium can influence political behavior only if the people have confidence in it. A lesson from the French experience is that crass partisan bias often destroys public trust.

Broadcasting and Media Control in the USSR [31]

In the USSR, radio and especially television play secondary roles in dispensing political information. Though radio developed in 1930, it was not officially given the job of reporting news until 1960, and even now most major decisions appear in print in *Isvestia* or *Pravda* before they are broadcast. Loudspeakers were the major broadcasting device until well into the fifties, and they are still the primary means of reaching people in rural areas.

Television was virtually unknown in the USSR before 1960, even though experimental transmissions were made as early as 1931. During the sixties, ownership leapt from twenty-five hundred sets in 1958 to about twenty-three million in 1968.[32] Color TV was inaugurated in 1967, and is spreading fast.

One reason for the early lag of radio and television in Russia was the cost of building the totally new power systems these media require. The size of the country and the lack of commercial incentive also hindered the growth

---

[30] Henry V. Ehrmann, *Politics in France* (Boston: Little, Brown, 1968), pp. 162–67.
[31] The following section draws from Mark W. Hopkins's chapter on "Radio Moscow and the Blue Screen," from his book *Mass Media in the Soviet Union* (New York: Pegasus, 1970), pp. 236–64.
[32] *Ibid.*, p. 250.

of radio and television. Because the media are young—and tightly controlled—much of the political potential of broadcasting is largely unexplored in the Soviet Union. Much of broadcasting's secondary status can be credited to the Kremlin's failure to recognize its potential advantages over newspapers.

Broadcasting Regulation. Television can be used to promote national unity, and the official role of Soviet television is to "encourage the acceptance of national goals and to help form a particular social culture" [33] (the Soviet version of the public interest). Thus, Soviet programs differ quite a bit from what we see on our screens. There is no violence such as that which appears on our familiar westerns and "cops-and-robbers" dramas, and the mindless comedies which fill so many hours of American schedules are nonexistent in the USSR. Soap operas and sensationalism are considered "enemies of the people."

The Committee on Radio Broadcasting and Television was established as an agency of the Council of Ministers in 1957 to regulate programming according to party doctrine. It is divided into several parts: the central editorial radio staffs and editorial television staffs; a combined radio and television editorial staff for local programming; and a conglomeration of smaller departments, including reference libraries, technical services, and correspondent networks. The local stations are subsidiary to the central committee. All broadcasting editorial offices, like the print media, work under party supervision.

Foreign Programming. The USSR both receives programs from other countries and broadcasts to them. Radio programs from the People's Republic of China, Western Europe, the United States, and Japan are heard on Russian stations. The practice of jamming to prevent foreign broadcasts ended almost completely in 1963. Instead of being blocked from the air, these messages are now answered with party-line counterpropaganda. Russia has her own foreign radio station, "Radio Peace and Progress," which broadcasts to Communist China, the United States, India, and Western Europe as the Kremlin's answer to "Voice of America."

Television and Its Environment: How They Affect One Another

The Influence of the Environment on Television

While government regulations impose some form of control on broadcasting in every country, there is another, more pervasive influence on what we see on our screens: the social environment itself.

[33] *Ibid.*, p. 240.

The mass media, and especially television, mirror their environment,[34] both social and material. A society's standards of behavior and its social and political institutions will influence the nature of the mass media. A free press is unlikely to survive in a society that rejects freedom of expression. A nation's leader will submit to press conferences and television interviews, as do American presidents, only if he sees himself as a public servant answerable to the voters.

In similar fashion, a nation's economy influences how its communications systems develop. America's capitalist system is mirrored in its major television stations: they are privately owned. The majority are affiliated with one of three major networks—the American Broadcasting Company, the Columbia Broadcasting System, or the National Broadcasting Company. Many are part of a smaller chain such as Metromedia or Westinghouse. For most of them, the only source of revenue is the sale of time to commercial advertisers. And the size of advertising revenues is directly related to the size of the audience a network's programs reach.[35] Thus, programs are selected to appeal to the largest market of viewers, not to the discriminating few who may want high-quality entertainment.

The influence of the profit motive, then, while contributing to television's fast technological development, has not been entirely beneficial. The networks have traditionally been reluctant to alienate or antagonize large segments of the viewing public, and this reluctance has contributed to the blandness of their presentations. Even editorially, television stations still tend to stay in the middle of the road, rarely expressing political views that might set them apart from other stations. Television editorials have almost invariably favored programs and viewpoints that no one is against. Only recently have "White-Paper"–type documentaries and magazine-format shows such as CBS's "Sixty Minutes" and NBC's "First Tuesday" allowed television reporters to express personal political opinions.

Television's Influence on Its Environment

Despite commercial restraints on TV programming, the medium has had a powerful impact on public opinion. For, while television is a product of its environment, it is also a powerful force for social and political change. The civil rights movement of the sixties presents an excellent example of the way in which the media and the movement worked upon each other to produce a revolution that might otherwise not have occurred.[36]

---

[34] Richard R. Fagen, *Politics and Communication* (Boston: Little, Brown, 1966), pp. 56–69.

[35] A hit network show can command anywhere from $50,000 to $100,000 for each one-minute advertising spot, while low-rated local programs on independent stations often cannot get more than a few hundred dollars for a one-minute message.

[36] William A. Wood's *Electronic Journalism* (New York: Columbia University Press, 1967), pp. 89–109, presents an excellent discussion of the cross-pollination between the movement and the medium, upon which our text is based.

Civil Rights and Television: Growing Up Together. In 1954 the Supreme Court decided that segregation in public schools was unconstitutional. This decision opened a new era for American blacks, and television played an important role in the ensuing turmoil. For TV brought the day's events into people's homes—and into their awareness—in a way never done by less immediate methods of communication. The sight of Eugene "Bull" Connors and his Birmingham police using electrified cattle prods, fire hoses, and nightsticks on unarmed civil rights demonstrators struck a responsive chord throughout middle America. It forced white viewers to take sides, arousing many people's natural sympathy for the underdog and winning for the movement millions of sympathetic friends in the white community. And coverage of the civil rights struggle on television roused the consciousness of millions of southern and northern blacks and forced them to join the movement for social equality. As William Monroe, head of NBC's Washington news bureau, summarized: ". . . television has been a central factor in the development of the Negro revolution. . . . [It] has accelerated it and forced a much speedier confrontation of events and ideas than otherwise would have been the case." [37] Television's coverage seems indeed to have played an important role in the passage of the 1964 Civil Rights Act and the 1965 Voting Rights Act.

The civil rights movement stimulated social reform by bringing the reality of social injustice into the homes of Americans, black and white. Television itself was changed by the social revolution—and not just because black faces appeared on the screen. The experience of reporting this major story—with the documentaries, commentaries, and news reports it involved—"helped television find itself, not only as a powerful technical instrument, but as a journalistic medium of maturity and guts . . . capable of adding to the vigor of a huge democracy." [38] So, in a sense, the two "grew up together."

The Indirect Influence of TV on the Social and Political Environment. The old Hollywood stereotype of the American Negro as seen in movies like *Porgy and Bess* undoubtedly influenced the thinking of many white Americans. Through the same method of unconscious stereotype, television is also a powerful device for passive learning. If a person is exposed to any given medium long enough, he tends to subconsciously absorb the attitudes and biases of that medium. This, along with television's portrayal of a tremendous amount of violence on children's programs, cartoons, and the news, has caused many critics to fear that people might begin to believe what they see on TV and accept violent behavior as normal and natural. [39]

[37] *Ibid.*, p. 103.
[38] William Monroe, "The Racial Crisis and the News Media," (Remarks at a meeting sponsored by ADL and the Freedom of Information Center, University of Missouri, November 16, 1965).
[39] Rose K. Goldsen, "NBC's Make-Believe Research on TV Violence," *Transaction* 8, no. 12. (October 1971): 28–35. For NBC's answer, see "In Defense of NBC 'Violence'" by J. Ronald Milavsky and Allen H. Barton in *Transaction* 9, no. 3 (January 1972): 30–31.

Early in 1972 the National Advisory Commission on Television Violence reported that large numbers of psychologically normal children might be influenced to more aggressive, violent behavior after being saturated with the make-believe violence of television.[40] The issue certainly warrants further research.

News Reporting. Americans prefer television's coverage of the news to that of the print media by nearly two to one. Believing that newspapers have a partisan editorial slant and that reporters can inject their own personal beliefs into their news stories and select which facts to emphasize and which to downplay, the public has more confidence in television news because it can *see* what is happening. Of course, biased television reporters and skillful film editors can just as easily slant the news, but the old adage that "seeing is believing" seems still to hold true.

Political scientists Harold Mendelsohn and Irving Crespi [41] say that television news reporting has already had a profound impact on our political process. They point to the 1968 Democratic convention in Chicago. The turmoil outside and inside the convention hall, which television so graphically captured, produced a public outcry, and this affected even the convention delegates. One result of this coverage has been a serious questioning of the traditional nominating procedures, which caused changes in both the Democratic and Republican conventions of 1972.

Mendelsohn and Crespi predict four pronounced political effects of the "televisation" of America. First, the nominating convention will decline in political importance, becoming a carefully controlled ceremony. Second, traditional political managers will continue to be replaced by public relations experts adept at using the mass media. Electronic campaigning (via radio and television) will antiquate the old traditions of stump speeches, hand-shaking, and baby-kissing. Third, party organization, no longer essential to a successful campaign, will become obsolete, making political machines a thing of the past.[42] And finally, the questioning of the political process which television has encouraged will lead to new political reforms of a more democratic nature. Although our nominating procedures are still healthy institutions, and are far from being stage-managed, it can hardly be denied that television has had a profound indirect impact on the American political process.

The Direct Influence of Television on Politics. Since television is such a powerful molder of public opinion, it is only natural that government, political candidates, and pressure groups should try to use the medium to

[40] John P. Murray et al., eds., *Television and Social Learning: A Technical Report to the Surgeon General's Science Advisory Committee On Television and Social Behavior* (Government Printing Office: HEW, 1972).

[41] Harold Mendelsohn and Irving Crespi, *Polls, Television, and the New Politics* (Scranton, Pa.: Chandler, 1970), pp. 297–317.

[42] See Epstein, *Political Parties in Western Democracies*, pp. 233–42, for more on the demise of the machine.

promote their own ends. While government control of broadcasts by the FCC is quite limited and extremely mild compared to the control wielded by most other governments, there has nevertheless been recent concern that the government may be taking unfair advantage of the media through other channels. How do the administration and other groups use the media to increase their own influence?

"Media Manipulation" by the Goverment. To the charge that governments seek to use the media to influence public opinion, the verdict must be "guilty." Presidents and prime ministers make televised announcements and hold live press conferences to inform the public, but they also want to present their positions in the most favorable light possible. President Kennedy held televised press conferences almost every month. Speaking freely and often humorously, he favorably impressed the public while presenting the government's position on the controversial issues of the day. Since these press conferences were news events, the networks, while performing a public service, also helped JFK's "image" to flourish on the screen.

It is only natural that all presidents do not feel comfortable or do well with the same media format. In contrast to JFK's glittering press conferences, Presidents Johnson and Nixon have avoided this format. Instead, both frequently used prime-time TV and radio broadcasts to make direct announcements to the public.

No network denies a presidential request for broadcast time (not only for fear of FCC reprisal, but also because the president's appearance on television is news, and it enhances TV's prestige), so that the chief executive can go before the American people at will. The government repays in kind. Unlike Fidel Castro, who has been known to harangue the Cuban people on television for nearly six hours, American presidents have not abused the public airwaves. Because of the public's habit of becoming bored with the familiar, it is unlikely that any administration will overuse the media in an attempt to manipulate the people.

A more serious concern than that of government taking too much air time has been the recent worry that the administration may be using its position of authority to deliberately misinform the public. This fear has been repeated again and again in recent years. Incidents such as the Tonkin Gulf Resolution, where evidence points toward President Johnson's knowingly misleading Congress in order to secure its support for an escalation of the Vietnam War, and the 1971 publication of the "Pentagon Papers" (which indicated that indeed the government had on occasion been guilty of saying one thing and doing another) all worked to sharpen the traditional "adversary" role of the press while at the same time disgruntling many government officials.

The questions raised by such incidents are complex. Is government obligated to keep the public informed of its policies, even when this involves classified information? If not—and few would argue that the people should be kept up to date on the touchiest foreign policy strategies—should the Senate and the House be kept in the dark about matters of national policy, and then be asked to act on the basis of their lack of information? Who should determine what is a security risk and what isn't? The information publicized in the Pentagon Papers seemed no longer to hold any threat to administration strategy, yet at the time of its disclosure, it had been hidden in the classified files.

The can of worms opened by these questions—the last one especially—is one which has nurtured many hard feelings on the part of both press and government alike.[43] The media argue that a role of the press in a nation where freedom of expression is a fundamental right is to "keep the government honest," and therefore the press should not be punished for exposing government manipulations of public opinion. But the government answers that the press is in no position to judge which information is vital to the security of the nation; that reporters might do irreparable damage by snooping in classified files; and that therefore the media should be reined. Whether a case of government manipulation or of dangerous irresponsibility by the press, the debate seems destined to continue for some time.

Muckraking. At the turn of the century, reform-minded journalists wrote books and novels to rally the public against the social and political abuses of the day. Upton Sinclair's *The Jungle* and Frank Norris's *The Octopus* are among the more famous books of that era. Today's television news documentary can also be a form of muckraking journalism, and, when used for this purpose, it has frequently produced spectacular results. In February 1971, CBS aired "The Selling of the Pentagon," which documented the military's use of public relations in gaining questionable defense appropriations. The show produced demands for reform, and a great deal of controversy. Geraldo Rivera of WABC-TV news in New York City created a major political embarrassment for the state government with a series of 1972 programs showing the poor conditions of many state mental institutions. The Rivera reports hit home, and were followed by public demands that the care of the retarded be improved. The list of television documentaries and news reports that have profoundly altered public opinion continues to grow, proving that what television chooses to stress or to minimize can directly affect public opinion, public policy, and political behavior.

Publicity for Interest Groups. The mass media are an important tool for pressure groups as well as government and journalists. Most interest groups today recognize that publicity is an important first step in gaining support for a cause. The Black Panthers and the Italian-American Civil Rights League have been extremely successful in winning media coverage with

---

[43] See the summary in "The Nixon Administration and the News Media," *Congressional Quarterly Weekly Report* 30 (January 1, 1972): 3–5.

newsworthy action and words. They realize that the exposure, even when negative, will make their views well known and gain them support.

In fact, it has been charged that television, because it publicizes the off-beat and the violent, encourages more of the offbeat and the violent. It is easy for militants and extremists to get on television, but more difficult for conservative pressure groups to make news. This gives radical groups a distinct advantage over more staid organizations in presenting their case to the public.[44]

Political Public Relations and Winning Elections

While television is important to interest groups and government, it is even more crucial to a politician seeking office. There are two approaches a candidate can take in using television to make his name familiar to voters. The first is news coverage: unpaid-for publicity, such as that used by interest groups, which gets on the air because it is deemed newsworthy. This includes discussion shows as well as films of candidates' rallies, and it gives an automatic edge to the incumbent—especially a presidential incumbent —who is considered more "newsworthy" than his opponents because of his position. While news coverage plays an important role in national and state campaigns, it is largely out of the candidates' hands.[45]

More important is the second means of publicity, which the candidate himself can direct: paid political advertising. This approach owes a great deal to the very complex contribution of professional public relations to politics. The extensive use of professional public relations experts in political campaigns is a recent development, paralleling the growing influence of television in American life. The California advertising firm of Whitaker and Baxter was the great pioneer in the art of political public relations: its early credits include the successful gubernatorial campaigns of Earl Warren and Goodwin J. Knight in the 1940s and 1950s.[46] Many of the techniques developed by Whitaker and Baxter then are still basic to political campaigns.

[44] This problem, which was certainly with us before television, will be discussed further in Chapter 10 on "Interest Groups."

[45] Joseph Napolitan relates the story of an exception to this rule. Eugene McCarthy, whose early showing in the 1968 Democratic primary elections was impressive, managed quite skillfully to use the free footage of news films by scheduling beach walks and similar "happenings" early enough in the day to allow reporters time to prepare stories for the 7:00 P.M. news programs. See *The Election Game and How to Win It* (Garden City, N.Y.: Doubleday, 1972), pp. 97–98.

[46] Stanley Kelley, Jr.'s *Professional Public Relations and Political Power* (Baltimore: Johns Hopkins Press, 1956) covers the activities of Whitaker and Baxter in great detail, and the discussion which follows is based on his account. Joseph Napolitan, a seasoned political consultant who believes firmly in the use of the mass media in campaigns, tells his very interesting story in *The Election Game*, also a primary source for the following section.

"The following dream is a paid political dream brought to you by Citizens for Ottinger."

Drawing by Dana Fradon; © 1970 The New Yorker Magazine, Inc.

Public Relations Tactics

The goal of public relations is the same in any field: to arouse interest and win support. Consequently, the techniques used in political public relations have much in common with any advertising methods. Clem Whitaker, of Whitaker and Baxter, admitted that he handled political campaigns in exactly the same way as he handled his commercial accounts, selling "men and measures" just as he sold "commodities."[47] Or, as one market researcher put it, the goal "is not necessarily [to give] consumers what they want, but rather to make consumers want what we . . . want them to want."[48]

[47] Kelley, *Professional Public Relations*, p. 39.
[48] Quoted in Dexter Mathews, *The Intelligent Buyer and the Tell-Tale Seller* (New York: Alfred A. Knopf, 1967), p. 11.

"I was packaged by Candidates Limited. Who packaged you?"

Drawing by Handelsman; © 1970 The New Yorker Magazine, Inc.

Planning a Campaign. This, many feel, puts the Whitaker-Baxter candidate on a par with dog food, soap suds, and canned ham. Political public relations tactics follow a set pattern. First, an issue or issues are selected for the candidate to stress. This decision hinges on what the public will buy almost more than on what the candidate believes to be right. In 1968 candidate Nixon straddled the Vietnam issue without proposing a plan for ending the war. A firm commitment on such a controversial issue, as George McGovern's 1972 defeat demonstrated, antagonizes too many voters. Public relations experts determine, through polls and public opinion samples, what the voters are thinking. They then tailor the campaign so as to avoid unpopular subjects or areas likely to alienate key voting blocs.

Once issues have been selected, the public relations team simplifies them into phrases that will draw the most positive response. In his campaign against the Truman administration's national health-insurance program, Clem Whitaker coined the phrase "socialized medicine." Since socialism held bad connotations in the America of the late forties, Truman's proposal was associated in the public mind with the "un-American." On the other hand, the system of private medical care was called the "American way," which set up a clear black-and-white classification.[49]

Finally, the campaign managers devise catchy slogans that will fix the candidate's name and personality in the public mind. "Keep Cool with Coolidge" was used in the 1924 presidential campaign; "In Your Heart You Know He's Right" was the slogan for Senator Barry Goldwater in 1964 (to which the Democrats replied, "Yes, Far Right"); and "Nixon's the One" was the Republican watchword in 1968.

But one can look at the "election game" from a less cynical perspective. In contrast to Whitaker and Baxter's "select; simplify; slogan" formula is Joseph Napolitan's pragmatic recipe:

First, *define the message the candidate is to communicate to the voters.*
Second, *select the vehicles of communication.*
Third, *implement the communication process.*[50]

Joe Napolitan represents the school of thought that believes the media is a necessary and legitimate tool for campaigning. He is not an advertising agent, and is opposed to out-and-out packaging of candidates. As a consultant, he advises campaigners on how to get the most mileage out of their own ideas and platforms, publicizing real programs rather than stuffed-doll images. He feels that the electronic media have made campaigning more honest rather than more plastic, as the public gets to see candidates whom they might otherwise not see. Instead of smoke-filled back rooms and party organization machinery, television campaigns put the candidate himself before the people.[51]

But in his three-part formula, where the "vehicles of communication" are primarily electronic, Napolitan's first step—defining the message—is closely akin to the Whitaker-Baxter "selecting" stage of the plan. Out of all the ideas or plans a candidate may support, only those that will arouse the least antagonism are chosen for public display.[52] Thus, all media campaigns —as, indeed, any campaign at all—depend on putting the candidate's best foot forward. How has television been used to do this in recent campaigns?

[49] Quoted in Kelley, *Professional Public Relations*, p. 39.
[50] Napolitan, *The Election Game*, p. 2.
[51] He pronounced this *apologia* in *The Election Game*, pp. 111–12.
[52] This is discussed in more detail in the "Strategies of Candidates" section of Chapter 12, "Voting Behavior."

Public Relations in Recent Presidential Campaigns

1960. Television came of age in the 1960 presidential election. The Democrats and Republicans spent a total of fourteen million dollars on radio and television advertising during that campaign, but the Democrats got far better mileage out of the media.[53] The Kennedy team took pains to emphasize their candidate's dynamic personality, dressing him in dark suits and using makeup to highlight his confident TV image. Vice-President Nixon, on the other hand, appeared less exciting; his "five-o'clock shadow" became perhaps the most famous in history.

Many observers think that Kennedy won the 1960 presidential election on the basis of his television image rather than on the issues he championed.[54] This set the trend for candidates of the Kennedy type (the virile, handsome, charismatic "media candidate") regardless of whether or not they were intellectually qualified for the office sought. Media candidates are not just an American phenomenon. In the 1960s Willy Brandt rode to power in West Germany with the help of his telegenic personality, and Harold Wilson led his Labour party to victory in the 1964 British elections partly because of the dynamic confidence he projected over television.[55]

1964. In 1964, the battle featured the advertising firms of Doyle Dane Bernbach (for the Johnson team) and Erwin, Wasey, Ruthrauff, and Ryan on the side of the Republicans. The incumbent Democrats were in a strong position throughout the campaign: they managed to further dignify their position at the expense of the Republicans. One of their commercials showed a little girl picking flowers in a garden. Moments later, the garden was blown to smithereens by a nuclear explosion, in a rather obvious comment on Senator Goldwater's hawkish war stance. Observers feel that one major reason for the Arizona senator's defeat was his refusal to be packaged and sold or to tailor his statements to what the marketing research team said he should say. While his stand was an honorable one, he took the political licking of his life.[56]

1968. Joe McGinniss, whose cynical view of electronic campaigns is evident from the title of his book, *The Selling of the President 1968*, amply documents much of the behind-the-scenes action on the Nixon side of that year's campaign.[57] Over eleven million dollars were spent in an effort to reach

---

53 See Edward L. Dryer, "Political Party Use of Radio and Television in the 1960 Campaign," for a good description. *Journal of Broadcasting* 8 (Summer 1964) : 211–17. Also, T. H. White's *The Making of the President, 1960* (New York: Atheneum, 1961).
54 White, *The Making of the President, 1960.*
55 Epstein, *Political Parties in Western Democracies*, p. 240.
56 See T. H. White's *The Making of the President, 1964* (New York: Atheneum, 1965).
57 McGinniss, *The Selling of the President 1968.*

every American home to change the popular image of Nixon. Handled by Harry Treleaven and the Fuller & Smith & Ross Agency, the campaign was tailored for television and geared to market research findings. The primary technique was a series of live, hour-long question-and-answer shows presented on a regional basis, which appeared to be spontaneous, but were actually carefully controlled. The result was the image of an outgoing, confident Nixon, in complete command of both himself and the issues facing the nation. Commercials focusing on crime, civil disorders, and the need for a new administration also enhanced this new image. The media campaign was skillfully packaged and highly effective in arousing voter interest, and the result bore this out.

The Democrats again hired Doyle Dane Bernbach to mastermind Hubert Humphrey's campaign. They mapped out a radio and television campaign costing six to seven million dollars, but ran short of funds in midstream. In September a smaller firm was hired to replace DDB, and it was nearly October before the Humphrey commercials got on the air. The party never had the money for an effective media campaign, and the Republicans won the election.[58] While the Democrats' weak use of television public relations was probably not the only reason for their defeat in 1968, it undoubtedly was a contributing factor.

Conclusion

The media have always been important in the political games of power, and their role has grown even more vital with the development of modern television. What of the future? Since television is now the prime source of political information for most of the Western world, it is unlikely that political campaigns will ever again do without it. (In fact, there is every likelihood that traditional stumping will gradually atrophy in favor of an entirely mass media campaign.)

While there is much that may seem distasteful in the specter of democracy's political battles being reduced to spot-appearances on television, the future is not all that bleak. While political public relations depends heavily upon simplification of issues, it can be argued that this very simplification enables problems and candidates to be made known to a significant number of voters who wouldn't otherwise be aware of them. The interest which public relations experts arouse may often be unenlightened, but it is just as genuine as the more sophisticated interest aroused by newspaper editorials and magazine articles. Television coverage may also increase popular participation in the political process by bringing out people who might not

[58] Napolitan, who acted as consultant for Humphrey in 1968, gives an excellent account of the tale in *The Election Game*, pp. 20–63.

otherwise bother to vote, and it tends to nationalize American politics by presenting the same issues at the same time to the entire nation, with a minimum of regional variation.

And although political public relations is often criticized for assuming that the average voter can be sold a candidate as easily as a candy bar, there are frequent glimmers that perhaps John Doe isn't *quite* so easily swayed. Britain's Harold Wilson and Canada's Pierre Elliot Trudeau, both charismatic leaders who looked good on television screens, had trouble at the polls in the later sixties and early seventies in spite of their images. And in the United States, a much-pronounced "media candidate" of the early 1972 Democratic presidential primaries, handsome Mayor John V. Lindsay of New York City, spent close to five hundred thousand dollars for a very skillful television campaign in Florida, but emerged with only seven percent of the votes. Political candidates are finding that even in the age of television, they must do more than project an image in order to win an election.

Suggested Readings

Agranoff, Robert, ed. *The New Style in Election Campaigns*. Boston: Hobrook Press, 1972. An up-to-date collection of readings on media management in election campaigns.

Berelson, Bernard, and Janowitz, Morris, eds. *Reader in Public Opinion and Communication*. 2nd ed. New York: The Free Press, 1966. Articles linking public opinion, communication, and mass media.

Deutsch, Karl W. *The Nerves of Government: Models of Political Communication and Control*. New York: The Free Press, 1966. An innovative study of the communications process in politics.

Downs, Anthony. *An Economic Theory of Democracy*. New York: Harper & Row, 1957. Parts II and III of this insightful work examine the impact of information availability and costs in a democratic society.

Fagen, Richard R. *Politics and Communication*. Boston: Little, Brown, 1966. An argument for the communications approach in the study of comparative politics.

Kelley, Stanley, Jr. *Professional Public Relations and Political Power*. Baltimore: Johns Hopkins University Press, 1956. A classic study in the area of public relations and politics.

McGinniss, Joe. *The Selling of the President, 1968*. New York: Trident Press, 1969. An account of the hard-sell techniques in the 1968 competition for the presidency.

Mendelsohn, Harold, and Crespi, Irving. *Polls, Television, and the New Politics*. Scranton, Pa.: Chandler, 1970. A review of the impact on politics of professional campaign management, polls, and television.

Milbrath, Lester. *The Washington Lobbyists.* Chicago: Rand McNally, 1963. A reexamination of the role of communications in the lobbying process.

Wood, William A. *Electronic Journalism.* New York: Columbia University Press, 1967. An argument claiming that media affects politics and politics affects media.

Wyckoff, Gene. *The Image Candidates: American Politics in the Age of Television.* New York: Macmillan, 1968. The manufacturing of a candidate image is dissected, analyzed, and evaluated.

Interest groups: Informal political participation
CHAPTER 10

No decade in this century, with the possible exception of the 1930s, was as socially restless as the 1960s. This restlessness was an international phenomenon, but it was especially evident in the United States. In the first half of the decade, the protests of blacks and their supporters provided the dominant theme. There were sit-ins and boycotts in the South to end segregation in buses, restaurants, and other public places and there were campaigns to increase black participation in the political process. In the middle of the decade, the Vietnamese War became the cause célèbre. Mass rallies and marches protested U.S. involvement in the war, and counter rallies and marches protested the protestors. At universities and colleges throughout the country, normal campus routines were disrupted by student demonstrations against the war, the draft, school-based military programs, and also against university policy related to curricular matters and admissions. Later in the decade a number of mass movements began to gain momentum. The more prominent ones included the ecology movement, organized by people who had become concerned about the destruction of our environment; the consumer movement, which gained new vitality and supporters largely as a result of the crusade of a young lawyer named Ralph Nader, who fought against a range of injurious and misrepresented goods and services marketed by American industry; and the women's liberation movement, a reawakening of women's longtime struggle for equal rights.

Such group actions are not new or rare occurrences in the history of the United States. Back in 1794, Pennsylvania farmers instigated the Whiskey Rebellion to protest an excise tax that had been imposed on their distillations. Before the Civil War abolitionists were active, and during the war there were draft riots. At the end of the nineteenth century Western farmers became Populists, supporting free coinage of silver, and such advanced programs as public ownership of transportation and communications facilities, and a graduated income tax. At about the same time, many women became suffragettes, fighting for political and economic rights. In 1932 a bonus army of unemployed war veterans marched to Washington, and in 1940 the "America Firsters" banded together to prevent U.S. involvement in World War II.

These are only a sampling of the interest groups that emerged and disappeared as part of the evolution of American society. Besides such relatively transient groups, there are many well-established interest groups that have exerted a powerful and continuing influence on our political and economic life for generations. To cite a few examples, the farmers' National Grange dates back to 1867; the American Federation of Labor since the 1880s; the National Association of Manufacturers, since 1895; and the American Civil Liberties Union since the 1920s.

Interests and Politics

Interest groups are especially numerous, vocal, and visible in the United States, but we have no monopoly on them. They are an element in the political life of every highly organized modern society, including France, Great Britain, Japan, India, West Germany, Italy, and other countries with Western-style democratic governments. Even in countries where social, economic, and political life is dominated by central planning, interest groups exist, though in a somewhat altered form. In the Soviet Union, for example, citizens have no legal right to organize private associations at will, and all legitimate organizations are rigidly controlled, with no real independence to criticize or alter government policy. However, certain unauthorized interest groups have developed a degree of cohesion, and they work outside the Soviet establishment to bring about changes in government policy and to defend the rights of their own people. One such group whose activities have been reported on this side of the Iron Curtain is made up of scholars and intellectuals who have persistently sought greater freedom of expression and inquiry for themselves and for their colleagues. Sometimes their efforts are rewarded with a limited victory, such as the release in 1970 of the Soviet geneticist, Dr. Zhores Medvedev, who had been held in a mental institution for his criticism of Soviet scientific policies and establishment scientists.

Another reform-seeking group are the Jews, who occupy an uncomfortably ambivalent position in the Soviet Union.[1] Although Judaism is recognized by the Soviet government as both a nationality and a religion, the Jews have no territorial republic as have all the other 107 nationality groups in the USSR. They have few places of worship and, unlike other religious groups, they are prohibited from publishing religious books, producing devotional materials, or providing rabbinical training. As an interest group, the Soviet Jews, like the Soviet intellectuals, have worked outside the government and its established channels. And, like the intellectuals, one of their most important strategies is to gain international publicity and support, and thus pressure the Soviet government into making concessions.

What Is an Interest Group?

The term *interest group* covers a wide spectrum of people and issues. In his landmark work, *The Governmental Process,* David B. Truman defines an interest group as "a shared-attitude group that makes certain claims upon other groups in society" by acting through the institutions of government.[2] Some interest groups are transient, while others are more permanently organized. Many are solely interested in influencing the government's public policy, while others are only sporadically concerned with political decisions. Some work directly through the executive or administrative agencies, while others work through the judicial or legislative sectors, or even through public opinion. But one crucial factor is common to all interest groups: they are all nonpublicly accountable organizations which attempt to promote shared private interests by influencing public policy outcomes that affect them.[3]

1 Ronald I. Rubin, "The Plight of Soviet Jews," *Thought* 43 (Autumn 1968) : 365–79. For further commentaries on the situation of Jews in the USSR, see William Korey, "The Legal Position of the Jewish Community in the Soviet Union," in Erich Goldhagen, ed., *Ethnic Minorities in the Soviet Union* (New York: Praeger Publishers, 1968), pp. 316–50; and Moshe Decter, "Soviet Jewry: A Current Survey," *Congress,* December 5, 1966, pp. 6–10.
2 David B. Truman, *The Governmental Process* (New York: Alfred A. Knopf, 1951), p. 37.
3 This general definition is reflected in Arthur Bentley's work, *The Process of Government* (Orig. ed., 1908; Evanston, Ill.: Principia Press, 1949), considered the forerunner of contemporary political science. The book attempts to tie together the common elements of modern interest groups.

How Interest Groups Differ from Political Parties.[4] It may seem to the reader that the definition of an interest group applies equally well to a political party. Party leaders are not elected by the general public, nor are they answerable to the people as a whole for their policy decisions; and political parties certainly try to influence public policy outcomes. But the two are not the same. For, unlike political parties, interest groups lie outside the electoral process and are thus not responsible to the public. While party leadership is not chosen by the voters as a whole, each elected candidate is, and so the survival of the party depends on the people's support. Private interest groups may try to influence the nomination of candidates who are sympathetic to their cause, but the candidates run under the party banner—not the interest group banner. Thus, interest groups differ from political parties in objectives, structure, and number.

Goals. The goal of the political party is to acquire political power through the election of its own candidates to the offices of government. The interest group, however, is concerned with specific programs and issues, and it has no official representatives of its own in the formal structure of government (although many lobby groups approximate this type of representation). The interest group tries to steer political parties and their elected officials toward certain policies, rather than enacting those policies itself. Interest groups often try to win the favor of all political parties. The conservationists want the support of both the Republicans and the Democrats in their fight to preserve national forests. But at times they may take a stand in favor of one party if they are convinced that party will further their objectives with greater vigor. In most recent elections, with the notable exception of 1972, labor unions have supported the national Democratic ticket.

Division of Labor. The division of labor between the representation of private interests and public policy making is most clearly defined in political systems such as ours, where only two parties compete for political domination, and each party contains a wide range of interests. But in nations such as Belgium and Israel, where many parties compete, minority parties may represent only the narrow interests of one small group, and the distinction may become blurred. Where do interest groups stop and political parties begin? Since it is the political party and not the interest group that provides the label under which candidates are elected by the people, the difference between private versus public accountability holds true even in nations with the most fractionalized party systems.

Nature of Memberships. Most political parties are interested in establishing a broad enough base of support to win an election, drawing into their ranks a coalition of different interests. Thus, their membership is character-

[4] See Chapter 11 for more on political parties.

istically much more varied than that of the interest group (with the exception, of course, of the very narrow special interest parties in some European nations). Consider, for instance, the Republican and Democratic parties of this country. The Republican party tends to be identified in the public mind with business and management, and in general it has a more conservative image than the Democrats. Yet its membership includes people in all income brackets and in all occupations, and some of its members are more liberal than many Democrats. The Democratic party, on the other hand, generally considers itself the more progressive party of the working man. Yet, men from financially well-established families like Averill Harriman and Ted Kennedy are Democrats.

In contrast to political parties, interest groups generally have a more selective membership. Members of a craft labor union are more likely than not to share similar living and working conditions and to have comparable educational and cultural backgrounds. Interest groups that have coalesced around a specific problem or issue, such as ecology or the banning of nuclear weapons, may draw their members from a wider spectrum, but even the memberships of these issue-oriented groups tend to share more similarities than broad-based political parties do.

Almost Unlimited Number. The central purpose of a political party is to nominate and elect its own candidates to government office and to perpetuate itself in power as long as possible. For several reasons, including the length of a ballot, the number of political parties must be limited; even in multiparty political systems, all the parties can usually be counted on the fingers of both hands. But interest groups are a different matter. There is no functional limit (such as the length of a ballot) on their proliferation, and some countries seem to offer a particularly fertile environment for their development. The United States has provided such an environment from the beginning of its national history. As Alexis de Tocqueville, a French political writer who visited this country in the 1830s observed: "In no country of the world has the principle of association been more successfully used or applied to a greater multitude of objects than in America." [5] De Tocqueville would have no reason to revise his opinion today. Even more than in his time, we must certainly lead the world in private associations.

As seen in Table 10-1, the list of groups involved in the 1970 Senate Pollution Hearings (incomplete though it is) cites several groups with a stake in this one issue. It is interesting to note that these groups are not limited to informal popular organizations, but also include several business firms, a law firm, and a research institute. Any private group, be it an oil company or a group of parents, acting together on behalf of an issue, is an interest group. This is why interest groups are so prolific. Considering that the

[5] Phillips Bradley, ed., *Democracy in America*, vol. 1 (New York: Vintage Books, 1945), p. 198.

Table 10-1
Nongovernmental Groups Providing Testimony on Air Pollution Legislation, Congressional Hearings, 1970

Atmospheric Sciences Research Center, State University of New York
Colorado Citizens for Clean Air
The Association of State and Territorial Health Officers
National Steel Corporation
United Steelworkers of America
Teller Environmental Systems
Southeastern Wisconsin Coalition for Clean Air
U.S. Chamber of Commerce
Manufacturing Chemists Association
Engelhard Minerals and Chemical Corporation
E.I. DuPont De Nemours & Co.
The American Trial Lawyers Association
Environmental Defense Fund
Citizens for a Quieter City, Inc.
Greenwald, Landrum and Baim (Attorneys)
Fels Research Institute
Ethyl Corporation
General Motors Research Laboratories
American Petroleum Institute
Standard Oil Company
Ford Motor Company
Air Transport Association of America
Campaign to Make General Motors Responsible
Airport Operators Council International
National Tuberculosis and Respiratory Disease Association
Federal Bar Association
National Air Conservation Commission
Stamp Out Smog Association
Chevron Research Company
Environmental Clearinghouse, Inc.
Automobile Manufacturers Association
National Coal Association
National Association of Electric Companies
Union Carbide Corporation

Source: U.S. Congress, Senate Committee on Public Works, Subcommittee on Air and Water Pollution. Hearings, Air Pollution, 1970. Ninety-first Congress, 2nd session.

pollution hearing was only one of the many held by congressional sub-committees during the 1970 session of Congress, that many issues never make it to the congressional hearing room, and that air pollution has only recently become a public issue, it can readily be seen that the number of interest groups in existence in the United States today must be far too large for us to count.

A Theory of Interest Groups: Who Belongs, and How Do Groups Hold Members?

In every highly organized technological society, the prevailing mode of life is maintained by a multitude of different industries: food processing, clothing manufacture, publishing, railroads, airlines, automobile production, petroleum processing, public utilities, radio and television, data processing, and metal refining, to name a few. There is a finely developed division of labor, with farmers, teachers, carpenters, artists, housekeepers, salesmen, writers, lawyers, doctors, clerical workers, plumbers, and innumerable other specialized producers contributing separate goods and services. The people who buy these goods and services need protection—from high tariffs, falsely labeled goods, and unlicensed practitioners. Within any society, there are differences in the cultural, economic, educational, and religious backgrounds of people. Ethnic backgrounds vary, especially in countries with large migrant populations such as the United States, and individuals have different systems of values, different modes of living, and different ways of assessing and solving problems. These varied categories of people and enterprises which make up society represent the kind of raw material from which interest groups are formed.

This inevitable characteristic of modern society supplies the basis for David Truman's theory of interest groups: wherever there are people, there exists the potential for an interest group, and the people will organize into such a group whenever it becomes necessary for them to take action.[6] The theory assigns to interest groups a central role in the working of a democratic government in modern society, and pays considerable attention to the pressure system of organized special interest groups which devote their time, effort, and resources to the attempt to influence governmental policies through official contacts. Because of our highly developed pressure system, the United States is often defined by theorists of Truman's school as a pluralist democracy in which a multiplicity of interest groups, all pushing their own claims and viewpoints, creates a balance of opposing interests which prevents any one group from establishing full dominance over the political system.[7] By this definition, government policy is viewed as the outcome of competition among many groups, who represent the varied interests of the people.

The U.S. system of interest groups does indeed include many rival pressure groups with enough political clout to affect the way a piece of legislation is written or enforced. But, in contrast to David Truman's theory, many observers have noted that the members of these groups tend to be drawn overwhelmingly from the middle and upper classes, and that group activities

---

[6] Truman, *The Governmental Process.*
[7] See Chapter 6 for a thorough discussion of both the pluralist and the elitist views of democracy in America.

are dominated by individuals with business-related interests.[8] The mere fact of competition among rival interest groups does not guarantee a democratic system. As E. E. Schattschneider noted, "The flaw in the pluralist heaven is that the heavenly chorus sings with a strong upper-class accent."[9] Many critics of our interest group system would agree that middle- and upper-class interests are disproportionately represented in comparison to the lower classes, who have relatively little voice in the informal pressure system.

Elitist interpreters argue that, if David Truman's group theory really operated, the poor would begin to organize in groups as soon as they became aware that they were poor and didn't want to be. Yet, with few notable exceptions (blacks since the early sixties, migrant workers, American Indians in certain areas), the poor, who seem to have so much to gain from collective action, have been slow in joining together to promote their common interests. When organizations or aid programs have been developed to tackle the problems of poverty, the impetus often has come from outside the community. As a result, the programs undertaken are often at odds with the ideas of the people in the community. Such was the case with some of the programs initiated under the Economic Opportunity Act of 1964, the central act of U.S. President Lyndon Johnson's "War on Poverty."

Left on their own, the lower classes have been more likely to act explosively rather than as organized groups, concerned with a reasonable means of handling their problems. They have a strong sense of grievance which has been demonstrated time after time through history. The storming of the Bastille during the French Revolution is one example of how poverty-nurtured resentments boiled over into violence. In recent U.S. history, the riots of the sixties in Watts, Harlem, and other large-city ghettos, reflected the anger that race-related poverty produced in many black Americans. The ghetto riots, while serving to publicize the grievances and anger that exist in certain poor communities, resulted in great destruction that hurt the people living in those communities more than anyone else. They cost their perpetrators a great deal without offering any real challenge to the power and influence of business and industry, strong labor unions, or other groups that the poor regard as stumbling blocks in the way of their objectives.

Is this lack of organizing impetus a characteristic of poverty? Not necessarily, according to Mancur Olson, Jr. In *The Logic of Collective Action,* Olson argues that *any* people who organize to promote a common interest are acting in an exceptional rather than a usual way.[10] Why? His argument stems from the nature of the goods that people hope to obtain from collective action.

[8] See Charles R. Wright and Herbert Hyman, "Voluntary Memberships of American Adults: Evidence from National Sample Surveys," *American Sociological Review* 23 (June 1958) : 284–92.

[9] E. E. Schattschneider, *The Semisovereign People, A Realist's View of Democracy* (New York: Holt, Rinehart and Winston, 1960), p. 29.

[10] For the entire discussion which we have drawn from, see Mancur Olson, Jr., *The Logic of Collective Action: Public Goods and the Theory of Groups* (New York: Schocken Books, 1965).

"Collective goods," or policies which affect everyone, cannot be reserved for the exclusive use of those who have invested money or effort in obtaining them. They are available to all at little or no cost above that expended to provide it for a few. For example, who benefits and who pays if a factory is made to remove pollution from the water it uses in its industrial processes? Everyone stands to benefit if the factory stops polluting rivers and lakes. This is therefore a collective good. However, it is the factory that must bear the costs of removing the pollution (although it probably will pass on the additional expense to consumers by raising the price of its products). Another type of collective good is the pay raise that a labor union may obtain from management. When a union succeeds in getting a company or industry to raise its wage rates or improve working conditions, the benefits apply not only to dues-paying members of the union but also to nonunion workers holding similar jobs.

Indifference to Organizing: The "Free-Rider" Syndrome and How It Is Overcome. Governments—local, state, and national—are the most obvious dispensers of all-or-nothing collective goods. Services such as street cleaning, garbage collection, police protection, and fire protection are provided by a city to accommodate not only city taxpayers but also nonresident visitors and others who contribute nothing to city revenues.[11] Typically, the attitude of citizens toward such collective goods is to pay as little as possible for them in taxes, while being highly critical of any shortcoming in the quality of the services supported by taxation. Few if any of us would pay anything for collective goods if we could get someone else to pay, and most of us particularly resent paying for such goods if we feel that someone else is getting them free when we are not.

If we can share collective goods for free, why do we often contribute our time and money? To overcome the "free-rider" temptation in all of us, governments and other institutions providing collective goods must often depend on coercion. Penalties, including fines and prison sentences, threaten people who attempt to evade taxes, and unions try to eliminate nonorganized free riders by inducing plants to become "union shops" which restrict employees to those with union memberships.

There are, of course, many occasions when people transcend their free-rider impulses to the extent that they will voluntarily contribute for the provision of some collective good. All blacks benefited from the civil rights movement regardless of whether they were members of NAACP (National Association for the Advancement of Colored People) or SCLC (Southern Christian Leadership Conference), but many joined these organizations nonetheless. And many people who stood nothing to gain at all gladly supported Cesar Chavez's table-grape boycott to improve the lot of California

---

[11] This is not to say, however, that the quality of the services are the same for all. In many regions, residents of poor areas sometimes complain that their school systems, garbage collection systems, and police protection are inferior to those in other, more affluent areas.

migrant farmers. The people who support subscription radio and television stations are another example of voluntary contributors. They offer their donations in full knowledge that the radio and television programs they are paying for will be enjoyed by an audience of free riders as well as subscribers like themselves. In their fund-raising campaigns, the subscription stations use hard-sell techniques that are aimed at guilt raising, reminding their audience that if too many of them remain free riders, subcription broadcasting will not survive. While such organizations raise enough money to keep themselves going, it is much easier to solicit support if the group can offer special benefits to its members only.

Exclusive Benefits as a Means of Attracting Members. Businesses, which are unusually well-organized interest groups, offer many examples of the ways that small and privileged groups work. These groups, which can be divided along industrial lines, include bodies like the American Association of Advertising Agencies, the Association of American Railroads, the National Association of Broadcasters, the American Petroleum Institute, the National Restaurant Association, the U.S. Copper Association, and the National Association of Tobacco Distributors.[12] According to Olson, the industrial groupings, each consisting of a relatively small number of firms voluntarily joined together, are able to offer special advantages to member firms and a favorable environment for group action. His point is borne out by the record of business success within the U.S. system of pressure groups.

Professional, consumer, and scholar associations, including the American Medical Association, the American Bar Association, the American Automobile Association, the American Association of University Professors, and the American Political Science Association, are another category of groups that have filled their ranks without resorting to coercion. To attract and keep their members they have relied also on special interest goods that are available on an exclusive basis only to members.[13] One of the most politically forceful of these groups has been the American Medical Association, which for many years has carried on high-powered lobbying activities and a massive public relations campaign to influence legislation and public opinion against a national health insurance program. Although many AMA doctors disapprove of socialized medicine strongly enough to firmly support the group's campaign against it anyway, the AMA offers many other inducements to its members. It publishes the *Journal of the American Medical Association*, the leading periodical for the profession which is circulated only to members. By means of the *Journal* and the AMA conventions which members may attend, members have access to information on the latest technical advances in the field, new products for medical use, and general

---

[12] Business organizations may also represent business as a whole. The Chamber of Commerce and NAM (National Association of Manufacturers) are examples.
[13] Olson, *The Logic of Collective Action*, pp. 132–67.

professional news, including opportunities for employment and research grants. As members, doctors may also receive help in defending themselves against malpractice suits.

Another powerful inducement for bringing in members that is available to the American Medical Association, as well as other groups such as the dental and bar associations, is the authority to establish the qualifications for licensing members of the profession. With such authority in the possession of professional associations, one may well understand why they need no closed- or union-shop arrangements to attract members. All of these inducements are organizational "by-products" and not the main areas to which a group's money and resources are directed. But without these inducements, it would be difficult for many interest groups to attract the members and the financial support to carry out their major programs.

Special interest goods can help to attract and hold members, and, in the case of professional and scholars' groups, they may serve the crucial role of disseminating up-to-date technical information among the members of a profession. However, the central concern of an interest group is directed outside the circle of members and is aimed at affecting the behavior of individuals and groups in the society as a whole through the public policy of government. In this sense, special interest goods are peripheral, and the success or failure of a group depends on other factors.

Effective Interest Groups: Ingredients for Success

A Receptive Environment

Interest groups are most likely to flourish in modern societies where occupational and other contacts put individuals in touch with a wide range of people besides their family, friends, and neighbors, and in which political participation is emphasized. The percentage of people who join organized groups differs greatly from one political culture to another.

In their study of different political cultures, Gabriel Almond and Sidney Verba noted that people in the United States, Great Britain, and Germany were more likely to participate in voluntary associations than were citizens of Italy and Mexico.[14] According to their findings, 57 percent of the respondents in the United States, 47 percent in Great Britain, and 44 percent in Germany were members of groups. In Italy and Mexico, the extent of participation was significantly smaller, amounting to only 30 percent and 24 percent respectively. Civic participation in every country increased with

[14] Gabriel Almond and Sidney Verba, *The Civic Culture* (Boston: Little, Brown, 1965). Another survey found 31 percent of the United States population actually belong to organizations that seek to influence public issues. See Robert E. Lane, *Political Life* (New York: The Free Press, 1959), p. 204.

educational level, and in all except the United States, more men than women were participants. Not all of the groups were political, of course, but some 24 percent of American, 19 percent of British, and 18 percent of German respondents were involved in political associations. By comparison, very few Italian and Mexican respondents participated in politically involved associations. One of the significant findings of the study was that in societies where many people join groups, people are most likely to have confidence in their own political judgments and to view political activism as a method of changing society.[15]

Whether interest groups will flourish in a society depends not only on politically oriented and motivated members, but also on the attitudes of the government, especially whether or not it sanctions group activism. There will be few interest groups where the government maintains close supervision over them, as does the Soviet Union, or where the government imposes many legal restrictions on such group political activities as lobbying or demonstrating. Even if a political system is relatively permissive about lobbying or demonstrating, it may frustrate poorly funded groups by failing to answer their demands in a meaningful way. Where the political system provides no effective legitimate channel for interest group activity, groups may resort to unconventional or extralegal behavior for strategic reasons. In the most extreme cases, they may even be driven to reject the system entirely, in favor of violence and revolution.

Financial Resources

All interest groups need money to carry out their programs. It pays rent for offices, enables them to hire a staff who will keep track of current developments, and it pays for promotional costs such as printing and mailing charges, newspaper space and TV and radio time, and travel and entertainment expenses. The costs can run high, especially for well-organized lobbies. A *Congressional Quarterly* report on lobby spending in 1970 listed the twenty-five lobbying organizations reporting the highest spending—between $73,000 and $341,000 paid out for such items as office expenses, gifts and contributions, printing and mailing costs, travel, and food and entertainment.[16] As Table 10-2 shows, the biggest spender listed was a veterans group, which that year was seeking a pension for 1,400,000 veterans. Other big spenders were postal interests concerned about the Postal Reorganization Act passed during 1970, farm groups, the AFL-CIO and several other labor unions, and hospital and medical associations. Two citizens' groups

[15] The best single work integrating this into political science theory is William Kornhauser, *The Politics of Mass Society* (New York: The Free Press, 1959).
[16] *Congressional Quarterly Weekly Report* 29, no. 32 (August 6, 1971) : 2.

Table 10-2
The Twenty-five
Top Spenders,
1970

Organization	1970
Veterans of World War I, U.S.A., Inc.	$341,244
National Association of Letter Carriers (AFL-CIO)	277,125
United Federation of Postal Clerks (AFL-CIO)	228,325
Council for a Livable World	214,626
AFL-CIO (National headquarters)	197,493
American Farm Bureau Federation	163,553
American Hospital Association	153,241
National Association of Home Builders of the United States	151,605
United States Savings & Loan League	149,794
Citizens Committee for Postal Reform, Inc.	138,545
Record Industry Association of America	123,286
Disabled American Veterans	117,134
National Committee for the Recording Arts	99,886
Livestock Producers Committee	96,945
American Medical Association	96,064
National Association of Postal Supervisors	94,661
National Council of Farmer Cooperatives	94,307
National Housing Conference, Inc.	92,549
Farmers Educational and Cooperative Union of America	80,738
Common Cause (and Urban Coalition Action Council)	79,347
National Cotton Council of America	79,036
American Legion	78,939
Brotherhood of Railway, Airline & Steamship Clerks, Freight Handlers, Express and Station Employees (AFL-CIO)	75,056
American Trucking Associations, Inc.	74,484
International Brotherhood of Teamsters, Chauffers, Warehousemen & Helpers of America	72,626

Source: Congressional Quarterly Weekly Report 29, no. 32 (August 6, 1971): 2.

among the top spenders were the Council for a Livable World, and the "people's lobby," Common Cause, which listed many social welfare and employment issues among its interests. As Figure 10-1 shows, business interest groups spent more than any other—a total of over $1,900,000 in 1970.

The figures, while indicative of spending by different groups, should not be taken too literally, since the groups' methods of reporting varied. However, they do indicate that a lobby must be able to command impressive financial resources to compete in the big leagues of government. But money is not the only key to success. An interest group must also be able to persuade a good portion of the public that its cause is just.

Figure 10-1
Breakdown of
Lobby-Group
Spending by Cate-
gory for 1970

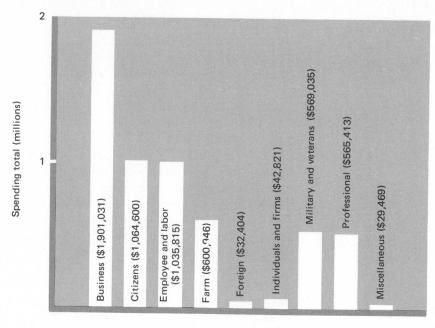

Source: From table in Congressional Quarterly Weekly Report 29, no. 32 (August 6, 1971): 3.

Public Support for an Issue

There is a saying that nothing can stop an idea whose time has come. Case studies of recently liberalized abortion laws tend to substantiate the saying, especially considering the hard-core resistance offered by small but dedicated antiabortion forces. Beginning in the late 1960s, Great Britain and a few states in the United States passed laws that made legal abortions available to many women. The most liberal piece of legislation, passed in New York State in 1970, made it possible for women to obtain legal abortions on demand. Less than a decade ago, such a law would have been unthinkable for most legislators. Why the radical change? A look at the abortion lobby in Great Britain provides some insight.

The British abortion law, though less liberal than the New York law, was enacted three years earlier, and its ambiguous terms, which permitted abortions if pregnancy threatened the present or future physical or mental health of a woman or children in her family, were interpreted liberally enough so that most women could obtain abortions without much difficulty.

The work of the thirty-year-old British Abortion Law Reform Association (ALRA) played an important role in passage of the bill.[17] The ALRA dates back to the thirties, when it recruited about four hundred members, mostly British working women. Dormant during World War II, it resumed political activity during the 1950s, but for many years the movement made little headway. Then the tragedy of the cruelly deformed Thalidomide babies born in the early 1960s caused many people to urge abortion on the grounds of fetal deformity, and ALRA picked up considerable support. During this period the ALRA organized a series of opinion surveys and publicized the results, indicating that both the public and the medical profession supported abortion reform. Gradually, the abortion lobby mustered support in Parliament, especially among the relatively young M.P.'s. In 1965 two abortion bills were presented in Parliament, and in 1966 a third abortion bill was introduced, which enlisted wide enough support to finally be enacted in late 1967.

Summing up the role of the ALRA in promoting the enactment of the Abortion Act of 1967, commentators noted that "the abortion lobby became successful when it was able to demonstrate to Parliament that despite religious opposition, public opinion had finally caught up with the views it had been expressing for thirty years. The lobby did not create this opinion, for many factors were at work, but it did influence opinion, hasten it, and organize it when the time was ripe." [18] The Thalidomide scandal, as well as such factors as the availability of "the pill," the general sexual liberalization of society, and the Women's Lib movement all contributed to changing public opinion on the abortion issue.

Strong Leadership

Leaders are the center of any group. They are the interpreters of ideas that attract supporters, and they provide these supporters with a plan of action. The leaders who ushered their nations into independence in the wake of World War II—Nehru of India, Sukarno of Indonesia, and Ho Chi Minh of North Vietnam, to name a few—each became the focus of their nations' independence movements, and, at least for a time, served as father figures to the newly independent nations.

As the names of certain nations are indelibly associated with their most outstanding leaders, so too, are the names of certain interest groups. A mention of the United Mine Workers Union evokes for many people the image of John L. Lewis, who headed that union from 1920 to 1960. An

---

[17] See Keith Hindell and Madeleine Simms, "How the Abortion Lobby Worked," *Political Quarterly* 39 (1968): 269–82, for the complete story upon which ours is based.
[18] *Ibid.*, p. 282.

independent and controversial leader, he fought hard for higher wages, better safety measures in the hazardous mining industry, and for union welfare funds (a field in which he pioneered). He was also a prime organizer of the Congress of Industrial Organizations (CIO). Similarly, the name of Ralph Nader has today become synonymous with the consumer movement, as has the name of George Meany with the AFL-CIO in recent years. With each of these movements, the personalities of charismatic leaders were crucial in shaping the movement and in sustaining it against challenges from opponents, rivals, and complacency, when, under the guidance of other leaders, the movements might have floundered. Strong leadership, then, can be crucial to the success of an interest group.

Flexibility

Most interest groups do not have sufficient influence to change the decisions of government on their own. Under these circumstances, it is advantageous at times for groups to form alliances. Some groups are flexible, while others are "purists" who are suspicious of entanglements and fear that any compromise on their part may end in a sellout of their interests by one of their partners. According to one study of relations among national interest groups, the two most important factors leading lobbies to cooperate with one another are a shared position on a basic issue and a similarity of legislative objectives extending over many years.[19] Interest groups do not seem to be as interested in a "logrolling" type of cooperation, where one group agrees to support another on one issue if that group agrees to return the compliment.

Cooperation and compromise can also be important for interest groups that do not lobby formally in government. A California group organized to save a small stretch of seacoast might hold different objectives than another state group dedicated to building mass transportation facilities in Los Angeles, but the two might well cooperate to support each other's causes. Compromise is sometimes advantageous: limited success is better than none. If the mass transportation group found that it had to settle for an expanded city bus route rather than a network of trains, that compromise would most likely be accepted as a step in the right direction.

Size

Insofar as there is strength in numbers, interest groups tend to gain strength as they increase in size. Other things being equal, a conglomerate group such as the AFL-CIO, with many millions of union members, has

[19] Robert L. Ross, "Relations Among National Interest Groups," *The Journal of Politics* 32, no. 1 (February 1970): 96–114.

more political impact than a small group such as the American Institute of Architects—just as the NAACP holds more power than a splinter black nationalist group dedicated to establishing a separate sovereign state for all black Americans. Of course, size is not all-important. The degree to which members within a group are united on issues also helps to determine the effectiveness of their tactics.

Cohesion

The AFL-CIO, while illustrating the strength of numbers, also provides a good example of how internal divisions can weaken the political force of an interest group. In national elections, for example, the top labor leadership has habitually supported the Democratic party (with the prominent exception of the 1972 election), but members feel no particular obligation to follow their lead. In the Eisenhower-Stevenson contest in 1956, for example, the Republican labor vote would probably have been large enough to have swung the election to Stevenson if union members had voted solidly behind the Democratic labor leaders. Similar divisions between leadership and membership on basic issues of interest group policy may be found in many other labor unions and professional associations, to say nothing of other types of interest groups.[20] This does not mean that interest groups are incapable of presenting a united front in the face of some challenge to their survival, but it is a reminder that members of a group often have different ways of perceiving the objectives of their group and different ideas as to how to achieve them.

Strategies of Interest Groups

Despite disagreements among group members, most private interest organizations manage to present a united front to the public. Public opinion is perhaps the most powerful ally that an interest group can enlist. Neither arm twisting nor friendly persuasion of legislators is effective in changing laws unless a majority of the public is receptive or, at least, not actively opposed to the changes. Nor, in fact, can mere changes in laws necessarily satisfy the objectives of interest groups who, according to David Truman,

[20] Comparing the policy preferences of leaders and members in the Oregon Education Association, Norman R. Luttbeg and Harmon Zeigler reported the results in "Attitude Consensus and Conflict in an Interest Group: An Assessment of Cohesion," *American Political Science Review* 60 (September 1966) : 655–66. According to their findings, members and leaders tended to differ on many matters, especially on the issues of whether the association should endorse political candidates and take sides on public issues, and whether liberals should be banished from the staff. The leaders were inclined to favor taking sides on candidates and issues while the rank and file were not.

want to establish, maintain or add to certain forms of behavior.[21] To be successful, an interest group's strategies must reach beyond direct attempts to influence legislators and administrators and encompass education, public relations, and a variety of other programs which will sway public opinion to their side.

Approaching the Lawmakers

Although lobbying is not the only strategy of interest groups, it is the one that receives the most attention. Unfortunately, the unscrupulous dealings of a few individuals have given lobbyists an unsavory image with the public.[22] While incidents of blackmail or bribery do occasionally occur (as they do in other areas of human endeavor), such tactics are anathema to the average lobbyist.

Lobbying Techniques. The approaches and techniques that are commonly used by lobbyists vary widely according to the types of interests they represent and the way in which they conceive their job. In "The Role of the Lobbyist," Samuel C. Patterson identified three types of lobbyists: the "contact man," the "informant," and the "watchdog." [23] The "contact man" promotes the interests of his group by establishing friendships with legislators to whom he can present his group's case on a person-to-person basis. The "informant" lobbies in public rather than in private meetings, offering testimony supporting his group's case at legislative hearings and disseminating published materials on their behalf. The "watchdog" keeps close track of what is happening in the legislature so he can alert his group to take action when the time is appropriate.

Criteria for Successful Lobbying. The success of a lobbyist's approach depends on several factors, one of which is the receptivity of legislators.[24] Surveying lobbyists' evaluations of their various techniques, Lester Milbrath found that those which were rated most effective by the lobbyists themselves involved direct communication between the lobbyist and the legislature. The highest-rated strategies included not only the personal presenta-

---

[21] Truman, *The Governmental Process.*

[22] See, for example, E. E. Schattschneider's discussion of the "contagion of conflict" in Chapter 1 of *The Semisovereign People.*

[23] Samuel C. Patterson, "The Role of the Lobbyist: The Case of Oklahoma," *The Journal of Politics* 25, no. 1 (February 1963) : 72–92.

[24] A classification of legislators was made by John C. Wahlke, William Buchanan, Heinz Eulau, and LeRoy C. Ferguson in "American State Legislators," *The Journal of Politics* 22, no. 2 (May 1960). Legislators were categorized as "facilitators," who are friendly toward lobbyists; "resistors," who are hostile toward lobbies; and "neutrals," who either have little knowledge about interest group activity or no deeply held bias in favor of or in opposition to interest groups. According to the study, "facilitators" tended to be open-minded in considering the arguments of all interest groups while the resistors tended to listen selectively to a few whom they considered worthy of their attention.

Table 10-3
How Washington
Lobbyists Rate
Their Techniques

Technique	Mean Rating
Means of Direct Communication	
Personal presentation of viewpoints	8.43
Presentation of research results	7.40
Testifying at hearings	6.55
Communication Through Intermediaries	
Contact by constituents	5.90
Contact by a close friend	3.76
Letter and telegram campaigns	4.55
Public relations campaigns	5.55
Publicizing voting records	2.05
Methods of Keeping Channels Open	
Entertaining	1.59
Giving a party	1.24
Bribery	0.10
Contributing money	1.88
Campaign work	2.28

Source: L. W. Milbrath, The Washington Lobbyists, *as prepared in Malcolm E. Jewell and Samuel C. Patterson,* The Legislative Process in the United States *(New York: Random House, 1966), p. 290.*

tions of viewpoints and "research results" made by the contact-man type of lobbyist to individual legislators, but also the lobbyist's testimony at legislative hearings. Rated less effective were the techniques—such as contacts by constituents and close friends, letter and telegram campaigns, public relations campaigns, and publicizing voting records—which involved no personal communication between the legislators and the lobbyists. The lowest-rated strategies were those of "keeping channels open" between interest groups and the legislators. Under this category would fall campaign work, social get-togethers, and financial contributions.[25] Table 10-3 summarizes the lobbyists' ratings of their techniques as tabulated by Milbrath.[26]

Approaching the Administration

The executive, as well as the legislative branch of government is a target for interest group pressure and persuasion. Antipollution groups, for instance, seek support from the Department of the Interior in their efforts to ban automobiles from the National Parks. As a general rule, interest groups

[25] Lester Milbrath, *The Washington Lobbyists* (Chicago: Rand McNally, 1963).
[26] A similar survey conducted by Harmon Zeigler and Michael Baer to measure the effectiveness of lobbying techniques in Massachusetts, North Carolina, Oregon, and Utah produced a comparable response, reported in *Lobbying: Interaction and Influence in American State Legislatures* (Belmont, Calif.: Wadsworth, 1969).

will approach a department of the government and not the president, who is not readily accessible to such groups and their lobbyists, although he may be aware of the pressures they apply and may be indirectly involved in deciding how to handle them. Interest groups tend to concentrate their attention on the department that specializes in their own area of interest. Farm groups deal with the Department of Agriculture; labor unions with the Department of Labor; public service companies with the Federal Power Commission; mining interests with the Bureau of Mines; telephone and broadcasting companies with the Federal Communications Commission, and so forth. As a rule, each department pays careful heed to the demands and arguments of groups in its own area of specialization, but in practice this is not always so easily done.

Bureaucratic Infighting and Interest-Group Competition. One problem interest groups come up against when approaching the executive agencies is the competition among the departments and bureaus of government. Each department must plan and administer its programs in relation to all the other agencies, which will be competing for public funds and promoting conflicting programs. For example, the competing demands for funds and conflicting priorities of cities may result in bureaucratic infighting between agencies of the Department of Housing and Urban Development and the Department of Transportation over a plot of land equally valuable as a lower-income housing site or an extension of a subway system. So, if an interest group succeeds in bending the ear of one government agency, this does not necessarily mean that the desired policy change is assured.

Nor are such interdepartmental conflicts of interest the only hazards that lie in the way when an interest group pursues its objectives in government officialdom. Each department is subjected not only to pressures from outside its sphere of operations, but also to the competing demands of interest groups within its sphere. The Federal Communications Commission is pressured by many groups with opposing viewpoints. Conservative interest groups have objected to what they regard as dangerous radicalism allowed by the FCC in the broadcasts of such noncommercial radio stations as Pacifica in San Francisco and WBAI in New York City and in some of the programming of public (noncommercial) television. But at the same time, groups with leftist leanings have accused the FCC of a conservative bias. Meanwhile, some government departments, such as Defense and State, have insisted that TV and radio news coverage is not fair to them and that the media have condoned violations of government-classified materials. Besides all these competing objections, the FCC has been subjected to criticism by those who feel there is too much violence in programs or that the morals of viewers, particularly children, are not being protected properly.[27]

When faced with a range of conflicting demands, a government bureaucracy has several options. It may choose to do nothing at all, in the hope

[27] See the discussion in Chapter 9, "Political Communication and the Media."

that the situation will resolve itself; it may try to work out a compromise that will not displease any group too much; or it may align itself on the side of one interest group, either because the alignment seems politically advantageous or simply because the officials of the government agency involved are in closest agreement with that group. (Of course, opinion within the agency itself is often divided, so whatever course of action is taken does not represent a monolithic policy stand.) In fact, at one time or another, many government bureaucracies have become identified with the interests of some powerful pressure group within their sphere of authority. The railroad interests of this nation in the late nineteenth century served the purpose of developing and integrating the country, and, as a result, had a powerful voice in many government departments. In other instances, government agencies have taken an initiative in organizing people with interests that deserve to be heard by the policy makers in government.

Techniques of Interest Groups. In dealing with the bureaucracy, interest groups employ about the same tactics as they do with legislators, including personal contacts with officials, the supplying of research and factual materials, public relations and publicity campaigns, and entertaining. Some kinds of pressuring such as letter-writing campaigns may be less effective with bureaucrats than with legislators, however, since the jobs in government administration are gained by appointment rather than election, and many are protected by tenure. One special occasion when interest groups may make their influence felt in the bureaucracy is at the time when candidates are up for appointment to top-level government posts, including positions in the president's cabinet. At such times, interest groups may demand the right to approve or disapprove a cabinet nominee who is to serve in areas that they regard as sensitive to their own interests. At times they exercise this right vigorously, as was the case when a newly elected President Nixon named Walter J. Hickel to be his first Secretary of the Interior. At the time, conservationist groups were generally opposed to Hickel's appointment, calling attention to his apparent willingness to give the interests of industrial development much higher priority than those of conservation. Because of such opposition, his appointment was held up for several days before it finally was cleared through Congress. Interestingly enough, many of Hickel's original opponents later developed respect for his diligence in protecting natural resources and became his supporters when he was asked to leave President Nixon's cabinet.

Approaching the Judiciary

In the United States interest groups also seek to realize their goals through the judicial process. Every year the state and federal courts hear numerous cases filed or supported by such interest groups as the American Civil Liberties Union, the Sierra Club, and the NAACP. The issue of government-enforced racial segregation is one of many that have been taken to the courts by interest groups. The legal staff of the NAACP, for example, through its chief attorney Thurgood Marshall (now an Associate Justice of the U.S. Supreme Court), successfully challenged the constitutionality of all state laws requiring racial segregation in public schools. In recent years the U.S. Supreme Court has dealt with several delicate and important social issues brought to it by interest groups, including school busing, women's rights, the death penalty, and abortion.

Interest groups have generally used two methods to pursue their goals through the judicial process. The first is to initiate suits directly on behalf of a group or class of people whose interests they represent (such suits are commonly referred to as "class actions"). The second method is for the interest group to file a brief as a "friend of the court" *(amicus curiae)* in support of a person whose suit seeks to achieve goals that the interest group is also seeking.

Interest Groups and the Government in Japan

In societies different from our own, interest groups have developed their own styles of approaching and pressuring their governments. Japanese interest groups, which have become a significant force in Japan only since World War II, have a number of interesting practices, some of which may sound familiar, but others very different from our own experience.[28] One of their favored strategies is a well-organized and very orderly mass demonstration, complete with banners, flags, and chanting. A Japanese peculiarity foreign to our political customs is the *chinjōdan*—a petition group representing a rural community, who come to Tokyo to plead their case in the offices of government officials and politicians. The *chinjōdan*, who sometimes bring gifts such as pears and tangerines, visit the capital city during December, January, and February, when the national budget is being put together. Many politicians like the idea of the *chinjōdan*, which offers them a convenient opportunity to contact their constituents without journeying to every village. However, these supplicants are not considered to be very effective as pressure groups, especially when compared to such well-organized and competently staffed organizations as the National Federation of Housewives Associations, which has been very effective in holding down the prices of such consumer items as dry cleaning and public baths; and the League for Government Compensation of Expropriated Lands, which has successfully pressured the government for very handsome settlements.

---

[28] For an excellent description of Japanese interest group techniques, see Nathaniel Thayer, *How the Conservatives Rule Japan* (Princeton, N.J.: Princeton University Press, 1969).

Other Tactics

Government is not the only target of interest-group action. Organized interests may often choose to confront management directly, or to take their case to the public with peaceful—or not so peaceful—appeals.

Appeals to Management. One of the most ubiquitous types of pressure-group action in modern America (and in many other nations) is the employee strike, directed against the management of a particular company or industry. The purpose of a strike is, of course, to halt production in the plant involved, and thus jeopardize the income and profits of the managers and owners so they will be willing to listen to their employees' demands for higher wages, shorter hours, more job security, better fringe benefits, and improved working conditions. Strikes are often enforced by picket lines, which are aimed at preventing anyone from going to work or taking over the jobs of the strikers. If the company serves the public, as does a retail store, the picket line may be used to bar not only nonstriking workers, but also customers from entering the establishment. Pickets don't even have to be striking employees; sometimes consumers may picket a business to protest some policy of the establishment. The inflation of the early 1970s drove many angry housewives in some cities to march in front of grocery stores, protesting the rising prices of food and urging other customers not to buy high-priced items, such as meat products. At about the same time, feminist groups were picketing bars and restaurants that refused to serve women.

Picketing is a double-edged strategy, intended to affect the policies of the management of an establishment and to influence public opinion in favor of the pickets and their objectives. Concern for public opinion is shared by virtually all interest groups, and some of their activities are aimed directly at the people.

Appeals to the Public. Even those interest groups with such advantages as a large membership, financial power, and influential government connections realize the importance of their public image and of getting the public to agree to—or, at least, not to oppose—their activities. For this reason, many interest groups invest considerable sums in public relations programs and publicity campaigns to explain how they contribute to the general welfare and why their programs and policies are good for the country. The International Ladies Garment Workers Union has bought prime advertising space to remind people of the low wages and intolerable working conditions which prevailed in the garment industry before it was unionized; and the American Medical Association has invested a considerable amount of time and money to convince the American people that socialized medicine is a disastrous alternative to privately arranged medical care.

Even while investing large sums in publicity, some interest groups maintain what is now popularly referred to as a "low profile"—preferring to promote their objectives without advertising themselves. In such cases, groups may rely on planted news stories that promote their objectives indirectly and behind-the-scenes pressure to prevent the publication of material that they judge to be detrimental to them. When the film "The Last Hurrah" was produced, for example, the National Association of Wool Growers was able to pressure the producers into suppressing a remark in the dialogue about nylon replacing wool. Other groups, including those concerned with reform or fund-raising, use their ads not only to promote their objectives, but also to solicit members and funds.

Demonstrations. While certain special interest organizations such as the American Cancer Society or the Heart Fund may have access to free advertising space and time, most interest groups do not, and most lack the funds to purchase such publicity. Under these circumstances, a group with limited finances and motivated members may decide to try nonviolent demonstrations as a way of publicizing and promoting their cause. The precedent for such demonstrations in modern times was provided by Mahatma Gandhi, who used this tactic against the British *raj* before India gained its independence in 1947. Gandhi, who derived his inspiration for nonviolent protest at least partly from an essay on civil disobedience, written by Henry David Thoreau in protest against the United States-Mexican War of 1846–48, provided a model for the American black leader, Martin Luther King, who headed the nonviolent civil rights movement during the 1950s and 1960s.[29]

In his "Protest as a Political Resource," Michael Lipsky calls such activity "an important aspect of minority-group- and low-income-group politics" and defines it as "a mode of political action oriented toward objection to one or more policies or conditions, characterized by showmanship or display of an unconventional nature, and undertaken to obtain rewards from political or economic systems while working within the systems."[30] According to Lipsky, the strategy underlying protest activity involves four groups: the protesters, who lack political power and the resources to acquire it; the people with whom the protesters must bargain to obtain the concessions they desire (called by Lipsky the "target groups"); the media; and third parties, whom the protesters try to persuade to get involved in the bargaining situation in ways that favor their cause (called by Lipsky the "reference publics").

Welfare recipients offer an example of a relatively powerless group, and their demonstrations in many cities to obtain such concessions as special clothing funds for school children illustrate the strategy of protest groups. The welfare demonstrators have welcomed press coverage and have directed their appeals and arguments as much to the general public as to city government officials who administer welfare programs. By publicizing their plight, they undoubtedly have hoped to pick up supporters with more influence than

---

[29] See Saul Alinsky's *Reveille for Radicals* (New York: Random House, 1969) which gives rules for organizing protest movements for groups with limited finances.
[30] Michael Lipsky, "Protest as a Political Resource," *American Political Science Review* 62, no. 4 (December 1968): 1144–58.

they themselves command to help them argue their case for changes in the welfare system. In New York City, a familiar example of such protest activity is the type of demonstration staged by tenants of low-rent buildings to protest such conditions as inadequate heat, plumbing problems, vermin, or filthy halls or to resist landlord attempts to empty the building of tenants paying legally controlled rents. By demonstrating, the tenants have generally desired to get press coverage and attract public support, and thus force the city to take action against the landlords to correct unsafe or unsanitary conditions or to interdict eviction proceedings.

In assessing the basic strategy common to all protest groups, Lipsky found a number of serious drawbacks. The strategy makes it necessary for protest leaders to deal with the conflicting requirements of four different groups: the protesters, who expect their leaders to "play the game" according to their own needs, rules, and mores; the press, which gives the most coverage to dramatic and unusual behavior and ideas; the public, who usually react most favorably to groups whose leadership displays moderation in making demands and presents an image of respectability; and public officials, who may be more interested in getting favorable press coverage and convincing the public of their zeal than in actually dealing with the problems of a relatively powerless minority (a course of action that could be costly and might offend more powerful interest groups concerned with other priorities and keeping tax rates low). As a consequence, the ultimate results obtained from protest activities often are unsatisfactory. Instead of stimulating genuine concern and leading to practical solutions, the protests may merely prod public officials into symbolic action. The officials may pay a visit to the neighborhoods where the protest originated, appoint a commission to study the situation, make a speech, or otherwise give the appearance of meaningful activity, until the spotlight of publicity moves elsewhere. Or, they may take swift and decisive action on one or two crisis cases while doing nothing to improve conditions for rank-and-file protesters. Another type of response is to discredit the objectives, leadership, or membership of the protesting group. Considering these drawbacks, Lipsky concluded that peaceful protest is often a frustrating form of political action which may fail to produce any improvements in the situations of the protesters, and which, as a result, may lead to political apathy or a rejection of conventional political channels as a means of working for change.

Violent Protest. A group that loses faith in the efficacy of conventional political channels and modes of action often sees violent protest as its only alternative. Although violent protest occurs more than we would like in this country, it is not a mode of action that interest groups normally use.[31] Rather, it is a reaction that requires a psychological buildup, nurtured by such tensions as poverty, discrimination, frustration, and a sense of personal

---

[31] Chapter 20 takes up at length the issue of violence in politics. For background on the history of violence in the United States, see Richard E. Rubenstein, *Rebels in Eden* (Boston: Little, Brown, 1970).

or social injustice. An outbreak of violence almost always begins spontaneously, as a result of an incident which sparks the pent-up anger of a frustrated group; and the momentum of mob behavior escalates the violence. The riots of the sixties in New York's Harlem, Los Angeles' Watts district, and black ghettos in other large cities typify the development of such violence. The ingredients for such explosions were squalor and frustration, aggravated by the uncomfortable heat of midsummer. The flint and tinder were the police and the blacks—mutually suspicious, antagonistic, and fearful. In New York, the riots began after a white off-duty policeman fatally shot a black youth who allegedly threatened him with a knife. Enraged, the people of Harlem marched on a police precinct station, and during the march, the rioting began. In Watts, the riots developed after two white policemen stopped a black youth for driving under the influence of alcohol; he resisted arrest and black onlookers claimed that the two policemen and their reinforcements physically maltreated the youth in the process of subduing him. The rioting that ensued lasted for about four days, claiming a toll of thirty-four lives, one thousand injuries, and about forty million dollars in property damage.

It was probably no accident that the riots came at a time when some racial barriers were beginning to crumble.[32] During the mid-1950s and 1960s, the civil rights legislation enacted by the United States Congress, and the formation of some two dozen new nations under black control in Africa, gave blacks reason to hope that the tide of history was turning in their favor. Consequently, their tolerance of programs that promised more than they actually delivered was limited, and they were more determined than ever to fight for what they considered to be their just rights. In his *Political Violence*, H. L. Nieburg views disorder as "intrinsically related to the social process." [33] According to him, "the widespread appeal to violence in a sense represents a strain toward social reintegration and legitimacy." It is not violence per se that is the problem, he maintains, "but the existence of conditions that divide our society and may make violence a pattern which may undermine the recuperative powers of the society."

Interest Groups: An Evaluation

Interest groups are an intrinsic part of every modern democracy. Yet, how well do they serve the needs of the average citizen? [34]

[32] See Chapter 19, "Minority Rights and Government Policy" for a more thorough discussion of the black civil rights movement.
[33] H. L. Nieburg, *Political Violence* (New York: St. Martin's Press, 1969).
[34] An excellent critique of the usual interest-group defense is given in George Beam, *Usual Politics* (New York: Holt, Rinehart and Winston, 1970). For another good discussion of the pros and cons of the interest-group system, from a more elitist perspective, see Chapter 8, "The Organized Interest: The Defenders of the Status-Quo," in Thomas Dye and L. Harmon Zeigler, *The Irony of Democracy*, 2nd ed. (Belmont, Calif.: Wadsworth, 1972).

How Well Do Interest Groups Articulate Ideas?

Every question of public policy involves a variety of different, and often conflicting, interests, most of which deserve a hearing if a democracy is to live up to the ideal of representative government. Some of these interests will be represented in the legislature, but there will be many that are not, especially in a two-party system like that of the United States. The existence of interest groups and pressure politics helps to assure that a wider range of interests will be taken into account by the legislative process. Take, for example, the question of whether the U.S. government should finance development of a supersonic transport (SST). From 1963 to 1971, Congress had periodically voted appropriations for the SST, which was promoted by the U.S. Department of Transportation on the grounds that our national prestige and our international preeminence in aeronautics were at stake, since Great Britain, France, and the USSR all had such projects. Naturally, the aircraft industry and its suppliers also favored government financing for development of this aircraft, since it was a very important source of jobs and income. Opposing the project was a coalition of interests who feared that its jet-engine exhausts would pollute the upper atmosphere, that its shock waves might damage land structures, and that its noise would be intolerable. The anti-SST forces also argued that its only real advantage over other air transports was higher speed—a dubiously practical value considering its tremendous cost and the fact that it would require airports of vast size, which would use up more of our dwindling land resources. The congressional controversy continued for years, with the pro-SST forces winning each round in the battle for appropriations. Then, in 1971, the opposition, which had gained considerable public backing, mustered enough congressional support to end governmental financing of the project.[35] The history of innumerable other legislative issues could, of course, illustrate just as well the role of interest groups in articulating a viewpoint and continuing to defend it for as long as the issue remains alive.

But many smaller organizations have neither the members nor the money to stage such an effective campaign. Unless they are able to form coalitions, they are unsuccessful in fighting challenges to their survival from larger, more powerful groups. For example, effective lobbying by the AMA helped to bring about a New York State ruling requiring all acupuncturists not licensed by the state to close down their practices. Since most of these practitioners were licensed in China and lacked the training to meet M.D. requirements here, the AMA in effect forced them to either relinquish their practices or go underground. Despite protests from patients claiming that acupuncture has relieved their long-time suffering from a variety of ailments, the state ruling remains on the books.

---

[35] Of course, a number of factors contributed to the success of the anti-SST forces. One important reason the bill passed was a 1971 congressional ruling requiring all major bills to be voted on in public with names recorded.

Interest Groups as a "Safety Valve"

In almost every nation, there are alienated citizens who feel they have been forgotten or discriminated against by the government. This attitude may be a symptom of youthful rebellion in some instances, but it is also found among minority groups more familiar with the flaws and inconsistencies in our system than with the opportunities and freedom it affords to many of its citizens. Interest groups often help to stabilize society by providing unhappy citizens with a "safety valve"—a legitimate outlet for their complaints and frustrations. Tenants subjected to the indignities of poor plumbing and roaches may organize to effectively voice their complaints rather than vent their frustrations by throwing rocks through the landlord's window. Of course, anyone who joins an organized group is largely committed to acting within the system. The truly alienated citizen wants radical change, and compromises between interest groups and government may not satisfy him. While organized interest groups are effective in keeping the peace within the confines of the system, they offer little to the forgotten man who has lost patience with gradual change.

Defining Issues and Arenas of Conflict

Individuals with interests in common do not constitute an interest group until they become aware of their shared attitudes, discontents, and problems, and are motivated to take action to maintain or improve their position. The Women's Lib movement started gathering momentum in the 1960s with a spate of books and articles expressing the dissatisfaction of some women with the conditions imposed by society on their sex. The leaders, ranging from moderates concerned with improving the legal status and employment opportunities of women to extremists who advocated a kind of sexual separatism to allow women to "find themselves," gave women a standard by which to measure their own feelings about themselves and the sexual role assigned to them by society. The movement also made it necessary for government officials and political candidates to develop political stands on the issue. Women's liberation groups organized support not only for such objectives as the ending of job discrimination, but also for the accessibility of birth control information, legal abortions, day care centers, and desegregation of traditionally male restaurants and bars.

But, do women's liberation groups and other organizations really speak for most of their members, or do they represent the interests of a small but vocal minority within the group? Interest group leaders, like leaders of political parties, often have stronger ideas on issues than their followers.[36] But political party leaders, especially in nations like the United States, must often compromise on issues in order to appeal to the largest possible ma-

[36] See Chapter 14, "Legislatures and Executives: Making and Applying Laws."

jority at election time. Interest group leaders, in contrast, must often take stronger or more extreme stands than many of their members would like in order to retain a favorable bargaining position. Strikes called by union leaders do not always have the full sympathy of the workers, many of whom are more interested in collecting their weekly paychecks than they are in bargaining for a new contract. And many women who are in favor of equal pay for equal work find the concept of abortion, as advocated by many women's lib leaders, to be totally anathema.

Interest Groups: Educators or Propagandists?

When important issues of public policy are being considered by Congress, it is customary to permit interested parties to offer testimony at committee hearings to support their stands on the issue. (In Great Britain, too, interest groups are officially recognized as basic sources of information by the parliamentary committees.) Earlier in this chapter, a partial list of experts who testified at congressional hearings on air pollution was presented. They served the purpose of presenting the legislators with important technical, scientific, and statistical information covering such areas as the economic and biological consequences of air pollution, the costs involved in reducing it, and the capability of industry to undertake such costs. Hearings of this type may help Congress to pass fairer laws that are more in tune to public needs. But the argument can also be made that the groups that get a hearing in Congress are limited to those with the influence to gain access to the formal governmental process; few grass-roots groups are so successful.

In addition to educating the government, interest groups often play a crucial role in developing public awareness and knowledge of issues. Certain groups, like the Consumers Union, specialize in helping people to use their money more knowledgeably. Others, like the AMA and some insurance organizations, have been sources of advice on such subjects as good health habits, proper nutrition, accident prevention, and planning for financial security. Critics of the interest-group system argue that by disseminating information, the groups are acting as propagandists rather than as educators. No interest group is going to publicize information which puts it in an unfavorable light; the information it offers to government and public is highly selective. The wool industry, for instance, may offer free brochures to the public on the care of carpets, but they are unlikely to include any helpful information regarding synthetic fibers.

Decentralizing Political Power

Interest groups compete with one another, and in the process, they may help to limit the power and influence that any one group can exercise within Congress or a governmental agency. The controversies aroused by the policies of the Pay Board and Price Commission established by President Nixon in

1971 to control inflation illustrate how interest groups challenge one another's influence. Until early in 1972, the pressure of organized labor prevented the Pay Board from challenging labor contracts that provided for wage increases above the established 5.5 percent allowed by the guidelines. When the Pay Board eventually took a stand against higher wage increases, the labor members of the board attacked the decision as "an unholy alliance" between the board's public members and its employer members. Soon after the Pay Board's stand, labor and consumer groups charged that businessmen who complied with wage controls were acting in violation of price guidelines. Labor, consumers, and employers each influenced the actions of the Pay Board. Thus, no one group dictated government policy.

But by dispersing political power, interest groups can also stalemate government action. Certain issues have been aptly characterized as "hot potatoes," because government action in either direction will arouse a loud outcry from one group. Typically, such issues are ardently supported and vehemently opposed by competing groups with enough voting power and influence on both sides to drive politicians to equivocation. In the 1972 presidential election, busing, abortion reform, and certain welfare issues were glossed over by both major parties for exactly this reason.

Private Citizens and Public Policy

The average citizen, on his own, has very little hope of making his opinions and demands count with legislators and government offices. But, through the interest-group system, it is possible to join forces with like-minded citizens to transform individual impotence into group power. In the middle-class section of Forest Hills in New York City in 1972, a group of outraged citizens protested city government plans to construct a large, low-income housing project in their community. They argued that such a project would change the safe character of the neighborhood and put an unfair burden on an already overcrowded school and transportation system. The controversy received extensive coverage from the press. While many people felt that those who objected to the project were arguing out of fear and prejudice rather than reason, the Forest Hills residents did succeed in making their case a central issue and forcing the city to temporarily shelve its plans. The experience of participating in pressure groups, whatever their objectives, appears to give individuals a sense of identification with the political process.

To an extent, an elite dominates our interest group system just as it does our political party system. A major reason is that the people with faith in their ability to join forces and effect change through the political process are more likely to be better educated than those with little interest or lack of confidence in the system. That large, well-financed groups wield more power in the political arena than smaller interests with limited funds is a fact of life. And, within interest groups, it is the most active, most vocal members who call the shots for the entire group.

Interest Groups: Do They Serve in Our Best Interests?

Interest groups are a part of modern society. Wherever there are people, there are interests. Thus, there always exists the potential need for an organized group through which the private citizen can voice his opinions on issues that directly affect him. Interest groups differ from each other in their structures and strategies as much as the people who join them. But they all share a common goal: to promote their needs by influencing the political decisions which affect them. Some interest groups, like ecology organizations and the Consumers Union, are intended to benefit the general public. Others, like the AMA and the Bar Association, offer services on a members-only basis. But, the services a group provides for its members are less important to its overall success than other factors, such as financial resources, a receptive social and political environment, an appealing issue, size, cohesiveness, strong leadership, and relations with other groups.

In two-party systems especially, issues tend to be muted by political candidates who try to appeal to as broad a segment of the voting public as possible. The result is a gap between the narrow interest of the individual voter and the general promises of an electoral campaign—a gap which interest groups attempt to fill by pressing for firm political actions on certain issues. But how well do interest groups serve the needs of the average citizen? The small businessman, the uninformed laborer, and minority groups with limited financial resources tend to get lost in the push and pull of larger interests and government. The successful interest groups, too, tend to be dominated by a vocal minority of well-educated, middle- and upper-class political activists. Despite this, the interest group system provides a crucial link between the private citizen and public policy. How well the system represents the average citizen depends, in some part, on the extent to which he is willing to actively defend what is important to him. No political group can survive unless its stands on issues are at least tacitly approved by the majority of its members. And while not everybody may be equally represented in interest groups, the system offers to everyone at least the potential for a hearing in the vast political arena.

Suggested Readings

Beer, Samuel H. *British Politics in the Collectivist Age.* New York: Alfred A. Knopf, 1966. A work containing several good sections on the role of pressure groups in contemporary Great Britain.

Ehrmann, Henry W., ed. *Interest Groups on Four Continents.* Pittsburgh: University of Pittsburgh Press, 1958. An examination of pressure-group operations in different cultural and societal settings.

Garceau, Oliver. *The Political Life of the American Medical Association.* Cambridge, Mass.: Harvard University Press, 1941. A classic study of the AMA as pressure group.

Key, V. O., Jr. *Politics, Parties, and Pressure Groups.* New York: Crowell-Collier & Macmillan, 1967. Part I is a comprehensive analysis of diverse groups in American politics.

Latham, Earl. *The Group Basis of Politics.* New York: Octagon, 1965. A work that helped to bring about a new look at the role of groups in politics.

Lowi, Theodore J. *The End of Liberalism: Ideology, Policy, and the Crisis of Public Authority.* New York: W. W. Norton, 1969. A critical, insightful, and stimulating analysis of the consequences of pressure-group politics in the United States.

Milbrath, Lester W. *The Washington Lobbyists.* Chicago: Rand McNally, 1963. A study that takes a positive view of the role of lobbyists in the political process.

Olson, Mancur, Jr. *The Logic of Collective Action: Public Goods and the Theory of Groups.* New York: Schocken Books, 1968. Olson creates an original model of the dynamics of group action and comes to some important conclusions.

Schattschneider, E. E. *The Semisovereign People: A Realist's View of Democracy in America.* New York: Holt, Rinehart, and Winston, 1960. The integral role of groups in the democratic process is provocatively discussed.

Truman, David B. *The Governmental Process: Political Parties and Public Opinion.* New York: Alfred A. Knopf, 1961. The role of pressure groups in congressional politics is thoroughly examined.

Zeigler, Harmon. *Interest Groups in American Society.* Englewood Cliffs, N.J.: Prentice-Hall, 1964. A thorough analysis of interest groups, interest-group theory, and the role of interest groups within democratic societies.

Party Roles in Democracies

In democratic systems, political parties fill several roles: they involve the people in the political process; they organize the machinery of government; they define issues and policy alternatives; and they structure and institutionalize political conflict. Further, as E. E. Schattschneider has pointed out: "The rise of political parties is indubitably one of the principal distinguishing marks of modern government. Political parties created democracy; modern democracy is unthinkable save in terms of parties." [3] It is evident that political parties are crucial to the functioning of a democracy—and, indeed, to almost every system of government. What are the roles played by political parties, and how do they go about performing these roles?

Mobilizing Voters. Every year at election time, on subways, buses, and television we see the familiar reminders: "Vote for the candidate of your choice." "Get out and vote!" But nobody is going to vote unless his interest is sufficiently aroused.[4] It is the job of the political parties to motivate the people to go to the polls and vote for the party ticket. In order to mobilize voters behind its candidates, a party wages a campaign that usually appeals to voters by stressing the candidate's fitness for office and the relevancy of the party's platform to the pressing needs of society. This has prodded critics to ask whether, if there are no pressing needs at the time of the campaign, if the economy is sound, and if the nation is at peace both internally and externally, political parties create artificial issues to fill this vacuum. Voter mobilization is unquestionably part of the party's role. But the way a party fulfills this role varies according to the mood of the public and the prevailing political system.

Socializing. In dictatorships such as Spain and Taiwan, where the party and the government are almost identical, the party is a conservative force, designed to uphold and perpetuate the existing social and political order. A major duty of the party is to strengthen the legitimacy of the established political system. A revolutionary party plays the opposite role. In the early years after the revolution in the People's Republic of China, for example, the political party attacked traditional social and economic values within

---

[3] *Party Government* (New York: Holt, Rinehart and Winston, 1942), p. 1. The problem with delineating party roles in this manner is that they are not necessarily related to the needs of the system. Sorauf acknowledges this problem in his paper "Political Parties and Political Analysis," in William Nisbet Chambers and Walter Dean Burnham, eds., *The American Party System: Stages of Political Development* (New York: Oxford University Press, 1967), pp. 33–53.

[4] As Anthony Downs points out in *An Economic Theory of Democracy* (New York: Harper & Row, 1957). See also the discussion on voting in William H. Riker and Peter C. Ordeshook, "A Theory of the Calculus of Voting," *American Political Science Review* 62 (March 1968): 25–42; and our own Chapter 13 on "Voting Behavior" for a more complete discussion.

the society in order to establish the legitimacy of the new values. Thus, the Chinese Communists had to challenge, destroy, and replace the traditional institutions of the Confucian social order before they could go ahead with their own political program. This even meant changing the family structure by creating giant agricultural communes where adults were assigned to work crews while children were cared for in central nurseries run by the party. By this action, the party hoped to take over the family's traditional socializing role and assume the lead in building China's new society.[5]

In stable democracies, political parties generally reinforce the status quo, though to a much lesser extent than in one-party governing systems. In the United States, the Democrats and Republicans may disagree on specific policies, but they are united in their basic belief in the free enterprise system and the democratic process. Thus, in democracies, too, political parties play the conservative role of reinforcing the system.

Organizing Government Policy.   Under democratic systems, the party that wins a majority of seats in the legislature or captures control of the executive branch fills the most powerful positions in the government. If the Democrats win a majority of Senate seats, they will be able to select the chairmen of Senate committees, and thus play an important role in the makeup of those committees. The minority party, likewise, decides who its representatives on the various committees will be. If the President is a Republican, his political orientation will largely determine who heads the major departments, who is appointed to federal court vacancies, and who mans the policy-making offices in the various federal agencies. In Great Britain, the party that wins a majority in the House of Commons is even more powerful: it decides who will be the prime minister and who will hold which cabinet post. Since the winning party largely decides who the policy makers will be, it is in a position to influence, if not determine, government policy. Control of the policy-making posts is one of the most powerful tools a political party can wield. (It is most powerful, we should note, in parliamentary democracies like Great Britain, where political advancement depends on party loyalty, and weakest in the United States, where party leaders have little control over political advancement.) Too much can be made of this weakness, however. Most American politicians do want, and for financial purposes, generally need the support of their party when they run for office. A congressman would much rather remain in the good graces of his party's leadership, for party backing is important in marshalling support for legislation, and it is the leaders who bestow good committee assignments and bad. American

[5] One of the best introductions to Chinese government and politics is O. Edmund Clubb, *Twentieth Century China* (New York: Columbia University Press, 1964). The opening chapters of John King Fairbank's *The United States and China* (New York: Viking, 1958) are also useful for an account of Communist China's handling of traditional social institutions.

lawmakers usually go along with their party until an issue comes up in which conscience or regional needs are more persuasive.[6]

Other Roles. Besides their primary political endeavors, many parties participate in community activities outside the political arena. European parties sponsor boy scout troops, youth recreation centers, senior citizen social clubs, adult education programs, and even health and life insurance plans. Such activities, it is hoped, will indirectly build up party loyalties which can be translated into votes on election day. Although American parties are rarely so involved in the lives of their constituents, they, too, have traditionally attempted to woo voters in a number of indirect ways. Nineteenth-century New York's infamous Tammany Hall served as a welcome wagon for European immigrants.[7] Political workers greeted new arrivals at the docks, helped them find housing and jobs, saw to it that they received proper medical attention, and attended to funeral arrangements for bereaved families. As the times changed, the parties changed with them. In recent years, American parties have organized urban and suburban "clubs" which appeal to the social and intellectual needs of professionals and white-collar workers.[8]

Parties help keep the political process running smoothly in other ways as well. They provide a training ground for future political leaders by allowing inexperienced politicians to hold minor party offices and learn the workings of the political system. They modify conflict by organizing diverse interests under one political umbrella, especially in systems such as ours, where each party covers a broad spectrum of ideologies. And by endorsing candidates for office and taking stands on political issues, the parties define and simplify the issues for the electorate while actively seeking solutions to the problems facing the nation. In England, for example, the Labour party actively championed the welfare state and was instrumental in bringing about socialized medicine and the widespread nationalization of British heavy industry. So successful were the Labourites in achieving their goals that the Conservatives were unable to reverse the decision.

In championing so controversial an issue, the British Labour party went out on a political limb where American parties are seldom found. In the United States, the parties rarely take a stand on a politically volatile issue.

[6] In the United States it has become apparent that in recent years southern Democratic congressmen have been voting less and less often with their fellow nonsouthern Democrats. See W. Wayne Shannon, "Revolt in Washington: The South in Congress," in William C. Havard, ed., *The Changing Policies of The South* (Baton Rouge: Louisiana State University Press, 1972).

[7] Examples of classic works on city machines in the United States include Charles Van Devander, *The Big Bosses* (New York: Crown Publishers, 1944) and Harold Zink, *City Bosses in the United States* (Durham, N.C.: Duke University Press, 1950). An account of a contemporary city machine in Chicago is given by Andrew M. Greeley, "Take Heart from the Heartland," *The New Republic* 163 (December 12, 1970): 16–19.

[8] Fred I. Greenstein, "The Changing Pattern of Urban Party Politics," *American Academy of Political and Social Science* 353 (May 1964): 1–13.

Instead, they seek moderate, compromising positions which will appeal to a broad majority of voters. Some critics of the American party system argue that in this way the parties shirk their political responsibilities.[9] Far better, to their way of thinking, are the parliamentary systems, especially that of England, which is often held up as the model of the responsible party system.

How Party Roles Differ in Presidential Democracies and Parliamentary Democracies

In democratic nations, each party theoretically draws up a platform, nominates candidates who will support it, seeks an electoral mandate and, if victorious, carries out its program. In evaluating the extent of these party responsibilities in the United States and elsewhere, two major factors must be considered: the degree of centralization in the party's organization and the extent to which a party actively participates in forming government policy.

Centralization.   The control party leadership can exert on its elected members varies widely among democratic systems. At one extreme is Israel, whose highly centralized system of candidate selection calls for each party to draw up a national list of nominees to the Parliament, or Knesset. Since Israel's system of elections uses proportional representation (described in Chapter 13), 120 candidates are nominated, but only the first 30 or 40 names on the ballot can be expected to win. Party leaders can easily condemn maverick candidates to political exile by relegating them to such a low place on the party list that they cannot be elected.

The British party system is not quite as centralized as Israel's, but its control is still quite effective.[10] Conservatives and Labourites select their parliamentary candidates on the local level, but the national party organization has the power to veto these candidates and deny them the party's backing. The Conservatives haven't used their veto power since the end of World War II; the Labourites vetoed five candidates in 1948–49. (The five mavericks ran anyway, as independents, but all were resoundingly defeated.) In addition, the British parties also have the power to force a candidate to

---

[9] The leading advocate of the idea that America does not, but should have, a more responsible party government is E. E. Schattschneider, who presents his arguments in *Party Government*. See also David S. Broder, *The Party's Over* (New York: Harper & Row, 1971) and John S. Saloma and Frederick H. Sontag, *Parties: The Real Opportunity for Effective Citizen Politics* (New York: Alfred A. Knopf, 1972). For a defense of the American party system as it is constituted see Pendleton Herring, *The Politics of Democracy: American Parties in Action* (New York: W. W. Norton, 1965). A convenient summary of the debate on whether or not America has a responsible party government is offered by Sorauf in *Political Parties in the American System*, Chapter 7.

[10] For a good comparison of American and British party systems, see Austin Ranney, *Pathways to Parliament* (Madison: University of Wisconsin Press, 1965).

run in an opposition party stronghold district, where he will most likely be defeated. Once elected, party members are still well advised to stay on good terms with party leadership, who bestow all assignments—good and bad. The degree of centralization any party can command is directly proportional to its power over a candidate's political career. Where candidates are dependent on party backing, they must toe the party line. This is not the case in the highly decentralized American party system.

In American political parties, the central organization has relatively little control over the actions of individual politicians. For the most part, congressional candidates are nominated by the rank-and-file in direct primary elections rather than by the party bosses. And while it is helpful for them to run with national party backing, such support is not vital. Franklin Delano Roosevelt's 1938 attempt to purge anti-New Dealers from the Democratic ranks ended in a fiasco. Out of all the Democratic incumbents whom F.D.R. actively campaigned against, only one—a New York City congressman— failed to win reelection. Most powerful senators and congressmen often have strong political organizations of their own at the state and local level which in no way depend on the support of national party leadership. The parties cannot consistently stop maverick candidates from winning elections. They can only hope to weaken the impact of their electoral campaign by withholding official endorsement.

Dictating Government Policy. One key to responsible party government is the extent to which the majority party can enact its legislative program. Here, the American party system is liable to its severest criticism from advocates of strong parties. In England and many other Western European democracies, the majority party must resign when it can no longer muster the votes to carry on its legislative program. In contrast, the problem in the United States is often one of identifying exactly where the majority lies. After all, is the platform of the presidential campaign binding on the members of the president's party in Congress? What if the party of the president is not the majority party in one or both houses? Furthermore, just what is and who determines the legislative program of a party that may control Congress, yet has no central leader like the president? Does Hubert Humphrey, George McGovern, George Wallace, or Edward Kennedy speak for the national Democratic party? Or, does the elected congressional leadership in each house of Congress have the right to speak for their party members when they are not represented in the White House? These are just some of the complex questions that must be answered if we are to determine the jurisdiction of the party program in the United States.

We can say, finally, that the legislative program is initiated centrally, with the president.[11] But it must be acted upon by various majorities within

[11] Samuel P. Huntington, "Congressional Responses to the Twentieth Century" in David B. Truman, ed., *The Congress and America's Future* (Englewood Cliffs, N.J.: Prentice-Hall, 1965).

the House and Senate, and by the 535 individual senators and congressmen, each of whom is ultimately responsible for his own vote, as he is for his own reelection. Is the president, then, to be blamed for failing to fulfill campaign promises, or does the fault lie rather with a party discipline that is too loose? Political critic E. E. Schattschneider argues that because our national parties are so decentralized, not one of them can agree on a strong national platform, and the result is that the American government is "a punching bag for every special and local interest in the nation." [12] But, on the other hand, many of us would prefer our senators and congressmen to vote according to their consciences rather than the dictates of a more distant party leadership.

Party Participation in Government.   True, a parliamentary system of government is more conducive to what Schattschneider regards as responsible party government than the American federal system. Our system, with its rigid set of checks and balances, can make it difficult for parties to bridge the separation of powers in order to enact platforms. But this is not entirely the fault of the American party system. It is inherent in the constitutional separation of powers between the executive and legislative branches. When the same party controls both the White House and Congress, a more substantial portion of the party platform stands a chance of becoming law. The 1965–66 Democratic Congress, under the presidency of Lyndon Johnson, enacted more than fifty major pieces of legislation. Among them were the nation's first auto safety standards act, Medicare, the Model Cities Program, and the Economic Opportunity Act. Granted that President Johnson had an almost unsurpassed way with Congress, but few European parliaments have passed so many sweeping social and economic reforms.

European parties, like European society historically, are generally organized on the basis of well-defined class or ideological lines. This, in itself, makes for a high degree of party centralization, because the party's members are already united in their basic political outlook. In the United States, such divisions have never been so distinct, and the American parties reflect this tradition. The parties are broad-based organizations that try to consolidate voters behind a platform that offers something to virtually everyone. This consolidation of interests helps preserve the American party system. By giving all vested interests hope that at least some of their demands will be met, the major parties retard the growth of narrow, special interest parties which could fragment American politics. The decentralized party system has adapted itself to America's heterogeneous society, and the parliamentary democracies of England and Western Europe serve their countries effectively too. The roles of a political party vary with a nation's political culture—the way a society views the political process and sees its particular place in the system. Nowhere does this become clearer than when we look at the role of the party in a Communist state.

[12] Schattschneider, *Party Government*, p. 209.

The Role of the Party in a Totalitarian State

The concept of "loyal opposition" is alien to Communist politics. While democratic systems acknowledge the right of differing political groups to try to alter the course of the nation, Communist systems claim that they already know the outcome of history. The party's job is not to question government policy, but to govern; its ultimate goal is not to gain control of the policy-making machinery, but to guide society from capitalism through socialism and into the classless society.

The Communist party in the Soviet Union almost has the quality of a fundamentalist religious order.[13] Unlike Western democratic parties, it offers a total and all-encompassing explanation of human history in the class struggle, and an equally dogmatic analysis of social evolution in dialectical materialism. The hierarchy of the party interprets Marxist-Leninist thought and applies it to whatever sociopolitical or economic crisis that might arise. The party's cadres go out among the people to enlist their support for the party's policies. Since the party leadership maintains absolute control over every aspect of government, there is a nearly absolute parallel between the structure of government and the party. In effect, the Soviet Communist party is a state within a state and a government within a government.[14]

USSR Communist Party Structure. In the Soviet Union, every level of government has its corresponding party organization. At the local level, each unit of government is controlled by a *soviet*—a legislative body whose members are elected by the people. For every soviet, there is a Communist party cell that nominates all candidates to local government. Higher up, the Supreme Soviet (the national legislature and, according to the 1936 constitution, the highest organ of the state) elects the members of the Presidium (an executive council that governs when the Supreme Soviet is not in session), and theoretically supervises the Council of Ministers, which is equivalent to a Western cabinet. But, corresponding to the Supreme Soviet is the Central Committee of the Communist party which dominates the Supreme Soviet (see Figure 11-1). The Central Committee is theoretically the highest Tribunal within the Soviet Communist party. Its members are elected by local, district, and regional party cells, and supposedly represent the will of the

---

[13] See Chapter 5's discussion; also, the analogy drawn in Thomas Ford Hoult, *The Sociology of Religion* (New York: Holt, Rinehart and Winston, 1958), p. 31.

[14] This may well be an artifact of all totalitarian Communist systems. See the argument given by Milovan Djilas, *The New Class: An Analysis of the Communist* (New York: Praeger Publishers, 1957); also his *Conversations with Stalin* (New York: Harcourt, Brace & World, Inc., 1962). Good accounts of the workings of the Russian Communist party and the Soviet government are John A. Armstrong, *Ideology, Politics, and Government in the Soviet Union* (New York: Praeger Publishers, 1967); Merle Fainsod, *How Russia is Ruled* (Cambridge, Mass.: Harvard University Press, 1963); and John A. Armstrong, *The Politics of Totalitarianism* (New York: Random House, 1961). On China, see A. Doak Barnett, *Cadres, Bureaucracy and Political Power in Communist China* (New York: Columbia University Press, 1967).

THEORY

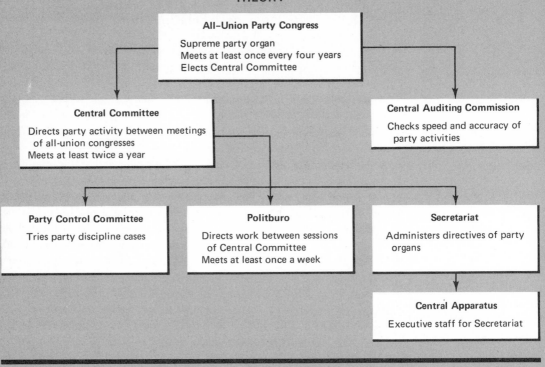

All–Union Party Congress

Supreme party organ
Meets at least once every four years
Elects Central Committee

Central Committee

Directs party activity between meetings
of all-union congresses
Meets at least twice a year

Central Auditing Commission

Checks speed and accuracy of
party activities

Party Control Committee

Tries party discipline cases

Politburo

Directs work between sessions
of Central Committee
Meets at least once a week

Secretariat

Administers directives of party
organs

Central Apparatus

Executive staff for Secretariat

PRACTICE

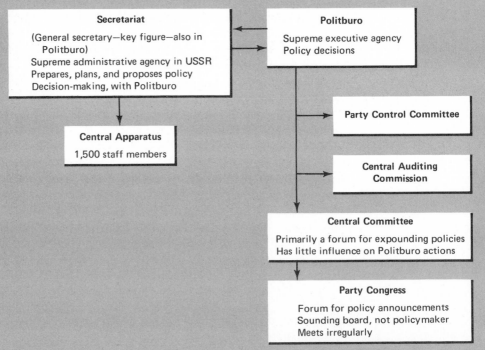

Secretariat

(General secretary—key figure—also in
Politburo)
Supreme administrative agency in USSR
Prepares, plans, and proposes policy
Decision-making, with Politburo

Politburo

Supreme executive agency
Policy decisions

Central Apparatus

1,500 staff members

Party Control Committee

**Central Auditing
Commission**

Central Committee

Primarily a forum for expounding policies
Has little influence on Politburo actions

Party Congress

Forum for policy announcements
Sounding board, not policymaker
Meets irregularly

Source: Gwendolyn M. Carter and John H. Herz, Major Foreign Powers, 6th ed. (New York: Harcourt Brace Jovanovich, 1972), p. 580.

Figure 11-1
Organization of the Communist Party in the Soviet Union: Theory and Practice

party's members. In practice, the Central Committee is normally a rather docile body which delegates most of its real authority to the Secretariat. (Corresponding to the Soviet Presidium, the Secretariat handles party affairs when the Central Committee is not in session.) And the Secretariat, in turn, is dominated by the Politburo, a body of approximately fifteen members, some of whom also serve on the Council of Ministers. While they may technically be referred further up, to the Central Committee, policy disagreements are normally confined to the Politburo. The various levels of the Communist party bureaucracy as well as the local cells are required to follow the policies of the Politburo, so that the entire Soviet Union is effectively governed by an oligarchy of approximately fifteen men. The Communist party bolsters and reinforces the state power, and its high degree of centralization is unmatched in any major Western political party.

Communist Party Membership. Communist parties, not only in totalitarian states but around the world, do not encourage mass membership for several important reasons. In the first place, party discipline decreases in direct proportion to growth in membership: ten thousand people are easier to control than a million. Moreover, they do not want inactive or rebellious members and periodically purge the party ranks of dead wood. Membership requirements are far more rigid than in Western political parties, and, once admitted, the party member must work hard.[15] He is responsible for turning out the vote in his area, explaining government policies to his fellow workers, and enlisting their support for those policies. Rather than seeking to change government policy, the loyal Communist party worker's job is to sell his fellow citizens on the leadership's policies.

Fascist Parties. Mussolini's Italian Fascist party and Hitler's Nazi party resembled the Communist party quite closely in organization. Like the Communists, the Fascists and Nazis had a highly centralized, elite party, and no political opposition was permitted. Both had youth organizations in order to recruit future party leaders, both conducted periodic purges to eliminate unreliable members, and both used secret police. Today, neo-Fascist and neo-Nazi parties still function in Italy and Germany. But they are small and unlikely ever to win control of their country's governments.[16]

The fundamental difference between the party system of a democratic nation and that of a Communist or Fascist state is obvious: the former allows parties to compete for political power, the latter doesn't. But, among democratic nations, party systems differ widely, according to the number of parties that compete in elections and the degree of competitiveness among them.

15 For more information, see the discussion later in this chapter.
16 See A. James Gregor, *The Ideology of Fascism* (New York: Free Press, 1969); and S. J. Woolf, ed., *The Nature of Fascism* (New York: Random House, 1969).

Classifying Party Systems

When we think of a democracy, we generally think of the Democratic-Republican system familiar to us. But the two-party system is actually in the minority among democratic nations. In general, the Western European democracies are multiparty states where from six to ten political parties may compete for power. At the other extreme are the one-party states. One easy way of categorizing party systems is by the number of active parties in a nation.

By Number of Parties

The One-party System. The one-party system, generally associated with totalitarian regimes of the left or right, is a twentieth-century phenomenon. The Soviet Union, the People's Republic of China, Spain, Greece, and about one-quarter of the emerging nations of Africa and Asia are one-party states.[17] All are characterized by a single party that controls every level of government, and is the only party legally allowed in the country.

The "people's democracies" of Eastern Europe are not, technically, one-party systems. Communist Poland, for example, has three legal political parties joined in a permanent national front. But the seats in the Sejm (parliament) are so divided that the Communists are assured a majority. The Polish Communists tolerate the other two parties, and Polish election laws do permit a certain degree of competition among individual candidates. But, since the Polish voter can only choose between candidates but not among parties, his franchise is essentially meaningless.[18]

---

[17] For a general discussion of the monoparty system see Samuel P. Huntington and Clement H. Moore, eds., *Authoritarian Politics in Modern Society: The Dynamics of Established One-Party Systems* (New York: Basic Books, 1970); and Carl J. Friedrich and Z. K. Brzezinski, *Totalitarian Dictatorship and Autocracy*, rev. ed. (Cambridge, Mass.: Harvard University Press, 1965). For the monoparty systems of the emerging nations see Gwendolen Carter, ed., *African One-Party States* (Ithaca, N.Y.: Cornell University Press, 1962); Aristide R. Zolberg, *Creating Political Order: The Party States of West Africa* (Skokie, Ill.: Rand McNally, 1966); Fred R. von der Mehden, *Politics of the Developing Nations* (Englewood Cliffs, N.J.: Prentice-Hall, 1964); and Rupert Emerson, *Political Modernization: The Single Party System* (Denver: University of Denver Press, 1963).
[18] The following works by Jerzy P. Wiatr are illuminating: "One-Party Systems: The Concept and Issue for Comparative Studies," in Erik Allardt and Yrgö Littunen, eds., *Cleavages, Ideologies and Party Systems* (Helsinki: Academy Bookstore, 1964), pp. 281–90; "Elections and Voting Behavior in Poland," in Austin Ranney, ed., *Essays on the Behavioral Study of Politics* (Urbana: University of Illinois Press, 1962), pp. 235–51; "The Hegemonic Party System in Poland," in Erik Allardt and Stein Rokkan, eds., *Studies in Political Sociology* (New York: The Free Press, 1969); and "Political Parties, Interest Representation, and Economic Development in Poland," *American Political Science Review* 69 (December 1970): 1239–45. See also, Jean L. Smith, *Germany Beyond the Wall* (Boston: Little, Brown, 1969), Chapter 9; and Andrew Gyorgy, "Satellite Parties in Eastern Europe," in Neumann, *Modern Political Parties*, pp. 284–301.

The Dominant-party System. The American South since the Civil War has until recently been the closest facsimile to a one-party system that America has had to offer. Eleven states in the American South were traditional Democratic strongholds: in these states, for many years, the Republicans were often so weak that they didn't even bother to run candidates for office.[19] Likewise, Republicans traditionally controlled much of New England and the midwestern farmbelt. It was rare for the Democrats to capture control of major state offices in these areas, and when they did they were rarely reelected.[20] But, a crucial factor separates these dominant-party systems, and their counterparts in Great Britain and France, from true one-party states: opposition parties in dominant-party systems are free to contest elections.

The dominant-party systems in the United States, Great Britain, and France exist only at the local or regional level. But some democratic nations, including India and Mexico, have dominant-party systems at the national level as well. Since winning independence in 1947, India has been governed solely by the Congress party, most recently under the leadership of Indira Gandhi. The party has consistently won three-quarters of the seats in the parliament, and has always held executive power. Although the Congress party is regularly opposed by parties advocating a variety of interests, the opposition is so disorganized that they haven't yet won a national election and have had to be content with scattered local victories. The Congress party's domination of the Indian national government is as complete as the Communist party's in Poland, but India is still a democratic state. Mexico has four major political parties, but here, too, one party—the Party of Revolutionary Institutions (PRI)—invariably wins 80 percent of the Congress and has never lost a presidential election.[21]

The Two-party System. Most familiar to us is the two-party system which, surprisingly, does not exist outside the English-speaking world. The term itself needs some qualification. The United States, England, Australia, and New Zealand all have one or more third parties. The English Liberal party and George Wallace's American Independent party of 1968 are good examples. But these parties are so small that they rarely have a controlling influence on overall government policy, leaving the two major parties with a fairly equal chance of winning. Governor Wallace received almost ten

[19] The classic study of the dominant party structure in the South is V. O. Key, Jr., *Southern Politics: In State and Nation* (New York: Alfred A. Knopf, 1949). Of course, the system has undergone a considerable change since then, and in the 1972 elections, President Nixon, a Republican, carried every southern state, and most by a considerable margin.
[20] See Duane Lockard, *New England State Politics* (Princeton, N.J.: Princeton University Press, 1959); and John H. Fenton, *Midwest Politics* (New York: Holt, Rinehart and Winston, 1966).
[21] Myron Weiner, *Party Politics in India* (Princeton, N.J.: Princeton University Press, 1957); and Robert E. Scott, *Mexican Government in Transition* (Urbana: University of Illinois Press, 1959).

million votes in the 1968 presidential election, but this was far from enough to even come close to an electoral victory. The impact of the Wallace movement on public policy, although indirect, has been quite noticeable, however, especially in the area of civil rights. Many believe that his strong showing among voters has had a strong impact on the federal government's school desegregation policy in the area of school busing.[22]

The Multiparty System. On the other end of the continuum from one-party nations are those with several competing parties. Often, this system is criticized as being unstable. The Fourth French Republic and the current coalition government of Italy are prime examples of the shortcomings of having many parties, as each has been unable to keep any government in power for more than a few months at a time. But while it is usually true that the existence of many political parties makes it harder for any one party to win a governing majority, this is not always the case. Since 1958, the Gaullist Union for the New Republic (UNR) has held a majority of seats in the French National Assembly against a badly splintered array of opposition parties. And in West Germany, the Christian Democrats or the Social Democrats usually come so close to winning a majority that they are able to form effective governments in alliance with one of the many smaller parties, usually the Free Democratic party (FDP). Despite these exceptions, multiparty systems generally do produce coalition governments. But these governments are not necessarily unstable.

The Netherlands has five major parties, none of which commands more than a third of the national vote. Yet, the Dutch government has been remarkably stable for a good reason: before a government is organized, the elected parties enter into prolonged periods of negotiations in which compromises are made that satisfy all the major factions. In Israel and Finland, stable coalition governments are formed in a similar way. The smaller parties in these nations represent narrow economic, ethnic, or religious interests rather than broad coalitions, but they are willing to enter into alliances with other parties that are flexible enough to see that these narrow interests are protected. Is a system where many parties compete for control of government preferable to our two-party system? Many political scientists think that the multiparty system is better adapted to the needs of a modern, industrial state than the two-party system, such as ours, which must necessarily gloss over the more fundamental differences among voters in order to gain the broad support needed to win an election.[23]

[22] Reg Murphy and Hal Gulliver carry the argument further, holding that Wallace's impact has been to slow down the enactment and enforcement of all civil rights laws. See *The Southern Strategy* (New York: Charles Scribner's Sons, 1971).

[23] George van den Bergh's *Unity in Diversity* (London: B. T. Batsford, 1955), pp. 35ff offers a good description and defense of the Dutch political system. Also interesting are Dankwart A. Rustow, *The Politics of Compromise* (Princeton, N.J.: Princeton University Press, 1955); and Amitai Etzioni, "Alternative Ways to Democracy," *Political Science Quarterly* 74 (June 1959): 196–214.

It is apparent that party systems can easily be classified according to how many parties thrive in one nation. But this method of grouping party systems into types is too general to be able to provide useful categories for political scientists. It tells us little about the varying degree of competitiveness among parties or, in the case of noncompetitive systems, the extent to which the party in power controls its society. Thus, in recent years, more sophisticated classification schemes have been devised which are able to delineate more precisely the differences among major party systems.

Competitive or Noncompetitive Party Systems

All noncompetitive party systems are repressive by democratic standards, as we consider the lack of choice among parties an abrogation of our political freedom. But, some one-party systems are more repressive than others. According to political scientists Joseph La Palombara and Myron Weiner,[24] noncompetitive party systems can be grouped into three distinct types: authoritarian, totalitarian, and pluralistic. Authoritarian describes countries like Franco's Spain, while totalitarian describes countries like Communist China and the Soviet Union. The difference between the two categories is the extent to which the party in power exercises its control. In the Soviet Union, the Communist party pervades every aspect of society. Franco's Falangists primarily dominate the government, leaving other institutions, like the Roman Catholic church, to exercise authority over their own respective social spheres. The third type, the pluralistic one-party system refers to nations like Mexico, where opposition parties are tolerated but completely overwhelmed by the dominant party. The Partido Revolucionario Institucional (PRI) in Mexico is regularly sniped at by parties of both the right and the left, but it still maintains control of the Presidency and the Congress.

LaPalombara and Weiner also developed a classification scheme for competitive party systems, and this has been further refined by political scientists Ronald McDonald and Douglas Rae.[25] Their scheme classifies party systems according to the number of parties having access to legislative power. McDonald and Rae consider the United States and Great Britain competitive two-party states, because access to the legislative branch is balanced. Each of the two major political parties receives at least 40 percent, but not more

---

[24] Joseph LaPalombara and Myron Weiner, "The Origin and Development of Political Parties," in LaPalombara and Weiner, *Political Parties and Political Development.*

[25] Ronald H. McDonald, "Electoral Systems, Party Representation, and Political Change in Latin America," *Western Political Quarterly* 20 (September 1967): 694–708; and Douglas W. Rae, *The Political Consequences of Electoral Laws* (New Haven, Conn.: Yale University Press, 1967), pp. 53–58; and "A Note on the Fractionalization of Some European Party Systems," *Comparative Political Studies* 1 (October 1968): 417. A convenient summary of classification systems is offered by David G. Pfeifer, "The Measurement of Inter-Party Competition and Systematic Stability," *American Political Science Review* 61 (June 1967): 457–67.

than 60 percent, of the seats in the legislature, and neither is strong enough to permanently dominate the other. In contrast, India under Indira Gandhi, and France under Charles de Gaulle are examples of dominant one-party states. Both the Congress party and the UNR consistently won at least 60 percent of the legislative seats and were the only parties in their respective nations that could reasonably expect to form a government. However, in both nations, the major party could conceivably lose its hold over voters to one of the opposition parties.

In the third broad grouping of types of party systems are the "multiple-party dominant" and the "multiparty loose" systems. In the former, three or more political parties compete, but one receives at least 40 percent of the vote. The dominant party usually allies itself with one or two smaller parties whose only hope for a share of power is to trade off their legislative votes for cabinet posts. The "loose" system has three or more parties, and as one would guess from the name, none receives even a 40 percent mandate. Especially in the years before 1967, Israel provided a good example of this type of party system. Here, two or three parties had to agree to join a coalition before a government could be formed. (Today, though the coalition system is still used, the Mapai Party is in such firm control that the system is more "dominant" than "loose.")

The Index of Fractionalization

In baseball, a team's standing in the league is based solely on its wins and losses. The team in first place is the team that wins the most games, whether those games have been won by one run or ten. But winning isn't everything in politics. Here, the margin of victory affects the degree to which a party can influence government policy. And these margins vary widely among party sytems. To measure objectively the varying degrees of competitiveness in major party systems, Douglas Rae has devised an index of fractionalization based on two factors: the number of political parties receiving shares of the popular vote and legislative seats; and the equality (or inequality) of the shares.[26] A one-party state such as the Soviet Union, where the Communist party receives a unanimous electoral mandate and all legislative seats, has an index score of 0.00; a two-party state in which votes and seats are split evenly down the middle would earn an index of 0.50; and if the ten parties in Israel were to divide the nation's votes evenly, the state would have an index of 0.90. In all, Rae studied twenty Western democratic nations, and arrived at the figures shown in Table 11-1.

Of all the democratic systems Rae studied, the English-speaking nations showed the least political fractionalization, which is in keeping with their tendency toward two-party systems. But, although it is tempting to make

[26] Rae, "A Note on the Fractionalization of Some European Party Systems," pp. 413–418.

Table 11-1
Index of Fractional-
ization for Twenty
Western Demo-
cratic Party
Systems, 1945–
1964

Nations [a]	Mean Fractionalization (shares of popular vote)	Mean Fractionalization (shares of legislative seats)
United States	0.50	0.48
New Zealand	0.54	0.49
Australia	0.56	0.49
Great Britain	0.58	0.52
Austria	0.61	0.56
Canada	0.66	0.62
Belgium	0.67	0.62
Luxembourg	0.70	0.66
Ireland	0.70	0.67
Sweden	0.70	0.68
Norway	0.73	0.67
West Germany	0.73	0.69
Iceland	0.73	0.71
Italy	0.74	0.71
Denmark	0.75	0.74
The Netherlands	0.78	0.77
France	0.81	0.77
Finland	0.81	0.78
Switzerland	0.81	0.79
Israel	0.81	0.80

[a] Ranked in order of increasing fractionalization.

Source: Douglas W. Rae, "A Note on the Fractionalization of Some European Party Systems," *Comparative Political Studies* 1 (October 1968): 417, Table 2.

generalizations from Rae's chart, there is no proven connection between the number of parties in a country and the degree of stability of its government. Israel, the most highly fractionalized of the twenty nations on our table, has effective political leadership. What are the correlates of stable, representative government? Why are some party systems competitive, while others are not?

Factors Affecting the Type of Party System

In the United States, we can count on a major Republican-Democratic battle every four years, while only one party dominates Mexican politics. Italy is plagued by a series of short-lived coalition governments, while England is stable. Much of the difference between party systems in various nations can be traced to the political culture, which is reflected in every country in the system of government. The party system, too, reflects a nation's culture—its history, its socioeconomic divisions, the number of ethnic and religious groups coexisting under the same government, and the sharpness of divisions between these groups.

Political Cleavages. All men may be created equal, but their beliefs and aspirations differ widely. An individual may be black or white, rich or poor, trusting or skeptical, doomed to his station in life or free to rise above it. These differences among people lead to divisions, or cleavages, within a society. How do these divisions influence political behavior? Douglas Rae and Michael Taylor have attempted to measure the relationship between a nation's social makeup and its party system.[27] As they see it, divisions in society stem from three kinds of criteria: traits such as race, religion, or ethnic identity; attitudes or opinions such as class bias, ideological commitment, or political preference; and roles, including occupation, or club membership. Societies with a high degree of social mobility, like the United States, have a relatively low degree of political division. These nations are mostly two-party systems, and practice consensus politics, whereby one of the two major parties is able to satisfy at least some of the demands of every significant social group. On the other hand, nations such as India and Israel, which are divided along caste, ethnic, and language lines, have sharp political cleavages. The political systems of these two nations, reflecting these divisions, abound with single-interest parties that appeal to only an isolated segment of the voters.

While Rae and Taylor's classification scheme provides a useful perspective for studying party systems, there are many exceptions—and cleavages themselves are often imprecise. For instance, some groups may be divided on one issue, only to be united on another. A Protestant group may oppose the Roman Catholic church on abortion reform, but support it on the question of increased old-age benefits. This degree of overlap indicates the extent to which the portion of people in favor of a given issue is the same as the portion opposing that same issue. Clearly, the greater the degree of overlap, the more stable a nation's political system will be, since the people will have more common interests. The greater the intensity of fragmentation, however, the more unstable the political system seems to become, for social divisions may grow so great that they cannot be bridged by a single government.

Ideology. The philosophical differences which have existed historically among many Western European parties appear to be on the decline.[28] In West Germany, for example, the Social Democrats are addressing themselves more to current issues than ideologies, more to policies than political doctrines. But European political systems have traditionally been described in ideological terms, and in many ways this is still the best explanation of

---

[27] Douglas W. Rae and Michael Taylor, *The Analysis of Political Cleavages* (New Haven, Conn.: Yale University Press, 1970).
[28] Epstein, *Political Parties in Western Democracies*, p. 287.

European political behavior.[29] With a few exceptions, European parties are committed to fairly rigid ideologies, which appeal to narrow rather than broad interests. Few parties are able to achieve government control alone, because their base of support is too narrow.

The Social Democrats and Christian Democrats in West Germany, and the Conservatives and Labourites in Great Britain are far more flexible. Like the Democrats and Republicans in America, they are "broker" or consensus parties that draw their leadership and support from several groups and play down their ideological differences. They all support the existing form of government. Their differences are largely over the means of achieving their goals rather than the goals themselves. The flexibility of these parties has been a major factor in producing political stability in England and Germany.[30]

The Electoral System. Party systems are influenced by a nation's electoral system as well as its cultural environment.[31] Electoral districts in which the one winning candidate must receive a majority of the votes favor the development of a two-party system; districts that elect more than one candidate tend to encourage the development of more political parties. Even small parties with a scattered national following can expect to capture at least a few legislative vacancies in proportional-representation systems, because seats are apportioned according to each party's percentage of the total popular vote. Since this system can result in a legislative amalgam where many parties have little control, coalition governments are often formed.

Although the electoral system can have much to do with a nation's party system, there are no hard-and-fast rules regarding the relationship between the two. The abolition of proportional representation in France has not given rise to a two-party system, and the multimember system used in many state and local elections in the United States (United States senators are elected from multimember districts) has never resulted in a proliferation of third parties.

Political parties differ from each other as much as the party systems in which they flourish. In addition to varying in ideologies and policies, they also differ in their organizational structures.

Types of Political Parties

One of the first political scientists to formulate a scheme for classifying political parties was Maurice Duverger. His relatively simple scheme put all political parties into one of three descriptive categories: mass, cadre, or

[29] A good discussion of ideologies is presented in Lyman T. Sargent, *Contemporary Political Ideologies*, 2nd ed. (Homewood, Ill.: The Dorsey Press, 1972).
[30] Anthony Downs maintains that in a democracy the logic of the system is such that "parties formulate policies in order to win elections, rather than win elections in order to formulate policies." *An Economic Theory of Democracy*, p. 28.
[31] See Chapter 13 for a more thorough description of electoral systems.

devotee. The mass parties include the Western democratic parties which vie for members by attempting to cut across social-class lines, and which seek the largest membership possible. European parties, while not as broadly based as the Anglo-American parties, are still mass parties because their membership is open. In contrast, cadre parties, like the Russian Communist party and India's Congress party, draw their support from the politically active elite. Generally asociated with totalitarian or developing nations, cadre parties have highly centralized organizations and expect the elite group which comprises their membership to be very active within the party. Duverger uses the term *devotee* for parties such as the Nazis under Hitler, where the party's formal structure is built around one man. This type of organization makes the leader as important as the philosophy he personifies.[32]

Maurice Duverger's system is useful for making some distinctions, but falls short in many instances. For example, how could Duverger explain the difference between the Democrats in the United States and the Mapai in Israel? Each is a mass party, but party leadership nominates Mapai candidates, while rank-and-file Democrats have the most powerful voice in the selection of party nominees. Because of the shortcomings of Duverger's classification scheme, political scientists Kenneth Janda and Fred Riggs have devised another way of categorizing party systems.[33] They label parties according to the ways they recruit members, raise funds, and make nominations. The Mapai party is leader-oriented because the party leadership alone nominates candidates. A party financed by members' dues is member-oriented, but if most of the support comes from private donors the party is interest-oriented. In all, Janda and Riggs have developed fifteen categories based on the variations and similarities in the internal structure of parties. But again, this classification scheme is imperfect because it fails to take into account variations in the ideology or the type of people who make up a party's membership. Political scientists Richard Rose and Derek Urwin do just this, categorizing parties according to whether the bulk of their membership is religious or anti-clerical; blue-collar or middle-class; united by race and ethnic identity, or mixed.[34] The numerous Christian Democratic parties in Western Europe are primarily Roman Catholic. The anti-clerical Italian Republicans and the Liberal Socialist parties draw their support from people who object to the alleged power of the church. Democratic Socialist parties have mostly trade union members and other wage earners; other parties are predominantly upper middle-class. Parties that are united by racial or ethnic identity are relatively rare in the Western world, but quite common

[32] Duverger, *Political Parties*, pp. 64–70.
[33] Kenneth Janda, "Retrieving Information for a Comparative Study of Political Parties," in William J. Crotty, ed., *Approaches to the Study of Party Organizations* (Boston: Allyn and Bacon, 1968), pp. 159–216; and Fred W. Riggs, "Comparative Politics and the Study of Political Parties: A Structural Approach," also in Crotty, pp. 45–104.
[34] Richard Rose and Derek Urwin, "Social Cohesion, Political Parties, and Strains in Regimes," *Comparative Political Studies* 2 (August 1969): 7–67.

in Asia and Africa. Mixed parties such as the Democratic and Republican parties in the United States cut across religious, social, and ethnic lines to draw at least some support from every significant group.

Broad Criteria for Party Categories

Political parties, evidently, can be classified in an almost unlimited number of ways. But, combining the three systems we discussed, we see that parties can be categorized according to four broad criteria:

Who Supports the Party? Broad-based parties such as the Democratic and Republican parties combine the political demands of different, and often antagonistic, parts of society. Narrow-interest parties, in contrast, articulate the interests of a single group. Parties that draw from all parts of society stand the best chance of winning control of a stable government, because their political appeal is as broad as the community itself. Generally speaking, narrow-interest parties do not have enough support to win power, unallied, through the democratic process. To win control of the government, they must either enter into coalitions or seize power by force.

What is the Party's Membership Policy? Political parties are either "open" or "closed" in their membership requirements. Broad-based parties generally have their doors open to anyone who wishes to join, while elitist parties operate more like an exclusive country club. They carefully screen prospective members, and in some cases require them to complete a lengthy period of apprenticeship. Some Democratic parties are technically open to anyone, but closed by virtue of their narrow appeal. A Belgian Jew, for example, would be unlikely to join with the Christian Democrats, even though he is free to become a member.

How Are Candidates Chosen? The way in which candidates are chosen varies so widely that meaningful distinctions are difficult. Broad-based parties generally give members the most voice in selecting nominees for office. This doesn't mean that political conventions are totally open, but rather that the party members have some say in who will run on the ticket. Where membership is exclusively one class, candidate selection is solely in the hands of the party hierarchy. Narrow-interest parties allow members to nominate candidates who are antagonistic to party leadership by petition. But these independent candidates rarely get elected, so the the party manages to keep a high degree of centralized control.

What Are the Party's Goals? The parties we are familiar with are concerned primarily with winning office and control of government. However, third parties such as the Liberal party in England or George Wallace's American Independent party in the United States realize the unlikelihood of their gaining legislative control, and have different goals. Their main concern is to "send a message" to the nation and influence public opinion. They exist to articulate a specific opinion and to see that this interest is protected by trading their political support for legislative favors. Finally, revolutionary parties, like the Communist party, are concerned with teaching the people a way of life, and use government power to change existing norms and established institutions. Their goal is to create a utopian society by employing the power of the state to convince its citizens to accept the party's concept of the ideal society.

Inherent in these broad criteria for classifying political parties is the assumption that the parties are aiming for a permanent standing in the political system. The nature of a party's appeal, its membership policy, candidate selection process, and political goals all center on the fact that the parties must hold some measure of support from the people. This support manifests itself in the form of members and money, both of which are vital to the survival of a party.

Recruitment and Financing

Political party leaders and members come and go, but the party itself remains. How do parties recruit new members? Where do their leaders come from? How do they obtain the financial backing necessary to carry on their activities?

Recruitment

The requirements for party membership vary widely among parties. The United States is unique in the Western world in that political party membership is defined by state law. A person joins a party in most states simply by registering at the local board of elections. This permits him to vote in his party's primaries, while imposing no other obligations on him. He doesn't pay formal dues, nor is he required to take an active part in campaigns by ringing doorbells, phoning voters, or stuffing envelopes. This is not the case in Europe: European countries regard political parties as private rather than public organizations. Parties set their own membership requirements and impose their own regulations on members. To join the Conservative party in England, a British citizen must sign a declaration testifying to his support of the party's goals and pay yearly dues amounting to about sixty cents. But this is not the only way a Briton can become a political party member. If he is a union member, he has a good chance of automatically becoming a Labourite. Many unions, on the continent as well as in England, divert a part of each man's dues to the labor party in their country, unless he specifically requests that his dues not be used for that purpose. Of course, most union members recruited in this manner are not likely to become actively involved in party affairs. In this respect, European labor parties resemble American parties with largely inactive memberships.

Role of Party Members. Political parties welcome active workers because they broaden the base of potential voter support. An active member can directly influence the voting patterns of his friends and relatives and reach countless others by ringing doorbells and circulating pamphlets. The very effective "grass roots" organization which helped George McGovern to win so many primary elections in 1972 is testimony to the political power of active supporters (although when broadened to a nationwide scale in the November elections, the results were markedly less impressive).

Why Do People Join Political Parties? For European union members, joining the labor party is often the path of least resistance. But there are other reasons why people choose to identify themselves with a particular party. Political scientist Samuel Eldersveld has found nine major reasons, ranging from the involvement of one's friends or relatives in a particular party to more self-generating motives.[35] Among these reasons lies the possibility that a particular candidate or issue may so capture the attention of a person that he is motivated to political action and so joins the party. Precinct workers may actively recruit party volunteers. Or, a citizen's participation in civic affairs may lead to political dealings with the local government, where one particular party is in office. Ideological commitment can also be a factor in motivating people to identify with a party, though this is true more in Europe than in the United States, where parties are less prone to ideological labels. Finally, people may become active in politics out of ambition for their own personal or professional advancement, or for political power itself.

Choosing Candidates. Despite Ronald Reagan's spectacular jump from Hollywood star to California governor, most candidates for public office come up through the party ranks.

How large a say does the party hierarchy have in deciding who will become a candidate? Lester G. Seligman's study of recruitment methods in the United States reveals that in "safe" districts, where people consistently vote for the same party, party officials do not play much of a role in candidate selection.[36] Usually, such districts have incumbent officeholders who will probably be returned to power, but when an office falls vacant, party factions are allowed to fight it out among themselves for control of the nomi-

[35] Eldersveld, *Political Parties*, pp. 118–134.
[36] Lester G. Seligman, "Political Recruitment and Party Structure: A Case Study," *American Political Science Review* 55 (March 1961): 77–86.

nation. In "unsafe" districts where the minority faces a difficult battle, party officials must go out and draft people to run. Generally, loyal party workers are given the dubious honor of leading the party to certain defeat, and they run out of a sense of obligation to the party as a result. Seligman finds that in competitive areas, party officials do not dominate in choosing candidates. Here, while party leaders as well as factions within the party tend to support favored candidates in the primaries, they are often upset by candidates supported by powerful nonparty groups, such as the unions.

Three means of choosing candidates exist outside of direct selection from the ranks by the established party leadership. Some candidates are self-recruited: they enter the primary on their own strength. These may be wealthy persons who hope to use massive advertising to compensate for their lack of organizational support, or persons who voice points of view that bring them a popular following, but not party backing. Candidates may also be recruited by cooptation: a party may ask a "big name" who is not formally identified with it to run as its candidate. This usually happens when the party has no strong candidate of its own, and hopes to capitalize on a popular new face. The Republican party's nomination of Eisenhower for president in 1952 is an example of very successful cooptation. Finally, candidates are persuaded to file for office as the agents of groups who hope to use the threat of such a candidacy to win concessions from the established party hierarchy. George Wallace's American Independent party candidates fall into this group, as would Ralph Nader if he succumbed to persuasions that he run for public office.

How Representative Are Party Leaders? How do our political leaders differ from each other? Are they representative of the party members who support them? Kenneth Prewitt recently studied the process by which eighty-seven San Francisco Bay area communities selected their local leaders.[37] His findings stress the role of social bias in the selection of political officials. Across the board, the city councilmen were wealthier and better educated than their respective constituencies. Prewitt finds that, consciously or subconsciously, the American political system tends to favor candidates from the upper socioeconomic classes.[38] If this finding is true, what effect does it have on the political opinions of leaders and their followers?

Political Opinions: Party Leaders and Rank-and-file. It is often argued that America's political leaders do not reflect and respond to the needs of their constituents, and that party platforms represent vague attempts to

[37] Kenneth Prewitt, *The Recruitment of Political Leaders: A Study of Citizen Politicians* (Indianapolis: Bobbs-Merrill, 1970). See our Chapter 6 for a discussion of the elitist view of American politics, which Prewitt represents. See also Donald P. Matthews, *The Social Background of Political Decision Makers* (Garden City, N.Y.: Doubleday, 1954) for a similar, if somewhat dated, presentation of the same point of view.
[38] See Prewitt, *The Recruitment of Political Leaders*, Chapter 1, "From the Many are Chosen the Few."

Table 11-4
Incidental Expenditures for the 1968 Republican Presidential Campaign

Item	Cost
20,500,000 buttons	$300,000
9,000,000 bumperstrips	300,000
560,000 balloons	70,000
400,000 posters	70,000
28,000 straw skimmers	30,000
30,000 brochures	
3,500,000 speeches & position papers	500,000
12,000 paper dresses	40,000
jewelry	50,000

Source: Herbert Alexander, Financing the 1968 Election (Lexington, Mass.: Heath Lexington Books, 1971), pp. 81–82.

wide political campaign in the United States. In 1968, the Republican, Democratic, and American Independent parties spent a staggering $300 million in the general elections of that year (see Table 11-4 for a breakdown of some of the Republicans' expenses). This figure includes expenditures in state primary elections as well as in the national election, and covers both the presidential and congressional campaigns of the major parties. A breakdown of campaign expenditures shows that the parties spent sixty cents on every voter who went to the polls, and that the Republicans outspent the Democrats by a margin of two-to-one.[41] In addition to incidental expenses such as buttons and bumper stickers, the costs of radio and television advertising contribute to the enormous financial pressure felt by political parties at election time—especially when they have few dues-paying members.

Methods of Financing Political Parties. Because we have no formal method for financing political parties, American parties are dependent, in great part, on voluntary contributions from wealthy donors. This is fortunately the exception, not the rule. Many other countries have official methods for raising financial support.

The Party Membership Fee. In Great Britain, India, Israel, and most continental European nations, political party members, like members of a private club, are required to pay dues in order to keep their membership active.

[41] Herbert Alexander, *Financing the 1968 Election* (Lexington, Mass.: Heath Lexington Books, 1971), p. 82. Other useful studies of political campaign spending and fund raising are Louise Overacker, *Money in Elections* (New York: Macmillan, 1932); and Herbert Alexander, ed., *Money for Politics: A Miscellany of Ideas* (Princeton, N.J.: Citizens' Research Foundation, 1963); Jasper B. Shannon, *Money and Politics* (New York: Random House, 1959); and Arnold J. Heidenheimer, ed., *Comparative Political Finance: The Financing of Party Organizations and Election Campaigns* (Lexington, Mass.: D. C. Heath, 1970).

To attract as large a membership as possible, the fee is deliberately kept low. While effective in this sense, the result is that the dues usually do not come close to covering operating expenses. Thus, parties must turn to external sources, and so the problem of fund raising, which is so familiar to American parties, is felt on a smaller scale in other nations, too. There are many different solutions. In West Germany and India, candidates are expected to contribute what they can to their own campaigns and their party's coffers. This favors wealthy candidates over politicians of only moderate means. Great Britain strictly limits the amount of money any single candidate can spend on a parliamentary campaign, holding candidates criminally liable for violations of campaign spending laws. While raising money still presents problems for political parties of these nations, however, the scale of their dilemma is nowhere near that of the Republicans and the Democrats. Our presidential campaigns, including the primary elections in the spring, require almost a year of speeches, appearances, and attention-getting gimmickry for at least one of the contenders. In contrast, European campaigns rarely last more than a couple of weeks to a month, so the expense is proportionally lower.

External Support.   Japan, Israel, France, and Italy, like the United States, have laws that restrict or sharply regulate political contributions from industrial corporations, labor unions, and similar economic interest groups. West Germany, Sweden, Finland, and Puerto Rico have an effective plan to use government funds to subsidize political parties. West Germany and Sweden, for example, funnel public tax revenues to their political parties in proportion to each party's electoral strength. Thus, the more votes a party receives, the larger its government subsidy will be. This system has been criticized for its obvious discrimination against new parties, however. The United States Congress has recently passed a similar plan (the Presidential Election Campaign Fund) which allows taxpayers to authorize the Internal Revenue Service to donate one dollar of their income tax payment to the party of their choice. Such a law, it is hoped, will encourage individual political contributions and reduce the current dependency of parties on large donors.

Party Financing in the United States.   The Corrupt Practices Act of 1925 is the basic statute governing expenditures and contributions in national elections. It prohibits direct contributions by corporations and labor unions, requires candidates to report all campaign expenditures, and limits the total any individual can contribute to a campaign. But labor unions and corporations can still funnel money to the parties through their numerous executives and officers. Or, corporations and unions may contribute to citizens' committees which, in turn, make donations to the parties. Finally, individual donors can give money in the names of their wives, children, and other relatives. The 1925 act becomes increasingly outdated as candidates turn more and more to expensive radio and television time as the fastest way to reach

"All right, Senator, let's try it again from where you look up with that quizzical little smile and say, 'Slush fund? Far from it! Why, staying in office has kept me poor as a church mouse.'"

the most voters. Campaign buttons and bumper stickers may cost money, but they are a drop in the bucket compared to the astronomical expense of mass-media politics. As campaign costs soar every year, the need for financial support becomes increasingly strong. An amendment to the Corrupt Practices Act requiring all political candidates to make public any contributions over $100 went into effect in April 1972. But earlier, in 1971, a bill was vetoed which would have limited political campaign spending to ten cents per eligible voter. The veto was not overridden, and despite talk to the contrary, there seems to be no immediate prospect for major campaign-spending reform by either of the major parties.

The American Party System: An Evaluation

Critics of the American party system argue that its lenient campaign-spending policies put candidate selection and election into the hands of the affluent few. Supporters say that this objection is irrelevant to the overall success of the system, because any winning campaign must cater to the needs of the majority in a substantial way. Our party system is also criticized for its ideological weaknesses, its vast decentralization, and its inability to enact major legislative reforms. But what system would be better adapted to the needs of American society? One-party totalitarian regimes are ideologically strong, but inimical to democratic ideals. Multiparty systems offer more of a political voice to minority groups, but can lead to unstable coalition governments. To change the American party system is to alter the balance of American political life—just as to impose a two-party system on Israel would be to change the whole political system of that nation. Imperfect as our two-party system is, a viable alternative for our political culture is hard to imagine.

Suggested Readings

Downs, Anthony. *An Economic Theory of Democracy*. New York: Harper & Row, 1957. One of the most innovative and influential analyses written in the last twenty-five years.

Duverger, Maurice. *Political Parties: Their Organization and Activities in the Modern State*. New York: John Wiley, 1954. A comparative treatment of political parties.

Eldersveld, Samuel J. *Political Parties: A Behavioral Analysis*. Chicago: Rand McNally, 1964. Both theory and empirical analysis of the political party in action are discussed.

Epstein, Leon D. *Political Parties in Western Democracies*. New York: Praeger, 1967. A comprehensive survey of political parties in democratic nations.

Fainsod, Merle. *How Russia Is Ruled*. Cambridge, Mass.: Harvard University Press, 1963. A comprehensive account of the Soviet party system.

Huntington, Samuel P., and Moore, Clement H., eds. *Authoritarian Politics in Modern Society: The Dynamics of Established One-Party Systems*. New York: Basic Books, 1970. A comprehensive collection of papers on one-party systems.

Key, V. O. *Parties, Politics, and Pressure Groups*. New York: Thomas Y. Crowell, 1964. An excellent analytic survey.

Michels, Robert. *Political Parties*. New York: The Free Press, 1949. The source for the "iron law of oligarchy" as developed in a study of socialist parties.

Ranney, Austin. *Pathways to Parliament*. Madison: University of Wisconsin Press, 1965. An excellent comparison of the American and British party systems.

Sorauf, Frank J. *Party Politics in America*. 2nd ed. Boston: Little, Brown, 1972. A comprehensive survey of the American party system.

Zink, Harold. *City Bosses in the United States*. Durham, N.C.: Duke University Press, 1950. Portraits of city bosses in the United States during the days of the city machine.

Zolberg, Aristide R. *Creating Political Order: The Party States of West Africa*. Chicago: Rand McNally, 1966. A discussion of party systems as they developed in colonial West Africa.

Voting behavior
CHAPTER 12

In modern America, the average citizen has a bird's-eye view of every stage of the political process. Television news programs cover not only the signing of treaties and bills, but also their subsequent effects of sending "our boys" to fight overseas, busing children to schools, and opening new public housing projects. Television, the newspapers, and the radio then report the people's reaction to these policies. We watch protesters picketing the White House, read about campus unrest, and hear the man in the street profess his support for a new arms-control agreement.

In a nation where everyone can daily observe the making and workings of government policy, one would expect the average citizen to show a high degree of interest in politics and the electoral process. Yet, analysis of American voting behavior tells another story (see Figure 12-1). A surprising number of Americans who have the right to vote simply do not exercise it. In the 1968 election, less than two-thirds of the 120 million persons of voting

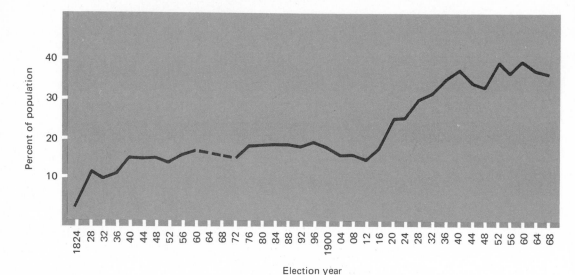

**Figure 12-1
Percent of Total
Population Voting
in Presidential
Elections, 1824–
1968**

Source: Robert A. Dahl, Democracy in the United States: Promise and Performance, 2nd ed. (Chicago: Rand McNally, 1972), Figure 9.1, p. 96.

age actually went to the polls. In 1972, only 55 percent of the potential voters exercised their right to vote. If these figures seem discouraging, it should be remembered that the degree of voter interest and involvement is even lower in nonpresidential election years. In these years, a turnout of one-third of the voters is considered a good showing.

Why is there such disparity between the number of Americans who have the potential to be involved in their democratic system and the statistics which show how few of these citizens actually vote? Apathy and indecisiveness are responsible. In the 1968 elections, more than half of the voting-age adults who never made it to the polls gave their reason for staying home as sheer lack of interest and dissatisfaction with the candidates.[1] Many people felt that their vote wouldn't make a difference, and many more felt that none of the candidates running for office suited their taste. Of the voters who did register their choice at the polls on election day in 1968, one in four had remained undecided up until two weeks before the election.[2] Only 5 to 7 percent of America's voting population is involved enough in politics to attend a political meeting, give money to a party or candidate, write a letter to a candidate, or actively canvass a neighborhood to stir up support for one candidate or party.[3]

[1] *Gallup Opinion Index* 42 (December 1968).
[2] *Ibid.*
[3] Lester W. Milbrath, *Political Participation* (Chicago: Rand McNally, 1965), pp. 16–22. See also Philip E. Converse and Richard Niemi, "Nonvoting Among Young Adults in the United States," in William J. Crotty, ed., *Political Parties and Political Behavior* (Boston: Allyn and Bacon, 1971), pp. 466.

The average American adult offers a sharp contrast to the democratic ideal of the concerned citizen, independent of mind, who carefully weighs the merits and faults of competing candidates before registering a seriously considered decision in the voting booth. But why shouldn't this be so? For most of us, political and social issues are far less important than such basic day-to-day or personal questions as "Will I pass the exam on Tuesday?" "Should we make a down payment on a new house?" "Should I get married?" Such matters are naturally the foremost thoughts in our minds, as they touch our lives more directly than any change in congressmen or state senators is likely to.

But to the politician, the political scientist, and the concerned citizen, these facts raise disturbing questions, especially since the national elections of almost every European state are able to draw considerably larger turnouts than American elections (see Table 12-1). Indeed, elitist scholarship argues strongly that the ignorance and apathy of large portions of the American electorate (portions that happen to coincide with the lower socioeconomic classes) encourage control by the already powerful, leaving few real policy choices to the people.[4]

The point is particularly disturbing when we consider what would happen if all these indifferent people did vote. If the United States elections were suddenly to draw 99-percent turnouts (as do the elections of the Soviet Union), the structure of our political system would probably be changed. The emergence of a new dominant voice in American politics could possibly change the stereotyped slot into which most of our presidents, senators, congressmen, and local politicos fit, along with the public policies they determine. It is quite possible that a consistently high voter turnout could give us the first successful third party in our history. Aside from such speculation, even a miniscule change in voting turnout could markedly change the outcome of many of our elections. In the years between 1834 and 1960, there were no less than six presidential elections in which minor vote shifts (less than 1 percent) could have reversed the outcome.[5] In 1960, a national shift of less than two-hundredths of 1 percent of the votes cast could have made John F. Kennedy a defeated candidate.

The Study of Voting Behavior

While whimsey, last-minute policy changes, rainy election days, and inaccurate polls (such as the predictions of a Dewey landslide in 1948) all contribute to making voting behavior very elusive to predict, the way peo-

[4] Thomas R. Dye and L. Harmon Zeigler summarize the arguments neatly in *The Irony of Democracy: An Uncommon Introduction to American Politics* (Belmont, Calif.: Wadsworth, 1970), Chapter 6. See also our Chapter 6.
[5] See Neal R. Pierce, *The People's President* (New York: Simon and Schuster, 1968), pp. 320–21.

Table 12-1
Voter Turnout in National Elections as a Percentage of Voting-age Population

Rank	Country	Voter Turnout	Year
1	USSR	99.6	1958
2	Bulgaria	99.2	1957
3	Czechoslovakia	98.1	1960
4	Romania	97.9	1957
5.5	East Germany	97.3	1958
5.5	Ivory Coast	97.3	1960
7	Albania	94.6	1958
8	Rwanda	98.7	1961
9	Hungary	98.5	1958
10	Italy	92.9	1968
11	Poland	92.8	1957
12	Nicaragua	92.7	1963
13	Gabon	92.6	1958
14	Netherlands [1]	92.1	1959
15	Indonesia	92.0	1955
16	Yugoslavia	91.4	1958
17	Austria	90.4	1959
18	France	89.4	1962
19	Israel	88.0	1961
20.5	Belgium [1]	87.6	1961
20.5	Guinea	87.6	1958
22	West Germany	86.9	1961
23	Iceland	86.6	1959
24	New Zealand	86.4	1960
25	Australia [1]	85.3	1958
26	Denmark	84.0	1960
27	Venezuela [1]	83.8	1958
28	Sweden	83.1	1960
29	Liberia	82.9	1959
30	Singapore	82.3	1959
31	Norway	78.8	1961
32	United Kingdom	78.0	1959
33.5	Canada	74.2	1958
33.5	Haiti	74.2	1957
35.5	Greece [1]	73.3	1958
35.5	Puerto Rico	73.3	1960
37	Netherlands Antilles	73.0	1958
38	Finland	72.8	1958
39	Turkey	72.5	1961
40	Cameroon	72.2	1960
41	Ireland	71.6	1957

Table 12-1
(Continued)

Rank	Country	Voter Turnout	Year
42	Japan	71.2	1960
43	Luxembourg	71.1	1954
44	Jamaica	70.6	1962
45	Cuba	69.1	1954
46	Burundi	68.4	1961
47	Madagascar	64.8	1959
48	United States	64.4	1960
49	Dominican Republic	63.6	1962
50	Argentina [1]	61.8	1960
51	Ceylon	58.8	1960
52	Senegal	58.5	1959
53	Uruguay	58.3	1962
54	Costa Rica	57.6	1962
55	Panama	56.2	1960
56	Philippines	55.1	1961
57	Malaya	54.8	1959
58	Burma	54.5	1960
59	India	52.6	1962
60	British Guiana	52.1	1957
61	Bolivia	51.4	1962
62	Tunisia	49.9	1959
63	Lebanon	48.0	1960
64	Ghana	43.9	1957
65	Mauritania	42.8	1956
66	Upper Volta	41.9	1956
67	Dahomey	41.1	1959
68	Nigeria	40.4	1957
69	Colombia	40.2	1962
70	Peru	39.2	1963
71	Chile	37.4	1961
72	Honduras	36.5	1957
73	Mexico	34.6	1961
74	Brazil	34.4	1960
75	Tanganyika	33.8	1962
76	South Korea	31.3	1960
77	Uganda	31.0	1961
78	Central African Republic	30.6	1956
79	El Salvador	29.3	1962
80	Paraguay	29.1	1963
81	Kenya	28.9	1961
82	Ecuador	28.4	1960

Table 12-1
(Continued)

Rank	Country	Voter Turnout	Year
83	Switzerland	28.0	1959
84	Syria	27.6	1961
85	Guatemala	27.5	1958
86	Mali	25.1	1956
87	Niger	24.1	1956
88	Portugal	18.5	1958
89	Sierra Leone	16.7	1957
90	Southwest Africa	11.0	1961
91	South Africa	10.4	1961
92	Rhodesia & Nyasaland	1.9	1958
96.5	Egypt	.0	
96.5	Iraq	.0	
96.5	Kuwait	.0	
96.5	Pakistan	.0	
96.5	Saudi Arabia	.0	
96.5	Spain	.0	
96.5	Sudan	.0	
96.5	Yemen	.0	

[1] Voting legally required.
Source: Bruce M. Russett et al., World Handbook of Political and Social Indicators (New Haven, Conn.: Yale University Press, 1964), pp. 84–86.

ple vote is still characterized by several recognizable patterns. These patterns have provided fertile ground for students of political behavior. Voting behavior analysis has become one of the most sophisticated areas of political science, and has armed itself with the trappings of computer analysis, polls, demographic and geographic surveys, and many other complicated techniques and formulas. In the United States, the Survey Research Center (SRC) at the University of Michigan has been collecting and analyzing data from most elections, both presidential and congressional, since 1948. Its publications constitute the most comprehensive body of data on the behavior of the American voter, focusing primarily on the process by which his voting preferences are formed.[6] Major national and international pollsters, including the Gallup and Louis Harris organizations in the United States, Marplan and National Opinion Polls in Great Britain, and *L'Institut Français de l'Opinion Publique* (IFOP) in France all do extensive research on what voters are thinking and how they are likely to vote and why. Any major candidate in this day and age will find it difficult to do battle in the

[6] Peter B. Natchez provides an excellent summary and critique of SRC findings and interpretations since the early fifties in "Images of Voting: The Social Psychologists," *Public Policy* 18 (Summer 1970): 553–88.

"I always wait until my husband decides on a candidate— then I vote for his opponent."

Reprinted by permission of Jack Markow.

political arena of his nation without being well-armed with information and predictions about his intended constituency. What are the factors that determine how a person will vote, and how do political candidates apply their knowledge of voter behavior to their campaign strategies?

Who Votes?

One of the most striking facts about American elections is the number of people who don't participate. Is this an American phenomenon alone, or is it a problem inherent in any democratic nation?

Who Votes in European Democracies?

Unlike the American voter, Europeans are very likely to cast their ballots on election day. England's 1972 turnout was 72 percent, while Germany's figure in the same year was a startling 91.2 percent. Italy averages close to a 90 percent voter turnout, while the French Fifth Republic has maintained a record of close to 80 percent in spite of the procedure that has voters report to the polls two or more times for every national election in the country's run-off system (described in Chapter 13).

Whether these figures can be offered as sound proof of the greater apathy of Americans, however, is debatable. Greater proportions of Europeans do vote, but they enjoy much looser regulations regarding eligibility and registration. In Italy, only criminals and minors are barred from the polls, and Italians don't have to register personally in order to vote; the government takes care of the details. (Government officials are always on hand at the polling place to take note of who shows up and who stays home on election day, which is another incentive for voting.) In Great Britain, where eighteen-year-olds have recently been granted the vote, it is the government and not the citizen who is responsible for keeping track of who is eligible to vote. Voters are registered automatically when they reach the age of eighteen.

In contrast, America's stiff residency laws and sometimes ponderous registration procedures can present quite an obstacle to the would-be voter. The citizen, not the government, carries the burden of making sure that any details such as change of name or residency are recorded in the official accounts. This involves the inconvenience of a special visit to the official place of registration several weeks before the election. If registration is cumbersome, its timing is impolitic. By the time that campaign excitement has begun to mount, the deadline for registration is long past. Once a person registers, he finds that elections are held on working days (in Germany, voting takes place on Sundays), and the lineup of local, state, and national candidates confronting him as he steps into the booth is often enough to baffle all but those who have memorized the sample ballots. It is no wonder that many eligible Americans never vote.

Nonvoting in America

But strict regulations and requirements and long lists of candidates are not the only reasons people stay away from the polls. Philip E. Converse and Richard Niemi have tried to discover the reasons for not voting, and have categorized them into three broad categories: accidental, motivational, and legal.[7]

Accidental Factors. Accidental factors include the kinds of last-minute inconveniences which keep even the well-intentioned voter from the polls. Flat tires, business emergencies, and sudden illnesses are all nonpolitical influences which prevent a certain number of voters from casting their ballots every election day.

Motivational Factors. Apathy and indifference are responsible for even more voters' failure to show up at the polls. According to Converse and Niemi, the lack of motivation which causes many people to decide not to vote can be the result of either external or internal influences.

---

[7] Converse and Niemi, "Nonvoting Among Young Adults in the United States," pp. 452–53.

External influences primarily involve the campaign's ability to arouse the voter's interest. For example, one of the clearest generalizations that can be made about voting in the United States is that turnout is higher in a presidential election than it is in an "off-year." The reason for this is that the high visibility of a presidential campaign, with its televised commercials, bumper stickers, and buttons, combined with the importance with which people view the office of president, provides an aura of excitement that interests many otherwise uninvolved citizens. The external stimuli which are so obvious during a presidential campaign simply do not exist when the voters are called on to choose between tax assessors, county supervisors, or local judges. Thus, voter turnout is markedly lower in these elections. Other external influences include interested friends or an active local party organization that persuade people to get out and vote.

While major elections always draw more voters than off-year contests, there are many citizens who take pride in their voting records no matter how dull the campaign or how minor the candidate. These voters will show up at the polls year after year and will go to the trouble of mailing absentee ballots if they must be away from home at election time. The difference between these voters and the voters who cast their ballots only when they have been caught up in a flashy national campaign is one of degree of "internalized motivation." Somewhere during their socialization process, the internally motivated voters have learned to feel a strong sense of civic responsibility. Through the influences of family, school, or friends, these citizens have learned that voting is the citizen's responsibility.[8] It is this "internalized motivation" which brings them to the polls.

Legal Barriers. In 1855, the territory of Kansas held elections for its legislature, with peculiar results. While only 2,000 Kansans were registered to vote, some 6,000 ballots were cast. Neighboring Missourians, who wanted the territory of Kansas to become slave territory, had travelled across the border on election day to make sure that the new Kansas legislature would be in sympathy with their wishes.

Obviously, there must be some legal restrictions in order to keep elections fair. Otherwise, not only could the Kansas experience of the Dred Scott days be repeated, but citizens with two residences, including college students who live in one state but attend universities in another, would be permitted to cast two or more ballots. Thus, residency laws prevent the United States citizen from voting in his state of residence unless he has lived in that state for a certain period of time and has registered well before election day. Other types of legal barriers to voting besides residency requirements include the restrictions that exist in every nation which prevent convicted criminals and persons confined to mental institutions from voting on elec-

---

8 William H. Riker and Peter C. Ordeshook argue that a sense of civic duty is the major factor in motivating voters to elections in "A Theory of the Calculus of Voting," *American Political Science Review* 62 (March 1968) : 25–42. See the discussion of how civic responsibility is taught through the socialization process in Chapter 8 of our text.

tion day. Maturity, too, is a universal requirement for voting in elections. In every nation, some sort of restriction prevents persons under the age of majority (usually 18 or 21) from voting.

A person will cast his vote on election day as long as legal restrictions, haphazard accidents, or inconveniences don't intrude, and as long as he is sufficiently interested in the election to stop whatever else he's doing and take a trip to the polling place. The question of what motivates people to vote, and why some groups of people are more likely to vote than others, is one which has received a great deal of attention from political scientists.

Why Do People Vote?

In his landmark work, *An Economic Theory of Democracy*,[9] Anthony Downs theorized that people will vote if the returns outweigh the costs. If the stakes seem important enough, the voter will go to the trouble of voting. Thus, the person whose property taxes stand to be raised if a new school bond is passed is much more likely to vote on the issue than his neighbor, who rents an apartment and stands no chance of being hurt by the tax since he owns no real estate. The cost of political information, both financial and personal, is also influential in determining whether a person will vote. The price of a newspaper, the sacrifice of turning off a favorite TV show in order to watch the news, and the time involved in attending a political meeting all tend to prevent political information from being distributed equally to everyone, because each person places a different value on his personal time and political awareness.

The result is that the poor and the uneducated in every society are the least likely to vote. In line with Anthony Downs's assessment, Gallup Associates drew a statistical profile of the American nonvoter from their analysis of the 1968 election.[10] According to the Gallup research, the typical American nonvoter is a woman who is in her twenties, is married to a blue-collar worker, and has little formal education. Why? Being relatively poor, she has few financial investments and probably feels she has little economic stake in the election outcome. Being poorly educated, the cost of getting political information, in terms of time taken from other interests and chores, is likely to outweigh the benefits she feels she derives from a knowledge of current affairs. Her lack of education also makes her part of a tradition in which her sex has stayed clear of politics. She is therefore likely to take voting less seriously than men do.

In contrast, the typical voter in almost every democracy is a person of opposite characteristics. He is a middle-aged white man, who is college educated and holds a white-collar job. He is more likely to vote in a na-

[9] Anthony Downs, "The Causes and Effects of Rational Abstention," *An Economic Theory of Democracy* (New York: Harper & Row, 1957), pp. 260–75.
[10] *Gallup Opinion Index* 42 (December 1968).

tional election if he lives in a city than if he lives in the country (except in France, where rural residents are more likely to vote than city dwellers). And he is more likely to vote if he identifies strongly with a political party than if he calls himself an Independent.[11]

Within these broad generalizations of characteristics of the typical voter and the typical nonvoter, it is possible to identify several specific factors that are likely to have an influence on whether a person votes or not. Although personality makeup is an important factor, income and education, race, age, sex, and area of residence all act in a predictable manner to help determine a person's inclination to vote or not to vote.

Income and Education. People who enjoy a large income are more likely to vote than those who are less affluent. And people who are well educated are more likely to vote than those who dropped out of high school. Are they in fact the same individuals? Not quite, for a wealthy person who did not finish high school is almost as likely to vote as a wealthy college graduate. Even though certain voters often combine these characteristics (good education makes it easier to earn a good salary), the two influence voting in rather different ways. One is a matter of having a stake in election outcomes, the other a broader question of interest and sophistication.

According to the Survey Research Center, the assembly-line worker living in a small town may see little difference between a Hubert Humphrey and a Richard Nixon.[12] He is accustomed to paying taxes, following rules and regulations, and making a barely adequate living through hard work. He is likely to see little difference in the way he will fare under a Democratic administration as opposed to a Republican administration, so he perceives that he has little stake in the election's outcome. In contrast, the president of a large corporation feels involved in the election. He sees a direct cause-and-effect relationship between who wins the election and his own personal life-style, which will be affected by changes in international monetary policy, personal and corporate tax reforms, government policy toward the organized labor he employs, interest-rate changes, and a score of other complex fiscal policies. Of course, the blue-collar worker may be affected by a change in the administration, but he is less likely to be aware of his stakes.

The difference between the upper-class voter and the lower-class nonvoter is primarily a feeling of efficacy. The assembly worker feels that his vote won't make any difference. The corporation president, on the other hand, believes that his participation is important to the political process, and that the difference between one candidate and the next is likely to be significant to him. While a change in the party in office is likely to have an impact on the life of the blue-collar worker, we can see why the corporation president

11 Although this last characteristic seems to be changing, see the discussion of Independents later in this chapter.
12 Angus Campbell, Philip E. Converse, Warren E. Miller, and Donald E. Stokes, *The American Voter* (New York: John Wiley & Sons, 1960), Chapter 17.

might feel that the stakes are more important to him. In his realm of experience, he has seen interest groups and private associations succeed in changing government policy, if only by successfully influencing the local school board to expand a school-bus route. In contrast, the blue-collar worker is likely to see American political life from the perspective of the "silent majority" subculture. His friends, neighbors, and family have never had any wealth to speak of and have never organized to successfully pressure the government.[13]

Many well-educated people (and not just wealthy corporation presidents) may have a broader interest in the results of an election beyond any personal economic stake in its outcome. More widely read and more sophisticated than the high-school graduate (or dropout), the college-educated person— whether wealthy or not—tends to be more interested, better informed, and more likely to participate in elections. As our discussion in Chapter 8 indicates, schooling helps to provide both a sense of the importance of political participation and a more abstract intellectual curiosity which makes people more likely to read papers, keep abreast of the news, and feel involved in the political events of their nation and local area.

There are, of course, many exceptions to these general patterns. Alabama's George Wallace had a strong following among people who might not statistically be expected to pay much attention to politics. Perhaps they felt that important matters were at stake for them—neighborhood schools, "small government," state control instead of federal "take-over." Many of Governor Wallace's very involved band of followers were neither highly educated nor wealthy, but they were certainly interested in Wallace's candidacy and were likely to participate by voting for him.

Race. If high income and educational background are important influences in getting people to the polls, it is not surprising to learn that a smaller percentage of blacks than whites exercise the right to vote.[14] For American blacks as a group have received less education and have brought home smaller paychecks than American whites. In the 1970 congressional elections, only 44 percent of eligible blacks voted, compared to 56 percent of eligible whites.

But income and education levels are only the most obvious influences that hinder blacks from voting. Subtler and perhaps more profound is a basic

---

[13] According to Seymour Martin Lipset, both organizing skill and a belief in the effectiveness of organization go hand in hand with higher income. See *Political Man* (New York: Doubleday, 1960), pp. 190–203. See also the discussion of who joins interest groups in our Chapter 10.

[14] Indeed, mysteriously stricter literacy requirements have, until very recently, contributed to the marked differences in voting turnout in some areas of the country. In 1960, before the Civil Rights laws of the mid-sixties, only 29 percent of southern blacks were registered—as opposed to 61 percent of their white counterparts. In 1970, the figures were 69 percent and 62 percent, respectively. Statistics are based on Table 569, "White and Negro Voter Registration in Eleven Southern States: 1960 to 1970," in the U.S. Bureau of the Census, *Statistical Abstract of the United States: 1971*, p. 365.

"... And this guide for the 18-year-old voter says a Pisces candidate has the dedication of a true idealist while a Scorpio tends to be tempestuous and mercurial."

"Grin and Bear It," by George Lichty; courtesy of Publishers-Hall Syndicate.

lack of confidence in the usefulness of elections. As long as our candidates for president, and most of our senators, congressmen, governors, and mayors remain white, many blacks feel that things will remain about the same no matter which side wins. As long as inequality based on race remains a social fact in the United States, blacks, Chicanos, Indians, and Puerto Ricans will likely have lower voter turnouts than whites.

Age. An important question in the 1972 presidential election was, "How will young people vote?" Many of the "older generation" who had watched the campus riots and demonstrations of the late sixties and early seventies wondered how the "radical" youth of America would react when given a legitimate political tool to wield on a national level.

Although the addition of 11 million persons to the electorate is a crucial event in any nation's history, the effect of this new force has not been as spectacular as some expected.[15] The results were predictable: young people rarely vote in great numbers, and when they do turn out, they vote much as their elders do. In the 1972 presidential election in the United States, only 48.3 percent of the newly enfranchised eighteen- to twenty-year-olds

15 William C. Mitchell predicted the "nonhappening" in Chapter 1 of *Why Vote?* (Chicago: Markham Publishers, 1971).

voted. And while these younger voters were somewhat more liberal than other voters (over half gave their support to George McGovern), the difference was nowhere near as significant as the Democrats had hoped. The British experience with the youth vote has been similar to that of the United States. In Great Britain, the 1969 Representation of the People Act lowered the voting age from twenty-one to eighteen, just as the United States' twenty-sixth amendment did in 1971. And just as in the United States, the 1970 national elections in Britain did not reflect any major shifts in the balance of the political parties which could be traced to the newly enfranchised young people.

Middle-aged people vote more often than do either the very young or the very old. In 1970 in the United States, two-thirds of America's voting-age population between the ages of forty-five and sixty-four turned out on election day, as compared with only one-third of the twenty-one- to twenty-four-year-olds. Why are the middle-aged most likely to participate in elections? The answer seems to be tied to their perceived stake in the election results. For the middle-aged person has reached a peak in earning power without having to retire yet. He is therefore the most likely of any group to be settled into a community whose affairs he feels involved in, and his voting record will reflect this. Both his job and his community are investments that he wants to protect.

Sex. Traditionally, men are more likely to vote than women in almost every society. In large part, this is due to the fact that women have only comparatively recently won the right to vote. (Switzerland's female population was enfranchised only in 1971). Since 1920, when female suffrage was granted in the United States, the gap between men's and women's voter turnout has been narrowing steadily. In 1968, the difference in turnout between the two groups was less than 4 percent.

Area of Residence. City dwellers are more likely to vote than rural residents. This probably reflects the easier accessibility of voting booths in the cities, where a relatively few blocks can comprise a voting district with the same population as a rural district of several square miles. In France, unlike Britain and the United States, rural areas traditionally turn out a higher percentage of voters than do cities. This is because in France, local politics in small towns is conducted on a much more intimate level than the highly depersonalized politics of the big city.

People who have lived in the same place for a long time are more likely to vote than are transients or newcomers, for long-time inhabitants of any community feel more involved in their neighborhood goings-on, and are therefore more likely to participate in groups and activities that will sustain their community.

Voter turnout in the United States is considerably lighter in the South than in the North and West, even in urban areas.[16] Traditionally lower participation in the South reflects a number of influences, including a lower standard of living for that region of the nation and a traditional lack of strong party competition in the area due to the once unquestioned predominance of the Democratic party. While many of the traditional characteristics of the South and its politics are rapidly changing, even the 1968 election showed a substantially lower turnout for the South than for other areas of the country. While the North and West averaged about 70 percent voter turnout, only 60 percent of southern voters reported going to the polls. Other nations are also characterized by regional differences in voter participation. In France, the areas south of the Loire River have a strikingly lower voter turnout than the northern areas of the country.

How Do People Vote?

When the white-collar, college-educated, city-dwelling middle-aged man who is the typical American voter gets into the voting booth, how does he behave? Without suggesting that every individual votes in a manner that can be scientifically predicted, it is possible to find some patterns in the way in which people vote.

Long- and Short-term Variables

The reasons that people vote as they do are many and complex. Deep loyalty to a political party, advice of a friend, fondness for one particular candidate and distrust of another, or feelings about a particular issue—each of these can have an overriding effect on a voter's election decision. The influences that determine the way a person will vote can be grouped according to the type of effect they have on the individual voter's political leanings. The result is a pattern of long-term and short-term variables. For example, many working-class Britons have always been Labourites and will continue to vote for the Labour party for the rest of their years. The same is true of many American Democrats and Republicans. An affiliation with a political party is a long-term influence: it affects the way a person votes for his entire lifetime. In contrast, there are short-term variables which may cause a person to vote one way or another for one election year but won't influence his ballot three or four years later. Many Frenchmen who voted consistently for Charles de Gaulle during the early years of the French

---

[16] William Flanigan discusses the reason for a lower southern turnout at greater length in *The Political Behavior of the American Electorate* (Boston: Allyn and Bacon, 1968), pp. 15–24.

Fifth Republic did not transfer their trust to the Gaullist heir, Georges Pompidou, in 1969. Similarly, in 1964 in the United States, many voters who would have normally support the Republican ticket defected to the Democrats because of fears about Senator Barry Goldwater's foreign policy. A particular candidate or a specific issue can have the effect of changing a person's vote for one election without causing any permanent shift in party loyalty.

Party Identification

American politics has operated on a two-party system since the mid-nineteenth century. There has been talk of developing an effective and permanent third party, but such a party has not yet come into existence. Indeed, most American voters seem satisfied with the two major parties; more than three-fourths of all adults express some degree of continuing loyalty to one or the other.

For some people, party identification is strong enough to be compared with a religious affiliation. It is heavily influenced by one's parents, and is instilled early in life. By the time they reach fourth grade, more than half of all school children consider themselves either Democrats or Republicans.[17] And close to 80 percent never change the affiliation they inherited from their parents.

Why does party identification remain such a stable element throughout so many people's lives? One reason is that what we learn as small children has a way of staying with us. Like a preference for certain foods learned in early childhood, a preference for one party is difficult to shake. Another reason is that it is easier to vote along party lines. To make a careful decision on every election choice in the complicated American ballot, the voter needs a great deal of information about candidates and issues. However, the amount of information he actually possesses is apt to be small. Party identification provides the easiest means of making a choice. It provides a shortcut for election decision making—a "standing decision."[18] The person who calls himself a Democrat is automatically predisposed toward any Democratic candidate, whether he realizes it or not. When asked how he feels about the Republican candidate, he will probably express suspicion of the person and his views.[19] The annual exhortations to "Vote Row A" or "Vote Row B," then, are more than simple slogans, for party identifica-

[17] Fred I. Greenstein, "The Benevolent Leader: Children's Images of Political Authority," *American Political Science Review* 54 (December 1960): 934–43.
[18] See Nelson W. Polsby and Aaron B. Wildavsky, *Presidential Elections: Strategies of American Electoral Politics*, 2nd ed. (New York: Charles Scribner's Sons, 1968), p. 23.
[19] See Richard W. Boyd, "Presidential Elections: An Explanation of Voting Defection," *American Political Science Review* 63, no. 2 (June 1969): 498–514.

tion is the most important variable in determining how a person will vote in the election booth.[20]

Party Identification in Europe. While American political parties have an overriding effect on the way most people vote, most European parties are even more influential in determining an individual's election choice. England in the years since World War II has been characterized by a very consistent split between Labour and Conservative supporters. Before 1970, the "swing" from one major party to another during national elections ranged only from about 1 percent to 3 percent. In 1970, an uncharacteristically high percentage of voters (5.3 percent—the highest since the war) abandoned the Labour party to support Conservative Edward Heath.[21] In voting for representatives in Parliament, one study of the mid-sixties showed that 71 percent of British constituencies could be counted on to return the same party to Commons.[22]

Great Britain and the United States both have two-party systems. What effect does party identification have in nations where there is a healthy competition among several political parties? One study compared party identifiers (as opposed to all voters) in the multiparty system of Norway to those in the American two-party system to determine how influential party identification was in determining voter decisions.[23] As could be expected, a significantly higher portion of Norwegian identifiers are likely to vote along party lines than are American Democrats or Republicans. The smaller political parties of Norway represent tighter-knit points of view. Thus, the party identifier in Norway is able to express a distinct personal ideology through his vote, unlike the Republican or Democrat in the United States.

Do the Norwegian findings mean that all political systems with several competing parties are characterized by a high party identification among their voters, and that the reverse is true of two-party nations? A comparative study of French and American voters found that while 75 percent of Americans classified themselves as either Republicans or Democrats, less than 45 percent of Frenchmen were members of one of their nation's many political parties.[24] The French party system, unlike that of Norway, is characterized by many short-lived splinter groups. The authors of the French-American study felt that the confusion caused by this complicated system

[20] Kenneth Prewitt and Norman Nie give a very clear discussion of partisan identification, independents, and the "normal vote" in "Review Article: Election Studies of the Survey Research Center," *British Journal of Political Science*, 1 (October 1971) : 484–96.

[21] Based on percentage of voters supporting either Labour or the Conservatives—not on total vote.

[22] Jorgan Rasmussen, "The Implications of Safe Seats for British Democracy," *Western Political Quarterly* 19 (September 1966) : 516–29.

[23] Angus Campbell and Henry Valen, "Party Identification in Norway and the United States," *Public Opinion Quarterly* 25 (Winter 1961) : 505–25.

[24] Philip E. Converse and Georges Dupeaux, "Politicization of the Electorate in France and the United States," *Public Opinion Quarterly* 26 (Spring 1962) : 1–23.

was the reason for France's low degree of party identification, but their findings do indicate that multiparty systems don't necessarily mean high voter identification with political parties.

Does party identification influence the European voter differently from the way it influences the voter in the United States? Leon D. Epstein argues that it does.[25] While a relatively high percentage of American voters identifies with a political party, Epstein feels that this party identification means something different in the American, as opposed to the European, setting. Many Americans are party members, but they cannot always be counted upon to vote according to their party preferences. On the other hand, Europeans, while less likely to be party members, are more likely to vote according to their party memberships once they have established such loyalties.

Who Belongs to What Party? Just as some groups are more likely to vote than other groups, or some people are more likely to be "liberal" than others so some people are more likely to identify with a particular party than others.[26] It has been found that party identification is often connected with characteristics such as social class, ethnic and religious groups, region, and age.[27] Groups of people with similar backgrounds who are likely to vote the same way are called voting blocs. In the United States, for example, the South is still more solidly Democratic than Republican (although this predilection is waning). Urban areas are also likely to be pockets of Democratic support as are the American black and Jewish communities, who are traditionally Democratic rather than Republican. Young people are consistently more likely to align themselves with the more liberal party, while older people are more likely to be conservative. In America, young voters are more often Democrats; in Britain, Labourites.

Perhaps the most important determinant of a person's party identification, though, is social-class membership. Even in nations such as the United States, where class divisions are very tentative compared to the traditional stratifications of many European nations, social class is the most pervasive single influence on a person's political outlook. In general, the blue-collar industrial worker is likely to vote for the party at the "left" of the political spectrum, while the middle and upper class tend to have more conservative political leanings.

One study compared the influence of social stratification on party membership in Great Britain, Australia, the United States, and Canada, and found that these nations could be ranked in this order according to their degree of class voting.[28] Why are Britons more likely to vote along class

[25] Leon D. Epstein, *Political Parties in Western Democracies* (New York: Praeger Publishers, 1967), pp. 78–85.
[26] See the discussion in Chapter 8 on public opinion blocs.
[27] William H. Flanigan gives an excellent discussion of American partisan blocs in Chapter 3 of his book, *The Political Behavior of the American Electorate*. We have drawn from his information in writing this section.
[28] Robert R. Alford, *Party and Society* (Chicago: Rand McNally, 1963).

lines than Americans and Canadians? The answer is complex, involving more than the fact that many blue-collar workers in Britain are automatically registered in the Labour party by their unions, or that Britain has a tradition of class consciousness.[29] Australia and Great Britain are relatively poor compared to Canada and the United States. Their educational opportunities and social mobility are more limited; they contain a relatively lower proportion of the middle class in their populations; and they are slightly less urbanized (although this is considerably more true of Australia than of Britain). Even more important, the populations of both Canada and the United States are divided along many other lines besides class. While Great Britain's and Australia's populations are relatively homogeneous, American and Canadian voters are divided into important racial, ethnic, religious, and sectional groups which are often just as influential in determining a person's politics as is the income he makes. In Canada, the conflict between the French- and English-speaking sectors adds an even further dimension to nonclass cleavages, and this undoubtedly contributes to the fact that Canadians are even less likely to vote according to class lines than Americans.

Given that relatively stable characteristics such as class, region, race and religion are important in determining which voting blocs will support which political party, it follows that a certain proportion of the voters can be expected to support each party at any given election. The term *normal vote* has been given to this relatively stable element of the vote.

The Normal Vote. In analyzing presidential elections in the United States between 1952 and 1964, the Survey Research Center was able to divide the total popular vote into two components—one showing the degree in which party identification influenced voter decisions; the other showing the effect of immediate variables such as issues and candidates.[30] They found that different people are influenced by party membership to different extents: while most American voters (close to 75 percent) classify themselves as either Republicans or Democrats, their degree of party loyalty varies considerably. Among strong Republicans and Democrats, over 95 percent will vote along party lines in a presidential election. But between the extremes of strong party identifiers in both parties falls a whole spectrum of weaker party identifiers and independent voters. Their votes, although less likely to go regularly to one party, do average out to a fairly constant "normal vote," that is, the percentage by which the vote would be divided if every voter voted for the party he is most sympathetic with.

Of course, the normal vote never absolutely determines the outcome of

[29] We have drawn from Leon D. Epstein's analysis in *Political Parties in Western Democracies*, pp. 85–93. Epstein concludes that class voting is likely to decline in all of these nations, as most of the factors connected with class divisions are on the downswing.

[30] See Angus Campbell, Philip Converse, Warren Miller, and Donald Stokes, "The Concept of the Normal Vote," *Elections and the Political Order* (New York: John Wiley & Sons, 1966), Chapter 2.

an election. If it did, the Democrats would always win, since traditionally more voters identify with them than with the Republican party.[31] But in the long run, the two usually balance out fairly evenly, as a greater percentage of Republicans can be expected to turn out at the polls, and the Republican party often has more financial support and thus greater access to the media. In the 1972 election, President Nixon had to attract a substantial number of people who normally vote Democratic in order to win.

The normal vote cannot be counted upon to bring the same results in every election. This can be seen by contrasting the defeat of one Republican candidate—Barry Goldwater—in 1964 with the victories of another Republican—Richard Nixon—in 1968 and 1972. In each case, the Republican candidate should have lost according to all the rules. But election outcomes, as we've seen, don't always follow the rules. In the first case many Republicans defected to the Democratic party; in the second and third cases, the normal minority Republicans were able to turn the tables. In an attempt to fit elections into a rational pattern according to the degree to which they conform with the normal vote, the Survey Research Center has developed a three-part classification of American elections.[32]

In the Kennedy and Johnson victories of 1960 and 1964, the elections roughly followed the pattern of the normal vote. That is, no overriding issues or candidate preferences were sufficient to cause large numbers of habitual Democrats to switch their votes to the Republican camp. This type of election is termed a "maintaining election." In contrast are the Eisenhower elections of the fifties. In both 1952 and 1956, the minority Republican party was able to draw enough support from the Democrats to elect its candidate. The Survey Research Center classifies such instances as "deviating elections," because in each case, the Republicans drew only temporary support from the Democrats. It was Eisenhower's personal appeal rather than a long-term change in party loyalty that caused many Democrats to change their vote.

A third general classification is the "realigning election." Here, voters permanently change their allegiance from one party to another. Franklin D. Roosevelt's 1932 victory in the midst of the Great Depression marked a permanent shift in the balance of the normal vote in America. Prior to 1932, the balance of American voters had been Republican; since 1932, the Democratic party has claimed the most support.

While such classifications as "maintaining," "deviating," and "realigning" elections can do little more than provide an overall framework from which to view American elections, they do give us a useful perspective. But the normal vote cannot give us much help in understanding or predicting the actions of voters who have no affiliation. What have political scientists learned about the Independent voter?

---

[31] Peter Natchez cites the figure of 56 percent to 44 percent in "Images of Voting: The Social Psychologists," *Public Policy* 18 (Summer 1970): 556.
[32] See Campbell et al., *The American Voter*, pp. 531–38.

Table 12-2
Shifts in Independents and Strong Party Identifiers, 1952–1969

Year	Independent	Strong Democratic	Strong Republican	Total Strong Identifiers
1952	23	23	14	37
1956	20	23	16	39
1960	23	21	16	37
1962	22	24	13	37
1964	23	27	11	38
1965 *	23			
1966	29	18	10	28
1967 *	31			
1968	28	23	9	32
1969 *	30			

* AIPO (Gallup) data were used for these years. Figures for other years are taken from Survey Research Center Studies.
Source: Based on data from Table 5.7 in Walter Burnham, Critical Elections and the Mainstream of American Politics (New York: W. W. Norton, 1970), p. 121.

The Independent Voters. In recent years, the United States has seen a sharp decline in strong party identifiers, and at the same time a corresponding increase in Independents—voters who are loyal to neither party. The 1950s were characterized by a relatively sharp polarization of American voters between strong Republicans and strong Democrats, with relatively few Independents in between. But the mid-sixties have brought what seems to be the beginning of an abrupt turnabout: between the years 1965 and 1966, the proportion of strong party identifiers (most notably Democrats) declined sharply, while the number of voters committed to neither party rose (see Table 12-2). The result is that, while in 1948 under 20 percent of voters called themselves Independents, today about 30 percent do so.[33]

Do these figures mean that the profile of the American voter has changed radically in recent years? Does a decline in party identifiers mean that fewer or more voters are involved in the political process? The answer is uncertain. In the 1950s, studies of the Independent voter indicated that the people who identified with neither party tended to be the ones who were least involved in and least informed about politics.[34] According to these sources, the rise in Independents would mean that the electorate is becoming less involved in politics. But efforts to pinpoint who the Independent voter is offer an interesting contrast.[35] They show that the Independent voters are drawn

[33] This section is based on Walter Burnham, *Critical Elections and the Mainstream of American Politics* (New York: W. W. Norton, 1970), p. 121.
[34] V. O. Key, and M. C. Cummings, Jr. *The Responsible Electorate: Rationality in Presidential Voting, 1936–1960* (Cambridge, Mass.: Harvard University Press, 1966), Chapter 1; and Campbell et al., *The American Voter*, pp. 143–45.
[35] See the discussion in Burnham from which we have drawn. *Critical Elections*, pp. 120–30.

Table 12-3
The "New Independents": Shifts in Proportion of Independents by Social Category, 1965–1967 [a]

Category	Percent Increase
Age 30–49	11
Highest Income ($7,000 and Over)	10
College Educated	10
Nonwhite	10
Age 21–29	10
White-Collar Occupations	10
U.S.	8
Age 50 and Over	6
Women	6
Grade-School Education	5
Middle Income ($5,000–$6,999)	5
Low Income (Under $3,000)	3
Farmers	2

[a] Based on published AIPO (Gallup) data.

Source: *Table 5.10 in Walter Burnham,* Critical Elections and the Mainstream of American Politics *(New York: W. W. Norton, 1970), p. 127.*

from the groups that have the highest rates of participation: the educated, the professional, and the upper-middle classes. It seems most unlikely that the groups that produce the most involved portion of American citizenry—the educated and the wealthy—are suddenly losing their interest in politics. But if the Independent is indeed the uninterested person who is least likely to vote, then this is exactly what has happened.

A more likely explanation is that the Independent may not be as uninvolved as we once thought he was, or that the type of person who is likely to be an Independent has undergone a change since the studies made in the mid-fifties. There seems to be considerable evidence to bear this out (see Table 12-3). Studies have shown that the percentage of people identifying themselves as Independents is higher among the young than the old, the college educated than grade- or high-school educated, whites than nonwhites, and men than women. By late 1969, 53 percent of college students called themselves Independents, and most of these classified themselves as "extremely liberal." [36]

The overall picture of the Independent voter seems to indicate a growing inclination of voters to make a rational decision to avoid commitment to either political party, not a sharp increase in ignorance and apathy. It also points toward a sharp decline in the influence of the two American political parties on voter decisions—which seems to be borne out to some extent by

[36] *Gallup Opinion Index* 48 (June 1969): 39; and *Gallup Opinion Index* 55 (January 1970): 14.

the high percentages of ticket-splitters during the 1972 elections (see the discussion that follows). Whether this indicates a permanent shift in the voting patterns of Americans, the beginning of a major change in the normal vote, or only a temporary movement by a number of voters is impossible to tell at this stage. It does mean that, as party identification declines, short-term influences are likely to have a more significant impact on voter decisions.

Short-term Variables

Which is more important to the voter—Edward Heath's stand on Britain's entry into the European Common Market, or the fact that he heads the Conservative party? John F. Kennedy's Catholicism or his membership in the Democratic party? The answer to what determines a vote depends largely on the divisiveness of the issues of an election year and on popular feeling about the candidate.[37] Party affiliation provides election guidelines for the voter when immediate variables don't intervene, but if the voter feels strongly enough about the opponents or the setting of one specific election, he is likely to disregard his party membership and vote for the opposition.

In every election, some voters will cross party lines and vote for a candidate or candidates in the opposite camp. Dividing one's vote between candidates of more than one party is called ticket-splitting. Analyses of ticket-splitting in presidential elections in the United States between 1900 and 1972 shows that this has been a growing trend. In their study of the 1968 national elections, Gallup Associates found a very high degree of ticket-splitting: 54 percent of their sample had voted for candidates of more than one political party.[38] Among the highest groups of ticket-splitters were the well educated, the upper classes, young voters (between twenty-one and twenty-nine years of age), and Independents. In 1972, in spite of Richard Nixon's landslide victory, the Democratic party was able to draw enough support both to keep control of Congress and add one governor to their ranks.

What are the reasons behind ticket-splitting? Cross-pressures between countervailing motives is the principal factor. The Republican who was a committed conscientious objector in 1964 had to make a choice between voting for his party or his principles; in many cases, his decision was to

[37] Peter Natchez and Irvin C. Bupp group elections according to the prevailing political climate. During *normal* periods, the electorate remains politically unaware; candidate personality and party ID are most important in determining the vote. But during a time of *crisis*—such as a depression or a war—voters are very aware of issues and their decisions depend primarily on this variable. See "Candidates, Issues, and Voters," *Public Policy* 17 (1968) : 409–37.

[38] *Gallup Opinion Index* 42 (December 1968) : 9. See also Richard W. Boyd's discussion in "Presidential Elections: An Explanation of Voting Defection" in *American Political Science Review* 63 (June 1969) : 498–514.

vote according to his principles on the national ticket and his party for state and local contests. The committed Democrat who was convinced that a Roman Catholic president would not be able to give primary loyalty to his nation had to make a tough decision in 1960; many (but not enough to swing the election) decided to vote for all of the Democratic candidates except the presidential hopeful.[39] The general rule is that the less committed the party identifier, the more likely he is to divide his vote.[40]

Although there are many variables that cause voters to divide their votes between parties, political analysts have found that most of the factors that lead to ticket-splitting and to a departure from long-term party identification are related either to the particular issues of a campaign or to the individual candidate.

Issue Orientation. In 1900, William Jennings Bryan based his candidacy on the Populists' call for a silver redemption standard for the dollar, identifying himself so strongly with that issue that even now, the mention of his name in a game of word association will most likely bring the response "cross of gold." Although Bryan lost, the case illustrates an election where one issue dominated voter decisions, at least to popular memory.

A political issue is a question about public policy which causes conflict. Any government actions or proposals will foster some conflict; the degree depends on the dimensions of public reaction. The issues that are the most decisive to any election are the ones which affect the most people most directly; and the way different issues affect different voters is a good measure of the diversity of the people. In the American presidential election of 1968, many young men of draft age decided their vote according to which candidate they thought would be most likely to end the war in Vietnam. Many black people voted instead for the candidate they saw as most likely to further racial equality, while a large number of workers in organized labor based their choice on the man they thought would be most sympathetic to organized labor. Domestic issues have traditionally had more impact on voter decisions than foreign affairs, although several elections (including Lyndon Johnson's victory over Barry Goldwater in 1964) have been dominated by foreign policy questions.[41]

[39] For a thorough discussion, see Philip Converse, "Religion in Politics: The 1960 Election" in Campbell et al., *Elections and the Political Order*, Chapter 2.

[40] Angus Campbell and Warren E. Miller carry this one step further, developing a four-part classification of voters according to their degree of commitment and their actual vote. The indifferent straight ticket, the indifferent split ticket, and the motivated straight-ticket voter are described in "The Motivational Bases of Straight and Split Ticket Voting," *American Political Science Review* 51 (June 1957): 293–312.

[41] In their book, *The Real Majority* (New York: Coward-McCann, 1970), Richard M. Scammon and Ben Z. Wattenberg identify four main types of issues which have dominated American elections and political strategies in the past decade. They include the "social issue" (crime in the streets, riots, drug abuse, et al.); the economy; the issue of ecology; and American international policy (primarily the Vietnam War). While their thesis is open to some dispute, the book provides excellent coverage and interesting reading.

Candidate Image. Charles de Gaulle of France, Pierre Elliott Trudeau of Canada, Willy Brandt of Germany, and John F. Kennedy of the United States are some of the more charismatic political figures of the past decade. Each inspired either strong loyalty or sharp distrust; very few people had neutral feelings about them.

Candidate orientation refers to a voter's attitudes about a particular candidate apart from his feelings about issues or his regular party affiliation. While its importance in influencing a voter's decision varies a good deal according to the strength of a candidate's image, candidate orientation is rarely very important in determining an election. Candidates for national office may spend staggering sums to build public images, but the fact is that candidate orientation is seldom the sole reason for voting a certain way and is rarely important in determining who wins an election.

The importance of a candidate's image to voter decisions varies according to the peculiarities of each election. In periods of economic depression, for example, the personalities of the candidates are likely to be secondary to the economic crisis. Candidate orientation is likely to be strongest when an incumbent is running for reelection: he is already a public figure, and voters will have firmer opinions about his capabilities.[42]

Some elections do hinge largely on who the candidates are. Dwight Eisenhower's winning smile deserves much of the credit for Republican control of the White House in the fifties, just as Charles de Gaulle's and Juan Peron's personalities dominated the politics and elections of France and Argentina for several years. Even in parliamentary democracies, where individual personalities ideally have little effect on the election of prime ministers because it is the party and not the candidate who receives the vote (see the discussion in Chapter 11), a candidate's image sometimes dominates elections.[43] Winston Churchill of England, David Ben Gurion of Israel, and Jawaharlal Nehru of India are cases in point.

With the growth of television as a campaign device, the image of the candidate seems to be growing even more important in parliamentary campaigns. In the 1970 elections both Harold Wilson and Edward Heath made appearances on television (once together), and their campaigns were oriented toward public appearances, walking tours, impromptu speeches, and public

[42] A basic fact of presidential politics is the advantage of the incumbent. In recent political history, one president to use this advantage successfully was Dwight D. Eisenhower, who after his first four years in office had become deeply revered and trusted. The importance of office is perhaps the incumbent's greatest advantage. Candidate orientation is thus a more important variable in presidential elections than in state or local contests, as the candidates' names are "household words" by the time of the National Conventions. Donald E. Stokes uses SRC data to trace the impact of candidate orientation, party identification, and issues as determining variables in the 1952, 1956, 1960, and 1964 elections. See "Some Dynamic Elements of Contests for the Presidency" in *American Political Science Review* 60 (March 1966) : 19–28.

[43] David E. Butler and Anthony King show how Conservative incumbent Sir Alec Douglas-Home's unpopularity, contrasted with the Labour party's candidate-oriented campaign, contributed heavily to Harold Wilson's election in 1964, in *The British General Election of 1964* (New York: St. Martin's Press, 1965) : 146–50; 370–71.

meetings which would afford them the greatest personal exposure on television and radio news broadcasts. Whether the images they projected by their appearances had much to do with the election outcome is debatable, but it is certain that they were calculated to influence the voters in a specific manner. The questions of how candidates use the information they have about the behavior of voters, who votes, and which groups vote which way provide an interesting insight into the practical applications that can be made of voting behavior studies.

Candidate Strategies: A Practical Application of Voting Behavior Studies

Campaign strategies, especially in two-party systems like those of the United States and Britain, are geared toward two goals: keeping "one foot on home base" by not alienating the normal party supporters, and at the same time trying to win over votes from the undecided and from as many of the opposition as possible. There are many forces at play in the ultimate decision of the voter. Party identification and the normal vote play a primary role in deciding elections. However, the image a candidate projects is more within his control. His image may also contribute to his victory or defeat, although its importance is often negligible, and it is often difficult to change a public image once established. The political and economic events of an election year—war, depression, treaties—also contribute to both the dimension and the direction of voter reaction. In a year when a major crisis has occurred, voter turnout is likely to be high; in a year when things have gone rather smoothly, voters may be relatively apathetic.

How does the candidate use these variables to plan his campaign strategy? In most cases, his campaign is designed to fit the opinions and needs of his constituency. Thus, he must be aware of pockets of party strength and resistance, what city dwellers are thinking versus the opinions of people in the suburbs, what districts contain the lowest rates of participation (and will therefore yield the smallest numbers of votes), and which stands on issues are likely to inflame large groups of people against his candidacy. Only when the candidate has some awareness of the direction and intensity of voter opinion will he be able to plan an effecive campaign. In this way he utilizes the knowledge of voting behavior which political science provides him with.

Voting Blocs and Campaign Strategies: A Conclusion

Any observer of the American election game who has witnessed liberal candidates wearing hard hats and conservative hopefuls making "peace signs" before an election will readily recognize the fact that people vote according to groups, and that these voting blocs play a major role in a campaign. Since the basic strategy is to win the support of the largest possible number of voters, a knowledge of what the people think is essential.

Voting blocs fall into roughly the same categories as the public opinion blocs discussed in Chapter 8. Class, ethnic, and geographic characteristics are the most important influences in opinion formation, and these provide general guidelines for predicting voting behavior. Urban and rural voters will oppose each other on a mass-transit bond; blacks and whites may vote differently on a school-busing issue. Every election victory is the result of a major coalition formed by several smaller blocs of voters. On a national scale, the Democrats have traditionally represented a coalition of labor, blacks, Catholics, Jews, and urban voters; the Republicans have received their support from a coalition of rural and farm voters, remaining Protestants, and nonunion workers.[44]

Robert Axelrod identifies three factors which determine a voting bloc's value, in terms of "vote power," to a political party.[45] They are the size of a group, its rate of turnout on election day, and its loyalty to a given party. A change in one variable will affect a group's contribution as a voting bloc. For example, the black contribution to the Democratic coalition increased from 5 percent in 1956 to 19 percent in 1968; this is primarily due to the increase in black voter turnout in that period. The result was that the "vote power" of the black voting bloc gained significantly. Blacks became a more important element in the Democratic coalition.

Once a candidate recognizes opinion patterns and the strength of the support he receives from various blocs within his constituency, he can use this knowledge to plan his strategies more effectively. In 1968 Richard Nixon reached large numbers of farmers who he knew would be receptive to his message through early-morning radio commercials. Black newspapers and "soul stations" carry political advertising to large numbers of black voters and sympathetic whites, and television spots preceding and following the Lawrence Welk show will reach a good number of older voters. In this way, the candidate can use even the mass media to aim a particular message toward a specific bloc of voters.

Through a knowledge of characteristic voting patterns of different regions, a presidential candidate may recognize that no matter how much

[44] Kevin Philips in his book, *The Emerging Republican Majority* (Garden City, N.Y.: Doubleday, 1970), largely masterminded the 1968 Republican National campaign strategy with his controversial theory of the emergence of a new alignment of Republican, conservative voting blocs. This alignment, he says, will consist of the following elements: 1) "sun belt conservatives"—the middle-class urban-suburban population of the South, the Southwest, and southern California; 2) "backlash urban voters," who have turned away from the Democratic party's commitment to racial equality; 3) "the heartland"— heavily Republican to begin with, it includes the Midwest, and the Mountain and trans-Appalachian border states; 4) "the old South"; and 5) "remnants of the Republican establishment."

[45] See "Where the Votes Come From: An Analysis of Electoral Coalitions, 1952–1968," *American Political Science Review* 66 (March 1972): 11–20.

time he spends in a state, he won't have a chance of carrying it—or, that a few more visits may be able to bring that state over to his side of the fence. An understanding of voting behavior can thus perform an immeasurable service in helping a candidate recognize which groups support him, which might support him, which won't even vote, and which he stands no chance of winning to his side.

Suggested Readings

Alford, Robert R. *Party and Society*. Chicago: Rand McNally, 1963. Voting patterns and preference in the United States, Great Britain, Canada, and Australia as drawn from interviews.

Berelson, Bernard, Lazarsfeld, Paul F., and McPhee, William N. *Voting*. Chicago: University of Chicago Press, 1954. One of the first of the behavioral-socio-political studies of the American electorate. Based on a survey of Elmira, New York.

Burdick, Eugene, and Brodbeck, Arthur J., eds. *American Voting Behavior*. New York: The Free Press, 1959. A first-rate collection of essays on the political behavior of the American.

Butler, David, and Stokes, Donald. *Political Change in Britain*. New York: St. Martin's Press, 1969. A definitive study of the British electorate.

Campbell, Angus et al. *The American Voter*. New York: John Wiley, 1960. A work on American voting behavior that forms the basis for other contemporary work, including opposition and reanalysis.

Flanigan, William H. *Political Behavior of the American Electorate*. 2nd ed. Boston: Allyn and Bacon, 1972. An up-to-date summary of findings on political behavior in the United States.

Key, V. O., and Cummings, Milton C. *The Responsible Electorate*. Cambridge, Mass.: Harvard University Press, 1966. An argument for the rationality of voters.

Lipset, Seymour Martin. *Political Man*. New York: Doubleday, 1960. An historical and contemporary analysis of the social bases of political behavior across nations.

Lubell, Samuel. *The Hidden Crisis in American Politics*. New York: W. W. Norton, 1970. An argument about the possibility of a new bias in political behavior during an American election.

Polsby, Nelson W., and Wildavsky, Aaron B. *Presidential Elections: Strategies of American Electoral Politics*. 3rd ed. New York: Charles Scribner's Sons, 1972. The strategies of parties are related to the behavior of the electorate.

Rokkan, Stein. *Citizens, Elections, Parties*. New York: David McKay, 1970. The social patterns of electoral support in Western politics are examined.

Representation
and electoral systems
CHAPTER 13

What gives government the right to take taxes from our pay checks? Why can the state ask eighteen- or nineteen-year-old men to take two or three years out of their lives to join the armed forces? To these questions, many of us would answer, "Government makes the laws; we have to obey." But is that really an answer? It doesn't explain who government is, why government has the right to make those laws, or why we must subordinate ourselves to the authority of the state.[1]

Ever since organized society developed, some six thousand years ago, various answers have been given to the question, "By what right can one

[1] For a provocative discussion which contends that men need not necessarily accede to the state's superior authority, see Robert Paul Wolff, *In Defense of Anarchism* (New York: Harper & Row, 1970).

man exercise authority over another?" Until the dawn of the modern age, around 1500 A.D., it was commonly assumed that government was divinely sanctioned. Chinese emperors asserted that they received their authority from heaven. Japanese emperors, Egyptian pharaohs, Incan chieftains, and the later Roman emperors went one step further and claimed the right to rule because they were living gods. For many centuries, the kings of Europe claimed to rule "by grace of God" and "by the divine right of Providence."

Today, the idea of a religious basis for government is not given much credence. (Imagine Americans believing their president ruled by divine right.) Instead, we believe that a democratic government's power comes from the consent of the governed: the people grant it authority to rule.

Government must rest upon more than military force or brute power. It depends upon the support of the people, even in dictatorships, where government can be overthrown by revolution. The most important way the people may express their wishes is through elections, and through the representatives who are put in office in those elections.

Representation: What It Is, and How It Works

Representation is basic to all modern governments. The word itself— *re-presentation*—means to make present again, implying that someone or something is symbolically, though perhaps not literally, present to participate in a given act or function. American government is considered representative because the people have a say in choosing the men and women who make law and government policy. Through his vote, the average American gives his representative the power to act in his name, to "represent" his vital interests, and to enact laws to protect his welfare, happiness, and security. But the concept of representation does not only apply to democratic government.[2] All government, figuratively, is based on *representation*—a word which has been given many different interpretations throughout history.

Theories of Representation

Thomas Hobbes's (1588–1679) answer to the question of why men form governments was that without government no man could be secure from

[2] Much of the discussion which follows is based on Hanna F. Pitkins's *The Concept of Representation* (Berkeley: University of California Press, 1967). An interesting essay tracing the etymology of the term *representation* is presented by Charles A. Beard and John D. Lewis in "The Representative in Perspective," in *The Representative: Trustee? Delegate? Partisan? Politico?*, ed. Neil Reimer (Boston: D. C. Heath, 1967), pp. 109–16. Reimer's book also presents an excellent bibliography on representation.

attack. Government began long ago when, to protect themselves, people renounced their personal independence and formed a "social contract" that authorized the sovereign to establish laws to protect everyone equally. Hobbes's government was founded on "consent of the governed"—with one exception. Once authority is given to a sovereign it can never be taken back; if the sovereign becomes a tyrant, the people cannot trade him in. Writing during the English civil wars, Hobbes felt that anarchy (the state of nature), where every man is free to do as he pleases is infinitely worse than even the most despotic government.

John Locke (1632–1704), the "father of democratic government," modified Hobbes's basic argument in several important ways.[3] In his *Second Treatise on Civil Government*, Locke declared that rulers must be responsible to the governed. His version of the social contract binds the government and the people to a set of mutual responsibilities: the people must obey the government only if it honors its obligation to protect them. If the government violates its trust, the people have the right to replace it. Locke's idea of representative government is much closer to modern democratic theory than is Hobbes's. All men were covered by Locke's approach, but since those with property had more to protect, they were afforded more protection.

Jean Jacques Rousseau (1712–1778) broke sharply from the traditions of Hobbes and Locke. Rousseau wanted nothing of his predecessors' social contract, and he felt that representation went hand in hand with inequality and loss of freedom. Man is an intelligent, rational being, and is quite capable of making decisions himself. Thus, the ideal was a city-state, where everyone could participate in deliberative assemblies of government, with no need of representatives who would only serve to disenfranchise the people. No one should speak for the people but themselves.

While the individual, and not the representative or ruler, was the basic unit of government, this did not mean that Rousseau favored anarchy. "Freedom," says Rousseau, "is obedience to a law we prescribe for ourselves. But society cannot subsist if every man makes his own law separately. Therefore all must make the law for all." [4]

Hobbes, Locke, and Rousseau represent quite a range of theories—from the allocation of all popular authority to the sovereign, to rule by the "general will," with direct popular participation instead of indirect representation. How do we interpret theories of representation today?

Representation in Western Democratic Society. When a president, senator, or minister of Parliament is voted into office, what obligation does he

[3] A basic discussion of the varieties of political thought is provided in Gerald M. Pomper, *Elections in America: Control and Influence in Democratic Politics* (New York: Dodd, Mead, 1970), Chapter 2.

[4] Quoted from John Plamenatz, *Man and Society*, vol. 1 (New York: McGraw-Hill, 1963), p. 401. This book forms the basis of our discussion of Rousseau.

have to the people who elected him? How much control should a voter have over the representative he elects? [5]

Standing for the People: Symbolic Representation. In one sense, the head of state is the "symbol" of the state: he represents his people by "standing for" them. An important reason that Franklin D. Roosevelt, Dwight D. Eisenhower, and John F. Kennedy were so popular was because they seemed to symbolize the spirit of the nation. In England, Queen Elizabeth "stands for" the people, and her life-style reflects the traditional power and glory of the nation. But few people today would be content to elect a representative to office purely because he or she symbolized the national or local character. More important in the voter's mind is how a representative will act for him, once he's in office.

Acting for the People: By Conscience or Constituents? When a congressman is elected from a farm district, is it his responsibility to vote for all bills that will help farmers, even though some of those bills may work to the disadvantage of the state or the nation? Should he act as the voice of the farmers in his district, or should he vote according to his conscience, even when it means going against his constituents? If a senator feels that busing of schoolchildren will improve racial equality, but his district doesn't want school busing, which way should he vote? After all, he has read the reports of the experts on the subject, while the people he represents aren't nearly as well informed. Should he act as an expert, or as a proxy for the less informed?

One answer to the dilemma was advocated by Edmund Burke (1729–1797), who believed that while a representative must act in the name of his constituents, he is not necessarily bound to act as they would wish him to act. As a minister of Parliament, Burke felt that he represented the entire British Empire, not just his district of Bristol. As such, he was responsible for acting in the best interests of the nation as a whole, even if that meant opposing the narrow self-interests of his district.[6] This idea did not violate the principles of representative government, Burke maintained, because if the people did not like the way their representative was acting, they could vote him out of office at the next election.

The opposite side of the argument is that a member of Parliament or a congressman is elected to act for his constituents and is morally obligated to act as they want him to act—even if it means going against his own better judgment. But while this theory comes closest to the ideal of "re-presenta-

[5] For a more detailed discussion of democratic representation see Roland Pennock and John W. Chapman, eds., *Representation* (New York: Atherton, 1968), Chapters 1–3; and Robert G. Dixon, Jr., *Democratic Representation* (New York: Oxford University Press, 1968), Chapters 1–3.

[6] For the original, see Ross Hoffman and Paul Levack, eds., *Burke's Politics: Selected Writings and Speeches of Edmund Burke on Reform, Revolution and War* (New York: Alfred A. Knopf, 1949), pp. 114–16. An extension of Burke's argument was that Parliament served *all* Englishmen, and this became a central controversy in the Revolutionary War. Parliament argued that by "virtual representation" all Englishmen in the colonies had an indirect voice in government. The colonists felt otherwise: "No taxation without (direct) representation." The rest is history.

tion," there are many problems in actually carrying it out. First and foremost is the representative's difficult in finding out *what* his constituents want, so that he can carry out their wishes. The average American congressman represents nearly half a million people, and the likelihood that he will speak to or receive mail from even 5 percent of that number is very slim, even on major issues.[7] Public opinions polls provide a somewhat better guide, but the public isn't tested on every issue that comes before Congress. And there is a wide range of public opinion on any issue. Which opinion represents the majority? In many cases, "I don't know" is the most common answer in a pollster's survey.

A representative, therefore, would find it very difficult to mirror the attitudes of his constituents, since it is virtually impossible to find out what most of those attitudes are. Yet, the congressman, senator, or minister of Parliament cannot help but pay attention—as best he can—to the voice of those he represents, as regular elections hold him responsible to his constituents. In sum, the question of whatever a representative should act as a Burkean leader or as a proxy for his people's will is a complicated one.[8]

How Representative Are Representatives? Even if a legislator were able to act as the voice of his district, he could easily be accused of being

[7] E. E. Schattschneider points out that those a congressman *does* hear from are most unlikely to be a representative sample of the constituency. His classic, *The Semisovereign People* (New York: Holt, Rinehart and Winston, 1960), shows that not all who "want" have equal access to express those wants to their congressman. (See especially Chapter 2.) On the selectivity of information received by congressmen—as reported by congressmen themselves—see Raymond Bauer, Ithiel de Sola Pool, and Louis A. Dexter, *American Business and Public Policy* (New York: Atherton, 1963). Warren E. Miller and Donald Stokes show how roll-call votes correspond to congressmen's perception of their constituency's feelings in "Constituency Influence in Congress," *American Political Science Review* 57 (March 1963): 45–56.

[8] So argues Anthony Downs in *An Economic Theory of Democracy* (New York: Harper & Row, 1957). See especially Part III. Joseph A. Schumpeter's classic discusses the representative's answerability. See *Capitalism, Socialism, and Democracy* (New York: Harper & Row, 1950).

unrepresentative on other grounds. If all of the state legislators of Alabama were white, most of us would agree that the state assembly would be an easy target for criticism, no matter how good a job it was doing.

Studies of American and British legislators show that most representatives are not at all representative in reflecting the social makeup of their districts. For the most part, lawmakers are middle- or upper-class professionals, overwhelmingly male, generally older than the average age of their constituents, and much better educated. WASPS (white, Anglo-Saxon Protestants) dominate both nations' legislatures.[9]

How can men in the United States with such backgrounds possibly represent the interests of women, blacks, or Mexican-Americans? In 1970, about 53 percent of Americans were women, while over 10 percent were black. But neither was represented in Congress in anywhere near that proportion. And the millions of people in low-income brackets and on public welfare had no representation at all. Some have suggested that the answer to this problem lies in having a representative government that corresponds to the characteristics of the general population. If the United States is 53 percent female, its legislative bodies must be 53 percent female. The proposed government must also contain blacks, Roman Catholics, Jews, and welfare recipients in proportion to their numbers in the population.

The proposal, while intriguing, is simpler on paper than in practice. In a democracy all citizens are equal before the law, but the correspondence theory would deny equal opportunity. If the quota for white males in Congress were filled, then any other white male who wanted to be a congressman would be denied the chance to run. If Chicano women were underrepresented, then they would have a "more than equal" opportunity to get into office. Another problem is determining which groups should be entitled to representation. Should the Gay Activist Alliance be represented in the legislature? What about ex-convicts, the mentally defective, vegetarians, and high-school dropouts?[10] Although their solutions may be unwieldy, the

---

[9] According to *Congressional Quarterly*, the average age of members of the Ninety-second Congress was 50.6 years, more than twenty years older than the average age of the American population. Of 535 members, 302 had legal backgrounds, 173 were businessmen or bankers, 72 were teachers, 47 were farmers, and 36 were journalists (with some overlapping). There were only 13 women and 13 Negroes. For studies of the makeup of British and American legislatures, see also Harold J. Laski, *The Personnel of the English Cabinet: 1801–1924* (New Haven, Conn.: Yale University Press, 1932); Charles S. Hyneman, "Who Makes Our Laws," *Political Science Quarterly* 55 (1940); Donald R. Matthews, *The Social Background of Political Decisionmakers* (Garden City, N.Y.: Doubleday, 1954); Norman Meller, "Legislative Behavior Research," *Western Political Quarterly* 13 (1960); John B. McConaughty, "Certain Personality Factors of State Legislators in South Carolina," *American Political Science Review* 44 (1950); and Kenneth Prewitt, *The Recruitment of Political Leaders* (New York: Bobbs-Merrill, 1970).

[10] Heinz Eulau proposes that correspondence theorists are mistaken to think that the "chosen" can ever resemble their "choosers." The very fact of having been selected makes a representative different from those he "represents" as his changed position sets him apart from them. See "Changing Views of Representation" in *Contemporary Political Science*, ed. Ithiel de Sola Pool (New York: McGraw-Hill, 1967), p. 80.

advocates of the correspondence theory have raised very important questions about *who* and *what* should be represented in government decision making.

Functional Representation and the Corporate State. An alternative to the correspondence-theory solution is the idea of functional representation, where the legislature is structured around the major social or economic interests in society.

Functional representation began in the Middle Ages in Europe, when people didn't think in terms of individual rights. A man was a member of a class (clergy, nobility, peasantry, town dweller) first, and a human being second.[11] The result was that, when legislative bodies first came into existence, they represented classes rather than men. Many European legislatures, such as the French *Etats-Generaux*, were representative of the clergy, the nobility, and the masses rather than the individual citizens as equals, and England's Parliament is still divided according to the aristocrats and the common man. Today, the idea that classes rather than the people as a whole should be represented has fallen into disrepute. In the only medieval legislative body still surviving today—the English Parliament—the House of Lords has been stripped of virtually all power. But the vestiges of medieval representation still exist and can be seen in the United States, West Germany, Australia, and Canada, where the upper houses originally represented units of government rather than the people.

In the twentieth century, the concept of functional representation was revived, and was tried in several nations. British political theorist and historian G. D. H. Cole led the movement.[12] He proposed that national legislatures should represent interests such as agriculture, organized labor, industry, and the arts and sciences instead of geographical districts. Each interest would be assigned seats according to its relative size and importance to the economy, and people would vote not as individuals, but as businessmen, laborers, or farmers.

One variation of Cole's idea has been used in the Irish Seanad (Senate).[13] Of sixty members, eleven are chosen by the prime minister, six by the universities, and the remaining forty-three are elected by the national legislature and county borough councils from lists of candidates drawn up by five vocational panels. These panels are based on occupational categories, and their choices represent cultural, educational, agricultural, labor, industrial, and commercial interests.

While the idea of vocations as the basis for representation ideally reflects

11 On this point see Robert R. Palmer, *The Age of the Democratic Revolution*, vol. 1 (Princeton, N.J.: Princeton University Press, 1959); and Maude V. Clarke, *Medieval Representation and Consent* (London: Longmans, Green, 1936).
12 G. D. H. Cole, *Guide Socialism Restated* (Philadelphia: J. B. Lippincott, 1920); and Fritz Nova, *Functional Representation* (Dubuque, Iowa: William C. Brown, 1950).
13 See Basil Chubb, ed., *A Source Book on Irish Government* (Dublin: Institute of Public Administration, 1964), especially pp. 203–10; and James D. O'Donnell, *How Ireland is Governed* (Dublin: Institute of Public Administration, 1965).

the division of a nation into business interests rather than units of government, the actual degree of functional representation in practice in the Seanad is very small. In the first place, the Seanad is much closer in its responsibilities and power to the ceremonial British House of Lords than it is to the United States Senate, so the duties of its members are largely advisory. And secondly, since the people who actually elect the nominees have political rather than vocational backgrounds, vocational interests usually receive second billing to political factors. Critics from the professions argue that "the degree to which [the system] has succeeded in introducing vocationalism into politics is considerably less than that to which it has introduced politics into vocational bodies." [14] So, while the Irish Seanad dabbles in functional representation, it can hardly be said to be a living example of this system.

The Irish Seanad is an interesting curiosity, but the corporate states created by Benito Mussolini in Italy and Antonio Salazar in Portugal carried the concept of functional representation to a more serious extreme in replacing people with economic interests. In 1926, Mussolini divided the seats in the Italian Chamber of Deputies among twenty-two state corporations, which represented the nation's economic interests. While the corporations were originally meant to speak for the workers, the government slipped farther and farther out of the grasp of the people. Soon the Fascist party controlled all of the corporations, and in 1939, the Chamber of Deputies was abolished and a chamber of corporations was established as the arm of the Italian Fascist party. By the time the corporate state reached its peak, Italy had a government of the corporations, by the corporations, and for the corporations.[15] The Portuguese also adopted a corporate state in 1935 under Antonio Salazar. Their regime still survives, but with no real popular participation.

A lesson from the twentieth century's flirtation with functional representation government based on economic interests rather than people is that this form of government lends itself to authoritarian control, because it automatically limits the people's right to representation. Even G. D. H. Cole rejected functional representation, after seeing how his idea worked in practice.

The Practice of Representation

Democracy comes from the Greek words *demos* and *kratia*. Literally, it means "people-power." The United States is not a democracy in this classic sense—it is a republic. *Democracy* means the rule by the people. In its literal application, however, this is physically impossible. So the Western world has adopted a republican form of government, where the people

---

[14] Chubb, *A Source Book*, p. 208.
[15] G. Lowell Field, *The Syndical and Corporate Institutions of Italian Fascism* (New York: Columbia University Press, 1938).

delegate to a few chosen representatives the right to act in their name, holding them accountable for their acts. Modern democracy is indirect, and the people themselves do not usually participate in making the laws. Who represents, and who is represented?

Electoral Districts. With the single exception of Israel, which is a one-constituency nation, every modern democracy is divided into geographical districts, or constituencies, which elect representatives.

There are two distinct types of constituencies.[16] Best known to Americans is the single-member district, where one assemblyman, one state senator, or one congressman is chosen to represent each electoral district. But many nations use multimember electoral districts, which elect more than one legislator at the same time. Multimember districts are most common in Western Europe, but they are also used in the United States. School-board members usually run on a city or countywide basis, and voters often choose three or four board members at a single election. It is seldom realized that United States senators represent multimember districts, but *two* senators are elected from each state. Because senatorial terms are staggered, however, people rarely have the opportunity to vote for two senators at the same time.[17]

Single-member or Multimember Districts: Which Works Better? Is the single-member or the multimember district better adapted to the task of representing its voters? Each system has both advantages and drawbacks.

It seems logical that multimember systems should encourage representation of smaller parties, since a list of several candidates from various parties allows the voter to choose separately according to party and qualifications. But multimember systems don't seem to work that way. Instead, there are often so many unfamiliar names on the ballot that the voter is likely to vote one of the major party lines instead of making a random selection from a smaller party. As a result, minority parties are often entirely shut out. While seeming to increase the voter's choice of candidates, multimember districts instead often favor the candidates backed by the strongest party. Thus they often permit a well-entrenched minority of the voters to control all the legislative seats from that district.[18]

16 For further discussion of single vs. multimember districts see Leon D. Epstein, *Political Parties in Western Democracies* (New York: Praeger Publishers, 1967), pp. 37–45; Frank J. Sorauf, *Political Parties in the American System* (Boston: Little, Brown, 1964), pp. 145–46; and Hugh A. Bone, *American Politics and the Party System*, 3rd ed. (New York: McGraw-Hill, 1965), pp. 150–53.

17 Actually, in 1962, 16 percent of American state senators, and 46 percent of state assemblymen came from multimember districts, as is shown in David Eisenberg, *State Legislative Redistricting* (Chicago: Public Administration Service, 1962), p. 20. Cleveland and Indianapolis still use multimember districts in city council elections, as do both of their states for electing assemblymen to their legislatures. See Howard D. Hamilton, "Legislative Constituencies: Single-Member Districts, Multimember Districts, and Floterial Districts," *Western Political Quarterly* 20 (June 1967): 321–40, for an examination of electoral districts in the United States.

18 Hamilton, "Legislative Constituencies." He came to this conclusion after studying multimember districts in the United States.

On the other hand, where multimember districts use proportional representation (PR), the result is the opposite: small parties are given voice in the legislature. In this system, each party wins seats in proportion to its percentage of the total vote. Although this system provides the closest thing to true representation of the different interests in the electorate, it has its drawbacks, too. Minority parties are given fair representation in the legislature, but this very fact often makes it virtually impossible for any one party to exercise any real control. The result is often highly unstable governments that are short-lived, unable to execute new policies, and often unable to exert any national leadership. The French Third and Fourth Republics, and Italy's series of temporary governments today are both typical of the worst of proportional representation. The average life expectancy of a post-World War II government in Italy has been about nine months. In general, the European nations using proportional representation have had unstable coalition governments that are incapable of providing decisive leadership.

The single-member system used in the United States and Great Britain is a "winner-take-all" system. Here, the candidate who wins the most votes gets into office, and the third place occupied by most minority-party candidates counts for nothing. Single-member districts favor two-party systems, for small parties can rarely hope to win enough seats to make a serious impact on government policy. The object of the game is to keep in the mainstream of political action. Parties who stray from the middle of the road usually win few supporters and so cut themselves off from a voice in the legislature.

But while single-member districts discriminate against small and unorthodox parties, they are more effective than proportional representation in another sense: they provide a more stable administration. Whichever party controls Congress or Parliament can claim a mandate from the people to put through its legislative program. Thus, while systems using proportional representation may give voice to a wider range of political opinion, it is the single-member districts that can usually provide a more effective government. Unfortunately, no one has yet figured out how to combine the advantages of both into the perfect electoral system.

Apportionment. Even if an electoral system were devised with the perfect balance between single-member districts and multimember proportional representation, it would still be possible to have an inefficient system of representation. If Congressman A and Congressman B each acted as a perfect representative, but A's district contained 300,000 people and B's contained 600,000, the two legislators would in fact be part of a very undemocratic system. The voters in A's district would be "twice as equal" as B's constituents because every *one* vote they cast would be equal to *two* votes from the second district.

Every democratic nation has some procedure by which legislative districts are apportioned, or drawn up according to the population to allow for the closest approximation of "one man, one vote." Ideally, districts should contain equal numbers of people, but this is not always the case, even today.

In Great Britain, a nonpartisan boundary commission supervised by Parliament adjusts districts after every census. The procedure sometimes allows for some shady manipulation. Since the commission's recommendations must be approved by Parliament, the majority party in the House of Commons has the opportunity to juggle the boundaries. As a result, pockets of opposition voters may find themselves divided among several majority districts, some of which are rather lopsided: disparities of as many as 60,000 people (in districts of under 100,000) have been reported within the past decade.[19] The United States does not have an unblemished record of fair and even apportionment either. Before the Supreme Court's 1964 "one man, one vote" ruling,[20] there were many serious inequalities. As recently as the 1960 election, one district in Michigan (the sixteenth) had close to 803,000 constituents, while another (the twelfth) had only a bit over 177,000. Each, of course, sent one representative to Congress. Until 1964, each state drew up its congressional districts in whatever way it saw fit, and gerrymandering (the practice of drawing constituency boundaries to the blatant advantage of the party in power) was often used. For the most part, however, gerrymandering was not widely practiced. If the party in power overplayed its advantage, the opposition might well return the compliment when it regained control. Thus a compromise system of "gentleman's agreements" was unofficially arranged: the seats of senior members of the minority party were usually protected against the perils of gerrymandering, and only junior legislators were faced with the threat of being mapped out of existence.[21]

Under our Constitution, a national census is taken every ten years to determine how many congressmen should represent each state. Originally, there was one representative for every 30,000 people, but the arrangement had to be revised, because with today's population, it would mean a House of more than 6,700 representatives. Today, the House is frozen at 435 members, and the quota for each state is proportional to its total population. Thus, in the ninety-second Congress, New York had 41 congressmen, but Rhode Island had only 2; Pennsylvania held 27 seats, but Vermont had only a single representative. This means in many instances that equal representation across state lines is impossible: Alaska and Vermont are each

[19] See R. L. Leonard, *Guide to the General Election* (London: Pan Books, 1964), p. 35; and also D. E. Butler, *The Electoral System in Britain since 1911*, 2nd ed. (New York: Oxford University Press, 1963).

[20] The *Baker* v. *Carr* ruling of 1962 established Federal jurisdiction over state apportionment cases. In 1964, the Warren Court extended this ruling, in the cases of *Reynolds* v. *Sims* and *Wesberry* v. *Sanders*, to apply to both the upper house of state legislatures and to congressional reapportionment. It determined that voters within a state are equal, and that their votes must be given equal weighting. Although the ruling aroused much controversy—on the grounds that state senates, like the national senate, should represent units of government rather than population—efforts to overturn the decisions were unsuccessful. See Gordon E. Baker, *The Reapportionment Revolution: Representation, Political Power, and the Supreme Court* (New York: Random House, 1966); also George W. Spicer, *The Supreme Court and Fundamental Freedoms* (New York: Appleton-Century-Crofts, 1967), pp. 163–72.

[21] Sorauf, *Political Parties in the American System*, pp. 145–46.

allowed one representative, yet Vermont's population is 110,000 more than Alaska's.[22] There is also a built-in inequality in any apportionment system's efforts to keep up to date in the fast-moving world of the last few decades. As Table 13-1 shows, in the ten years between the 1960 and the 1970 census, populations had shifted enough so that in one state (California), the difference in population between the largest and smallest congressional district was 106.3 percent.

Representatives. Who "acts for" the people in the offices of government? A representative may be symbolic, as is a king or dictator. He may be a head of state such as a president or a prime minister. He may be a judge

[22] *Congressional Quarterly Weekly Report* 30, no. 28 (July 8, 1972): 3.

Table 13-1
Range of the Largest and Smallest U.S. Congressional Districts before and after 1970 Census Redistricting

State	Variance [a]	
	After Redistricting	Before Redistricting
Michigan	0.0026%	39.9%
South Dakota	0.013	10.0
Utah	0.020	3.2
Georgia	0.10	53.4
Oklahoma	0.11	16.7
Florida	0.12	47.6
Colorado	0.12	55.9
Nebraska	0.15	0.15
New Jersey	0.15	51.5
New York	0.16	87.1
Idaho	0.20	24.6
Arizona	0.22	12.8
Oregon	0.22	30.0
Indiana	0.23	29.5
Rhode Island	0.24	19.6
Arkansas	0.26	23.2
Louisiana	0.31	32.9
Maine	0.46	0.46
Washington	0.48	31.7
Ohio	0.50	38.1
Missouri	0.62	48.8
Iowa	0.65	29.1
Virginia	0.67	50.9
Wisconsin	0.70	32.7
Alabama	0.78	21.3

Table 13-1
(Continued)

State	Variance [a]	
	After Redistricting	*Before Redistricting*
West Virginia	0.78	14.8
New Hampshire	0.88	4.8
New Mexico	1.24	1.24
Illinois	1.32	64.6
Kentucky	1.34	40.3
Minnesota	1.39	64.1
Montana	1.40	3.6
Kansas	1.56	16.2
Tennessee	1.58	10.8
Massachusetts	1.60	35.9
California	1.65	106.3
Pennsylvania	2.23	54.2
Maryland	2.56	68.5
North Carolina	3.72	27.9
Hawaii	3.96	3.96
Mississippi	4.08	24.8
Texas	4.99	54.4
South Carolina	8.17	21.4

[a] Refers to difference in population between the largest and smallest congressional districts.

Six states elect one representative at large and are thus not listed above: Alaska, Delaware, Nevada, North Dakota, Vermont, Wyoming.

Four states did not redistrict after 1970 census: Hawaii, Maine, Nebraska, New Mexico.

Connecticut has not yet redistricted. The variance of old districts is 16.8 percent.

The Hawaii figure is based on registered voters per congressional district. If total population figures were used, the variance would be 11.86 percent.

Source: Table in Congressional Quarterly Weekly Report, *30, no. 28 (July 8, 1972):* 3.

or an administrator who is representative in the sense that he is expected to be impartial, and not to represent any special group but to act in the interests of the whole. But the type of representative that automatically comes to mind in connection with the word is the legislator.

In all modern democracies, the lower house of the legislature is elected by the people directly. Historically, bodies such as the United States House of Representatives, the English House of Commons, and the German Bundestag were supposed to be the instruments which the average citizen could use to register his will, and were accordingly given a major share of lawmaking responsibility. (For example, laws dealing with public funds must always originate in the lower house.) The lower house provides the closest representation on a national scale.[23]

There is considerably more variation in the duties of the upper houses of legislatures. In England, Canada, India, and Sweden, where membership is hereditary, appointed, or indirectly elected, upper houses are mostly ceremonial, with no real responsibility. But in the United States, West Germany, and Australia, the upper houses are very powerful. Members of the West German Bundesrat are chosen by the popularly elected state legislatures, and American and Australian senators are directly elected by the people.[24]

Legislators, heads of state, judges, and administrators are all part of the republican system of government, where the people's participation in actual decision making is only by proxy. But while indirect democracy is necessary because populations are enormous and many people never bother to participate, it has not always served the best interests of the people.

"Direct Democracy": The Initiative and Referendum. At the end of the last century, it was beginning to look to some people as though republican government couldn't work. The California legislature seemed to represent the Southern Pacific Railroad more than it did the people of that state; the New York City Board of Aldermen was popularly known as "the forty thieves"; and the United States Senate was caricatured by writers and cartoonists as a rich man's club. The people's unhappiness was reflected in books like Frank Norris's *The Octopus*. Americans disgusted with a democracy that was too indirect introduced a series of reforms to bring government back to the people, and the "progressive era" was born. During this period, practically every American state adopted the initiative, the referendum and plebiscite, and the direct primary in one form or another.

The Initiative. Designed to bypass corrupt legislatures, the initiative allows the people themselves to place proposed laws or constitutional amendments on the ballot. Generally, a specific percentage of voters must sign a petition supporting the law, and as soon as enough signatures have been collected, the proposal is placed on the ballot for the next election. The number of signatures needed to place an initiative proposal on the ballot is deliberately kept low in order to encourage the use of this procedure, which broadens participation in government.

The Referendum and Plebiscite. Often used synonymously, the referendum and the plebiscite are actually two separate things. The referendum is a simple "yes" or "no" vote on a proposal placed on the ballot by a legislature or, more commonly, by a constitutional convention. Most American states and Switzerland use the initiative and the referendum as separate

---

[23] Legislative, executive, judicial, and administrative roles and duties will all be discussed in Part IV of this book.

[24] United States senators were elected by state legislatures until the passage of the seventeenth amendment in 1913.

processes by which the people can make and pass their own laws, although in some American states the referendum is used simply to test public opinion, and is not necessarily binding upon the legislature.

The plebiscite is also a "yes" or "no" vote, but it technically refers only to constitutional amendments. Some states in the United States, most European nations, and Australia and Japan use the plebiscite to amend or alter their constitutions.

Direct Primary Elections. A more familiar institution which had its origins in the "progressive era" is the direct primary election, which will be discussed in greater detail later in this chapter. It was adopted in the hope of breaking the power of political bosses such as Tammany Hall's Charles Francis Murphy, Cincinnati's George F. Cox, and San Francisco's Abe Ruef. In order to keep candidate selection out of smoky back rooms, the primary requires that nominees for office be chosen by the rank-and-file voters of each party in a special election. It is used in practically every state to select candidates for the legislature, and about one-third to one-half of the states also use it to select delegates to the national presidential nominating conventions.

Does Direct Democracy Work? Despite efforts of turn-of-the-century reformers, few long-lasting changes have resulted from the initiative, referendum and plebiscite, and the direct primary. Except for a few hotly contested issues, referenda rarely arouse more than a 15–20 percent response from the polling booths, and a general rule of thumb is that initiative propositions requiring outlays of money are turned down. A high percentage of voters automatically votes "no" to all referenda, feeling that that government "is best which does least." [25]

The direct primary, although probably the most publicized reform, has also had imperfect results in reaching its goals. Voter turnout for the primaries tends to be far less than the turnout at the general election, and the system gives organization-supported candidates a decisive advantage. The party faithful will usually vote for the organization's choice, but the independent voters cannot be relied upon to support the less-established candidates. One result has been the charge that the direct primary, instead of undermining boss control of political nominations, merely gives boss-controlled candidates the *appearance* of winning a popular mandate from the party rank-and-file. The question is open to endless debate. Suffice it to say here that political machines *have* declined (although this decline is due more to the mobility of modern America than to the institutions of direct

[25] John E. Mueller, "Voting on the Propositions: Ballot Patterns and Historical Trends in California," *American Political Science Review* 63 (December 1969): 1197–1212; and Raymond E. Wolfinger and Fred I. Greenstein, "The Repeal of Fair Housing in California: An Analysis of Referendum Voting," *American Political Science Review* 62 (September 1968): 753–69.

democracy) [26] and that few of us today would willingly give up our right to direct primary participation.

Elections: Choosing Representatives

"It is an unquestionable truth that the body of the people in every country . . . do not possess the discernment and stability necessary for systematic government." Thus argued Alexander Hamilton at the New York State convention that ratified the United States Constitution. Although government of the people, by the people, and for the people is today a primary article of American faith, it has not always enjoyed such universal favor.

From the time of Plato, the case against democracy has rested on the familiar elitist argument. The people do not have the intelligence or the training to govern themselves, and thus, power should be held by an intellectual elite (or "natural aristocracy" as Thomas Jefferson called them) who do have those capabilities. The writers of the Constitution feared popular government. Alexander Hamilton and James Madison felt that man was naturally inclined toward evil, and pure democracy would give this evil free rein. The masses would tyrannize men of property and education. Democracy in its modern sense did not come of age until the 1820s and the election of Andrew Jackson, when property qualifications for voting were abolished.[27]

Has this change from "natural aristocracy" to representative democracy been for the better, or was Alexander Hamilton right? Popular rule has not always given us the wisest selection of officials.[28] Many historians would argue that Warren G. Harding and Ulysses S. Grant can scarcely be ranked with George Washington and Thomas Jefferson. But if democracy is imperfect, it is still a good way for the people to protect themselves from misuse of government power (and many "great" presidents, including Lincoln and Wilson,

---

[26] An excellent discussion about the rise and fall of the great urban political machine is given in Fred Greenstein, *The American Party System and the American People*, 2nd ed. (Englewood Cliffs, N.J.: Prentice-Hall, 1970). See Chapter 4, "Local Parties: Old-Time Machines and Modern Variants." For an entertaining firsthand account of the city machine and its workings, see William L. Riordan, *Plunkitt of Tammany Hall* (New York: Alfred A. Knopf, 1948. Original publication, 1905).

[27] But it was not generally accepted until the mid-century. Alexis de Tocqueville, who visited the New World during this period and recorded his impressions in *Democracy in America*, constantly referred to "the omnipotence of the majority" in the United States, whose effects he greatly feared. Volume I, part II discusses democracy in the United States—its origins, advantages and disadvantages, and probable future. (Garden City, N.Y.: Doubleday, 1969; Anchor edition, translation based on 1848 edition.)

[28] For a summation of the pros and cons of popular democracy, see Pomper, *Elections in America*, Chapter 2. George D. Beam's *Usual Politics* (New York: Holt, Rinehart and Winston, 1970), discusses the difference between substantive and procedural democracy, and finds that most Americans are more concerned with whether or not they can vote than with substantive issues, such as the actual existence of equality in America.

have been elected popularly). As John Stuart Mill observed, "Men, as well as women, do not need political rights in order that they may govern, but in order that they not be misgoverned." [29] Popular elections are a proven means for modern societies to establish legitimate and relatively stable governments, protect the people's needs, and choose or peacefully dismiss representatives.

Free Elections: What Are They?

Americans are fond of contrasting elections in the United States with those in the Soviet Union in order to point up the differences between free elections and "phony" elections. But the Russians just as logically argue that Soviet elections also represent the "will of the people." Is there a model of a free election with which American and Russian elections can be compared? While it is true that what we consider to be a "free election" depends considerably upon our ideological persuasion, political scientists have compiled an objective list of what they consider to be the six most important requirements for a free and meaningful election.[30]

Two or More Competing Political Parties. In order to have a meaningful choice, the voter must be permitted to choose freely between candidates with different stands on various issues. The Soviet Union, where only Communist party candidates are allowed to run for office, fails to meet this basic requirement. But it might also be remembered that many New Left thinkers criticize the American party system on similar grounds: they argue that our elections do not offer a meaningful choice because both Democrats and Republicans support the capitalist economic system. It is true that the Democrats and Republicans both endorse capitalism, but their stands on domestic and foreign policy questions often differ (as George McGovern's and Richard Nixon's positions on the Vietnam War revealed in 1972), so that within the capitalist frame of reference the voters are allowed a choice. And if this choice is not distinct enough, there are socialist and other minority parties on the ballot, and the voter is free to bypass the major parties in their favor.

Freedom to Campaign and Debate the Issues. In a free election all political parties and legally qualified candidates must have the opportunity to air their views and seek the support of the public. In practice, this means that newspapers, magazines, radio, and television must make advertising space and time available to all parties.

[29] *Considerations on Representative Government* (New York: Liberal Arts Press, 1958), p. 144

[30] The discussion which follows is based on Pomper, *Elections in America*, pp. 263–66. See also the views of W. J. M. Mackenzie in his *Free Elections* (New York: Holt, Rinehart and Winston, 1958), Chapter 20; and of Robert Dahl in *A Preface to Democratic Theory* (Chicago: University of Chicago Press, 1956).

The question of "equal opportunity" to campaign has prompted some political theorists to suggest that truly democratic elections require some sort of financial subsidy to parties and candidates that are too poor to compete with the major parties and their candidates. The Socialist Labor and the Socialist Workers parties, for example, do not have the money to buy television time, and therefore their campaigns are too limited to ever win a major election. But while the proposal may sound reasonable, it raises some very difficult questions. Does democracy require that unpopular parties be subsidized out of public taxes? Should minor parties receive more government money just because they need more? Where do parties stop and interest groups start? There is no easy way to even the odds against minority parties, so it is unlikely the United States will ever provide truly equal opportunity to campaign.

Universal Adult Suffrage and Equal Weighting of Votes. Democracy requires that the right to vote be universal (within limitations), with every person's vote counting equally in choosing representatives. As we saw in Chapter 12, all nations restrict the right to vote in some degree, even if only to keep convicted murderers from the polls. Most of these restrictions do not violate basic democratic principles, but some do. Nations such as South Africa and Rhodesia, which deny the vote to members of nonwhite races, cannot be considered to have free elections. Nor is it permissible to give one man as many as three votes (as was done in Kenya for a time) simply because he is better educated or wealthier than the average voter. All electoral districts must be roughly equal to all other electoral districts within the jurisdiction of the state.

The Ballot Must Be Easy to Understand. Precautions to make sure that there is free competition among candidates and universal suffrage among voters are of little good if, once the voter draws the curtain behind him in the voting booth, he is confronted with such a tangle of names, offices, and propositions that he can't figure out how to register his choices. An overly complex ballot can be almost as useless as a ballot printed in the wrong language. Fortunately, most nations have devised their own systems which allow the voter to understand the ballot with relatively little trouble, even in a complicated election year. In the United States, we list candidates according to party and office; in other nations such as Israel, the ballot is arranged according to party lists.

Free Choice and an Honest Count. Absolutely crucial to a free election is the right of the voter to cast his ballot without fear of reprisal. Before the introduction of the secret ballot, or Australian Ballot, in the 1870s, American voting was often in public view. The problem with public votes is obvious: people who voted against their bosses' candidates often lived to regret it. With the secret ballot, however, no one need know how his neighbor votes, and everyone is free to vote according to his conscience.

Elections must also be honestly administered. To avoid fraud (such as voting several times in several different precincts, or "voting the graveyards"), there are lists of all registered and legally qualified voters, and a citizen may be required to give positive identification before being permitted to vote. And when the polls have closed, election results must be honestly counted and publicly posted. (Today, most votes in the United States are tabulated by machines which make the count more reliable—but even machines sometimes fail.) For the most part, elections are fair and accurate. Mistakes seldom occur on a large enough scale to change a victory to a defeat.

The Candidate Can Claim a Mandate. In the United States, the candidate who wins a presidential election (even if he does not obtain a majority of the popular vote) claims to have received a mandate to carry out his platform. For an election to be meaningful the winning party must have the backing of a large proportion of the people, and those people must have clearly understood who and what they were (and were not) voting for.

In European nations using proportional representation, it is much more difficult for any one party to win a "working majority." To control a legislature, a party must often enter into a coalition with the opposition. This can greatly dilute the claim to a clear mandate, and the result is often an ineffective government.

A Contrast: The Soviet Electoral System

Using these six criteria as a model of a free and meaningful election, we can see that the United States and most Western European nations generally meet the requirements. How does the Soviet Union differ? According to its constitution of 1936, all citizens of the age of majority —no matter what their race, religion, nationality, sex, social class, wealth, or past political activity—are guaranteed the right to vote, and 99.9 percent of eligible voters participate in the national elections. On paper, at least, no system could be more democratic than Russia's. But is it so democratic in operation?

One-party Control. The Supreme Soviet is the highest governing authority in the Soviet Union, and election laws specify that its candidates may be nominated by Communist party cells, collective farms, factory labor organizations, youth organizations, and cultural societies.[31] In practice, it is not the organizations in general but only the party members who do the nominating. Except for the lowest levels of government, the Soviet nominating system produces only a single candidate for each office, and chances are four to one that candidate is a member of the Communist party. Once nominated, candidates campaign actively, holding rallies and addressing the people over radio and television. But there is really no contest. If a voter approves of all the candidates, he folds his ballot and drops it in the box. But if he disapproves of one or more candidates, he must retreat behind a screen in order to mark the ballot. He may not write in the name of an alternate candidate; he is allowed only to scratch out the name of the person he disapproves of. As only the bravest voters would draw attention to themselves by retreating behind the screen, virtually every candidate wins office with 99.9 percent of the popular vote—a "mandate" which any democratic candidate would envy!

In Western eyes, Soviet elections may seem a waste of time, but the Russians can and do defend them. The Communist party, they argue, truly represents the will of the Russian people, and since no one has the right to oppose the people's will, no one should oppose the party. If one accepts this somewhat circular reasoning, then the Russian electoral system is democratic, and Soviet elections renew and strengthen the Communist party's popular mandate. But the Western idea of democracy and popular elections is quite different. How do democratic elections work?

---

[31] For thorough discussions of the Soviet nominating and electoral system, see Randolph L. Braham, *Soviet Politics and Government* (New York: Alfred A. Knopf, 1965); Derek J. R. Scott, *Russian Political Institutions* (New York: Praeger Publishers, 1966); and L. G. Churchward, *Contemporary Soviet Government* (London: Routledge and Kegan Paul, 1968).

Choosing the Candidates: The First Step in an Election

If every four years, Americans were asked to go to the polls and register their choice for president, but no candidates were endorsed by any political party and no one was listed on the ballot, what would happen? Aside from the almost automatic reelection of anyone who had already made it to office (because his would be the only familiar name), the result would most probably be such a splintered vote that no elected president could really claim the support of more than a tiny slice of the public—or a landslide victory by a "joke" candidate such as Alfred E. Newman or Pat Paulson!

A necessary first step in any election is choosing which candidates to put before the public. This process is crucial to all democratic electoral systems. The United States, with over ninety thousand separate governing units, has the most elaborate, cumbersome, and costly nominating system of any democratic nation. It might therefore be instructive to take a look at some other nominating systems before discussing our own.

Nomination by Petition. Great Britain, France, Japan, Canada, Australia, and New Zealand use a petition system to nominate candidates. In England, almost any citizen over twenty-one years of age is free to run for election to the House of Commons. All he must do is obtain a nomination petition listing his name, address, occupation, and the parliamentary district, register the signatures of ten legally qualified voters from that district, and make a deposit of £150. The fee is returned to the candidate if he polls at least one-eighth of the vote in the general election; otherwise, it is kept by the government. This is designed to discourage half-hearted candidates from clogging the ballots.

As we see, anyone with £150 and ten friends can run for election to the House of Commons, but that does not mean that such a nominee is an official candidate. In Great Britain, nomination is simply placing a candidate's name on the ballot, as opposed to candidate selection, which is the process by which the Conservative, Labour, or Liberal party endorses one of those candidates.[32] The official selection of candidates is done by local party organizations, who gather at private meetings to decide who to endorse (see Table 13-2). There are no national nominating conventions or primary elections in England (although the national party organization does endorse the local choice). Instead, hopefuls campaign intensely within each local organization to win party backing.

Nominations in the United States. Most candidates for office in the United States are nominated by direct primary elections—with the exception, of

---

[32] A good description of the British nominating system is provided in Austin Ranney, "Candidate Selection and Party Cohesion in Britain and the United States," in *Approaches to the Study of Party Organization*, ed. William J. Crotty (Boston: Allyn and Bacon, 1968), pp. 139–56.

course, of the presidential and vice-presidential candidates who are nominated by delegates at a national convention. Delegates to this convention are often elected in primaries (just as candidates may be nominated in primaries), but this varies from state to state. Since election laws are made and enforced by each state, there is no one national procedure.

The Party Caucus. Before the direct primary was introduced around the turn of the century, the party caucus was the chief means of selecting candidates at all levels and choosing delegates to state and national con-

Table 13-2
Selecting Candidates in Britain and the United States

Selection Stage	British Procedures	American Procedures
1. Preliminary local party selection	1. "Short lists" drawn up by small screening committees after considering and/or soliciting possibilities. Almost always done in secret.	1. Where local parties are strong, organization's choice is made after considering and/or soliciting possibilities. Almost always done in secret. Where local parties are weak, changing congeries of local factions push several different aspirants, and there is no organization choice.
2. Final local party selection	2. By small representative councils elected by dues-paying local party members. Usually done in secret. (Conservatives also have final ratification by a meeting of all local dues-paying members.)	2. Same as 4.
3. National party endorsement	3. A national agency must endorse the local selection before he or she may appear publicly as the party's official candidate.*	3. None
4. Legal nomination	4. Nomination paper entered with constituency returning officer. Ten signatures of qualified voters in constituency required. £150 deposit, returned if candidate polls over ⅛ of general election vote. No party designations on the ballot.	4. Winner of each party's direct primary election in state or district automatically goes on the ballot as his party's official nominee. (Four states nominate senatorial candidates by state conventions of locally selected delegates.)

* In the Conservative and Labour parties, but not in the the Liberal party.

Source: Austin Ranney, "The Structure and Functions of the Party Organization," in Political Parties and Political Behavior, ed. William J. Crotty et al. (Boston: Allyn and Bacon, Inc., 1971), p. 253.

ventions. Party organizations would caucus in private meetings, usually held behind closed doors, to select these candidates and delegates. Today, while precinct and county caucuses are still widely used, especially in choosing delegates, the state caucus is not nearly as powerful as it once was, and has been largely replaced by the primary elections. Besides choosing delegates to the presidential convention in about half of the states, its only real area of authority is in drawing up the party's platform—which, as we have already noted, is not necessarily binding upon the candidates. On the national level, of course, the presidential nominating convention is still very much alive.[33]

The Primary Election. In most states, candidates for the House, the Senate, governorships, and other offices must win a plurality in a primary election before becoming official candidates. To enter a primary, a candidate must file a petition stating his name, legal residence, and the office he is seeking, along with the signatures of a specific number of party supporters. Two types of primaries are used in the United States. The closed primary is used in Illinois, Florida, New York, and in many other states. It allows only registered members of the party to participate: Democrats may not vote in the Republican primary, Republicans may not vote in the Democratic primary, and registered independents may not vote in either primary. The open primary, used in Wisconsin and in several other states, allows any voter to participate in any party primary: Republicans may cross over and vote in the Democratic primary, and vice-versa. The main problem with the open primary is that if voters decide to cross over in large enough numbers, one party could determine the outcome of the other's primary election. Therefore, the open primary cannot be relied upon to reflect the true feelings of the party rank-and-file.[34]

The direct primary is the chief means by which the major American parties select their standard-bearers, and in some ways it helps to democratize our system of nominations. A candidate who opposes the party line can frequently upset the party organization's candidate if he is able to exploit a sensitive public issue. In the 1972 presidential primaries, George Wallace spoke out against school busing and, by voicing the general disquiet of many voters, proved himself to be a solid vote-getter. Had he not been injured in an assassination attempt, he might have collected enough convention delegates to have slowed or halted George McGovern's push for the nomination. Primary elections allow presidential hopefuls to enlist grass-roots support in their bid for candidacy, thus bringing the people —at least ideally—into the candidate-selection process.

But the primaries have their drawbacks too. First, they impose a heavy financial burden on both the candidates and the party. To mount an ef-

[33] A very useful discussion of this phenomenon may be found in Paul T. David, Ralph M. Goldman, and Richard C. Bain, *The Politics of National Party Conventions* (Washington, D.C.: Peter Smith, 1960).

[34] Epstein, *Political Parties in Western Democracies*, pp. 43–45.

fective campaign, a candidate must buy office space, billboards and bumper stickers, and media time, along with all the advisors and assistants that go with them. Access to wealth is almost a prerequisite for a successful primary campaign. Secondly, many political scientists feel that the primaries have weakened the political system.[35] By appealing directly to the rank-and-file voters, candidates need not depend on official party support, and can thus afford to be independent. Neither the Democratic nor the Republican party can effectively discipline wayward candidates or officials who ignore official policy decisions.

The Nominating Convention: Choosing the Presidential Candidate.[36] Delegates to national nominating conventions, whether chosen in party caucus or elected in primaries, may be legally bound or personally committed to a particular candidate, united behind a favorite son, or uncommitted. Generally, a "committed delegate" is committed on the first ballot only, and is free to vote as he or she pleases thereafter.

Nomination at the national convention hinges upon winning a majority of delegates' votes. It is quite possible that when the convention opens, no candidate will have the required number of committed delegates to win the nomination on the first ballot. In this case, it may take several votes before one of the front-runners—or in the case of a tie, a compromise "dark horse" candidate—is chosen to head the ticket. In 1844, for example, James K. Polk was nominated to lead the Democratic party on the ninth ballot —even though Martin Van Buren had come to the convention with most of the delegates committed to support his own nomination. In the past, coalitions and behind-the-scenes bargains often played an important part in settling on a compromise candidate. Today, they are still major strategies in enlisting the support of fringe groups for the final party ticket, although coalitions and bargains are usually arranged before the first ballot, so that voting rarely continues to a second or third one.[37]

Bypassing the Convention: The Petition. As in Europe, candidates who fail to win the nomination of one of the major parties can get on the American ballot by petition. In the 1968 election, George Wallace and his American Independent party got on the ballot of every state through the

[35] See V. O. Key, Jr., *American State Politics: An Introduction* (New York: Alfred A. Knopf, 1956), Chaps. 4–6; Sorauf, *Party Politics in America*, Chap. 9; Austin Ranney, "The Representativeness of Primary Electorates," *Midwest Journal of Political Science* 12 (May 1968): 224–38; and Austin Ranney and Leon D. Epstein, "The Two Electorates: Voters and Nonvoters in a Wisconsin Primary," *Journal of Politics* 28 (August 1966): 598–616. Austin Ranney's "Turnout and Representation in Presidential Primary Elections," *American Political Science Review* 66 (March 1972): 21–37, points out the difference between primary and general election campaigns.

[36] One of the best references on this topic is Nelson Polsby and Aaron Wildavsky, *Presidential Elections*, 3rd ed. (New York: Charles Scribner's Sons, 1971).

[37] William A. Gamson, in "Coalition Formation at Presidential Nominating Conventions," takes the view that deals among power brokers, and promises of cabinet positions, federal patronage, and other "payoffs," are the main force behind final convention choices. *American Journal of Sociology* 68 (1962): 157–71.

petition process. The number of valid signatures required to get on the ballot varies widely from state to state. In New York, an independent candidate or party must get only 3,100 signatures—at least 50 in each of the state's sixty-two counties. In California, 66,000 signatures must be gathered on a statewide basis.

The Election: Frequency and Timing

Once the candidates have been nominated, the formal campaign can begin. Here, too, the United States holds the record: it not only spends the most money on its political campaigns,[38] it also has the longest campaigns of any Western democracy. While most European nations limit their campaigns to three or four weeks, American primary elections, conventions, and eight weeks of formal campaigning force presidential hopefuls to spend a good part of the year on the campaign trail. Suggestions are regularly made that American election campaigns be shortened. Yet the campaign has become an American institution, and it is unlikely that it will be greatly revised in the near future.

Election Timing in Presidential Democracies. In presidential democracies such as the United States and Mexico, elections are fixed at regular intervals by constitutional law. In general, members of the lower house of the national legislature are elected for the shorter period of time. In America, a new House of Representatives is elected every two years, the reasoning being that the representative should remain close to his constituents. A short term of office gives the people the chance to remove any congressman who drifts too far from fulfillment of their needs. Members of the upper house are elected for a much longer term. The original rationale is that their distance from the people allows them to stabilize the actions of the lower house, which might be carried away by momentary concerns. United States senators, therefore, are elected for six-year terms, with one-third of the Senate up for election every two years.

Normally, the chief executive of a presidential democracy is elected every four years, with limitations often placed on his ability to succeed himself. In the United States, the president may serve only two full consecutive terms. Franklin Roosevelt's more than twelve years in office caused complaints of monarchy and demands for reform, so that Americans today are assured a new administration every other presidential election year.[39]

Elections in Parliamentary Democracies. Great Britain, and the many nations who pattern their governments after her, has a far more flexible

---

[38] Some $300 million was spent in national and state elections in 1968.
[39] With the exception, of course, of the case where a president dies in office after two years of his term have elapsed, and his successor may then be reelected twice.

system. Parliamentary constitutions simply provide that a general election to select a new parliament (and hence a new administration) must be held at least once every five years (every four years in Germany), and may be held at any time *during* that period. An incumbent government's ability to call an election when it wishes gives it a marked advantage over the opposition party. When Labour's Harold Wilson won only a narrow majority in the 1964 British general elections, he waited until the economy had improved before calling for new elections. Taking advantage of his government's upsurge in popularity, Wilson increased his parliamentary majority in 1966 to a comfortable margin—and rested on his laurels until 1970, when he miscalculated and lost to Edward Heath.

Which system works best—presidential elections at set intervals, or parliamentary systems where the administration can call the shots? Each has its advocates. Many political scientists argue that the parliamentary system is superior: if a national scandal or crisis develops and the prime minister's party can no longer control Parliament, then new elections must be held and a new mandate sought. Government is always "on its toes," and so is kept responsive to the people. In presidential democracies, nothing (save impeachment) can hasten the demise of a corrupt or incompetent government, and the people must wait patiently until the next election before turning the culprits out of office. Moreover, national elections in presidential democracies often fall during lulls—periods of apathy between national crises, when no crucial issues exist.[40] But, on the other hand, few can deny the enormous advantage a prime minister holds over his opposition. On the whole, the two systems seem to have both strengths and drawbacks which make each best suited to its own political system.

Indirect Elections: The Electoral College [41]

Americans are so used to the idea of directly electing their public officials that they often forget that they do not directly elect the most important officer of their government. Switzerland, Uruguay, and the United States all elect their chief executives indirectly, by means of electoral colleges. And France, Holland, and Sweden choose the upper houses of their national legislatures indirectly. Indirect elections operate by people voting for electors who, in turn, vote for the candidates.

The American citizen who voted for George McGovern or Richard Nixon in the 1972 presidential election did not actually cast his ballot for the man

---

[40] This point is discussed in Pendleton Herring, *The Politics of Democracy* (New York: Holt, Rinehart and Winston, 1940), pp. 290ff.

[41] For an excellent discussion of the electoral college and its proposed reforms, see Polsby and Wildavsky, *Presidential Elections*, Chapter 5. Also see Lawrence D. Longley and Allan G. Braun, *The Politics of Electoral College Reform* (New Haven, Conn.: Yale University Press, 1972).

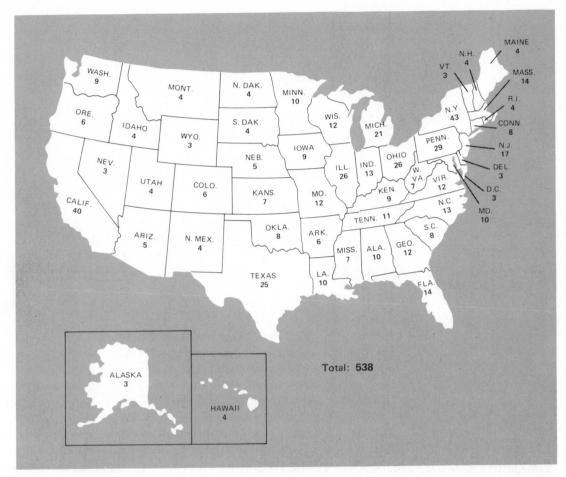

Figure 13-1
Electoral College
Votes, by State
(1970)

whose name appeared on the party ticket. Instead, he voted for a slate of electors who were morally pledged, but not legally obligated, to vote for the candidate whose name appeared on the ticket. Each state has an electoral vote equal to its total number of representatives and senators in Congress [42] (see Figure 13-1), and the candidate who receives the most popular votes in each state normally receives *all* the electoral votes of that state. As a result, candidates' campaigns tend to focus on the large states with the most electoral votes.

Is the use of the electoral college instead of direct popular voting compatible with democracy? The question has raised serious concern in recent years. In 1860, Abraham Lincoln received only 40 percent of the popular vote, but was elected by a majority of the electoral college. And in 1968, Richard Nixon finished only half-a-million votes ahead of Hubert Humphrey in one

[42] With the exception of Washington, D.C., which has in effect three electors assigned to it by the 23rd amendment.

of the closest popular elections in American history, yet won the electoral college hands down—301 to 191. The electoral college vote often bears little numerical relationship to the actual popular vote (see Table 13-3). A second major objection to the electoral college is that the electors are only morally —not legally—committed: they can conceivably throw their support to any of the candidates listed on their state's ballot. (In 1968, a South Carolina elector who was supposed to vote for Nixon actually cast his ballot for Wallace.) And finally, in the event of an electoral tie, the House of Representatives is obligated only to choose one of the *three* highest finishers, with no obligation to choose the candidate with the most popular votes.

The electoral college was originally intended to reduce the president's dependence on the masses, and to allow the educated elite to choose the best qualified man for the presidency. But while this rationale is logical from the perspective of eighteenth-century thought, it doesn't fit nearly as well with modern democratic thinking. The electoral college is in many ways an anachronism, and many feel that it should be abolished and the president elected by popular vote.

Major Systems of Elections

Almost every nation uses a different system to choose its government. The size and type of electoral district, the number of parties and the strength of each party, the nomination procedures, and the timing of elections are only a few of the variables that form an electoral system.

Confronted with the almost infinite variety of ways of electing representatives, political scientists have found that one of the easiest ways of bringing order to chaos is to classify them from the bottom up, according to the type of constituency. Thus, the two main species of electoral system are single-member and multimember. Within each, there are variations according to the type of ballot used and the method of deciding who wins. Plurality and absolute majority victories, and preferential, runoff, or single-vote ballots are used in single-member systems. And a range of ballots—from nontransferable to preferential and from cumulative to limited votes—and proportional representation systems are used in multimember systems.

Single-member Systems.[43] Single-member systems are designed to produce a simple plurality or majority victory for one candidate from each district. A nation is divided into relatively equal constituencies, and one representative is chosen from each district. This is the system used for electing our House of Representatives, the British Parliament, the French National As-

[43] The discussion which follows is based on E. Lakeman and J. D. Lambert, *Voting in Democracies* (London: Faber & Faber, 1955); and, George van den Bergh, *Unity in Diversity: A Systematic Critical Analysis of All Electoral Systems* (London: B. T. Batsford, 1956).

Table 13-3
Electoral vs. Popular Vote Support for U.S. Presidents, by Percent, 1824[a]– 1972

	Elected President	Percent Popular Vote	Percent Electoral Vote
1824	John Q. Adams (Dem-Rep.) [b]	31.9 [c]	32.1
1828	Andrew Jackson (Dem.)	56.0	68.1
1832	Andrew Jackson (Dem.)	54.5	76.5
1836	Martin Van Buren (Dem.)	50.9	57.8
1840	William H. Harrison (Whig)	52.9	79.6
1844	James K. Polk (Dem.)	49.6	61.8
1848	Zachary Taylor (Whig)	47.3	56.2
1852	Franklin Pierce (Dem.)	50.8	85.8
1856	James Buchanan (Dem.)	45.6	58.8
1860	Abraham Lincoln (Rep.)	39.8	59.4
1864	Abraham Lincoln (Rep.)	55.1	91.0
1868	Ulysses S. Grant (Rep.)	52.7	72.8
1872	Ulysses S. Grant (Rep.)	55.6	87.2
1876	Rutherford B. Hayes (Rep.)	47.9 [c]	50.1
1880	James A. Garfield (Rep.)	48.3	58.0
1884	Grover Cleveland (Dem.)	48.5	54.6
1888	Benjamin Harrison (Rep.)	47.8 [c]	58.1
1892	Grover Cleveland (Dem.)	46.0	62.4
1894	William McKinley (Rep.)	51.0	60.6
1900	William McKinley (Rep.)	51.7	61.2
1904	Theodore Roosevelt (Rep.)	56.4	70.6
1908	William H. Taft (Rep.)	51.6	66.5
1912	Woodrow Wilson (Dem.)	41.8	81.9
1916	Woodrow Wilson (Dem.)	49.3	52.2
1920	Warren G. Harding (Rep.)	60.3	76.1
1924	Calvin Coolidge (Rep.)	54.0	71.9
1928	Herbert Hoover (Rep.)	58.2	83.6
1932	Franklin D. Roosevelt (Dem.)	57.4	88.9
1936	Franklin D. Roosevelt (Dem.)	60.8	98.5
1940	Franklin D. Roosevelt (Dem.)	54.7	84.6
1944	Franklin D. Roosevelt (Dem.)	53.4	81.4
1948	Harry S. Truman (Dem.)	49.5	57.1
1952	Dwight D. Eisenhower (Rep.)	55.1	83.2
1956	Dwight D. Eisenhower (Rep.)	57.4	86.2
1960	John F. Kennedy (Dem.)	49.7	58.0
1964	Lyndon B. Johnson (Dem.)	61.1	90.0
1968	Richard M. Nixon (Rep.)	43.4	56.0
1972	Richard M. Nixon (Rep.)	61.3	96.8

[a] First popular election, 1824.
[b] Election decided in House of Representatives.
[c] Victor failed to win a plurality of the popular vote.

sembly (since 1958), and the lower houses of the Canadian and Indian parliaments. Contrary to the arguments of famous political scientist Maurice Duverger,[44] the single-member system does not automatically produce a two-party system (both France and India have several parties), though it does favor such a system. The main disadvantages of the single-member system are that minority parties are underrepresented, and that new political parties are discouraged.

Plurality Victory. Single-member systems may provide for a majority victory or a plurality victory. In the United States and most English-speaking countries, elections are won by a plurality, or "first past the post." In many cases, of course, the first past the post also wins an absolute majority, but if a third or even fourth party takes a sizeable enough chunk of the vote—as did George Wallace in 1968—then the winner can claim only a plurality.

Majority Victories: Runoff and Preferential Ballots. In contrast to the American system,[45] France and Australia require candidates for legislative and executive posts to win an absolute majority of the vote. The French use a system of runoff elections which continue until one candidate wins a majority. In the first stages of the French presidential election of 1969, Georges Pompidou received a large plurality, but not a majority, of the popular vote. Thus, a runoff election was scheduled, barring all candidates who failed to receive at least 10 percent of the first vote. Pompidou's original field of six opponents was narrowed to only Alain Poher, and in the runoff Pompidou won a clear majority.

Another, more complicated version of single-member majority elections is found in Australia, where a preferential ballot is used. Here, voters rank all of the candidates for the legislature in order of preference: if five candidates run for the same office, the voter will number his ballot from one to five. If no one receives an absolute majority of first-place votes, then the lowest candidate is dropped and his votes are distributed among the survivors in a second election. This Darwinian process of survival of the fittest continues until one candidate finally receives a majority of the total vote. The method eventually produces a true mandate, but it is time-consuming, costly to administer, and cumbersome.

The chief advantage of the single-member system is that it enables the winning candidate or party to claim some sort of clear mandate from the electorate, because the victor always claims the most votes. Since it is a winner-take-all system, it tends to promote stable governments where one party has uncontested control. But all of the single-member systems are open to criticism because they underrepresent minority groups.

Multimember Systems. Multimember electoral systems can be extremely complex, with a number of significant variations. Multimember elections are often equated with proportional representation, but the two are not the

---

[44] Maurice Duverger, *Political Parties* (New York: John Wiley & Sons, 1954).
[45] Except in the U.S. South, where primary elections often have runoffs because there are so many candidates that one can't win a majority.

same. While proportional representation requires a multimember system, a multimember system does not necessarily use proportional representation. All systems of multimember representation are designed to give minority political viewpoints some share of political power and representation, thereby producing a legislature which can reflect the nation's political makeup. But they do not succeed equally well.

Single, Nontransferable Vote. The simplest form of multimember balloting is the system of "block-voting" used in elections to the Turkish national assembly (and in a number of American municipal and judicial elections): the citizen votes for as many candidates as there are offices to be filled. For example, if a given district is entitled to three representatives on the city council, the voter of that district will cast his ballot for any three of the five (or six, or nine) candidates. The three candidates who win the most votes are elected. This is also known as the single, nontransferable ballot, since the voter casts a single vote for a number of candidates, and that vote may not be transferred to other candidates.

Preferential and Cumulative Ballots. Another variety of the multimember system uses a transferable vote, through preferential or cumulative ballots. The preferential multimember ballot is similar to the Australian single-member system. If three city councilmen are running for office, the voter will indicate his first, second, and third choices on the ballot. In order to win, a candidate must obtain either a majority of first-choice votes or an electoral quotient (which is determined by a complex mathematical formula). If one or more of the candidates doesn't win a clear victory on the first round, then the candidate with the fewest first-place votes is dropped and his second-choice votes are distributed among the survivors. This process continues until three candidates have been declared elected. Its chief drawback is the complexity of tabulation, and it is used only to a limited extent in Switzerland and Finland.

In the cumulative system (also used in Switzerland and Finland), the voter may cast as many ballots as there are offices to be filled, but here he has the option of giving all his votes to a single candidate. If a voter is to select three city councilmen, he may cast all three votes for candidate A; one vote each for candidates A, C, and D; one for C and two for A; or any other combination he chooses. By using all his votes on one candidate, he can best ensure that his favorite will win.

Limited Vote Systems. Some multimember systems use a limited vote ballot, where the voter has fewer votes than the number of seats to be filled. If three candidates are running, the voter is allowed to cast ballots for only two. This is designed to give minority political groups a better chance of winning. Its practical effect is to artificially reduce the voting strength of the major parties, but it does not necessarily produce a legislature representative of the actual strength of political groups.

Multimember Proportional Representation.

What would happen if American blacks organized an official political party? How would it fare under the American electoral system? Assuming that every qualified black voter supported the new party, it could expect to receive about 11 percent of the national vote. But many of these votes would be squandered in white congressional districts, where the support of even a third of the people would count for nothing. The new black party would probably have very little impact on Congress, because black voters are in the majority in only a few congressional districts. The Ninety-second Congress contained thirteen blacks, and even with the new party this number would remain quite stable. However, if the House of Representatives was reorganized so that congress-men were elected by a proportional representation system from multimember districts, the picture would change considerably. Out of 435 seats, the black party could expect to win close to 50 seats—not just 13. As a remedy to such situations where major minority groups are underrepresented, the system of proportional representation was developed in the late nineteenth century. It has since gained wide popularity, and has been adopted in some fashion in most of the democratic states which have emerged in the twentieth-century.[46] It is now in use in the Scandinavian nations, Israel, Japan, South Africa, Ireland, and most of Western Europe. Two main types of ballot are used in proportional representation: The party list and the single, transferable vote.

Party Lists. Israel is the best example of the party list electoral system. The nation is not divided into districts, and all 120 members of the Knesset, or parliament, are elected at large. Each of the ten political parties draws up a list of 120 candidates consecutively numbered from 1 through 120. Position numbers for the ballot are assigned by the party, and independent candidates cannot get on the ballot.[47] On election day, the voter must cast his ballot for one list on a take-it-or-leave-it basis. There is no way to split the ticket, or even to change the order in which candidates are listed. The rationale is that the Israeli voter is more interested in his party's political stand than he is in the personality or ideology of the candidates. The individual legislator counts for little; it is the party that matters.

After the votes have been counted, each party is awarded seats in the Knesset in proportion to its percentage of the popular vote. Thus, if the Mapai (Labor) party wins 30 percent of the vote, it wins thirty-six seats; if the Gahal (Nationalist) party wins 25 percent of the vote, it wins thirty seats. In both cases, the first thirty-six and thirty names on each party's list are declared elected. Accordingly, the seasoned politicians are given the best positions on each list; newcomers get the least secure spots. The party-list system produces a legislature which accurately reflects the political divisions of the nation, but it can easily produce unstable coalition governments.

[46] Arguments in favor of proportional representation are offered in C. G. Hoag and G. H. Hallett, *Proportional Representation* (New York: Crowell-Collier and Macmillan, 1926); opposing arguments are offered in F. A. Hermens, *Democracy or Anarchy?* (Notre Dame, Ind.: Review of Politics, 1941); and Herman Finer, *Theory and Practice of Modern Government* (New York: Holt, Rinehart and Winston, 1949), pp. 556–58.
[47] In the party list systems of Finland, Chile, and Denmark, independent candidates *are* able to get on the ballot if enough voters sign a petition on their behalf.

With ten parties in the field, the chances of one winning the sixty-one seats needed for a legislative majority are remote.[48]

The Single, Transferable Ballot. The single, transferable ballot has the advantage of offering the voter full freedom of choice. But this is gained only at the cost of a very complex procedure. The voter is given all of the options of the preferential and cumulative systems combined. He may split his ticket among several parties, change the order of candidate lists (some nations limit the voter's right to move his favorite candidates to the top of the party list by restricting him to three or four preferences), or he can bunch his vote among one or a few favored candidates. The result, of course, is that counting the votes is no simple matter. In order to win, a candidate must receive a complicated electoral quotient, and in order to determine this quotient, voters must rank candidates by order of preference, often in several ballots. Low-ranking candidates are eliminated and their votes are transferred to second-, third-, or fourth-choice candidates until every legislative seat is filled. While the single, transferable ballot has the advantage of giving an accurate reflection of what the voter wants, it makes tabulation and administration of elections extremely difficult and costly. This system is used for choosing the Senate of Ulster (Northern Ireland), and also the Senates of Australia and South Africa.

Electoral Systems: Which Works Best?

Of all the systems used for electing representatives, which works best? [49] The question cannot be answered in simple terms, for the word *best* is at most a very subjective term which depends on one's view of what a system of representation should do. No one system has all the advantages. The tendency to favor large, well-established parties at the expense of newer and smaller parties is most pronounced in single-member systems, but is also true of multimember systems. Even proportional representation does not significantly help small parties unless they have strong regional bases of support. And while proportional representation works best in terms of accurately representing groups, it often goes hand-in-hand with unstable governments. In proportional representation, the more legislators who are elected from a given district, the greater is the proportionality. Thus, Israel, a single-constituency nation, has the truest system of proportional representation. But Israel also has more parties than any other democratic state, and is the most politically splintered.

Single-member districts, in contrast, are often accompanied by two-party

[48] Oscar Kraines, *Government and Politics in Israel* (Boston: Houghton Mifflin, 1961), pp. 86–95.
[49] Douglas W. Rae gives the pros and cons in much greater detail than we can here. See *The Political Consequences of Electoral Laws* (New Haven, Conn.: Yale University Press, 1967).

competition, with the result that one party can more easily win a clear mandate, and thus the effective control of the state. But small parties are denied a voice in the government. If one prizes stability over a wide representation of ideologies, then the single-member electoral system works best. But if the official representation of several political beliefs is more important than stability, then the multimember proportional representation system wins out. Both systems depend upon intelligent voter participation, and neither works in isolation from the pressures of interest groups throughout the society.

Suggested Readings

Clarke, Maude V. *Medieval Representation and Consent.* London: Longmans, Green, 1936. A fascinating presentation of pre-democratic concepts of government and representation.

Hermans, Ferdinand A. *Democracy or Anarchy?* Notre Dame, Ind.: The Review of Politics, 1941. A classic attack on the system of proportional representation.

Hoag, Clarence G., and Hallett, George H. *Proportional Representation.* New York: Crowell-Collier and Macmillan, 1926. A classic defense of the system of proportional representation.

Longley, Lawrence D., and Braun, Allan G. *The Politics of Electoral College Reform.* New Haven, Conn.: Yale University Press, 1972. An excellent presentation of the malapportionment built into the electoral college system and who benefits from it.

Mathews, Donald. *The Social Background of Political Decision-Makers.* Garden City, N.Y.: Doubleday, 1954. A comprehensive survey of the various social backgrounds of American politicians.

Mill, John Stuart. *Considerations on Representative Government.* Currin V. Shields, ed. New York: Bobbs-Merrill: 1958. A classic statement of the democratic theory of representation.

Pennock, Roland, and Chapman, John W., eds. *Representation.* New York: Atherton, 1968. A collection of papers on the concept and scope of representation in democratic societies.

Pitkin, Hanna F. *The Concept of Representation.* Berkeley: University of California Press, 1967. An analytical treatment of the notion of representation.

Prewitt, Kenneth. *The Recruitment of Political Leaders.* New York: Bobbs-Merrill, 1970. An examination of the process and meaning of political recruitment, with empirical data from a multi-city survey.

Rae, Douglas W. *The Political Consequences of Electoral Laws.* New Haven, Conn.: Yale University Press, 1967. A contemporary analysis of how rules and institutions affect representation.

FOUR

The Institutions of Government

Legislatures and executives: Making and applying laws
CHAPTER 14

One of the hallmarks of man's progress from "barbarism" to "civilization" has been the division of labor and the development of specialized fields of endeavor. Surprisingly, government has been among the last institutions to be affected by this progressive compartmentalization of tasks and knowledge. The development of separate legislative, executive, and judicial branches was still only rudimentary—and not very meaningful—at the same time that the populations ruled by governments were divided into distinctive groups like farmers, soldiers, clerks, blacksmiths, and fishermen. The Athenian assembly combined legislative, executive and judicial roles. Medieval parliaments were, for the most part, mere extensions of the monarch's will, and until the 1640s, he and his ministers exercised all the powers of government from the enactment of laws to their execution and enforcement. Today, many primitive tribes are still governed by one chief who handily combines all the powers of an active government.

With the Puritan Revolution in England, the idea developed that government was a partnership between "king, lords, and commons," and that each partner had a distinct function to perform. During the "Age of Enlightenment" in the eighteenth century, political theorists such as Montesquieu, Voltaire, and Jefferson declared that liberty could only be secured if government were divided into three distinct branches, each having the ability to check and balance the others. With few exceptions, modern governments are divided into these three branches. Theoretically at least, the legislature enacts laws (rule initiation) that allocate values for society; the executive branch enforces the statutes (rule application) passed by the legislature; and the judicial branch interprets the law (rule adjudication) and imposes sanctions upon those who violate it. But these responsibilities often overlap, and the separation of powers is not always clear-cut.

Presidential versus Parliamentary Democracies: The Executive and the Legislature

Presidential democracies most clearly show the separation of power between the executive and legislative branches, for in this form of government the head of state is elected directly by the people rather than by legislative mandate and is therefore not responsible to the legislature. Parliamentary systems, on the other hand, fuse legislative and executive powers. But even in our political system, the division of authority is not as sharply defined as we might assume, and legislative initiative often starts with the executive branch.

Our presidential system of government, like our two-party system, is not shared by many other democratic nations. Only the United States and a handful of Latin American countries vest one president with executive powers. The separation of powers between the executive and legislative branches is outlined in the Constitution to provide, at least in theory, a system of "checks and balances." A president can veto bills passed by Congress; Congress, in turn, can refuse to enact the president's program. In neither case does a government stalemate lead to the president's resignation or new congressional elections. The division of power is also guaranteed by a constitutional provision prohibiting any elected official from holding office outside his branch of government. A congressman must resign his seat in the legislature to accept a cabinet post; a judge is expected to leave the court if he plans to serve as a presidential advisor. This is not the case in parliamentary systems.

The parliamentary system, which is the most commonly used democratic form of government, fuses rather than separates executive and legislative powers.[1] In Great Britain, for instance, the prime minister and his chief executives must be elected members of Parliament. Executive power in Great Britain, as in Germany and France, hinges on the degree of cohesion between the executive branch and the legislature. When a chancellor or prime minister fails to get his programs through the legislature, he must resign or call for a new electoral mandate for his party. Unlike presidential democracies where it is not unusual for a president to control a minority in Congress, the prime minister in a parliamentary system must have majority control in the legislative branch; a split between the executive and legislative branches in a parliamentary system can topple the government. And in select parliamentary systems, the prime minister must respond to legislative inquiries. The executive branch is held accountable to the legislators in many European countries like Great Britain during a time set aside for these inquiries known as the Question Period. The British House of Commons uses the Question Period to allow members of the opposition party to officially ask the majority party and the prime minister questions relating to the conduct of government. In spite of these differences, however, the various branches of government in presidential and parliamentary democracies share many organizational and functional similarities.

The Legislatures

Variations

The main purpose of all legislative bodies, at least in theory, is to formulate the laws that govern society. In practice, the degree to which the legislature is free to act as law-initiator varies widely among political systems. Political scientist Robert C. Fried distinguishes six different types of legislatures.[2] *Dictatorial legislatures*, such as the French Convention of 1792–1795, are omnipotent bodies that directly rule the country. The executive and judicial branches of the French government were abolished under this "Reign of Terror"; the convention initiated, applied, and enforced all laws of the land. The modern nations of the Union of South Africa and Southern Rhodesia have *oligarchic legislatures* that perpetuate the dictatorial rule of the powerful elite whom they represent. *Strong legislatures*, generally found in parliamentary systems with coalition governments, such as modern Italy, dominate the ministry and the party leadership. *Independent legislatures*,

[1] A good description of parliamentary government is Lord Campion and D. W. S. Lidderdale, *European Parliamentary Procedure* (London: Interparliamentary Union, 1955); and Roland Young, *The British Parliament* (Chicago: Northwestern University Press, 1962).

[2] Robert C. Fried, *Comparative Political Institutions* (New York: Macmillan, 1966), Chapter 2. This book provides a useful introduction to all the institutions of government.

Legislature	Sitting Days (annual average)	Length of Sitting (daily average in hours and minutes)	Length of Sitting (annual average in hours)
England			
House of Commons 1954–1958	161.6	7:54	1280
French Fourth Republic			
National Assembly, 1954	132.0	6:02	796
Federal Republic of Germany			
Second Bundestag, 1953–1957	55.8	7:37	425
United States			
House of Representatives, 1954–58	125.8	4:13	532

Source: Compiled from data in Gerhard Loewenberg, "The Remaking of the German Party System," Polity 1 (1968): 513.

Table 14-1
Frequency and Length of Public Sessions of Legislatures

exemplified by the Congress of the United States, are directly responsible to the electorate and exercise lawmaking powers on their own.[3] *Weak legislatures,* including Britain's Parliament and the Fifth French Republic's Assembly, are dominated by strong party leaders who occupy all executive posts. The *captive legislatures* of totalitarian governments, like the Supreme Soviet of the USSR, have no real power of their own and serve primarily to legitimatize the decisions of the party leadership.

Legislatures differ not only in degree of political power, but also in the lengths of their sessions. Captive legislatures, with little to debate and no power to introduce bills independently of the executive branch, seldom meet for more than a few weeks at a time. Among democratic legislatures, the duration of sessions varies widely, as Table 14-1 indicates. These variations are due to a number of factors, including the method by which bills are considered in each legislature and the particular majority required to end debate.

The Role of the Legislature

Democratic legislatures differ in power, structure, and organization, but they all perform the same general functions.[4] They initiate laws, propose constitutional amendments, ratify treaties, control tax revenues, and act as a check on the other branches of government. Usually, political power is divided within the legislature itself between a lower and an upper house. The British House of Commons, the United States House of Representatives, and the French National Assembly are lower houses. Their members out-

[3] Congress, in fact, often competes with the executive branch for power. For differing ideas on what Congress *ought* to be doing, see John S. Saloma III, *Congress and the New Politics* (Boston: Little, Brown, 1969).
[4] See K. C. Wheare, *Legislatures* (New York: Oxford University Press, 1963).

number those of the upper houses (435 congressmen to 100 senators in the United States), serve shorter terms (only two years for U.S. congressmen, six for U.S. senators), and usually represent voters from a narrower geographic area. The lower house usually controls the "purse strings." Bills concerning tax expenditures must originate there, giving representatives of the lower house effective control over most government activities.[5] The upper houses in federal states like the United States, West Germany, and Austria have power equal to or greater than the lower houses. Members represent the voters of an entire state or province, and have authority to approve executive appointments, ratify treaties, and impeach public officials. In nonfederal states like Great Britain, the upper house represents the country's social elite and because of this can be considered a holdover from medieval times. The British House of Lords performs mostly ceremonial functions while the real legislative power lies in the lower house, the House of Commons. Not all democratic nations have bicameral legislatures: Israel, Denmark, and New Zealand vest all legislative responsibility in one house. But, bicameral or unicameral, democratic legislatures all perform similar roles.

Lawmaking. The primary job of all democratic legislatures is that of rule initiation: making the laws that govern society. This task involves a complex process that varies little from country to country.[6] The journey of a bill from inception to enactment is a long and arduous one, and most bills introduced in a legislative session never survive it. During the first session of the U.S. Ninety-first Congress (January-December 1969) 21,553 bills were introduced in the House and Senate; only 150 became public law.

How does a bill become law? The first step is to draft and introduce the proposed bill. In the West German Bundestag, individual legislators may not introduce bills on their own, but must join a *fraktion* (a group of fifteen members) to propose legislation. But in most democratic legislatures, any member may introduce a bill. Rule initiation in the United States often originates in the executive branch, with an agency drafting a proposal and finding a sympathetic legislator to introduce the bill in Congress. When a senator or congressman wants to propose a bill of his own, his staff usually does the actual writing, with the aid of the Office of the Legislative Council to check on the proper wording. In parliamentary governments, the executive branch may introduce legislation directly since cabinet members hold seats in the legislature. The Swiss save time by introducing all bills in both houses simultaneously, and while this is not always the case in the United States, here, too, high priority bills are usually introduced in both houses at the same time.

Formal introduction of a bill in the U.S. Congress begins when the pro-

[5] Norway is an exception; *all* bills must originate in the lower house.
[6] For basics on the American lawmaking process see Lewis A. Froman, Jr., *The Congressional Process: Strategies, Rules, and Procedures* (Boston: Little, Brown, 1967).

posal is registered with the clerk of the House or Senate and referred to the appropriate committee.[7] Most bills are tabled, or laid aside by the committee after brief consideration, never to be heard of again. However, when the committee thinks a bill has merit, it is sent to a subcommittee for further investigation. Public hearings, which can last for months if a controversial measure is up for discussion, may be held on very important bills. When staff investigations or public hearings are concluded, the bill is then reviewed by the full committee. At this point, the committee may modify certain sections of the bill before voting for or against its passage. If the bill is approved, it goes to the House Rules Committee or Senate majority leader and is then placed on the calendar of the appropriate house for floor consideration.

Once on the floor, the bill is again debated, amended, and revised before it is voted on by the House or Senate.[8] If a majority of each house carries the bill, the Senate and the House then create a conference committee, where differences between the two versions are ironed out.[9] The agreed-on bill then goes back to the House and Senate for a routine revote, where it rarely encounters any controversy. The legislation is then signed by the heads of both houses and sent to the president for his action. If he signs the bill, it becomes law. If he rejects it, Congress needs a hard-to-achieve two-thirds majority to override his veto. (See Figure 14-1 for the stages through which a bill must pass before it reaches the president's desk.) If the president neither signs the bill nor vetoes it, it automatically becomes law in ten days—if the Congress is still in session. But if Congress adjourns before the ten days have elapsed, the bill does not become law. This latter approach is known as the "pocket veto."

Investigate and Inform. One of the most controversial powers held by legislatures is their right to hold investigations. Critics of congressional hearings claim that witnesses are not allowed to defend themselves properly on cross examination, and suffer public censure no matter what their testimony. The worst abuse of congressional investigations in U.S. history came during the McCarthy hearings, which dealt with the alleged subversion of the federal government. These hearings made political leaders and the general

[7] The Speaker of the House has the discretionary power to determine which committee will consider each piece of legislation. Bills he likes are naturally sent to committees he feels will be agreeable to them, while those he doesn't like may be more likely to land in less fertile soil.

[8] The rules of debate vary greatly in the House and Senate. In the House, strict rules limit debate to a relatively brief period—seldom more than one or two days. The amount of debating time is determined by a special rule for each bill, which is recommended by the House Rules Committee and adopted by the House. The debating rules of the Senate allow each senator unlimited debating time. Some senators, in an attempt to prevent a bill from coming to a vote, have abused these rules by engaging in filibusters. A cloture petition, which must be approved by two-thirds of the senators present (assuming a quorum), can stop a filibuster.

[9] One of the best reference works on the role of the conference committee is Gilbert Y. Steiner, *The Congressional Conference Committee* (Urbana: University of Illinois Press, 1951).

Figure 14-1
Steps in the Passage of a Typical Bill

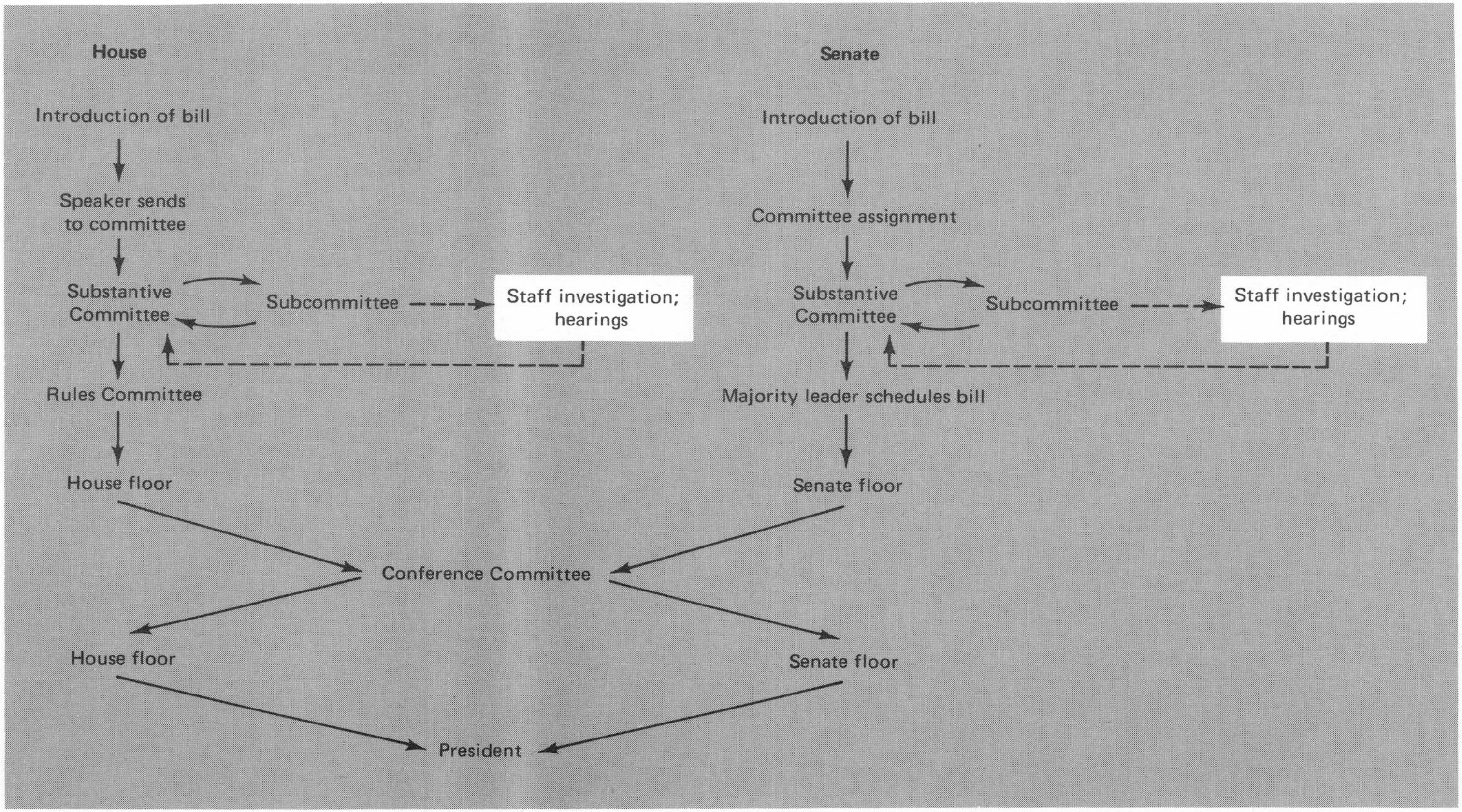

House

Introduction of bill → Speaker sends to committee → Substantive Committee → Subcommittee → Staff investigation; hearings

Substantive Committee → Rules Committee → House floor → Conference Committee → House floor → President

Senate

Introduction of bill → Committee assignment → Substantive Committee → Subcommittee → Staff investigation; hearings

Substantive Committee → Majority leader schedules bill → Senate floor → Conference Committee → Senate floor → President

public wary of unchecked investigations that could further abuse the system. But all legislatures need the proper information on which to base their decisions, and few of us would question the value of committee hearings on issues such as air pollution control or traffic safety. Another important source of congressional information is the standing committee or subcommittee. Members of the Senate Finance Committee or the Far Eastern Affairs Subcommittee, for example, must keep abreast of developments in their areas of expertise, for they are sources of information for the Senate as a whole.

Judicial Role. Most legislatures have the power to impeach national officials, but this power is seldom used. Removal from office is a two-step process in the United States: the House hears evidence and decides by majority vote whether to impeach the official. If the answer is yes, the Senate sits as a court. Conviction requires a two-thirds vote by the Senate. Since 1789, the House has impeached nine federal judges, a president (Andrew Johnson), a senator, and a cabinet officer; the Senate acquitted all but four judges. No president has been impeached, however, since Andrew Johnson in 1868.[10] The French National Assembly, sitting together with the French Senate, can impeach the president of the republic and the ministers of state, but they must then be tried by France's High Court of Justice. In Great Britain, of course, Parliament has no need to exercise its power of impeachment, since the legislature can topple any government by simply refusing to pass its programs.

Approving Executive Appointments. An important check legislatures have on the executive branch is the power to approve executive appointments. The upper house of the democratic legislature generally has power of approval over the nation's ambassadors, judges, bureaucratic heads, and certain military personnel. In the United States, the Senate usually approves the president's choices, but the rejections of Clement Haynsworth's and Harold Carswell's appointments to the Supreme Court early in Nixon's first term are notable recent exceptions.

Amending the Constitution. In most European nations, constitutional amendments are proposed by the national legislature, then submitted to the voters for a referendum. The pattern is somewhat similar in the United States. Congress has the power to propose constitutional amendments by a two-thirds vote, but if a proposed amendment is to be adopted, it must be ratified by three-quarters of the states, acting either through their legislatures

---

[10] A good analysis of the legal problems involved in impeachment is Raoul Berger, *Impeachment: The Constitutional Problems* (Cambridge, Mass.: Harvard University Press, 1973). Michael Benedict has recently studied the causes and course of Andrew Johnson's impeachment. See *The Impeachment and Trial of Andrew Johnson* (New York: Norton, 1973).

or through specially convened state conventions. Amendments to the U.S. Constitution can also be proposed by a constitutional convention, which can be called by the Congress upon a request by two-thirds of the states. For the most part, constitutional amendments are rarely adopted—the difficult procedure for their passage being a major reason why. The United States, for example, has amended its Constitution only twenty-six times since 1789.

Ratifying Treaties. The Soviet Union under Stalin, France under de Gaulle, and England under Churchill each had a foreign policy that seemed to be largely the extension of one man's personality. But then, as now, legislatures must approve all formal treaties with foreign governments before they go into effect. Stalin, de Gaulle, and Churchill all seemed to have personal control of the reins of government because they had the wartime support of their assemblies behind them. The upper house of the legislature usually has power to ratify treaties, and in democratic nations such ratification is by no means automatic. Woodrow Wilson found this to be so when he took his League of Nations plan to the Senate for approval after World War I and it was rejected. In the United States, the Constitution requires a two-thirds vote in the Senate to approve a treaty, making it easy for a determined minority to block ratification. Nevertheless, denial of ratification is infrequent.

Financial Control. The "power of the purse" varies widely among legislatures.[11] Executive budgets in the United States and the Scandinavian countries are drawn up and submitted to the legislatures as suggestions, and the lawmakers may then follow executive recommendations at their own discretion. The taxes to finance the budget and the appropriations requested by the chief executive for the various departments and agencies of government must be voted on by the legislature, which rarely approves his entire budget. This power to withhold revenue or reduce appropriations has been dubbed the "watchdog function" of the legislature. Every year the president of the United States, with the assistance of the Office of Management and Budget, submits a budget to Congress which allocates funds to each of the departments and agencies of the federal government. And, just as a child must explain to her parents the reasons she needs a larger allowance, the heads of these departments and agencies must justify the appropriations request to the proper congressional committee. During these hearings, the department or agency must account for past spending, explain what the agency is currently doing, and how it plans to use its funds in the future. Committee members may challenge the department head on misappropriation of government funds, and may compel the executive branch to justify its bud-

[11] For discussions of the extent of legislative control of finances in the United States, see Richard F. Fenno, Jr., *The Power of the Purse: Appropriations Politics in Congress* (Boston: Little, Brown, 1966); and John F. Manley, *The Politics of Finance: The House Committee on Ways and Means* (Boston: Little, Brown, 1970).

"Then Congress started slashing the research-and-development funds."

get allocations. In this way, Congress ensures that its appropriations are well spent and that the agencies of government are being run honestly and efficiently. But Congress often does not have the last word over the budget. A president can veto an appropriation if he thinks it is excessive. If Congress overrides his veto, the president may simply refuse to spend the extra money, as President Nixon did early in his second term. The legality of this action has been challenged, however, and Mr. Nixon's refusal to spend funds appropriated by Congress is being contested in the courts.

In countries with a cabinet system, like Great Britain and Switzerland, the budget is approved or rejected in its entirety by the legislature.[12] If it is rejected, either the cabinet must resign or parliament must be dissolved. In West Germany and France, the executive branch of government has greater power of the purse than the legislature. The German chancellor may go over the heads of legislators to authorize expenditures, and a French president can use an executive order to put his budget into effect even without legislative approval. Of course, even in the United States, in unusual circumstances, a powerful president might spend money not authorized by Congress and then challenge the legislature to refuse to allocate the needed funds. President Lincoln, for instance, spent vast amounts of money at the beginning of the Civil War without first securing congressional approval. And in 1907, in order to demonstrate to the great powers, including

[12] The Swiss legislature is allowed to modify the budget, but it usually either accepts or rejects it entirely.

Japan, the fighting strength of the U.S. Navy and to show the American people how important the navy was to the country's defense, Teddy Roosevelt sent the fleet halfway around the world, knowing there wasn't enough money to bring it home. Congress had little choice but to allocate funds for the return trip.

Who Holds Power in the Legislature: Structure and Operation

In presidential systems, the legislature and the executive are both directly responsible to the voters; in parliamentary governments, cabinet members are ministers of Parliament, and the executive is answerable to the legislature. There is no way for Congress to remove a president short of impeachment; but in Great Britain, a simple vote of no confidence can cause the government to fall. This is not a common occurrence, however. In the twentieth century no government which has had a majority in the House of Commons has fallen because of a vote of no confidence. Two-house (bicameral) legislatures and one-house (unicameral) legislatures differ in organization. Despite these differences, however, most legislatures, like most social institutions, share a similar overall structure.

Bicameralism. About two-thirds of modern democratic legislatures are divided into two distinct houses. (For a description of legislatures of selected countries with various forms of government, see Table 14-2.) Bicameralism in parliamentary systems can be traced back to the social structure of medieval society: the early parliaments represented the common people in the lower house and the aristocracy in the upper house. As democracy grew, the lower house increased its power, while the power of the upper house declined along with the leveling of the aristocracy. In federal nations, like the United States, the upper house was designed to represent units of government, and to act as a check on the popularly elected lower house. The early Senate had much in common with the House of Lords in England. It was elected by the state legislature and was intended to consist of men from the upper social classes who would preserve the rights of the nation's landed gentry and check the less rational masses. Although the Senate is popularly elected today, it still allows the states with a minority of the country's population to cast a majority of the votes. This situation is not questioned because of our acceptance of the fifty states as separate and unitary political entities.

Although the parliamentary system gives little real power to the upper house, this generalization does not hold true in all bicameral legislatures. The French Senate, indirectly elected by the National Assembly and local and provincial councillors, has the power to veto bills passed by the Assembly, although the Assembly can override that veto. The German Bundesrat is chosen by the states comprising the federal republic, and it can check

Table 14-2
Legislatures and Forms of Government

Country	Estimated Population	Form of Government	Unicam	Bicam	Upper House Number of Members	Upper House Length of Term (in years)	Lower House Number of Members	Lower House Length of Term (in years)
Albania	2,019,000	Communist	X		240	4		
Australia	12,500,000	Parliamentary		X	60	6	125	3
Canada	21,400,000	Parliamentary		X	102	Life to 75	264	5
France	51,100,000	Parliamentary		X	283	9	487	5
East Germany	16,200,000	Communist	X		434	4		
Federal Republic of Germany	58,600,000	Parliamentary		X	41	—[a]	496	4
Haiti	4,867,000	Presidential Dictatorship	X		58	6		
India	554,600,000	Parliamentary		X	240	5	521	5
Republic of Ireland	3,000,000	Presidential		X	60	5	144	5
Israel	2,900,000	Parliamentary	X		120	4		
Italy	53,670,000	Parliamentary		X	322	5	630	5
Japan	103,540,000	Parliamentary		X	250	6	486	4
Lebanon	2,800,000	Parliamentary	X		99	4		
Liberia	1,170,000	Presidential		X	18	6	52	4
Mexico	50,700,000	Presidential		X	60	6	213	3
Morocco	15,700,000	Monarchy	X		240	6		

Country	Estimated Population	Form of Government	Legislative Type Unicam	Legislative Type Bicam	Upper House Number of Members	Upper House Length of Term (in years)	Lower House Number of Members	Lower House Length of Term (in years)
Netherlands	13,000,000	Parliamentary		X	75	6	150	4
New Zealand	2,763,107	Parliamentary	X		84	3		
Norway	3,879,000	Parliamentary		X	38	4	112	4
Poland	32,807,000	Communist	X		460	4		
Portugal	9,600,000	Parliamentary		X	130	4	Corporate Chamber (Advisory)	
Romania	20,253,000	Communist	X		465	4		
Spain	33,290,000	Dictatorship	X		570	4		
Sweden	8,046,000	Parliamentary	X		350	3		
Syria	6,200,000	Military Junta	X		1743	Chosen by President		
Turkey	35,600,000	Parliamentary		X	184	6	450	4
United Kingdom	56,000,000	Parliamentary		X	c1000	Life	630	5 (Max.)
USSR	242,768,000	Communist		X	767	4	750	4
USA	204,600,000	Presidential		X	100	6	435	2

[a] Members of the West German Bundesrat are appointed and recalled by the ten state governments they represent. They have no fixed term of membership.

the popularly elected Bundestag. The House and the Senate in the United States cannot override each other's veto, and often conflict with one another as much as they do with the executive branch.[13]

The Committee System. Virtually every legislature has a number of standing or permanent committees, and may from time to time create special ad hoc committees to study urgent matters. The British House of Commons has five standing committees, plus another committee to handle matters pertaining to Scotland. However, it is in the United States Congress that the committee system has been most fully developed.[14] The House of Representatives has twenty-one standing committees; the Senate, seventeen—and they often make the news. We often hear of the more prestigious of these committees, such as the House Ways and Means, and Foreign Affairs, and we know that a good committee assignment is a boon to a freshman congressman's career.

What purposes do these committees serve? Their major function, of course, is to screen the thousands upon thousands of bills that are introduced at every session and pick out the few that merit serious study and consideration. Secondly, legislatures are so large that bills cannot be drafted by the entire membership; in order to work out an agreement on the precise wording and scope of legislation, proposals must be referred to relatively small groups of lawmakers who will iron out differences and submit polished bills for the consideration of the whole membership. It should not be surprising, therefore, that the bulk of legislative work is not performed on the floor of the House or Senate but is done in committee and subcommittee rooms. The committees are "where the action is."

The decision makers who hold the power over committee assignments vary according to political party and legislative body. Republican congressmen receive their committee assignments from the party's Committee on Committees, which is made up of one congressman from every state with Republican representatives. Democrats receive their assignments from the senior Democratic members of the House who serve on the Ways and Means Committee. All assignments are automatically approved by the House. In the Senate, the steering committees of each party determine where its members will serve. The senators with the most seniority serve on the steering committees and generally give preference to other senior members. When Lyndon Johnson was Democratic Senate Leader in the late 1950s, however, he made

---

[13] For a description of the structure of Congress, see Richard F. Fenno, Jr., "The Internal Distribution of Influence: The House," and Ralph K. Huitt, "The Internal Distribution of Influence: The Senate," both in *Congress and America's Future*, ed. American Assembly (Englewood Cliffs, N.J.: Prentice-Hall, 1965).

[14] An excellent account of the committee system is given in Charles L. Clapp, *The Congressman: His Work as He Sees It* (New York: Anchor Books, 1963), Chapters 5–6. Woodrow Wilson's study points out the power and distinctiveness of the U.S. committee system. See *Congressional Government: A Study in American Politics* (New York: World Publishing, 1965).

an astute political move. He changed the rules of the steering committee so that every freshman Democrat was entitled to one good committee assignment. Johnson's plan allowed the junior member to take part in the substantive work of an important Senate committee before a senior member could receive a second major committee assignment. Needless to say, this action earned him the gratitude of many freshman Democrats.[15]

Standing Committees. In Great Britain and France, standing committees are not as specialized and lack the political influence of their American counterparts. The standing committees in the British Parliament are designed to be flexible and broad, and have traditionally played a less critical role than the American committees. They work out the details of a bill after the House of Commons has approved it, rather than sitting in judgment on the bill before it reaches the House floor. However, the age of specialization has been felt in Britain too, and parliamentary reforms initiated by the Labour party in 1966 have increased the degree of committee specialization. Education, overseas aid and development, race relations, science and technology, nationalized industries, and Scottish affairs all rate permanent committees in Commons. The counterpart in the French National Assembly is the commission—again not as compartmentalized as the American committee. In studying a bill, the commission assigns only one member—called the rapporteur—to the task, rather than working collectively as in the United States and Britain. In the United States, specialization is the name of the game. The larger committees, such as the Senate Foreign Relations Committee, may have as many as ten subcommittees. All told, there are 125 subcommittees in Congress as compared to only six in each legislative chamber of France.

Standing committees in Congress are balanced so that they will represent both political parties and the states or geographic regions with the greatest interest in the committee's area of specialization. For example, Nebraska has a man on the Agricultural Committee, and New York is usually represented on the Education and Labor Committee. Each standing committee is bipartisan, made up of Democrats and Republicans in direct proportion to each party's representation in that house of Congress. If the House is sixty percent Democratic, the House Ways and Means Committee will be too. The work of most standing committees—Judiciary, Agriculture, Foreign Relations —is obvious from their names. The House Rules Committee controls the order in which legislation is brought to the floor for debate; the rules to govern floor debate, including the amount of time allotted; whether or not to allow amendments to the bill; and when to schedule a vote on passage. Through these powers this committee has enormous legislative influence. The Ways and Means Committee, in addition to doling out committee assignments, handles all bills related to taxes and public revenues.

---

[15] For a full account, see Ralph K. Huitt, "Democratic Party Leadership in the Senate," *American Political Science Review* 55 (June 1961) : 333–44.

Select and Special Committees.   Unlike standing committees, select and special committees are temporary; they are created to handle specific issues that have arisen, like the Senate investigation of the Watergate break-in. These committees hold legislative investigations of labor-management relations and periodic hearings on organized crime. Once their work is completed, they are disbanded. Most democratic legislatures, like the United States Congress, use special committees to study less permanent issues.

Joint and Conference Committees.   In the U.S. Congress, joint committees, composed of members from both the House and Senate, study legislation currently under consideration in both houses. This type of committee has been used only sparingly, though some, like the Joint Economic Committee, conduct vital business. Conference committees are called in cases where different versions of the same bill have been passed by the two houses, and neither house is willing to accept the other's version. The purpose of the conference committee is to work out a compromise.

Legislative Leaders.   While committees receive more attention in the U.S. Congress than in other legislatures, presiding officers are the center of power in almost every democratic legislature. (The vice-president of the United States is a major exception. As David Maxey put it, "Vice-presidents are elected by a constituency of one," [16] and this is reflected in their role as presiding officer of the Senate. They are powerless, except to cast a tie-breaking vote.) Most presiding officers are chosen by their colleagues and hold positions with substantial political influence. They recognize speakers, rule on procedures, place motions before the legislature, and have a say in what committee considers a given piece of legislation as well as a significant voice in who serves on a particular committee. Party leaders and whips influence their parties' stands on pending legislation and voting within the parties' congressional and senatorial ranks.[17] How, then, can they direct operations of an entire legislative body with any degree of fairness?

Majority Leaders.   The majority leaders of the United States House and Senate are the spokesmen of the controlling party in each house, and both are elected by party caucus. They formulate party stands on upcoming legislation, determine the order in which bills come to the floor, negotiate compromises, and have a considerable voice in committee appointments. Their positions accord them substantial power within their parties and the legislature—power that is bolstered by prestigious committee memberships achieved after several years on Capitol Hill.

Minority Leaders.   The U.S. House and Senate minority leaders are also elected by party caucus, and serve as spokesmen for the party with the minority of legislative seats. Like majority leaders, they formulate party

[16] David Maxey, "Agnew Sitting Pretty," *Life Magazine* 73, no. 17 (October 27, 1972) : 38.
[17] A good survey of the role played by party leaders in Congress is Randall B. Ripley, *Party Leaders in the House of Representatives* (Washington, D.C.: The Brookings Institution, 1967).

stands and direct their parties' strategies on the floor. But, since they influence fewer votes, they are not as powerful in the legislature as their counterparts in the majority party, whom they often criticize.

Speakers. In the United States the Speaker of the House is its presiding officer. In Great Britain, the Speaker of the House of Commons is chosen by both major parties in the legislature. Once elected, he must sever all party connections and refrain from taking part in debates. The Speaker of the United States House of Representatives, in contrast, is like a father umpiring at his son's Little League game: he is allowed to hope for the best for his son (party), but his rulings are expected to be impartial. The Speaker is expected by both parties to use his considerable powers to partisan advantage. Yet, as presiding officer, he must rule impartially on points of order and give the minority party equal chance to voice their views. The Speakers of most European legislatures are far less partisan than their American counterparts. And many political critics from abroad are quite skeptical about how successfully one man can fulfill the conflicting duties of party leader and neutral presiding officer. Despite this apparent conflict, the majority party rarely complains of poor leadership, and the minority party seldom faults him for being unfair.[18]

Whips. Both the U.S. House of Representatives and the Senate have majority and minority *whips*—a term which is British in origin. In fox hunting, the "whipper-in" keeps the hounds from straying from the pack; in the legislature, the party whip keeps discipline within the party ranks and rounds up support for party policies. He serves as an important liaison between the leadership and the ranks, informing members of how the leadership would like them to vote, assessing projected vote totals, and, in turn, telling party leaders how much "watering down" a piece of legislation needs in order to stand a chance of passing. The accuracy of the whip's vote-count for a given piece of legislation will often determine whether a bill will ever make it to the floor. Senate whips are chosen by party caucuses which endorse the choices of the party leaders. In the House, Democratic whips are chosen directly by the floor leaders, and Republican whips by the Committee on Committees.

Seniority and Power. Almost all institutions in our society have some sort of official or unofficial seniority system. Older children are allowed to stay up later than their younger siblings, senior vice-presidents are usually next in line for corporation presidencies, and four-star generals have achieved their status only by working their way up through the ranks of officer. In our legislature, too, majority and minority leaders and committee chairmen are traditionally veteran members of Congress. One of the main reasons Congress maintains the seniority system is that it helps to prevent intraparty

[18] For a discussion of the extent to which American speakers are bipartisan, see William J. Keefe and Morris S. Opul, *The American Legislative Process*, 2nd ed. (Englewood Cliffs, N.J.: Prentice-Hall, 1968), pp. 42–43.

conflicts over committee chairmanships at every new legislative session. But, since the 1950s, the system has come under a good deal of criticism. Many argue that the seniority tradition favors one-party districts and states that always return the same man to the Senate. And freshmen congressmen often end up on a committee that they are totally unsuited for, simply because they are "low men on the totem pole." (Congressman Herman Badillo, who represented a black and Puerto Rican district of New York City found this out in 1971 when he was assigned to the House Agriculture Committee. Badillo was finally reassigned to the House Education and Labor Committee, but only after considerable wrangling.) For the most part, though, efforts are made to give every committee regional balance and to give major interests representation on the appropriate committees.

Prior to 1910, the Speaker of the House made all House committee assignments on the basis of seniority. But complaints and reforms have changed the picture considerably. Today, both House and Senate committee assignments are made by groups of party leaders, and a serious effort is usually made to fit a person's assignment to his background. In general, the only time seniority is used is when two equally qualified persons vie for the same committee assignment.[19] Of course, once a senator or congressman has made it to the committee of his choice, he is most unlikely to be reassigned to a new or unfamiliar post. If this were the case, no committee member would be able to accumulate any expertise in a special area, and the committee system as a whole would suffer.

Despite these reforms in the committee assignment process, seniority is increasingly applied in the selection of committee chairmen (see Figure 14-2).[20] In 1972, by decision of party caucus, committee chairmen were elected. Nonetheless, each case resulted in a victory for seniority. A committee chairman holds a position with substantial political influence. He decides when his committee will meet, what bills they will consider, whether or not hearings should be held on a given piece of legislation—and his decisions are rarely overridden by his own committee. Defenders of the seniority system argue that any other method of choosing committee chairmen would be equally discriminatory to some members, and that this system offers stability and continuity in the distribution of congressional influence. If Congress were not based upon the seniority system, every election would bring intraparty power-grabs. Under the seniority system this never happens; the transfer of committee leadership is automatic. It also places experienced people in committee leadership positions, and this experience often makes the committee chairman an expert in his field. Wilbur Mills of the House Ways and Means Committee, for example, is an extremely competent committee leader.

[19] Clapp, *The Congressman*, pp. 221 ff.
[20] Nelson Polsby, Miriam Gallaher and Barry Spencer Rindquist, "The Growth of the Seniority System in the United States House of Representatives," *American Political Science Review* 63, no. 3 (September 1969) : 787–807.

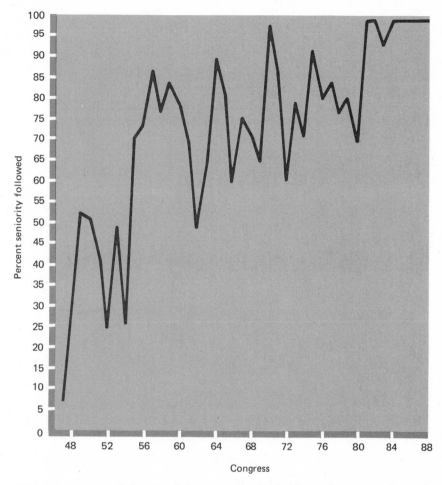

Figure 14-2
Percentage of
House Committees
Using Seniority to
Select Chairmen,
1881–1963
(Eighty-eighth
Congress) *

* Percentages were calculated as follows: seniority divided by total committees for each Congress.

Source: Nelson W. Polsby, Miriam Gallaher, and Barry Spencer Rindquist, "The Growth of the Seniority System in the U.S. House of Representatives," American Political Science Review 63, no. 3 (September 1969): 793.

An extensive study of the seniority system by political scientist Barbara Hinckley concludes that the system does not produce any appreciable regional bias, and, perhaps more importantly, that on balance senior chairmen are neither more nor less conservative than their younger committee colleagues. Hinckley suggests that although seniority remains a controversial tradition, original committee assignments and reassignments may be as important as seniority in determining future chairmanships.[21]

[21] Barbara Hinckley, *The Seniority System in Congress* (Bloomington: Indiana University Press, 1971). For a similar discussion of the pros and cons of the modified seniority system in Congress, see Nelson W. Polsby et al., "The Growth of the Seniority System in the United States House of Representatives."

In spite of the power held by the majority and minority leaders, Speakers, whips, and committee chairmen, few of us can name all of the people who hold these important positions. In contrast, none of us would have trouble remembering the last three presidents of the United States, or the current prime minister of Britain and chancellor of Germany. The degree to which political power is divided between the legislative and executive branches varies from country to country.

Executives and Executive Powers

While President Nixon and Britain's Prime Minister Heath do approximately the same job, the United States has no parallel to Queen Elizabeth, except perhaps Uncle Sam. The queen is a symbol of national unity with no real political power—a figurehead rather than a leader. The actual decision maker in England's executive branch is the prime minister, who is the chief of government, even though he is not the chief of state. Most parliamentary systems, with the exception of France, divide the executive function similarly: a president or monarch performs ceremonial functions, while the prime minister or chancellor is the actual working head of government. Presidential democracies, in contrast, vest all executive responsibilities in one leader.

While chief executive officers of all sovereign nations are equal under international law, their extent of real political power varies greatly.[22] At one extreme is the totalitarian dictator: Joseph Stalin, Adolf Hitler, Benito Mussolini, and Francisco Franco are notable examples. This type of leader rules the country single-handedly, dominating all branches of government at once. The independent executive found in presidential democracies has considerable power too, but nothing to compare to that of the dictator. He cannot be forced to step down from office just because he fails to get his programs through the legislature; to oust him, the people must wait until the next scheduled election. On the other hand, he *is* subject to effective checks by the legislature and, on occasion, the courts. President Lyndon Johnson, for example, faced an increasingly hostile Congress during most of his last term, yet he did not relinquish the presidency until it was time for new elections. Captive executives, like the prime minister of the Soviet Union, are completely controlled by another power—in this case, the Presidium of the Communist party. They carry out the bidding of the party leadership, and their power stems from their party positions rather than from their offices in the executive branch. Executives such as the prime minister of Great Britain fall in between the independent and captive status. Edward Heath is more under Parliament's thumb than Richard Nixon is under Congress', but he is by no means close to being "captive."

[22] Our discussion relies primarily on Fried, *Comparative Political Institutions*, pp. 18–27.

Who Is the Executive?

In the United States, we hail to only one chief. Our president makes all cabinet appointments (with Senate approval), and has final and ultimate responsibility for all policy decisions. Many Latin American countries also give all executive power to one person. President Allende of Chile, the first Marxist ever to be popularly elected in a Western Hemisphere democracy, is his nation's sole executive leader. Yet in Chile, as in any presidential democracy, his policy decisions are subject to challenge from the legislature.

The Plural Executive. Although we are accustomed to thinking that our government is headed by a single executive, this is not the case at all levels. Executive power is often divided among several people at the state level. The attorney general, the comptroller, and, in some cases, the lieutenant governor are elected independently of the governor, and exercise important executive powers of their own. Another type of plural executive—the council system—is used at the national level in Switzerland,[23] where a seven-man Federal Council is elected to a four-year term by the legislature. Although the council does have the president and vice-president to lead discussions and perform ceremonial duties, these men have no political power over their colleagues. Policy decisions must be made by majority vote.

Cabinet Government. The most common plural executive structure is the cabinet. Great Britain's system is a classic example. Technically, it is a plural executive with decision-making powers shared by the prime minister, the ministry, and the cabinet. But in practice, it generally operates much like the single executive system.[24]

The monarch, as official head of state, initiates the new administration by formally inviting one of her subjects to become prime minister and assume the responsibility of forming a government. (The majority leader in the House of Commons is traditionally chosen for the position.) As such, he appoints the twenty-four executive department heads, parliamentary secretaries, legal officers, ministers without portfolio, and parliamentary whips who make up the ministry. They are generally all members of the prime minister's party, and are chosen to represent every significant group within the party. The actual cabinet consists of eighteen to twenty-three of the most trusted ministers, and is charged with the formulation of government policy. Theoretically, the prime minister is *primus inter pares* (first among equals), and must carry out decisions reached by the whole cabinet even

[23] See George A. Codding, Jr., *The Federal Government of Switzerland* (Boston: Houghton Mifflin, 1961), Chapter 6.
[24] See W. Ivor Jennings, *Cabinet Government* (New York: Cambridge University Press, 1959); Byrum E. Carter, *The Office of Prime Minister* (Princeton, N.J.: Princeton University Press, 1956); and Anthony King, ed., *The British Prime Minister* (New York: St. Martin's Press, 1967).

when he is personally opposed. But, like an American president, the prime minister can dismiss a cabinet member at any time, and those who oppose his decisions are expected to resign. Conceivably, a cabinet that is strongly united against the prime minister could force a change in government policy or even the prime minister's resignation. But this happens rarely, and hasn't occurred since Neville Chamberlain was ousted from party leadership in 1940.

The chancellor of West Germany, in many ways, is even stronger than the British prime minister. Like his English counterpart, he is majority leader in the lower house (Bundestag). But his cabinet appointments are not subject to legislative confirmation, and, once in office, he doesn't necessarily have to resign just because his party fails to secure a majority in the house at election time.[25] He can then form a coalition government with a minor, splinter party and continue as chancellor. His dominance in the West German government is further assured by other powers that come with his office. If he cannot get his programs through the Bundestag, he may call a six-month "state of emergency" and secure legislative enactment with the approval of the upper house alone; he may veto any appropriations increase made by the Bundestag; and, if the Bundestag rejects his budget, the budget from the previous year is carried over automatically. The cabinet system can thus be stretched to allow the executive greater dominance over Parliament than a president has over his legislature. But which system makes for a stronger national leader?

The Roles of the Executive

Richard E. Neustadt, a leading authority on the American presidency, has written that "from outside or below, a President is 'many men' or one man wearing many 'hats,' or playing many roles . . . the President himself plays every 'role,' wears every 'hat' at once." [26] Not only the president, but most modern chief executives wear more than one "hat." The unique powers of the presidency, however, put the man in the White House in an uncommonly strong position. He is elected independently of the legislature, and, as such, is the direct choice of the nation as well as the choice of his party. In addition, he has several executive roles that are his alone: official chief of state, head of government, party leader, commander-in-chief of the armed forces, chief diplomat, chief executive, and chief legislator. These powers reinforce each other to make the presidency the most respected office in the nation. Great responsibility also comes with these broad powers. And, in the last analysis, there is no one to whom he can pass the blame for mismanaged

[25] The same is true in Canada, where Pierre Trudeau failed to win a majority in the 1972 elections but decided to stay on, if only temporarily, on the strength of his hairline plurality and the implicit support of a third party.
[26] Richard E. Neustadt, *Presidential Power* (New York: New American Library, 1964), p. viii.

affairs. As the sign in Harry Truman's oval office so aptly put it: "The buck stops here." Since 1789, the powers of the president have grown enormously,[27] as have those of the chief executives of all other nations.

Chief of State. The president is the surrogate and spokesman for the American people. He is the visible symbol of the nation, and must perform numerous "ribbon-cutting" ceremonies usually saved for kings and queens and figurehead presidents in other nations. While the vice-president or the president's wife are sometimes sent to dedicate major public works projects or christen boats, tradition still demands the president's appearance at many of these occasions. And, like prime ministers and chancellors, he must personally greet visiting dignitaries, entertain the diplomatic corps, and represent his country at some important international conferences.

Head of Government. Every head of government—president, prime minister, chancellor—is responsible for carrying out legislative decisions and enforcing court orders. He must also supervise the bureaucratic machinery at the national level, making the responsibilities of his job staggering. President Nixon, for instance, is responsible for eleven major departments of government, more than one hundred executive bureaus, five hundred administrative offices, and six hundred divisions employing nearly three million civil servants. One American worker in sixty is a federal employee (compared to one in two thousand in Washington's day), and the president is—at least in theory—each federal worker's boss.[28] To aid the president in this enormous task, the Executive Office of the President, now employing some twelve hundred fulltime workers, was formed in 1939 to conduct the day-to-day supervisory functions of running the bureaucracy. The cabinet, while responsible for some government administration, has become more an advisory body.[29]

Party Chief. Although the president is chosen directly by the people, he is still leader of his political party, as are the British, French, and German heads of government. The chief executive is expected to take the lead in raising campaign funds, and in endorsing and campaigning on behalf of his party's candidates for local, state, and national office. More importantly, he is expected to play a major role in formulating his party's legislative program. The president is not as powerful a party leader as the prime minister in a parliamentary government because of the lack of centralization and discipline in the American party system. Edward Corwin clearly shows that party leadership is not always as strong as it might be in the United States

[27] Our discussion follows Edward S. Corwin, *The President: Office and Powers* (New York: New York University Press, 1957).

[28] Sidney Hyman, *The American President* (New York: Harper, 1954), pp. 9–10. See Chapter 15 on the bureaucracy for more details.

[29] Richard F. Fenno, Jr., *The President's Cabinet* (Cambridge, Mass.: Harvard University Press, 1959).

when he writes of the Franklin Delano Roosevelt administration: "The President's [Roosevelt's] death on April 12 brought to a close a constantly renewed feud of more than two years' duration with Congresses in which his own party was in the majority." [30] Lyndon Johnson, with his long experience in Senate leadership, is perhaps the best example of a president who was able to marshal party support behind his legislative program. But even in Johnson's case, the tide of political events eventually turned the legislature against him.

Commander-in-chief. The Cuban missile crisis began when President Kennedy learned that the Russians were erecting missile silos in Cuba—a strategic move which the president believed threatened both our nuclear superiority over the Soviet Union and our credibility. [31] He had to act quickly, and in so doing brought us to the brink of war by imposing a naval blockade on Cuba. Kennedy's assumption that the implied threat of military action would force Khrushchev to back off worked effectively. But Kennedy acted without congressional authorization, and many people, especially after the escalations of the war in Vietnam in the sixties, feel the president should not have that prerogative. The United States Supreme Court, however, has consistently upheld the right of the president to deploy the armed forces unilaterally when our national security is threatened.

Chief Diplomat. Golda Meir, Indira Gandhi, Chou En-lai, Richard Nixon— these are the names in the news, the people who formulate their nations' foreign policies. Presidents, premiers, chancellors, and prime ministers by any other name are still the official channels of communication between their countries and foreign governments. When De Gaulle decided to open trade relations with Mainland China, he did so without consulting his legislature. In the United States and West Germany, the legislature must ratify treaties, but the president and chancellor can enter into executive agreements with nations without legislative approval. For the most part, legislatures concede that foreign affairs are primarily an executive function, and generally go along with the decisions of the chief executive. Few complained that President Nixon exceeded his bounds when he went to the People's Republic of China to negotiate with Chou En-lai.

Dispenser of Appointments. Since the introduction of the merit system in the U.S. civil service at the turn of the century, the power of patronage has been considerably diminished. All federal judges and legal officers are appointed by the president, as are diplomatic officers, and upper-echelon management personnel in the federal departments, agencies, offices, bureaus, and divisions. All in all, the president still has thousands of jobs to dispense

[30] Corwin, *The President*, p. 277.
[31] An excellent account of the president's role during international crises is offered in Robert F. Kennedy, *Thirteen Days* (New York: W. W. Norton, 1969).

every year. One of the key ways a president can enforce party discipline within the congressional ranks is by his influence in patronage appointments. Although the power of patronage is not as important as it once was, it carries enough weight so that few legislators willingly incur the wrath of the party leadership.

To a large extent, the success of a president's program is determined by the kind of people he appoints to office, for these appointees can bring either creative leadership or routine administration to their jobs. In making appointments, a president considers a candidate's experience, talent, and temperament to manage the responsibilities of office. His decision is also influenced by how many votes an appointee will bring to the administration, the political debts he must pay, and the responsibility to call upon prominent political and national leaders to serve the office of the president.

Chief Legislator. The president is not only responsible for executing the laws passed by Congress, but he is also vested—both formally and informally—with considerable lawmaking powers.[32] For example, he can unilaterally declare a state of national emergency in a depressed area, as President Nixon did during the floods in South Dakota in the spring of 1972. In some instances, he can create new offices and agencies: President Nixon's Wage and Price Boards were not created by Congress specifically, but established in accordance with economic powers previously granted to the president by the legislature. Congressional rulings give the chief executive broad discretionary powers in interpreting and implementing law. In many cases, Congress passes very general legislation and leaves it up to the president to fill in the details. Finally, the president initiates legislation himself. He submits a State of the Union message and a National Budget to Congress every year. These messages usually spell out the general direction of his administration for the coming year and suggest programs and laws that he believes are in the best and most urgent interests of the nation. President Kennedy asked Congress for civil rights legislation and tax reductions; President Johnson called for a War on Poverty; and President Nixon asked for a national welfare program and federal revenue sharing with the states.

The ever-increasing trend for the president to initiate legislation is due to several factors. First, during the last few decades so many government programs have been initiated that now most new proposals relate to the improvement of existing programs. In most cases executive agencies administer these programs and are intimately familiar with the parts that require legislative action. It makes a great deal of sense, therefore, for these administrative agencies to suggest legislation to the president, who in turn considers it and presents it to Congress. Secondly, the president's coordination of the budgets of all administrative agencies allows him to shape public programs by controlling their funds.

[32] See Wilfred E. Binkley, "The President as Chief Legislator," *Annals of the American Academy of Political and Social Science* 307 (September 1956): 92–105.

Congress often finds it hard to ignore presidential requests, especially if the president is popular with the people. Thanks to television, a president can enlist the support of millions of Americans by appealing to them directly in a single hour-long speech. And, public opinion is often a powerful persuader with many congressmen who hope to "coattail" to reelection on the same ticket with a popular president. In a more direct manner, the president can appeal to a legislator's sense of party loyalty, or promise him patronage or support in the next election. And when all else fails, the president can always fall back on his executive veto. The threat of a presidential veto is sometimes enough to persuade Congress to frame legislation more to the president's liking.

But presidential powers alone do not make a powerful president. Many people believe that Franklin Roosevelt wound up with a rebellious Congress during his last term because he overstepped the limits of his office. Dwight Eisenhower came to the presidency with a military background, which had prepared him to give orders rather than to negotiate and bargain, and as a result he had little success with Capitol Hill. Our unique system of checks and balances puts many legislative and judicial controls on the presidency, and each president must determine for himself how far the other two branches will go to thwart his decisions.

Limitations on the Executive

In part the President is an office . . . whose head knows what is going on in government and has something to say about it. Secondly the President is an office whose head knows what is going on but has nothing to say about it. Thirdly, the President is an office whose head does not know what is going on and has nothing to say about it. There is a little of the first in the presidency, a good deal of the second, and a great amount of the third.[33]

Most presidents would agree with Alfred de Grazia's assessment. While many executive leaders in Europe may serve unlimited terms, the U.S. president can only serve two terms. As a lame-duck, he is invariably weaker during his second term, as other party leaders begin vying for the political limelight. And, although a rare occurrence, the Supreme Court *can* declare presidential actions unconstitutional, leaving the president little choice but to go along with the ruling. This happened in 1952, when the Court ruled President Truman's seizure of strike-bound steel mills to be unconstitutional. And Congress, too, can tie a president's hands by simply refusing to enact his legislative program.

While Britain's prime minister can dissolve Parliament and call for new elections, the president has no such power (much as he might appreciate

[33] Alfred de Grazia, as quoted in *Congress and the President,* ed. Ronald C. Moe (Pacific Palisades, Calif.: Goodyear Publishing, 1971), p. 91.

it at some moments). John Kennedy's civil rights bill was bottled up in the uncooperative House Rules Committee for months, and it finally took the tragedy of his assassination to uncork it. And the expression "he who holds the purse strings controls the nation" holds true to a large extent in the United States. A West German chancellor and a French president have ultimate spending power, but a recalcitrant United States Congress can withhold government funds with impunity, thus blocking many of the president's activities. "One word from me," as Harry Truman declared about his experiences as president, "and everyone does as he pleases!"

Congress and the President: Separation of Powers?

"The accumulation of all powers, legislative, executive, and judiciary, in the same hands," James Madison wrote in *The Federalist*, no. 47, "may justly be pronounced the very definition of tyranny." All democratic systems hold that power must be balanced internally to prevent one man or group of men from seizing all political control. Checks and balances, John Adams declared, is as effective as "setting a thief to catch a thief," and he was confident that interbranch jealousies would ensure that each branch would confine the other to the political limits set down in the Constitution. In recent years, many political scientists have voiced the fear that, despite the numerous limitations imposed on presidential authority, the breadth of responsibility required to run a modern nation as large as the United States has caused the office of the presidency to become too powerful.[34] How valid are these fears? Certainly, the relationship between Congress and the president has changed profoundly in the last century. But does this new relationship constitute a threat to our system of democracy?

Has the legislature lost its initiative? Samuel P. Huntington has noted some startling statistics. From 1882 to 1909, Congress was responsible for shaping more than half (55 percent) of all significant pieces of legislation; between 1910 and 1932, the figure dropped to 46 percent; and from 1933 to 1940, Congress was primarily responsible for initiating a mere 8 percent of all major laws. "Since 1933," Huntington writes, "the initiative in formulating legislation, in assigning legislative priorities, in arousing support for legislation, and in determining the final content of legislation enacted has clearly shifted to the executive branch."[35] This situation has significantly altered the traditional separation of powers between the legislative and executive branches, and has produced a variety of studies both decrying

[34] For a summary of recent research in the area of congressional-presidential relations see Ralph K. Huitt and Robert L. Peabody, *Congress: Two Decades of Analysis* (New York: Harper & Row, 1969), Chapter 1.

[35] Samuel P. Huntington, "Congressional Responses to the Twentieth Century," in *The Congress and America's Future*, ed. American Assembly, pp. 23–24.

"Since most of our power was usurped by the Executive branch, I find I have more free time to devote to getting myself re-elected."

the fall of Congress and defending the increased legislative responsibilities of the presidency.

One of the reasons for the decline of Congress as policy initiator is America's rapidly changing social needs.[36] Congressmen, for the most part, are trained in law or business. Few have the background or the training to deal with such problems as pollution, weapons systems, and the urban blight—problems that weren't even recognized in the America of their youth. As a result, Congress often follows the legislative lead of the executive agencies, staffed with experts who have a wealth of information at their disposal.

[36] For examples, see Richard A. Cooley and Geoffrey Wandesforde-Smith, *Congress and the Environment* (Seattle: University of Washington Press, 1970) which treats Congress's role in antipollution legislation; and Frederic N. Cleaveland and associates, *Congress and Urban Problems* (Washington, D.C.: The Brookings Institution, 1960) which offers seven case histories of urban legislation enacted by Congress.

The committee system is a basic underlying reason for Congress's slowness in responding to the changing needs of society. Many critics fault the established committees (such as agriculture, armed services, education and labor, etc.) for their reluctance to yield power and influence to new groups. [37] Despite the transformation of America in the past few decades, there are still no major congressional committees on urban affairs or the environment. Critics argue that Congress is not structurally equipped to initiate new laws in these areas. Congress will, however, most likely create more committees to handle urban and environmental legislation as such issues become of greater and greater importance to voters.

At other times in our history, one branch has dominated the other. Right now, we seem to be in a period of strong executive leadership and congressional quiescence. But what the next decade will bring is a matter for speculation and observation.

One area in which the president is most likely to maintain his authority is foreign policy.[38] There are two basic reasons for this. First, foreign policy decisions require vast amounts of technical information that are not available to Congress. Much of this information involves delicate negotiations with foreign powers, which no executive leader wishes to be made public. Secondly, many foreign policy matters—especially those of a strategic or military nature—require decisions that must be made within days or even hours. Congress simply needs too much time to reach a decision. What would have happened if President Kennedy had first asked Congress whether he should blockade Cuba during the 1962 missile crisis? While Congress debated, the crisis might have become even more acute.

While some students and scholars have expressed fear that the president has too much authority, many others believe that the executive branch should be given more powers. Louis W. Koenig argues that the president is the only public official truly representative of all the people, and that he should be given the power to carry out his popular mandate.[39] Koenig points out that presidents have pushed for civil rights while Congress fought to maintain the status quo; presidents have struggled with major economic crises while Congress frustrated their policies; and presidents have maintained our national security while Congress engaged in criticism. Congressmen—remote from the people, representative of powerful and well-established interests, and bowed under by the weight of the seniority system—are unable, according to Koenig, to respond to the real needs of the average American voter. Koenig would like to see the president's two-term limitation

---

[37] See Cooley and Wandeforde-Smith, *Congress and the Environment*. Also, Cleaveland, *Congress and Urban Problems*. For a scathing denunciation of the U.S. committee system, see Ralph Nader, *Who Rules Congress?* (New York: Grossman Publishers, 1972), pp. 52–83.

[38] James A. Robinson's *Congress and Foreign Policy Making* (Homewood, Ill.: Dorsey Press, 1962) gives this area a lucid treatment.

[39] Louis W. Koenig, "More Power to the President (Not Less)," *Congress and the President*, ed. Ronald C. Moe, pp. 69–73.

seventy, so that younger leaders can be free to move up to positions of congressional leadership.[40] He, too, calls for reforms in the seniority system, suggesting that committee chairmen should be chosen in open elections. And he offers various proposals aimed at allowing Congress to better avail itself of the technical expertise now at the disposal of the executive agencies. In this way Congress and the president will both play an active part in solving some of the problems of the modern age.

The balance of powers established in our Constitution is becoming harder and harder to maintain in modern America. The complexity of our growing society, the speed at which events move, and the necessity for quick and decisive action have all combined to increase the importance of the presidency. One man can reach a decision faster than 535 congressmen, and it seems likely that Congress will continue to play less of a part in laying the groundwork for potential legislation. But the president must still secure congressional approval for his programs; and Congress still holds the purse strings to finance his policies. The president has not *become* the government, and his authority can still be checked by the legislature.

[40] Nelson W. Polsby, "Strengthening Congress in National Policymaking," in *Congressional Behavior,* ed. Nelson W. Polsby (New York: Random House, 1971), pp. 3–13

Suggested Readings

Burns, James M. *The Deadlock of Democracy.* Englewood Cliffs, N.J.: Prentice-Hall, 1963. An argument stating that Congress is slow, unresponsive, and actually split into four separate wings: congressional Democrats, congressional Republicans, presidential Democrats, and presidential Republicans.

Fenno, Richard F., Jr. *The President's Cabinet.* Cambridge, Mass.: Harvard University Press, 1959. A succinct study of the role of the Cabinet under various administrations.

Huitt, Ralph K., and Peabody, Robert L. *Congress: Two Decades of Analysis.* New York: Harper & Row, 1969. A review of what is and is not known about Congress.

Jennings, Ivor. *Parliament.* New York: Cambridge University Press, 1939. The classic study of British Parliament.

————. *Cabinet Government.* New York: Cambridge University Press, 1947. The classic study of the British executive system.

King, Anthony, ed. *The British Prime Minister.* New York: St. Martin's Press, 1969. An excellent collection of articles on the British chief executive.

Moe, Ronald C., ed. *Congress and the President.* Pacific Palisades, Calif.: Goodyear Publishing, 1969. A collection of recent articles on the American legislative and executive branches of government.

Neustadt, Richard E. *Presidential Power*. New York: John Wiley, 1960. An examination of the presidency and how it functions, with case studies of recent administrations.

Polsby, Nelson W., ed. *The Modern Presidency*. New York: Random House, 1973. A collection of journalistic analyses of the presidency, from FDR to Nixon.

Reedy, George E. *The Twilight of the Presidency*. New York: NAL-World, 1970. An argument that the presidency has become isolated from the real world and is subject to costly errors as a result.

Saloma, John S., III. *Congress and the New Politics*. Boston: Little, Brown, 1969. An examination of the changing relationship between Congress and the President.

Wahlke, John C., et al. *The Legislative System*. New York: John Wiley, 1962. A study of legislators and the legislative process in four American states.

Wheare, K. C. *Legislatures*. New York: Oxford University Press, 1963. An introduction to legislatures in modern democracies.

Administration
and the bureaucracy
CHAPTER 15

As the United States changed from a rural, agricultural society to one that is urban and industrial, the administrative requirements of government grew to enormous proportions. The federal government alone now maintains more than eighteen thousand separate departments, agencies, bureaus, branches, corporations, administrations, commissions, and authorities. The various state, county, and municipal governments also maintain their own vast bureaucracies.

In fact, the federal government is the largest single employer in the United States. In 1969 nearly three million civilians worked for the U.S. government; these people made up fully 3.9 percent of the civilian labor force. When combined with the number of workers employed by the various local governments, the percentage rises to an astounding 16.7. Clearly, government has a tremendous and direct impact on the economy. For example, out of every $3 spent on construction in the United States, $1 is spent by either the federal or local governments. Twenty-five percent of the money spent for goods and services comes directly from the various governments, and for every $4.30 of personal income in the United States, $1 comes from direct government payments. The scope and impact of modern government would have been unthinkable only a century ago. What factors contributed to the rise and development of this twentieth-century phenomenon?

Government, like Topsy, "just growed and growed." Before the Civil War, the economy was predominantly agricultural, and although industry was beginning to have a direct impact on day-to-day life, a consumer-oriented, nationwide economy scarcely existed. Most Americans still lived close to the subsistence level. They made their own clothes, built their own furniture, and grew much of their own food. They made few demands on the institutions of society, which were then local in scope and nature.

The rapid industrialization that followed the Civil War radically changed that picture. Modern industry, aided by modern science and technology, provides a wide variety of goods, such as radios, television sets, sewing machines, and automobiles, that few of us could make ourselves. We depend on modern industry to meet our needs for these products. Along with this transformation in industrial growth came a demand for new government services to protect the public against industrial abuse. The Interstate Commerce Commission (ICC) was established for just this reason—to correct the inequitable practices of the railroads. Railroad management, through the use of rebates, long haul-short haul discrimination, and other unfair practices, favored the larger shippers over the smaller ones. Groups who felt they were at a disadvantage demanded that the government step in to regulate the railroads, and in 1887 Congress created the ICC for that purpose. Most of the regulatory agencies and commissions were founded to correct similar abuses. Agencies such as the Federal Communications Commission (FCC) and the Social Security Administration (SSA) were created to regulate vital economic activities and to provide basic social services.

Government bureaucracy, therefore, has grown by leaps and bounds, precisely because only government can meet the needs of highly complex societies. As regulator, as adjuster between interests, as countervailing power in a complex society with big business and labor, the role of government has grown along with the private interests of society.[1]

---

[1] A good description of big government is Paul H. Appleby, *Big Democracy* (New York: Alfred A. Knopf, 1945) ; and Peter M. Blau, *Bureaucracy in Modern Society* (New York: Random House, 1956). For the reasons behind the growth of bureaucracy see Charles E. Jacob, *Policy and Bureaucracy* (Princeton, N.J.: Van Nostrand, 1966) ; and Kenneth E. Boulding, *The Organizational Revolution* (New York: Harper & Row, 1953).

The Bureaucracy: What It Is

What Is Bureaucracy?

When the term *bureaucracy* is mentioned to the average citizen, he thinks of the red tape he must cut through to obtain a service or information. Actually the term refers to any large-scale organization of appointed officials, whose primary function is to implement the policies of the decision makers. Ideally, a bureaucracy is a rational system or organized structure, designed to permit the efficient and effective execution of public policy. In order to do this, a bureaucracy operates in accordance with a fixed set of rules and procedures. It has a clearly recognized chain of command (or hierarchy of authority) through which responsibility flows from the top down. The job of the bureaucracy is, in short, to apply the broad policy guidelines of legislative action to particular situations. It is a method of organization that enables government to operate with some uniformity—and, therefore, predictability—and in a manner that is both rational and subject to internal supervision and control.[2]

Bureaucracy is by no means confined to government. At a time when most Western governments were little more than loose confederations of competing feudal powers, the Roman Catholic Church had an impressive and influential administrative system. Through a recognized chain of command, authority flowed from the pope down to the humblest parish priest. Until the advent of strong monarchies, this organizational pattern was the envy of secular rulers. Armies are also characterized by their rigid bureaucratic structures, which are based upon the military chain of command. Bureaucracy is equally pervasive in most civilian institutions, including schools, hospitals, large corporations, and so on. Corporations such as United States Steel and General Motors have clearly defined chains of command, and they organize their necessary functions into specialized departments and offices. Most big corporations, for example, have an office of public relations whose purpose is to generate favorable publicity for the company. These offices are usually subdivided into such areas as minority-group relations, charitable activities, and lobbying activities.

Virtually all of us, at one time or another, have been subject to or part of a bureaucratic organization—and they give no indication of disappearing from the social scene.[3] Government bureaucracies are more complex than private bureaucracies, if only because government's responsibilities are so much more extensive.

[2] John M. Pfiffner and Robert V. Presthus, *Public Administration,* 4th ed. (New York: Ronald Press, 1960), p. 40. See also Marshall E. and Gladys D. Dimock, *Public Administration,* 4th ed. (New York: Holt, Rinehart and Winston, 1969).
[3] On this point see James G. March and Herbert A. Simon, *Organizations* (New York: John Wiley & Sons, 1958); and Robert Presthus, *Organizational Society* (New York: Random House, 1962).

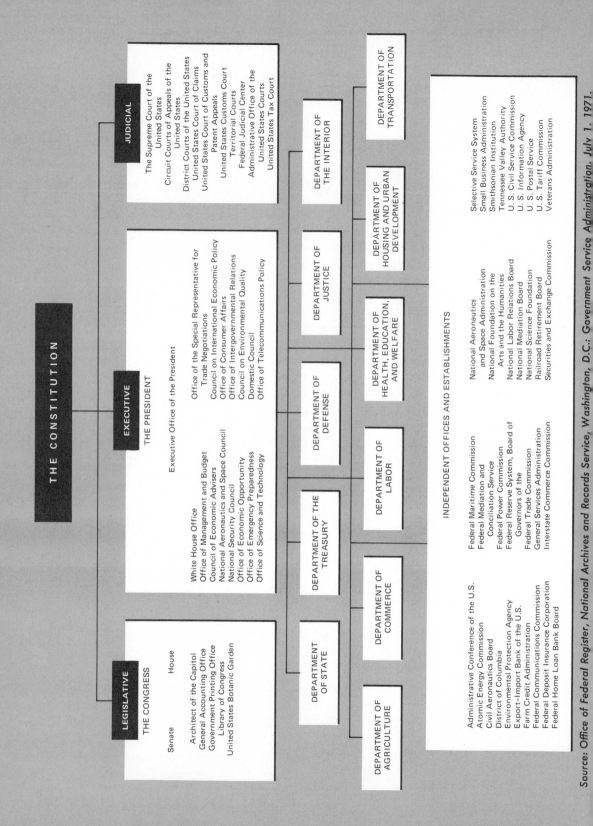

THE CONSTITUTION

LEGISLATIVE

THE CONGRESS

Senate   House

Architect of the Capitol
General Accounting Office
Government Printing Office
Library of Congress
United States Botanic Garden

EXECUTIVE

THE PRESIDENT

Executive Office of the President

White House Office
Office of Management and Budget
Council of Economic Advisers
National Aeronautics and Space Council
National Security Council
Office of Economic Opportunity
Office of Emergency Preparedness
Office of Science and Technology

Office of the Special Representative for Trade Negotiations
Council on International Economic Policy
Office of Consumer Affairs
Office of Intergovernmental Relations
Council on Environmental Quality
Domestic Council
Office of Telecommunications Policy

JUDICIAL

The Supreme Court of the United States
Circuit Courts of Appeals of the United States
District Courts of the United States
United States Court of Claims
United States Court of Customs and Patent Appeals
United States Customs Court
Territorial Courts
Federal Judicial Center
Administrative Office of the United States Courts
United States Tax Court

DEPARTMENT OF STATE

DEPARTMENT OF THE TREASURY

DEPARTMENT OF DEFENSE

DEPARTMENT OF JUSTICE

DEPARTMENT OF THE INTERIOR

DEPARTMENT OF AGRICULTURE

DEPARTMENT OF COMMERCE

DEPARTMENT OF LABOR

DEPARTMENT OF HEALTH, EDUCATION, AND WELFARE

DEPARTMENT OF HOUSING AND URBAN DEVELOPMENT

DEPARTMENT OF TRANSPORTATION

INDEPENDENT OFFICES AND ESTABLISHMENTS

Administrative Conference of the U.S.
Atomic Energy Commission
Civil Aeronautics Board
District of Columbia
Environmental Protection Agency
Export-Import Bank of the U.S.
Farm Credit Administration
Federal Communications Commission
Federal Deposit Insurance Corporation
Federal Home Loan Bank Board

Federal Maritime Commission
Federal Mediation and Conciliation Service
Federal Power Commission
Federal Reserve System, Board of Governors of the
Federal Trade Commission
General Services Administration
Interstate Commerce Commission

National Aeronautics and Space Administration
National Foundation on the Arts and the Humanities
National Labor Relations Board
National Mediation Board
National Science Foundation
Railroad Retirement Board
Securities and Exchange Commission

Selective Service System
Small Business Administration
Smithsonian Institution
Tennessee Valley Authority
U. S. Civil Service Commission
U. S. Information Agency
U. S. Postal Service
U. S. Tariff Commission
Veterans Administration

Source: Office of Federal Register, National Archives and Records Service, Washington, D.C.: Government Service Administration, July 1, 1971.

Figure 15-1
The Government
of the United
States

The Organization of the Federal Bureaucracy in the United States

While the basic purpose of all bureaucratic structures—the management and regulation of their specialized areas of concern—is essentially the same, bureaucratic organization and methods of functioning vary widely from country to country.

The Cabinet Departments. In the United States, the eleven cabinet departments—employing between 85 and 90 percent of all federal civil servants —share a common anatomy, even though they may differ in size and scope of operations. Each is headed by a secretary who is appointed by the president (with the consent of the Senate) and serves at his pleasure. The undersecretaries and assistant secretaries are also political appointees. (This differs, for example, from the system used in Great Britain, where officials up through the equivalent of our undersecretaries are members of the permanent civil service.)

The basic function of the cabinet departments is to carry out legislative and executive policies. For example, the Department of Health, Education, and Welfare (HEW) is charged with enforcing the integration of public services, in accordance with the terms of the 1964 Civil Rights Act. This is no simple matter, however, for the cabinet department must determine the best way to interpret the intent of Congress at the time the act was passed. Very often, when a controversial issue is involved, the only way Congress can muster even the barest majority to pass the legislation is by couching it in the most general, and politically nonoffensive, terms. Thus, the legislation that a cabinet department must enforce often only sets broad guidelines for action and the bureaucracy has broad latitude to establish specific working policy that suits its own interests or those of the chief executive. Walter Hickel, for example, broke with the president and espoused strong conservation programs, a stance which eventually led to his departure from the cabinet.

The cabinet departments are subdivided into bureaus that are headed by career civil servants rather than political appointees. For example, the Bureau of Labor Statistics is part of the Department of Labor, and the Bureau of the Census is part of the Department of Commerce. Here the day-to-day work of the departments is carried out, and bureau chiefs possess a great deal of discretionary authority, even though they must work within a certain framework of statutory law and executive policy. In addition, the cabinet departments maintain local offices in each state, and ideally uniform policies prevail at all departmental levels. Figure 15-1 illustrates the organizational lines of the federal government and gives some idea of its scope.

Federal Agencies. Some of the various agencies of the federal government, like the cabinet departments, are accountable to the president. Each is headed by a single administrator whom the president appoints and can remove. Sometimes created in response to a particular lobby, the agency performs a single, highly complex function that may be more political than administrative. For example, the United States Information Agency (USIA) is frankly ideological; its function is to portray the United States in the most favorable light possible and win foreign support for American policies. At the other end of the spectrum is the National Aeronautics and Space Administration (NASA) which was organized to coordinate America's explorations into space.

Federal Corporations.   Government-owned corporations are combinations of government agencies and private business enterprises, which serve vital needs that private enterprise cannot meet. Although corporation heads are appointed by the president and, in many cases, confirmed by the Senate, they exercise a good deal of autonomous power. They can, for example, use their own judgment to handle and reinvest the funds that the legislature has appropriated. The United States Postal Service, the Tennessee Valley Authority (TVA), the St. Lawrence Seaway Development Corporation, and the Export-Import Bank are a few of the more important federal corporations currently in operation. The TVA and St. Lawrence Corporation undertook massive public works construction; very few private corporations could have financed their costs. Similarly, no private corporation would be willing to underwrite the Post Office's huge deficits. Federal corporations operate under the basic guidelines set down by Congress, and, since few of them are profitable, they depend upon annual legislative appropriations. They are therefore liable to congressional criticism of their organizational structure and policies.

Independent Regulatory Agencies.   These agencies are charged with the economic regulation of private businesses that directly affect the public welfare.[4] They have quasi-judicial and quasi-legislative authority that derives from Congress. For example, Congress has given the Federal Communications Commission (FCC) the power to regulate the electronic communications media; its power to renew or revoke licenses backs up its regulatory authority. Moreover, the decisions of these agencies are enforceable in the courts and are rarely overturned by the judiciary. Their independence from political pressures and presidential influence is augmented by the fact that the commissioners, though appointed by the president with the advice and consent of the Senate, cannot be removed by him until their fixed terms expire.

Recently these agencies have been the target for a great deal of criticism. Ralph Nader and others have charged that they are overly influenced by the very industries they should be controlling. Many commissioners are

[4] For a good discussion of the regulatory commissions, see Marver H. Bernstein, *Regulating Business by Independent Commissions* (Princeton, N.J.: Princeton University Press, 1955).

West Germany. Frederick the Great of Prussia, who ruled from 1740 to 1786, was the first to establish universities to train government bureaucrats; William I, who was proclaimed emperor of a united Germany in 1871, followed suit. Between 1871 and 1918 the German Empire's bureaucracy and its civil service were accountable only to the emperor, through the chancellor and cabinet—and not to the Reichstag.

The German federal government of the Weimar Republic had very few functions; and the same is true for the current West German Federal Republic. Theoretically, it is responsible for controlling foreign affairs, collecting taxes, defense, transportation, the postal service, some social insurance programs, and intelligence activities. But in practice, the federal government controls only one domestic program—unemployment insurance. It also operates jointly with the Länder (state) governments to collect taxes; all other domestic programs are administered by the Länder, under federal control. If we followed this system in the United States, the state governments rather than the Department of Labor and the Justice Department would be charged with enforcing the Taft-Hartley Act.

Great Britain. Britain, unlike France, has strong traditions of local self-government and dispersion of authority. This pattern of administration, which is also common to the United States, relates to the Anglo-American experience with representative government, which encouraged legislative control of administrative authorities. During the nineteenth century, the growth of British government at the local level also encouraged the dispersion of administrative authority; it was not until the twentieth century that the central government began to participate in local affairs.

Curiously, Great Britain was rather late in developing a modern bureaucracy.[7] Until the Northcote-Trevelyan Report calling for major reform was issued in 1854, the bureaucracy was rife with corruption and nepotism. Positions in the bureaucracy, for instance military commissions, were openly bought and sold. By 1870, however, a merit civil service based on competitive examinations had been established.

Departmental heads, or ministers as they are called in Britain, are accountable to Parliament for the conduct of their departments and, along with their cabinet colleagues, make departmental policy. However, the real bureaucratic power is in the hands of the permanent secretary (a career administrator) and the career deputy secretaries, undersecretaries, and assistant secretaries who serve under him. Thus, even though the British and American bureaucracies share the same tradition of decentralized administrative authority, control over the bureaucracy is much tighter in Britain than in America. English bureaucrats feel that their primary loyalty belongs to their departments rather than to a political party or leader; and so they faithfully carry out the ministry's policies and seldom initiate policy on their own.

[7] For a good account of the British bureaucracy see C. H. Sisson, *The Spirit of British Administration* (London: Faber & Faber, 1959).

Characteristics of Bureaucracies

The bureaucrat has often been pictured as the plodding counter of paper clips who spends his time passing the buck and figuring out how much his pension will amount to. As is the case with most caricatures, this one contains some germs of truth, but is far from accurate. The first scholar to make a systematic analysis of bureaucracy and bureaucrats was the German sociologist Max Weber (1864–1920). His classic studies provide the starting point for a current examination of bureaucracy.

Weber's Six Characteristics of Bureaucracies. Weber's analysis was based on the German bureaucratic model, but his principles have much wider application. Peter M. Blau, in his study of Weber's theory of bureaucracy, points out that Weber considered the following to be distinctive features of formal organizations that are bureaucratically organized:

1. Organizational tasks are distributed among the various positions as official duties. Implied is a clear-cut division of labor among positions which makes possible a high degree of specialization. Specialization in turn promotes expertness among the staff, both directly and by enabling the organization to hire employees on the basis of their technical qualifications.

2. The positions or offices are organized into a hierarchical authority structure. In the usual case this hierarchy takes on the shape of a pyramid wherein each official is responsible for his subordinates' decisions and actions as well as his own to the superior above him in the pyramid and wherein each official has authority over the officials under him. The scope of authority of supervisors over subordinates is clearly circumscribed.

3. A formally established system of rules and regulations governs official decisions and actions. In principle, the operations in such administrative organizations involve the application of these general regulations to particular cases. The regulations ensure the uniformity of operations and, together with the authority structure, make possible the coordination of the various activities. They also provide for continuity in operations regardless of changes of personnel, thus promoting a stability lacking in many other types of groups and collectivities, such as social movements.

4. There is a specialized administrative staff whose task it is to maintain the organization and, in particular, the lines of communication in it. The lowest level of this administrative apparatus consists of the clerical staff responsible for keeping the written records and files of the organization, in which all official decisions and actions are embodied. Whereas the "production" staff contributes directly to the achievement of the organization's objectives, whether this involves producing cars, collecting taxes, fighting wars, or curing patients, the administrative staff contributes to goal achievement only indirectly by keeping the organization itself going.

5. Officials are expected to assume an impersonal orientation in their contacts with clients and with other officials. Clients are to be treated as cases, the officials being expected to disregard all personal considerations and to maintain complete emotional detachment, and subordinates are to be treated in a similarly impersonal fashion. The social distance between hierarchical levels and that between officials and their clients is intended to foster such formality. Impersonal detachment is designed to prevent the personal feelings of officials from distorting their rational judgment in carrying out their duties.

6. Employment by the organization constitutes a career for officials. Typically an official is a full-time employee and looks forward to a lifelong career in the agency. Employment is based on the technical qualifications of the candidate rather than on political, family, or other connections. Usually such qualifications are tested by examination or by certificates that demonstrate the candidate's educational attainment—college degrees, for example. Such educational qualifications create a certain amount of class homogeneity among officials, since relatively few persons of working-class origin have college degrees, although their number is increasing. Officials are appointed to positions, not elected, and thus are dependent on superiors in the organization rather than on a body of constituents. After a trial period officials gain tenure of position and are protected against arbitrary dismissal. Remuneration is in the form of a salary, and pensions are provided after retirement. Career advancements are "according to seniority or to achievement, or both." [8]

Do the bureaucracies that we know today fit Weber's description? Many citizens would reply negatively, but even with their drawbacks, bureaucracies still provide the most efficient and uniform method of administration yet devised. In considering bureaucracies, we will also use studies that have considered the American bureaucratic experience.

Goodnow and Wilson. At the turn of the century, Frank J. Goodnow and Woodrow Wilson made significant studies of the American bureaucratic system.[9] Bureaucracy in the United States, they noted, must work within the framework of our democratic society. But how can professional civil servants, who are not directly accountable to the electorate, be reconciled with the goals of democracy? Wilson and Goodnow set up the theoretical base that allowed turn-of-the-century political scientists to accept the ideals of democracy together with the efficiency of a professional civil service. They made a clear distinction between political (policy making) and administrative (enforcement) officials. In order to ensure that our democratic system is always run by elected officials, Goodnow concluded that the political officials must always control the administrative officials. This subordination must be clearly defined on an individual and agency level. Administrators,

[8] Peter M. Blau, "The Study of Formal Organization," in *American Sociology*, ed. Talcott Parsons (New York: Basic Books, 1968), pp. 57–59. The phrase at the end of Blau's analysis is quoted from Max Weber, *The Theory of Social and Economic Organization* (Glencoe, Ill.: The Free Press, 1947), p. 334.

[9] Frank J. Goodnow, *Politics and Administration* (New York: Macmillan, 1900); and Woodrow Wilson, "The Study of Administration," *Political Science Quarterly* 2 (June 1887): 197–222.

then, never initiate policy: they merely follow the policy guidelines laid down for them by the political leaders.

Political scientists today feel that these distinctions are not applicable to modern government. Administrative officials, they note, when given only the broadest policy guidelines by Congress and the president, must make policy decisions. Many of these decisions are made on the basis of the administrators' expertise in their fields, which, because of our highly specialized government, political leaders do not always have.

The overlapping of administrative and political functions, therefore, is a result of the demands of modern government and not of the desire for power of professional civil servants. It is clear that the United States of the 1970s can no longer look to Weber or Goodnow and Wilson for an analysis of modern bureaucracy. We must go further.

Beyond Weber. Weber's bureaucracy served a highly stratified, authoritarian society—one in which the average citizen did not "talk back" to bureaucrats. Late twentieth-century America is a far different place, and private citizens and legislators do not hesitate to criticize bureaucrats or call them before investigating committees to explain their actions. These investigations, however, can be carried to extremes, as the excesses of Senator Joseph McCarthy in the 1950s illustrate. McCarthy's almost fanatical crusade against communism eliminated from public service such people as an entire generation of experts on Chinese affairs and culture. Bureaucrats in sensitive political posts try to keep themselves attuned to prevailing public and congressional opinion. They do not—indeed, they cannot—function solely on the basis of precedent and "paper rules and procedures." [10]

Finally, anyone who has had to deal with a bureaucracy can testify to the fact that it is not as impersonal, predictable, and precise as the Weberian ideal would have it. Bureaucrats themselves are psychological beings and seldom act in the sterile manner implied by Weber. In a bureaucracy, as in other organizations, improvisation, informality, and unpredictability in the decision-making process are common.[11]

The Civil Service

To be a civil servant simply means to work for the government in a non-military capacity. Clearly, the man who delivers your mail, collects your garbage, or checks housing violations is not a political official, nor is he in a position to initiate policy as are some career bureaucrats. The civil services of most countries use some sort of merit system—usually based on com-

[10] Jacob, *Policy and Bureaucracy*, pp. 38–43. See also Anthony Downs, *Inside Bureaucracy* (Boston: Little, Brown, 1967) ; Charles S. Hyneman, *Bureaucracy in a Democracy* (New York: Harper & Row, 1950) ; Herbert A. Simon, *Administrative Behavior*, 2nd ed. (New York: The Free Press, 1957).
[11] Presthus, *Organizational Society*, Chapters 6–8. See also Robert K. Merton, "Bureaucratic Structure and Personality," *Social Forces* 17 (1940) : 560–68.

petitive examinations—for recruitment, promotion, and tenure. The employee is protected, in most cases, against dismissal for political or personal reasons, and he usually retires with some kind of pension. In the United States and Great Britain, civil servants are forbidden to play conspicuous roles in political activities. In 1972, however, a federal court ruled that a portion of the Hatch Act, which forbids political activity, is illegal on the grounds that it deprives civil servants of the political rights enjoyed by other citizens.

While civil service positions—particularly in the United States—seldom pay significantly more than comparable positions in private industry, they do have the important benefits of job security and health and welfare benefits. Unlike employees in private industry, government workers cannot be fired if there is a downturn in the economy and, moreover, many of them perform services that are needed no matter what the general economic situation. For example, there is always a "demand" for garbage collectors, firemen, policemen, and teachers. During the Depression, civil service positions were prized possessions, and postmen and garbage collectors were envied by much more skilled—but unemployed—individuals. Advancement in the ranks is not based on personal favoritism as is often the case in private industry, but is determined by the results of competitive examinations and job performance as measured by objective criteria. (For a closer look at the reasons why people join the civil service in the United States, see Table 15-1.)

The United States. The Civil Service Commission, a bipartisan group of three members, administers our federal civil service. At the present time, more than 75 percent of federal employees are covered and protected by the civil service laws. An individual wanting to become a civil servant first takes an examination and then is classified—according to the results—at a particular grade level (called the GS rating). These range from grades for unskilled or clerical workers to those for highly skilled professionals or administrators, such as engineers, doctors, or lawyers. Each grade level carries with it a specific salary range and requires specific skills.

Great Britain. British civil servants, like their American counterparts, are chosen through competitive examinations. The British system is divided into four different job levels—clerical, subclerical, executive, and administrative. The lower civil service levels are open to grade-school graduates, but few of the civil servants who hold these positions rise in the hierarchy. Executive and administrative jobs are open only to secondary and university graduates. Entrance examinations for the higher posts are based on the curricula of the schools attended. Those who go into these ranks are embarking upon lifetime careers; they are not just taking jobs, as is often the case in the United States. This is why general education is considered more important than specialized training for specific posts. These positions are extremely well paid and carry great social prestige. Permanent secretaries, for example, are generally knighted upon retirement, and many are admitted to the peerage.

Table 15-1
Reasons Given by
U.S. Federal
Employees When
Asked Why
They Had Become
Civil Servants

Security and fringe benefits	76%
Good financial reward	16
Specific job opportunities	13
Self-advancement, desire for success	10
Unable to work or succeed elsewhere	10
Physical environment, working conditions	9
Interest in work	8
Opportunity to be of service	8

Source: Compiled from data in Franklin P. Kilpatrick, Milton C. Cummings, Jr., and M. Kent Jenkins, The Image of the Federal Service (Washington, D.C.: The Brookings Institution, 1964), p. 231.

France. The French system resembles the British in many ways; it, too, emphasizes general education and is divided into four ranks. Its Ecole National d'Administration, which prepares civil servants for higher administrative positions, is the system's distinctive feature. The civil service is prestigious, attracts some of society's most talented people, and is very nearly the preserve of the upper-middle and upper classes. Very few working-class people ever rise above the lower ranks.

West Germany. The development of a German civil service actually antedates unification. Frederick the Great of Prussia developed the world's first truly modern bureaucracy in the eighteenth century, which evolved into an official class that was self-perpetuating. Career civil servants faithfully executed ministerial orders, without hesitation or criticism. The West German civil service of today carries on this tradition, to some extent, and the distinction between the upper and lower ranks is even greater than it is in France and Great Britain. Moreover, entrance into the upper ranks is limited to graduates of certain schools who must also be trained in law. The highest level, Beamte, has always carried great social prestige and deference with it, although this is lessening in Germany today. Traditionally, those in the Beamte class have been drawn from the upper classes, and a career in the civil service was often a family tradition. This is still true, although not to the extent that it was in the past.

The Role of the Bureaucracy in Modern Governments

General Functions

The functions of modern government bureaucracies include administering, servicing, regulating, licensing, information gathering, and "housekeeping" chores. All government bureaucracies perform at least two of these six basic functions, with some bureaus specializing, and some carrying out multiple functions.[12]

Administration. The primary function of most government bureaus can be defined, simply, as the execution and enforcement of the laws enacted by the legislature and the policies promulgated by the executive. For example, the United States has a policy of channeling federal funds to the states to defray the cost of various welfare and educational programs. HEW administers this policy by deciding how much federal money each state is entitled to and seeing to it that the money is used for its intended purpose. Great Britain has a policy of providing free medical care to all its citizens. The British National Health Service administers this policy by overseeing medical training, assigning patients to doctors, running the hospitals, and so on. Administration, therefore, is the implementation of public policy, and, because it involves policy decisions, it also entails rule making. In conjunction with their administrative duties, departments often initiate campaigns to publicize their work and to educate the public as to a program's benefits and purposes. In many countries there are also continuous programs of education in such areas as traffic safety, fire prevention, and conservation of natural resources.

Patterns of administration vary from country to country. In the Soviet Union, for example, administrators have no voice in policy-making decisions or rule making; they exist solely to execute and implement policies decided upon by the party leaders. Therefore, administrators are nonpolitical. However, they work within a specific, carefully defined, ideological frame of reference. The administration is controlled tightly by having party members in policy positions wherever possible. If a technically skilled bureaucrat (sometimes known as a technocrat) is absolutely essential for a particular spot, he is sure to be supervised by party members. In addition, the Ministry of Finance supervises the financial management of the various bureaucratic departments; and, on a lower level, people's control committees (local party watchdogs) have the power to oversee the administration of local bureaucratic units to guard against inefficiency or wrongdoing. Nonparty bureaucrats who perform their jobs well and do not meddle in politics will be allowed to work without interference; however, unlike their Western counterparts, they will never shape policies or programs. The most important aspect of administration in the Soviet Union—and in all Communist countries—is the control and direction of the nation's economy. The Soviet Council of Ministers sets economic priorities, and decides how they will be met. These decisions determine how much meat the average citizen will eat,

---

[12] The following section is based on Charles E. Lindblom, *The Policy-Making Process* (Englewood Cliffs, N.J.: Prentice-Hall, 1968); Harold Seidman, *Politics, Position, and Power: The Dynamics of Federal Organization* (New York: Oxford University Press, 1970); and Peter Woll, *American Bureaucracy* (New York: W. W. Norton, 1963).

what his chances of buying a new pair of shoes will be, how much he will earn, and so on.

The key feature of French administration is that it is centrally controlled, and that local levels of government merely carry out the directives that come from Paris. Thus, many functions that are handled at the local levels in the United States are directed by the central administration in France. These include such diverse services as education, justice, unemployment compensation, health programs, and the Renault Auto Works. The government also has a monopoly on television and keeps a tight rein on news coverage.

In England, executives and administrators oversee the day-to-day operations of their departments, and higher administrative officials help draft proposed legislation as well as help their ministers answer questions from Members of Parliament. Since England is a democratic socialist state, such basic services as steel plants, coal mines, railroads, and telegraph and telephone lines are run by government-controlled corporations that make policy decisions normally reserved to the private sector in the United States.

Services. Many government agencies are created to serve the general public or specific groups. The United States Weather Bureau is, perhaps, the best example of a service agency. While those of us who have been caught without an umbrella on a day when the Weather Bureau promised no rain may not think much of the service, it is, nevertheless, vital to farmers and fishermen. The U.S. Department of Agriculture conducts research in pest control, land management, and livestock improvement, dispenses surplus food to the poor, and provides important information about nutrition to the general public. The Small Business Administration, a subdivision of the U.S. Department of Commerce, provides low-interest loans to those who might be judged poor risks by the commercial lending institutions. In Great Britain, most health care is dispensed by the government. In Sweden, the government runs an extensive job-finding service. And in the Soviet Union, the government provides free education at all levels to those who qualify.

Regulation. The regulatory functions of government are also designed to safeguard the general public's welfare. In the United States, the Securities and Exchange Commission, for example, protects the investor by establishing guidelines for the registration of new issues, as well as the buying and selling of stocks and bonds. Great Britain has had legislation on the books since 1819 regulating working conditions in factories, and similar legislation exists in most industrialized countries. This legislation is enforced by particular agencies. The U.S. Department of Labor, for example, oversees elections in unions to ensure that they are conducted fairly. The recent election of a reform candidate to the scandal-ridden United Mine Workers' Union shows how successful the Department of Labor's regulating powers can be. In Germany, the enforcement of federal law by the Länder governments is supervised by the Bundesrat (the upper house of the national legislature), and federal administrative courts are empowered to compel the Länder governments to enforce national law. In all instances, the regulation powers are backed by the potential of force. In the United States, for example, the regulatory agencies can issue "cease and desist" orders. While offenders may challenge these orders in court, most voluntarily choose to comply.

Licensing. Licensing is closely related to regulation. It enables governments to impose minimum standards and qualifications in certain areas. For example, if you want a license to drive a car, practice medicine or law, sell real estate, teach in the public schools, or work as a barber, you must meet certain government standards. In the United States and other federal countries, these standards are usually set by the individual states. In countries such as France or Great Britain, the national government sets the standards and administers the tests. Even in the United States, however, some licenses are issued by the federal government. For example, an FCC license is needed to operate a radio or television station.

Information Gathering. Information is needed for two major purposes: to determine whether a law has been violated, and to make policy decisions that are rational and based on factual evidence. For example, if a U.S. citizen complains that his civil rights have been violated, an investigation —usually by the Civil Rights Division of the Justice Department—has to be made before any action can be taken. And the Environmental Protection Agency must know the exact state of air and water pollution before it can issue orders concerning violations. Similar investigations are conducted by all modern states. The French government made an extensive study of the nation's food distribution system before deciding to tear down the old *Les Halles* (wholesale food market) in the center of Paris and move it to the suburbs.

Some agencies only act when there has been a complaint. Others, like the Food and Drug Administration (FDA), are constantly making investigations on their own initiative. The FDA does not allow a drug to go on the market—regardless of whether a complaint has been made—until it is satisfied that the product is safe and effective. Sometimes the problem of invasion of privacy arises when organizations, such as the FBI, investigate the activities of alleged subversives and question their friends, neighbors, and family members. The line between investigation necessary to protect the public interest and invasion of privacy is a fine one, and it is often difficult to tell where one leaves off and the other begins.

"Housekeeping" Chores. These are the tasks that make it possible for the above functions to be carried out, and include such things as running personnel departments, and ordering and keeping track of supplies.

Improving Bureaucratic Efficiency

Reorganize the Bureaucracy. One technique for improving bureaucratic efficiency and effectiveness has been to shift authority to higher levels of executive power. Those who advocate this shift claim that a broader range of interests and knowledge will go into policy-making decisions if those who make the decisions have wide constituencies. The assumption here is that individual bureaus and agencies often become parochial in outlook and, over a period of time, tied to one social group or economic interest. For example, if a bureaucrat has spent most of his working life at the Bureau of the Mines, it would be reasonable to expect him to believe that mining is the most important industry in the country and that the interests of mine operators should come first. Other motives for this kind of reorganization include saving money by eliminating duplication of effort and grouping related activities into cohesive units. But the main objective for this move is to serve the public interest, however defined, by vesting decision-making powers in people who have broader political and social outlooks.

However, new voices are now being heard which question the wisdom of concentrated power. Many believe that the old-fashioned system of giving at least some power to representatives of particular groups was not altogether undesirable. The older system, they claim, made bureaucracy more responsive and, conversely, the new system contributes to the public's feeling that the bureaucracy is a vast system that it cannot relate to. Dispersion of authority, they point out, keeps the heads of the various agencies "on their toes," because they must constantly compete with each other for official

"For heaven's sake, you'll get your appropriation, General! But first we have to go through our deliberations, don't we?"

Drawing by Handelsman; © 1972 The New Yorker Magazine; Inc.

favor. Moreover, in concentrating power at higher levels, those with specialized knowledge of a particular area (for example, bureau chiefs) often find themselves overruled by department heads who do not have their professional competence. While the number of these critics has increased, a clear alternative to the hierarchical system has yet to emerge.

Quantitative Data Systems. The attempt to quantify problems—so popular in so many areas of modern life—has been extended to bureaucratic management. Robert McNamara, Secretary of Defense under Presidents Kennedy and Johnson, used this approach when he was at the Ford Motor Company, and he introduced it to the Department of Defense, with a fair amount of success. The program uses sophisticated techniques of quantitative measurement and empirical analysis to find the objectives and the costs and benefits of each program. In the Department of Defense there was a particular concern with the costs of elaborate weapons systems, and McNamara attempted to relate cost to national security. This approach has a great deal of political appeal, since the saving of money is always popular with the public.

The system that McNamara introduced is called PPBS—the Planning, Programming, Budget System. It is

designed to provide executive agencies with a means of clearly identifying and ranking their major goals, and at the same time to supply a more accurate measure of the cost of alternative ways of achieving these objectives.[13]

This method enables economists to gauge the relative merits and effectiveness of various government programs, and allows for better control, coordination, and evaluation of existing programs. President Johnson was so impressed with the results at the Defense Department that he extended the system to civilian agencies in 1965. Although hailed as the first step in the creation of an exact science of administration, the system did have technical and political complications.[14]

PPBS works well only in those areas where goals can be measured in quantitative terms; in programs that are not as clearly measurable, PPBS falls short of success. The Defense Department, for example, tried to use PPBS to weigh the effects of its pacification program in Vietnam. It was reasoned that one of the most reliable ways it could judge whether its expenditures on the war were rational or wasteful was to quantitatively measure the percentage of land and people that were won over to South

[13] Francis E. Rourke, *Bureaucracy, Politics, and Public Policy* (Boston: Little, Brown, 1969), p. 123.
[14] David Novick, ed., *Program Budgeting* (Cambridge, Mass.: Harvard University Press, 1965) ; see also Austin Ranney, ed., *Political Science and Public Policy* (Chicago: Markham, 1968), pp. 55–82.

Vietnam. But not everyone in the United States accepted the objectives of the pacification program, and it became increasingly clear that the United States involvement in the war could not be so simply measured. McNamara, or any department head for that matter, could not base his policy decisions solely on a program like PPBS. Moreover, no quantitative system permits comparisons of the relative benefits of various programs; the choice among them is and will remain political and social in nature. At present, PPBS has been greatly de-emphasized in the federal government, although many state and local governments are continuing to test the system's applicability.

Encourage Creativity. The lack of energy and enthusiasm in bureaucracy is a frequent complaint and cause for concern. This was not always the case. The programs developed during the New Deal, for instance, changed the social face of this country, and people came to look to government for a redress of grievances. And the new programs developed in the 1960s extended the social role of government and its identification with the problems of the underprivileged. For these reasons, bureaucracy has traditionally been more popular with liberals than with conservatives.

However, this appears to be changing, and many critics now claim that the bureaucratic engine is running down and is becoming tied to convention. For example, those interested in improving the education of black and Puerto Rican children in New York City claim that the Board of Education has been a major stumbling block in the development of new approaches and programs. Critics of both the right and the left claim that bureaucrats are rigid in their points of view, reluctant to try new methods, and even more reluctant to abandon methods that have not worked.

Therefore, methods designed to spark imagination and vitality have been proposed. These suggested reforms include "lateral entrance," which is designed to bring in knowledgeable outsiders at all levels of bureaucracy rather than filling all vacant spots from within. While this method may bring in a freshness of viewpoint, it does have drawbacks. Outsiders tend to lack necessary experience, and bringing in large numbers of people who have not served time in the ranks is bound to lower the morale of the permanent staff. Another suggestion is to allow permanent officials to work outside their own agencies for stated periods. The current structure of bureaucracy discourages sabbaticals; the individual knows that his career will probably be hurt if he takes any extended time away from his job. The quickest and most nearly complete way to get a new approach is to establish a new agency. This allows a whole new staff to be recruited and eliminates some of the problems of dealing with vested interests; moreover, administrative procedures have not become fixed, and greater flexibility is therefore possible. The Office of Management and Budget, created in 1970 to supervise the preparation and administration of the federal budget, is a good example of such an agency. An agency can also consult with outside organizations for advice and, in some cases, for direction in operating selected programs.

Despite the many efforts to improve the bureaucracy, it is bound to remain as imperfect as the human beings who control it. Moreover, considering the complexity of modern life, the bureaucracy is bound to remain large-scale. This conclusion has given rise to a fear of its power—a fear of "administocracy."

The Bureaucracy: Administrator or Policy Maker?

The Rise of Administocracy. The early theorists of bureaucracy (Weber, Goodnow, Wilson) assumed that professional bureaucrats would never make public policy, but merely execute the will of elected officials. And, indeed, nonpartisan administration was the original motivation behind the development of a merit civil service. However, as Guy S. Claire has warned, most Western nations have developed—however unwittingly—administocracies (defined as an aristocracy of administrators) whose personnel are not publicly accountable, but who nevertheless make policy.[15] While a return to the nineteenth-century spoils system is neither possible nor desirable, the question of whether a democracy can afford to allow nonelected and nonresponsible administrators make decisions that will affect the lives of the people must be considered. First it is necessary to define the specific ways in which bureaucracies affect policy making.[16]

Adjudication. Many regulatory agencies maintain administrative courts that operate much like regular courts, and whose edicts and awards are enforceable in the regular courts. Most states, for example, have administrative tribunals that grant workmen's compensation awards. All parties to such an action are entitled to legal counsel, and may offer evidence in their own defense. The FDA can order a drug off the market; and the SEC can ban trading in a particular stock. Two major questions have been raised in this connection. Some maintain that these tribunals' cease-and-desist orders, edicts, and so on should be made by the regular courts: if a cosmetic is harmful, should not the courts—and not the FDA—make this decision? Proponents of the administrative courts answer this objection by pointing out that the courts, by their own admission, often lack the expertise to judge in highly technical matters. The second question is raised by those who doubt the wisdom of giving so much power to the administrators. These critics feel that even though the law has empowered an agency or department to "regulate in the public interest, convenience, or necessity," the

---

[15] Guy S. Claire, *Administocracy* (New York: Crowell-Collier, 1934); John D. Millet, *Government and Public Administration* (New York: McGraw-Hill, 1959); Emmette S. Redford, *Democracy in the Administrative State* (New York: Oxford University Press, 1969); and Rourke, *Bureaucracy, Politics, and Public Policy.*

[16] Based on Jacob, *Policy and Bureaucracy*, pp. 44–46.

creation of administrative courts means that Congress has given administrators a blank check.

Discretionary Implementation. When a legislature enacts a law, the bureaucracy must enforce it, and when statute law is specific, this is a relatively simple matter. However, this is not usually the case. For example, the United States Congress may pass a law requiring that our waterways be cleaned of pollution. This law enables the Environmental Protection Agency (EPA) to do whatever is necessary to achieve this goal. The EPA must then make certain decisions because every waterway cannot be cleaned up at once, and each one entails different ecological as well as political problems. Deciding how to go about achieving the general goal, then, becomes the responsibility of the EPA. It may decide to hold off for a while on one company that is in the process of developing a water treatment system for waste, but may be more stringent with a second company that is making no attempt to deal with waste. In the case of a third company, EPA may decide to postpone action for a while because this company employs an entire town, and economic problems must be considered. In granting agencies the prerogative of deciding how to implement a law or policy, they are being permitted to make law for society.[17] Defenders of discretionary implementation point out, however, that no code of law can anticipate all circumstances that might arise and that administrators must therefore have some leeway. Furthermore, administrators can always be overruled by public or legislative pressure or by executive edict.

Rule Making. The rule-making authority of regulatory agencies is related to discretionary implementation. If an airline wishes to raise its fares, the FAA must grant its permission. Similarly, higher rates for telephone use must be approved by the Public Service Commission (PSC).

Perhaps the best recent example of bureaucratic rule making was the fight to force cigarette manufacturers to place health hazard warnings on their cigarette packages and to include them in advertisements. For several years, the Federal Trade Commission (FTC) and HEW's Public Health Service had been urging such practices. Congress had been reluctant to go along, however, primarily because of pressure from the tobacco industry. In 1965 the Advisory Committee on Smoking and Health and the Surgeon General (the nation's chief public health officer) concluded that heavy cigarette smoking increased the likelihood of contracting lung cancer and shortened one's life span considerably. The report disturbed the public, and public pressure on Congress increased. Since January of 1966 cigarette manufacturers have been required to print danger warnings on all packs.

Meanwhile, the tobacco industry tried, unsuccessfully, to discredit the

---

[17] For the policy-making role of career civil servants, see John J. Corson and R. Shale Paub, *Men Near the Top* (Baltimore: Johns Hopkins University Press, 1966); and Louis C. Gawthrop, *Administrative Politics and Social Change* (New York: St. Martin's Press, 1970); and Emmette S. Redford, *Ideal and Practice in Public Administration* (Montgomery: University of Alabama Press, 1970).

Surgeon General's Report, and organizations such as the American Cancer Society were agitating for still firmer antitobacco legislation. In June of 1967, the FCC entered the crusade. Citing the fairness doctrine, it ordered all radio and television stations accepting cigarette commercials to make free time available for antismoking commercials. Soon the American Cancer Society was producing one-minute antismoking announcements.

In 1969 the FCC banned cigarette advertising on radio and television. And, in January 1971, President Nixon signed an FTC-sponsored bill requiring cigarette companies to print health warnings on all advertising copy as well as on every pack of cigarettes. A. Lee Fritschler, who wrote an excellent brief monograph on the subject, reached the following conclusion:

The initiation and continuation of the cigarette controversy were possible because of both the political power and delegated authority possessed by bureaucratic agencies. Had the decision on cigarettes and health been left to Congress alone, it is safe to assume that the manufacturers would have triumphed, and no health warnings of any kind would have been required. The cigarette-labeling controversy is a clear example of agencies' power to influence and even formulate public policy.[18]

Here was a vivid case of federal agencies openly lobbying for a particular policy. (It must also be pointed out, however, that the tobacco industry and the American Cancer Society and other health groups did a good deal of lobbying themselves.) Their pressure—which translated itself into public pressure—had the desired effect on Congress. While most people would agree that the public interest was served in this instance, there is a broader question to be considered. What happens when an overbearing bureaucracy tries to promote a program that many would consider harmful? There is no simple answer to this problem, but it is one that we will probably have to grapple with increasingly in the years to come.

Advisory Roles. The growing complexity of modern life has caused legislatures and executives to rely more and more heavily upon the technical expertise of bureaucrats. Congress may decide that unsafe mines should be shut down, but only mining experts can determine exactly what conditions make a mine unsafe. Many laws require administrative interpretation. For example, Congress may outlaw deceptive advertising, but the determination of what *is* deceptive is made by the FTC. Bureaucrats do not usually have to convince legislators to take their advice; the lawmakers are often only too happy to have the technical assistance of specialists. This is yet another way in which bureaucrats influence the formulation of public policy.

Conflicts can arise, however. For example, former Secretary of Defense McNamara, a political appointee, was intent upon cutting costs where possible. He ran into a wall of opposition from military men, who claimed

---

[18] A. Lee Fritschler, *Smoking and Politics: Policymaking and the Federal Bureaucracy* (New York: Appleton-Century-Crofts, 1969), pp. 139–40.

that they alone knew the technical side of security needs. McNamara's relationship with the military high command was, as can be imagined, frequently stormy. Similarly, in 1948, President Truman was under intense pressure by State Department experts not to recognize Israel when it became an independent state. For a time he wavered under their pressure, but then made the decision to extend recognition. Both McNamara and Truman realized that some decisions are, by their very nature, political and that only a politically responsible official ought to make them.

The bureaucracy's role of adviser is not peculiar to the United States; rather, it is an inevitable feature of the modern industrial state. In France, for example, laws and presidential decrees are drawn up and promulgated with the active assistance of the bureaucracy (particularly the Council of State), and career executives thus have the opportunity to shape policy. Again, however, if their policies are directly opposed by the ministry or the Assembly, they will not be incorporated into official government policy.

Bureaucrats play a large role in the framing of legislation in West Germany. Since federal bureaucrats do not have to supervise field or branch offices, they can devote their energies to policy matters. In fact, they are often successful in convincing their political superiors to accept their way of thinking on issues.

Is Administocracy a Threat? Although the U.S. Constitution mandates a relatively clear separation of powers, many fear that the lines between the branches of government are becoming increasingly blurred. In considering this question, it is, first of all, important to remember that an absolute separation of powers is difficult, if not impossible, to maintain in a modern industrial society.[19] The fact that an administrative agency's activities sometimes overlap the responsibilities of the legislative and judicial branches of government does not necessarily mean that it is exceeding its authority. Nevertheless, many Americans are apprehensive about the development of a power elite of bureaucrats; it is feared that they will play too dominant a role in the decisions which they are concerned with. (Indeed, a decisive power of initiative is now in the hands of executive officials.) Liberals are afraid of the power of the defense establishment, and conservatives fear government's social and economic roles. Both groups can exaggerate their fears and criticisms, but the overall question must be considered.

Criticisms. John Kenneth Galbraith has observed that bureaucracies tend to take on lives of their own that are totally divorced from the world around

[19] For good discussions of this problem see Dwight Waldo, *The Administrative State* (New York: Ronald Press, 1948); Frederick C. Mosher, *Democracy and the Public Service* (New York: Oxford University Press, 1968); Louis C. Gawthrop, ed., *The Administrative Process and Democratic Theory* (Boston: Houghton Mifflin, 1970); Norman J. Powell, *Responsible Public Bureaucracy in the United States* (Boston: Allyn and Bacon, 1967); Rourke, *Bureaucracy, Politics, and Public Policy*; Gordon Tullock, *The Politics of Bureaucracy* (Washington, D.C.: Public Affairs Press, 1965); and Aaron B. Wildavsky, *The Politics of the Budgetary Process* (Boston: Little, Brown, 1964).

them.[20] The fear is that a bureaucracy will become concerned primarily with self-preservation and the enhancement of its own position and that it will become isolated and insulated from the needs of society. As Galbraith writes, it

will develop a life and purpose and policy of its own. . . . A bureaucracy is governed not by the truth but by its own truth. It defends its truth against the reality. Those who question its truth are discounted for eccentricity.[21] This, in his opinion, explains our foreign policy failures in Cuba, the Dominican Republic, and Vietnam. To justify their roles, the Departments of Defense and State insistently viewed the rise of communism in these countries as threats to our national security. While Galbraith's analysis is open to question, we do have to consider whether bureaucracy has become a master of society rather than its servant.

Others criticize bureaucracy on the grounds that its members are not representative of the people.[22] This is often true of European bureaucracies, for in most European countries a university education is all but impossible for a working-class youth and difficult for a middle-class one. The American bureaucracy is largely middle class, but then most Americans are too, so the civil service is far more representative of our society. We can be faulted, however, for not having greater numbers of women, blacks, Chicanos, and working-class people in high-ranking positions. The government's minority hiring practices are better than private industry's, and, bowing under the pressure from feminist and civil rights groups, government is attempting to bring in still greater numbers of women and minority-group members. It is somewhat unrealistic to expect modern bureaucracies to be truly representative of the general population, because their functions often require high degrees of employee skill and education. Bureaucrats will probably continue to be drawn from the ranks of the various educational elites, regardless of sex or ethnic origin.

A number of suggestions have been put forth to make modern bureaucracy more responsive to the public. For example, the president could appoint all policy-making personnel. This plan has unfortunate side effects, however. It would inject partisan politics into technical decision making and would remove career executives from the merit civil service system. Others have suggested that bureaucrats be elected, but it is clear that voters do not always choose a candidate on his technical qualifications. Those who defend the merit system that we have claim that its internal checks are sufficient to ensure a responsible bureaucracy.

---

[20] See John Kenneth Galbraith, *The New Industrial State* (Boston: Houghton Mifflin, 1967).

[21] John Kenneth Galbraith, "Who Needs the Democrats?" *Harper's* 241 (July 1970): 43–62.

[22] See V. Subramariam, "Representative Bureaucracy: A Reassessment," *American Political Science Review* 61 (December 1967): 1010–19.

The Case for the Bureaucracy: The Benefits of Technocracy. Modern bureaucracy may be coldly impersonal, may become clogged with red tape, and may be somewhat inefficient, but its benefits still outweigh its liabilities. The bureaucracy takes the administration out of the partisan political arena, establishes rational and consistent working rules, provides policy makers with necessary technical know-how, and is a stable and reasonably efficient machine that is not dependent upon the will or personality of a charismatic leader for its effectiveness. These are not qualities to be dismissed lightly. Bureaucratic organization makes the lines of authority—and, thus, managerial responsibility—clear, and its rules (based on statutory law as well as administrative precedent) help to guide and regulate a highly complex industrial society. Moreover, bureaucracies impartially render needed social services that no private organization can provide. The Social Security Administration, for example, provides services and funds to any qualified individual no matter what his politics.

Bureaucracies do not exist in isolation, but within the framework of the state. They must compete with other power centers, keep the favor of elected officials (both legislative and executive), and please the public, in addition to satisfying legal requirements. Thus, there are direct and indirect constraints upon bureaucratic power.

Checks on the Bureaucracy.

The chief executive exercises the most important check on the bureaucracy. A direct order from the president to change a departmental policy will usually prove effective; bureaucrats may stall, but eventually they have to give in. For example, when HEW ignored a Nixon administration request that it go slow on implementing forced school busing in a southern state, the president ordered the Justice Department to intervene by obtaining a court order to block HEW's directive.

The legislatures also possess restraining powers. In the United States, Congress can compel a bureaucracy to change an administrative policy by writing a new law or by revoking an agency's cease-and-desist powers. Then there is the all-important power of the purse that the English Parliament as well as the United States Congress holds: the mere threat of a withholding of funds can force an agency to change a policy. For example, OEO had to abandon some of its more radical—or, at least, controversial—programs because of legislative disapproval.

Every year department and agency heads must appear before the appropriate committee of Congress to defend their budgetary requests. Congress, on the basis of budget and other investigatory hearings, can change statute law to force the bureaucracy to change its course. For example, in 1946 Congress enacted the Administrative Procedure Act, which required that judicial standards be applied to all administrative proceedings in order to protect the constitutional rights of the people appearing before such panels. In essence, this means that representatives of a railroad called before the ICC can have legal counsel; they can also offer evidence in their own behalf, and cross examine witnesses testifying against them. Congressional investigations give citizens assurance that, at least sometimes, government is on their side. Committee investigations, like the Ervin Committee (1969–71), looking into government invasions of privacy, give citizen complaints an institutional voice and a great deal of power. Once Congress has changed statutory law, the bureaucracy must enforce the new law.

Individual legislators indirectly exercise restraints by becoming experts on particular subjects. For example, it is generally acknowledged that Congressman Wilbur Mills (Democrat-Arkansas), Chairman of the House Ways and Means Committee, is a leading expert on taxation. Similarly, Senator Sam J. Ervin, Jr. (Democrat-North Carolina), Chairman of the Senate Watergate Investigating Committee, is well-known for his expertise in constitutional law. In general, the committee system supports the tendency of congressmen to become experts in the areas that their committees are responsible for.

It must be noted, however, that many bureaucrats have become astute at handling Congress, cultivating particular legislators, and provoking conflict among legislators or between the legislature and the executive. For example, the late Congressman Mendel Rivers of South Carolina was Chairman of the House Armed Services Committee and was one of the military's staunchest supporters. It was a rare military request that did not get a sympathetic response from him, whatever its cost to the taxpaying public. Coincidentally—or not so coincidentally—the military located several of its installations in his district of South Carolina, providing many jobs for the local population and thus ensuring their support for the congressman. He also had an Air Force plane at his disposal and received red-carpet treatment at military installations around the world.

Then there are the courts. They have final authority to decide whether the administrative agencies are enforcing statutory law correctly. This authority is based on their power to review administrative decisions and to reexamine the evidence that the original decision was based upon. If the courts decide that administrators have misinterpreted the evidence, misread the law, or gone beyond their legitimate authority, they will reverse the administrative decision. The courts have frequently ruled against the government in cases of economic regulation and antitrust proceedings. In 1973, for example, the director of the Office of Economic Opportunity was ordered to take no further action on his plans to disband the agency because his appointment had never been submitted to the Congress for approval. It is therefore fair to say that the American constitutional system provides enough checks which, if vigilantly applied, make it extremely difficult for the bureaucrat to become Big Brother.

Competition among agencies is another more subtle, but equally effective way in which bureaucratic power is held in check. The various military services, for example, regularly compete with each other for funds, each claiming to be the most vital service. This interservice rivalry has enabled civilian authorities to keep a check on the military.

Not only do various agencies compete with each other, but the personalities of the individual bureaucrats are often in conflict. The authors of *The Federalist Papers* foresaw that this could be turned into a valuable check upon unrestrained power:

Ambition must be made to counteract ambition. The interest of the man must be connected with the constitutional rights of the place . . . the constant aim is to divide and arrange the several offices in such a manner that each may be a check on the other—that the private interest of every individual may be a sentinel over the public rights.[23]

The case of Walt Disney Productions' attempts to develop a resort in California's Mineral King Valley illustrates this principle well. The Forest Service (a subdivision of the Department of Agriculture) had supported the project. The Sierra Club opposed it on the grounds that it would do irreparable damage to a wild, unspoiled area. The Park Service (a subdivision of the Department of Interior) sided with the conservationists, and Secretary of Interior Udall backed them up. This led to an angry confrontation between Udall and Secretary of Agriculture Freeman in December 1967. It should be noted that the two services disagree frequently, and conservationists charge that the Forest Service is more inclined to serve the interests of particular groups than those of the general public. Secretary Freeman took the position that ecological damage would be minimal. In January of 1968 the Bureau of the Budget silenced Udall's criticisms, and the Forest Service approved Disney's master plan. However, the thirty-year development permit was not issued, and, before work could begin, the Sierra Club filed a class-action suit for an injunction against the project. They won a preliminary injunction, but this was overturned by a federal appeals court that ruled, in September 1970, that the club had no legal standing to sue. An appeal to this decision is still pending. Whether or not the project finally goes through, the battle over it is a good example of how an administrative action was brought to the public's attention by an open interagency conflict.

Bureaucracy can be reformed from within or without government. Public-interest pressure groups like John Gardner's "Common Cause" and Ralph Nader's "Raiders" have directly fought government and industry abuse and won. Nader's first and perhaps most famous bout with the bureaucracy came during congressional investigations of automobile safety.

Publicity provides another important way to check the bureaucracy, and this is where the media come in. The media have power to reflect and shape

---

[23] See Roy P. Fairfield, ed., *The Federalist Papers* (Garden City, N.Y.: Doubleday, 1961), p. 160.

public attitudes by bringing certain facts to light. This was most dramatically done in a 1971 television special "The Selling of the Pentagon," which criticized the Defense Department's public relations programs. Another example of the power of the mass media occurred when the New York City Fire Department announced that it would close some firehouses and consolidate others to save money. Demonstrations against this plan were organized, and the television cameras were soon filming small children carrying signs that said "save our lives—don't take away our firehouse." The sight did not enhance City Hall's image, and the fire department's policy was soon reviewed. Vigorous investigative reporting also helps to control bureaucratic abuses in domestic and foreign affairs. Jack Anderson's revelations that the United States was siding with Pakistan in the India-Pakistan conflict —when the State Department was claiming official neutrality—was very embarrassing to all involved.

The problem of how to keep bureaucracies in check is by no means confined to the United States. The roles of bureaucracies and the controls placed upon them vary considerably from nation to nation.

Supervisory control over the German administrative bureaucracy is exercised by the Supreme Administrative Court, whose decision can be appealed to civil constitutional courts. This court makes basic interpretive decisions that are often reserved to bureaucratic departments in other nations. For example, the Supreme Administrative Court has ruled that the receipt of welfare assistance is a right of German citizens, and that young men may refuse military service on moral grounds without demonstrating a belief in a set of established religious principles.

Largely as a result of the weakness of the French executive, the bureaucracy in France developed three grands corps (elite departments) that are designed to prevent corruption and abuse of power. The Finance Inspectorate, the Court of Accounts, and the Council of State are charged with the task of ensuring administrative honesty and efficiency. Of the three, the Council of State is by far the most important. It is, in reality, an administrative court and stands as the final court of appeals for the nation's twenty-three other administrative courts. The council rides herd on the bureaucracy, resolves administrative disputes, and has been so successful in defending the rights of the French people against the arbitrary acts of government officials that it has merited widespread popular respect and trust. In fact, the Council of State has built up a large body of administrative case law that makes the French bureaucracy one of the most consistent and efficient bureaucracies in the Western World.

Sweden's method of controlling the bureaucracy, which developed in the early eighteenth century, is becoming increasingly popular; Denmark, Finland, Norway, New Zealand, and the State of Hawaii have already adopted it. The ombudsman, or parliamentary commissioner, is elected by, but is not a member of Parliament. He has broad powers to investigate citizens' (and civil servants') complaints of discrimination, arbitrary behavior on the part of administrators, and negligence. He also has the power to mediate conflicts, make recommendations, and even, when he deems it necessary, prosecute. Thus, he acts to make officials live up to their responsibilities.

Unlike other European nations, the British have not felt the need to develop administrative courts to enforce policy decisions. Rather, they rely upon the regular courts to enforce bureaucratic edicts. There are no administrative courts in the Soviet Union, and the bureaucracy is controlled and policed by units of the Communist party.

In all of these countries, interagency conflicts also check bureaucratic power, and in all except the Soviet Union, the media serve as watchdogs for the public.

Conclusion

In the United States, bureaucratic agencies are involved in such essential tasks as policy initiation and the interpretation of broadly framed legislation. Our government is, to a large extent, administered by bureaucratic experts who take Congress' and the president's broad policy guidelines and fill in the specific working details. The complexity of governments around the world increases the presence of large-scale bureaucracies. But this is not necessarily a bad thing. For it is clear that it takes a complex bureaucracy to deal with the problems of a complex industrialized society; without it, modern government would come to a screeching halt. We must continue to search, however, for ways to improve and continually vitalize what is, in most cases, a sound bureaucratic structure.

Suggested Readings

Altshuler, Alan A., ed. *The Politics of the Federal Bureaucracy*. New York: Dodd, Mead, 1968. A collection of papers emphasizing the interaction of the federal bureaucracy with the political system.

Blau, Peter M. *The Dynamics of Bureaucracy: A Study of Interpersonal Relationships in Two Federal Agencies*. 2nd ed. Chicago: University of Chicago Press, 1963. A work that emphasizes the actual behavior of personnel rather than the operation of the administration.

Downs, Anthony. *Inside Bureaucracy*. Boston: Little, Brown, 1967. A rigorous model of the bureaucratic process.

Goodnow, Frank J. *Politics and Administration: A Study in Government*. New York: Russell and Russell, 1967. A classic in the field, with emphasis on administration in a democratic polity.

Heady, Ferrel. *Public Administration: A Comparative Perspective*. Englewood Cliffs, N.J.: Prentice-Hall, 1966. A comparative perspective on public administration in Western and non-Western nations.

La Palombara, Joseph, and Riggs, Fred W., eds. *Bureaucracy and Political Development*. Princeton, N.J.: Princeton University Press, 1963. An excellent collection of papers that focus on the role of the bureaucrats in developing nations.

Ranney, Austin, ed. *Political Science and Public Policy*. Chicago: Markham, 1968. A collection of articles on the policy-making process.

Simon, Herbert A. *Administrative Behavior*. 2nd ed. New York: Macmillan, 1957. A study that lay the foundation for much of the contemporary work done on bureaucratic organizations.

Rourke, Francis E. *Bureaucracy, Politics, and Public Policy*. Boston: Little, Brown, 1969. An introduction to the role of bureaucracy in the policy-making process.

Weber, Max. *Theory of Social and Economic Organization*. Translated by A. M. Henderson and Talcott Parsons. Glencoe, Ill.: The Free Press, 1958. Probably the most influential study of public administration ever written.

Legal systems and the courts
CHAPTER 16

The yearning for "equal justice under law" is one of mankind's oldest aspirations. Justice Oliver Wendell Holmes once remarked, "My freedom to swing my arm stops where the other man's nose begins." Because man is a social being, his freedom of action must have its limits if the freedom of all is to be preserved. But who decides what these limits are? Without a legal system, force alone would settle disputes. Even in primitive societies, two parties who disagree often look to an objective third party to provide a solution. Modern nations depend upon laws to regulate human relations, and courts help to maintain order by enforcing these laws.

However, courts and laws may favor certain groups over others. In recent years, many modern societies have become concerned with assuring equal treatment under law for men and women of all races, religions, and economic means. Both lawmakers and courts play important roles in establishing this equality.

For example, federal antilynching laws have nearly eliminated this vicious crime, which was fairly common in the southern states at the turn of the century and in which 85 percent of the victims were black. Similarly, racial segregation gradually gave way to the persistent and patient legal work that ended in the Supreme Court's landmark ruling in *Brown* v. *Board of Education of Topeka* (1954). This decision, the first of many to establish the principle that racial segregation is a violation of the U.S. Constitution, produced a revolution in American race relations. Some violence did take place, and the battle is by no means over. But to appreciate the importance of law to the civil rights movement, compare the position of the American black to that of the South African black. In South Africa, the whole legal system supports segregation, making its peaceful elimination difficult.

Thus, we see that the law does more than resolve private conflicts among individuals and social groups, granting rights and privileges and imposing duties and responsibilities. Law is also an expression of society's goals and aspirations. The passage of child labor laws, for instance, expresses society's determination to eliminate a practice it has come to regard as a social evil. Changes in the law—in regard to the legality of labor unions, for example —indicate changes in the thinking of the people as a whole with respect to specific questions. Although the law is often slow to catch up with changing mores, it usually does catch up with them in democratic societies because the legislators, who represent the people who elect them, change the laws to suit the voters' new goals and desires. Not everyone agrees about using law to bring about social change, however. Some suggest that Americans place too much of a burden on the law and endanger its status by expecting it to resolve all social and political problems.

No legal system is perfect; complaints about the law have been heard down through the centuries. Shakespeare complained of the law's "delay"; Dickens called it an "ass"; and Karl Marx scorned it as an instrument of bourgeois oppression. But despite its inequities and frustrating slowness, organized society could not exist without the restraints and guarantees of a legal system. In this chapter, we shall examine what the law is, how different legal systems have developed and how they operate, how the United States court system functions, and what social and political roles the courts play.

The Nature of Law

What Is Law?

For our purposes, law may be defined as "that which must be obeyed and followed by citizens, subject to sanctions or legal consequences," [1] However,

[1] *Black's Law Dictionary* (St. Paul, Minn.: West Publishing, 1968), p. 1028.

this definition is, in many ways, too narrow, for when people speak of law they often mean many things other than government regulation. For example, the term may refer to moral or religious law. Although we will not go to jail if we cruelly hurt others' feelings, we may have been taught that it is immoral to do so. The devout Roman Catholic feels bound to obey his church's law (called canon law) as well as secular laws. The Orthodox Jew likewise follows the precepts of the Torah (the first five books of the Old Testament), as interpreted by the rabbis in the Talmud.

Terms such as *higher law* or *natural law* have appeared in political and social philosophy since the beginning of recorded civilization. In the Western tradition, the concept of a "higher law" grew out of a mingling of Stoic philosophy and the Judeo-Christian tradition. Higher law was attributed to God or the Creator and was thus higher than laws made by men. Our own system depends upon the idea that people are "endowed by their Creator" with the rights to life, liberty, and the pursuit of happiness, and the right to own property and enjoy the fruits of one's labor—rights that no just government can take away. Many argue that this so-called higher law takes precedence over the laws enacted by man, and some justify their defiance of society's laws by citing their adherence to the higher law of nature. Mahatma Gandhi in India and Martin Luther King, Jr. in the United States claimed that their actions, which were violations of existing man-made laws, were morally correct because they conformed to the higher edicts of natural law.[2] However, to narrow the focus of our discussion in this chapter, we will restrict ourselves to the definition of law cited at the beginning of this section.

Types of Law

Our complex society requires many types of law. For example, admiralty and maritime law governs conduct on the high seas, regulates neutral shippers in war zones, establishes the rights of salvage, and provides for aid to ships in distress. Patent law, on the other hand, deals with the rights of inventors and with copyrights, which govern ownership and use of printed materials. There are five major branches of law that deserve closer examination.[3]

Criminal Law. In these days when fear of crime is a persistent feature of our lives, it is the workings of the criminal law system that we hear, read, and think most about. Modern criminal law is statutory (or code) law and covers a specific category of wrongs committed against persons or insti-

---

[2] For differing definitions of law, see George W. Patton, *A Textbook of Jurisprudence,* 2nd ed. (New York: Oxford University Press, 1948), Chapter 3; and Roscoe Pound, *Outlines of Lectures on Jurisprudence* (Cambridge, Mass.: Harvard University Press, 1943). See also Felix S. Cohen, *Ethical Systems and Legal Ideals* (Ithaca, N.Y.: Cornell University Press, 1933).

[3] See Patton, *Jurisprudence,* Chapter 3.

tutions. Acts defined as criminal are considered social evils and are threats to the entire community because they disturb the public order or threaten the public welfare. Consequently, the state rather than the aggrieved party is always the prosecutor (plaintiff). Criminal codes are usually divided into two classes. Misdemeanors are minor offenses (for example, public drunkenness, gambling, prostitution, traffic violations) and are normally punished by fines. Major crimes, called felonies (for example, rape, murder, robbery, extortion), are punished by heavy fines, imprisonment, or both. In most societies, the punishment depends upon the gravity of the offense, the age of the accused, and the defendant's record. In the United States, some criminal offenses (such as kidnapping and interstate car theft) are federal in nature; others (murder, rape, and mugging) are mainly state concerns; and a few (bank robbery and drug traffic, for instance) violate both state and federal criminal laws.

Civil Law. Many legislative acts (statutes) govern civil rather than criminal matters. Marriage and divorce, custody of children under eighteen years of age and inheritance, bankruptcy and the conduct of business are civil concerns. Not every contingency is covered by a statute, however, and in the English-speaking countries, statutory law is supplemented by common law (judge-made law based on precedent) and equity law. Civil law is distinguished from criminal law in that it provides redress for private individuals or corporations who feel that injuries have been done to them. Because civil offenses are held not to endanger the peace or welfare of the community, the private individuals themselves prosecute. The government merely provides the courts to resolve the disputes according to statutory, common, or equity law. Where a statute does not exist (and statutory law is expanding continually), the common law, dating back to medieval England, is applied. It operates on the basis of *stare decisis* (literally, "let the decision stand"), also called precedent. The lawyer in a given case will study similar cases that have occurred in the past, and if the decisions appear to be favorable to his own case, he will ask the presiding judge to make a similar ruling in this case. All other things being equal, the judge will usually honor precedent. However, a judge is not compelled to apply precedent in every case; an intelligent judge understands that new decisions must often take changing conditions into account.

Unfortunately, both common law and statutory law have one major drawback: they can only provide redress (usually a monetary award) after an injury has been done; they cannot prevent it. If striking workers damage private property, statutory law can make them pay the property owners, but it cannot prevent them from destroying the property. Equity (or chancery) law was developed in England to remedy this defect. Arising as an appeal to the "king's conscience," it traditionally dealt with property matters (for example, estates, inheritances, and real estate). Only one feature of it, the injunctive process, is still used widely. An injunction is a court order requiring the person or persons to whom it is directed to do or not to do a particular thing. Equity law can therefore be described as preventive law.

Constitutional Law. Written constitutions are usually general documents that describe the organs of government, establish their powers, and specify individual guarantees of freedom. General legislation and court interpretation must fill in the details. An important role of the courts, under a constitutional system of government such as ours, with the recognized authority of judicial review, is to make sure that statutory laws and their administrative interpretations do not violate the spirit or meaning of the constitution. Revolving around constitutional provisions and safeguards, the nature and extent of government power, the rights and privileges of citizens, and the relationships between branches of government, the body of constitutional law in the United States is mainly composed of the judicial decisions which interpret the various sections of the Constitution.

In the United States, with its traditional acceptance of judicial review, the ultimate responsibility of interpreting the Constitution rests with the U.S. Supreme Court. The Supreme Court's interpretations of the Constitution change with time. Economic, social, and political conditions are in a constant state of flux, and the men who become justices of the court naturally reflect the times in which they live and, to a lesser degree, the judicial philosophy of the president who appointed them. Thus, the cliché, "The Constitution is what the Supreme Court says it is," is not unfounded. In 1896, for example, the Court ruled, in *Plessy* v. *Ferguson*, that state laws requiring racial segregation in public transportation did not necessarily violate the Fourteenth Amendment, which provides for equal protection under the laws, as long as the transportation facilities for whites and blacks were physically equal. Fifty-eight years later the court reversed itself and ruled that separate public education facilities for whites and blacks are *inherently* unequal, even if physically alike. The Constitution didn't change, but society's conception of individual rights did. If the judicial process is to remain vital, it must adapt to these changes. What was acceptable in the 1890s proved intolerable in the 1950s. Constitutional law (indeed, law itself) is not static, but a living, growing institution.

Administrative Law. A relatively recent development, administrative law includes the regulatory orders enacted by appropriate government agencies. This form of law is more highly developed in continental Europe than it is in Great Britain or the United States. Essentially, administrative law develops when regulatory agencies interpret the statutory law that Congress has enacted. For example, federal antitrust laws prohibit business practices that tend to reduce competition. But what practices do reduce or inhibit competition? Initially, the Federal Trade Commission must decide. As the agencies interpret the meaning of Congress' laws, they begin to build up a body of administrative case law that binds the commission in its future decisions. Although administrative rulings may be appealed to the federal courts, these courts are reluctant to interfere and will do so only when the statute in question seems to have been grossly misinterpreted. The federal government now codifies administrative rulings, and a fairly substantial body of administrative law has grown up in the past half century.

International Law. International law consists of international treaties and conventions, and long-established customs recognized by most nations. It is a very special body of law, because it cannot be enforced in the same way as national law.[4] Treaties and agreements among nations may be signed, but their effectiveness depends mainly on voluntary compliance and reciprocal benefit, and threat, coercion, or deprivation. More importantly, neither domestic nor international courts are always able to ensure that judicial decisions will be executed. Matters are further complicated by the fact that not all states subscribe to existing rules of law. For example, while the United States and the USSR comply with the limited Nuclear Test Ban Treaty, which they and several other nations signed in 1963, neither France nor China is a party to the treaty and each continues nuclear testing in the atmosphere. Hence, in 1973 Japan could do no more than protest the radioactive effects of Chinese tests; and, in the same year, Australia and New Zealand vowed to station important statesmen in the area of announced French tests in order to dissuade France from conducting them.

To be sure, there is an International Court of Justice at the Hague, but it hears only those cases that states bring to it voluntarily. Thus, the system can work only when the individual nations respect the rules. Unfortunately, many do not. For example, a number of nations (including Chile, Peru, Korea, and Iceland) have declared that they will not recognize the traditional three-mile limit for sovereignty over coastal waters. International law is a legal system, in that it has built up a fairly uniform body of law over the centuries; but it lacks the cohesion and enforceability we are accustomed to in domestic law.

Legal Systems

Legal systems consist of two major elements used to govern society: a uniform body of law and an enforcement apparatus. In primitive cultures, the system is oral and consists of the mores, traditions, and beliefs that govern behavior. In modern society, legal systems are codified, that is, embodied in written laws. Committing the systems to writing makes them more precise in intent and thus usually more uniform in application. Codified law is less likely to be dependent upon the whim of the official enforcing it.

---

[4] See Chapter 18 for a fuller discussion of international law.

Legal codification began in ancient times and has been a major feature in the development of civilization. The Ten Commandments and the Code of Hammurabi—still influential—are among the earliest examples of law codes. However, the supreme legal achievement of the ancient world was Roman law. Its concepts, based on the idea that "right reason" should govern man's affairs, were so universal, flexible, and logical that they are still in use in much of the world today.[5]

Rome's first great law code, the famous Twelve Tables, dates from about 450 B.C. This was a codification of early customary law. On this foundation the Romans developed two major legal frameworks that were used throughout their empire. One body of laws, called the *jus civile*, governed the conduct of Roman citizens; the other, the *jus gentium*, applied to the non-Roman subjects of the Roman Empire. The development of the Roman legal tradition rested on the assumption that law and justice depended on the establishment of extensive legal codes to cover all aspects of social life. The jurist's task was not to argue each case on its individual merits, but rather to search through the legal codes to find the relevant laws.

As new needs arose, new laws were drawn up. When the Roman Empire collapsed, the decline of Roman law was a major factor in the general decline of civilization. However, its precepts were not forgotten. They were used by the Catholic church—the new center of power—in its canon law and, in the East, by the Byzantine Emperor Justinian. The celebrated Code of Justinian (*Corpus Juris Civilis*), based on Roman law and dating from approximately A.D. 533, is the foundation that Europe's modern legal systems (with the important exception of Great Britain's) were built on. After a long intermediate period during which the more primitive Germanic and Salic systems were used, Roman law was revived in the twelfth century, partly because of the work being done in medieval universities by legal scholars. Modern European law, then, is mostly an amalgamation of Roman, feudal, and ecclesiastical law.

The English Common Law

Development. The English common law began to develop after the Norman Conquest in 1066 and during the reign of Henry I (1100–1135).[6] At this time, feudal lords, and the church dispensed justice. Henry began the practice of tightening royal control over the administration of justice. In this way, he made it more uniform and less subject to the whims of the barons. It

[5] See W. W. Buckland and A. D. McNair, *Roman Law and Common Law* (New York: Oxford University Press, 1936); B. Schwartz, ed., *The Code Napoleon and the Common Law World* (New York: New York University Press, 1956); and Stanley Rothman, *European Society and Politics* (Indianapolis: Bobbs-Merrill, 1970), Chapter 20.

[6] A good history is T. F. T. Pluckett, *A Concise History of the Common Law*, 2nd ed. (New York: Lawyer's Cooperative, 1936); and Oliver Wendell Holmes, Jr., *The Common Law* (Boston: Little, Brown, 1881).

was Henry II (1154–1189), however, who did the important work of legal reform. New legal remedies (such as trial by jury), new modes of litigation, and new forms of action were created. The principles of the grand jury were also developed at this time. Itinerant royal judges began traveling throughout the kingdom, and the feudal and ecclesiastical courts thus lost influence. Over time, the itinerant judges came to use similar principles to decide similar cases in different parts of the kingdom, and there emerged a judge-made body of law which was "common" to all of England. Eventually, the new system led to a regular system of royal courts. Henry's new justice was popular and eagerly sought by a people accustomed to cruelty, violence, and oppression. The royal writ, in a society only slowly emerging from barbarism, at least afforded occasional help and remedy to the defenseless.

By the opening of the thirteenth century, this entire structure of royal justice rested upon the shoulders of the humble "J.P." A local citizen appointed by the Crown, the justice of the peace was supposed to take custody of prisoners until the king's judges arrived to try them. As time passed, the J.P. began to take on limited judicial functions. For example, he had authority to try minor infractions of law and supervise local police functions; later he was allowed to perform civil marriage ceremonies. The traveling royal justices, the common law courts, and the justices of the peace laid the foundation for the development of English common law.

Features. The responsibility of the traveling judges and the royal courts was to see that royal edicts and statutes were being faithfully administered and enforced. However, royal edicts were quite limited in their scope, and they did not cover all contingencies. The common law developed to fill the gaps left by these edicts. In administering justice, the judges and courts were forced to improvise. Most of the early judges had a clerical education and were familiar with Roman law as interpreted by the church. Accordingly, when royal law proved inadequate to the case at hand, the judges applied Roman and canon law provisions. If these were not applicable, they relied upon their own common sense and judgment, as well as the common practices of the English people. Over the centuries, a substantial body of common law developed—an amalgam of Roman law, church law, and local English customs.

Common law has three distinctive features. First, it is case law. That is, it is based upon individual legal decisions rather than upon a comprehensive code of statutes. Second, common law was made by judicial decision (it is "judge-made" law), and thus has great flexibility. Judges can easily reinterpret or modify previous rulings and principles to fit new social and economic circumstances and institutions. Third, common law relies heavily on *stare decisis,* or precedent. As we have said, precedent is the use of past judicial decisions to decide current cases. Of course, judges do not rely only upon precedent. Because no two cases are exactly alike, a judge can pick on the smallest point of difference to justify a ruling that breaks precedent. In this way, common law is kept relevant to changing social needs. With the rise of Parliament as a dominant institution in seventeenth-century England, statute law supplemented (and in some cases supplanted) specific provisions of the common law. Today when the two conflict, statute law always takes precedence.

Significance. Despite the fact that common law has declined somewhat in importance, its influence is still considerable. Tangibly, it has remained important in the legal systems of the United States, Canada, Australia, New Zealand, and a number of former British colonies. In many instances, statute law is a formal enactment, with minor modifications, of existing common law provisions. In England, where there is no uniform code of law, the common law occupies a central place in the legal system. The intangible effects of common law, however, may be even more important, for it shaped the development of English society and politics and gave distinctive habits of thought to all English-speaking societies.

Code (Roman) Law

Development. The legal systems of continental Europe (France, in particular) developed very differently from that of England. Feudalism was stronger in France than anywhere else, and until the thirteenth century the feudal lords were virtually independent of royal control. Exceptionally poor communications strengthened the local lords still further, so that they were able to dispense justice within their territories and ignore royal justice. Thus, national unification was the essential ingredient in the development of a uniform system of justice. Unifying the country was a long, drawn-out process, with the local lords resisting the central government every inch of the way. The process was finally completed under Louis XIII's reign (1610–1643), mainly because of his brilliant adviser, Cardinal Richelieu. However, this success did not lead automatically to the desired uniform justice.

The French parlement (not to be confused with a legislative body) was the only institution approaching a national court system. Originating in Paris in the fourteenth century, parlements were royal bodies that registered royal decrees and edicts throughout the provinces; no law could be enforced until it was registered with the parlements. But they were not courts in the Anglo-American understanding of the term. Unfortunately, the provincial parlements were extremely jealous of their prerogatives and parochial in their point of view, and, as a result, they modified royal laws to conform to local traditions. The financial troubles of the French kings compounded the problem, for they were forced to sell judicial offices. Turning these offices into a form of private property weakened royal control over the administration of justice.

Roman law, meanwhile, was enjoying a revival, because of the work of legal scholars and changing conditions in Europe. Royal governments were asserting themselves throughout Europe, and commerce was being revived on a large scale. It was becoming obvious that some form of centralized justice would be needed for this new age. French jurists, in particular, were beginning to see the value of Roman law to solve their problems. The main advantage was that it could be universal. Rules were reduced to writing; though they were precise, they were flexible, because the original Roman law had been used to rule a widespread empire. If this law could work so well for the ancient world, why not introduce it into France? Many of its principles, in fact, were already in use because of canon law. The job that remained was codification.

Codifying the law was Napoleon's lasting contribution to the rationalization of justice for France and, eventually, for most of Europe. The Code Napoleon (1804) was the first modern codification of European law. Feudal laws were bypassed, and the emancipation of civil law from religious influence—begun during the French Revolution—was maintained. The new code followed Justinian's Code, but reinterpreted it in the light of French needs. Although it preserved many of the gains of the revolution, such as the elimination of torture and arbitrary arrest and imprisonment, as well as the guaranteeing of civil liberty and civil equality, it reflected Napoleon's authoritarian views as well. These views are seen in the provisions concerning family life: the father's authority was firmly established, and the status of women was depressed. Nevertheless, the code was a great step forward, because it was far more equitable than the system of justice under the *ancien régime* and provided the necessary framework within which France could adapt to a modern, industrial age. Napoleon's invasions of Belgium, Spain, Italy, and Germany brought the code to these countries, and their legal systems are still based upon it. It is also in use in Louisiana, and European colonists carried it to Asia and Africa later on in the nineteenth century. The tight centralization of French life today is a reflection of its basic philosophy.

Features. Today, most of the world's people live under some form of Roman law as interpreted by the Code Napoleon.[7] Most code law is detailed, precise (unlike the more loosely written laws in the common law countries), comprehensive, and understandable by laymen. Judges are not expected to "make" law, merely to apply it. Precedent carries little weight. Another important feature of Roman law is that the judiciary is not independent of the executive (as it is in the Anglo-American system). Therefore, its powers of judicial review are quite limited—either shared with the legislative branch or assigned to a special national court. In Italy, for example, only the *Corte Constituzionale* can rule on the constitutionality of legislation, and the regular supreme court must assume that laws are constitutional unless this court rules otherwise.

[7] Schwartz, *The Code Napoleon.*

Common Features of Both Legal Systems

The differences between the common law and the Roman system are self-evident. The former is general and largely judge-made, and it relies on precedent and custom. The latter is specific and is largely the product of the legislature. Each grew within a different historical context and thus developed to serve different needs.

The differences between these two systems should not obscure their similarities, however; in fact, they are becoming more and more alike. As the volume of statute law increases in the English-speaking nations, the importance and relevance of common law decreases. More and more, the details of legislative enactment are being outlined by administrative agencies, whose codified rulings are now an integral part of the legal system. Both systems are inspired by Roman law traditions, the Judeo-Christian moral code, and Western concepts of natural law and natural rights. In both systems, the law is relatively uniform in its application, universal in its scope, and amenable to change. Both systems seem to work about equally well, and both share a common set of problems. They protect the rights of the accused in criminal proceedings, although in varying degrees, and have internal systems of checks and balances designed to counter abuses of law or judicial process. And both are struggling with the problems of how best to protect the citizen from arbitrary actions of government. Both legal systems will continue to change, but both should be able to serve their societies as well in the future as they have in the past.

The Courts, the Bench, and the Bar

As legal systems developed, so did judicial systems, for it is these systems that handle the day-to-day administration of the law. The organization of a judicial system is always hierarchical, which means that the courts are ranked in a specific order. The different courts have specific jurisdictions; that is, they generally hear different kinds of cases and have authority in specific geographical areas.

The United States Court System

Our court system is unique in that it is the only truly federal court system in the world today. Some other countries have federal systems of government —Canada, Australia, Switzerland, and West Germany, for example—but none of them has a federal court system. Although Canada, Australia, Switzerland, and West Germany have federal supreme courts that supervise the conduct of the various local courts, most litigation (lawsuits or legal contests) in these countries originates in the state and local courts. Thus, federal courts primarily hear appeals covering alleged violations or mis-applications of national law by the local courts. Such a court structure contrasts sharply with that of the United States, where the federal courts have jurisdiction within the states and where infractions of federal law are tried in federal rather than state courts.[8]

The National Court Structure. The federal district court is at the base of the national court system. Congress has divided the nation, including the District of Columbia and the Commonwealth of Puerto Rico, into ninety-three federal court districts, none of which may extend over state lines. Thus, each state has at least one federal district within its borders. The more populous states may have several; New York, for example, has four. The district court is a trial court and has jurisdiction over all violations of federal law, both civil and criminal. It is here that defendants accused of federal crimes such as kidnapping, bank robbery, and interstate auto theft are tried. All cases concerning federal crime are heard by a federal jury, unless defendant waives his right to a jury trial, in which case he is tried by a judge. In many cases, where the accused is charged with violating state law as well as federal law, the defendants are turned over to state criminal courts for trial. Bank robbery, kidnapping, and auto theft violate both state and federal laws, and federal prisoners must face state criminal proceedings as well. Jury trials are also permitted in most civil cases that come before the federal district courts, which handle approximately 10 percent of the nation's legal business.

All federal district court decisions, except acquittal in a criminal case, can be appealed to a United States Circuit Court of Appeals. At present, there are eleven Circuit Courts of Appeals presided over by approximately ninety-five judges. (The United States is divided into ten judicial circuits, which cross state boundaries; in addition, there is a Circuit Court of Appeals for Washington, D.C.) Besides hearing appeals from the district courts within its circuit, a Circuit Court of Appeals may also review the rulings of administrative tribunals and commissions such as the Federal Trade Commission, the Federal Aviation Administration, and the Food and Drug Administration. Each Circuit Court of Appeals consists of three to nine judges, depending on need, and arguments are heard by panels of three judges. For the most part, these courts do not question the facts of the case, but consider only whether or not the law has been misinterpreted or misapplied. The Circuit Court of Appeals bases its majority-vote verdict on the appeal primarily upon the briefs submitted by the attorneys for both parties to the dispute; oral arguments are quite limited.

[8] W. J. Wagner, *Federal States and Their Judiciary* (New York: Humanities Press, 1959). On the United States court system see H. J. Abraham, *The Judicial Process*, 2nd ed. (New York: Oxford University Press, 1968); Thomas P. Jahnige and Sheldon Goldman, eds., *The Federal Judiciary System* (New York: Holt, Rinehart and Winston, 1968); and Alpheus Mason and William M. Beaney, *American Constitutional Law: Introductory Essays and Selected Cases*, 4th ed. (Englewood Cliffs, N.J.: Prentice-Hall, 1968).

There are also a number of specialized federal courts. The Court of Claims hears disputes concerning the income tax laws, as well as claims that the federal government has failed to live up to its contracts. The Tax Court of the United States hears cases dealing with income tax laws. The Customs Court handles civil claims against United States customs officers. The Court of Customs and Patent Appeals hears appeals from the Customs Court and has original jurisdiction in cases of patent or copyright infringement. Appeals from these courts can be carried to the United States Supreme Court. Finally, the United States Court of Military Appeals is an appellate court for those convicted by military court martials. Its decisions can be appealed directly to the president, in his capacity of commander in chief of the armed forces.

At the pinnacle of the federal court system stands the United States Supreme Court, consisting of one chief justice and eight associate justices. The Supreme Court has original, but not exclusive, jurisdiction in cases involving the diplomatic personnel of foreign nations, as well as in cases "in which a state shall be a party." In all other instances, its jurisdiction is entirely appellate, although the Constitution provides that the Supreme Court's appellate jurisdiction may be altered by Congress. The nation's highest court, unlike a U.S. Circuit Court of Appeals, is not obliged to hear every case presented to it, and it accepts for review only a small fraction of the appeals it receives (approximately one in ten). The Supreme Court will generally not agree to hear an appeal unless the case involves a substantial constitutional question, a treaty, or some significant point of federal law. Here we see the importance of precedent; a substantial constitutional question is important because the court's ruling will establish a precedent for future decisions. In addition to hearing appeals from the lower federal courts, the Supreme Court will also review cases that come from the state supreme courts if a substantial federal constitutional issue is in question. For example, if a state supreme court declares a federal statute unconstitutional, it is almost certain that the U.S. Supreme Court will hear the case.

The State Court System. Each of the fifty states maintains and operates its own court system. As 90 percent of the nation's legal business is handled in the state courts, most of the cases that come before them are civil in nature. Generally, state trial courts operate at the county level, though a number of sparsely populated rural counties may be combined into a single court district with civil and criminal sections. These courts have original jurisdiction in all civil and criminal cases, and can hear appeals from local justice of the peace courts and magistrate's courts. Only about one-quarter of the states have appellate court divisions to hear appeals from the lower courts; however, as the volume of legal business grows, more and more states are adding appellate divisions to their court systems. In most states the appellate court is known as the supreme court; but in New York, Kentucky, and Maryland the supreme court is actually a lower court, and the Court of Appeals is the highest state court.

At the local level, justice of the peace courts are found in rural counties. They try minor civil and criminal infractions—primarily small civil claims and misdemeanors. In urban areas, there are magistrate's or police courts that have jurisdiction over minor traffic cases, violations of city ordinances, and misdemeanors such as public drunkenness. For the most part, these local courts operate without juries, because serious cases are handled by the state courts. Most of the penalties they impose are fines or short jail terms. There are also some specialized state courts, such as claims courts and probate courts, which handle wills and estates.

Judges: Selection and Tenure. To a great extent, the success of the court system depends upon the quality of persons selected to fill the bench. A judge is expected to be knowledgeable in the law, scrupulously honest, and thoroughly impartial. Considering how much is expected of judges, it is surprising that the law has so little to say about their qualifications. For example, the U.S. Constitution does not require that Supreme Court justices have prior experience on the bench or even hold law degrees. A president could, theoretically, nominate a man to the Supreme Court even if he has never set foot inside a court room or opened a law book. He is highly unlikely to do so, however, because there are a number of traditions and customary practices governing the selection of judges [9] and because Senate confirmation of such an individual would be unlikely.

The Federal Judges. Nearly all federal judges are nominated for the federal bench by the president and are appointed with the advice and consent of the Senate. Federal judges hold their positions during "good behavior," which generally means that they serve for life, unless impeached and convicted for criminal behavior. The purpose of a "lifetime" appointment is to free the judges from executive and other political pressure. To further ensure an independent judiciary, the Constitution provides that a federal judge's salary may not be reduced as long as he is in office.

Traditionally, federal judges are lawyers. Some undoubtedly owe their appointments to political favors, but they are usually knowledgeable in the law. Moreover, safeguards do exist to assure their qualifications. In the first place, the Attorney General will draw up a list of eligible candidates; as vacancies occur, the president selects a few names from that list. Before the names are made public, it has been the practice for the president to consult with the American Bar Association, which rates the judges. Although the president is not obliged to take the ABA's advice, he is usually influenced by it. At the same time, the FBI inquires into the candidate's past and present activities. Finally, if a judgeship is vacant in a state that has a

---

[9] Judicial appointments are discussed in Joel B. Grossman, *Lawyers and Judges* (New York: John Wiley & Sons, 1965). See also Laurence M. Hyde, "Judges: Their Selection and Tenure," *Journal of the American Judicature Society* 30 (February 1947): 152–59.

senator of the president's political party, the unwritten rule of senatorial courtesy requires the president to clear his choice with that senator. In fact, the president will often ask a senator for recommendations, and no one unacceptable to him will be named. Of course, if neither of the senators from that state belongs to the president's party, he is under no obligation to consult them.

Some presidents, Eisenhower for example, have argued that the federal judiciary should be nonpartisan, or at the very least bipartisan. Eisenhower appointed some Democrats to the federal bench (including Supreme Court Justice William J. Brennan), and made an effort to achieve a balance between judicial liberals and judicial conservatives. This is the exception rather than the rule, however; most presidents appoint men of their own political party who share their judicial philosophy. President Johnson, for example, appointed Thurgood Marshall—a liberal who believes that the Court should take an active role in promoting social justice—to the Supreme Court. President Nixon, in contrast, has appointed four justices whose general political philosophy is conservative and who believe that the Warren Court went too far in protecting the rights of the individual, to the detriment of society as a whole.

The State Judges. Unlike federal judges, many state judges are popularly elected, for terms ranging up to fourteen years. Both parties often nominate the same slate of judges, so that judicial elections have become largely nonpartisan affairs; only rarely do party fights for a judicial office take place. Most state parties will not nominate candidates unless the state bar associations have passed on their fitness. Generally, the party in power tries to select judges whose judicial philosophy is consistent with the party's general political philosophy. Often, however, a person's past behavior is not a good predictor of what his behavior will be as a judge.

The Judge's Role in the Adjudication Process. What role should the judge play once he dons his black robes and takes his seat on the bench? Should he act as an umpire, passively watching the legal drama, confining his responsibility to simply ruling upon disputed points of procedure? Or should he actively direct the course of the trial, question witnesses, elicit evidence, and comment on the proceedings as they unfold? The idea of judges playing such a role would, undoubtedly, seem strange—if not harmful —to those of us who have been raised within the common law framework. Yet, in code law countries, judges play just such an active role, and this is one of the crucial differences between the common law and code law systems.[10]

---

[10] On this point see Abraham, *The Judicial Process*; Rothman, *European Society and Politics*, Chapter 20; and Herbert Jacob, *Justice in America* (Boston: Little, Brown, 1965).

The Anglo-American Adversary and Accusatorial Process. English and American courts are passive institutions, in that they do not look for injustices to correct, and they do not apprehend or search out lawbreakers. Instead, they wait until a law is challenged or broken by someone, and the case then works its way up the court system. Congress cannot get advisory opinions from the federal courts about the constitutionality of a certain piece of legislation before enacting it.

The Anglo-American system of justice operates on a set of principles that, together, make up the adversary and accusatorial process. In the adversary process, two sides (plaintiff and defendant) are vying for a favorable decision from an impartial court. The operating principles are as follows. First, the courts will not accept a case that does not involve a real conflict of interest; in other words, the plaintiff must demonstrate how, and in what ways, the defendant has damaged his personal or property interests. Second, once a case has been accepted for trial, the presiding judge acts solely as an umpire. Both parties will present their evidence, call and cross-examine witnesses, and try to refute each other's arguments. The judge may rule only on the evidence and testimony that is admitted, see that proper legal procedures are followed, and rule on disputed points of procedure. After both sides have presented their cases, the judge will base his ruling on his understanding of the facts as well as upon the relevant law. If a jury is hearing the case, the judge will instruct the members as to the weight of the evidence (those factors that they may or may not consider). The judge makes an appropriate decision after the jury gives its verdict.

In criminal cases, the police investigate the facts of a crime and make a report to the public prosecutor. If evidence exists to link a particular individual to a crime, the prosecutor will usually present such evidence before a grand jury. A grand jury is a body of persons chosen to inquire into or determine the facts concerning a crime or an accusation submitted to them. It does not decide on the validity of the evidence presented before it, but merely rules on whether or not sufficient evidence exists to make the accused stand trial. If the decision is affirmative, the accused is indicted. The actual trial proceeds much like a civil one; the government is the plaintiff, the accused is the defendant, and the court is a neutral observer of the contest.

Many of the decisions made by the Warren Court led to increased protection of the rights of the accused. In addition, evidence acquired in searches not sanctioned by court warrants, or through wiretapping, has been ruled inadmissible. Some people feel that such provisions threaten the rights of the law-abiding citizen by making it easier for criminals to avoid conviction. Some legal observers believe that we are entering a more restrictive era. But the cries for "law and order" are not only heard in the United States. A recent article in *The New York Times* described a similar trend of opinion in Great Britain. The British system of justice, long regarded as a hallmark of fairness and honesty, is under attack by prosecutors, police officials, and the general public.[11]

The Modern English Court System

The court system in operation in England today was established by the Judicature Act of 1873. For the most part, this system continues common law traditions [12] and is divided into civil and criminal branches.

Selection and Tenure of Judges. All English judges are appointed by the Crown. Actually, however, the monarch acts only upon the advice of the prime minister, and his choices are based upon the recommendations of the lord chancellor, who presides over the House of Lords and is usually a cabinet member. To encourage independence, British judges are given life-time tenure. And like U.S. federal judges, they cannot be removed unless convicted of wrongdoing or criminal behavior. By tradition, the English bench is supposed to be above party politics and is not supposed to make policy—a tradition bolstered by the fact that there is no judicial review in Great Britain. English courts interpret Parliament's laws to apply them to specific cases, but Parliament can overrule the courts simply by passing a new law. An English court cannot declare an act of Parliament to be unconstitutional. Judicial review would be difficult in England, also, because there is no written constitution. Therefore, the judiciary is weaker in relation to the legislature than it is in the United States.

Lawyer's Role. Although the United States and England share a common legal heritage, there are important differences between their systems. One of the biggest distinctions is that in England the Crown hires lawyers to prosecute individual cases. There are no professional prosecutors to parallel the district attorneys in the American system. Another difference is in the degree of specialization within the legal profession. American lawyers are law school graduates who have successfully passed the bar examination of the state in which they wish to practice. After passing the examination, they may take on any type of case or legal work, without restriction. Of course, American lawyers do specialize—some handle corporation law, others specialize in criminal cases, and some devote their time to civil rights cases; but they do so by choice, not because they are obliged to. In England, the

---

[11] Alvin Shuster, "British Criminal Justice Assailed," *The New York Times*, August 7, 1972.

[12] For good descriptions see Richard N. Jackson, *The Machinery of Justice in England* (New York: St. Martin's Press, 1960); Abraham, *The Judicial Process*; Rothman, *European Society and Politics*, Chapter 20; and H. G. Hanbury, *English Courts of Law* (New York: Oxford University Press, 1953).

legal profession is more specialized. Barristers and solicitors, the two major types of lawyers, receive different training and do different work. A solicitor attempts to solve legal disputes without courtroom process. Failing this, a solicitor refers his client to a barrister, who is the courtroom lawyer in the English legal system.

The Modern French Court System

French courts, unlike the English ones, are not divided into separate criminal and civil divisions. Instead, France maintains separate systems of regular and administrative courts.[13] In 1959, de Gaulle's government restructured the judicial system substantially.

French juries are quite different from their Anglo-American counterparts. In the Anglo-American system, the judge rules on points of law and procedure, whereas the jury judges the facts and makes an independent verdict. French judges also rule on points of law and procedure, but at the conclusion of the trial they retire *with* the jury to consider the verdict and the sentence. Obviously, there is great pressure on the lay jurors to go along with the superior—or at least professional—knowledge and judgment of the judges. Verdicts require at least an eight to four vote, which means that three judges and five of the jurors must agree. American jury decisions, by contrast, must be unanimous in most states. (In two recent decisions, the U.S. Supreme Court has sustained state jury procedures that allow for less than a unanimous vote in criminal cases.[14] However, a unanimous agreement is still required in federal criminal cases.)

Role of Judges in Adjudication: The Inquisitorial Process. In code law countries, the judge plays a radically different role from the one he plays in common law countries. Suppose a robbery is committed. The police —as in England or the United States—conduct a preliminary investigation. They then notify the public prosecutor (*procureur*), who is himself a high police official, that they suspect Mr. X of being the robber. If the prosecutor agrees, he will forward the charges, and the evidence on which they are based, to an investigating judge (*juge d'instruction*). There is no parallel office in the Anglo-American system. The investigating judge is a professional magistrate who represents the Ministry of Justice, and who conducts an inquiry (*enquête*) into the case. Unlike the American grand jury, which simply rules on whether enough evidence exists to indict the accused, the French investigating judge conducts his own exhaustive inquiry with the

[13] See René David, *French Law: Its Structure, Sources, and Methodology*, trans. Michael Kindred (Baton Rouge: Louisiana State University Press, 1972).
[14] See *Johnson* v. *Louisiana*, 406 U.S. 356 (1972); and *Apodaca* v. *Oregon*, 406 U.S. 404 (1972).

cooperation of the police. Thus, his role is active rather than passive. He will usually visit the scene of the crime, interview the victim or witnesses, and interrogate the accused. When testimony conflicts, the judge can call the witnesses to his office and question them until he is satisfied as to who is telling the truth.

When the inquiry is complete, the investigating judge decides whether or not he thinks the accused is guilty. If he does, he will send the case to trial. The dossier that he has compiled becomes the core of the prosecution's case, and the resulting trial is often little more than a public affirmation of the evidence gathered by the judge.

The major differences between Anglo-American and French criminal procedures, then, are that (1) the decision to indict is not made by a grand jury but by a judge, and (2) the weight of evidence is not controlled by the adversaries (plaintiff and defendant) but by the court, which can take the initiative in acquiring needed evidence.

Another major point of difference in the two systems is that in the Anglo-American system the accused is presumed innocent until proven guilty; in France the assumptions are reversed. This makes an enormous difference in the trials. In an American or English court, the burden of proof is on the prosecution, and the defendant need not say one word in his defense; the prosecutor must prove guilt "beyond a reasonable doubt." In France and other code law countries, the accused bears the burden of having to prove that the investigating judge is wrong. However, the Napoleonic Code does make some provisions for the protection of the accused, and the system is by no means arbitrary.

Lawyer's Role. Unlike a British or American trial lawyer, the French *avocat* does not question witnesses (the court does that). Instead, he tries to show logical or factual mistakes in the opposition's argument or case, attempting to sway the sympathy of the lay jury by his oratory. In short, his work is roughly equivalent to the summation argument of an American trial lawyer. In addition to the *avocat*, there are sixty *avocats aux conseils* in France. These men are the cream of the French legal profession; they alone may argue cases before the Court of Cassation and Council of State. For the most part, the role of the French lawyer is not as vital or creative as that of his English or American counterparts. The court, not he, takes the initiative in discovering the facts of the case.

Law in the Soviet Union

The Legal System. The basic concepts of Soviet law and the workings of the Soviet judicial process are quite different from those of the Western democracies,[15] even though they are similar in strictly criminal—as opposed

[15] See Harold J. Berman, *Justice in the USSR* (New York: Vintage Books, 1963).

to political—matters. Soviet law takes as its starting point the idea that the legal system exists to serve the state. Therefore, it is reasoned, class justice is given to the proletariat. Marxism states that the bourgeois legal systems exist to promote the interests of the capitalists. Believing this to be so, the Soviet Union designed its legal system, at least theoretically, to serve the working class.

However, abstract theories are always modified in practice, and Soviet law is no exception. For example, because most property is owned by the state, Russian law is preoccupied with offenses against the state. Rules are often intentionally vague; in fact, they usually aren't published. Although there is no distinct area of private law, Soviet law codes are still tied to Russia's past. All Soviet law draws upon several sources: Russian traditions, Communist ideology, and Roman law, which came to Russia with the Byzantines.

Nearly all nations have laws against political sedition and subversion. However, if an individual, or group of individuals, is brought to trial for such a crime in a democracy, his trial will be handled by a court system that is relatively independent of government agencies and pressures. Such a trial would be impossible in the Soviet Union because judges are appointed by the party; individuals accused of political crimes are invariably convicted. America has also had political trials (some would include the trials of Angela Davis, Daniel Ellsberg, and Father Philip Berrigan), but even then, the accused are tried in open court for specific violations of the criminal codes, and conviction is uncertain (as Davis's retrial and Ellsberg's dismissal show).

The five-judge regional courts are the highest courts within the individual Soviet republics. (There are no jury trials in the Soviet Union.) These courts have appellate jurisdiction over the courts of original jurisdiction, or People's Courts, and original jurisdiction over criminal offenses. Their judges are elected for five-year terms (there is no judicial tenure) by the Soviet of their region, and judicial posts go to loyal party members. Each of the Union Republics has its own supreme court of five judges, elected for five-year terms by the Supreme Soviet (legislature) of each republic. The supreme courts have appellate jurisdiction over the regional courts of the republic, and they try political cases. Alongside the formal court system is a second system called the procuracy. It has several levels, with a procurator-general at the top. His chief role is to assure that actions taken by state organizations conform to Soviet legal-political requirements.

At the pinnacle of the Soviet court system is the Supreme Court of the USSR, whose judges are chosen by the Supreme Soviet of the USSR, and who also serve five-year terms. Decisions of republic supreme courts can be appealed to the Supreme Court of the USSR, which also has original jurisdiction in disputes between the republics and over serious political crimes, such as a publicly expressed desire to leave the country. The Supreme Court of the USSR is divided into specialized panels of judges, each handling a different area of law. They have no power of judicial review, and they have never ruled against the government.

The Administration of Criminal Justice. In criminal matters, the Soviet system basically follows Roman law as used in Tsarist times. Unlike the French system, however, the Communist system still uses severe interrogation methods. The key figure is the public prosecutor of the USSR, who is elected for a seven-year term by the Supreme Soviet and who works closely with the ruling party presidium. The public prosecutor, in turn, appoints prosecutors for each union, regional, and local court in the Soviet Union. These prosecutors are directly accountable to the public prosecutor of the USSR and to no one else. Like the French investigating judges, they investigate crimes, bring the guilty to justice, and see to it that the rights of the accused are protected. When a case has no political overtones, the Soviet system works as fairly as those of other code law countries. Indeed, public prosecutors often request that guilty sentences be reversed when new evidence is brought to light and will often intervene with the courts to have severe sentences reduced. However, the prosecutor must also see to it that local court decisions do not deviate from national law. If the prosecutor does not approve of a decision, it is appealed promptly to the next highest court, and the position of the government is nearly always sustained.

When a trial is political in nature, methods of interrogation and the conduct of trials are much harsher than in criminal cases. Since most Soviet judges believe that the welfare of the individual must be subordinate to that of the state, they justify severe methods of psychological pressure. Arthur Koestler's *Darkness at Noon* gives a fascinating description of the process. However, his book concerned the trials of the 1930s, which represent the height of Stalin's brutality and tyranny. The Soviet Union has become much more liberal since then and the methods that Koestler details so movingly have been abandoned in most cases. Nevertheless, the basic point still remains that justice within a totalitarian system must serve the state first.

Although the Soviet government does have full control of the court system, there are checks on how it is used. Concerned with world public opinion, Communist leaders often restrain themselves if they feel that the political backlash will be too strong. For example, when a group of Leningrad Jews were sentenced to death in 1970 for hijacking a plane in a futile attempt to flee the country, the world outcry forced the government to back down and commute the sentences. Similarly, Alexander Solzhenitsyn, the Nobel Prize-winning writer, has not been put on trial even though party leaders consider his writing subversive. They realize that world opinion would be outraged, and they act accordingly.

The Role of the Courts

General Adjudication

In democratic societies, the courts' primary function is to uphold the constitutional system under which the state operates. Protecting a particular political group is secondary and must fit into the constitutional framework. Traditionally, the court is expected to be above party politics; in reality, of course, politics cannot be excluded completely. However, the process works both ways, and court decisions affect political actions.

In the United States, for example, we look to the courts to strike down laws that violate the terms of the Constitution, and we expect the justices to leave their personal feelings and beliefs out of their interpretations.[16] Judicial review is more highly developed in the United States than in any other country. As a result, Americans expect more of their courts than do most other people.

However, this function is not completely absent from the courts in other Western democracies. In Switzerland, for example, when cases from the cantonal (state or province) courts come before the Federal Tribunal (their supreme court), the tribunal determines if a cantonal law violates the federal constitution. However, the tribunal does not pass on the constitutionality of laws passed by the Swiss Parliament. France, Italy, and West Germany have set up constitutional courts, but these do not operate on the principles of judicial review as we understand it. Rather, they give their opinion on a law's constitutionality when asked, before a law is passed. Doing so indicates that the executive and legislative branches of government want their laws and decrees to be legal. These courts usually have other functions as well. For example, they may interpret constitutional provisions or rule on the status of various kinds of statutes. Therefore, though not as strong or independent as the United States Supreme Court, they, too, act to safeguard their constitutions.

Interpreting the Constitution. The United States Supreme Court's power of judicial review is not mentioned specifically in the Constitution, and throughout much of our history the doctrine that the Supreme Court has this prerogative has been vehemently challenged.

The doctrine was first considered and debated at the Constitutional Convention of 1787. Delegates to that convention suggested that, when in doubt, legislators might call upon the judges for an opinion on a proposed law's constitutionality. James Madison stated that a "law violating a constitution established by the people themselves would be considered by the judges as

---

[16] This conception is expressed in Fred V. Cahill, Jr., *Judicial Legislation* (New York: Ronald Press, 1952), Chapter 1; and in Jack W. Peltason, *Federal Courts in the Political Process* (New York: Random House, 1955), Chapter 3.

null and void." However, this position was challenged by those who believed that such a power would give the Court a double check and compromise its neutrality. Others felt that it would violate the principle of separation of powers. Elbridge Gerry stated that it would make "statesmen of judges." As things turned out, his remark was quite prophetic. At the close of the convention, judicial review had not been explicitly provided for. However, Alexander Hamilton supported the idea and, in *The Federalist* no. 78, written to promote ratification of the Constitution, he specifically stated that only the courts could limit legislative authority. John Marshall agreed with this position; in fact, he went on record in favor of it nearly fifteen years before the landmark decision *Marbury* v. *Madison* (1803). Therefore, his assertion of the doctrine of judicial review in that case should have come as no surprise.

The doctrine has never been universally popular, however; strong-willed presidents, in particular, have tried to resist the authority of the court. Thomas Jefferson, Andrew Jackson, Abraham Lincoln, and Franklin D. Roosevelt all differed sharply with equally strong-willed judges.

The background to *Marbury* v. *Madison* is as follows.[17] President John Adams, a Federalist, had appointed William Marbury, a Washington, D.C. justice of the peace shortly before leaving office. For some unknown reason, however, Secretary of State John Marshall had neglected to deliver the commission to Marbury. Marshall's successor, the Republican [18] James Madison, refused to deliver the commission. Marbury brought suit in original jurisdiction before the Supreme Court, asking the Court to issue a writ of *mandamus* commanding Madison to deliver the commission. If Marshall and the Supreme Court issued the writ, and Madison refused to deliver the commission, the prestige and authority of the Court would be dealt a severe blow. If, however, Marshall refused to issue the writ, he would in effect call into question the legitimacy of the hasty judicial appointments made to federalists in the final days of the Adams administration. Marshall's solution was nothing short of brilliant, for it not only criticized Madison and Jefferson, but also established explicitly the principle of judicial review. On the one hand, Marshall ruled that Marbury was entitled to his commission and that Madison should have given it to him. On the other hand, however, he stated that the Supreme Court had no authority to issue a writ of *mandamus* in a case brought to it in original jurisdiction and, because Section 13 of the Judiciary Act of 1789 implied otherwise, that part of the act was unconstitutional. The decision infuriated President Jefferson, for he understood

[17] Robert K. Carr, *The Supreme Court and Judicial Review* (New York: Holt, Rinehart and Winston, 1942); Robert H. Jackson, *The Struggle for Judicial Supremacy* (New York: Vintage Books, 1941), pp. 24–28; and Robert G. McCloskey, *The American Supreme Court* (Chicago: University of Chicago Press, 1960), pp. 40–47.
[18] The Republican party of 1803 was not the Republican party of today, which dates only to 1860. The former, roughly equivalent to the English Whigs of that time, was more liberal than the Federalist party.

all too well how cleverly Marshall had escaped the trap and asserted the authority of the Court into the bargain. He realized that the precedent for judicial review had been laid, and called it "both elitist and undemocratic."

From 1803 to 1857, the Supreme Court did not invalidate any act of Congress. In the latter year, it threw out the Missouri Compromise of 1820 that had barred slavery in the old Northwest Territory. This touched off a political storm that was to make Abraham Lincoln president. In the twentieth century, the doctrine has been used extensively. The court itself, however, has always been divided on how it should be used. Judicial activists, led by Hugo Black,[19] William O. Douglas, and Earl Warren, have argued that the Supreme Court must be vigilant in its protection of the Bill of Rights' guarantees. When the Court doubts the constitutionality of a law, the Court should strike it down. William Rehnquist is also an activist—an activist in favor of conservative decisions to expand the government's authority in such areas as wiretapping. Advocates of judicial restraint, led by justices Felix Frankfurter, Byron White, and Warren Burger, have argued that only Congress should make public policy, and that unless a legislative act clearly violates the Constitution, the law should stand. By 1973 the Court was about evenly divided, although the advocates of restraint were in the ascendancy. However, the pendulum has swung back and forth in the past, and will undoubtedly continue to do so.

Interpreting the Law. The responsibility of interpreting laws passed by the legislature is closely related to that of protecting the Constitution. In the past two decades, the Supreme Court has used this power often. For example, in race relations, the court has ruled that state laws or the use of state power providing for racial segregation violates the Fourteenth Amendment's "equal protection of the laws" provision. Another illustration is the court's ruling in *Pennsylvania* v. *Nelson* (1956), which threw out all state antisubversion laws aimed at protecting the federal government from sedition on the grounds that the 1940 Smith Act (federal) pre-empted them. Even though many critics in and out of Congress complained that mere passage of a federal statute should not inhibit a state from passing legislation in the same area unless Congress specifically indicated so, the court's interpretation stood.

There is no question that decisions like these can be reasonably interpreted to be judicial lawmaking of considerable magnitude. Many people have complained—and will continue to do so—that judges have no right to substitute their judgment for that of Congress, which, after all, is elected by the people. However, the other side has an equally compelling case. No law can cover all conditions that may arise, or can be so clear that no interpretation is needed. It is true that the Constitution can be amended, but practically, this is a difficult task. Therefore, the final word on what the law means will continue to come from the courts.

---

[19] Black was an activist on Bill of Rights issues, not across the board.

The Supreme Court's Political Role. In this country, the Supreme Court's rulings have often become political issues. This is not true in other countries, simply because their courts do not have the authority and independence that our courts have. When the Supreme Court of Franklin Roosevelt's day ruled that many New Deal laws were unconstitutional, he referred to the justices contemptuously as "nine tired old men." President Nixon, in the 1968 campaign, charged that the Warren Court's liberal decisions had added to the crime problem and, by implication, had endangered the safety of society. It should be obvious by now that the justices do play important political roles. Moreover, the appointment of just one new justice can make an enormous difference. Suppose the Court frequently splits its decisions five to four. A new justice who sides frequently with the minority obviously turns it into a majority. Therefore, it is important to know whether, and to what extent, judges let their personal beliefs interfere with their decisions. Are their ideological views incompatible with the idea of the Court as an "impartial dispenser of justice"? [20]

The Role of Judges. However conscientiously a judge may try to keep his personal beliefs out of his decisions, his own outlook and background no doubt play some part in his work. Most Supreme Court justices are and have been white, Protestant, and from upper- or upper-middle-class families,

[20] For discussions of the political roles of the courts—especially the Supreme Court—see Alexander M. Bickel, *The Supreme Court and the Idea of Progress* (New York: Harper, 1970), and *The Least Dangerous Branch: The Supreme Court as the Bar of Politics* (Indianapolis: Bobbs-Merrill, 1962) ; Samuel Krislov, *The Supreme Court in the Political Process* (New York: Macmillan, 1965) ; Glendon Schubert, *Constitutional Policy* (Boston: Boston University Press, 1970) ; Glendon Schubert, ed., *Judicial Decision Making* (New York: The Free Press, 1963) ; Charles Warren, *The Supreme Court in United States History*, 2 vols. (Boston: Little, Brown, 1922) ; and William F. Swindler, *Court and Constitution in the Twentieth Century*, 2 vols. (Indianapolis: Bobbs-Merrill, 1970).

most of whom can trace their origins to the British Isles.[21] Those critics who claim that the judicial system is too conservative state that the judges cannot possibly identify with the needs of the poor or racially oppressed. But others argue that selecting judges from lower-class and minority groups will not insure fairness; it will merely replace one set of prejudices with another.

There are other, more concrete, factors that affect a judge's rulings. Southern jurists have been, traditionally, more conservative on racial matters. However, there are exceptions. One of the strongest champions of civil rights was Alabama's Hugo L. Black, who had been a member of the Ku Klux Klan during his youth. Similarly, eastern judges are expected to be more responsive to the needs of large industry than judges from farm states. Here, too, however, there are no hard-and-fast rules. Occupational background may also affect decision making; for example, former corporation lawyers may be more sympathetic than others to the problems of business. Some justices, like Louis D. Brandeis (one of five Jewish justices) and Thurgood Marshall (the only black justice), were active in reform and civil rights causes and brought their liberalism to the bench. Others who have served on state courts, believe that states' rights should be strengthened.[22]

The two most important influences on voting, however, seem to be political party affiliation and the justice's conception of the judicial role in the American system of government. Although we should be wary of generalizations, recent studies indicate that Democratic justices are much more likely to support liberal stands than are Republican justices.[23] Democrats tend to be judicial activists and to see the Supreme Court as a defender of oppressed minorities and economic groups. They are more likely to distrust state power and to favor an increase in federal authority, while also seeking to protect individual rights under the Fourteenth Amendment against state authority. Republicans, on the other hand, usually favor judicial restraint, are more likely to uphold state authority within the federal system of government, and are less likely than Democrats to apply Bill of Rights guarantees. There are, of course, exceptions to this pattern. Former Chief Justice Earl Warren, for example, was a Republican and was thought to be a "middle-of-the-roader." But President Eisenhower was often surprised and frequently exasperated by the Warren Court's liberal, ground-breaking decisions.

The Supreme Court justices undoubtedly keep abreast of changes in public attitudes, and these new modes of thinking probably influence their de-

[21] John R. Schmidhauser, "The Justices of the Supreme Court: A Collective Portrait," *Midwest Journal of Political Science* 3 (1959): 1–57, and *The Supreme Court* (New York: Holt, Rinehart and Winston, 1960).

[22] Joel B. Grossman, "Social Backgrounds and Judicial Decision Making," *Harvard Law Review* 79 (1966): 1551–64.

[23] Stuart Nagel, "Political Party Affiliation and Judges' Decisions," *American Political Science Review* 60 (1961): 843–50. For related studies on judicial philosophy and behavior see Wallace Mendelson, *Justices Black and Frankfurter, Conflict in the Court*, 2nd ed. (Chicago: University of Chicago Press, 1966); Walter F. Murphy, *Elements of Judicial Strategy* (Chicago: University of Chicago Press, 1964); and Glendon Schubert, *The Judicial Mind* (Evanston, Ill.: Northwestern University Press, 1965).

cisions.[24] However, many justices see the Court's role as standing firm on certain constitutional principles, despite fluctuations in public opinion. Justice Jackson put it this way: "One's right to life, liberty and property, to free speech, a free press, freedom of worship and assembly, and other fundamental rights may not be submitted to vote; they depend upon the outcome of no election."

In the 1936 election, after the Court had struck down several important laws designed to alleviate the Depression, President Roosevelt was given the greatest mandate in the nation's history. In the following year, he submitted legislation that would have had the effect of expanding the Supreme Court to fifteen members and would have allowed every sitting justice over the age of seventy to retire at a sizeable pension. The plan failed because the people felt that Roosevelt was going too far in attacking the constitutional principle of an independent judiciary, but it did force the Court to look beyond its own narrow world and accept the fact that basic social change could not be postponed indefinitely. Most legal scholars believe that the electoral liberal triumph of 1936 and the controversy over the "court packing" scheme led directly to the Court's becoming more restrained in dealing with New Deal legislation.[25] As one jokester put it, "A switch in time saves nine."

Still another influence on a Supreme Court justice is his colleagues' opinions. Both Chief Justices John Marshall (1801–1835) and Earl Warren (1953–1969) were able to convert some of their colleagues to their judicial philosophies, by the force of their personalities as well as their judicial reasoning. This has been true of other Supreme Court justices who have not been chief justices: for example, Felix Frankfurter, Hugo Black, and William O. Douglas. In short, many factors—some conscious and some subconscious—determine how and why a given judge will vote on any particular issue. It is impossible to point to any one factor as the decisive one; legal and political scholars disagree among themselves as to the influences on the judicial mind.

Political Impact of the Court

Our legal system—in theory and practice—poses a basic conflict. On the one hand, a justice is expected to be impartial; on the other hand, the importance of the Court gives him considerable political power. And in the twentieth century, his power is increasing. The view of judicial impartiality is giving way to the views of the legal realists.

Legal Realism. Inspired by Oliver Wendell Holmes, Jr. and Louis D. Brandeis, "legal realists" such as Jerome Frank, Thurman Arnold, and Ed-

[24] On this point see Benjamin N. Cardozo, *The Nature of the Judicial Process* (New Haven, Conn.: Yale University Press, 1921); and Robert H. Jackson, *The Supreme Court in the American System of Government* (Cambridge, Mass.: Harvard University Press, 1955).
[25] C. H. Pritchett, *The Roosevelt Court* (New York: Macmillan, 1948); and E. V. Rostow, *The Sovereign Prerogative* (New Haven, Conn.: Yale University Press, 1962).

ward S. Robinson recognize that judges, in the course of making decisions, must inevitably make policy to some extent. The decisions and policies that they lay down will be influenced partly by their own social backgrounds, convictions, and philosophy. In short, law is not an absolute verity interpreted by infallible oracles; rather, it is a changing and growing human institution, and those who interpret it can be misguided. Moreover, the legal realists argue that jurists should not be afraid to make policy, should not shy away from blazing new trails. The law, they hold, must evolve as the needs of society do, and the judges are catalysts for this legal progress.[26] Perhaps the Warren Court exemplified the principle of legal realism best; its policy-making role, therefore, deserves closer examination.

The Warren Court. Earl Warren's court was as active as it was controversial, and in three key areas—civil rights, criminal rights, and legislative reapportionment—it substantially rewrote constitutional law.[27] In the opinion of some, as ninety-six southern congressmen put it, the Court overturned "the established law of the land" and implemented its "personal political and social philosophy."

Civil Rights. The Supreme Court's decision in *Brown* v. *Board of Education of Topeka* (1954) led to crucial changes in American race relations. In a unanimous ruling, the Court accepted the sociological argument of Thurgood Marshall (then attorney for the NAACP) that segregated public school facilities were "inherently unequal" because they stigmatized black children and thus deprived them of the Fourteenth Amendment's guarantee of equal protection of the law. Racial segregation, which had been established in law for over half a century, was struck down as an American legal institution. One year later, in *Brown* II (1955), the process of desegregation in the public schools was ordered to proceed "with all deliberate speed." This was a fundamental alteration of American public policy. Southern whites vowed massive resistance, and in 1958 federal troops had to be called out to implement court-ordered desegregation of Central High School in Little Rock, Arkansas. But the Court refused to back down.

America's blacks, encouraged by this legal support, attempted to gain equal treatment in other areas. By 1963, passive resistance had given way to massive confrontation. In *Lombard* v. *Louisiana* (1963), the Warren Court supported by implication the sit-in tactic, ruling that blacks who had refused to leave a segregated lunch counter could not be prosecuted for attempting to exercise their constitutional rights. Disobedience to an unconstitutional act could not be punished. The sit-in had become a major

[26] See Roscoe Pound, *An Introduction to the Philosophy of Law* (New Haven, Conn.: Yale University Press, 1922); Julius Stone, *The Province and Function of Law* (Cambridge, Mass.: Harvard University Press, 1950); W. F. Murphy and C. H. Pritchett, *Courts, Judges, and Politics* (New York: Random House, 1961); and Victor Rosenblum, *Law As a Political Instrument* (New York: Random House, 1955).

[27] For a good account of the Warren Court's decisions, see Archibald Cox, *The Warren Court* (Cambridge, Mass.: Harvard University Press, 1968).

weapon in the civil rights struggle. In 1964 Congress followed the Court's lead when it enacted the Civil Rights Act, which barred segregation in public accommodations such as hotels, motels, restaurants, and theaters. The Court, of course, was not the prime mover of this legislation, but it did give the initial impetus, and its rulings in this area set the tone of public policy.

Criminal Justice. The Warren Court's rulings in the area of criminal justice and procedural rights in state criminal cases were even more disturbing to many Americans. An important case in this area was *Mapp* v. *Ohio* (1961), in which the Court ruled that, except in unusual circumstances, evidence seized by police without a warrnat was inadmissible in a state court.[28] In 1963, *Gideon* v. *Wainwright*, the Court held that, unless they waive the right, indigent defendants must be provided with legal counsel in all state criminal proceedings where the defendant is accused of a serious crime. This decision did not produce a public outcry because it was, after all, in the best traditions of American fair play. But subsequent Court rulings aroused more public debate. In *Escobedo* v. *Illinois* (1964), the Supreme Court forced a major revision of state criminal procedure. In a five-to-four decision, it ruled that a suspect could not be denied the right to have a lawyer with him during police questioning, and that any confessions obtained without an opportunity provided to get counsel, unless counsel was knowledgeably waived, could not be used in a state criminal case. Justice White bitterly dissented from the majority ruling in the Escobedo case; he asserted that it was an "unworkable" ruling. If the Court continued along its path, he quipped, it would soon be demanding that criminals obtain counsel before committing their offenses, so as to better avoid capture and prosecution.

One of the Court's most controversial rulings came in 1966 in the case of *Miranda* v. *Arizona*. The majority (five to four) ruled that as soon as a suspect is detained by the police he must be told that he has the right to remain silent and is entitled to have a lawyer present during police questioning. Once again the Court had upset local criminal procedures, and once again its ruling was unpopular. Justice White declared that the Supreme Court was writing "new law and new public policy," and had usurped its proper role in the constitutional system. Justice Harlan joined in the dissent, angrily asserting, "The Court is taking a real risk with society's welfare in imposing its new regime on the country."

Legislative Reapportionment. Equally controversial was the Supreme Court's "one man, one vote" ruling. Until 1962, state legislative districts had been gerrymandered [29] notoriously, and yet the Supreme Court had consistently refused to provide a judicial remedy for cases in this area. The court had always maintained that the states and Congress should be the sole

---

28 Stolen evidence could not be used in a federal criminal case as a result of the Supreme Court decision in *Elkins* v. *United States* (1960).

29 To gerrymander is to divide a state or county into election districts so as to give one political party a majority in many districts, while concentrating the voting strength of the other members into as few districts as possible.

"Before we begin, it is my duty to tell you that anything you say may be used against you."

Drawing by Ed Fisher;
© 1971 The New Yorker
Magazine, Inc.

judges in this political area. However, in *Baker* v. *Carr* (1962), the Warren Court broke precedent and said that the failure of a state to reapportion its legislature could be examined by a federal court under the Fourteenth Amendment. This decision began a reapportionment struggle that is still in progress. *Reynolds* v. *Sims* (1964) applied a "one-man, one-vote" principle to both houses of a state legislature; *Wesberry* v. *Sanders* (1964) barred unequal apportionment in federal congressional districts; and *WMCA, Inc.* v. *Lomenzo* (1964) authorized the federal courts to supervise legislative reapportionment to root out "built-in bias."

Not unexpectedly, these rulings were unpopular in rural America; once again the Court was accused of making law and public policy. In the Congress, in 1965, Senator Everett M. Dirksen proposed a constitutional amendment to negate the effects of these reapportionment rulings; it was opposed by Senate liberals and failed by seven votes.

The Warren Court, then, overthrew the legal foundations of the Jim Crow system, wrote a new manual for the handling of criminal cases, and attempted to redraw the legislative map. With the possible exception of the Marshall Court, it was the most active, ground-breaking Court in American history.

Limitations on the Court

Despite the fact that the Warren Court's decisions made basic changes in American society, the Supreme Court cannot just rewrite the law. Institutional as well as noninstitutional checks upon its authority do exist. For one thing, the Court hears only a handful of the cases brought before it. Once the Court has ruled, moreover, Congress can propose—and the states may enact—constitutional amendments to reverse Court rulings. The Sixteenth Amendment, for instance, reversed a Supreme Court ruling that said that the federal income tax was unconstitutional. Congress can also redefine the authority of the Supreme Court, removing whole areas of litigation from the Court's appellate jurisdiction. In addition, the Court must rely upon the chief executive to enforce its rulings, and he can always refuse. In the famous words of Andrew Jackson, "John Marshall has made his decision, now let him enforce it." If Eisenhower had not sent federal troops to Little Rock in 1958, its schools would not have been desegregated despite the Court's 1954 ruling. Moreover, lower federal courts have been known to ignore or evade Supreme Court rulings with which they disagree. Federal judges are somewhat immune from pressures from the higher court or the executive because they have tenure. Finally, no law and no court order can be enforced well, or for long, unless it has substantial popular support. The Supreme Court cannot afford to get too far ahead or too far behind public opinion.[30] The Court's leftward swing in 1937, and the Burger Court's apparent rightward swing illustrate the importance of public opinion to the Court.

The federal courts are thus an integral part of the policy-making apparatus of government—not just mechanical interpreters of law. They are involved in the political process in three distinct ways. First, judges are selected on the basis of their political party affiliation and judicial philosophy. Second, judicial decisions in areas like civil rights and economc matters are influenced by politics. Groups whose welfare depends on the Court's decisions will try to influence the Court to adopt their point of view; and groups that do not succeed with the president or Congress hope that they will have better luck with the courts. Finally, Supreme Court decisions *technically* bind only those parties in the case decided by the Court. By extension, however, such rulings set precedents for similar cases, but the lower courts must decide how and in what ways previous rulings affect the cases that they are considering. And, in this respect, lower court judges have a good deal of latitude. As Jack W. Peltason puts it:

> *The subordinate judge's task of applying the Supreme Court's mandates is no more mechanical than is the Supreme Court's of applying the Constitution's mandates. The high court decisions which are supposed to guide and control the subordinates are frequently just as ambiguous as is the*

[30] See Theodore L. Becker, ed., *The Impact of Supreme Court Decisions* (New York: Oxford University Press, 1969) ; Walter F. Murphy, "The Framework of Judicial Power," in *Introductory Readings in American Government*, ed. Robert J. Ross and William C. Mitchell (Chicago: Markham, 1971) ; Jay A. Sigler, "The Judicial Institution," in *The Performance of American Government*, ed. Gerald M. Pomper (New York: The Free Press, 1968) ; Kenneth Vines, "Federal District Judges and Race Relations Cases in the South," *Journal of Politics* 26 (1964) : 337–57; and Peltason, *Federal Courts in the Political Process*.

Constitution or statute which is supposed to guide the Supreme Court, and they admit of many interpretations. Hence, just as it is said that the Constitution is what the judges say it is, so it can be said that a Supreme Court decision is what the subordinate judges who apply it say it is.[31]

Judicial decisions are no more final and binding than a statute; like statutes, they can be changed or reversed. The courts are moved by politics just as legislatures and presidents are; all three institutions are part of the same political system.

[31] Peltason, *Federal Courts in the Political Process*, p. 14.

Suggested Readings

Abraham, Henry J. *The Judicial Process.* 2nd ed. New York: Oxford University Press, 1968. An introduction to the judicial process in the United States from a comparative perspective.

Allen, Carleton Kemp. *Law in the Making.* 6th ed. New York: Oxford University Press, 1958. A work that emphasizes the development of major legal systems.

Berman, Harold J. *Justice in the USSR.* Rev. ed. New York: Vintage Books, 1963. An analysis of the Soviet system of justice.

Cox, Archibald. *The Warren Court.* Cambridge, Mass.: Harvard University Press, 1968. An eminent scholar discusses the impact and approach of the U.S. Supreme Court under Chief Justice Earl Warren.

Danielski, David J. *A Supreme Court Justice Is Appointed.* New York: Random House, 1964. An examination of the process and politics of judicial appointments.

Mason, Alpheus, and Beaney, William M. *American Constitutional Law: Introductory Essays and Selected Cases.* 4th ed. Englewood Cliffs, N.J.: Prentice-Hall, 1968. An excellent basic introduction to constitutional law.

Shubert, Glendon. *Judicial Policy-Making.* Glenview, Ill.: Scott, Foresman, 1955. A systems-theory approach is used in reviewing the roles of the court in policy making.

————, ed. *Judicial Decision-Making.* New York: The Free Press, 1963. An excellent collection of behavior-oriented articles dealing with the judicial process.

Unitary and federal models of government

CHAPTER 17

Just before April 1 of each year, nearly $600 million is withdrawn from five banks in Chicago. This signals no financial crisis, nor is it an April Fool's prank. It is a legal and very profitable tax dodge, one that deprives the state of $3 million per year in tax money.[1] Illinois has a stiff tax on personal property. April 1 is assessment day, and any money on deposit in local banks can be taxed. But what if the money isn't there on April 1? In Chicago, it usually isn't. Large corporations convert their deposits into government bonds (which are tax-exempt) or move the money to banks across the state line. Then, after April 1, the $600 million magically reappears.

[1] This discussion comes from the *Wall Street Journal*, July 17, 1972, pp. 1, 23.

There are many similar stories. For years, the Southern Pacific Railroad bought switch locomotives from a General Motors plant in Illinois. But the railroad *officially* received the cars in its yard at Pine Bluff, Arkansas. Unlike Illinois, Arkansas had no state sales tax, and the company saved thousands of dollars. The state of Nevada is another favorite of businesses eager to avoid taxes. California companies, for instance, keep their inventories in Nevada and ignore local excise taxes.

These incidents pose a critical problem. How can we expect equal treatment under the law when we have so many state and local governments with inconsistent and often conflicting regulations? The federal system seems to encourage not only the loopholes, but all sorts of bureaucratic confusion. Suppose we care about water pollution. We learn that our state government is allowing companies to ruin a beautiful river which runs through more than one state. Should we expect and demand federal action against the polluters? Some people might claim that to do so violates our state's right to control its own affairs. Others ask whether this privilege is more important in a free society than its results—in this case, a polluted river. Some states insisted that they had the right to maintain segregated schools; in 1954, the U.S. Supreme Court held that they did not.

Some social welfare programs become too expensive for city or state governments. Help from the federal government may seem to be the obvious solution. But if the federal government pays for day-care centers in New York City, does it have the right to dictate educational policy? To hire and fire teachers? To decide which families are eligible for day care? Some citizens believe that these are matters for local initiative; others would prefer to have nation-wide standards imposed by the federal government. There are no simple answers to these questions, and they can lead to bitter controversy. In a complex technological society, all levels of government are asked to provide more and more social services, both efficiently and fairly, And the same problem keeps coming up, both in federal systems like ours, and in unitary systems like most countries': can the central government enforce national priorities without crushing local influence and minority viewpoints? This is one of the most serious and delicate political questions of our age.

Divisions of National Authority

To operate effectively, governmental authority should ideally be divided among central and local units. That way, the central government would not be overburdened by local problems that could more easily be solved by each community; at the same time, a centralized authority would assure equal treatment of each locality.

Whether nations choose to follow this ideal model depends on their own needs. A small country like Luxembourg does not require as complex a national government as the Soviet Union or the United States has. Nations divide central and local authority in two major ways: most have unitary systems of government; a few, like the United States, operate under federal systems. Before the present U.S. Constitution went into effect, we followed still a third form of government—a confederation.[2] In a confederation, states would have most of the power and would delegate very limited authority to the central government. No confederations are in existence today, however.

The Unitary System

Unitary governments have centralized administrative control. Although local and regional governments exist, their authority is quite limited, for the national government can dictate local policies at will. This is not the case in federal nations.

Most modern nations have unitary governments. Some countries (such as Ireland, Egypt, and Costa Rica) prefer the unitary model because their populations are fairly homogeneous; they do not need to protect the local prerogatives of many different minorities. Other nations have chosen to adopt unitary governments after periods of national disunity: the French people installed the Fifth Republic—with vast powers concentrated in the presidency, occupied by Charles de Gaulle—after experiencing the turmoil of the Fourth Republic. The new nations of Asia and Africa have used the unitary system in order to break down tribal divisiveness, hoping that national unity can be promoted through a strong central government.[3] In these states, as in other unitary countries, the basic principle of this form of government applies: all authority flows from the top down.[4]

Federal Systems

In a federal system, the central government and local governments share power. Usually, national defense, foreign policy, commerce, and monetary policy are controlled by the national government (sometimes called the "federal," or "central," government), while local officials take charge of such matters as education, sanitation, and policing. State and local governments have no veto power over the federal government, except in Switzerland, where

[2] Christopher Hughes, *Confederacies* (Leicester, England: University of Leicester Press, 1963).

[3] See Gwendolen M. Carter, ed., *National Unity and Regionalism in Eight African States* (Ithaca, N.Y.: Cornell University Press, 1966); and David P. Currie, *Federalism and the New Nations of Africa* (Chicago: University of Chicago Press, 1964).

[4] Ivo D. Duchacek, *Comparative Federalism: The Territorial Dimension of Politics* (New York: Holt, Rinehart and Winston, 1970), pp. 114–19.

a vote of eight of the twenty-two cantons can veto national legislation. Each state or local government can make laws without the approval of the other, although in certain cases federal courts, such as the federal district courts and the Supreme Court in the United States and the High Court in Australia, can rule that local statutes are contrary to national law and thus invalid.

Federalism exists in relatively few nations (see Figure 17-1). It is most often found in large countries, such as Canada and West Germany, where there are people from several racial or ethnic groups. Often the federal system will unite a nation that has strong minority groups who are anxious

Figure 17-1
Federal Systems of the World

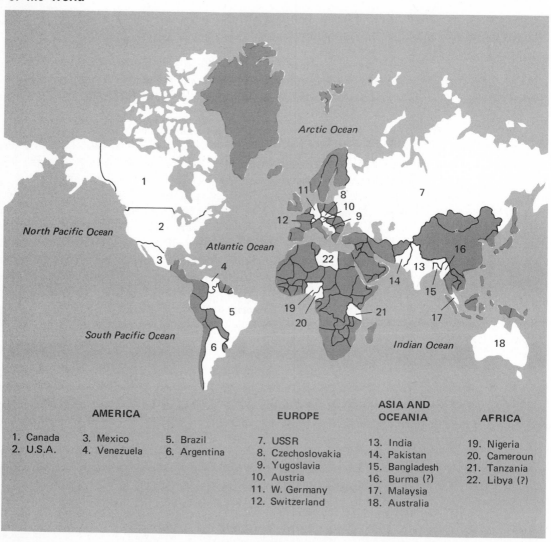

AMERICA		EUROPE	ASIA AND OCEANIA	AFRICA
1. Canada	3. Mexico	5. Brazil	7. USSR	13. India	19. Nigeria

1. Canada
2. U.S.A.
3. Mexico
4. Venezuela
5. Brazil
6. Argentina

7. USSR
8. Czechoslovakia
9. Yugoslavia
10. Austria
11. W. Germany
12. Switzerland

13. India
14. Pakistan
15. Bangladesh
16. Burma (?)
17. Malaysia
18. Australia

19. Nigeria
20. Cameroun
21. Tanzania
22. Libya (?)

Source: Ivo D. Duchacek, *Comparative Federalism: The Territorial Dimension of Politics* (New York: Holt, Rinehart and Winston, 1970), pp. 196–97.

to preserve their own identities. This has been the case in India where there are many distinct peoples—each with their own history, culture, and language. Some of the Indian states would not have joined the federal union unless it allowed enough local control so that they could maintain their own cultures.

Unitary Systems of Government

As we have said, unitary national governments have significant control over local authorities. They usually touch people's daily lives in more ways than a federal government would. For example, in France, elementary school curriculums are drawn up by the central ministry in Paris in order to reduce regional differences. Most unitary states have a national police force and exert total control over local militia units. Generally, there is only one court system, whose judicial officers are appointed by the national government.

Unitary governments might appear to be monolithic and awesome in their power. In reality, some central governments in unitary countries are quite authoritarian, while others, like that of Great Britain, follow the traditional republican model of democracy. Perhaps the most important difference among unitary systems is the degree of local authority allowed, which varies considerably from nation to nation.

Local and Regional Governments

Even in a unitary state, the central government cannot run all local affairs. Complete direction from the capital would be very unwieldy, and unwise decisions would probably result. Local units of government obviously must be given some areas of responsibility, but each nation has its own formula for the amount of local autonomy it will allow.

France, for example, holds a tight rein over its local governments.[5] The nation is divided into ninety-five départements, each run by a prefect appointed by the President of France and answerable to the Minister of the Interior. For every département, there is a popularly elected council with representatives of the arrondissements and communes (local communities). The councils can legislate on health, welfare, and sanitary matters and can vote a departmental budget; but virtually all of their actions can be vetoed by the prefect. He prepares the budget and can raise and spend money on matters of national law without council approval. Elected officials are left with little meaningful power.

[5] Our discussion follows B. Chapman, *Introduction to French Local Government* (London: Allen & Unwin, 1953); and Mark Kesselman, *The Ambiguous Consensus: A Study of Local Government in France* (New York: Alfred A. Knopf, 1967).

By contrast, in Great Britain, local governments maintain substantial authority.[6] All the counties and boroughs (cities) elect councils with standing committees for each area of administration. The councils control policing, education, and health and welfare matters. Parliament can always step into local affairs and override these officials; in practice, however, it intervenes only in emergencies, because the British people place a high value on local autonomy.

The Threat of Local Autonomy

Granting home rule to local communities can be a risky enterprise for the central government. In the developing countries especially, there are racial, ethnic, and religious minorities who claim the right to autonomous control over their own settlements. In some cases, they demand independence from the larger nation.

Generally, old and established unitary governments can allow more local self-determination than can newly created states. The young nations of Asia and Africa are often beset with economic instability and historic rivalries between minority groups. As a result, they sometimes see any plea for home rule as a movement for secession. If the Kurdish tribesmen of Iraq insist upon local autonomy from Baghdad, will they next push for independence from Iraq? How much governmental power can Cyprus deny its Turkish minority without risking civil war?

Only a secure government can allow effective decentralization. Yet in recent years, even established Western nations like Great Britain and Belgium have been shaken by demands for greater autonomy for minority groups—Catholics in Northern Ireland and Walloons in Belgium. The unitary system, with its concentration of power in a central government, might seem more likely to raise the fears and suspicions of alienated minorities. But these tensions exist in all parts of the world, in both unitary and federal nations. Such anxieties have led to violence and civil war in many states, both unitary and federal.

Pros and Cons of the Unitary System

The centralization of power in a unitary state can be a mixed blessing for its citizens. Clearly, the danger that movements for home rule may erupt into warfare is a serious drawback of unitary government. Such a concentration of governmental authority also suggests a wider problem. Many citizens feel that it is pointless to become active in local affairs if all power

[6] Our discussion follows H. Finer, *English Local Government* (London: Methuen, 1950); and E. C. R. Hadfield and J. C. MacColl, *British Local Government* (London: Hutchinson's University Library, 1948).

radiates downward from the capital; this feeling can turn into widespread alienation from the government and national political institutions. Furthermore, with national leaders so far removed from community problems—and citizens too disenchanted to make their views known—wise policy making may prove difficult.

On the other hand, the centralization of power in a unitary state can be a significant advantage in facing the problems of modern society. Clear lines of authority can be useful. In unitary systems, the central government can marshal economic resources and coordinate planning and development; its broad taxation powers make the task of financing social welfare legislation much easier. This may explain why many federal nations have become more centralized in recent years. In the United States, India, and West Germany, the federal governments have established national economic policies and have bankrolled social welfare programs.

The critical issue is whether federal systems provide a more workable solution to contemporary needs than the unitary systems. Do the advantages of allowing greater leeway to local communities outweigh the bureaucratic confusion and paralysis that can sometimes result in a federal system? Can federal governments mobilize sufficient resources to cope with national problems? Are people any less alienated from political institutions in federal states than they are in unitary states? The answers to such questions will suggest whether federalism is actually an improvement over the unitary system of government.

Federal Government: Structure and Organization

Advocates of federalism consider it preferable to the unitary model because it preserves local diversity, while simultaneously allowing the central government enough power to run the country. In reality, however, there is a great deal of variation in the *governing* of federal nations.[7] Some countries, such as the Soviet Union and Mexico, have become so centralized that some scholars wonder if they can still be called federal.

Because of the wide range of governmental models that are possible within the federal system, opinions often vary as to which governments are correctly labeled as federal. Nevertheless, many political scientists agree that a true federal government must meet ten tests. If it fails more than two or three, it is questionable whether it can properly be called a federal state.[8]

---

[7] The best comparative studies are Arthur W. Macmahon, ed., *Federalism: Mature and Emergent* (New York: Doubleday, 1955); Duchacek, *Comparative Federalism*; Valerie Earle, ed., *Federalism: Infinite Variety in Theory and Practice* (Itasca, Ill.: Peacock Publishers, 1968); and William H. Riker, *Federalism: Origin, Operation, Significance* (Boston: Little, Brown, 1964).

[8] See Duchacek, *Comparative Federalism*, Chapters 7–8.

1. The federal government has exclusive control over foreign policy.

2. Member states may not secede or unilaterally break their ties to the national union.

3. The national government may exercise its authority independently of the states and can impose its will without their direct approval or resources.

4. The constitution cannot be amended without the approval of the states.

5. The national government may not unilaterally change the boundaries of a member state.

6. Some significant powers must be reserved for the states.

7. The national legislature is bicameral, and the states are equally represented in at least one house.

8. A dual court system exists; each level of government has courts to enforce its own laws.

9. A national court interprets the constitution and can decide conflicts between state and national governments.

10. Authority is clearly divided between federal and state governments.

A true federal government, according to these standards, rests on a delicate balance between centralized power and local autonomy. This balance is being severely tested in many nations by the demands of contemporary society. Nevertheless, more than twenty countries in the world community retain the federal system. For these nations, the advantages of the federal model justify its continuance.

Why Form a Federation?

There are four basic reasons for starting a federal union.[9] The first is to escape the danger of military attack. By combining their resources, a number of small and weak states can defend themselves against a more powerful nation. On the other hand, federations are sometimes formed because member states are interested in aggressive expansion. The pooling of diplomatic and military resources of the states made Bismarck's Germany a major power. Federal unions can be created for economic reasons as well. Chad, the Central African Republic, and the Congo-Brazzaville formed the Union of Central African States in 1968 in an unsuccessful attempt to build a united market and production area. In some cases, a particular social class within a nation will prefer a federal system in the hopes of gaining

[9] See Riker, *Federalism*, pp. 12–16. Also useful, on the American system specifically, is Aaron Wildavsky, ed., *American Federalism in Perspective* (Boston: Little, Brown, 1967). Morton Grodzins's essay, "The Federal System," in the Wildavsky reader is especially helpful.

economic advantage. Charles Beard saw America's Constitution of 1787 as an attempt by the Founding Fathers to defend their property interests by strengthening the central government.[10] Finally, federalism is often the only way to protect national unity brought about by force of arms. After the termination of British colonial rule, India set up a federal system that allowed states like Bengal, Punjab, Marathastan, and Rajastan to maintain their own cultures while joining in the Indian nation. These states were jealous of their identities and would not have entered the federal union without a guarantee of local autonomy.

The Units of Government in a Federal System

Federalism protects local autonomy by creating different levels of government, each with its own responsibilities. In many federal states, there are three levels: the national (or federal) government; the state or provincial governments; and local governments. These units often form a pyramid: there are many local governments at the base, fewer state governments above them, and one central authority at the top. Countries with unitary systems are often divided similarly, but the lower levels of government wield little power.

County and Municipal Government. The basic units of local government, the county and the city (or a comparable unit in countries besides the United States), are generally created by the states or provinces. They operate under the terms of a charter granted by the state legislature, which outlines their structure and responsibilities. Generally, these charters can be amended *at will* by the state legislature.[11] For example, a state government can force a city to build a new sewer system or give police a salary increase.

Local government has five basic functions: (1) public safety, including maintenance of police and fire departments and public health offices; (2) assistance programs for the aged, handicapped, chronically ill, and needy children; (3) regulatory functions, such as zoning, consumer protection, and traffic safety; (4) public services, including schools, parks, and libraries; and (5) proprietary functions, such as owning and operating gas and

10 See Thomas R. Dye and L. Harmon Zeigler, *The Irony of Democracy: An Uncommon Introduction to American Politics* (Belmont, Calif.: Duxbury Press, 1971), pp. 23–55. The pioneering work on this subject is Charles A. Beard, *An Economic Interpretation of the Constitution* (New York: Macmillan, 1935). A criticism of Beard's thesis is A. C. McLaughlin, *A Constitutional History of the United States* (New York: Appleton-Century, 1935).

11 Good studies of municipal government and problems are Charles R. Adrian, *Governing Urban America* (New York: McGraw-Hill, 1955); and Advisory Commission on Intergovernmental Relations, *Metropolitan America: Challenges to Federalism* (Washington, D.C.: Government Printing Office, 1966). See also Chapter 21 of this textbook.

electric utilities. Many European cities own utilities, but few American cities do. On the other hand, a German city is likely to operate markets, theaters, and other enterprises that are privately owned elsewhere.

There are both advantages and disadvantages to making decisions on a local level.[12] One advantage is that the citizen is closest to his local government; he may influence officials and can see how a decision is made and what its effects are. Often, local governments can experiment with new programs more easily than larger units; the costs of failure are likewise lower. On the other hand, local governments may lack the money to finance social welfare programs, and their officials are sometimes poorly trained and occasionally corrupt. Local decision making can lead to duplication of services and poor coordination. When this happens, the responsibility for straightening out the bureaucratic mess may fall on the state government.

State and Regional Government. The relationship of the states or provinces to other levels of government varies in different federal systems. Generally, these units have their own governments and handle local problems within the limits of federal law.

In West Germany, each of the ten Länder (states) has its own constitution and government.[13] The Landtag (state legislature) can affect the conduct of foreign policy because it elects members of the Bundesrat (the upper house of the national legislature). The Landtag also can legislate on all local matters.

States in the Indian federation are given control over certain legislative areas, including education, agriculture, public health, forests, and fisheries.[14] There are also many areas (including marriage and divorce, civil law, and bankruptcy) in which states and the national government share authority. India is unique among federal states because its national government can proclaim a state of emergency, suspend the constitution, and take over the government of any state. In 1959, "president's rule" was declared in the state of Kerala after riots and disorders had wracked the state, and again in 1968, when political clashes led to a similar takeover in West Bengal.

Each of America's fifty states has its own government, which can legislate in any area not reserved to the federal government or to the people. Usually, education, welfare, civil law, property taxes, and licensing of professions are all state functions. However, in recent years, the federal government has expanded its activity in the areas of civil law, welfare, and economic regulation. In the early 1970s, for example, President Nixon threatened to withhold federal aid to school districts that did not meet federal standards for racial balance. Such federal action reduces the states' powers.

---

[12] William C. Mitchell, *Public Choice in America* (Chicago: Markham, 1971), pp. 284–87.
[13] See Peter H. Merkl, *The Origin of the West German Republic* (New York: Oxford University Press, 1963).
[14] See M. V. Pylee, *India's Constitution*, 2nd rev. ed. (New York: Asia House, 1967); and Norman D. Palmer, *The Indian Political System* (Boston: Houghton Mifflin, 1961).

National or Federal Government. Originally, the national government in a federal union was expected to handle problems the states could not solve themselves. Thus, central governments today regulate the nation's economy, control national defense and foreign policy, and guarantee the civil rights of citizens.

All federal governments insist that national law take precedence over state law. Members of the national legislature are usually elected directly by the people, rather than by members of state governments. The national executive is not under the control of the state government officials either. In presidential federal states, he is elected by the national citizenry; in parliamentary states, he is the leader of the majority party in the national legislature.

From its very beginning the United States has engaged in a long and stormy debate over the proper role of the federal government. Southern attachment to "states' rights" led to a clash with President Lincoln over the issue of slavery, and the nation erupted into civil war. In the 1960s, controversial U.S. Supreme Court decisions under Chief Justice Earl Warren prompted a campaign to curb the power of the federal courts. Senator Everett Dirksen even went so far as to try to call a Second Constitutional Convention to reverse the decisions of the Warren Court on legislative apportionment. Although he was unsuccessful, the debate about the limits of federal power continued into the 1970s. Some political leaders insisted that the concentration of power in Washington was perverting American federalism and endangering the well-being of the nation. At the same time, local governments and citizens continued to rely on a strong federal government for help in solving complex—and expensive—problems.

Federalism in Practice

There is often a gulf between the way a federal system purports to function and how it actually operates in practice. Although the division of authority may seem clear-cut on paper, it is seldom so well-defined in reality. Federal and state functions overlap in many areas, and no federal nation follows a textbook model of federalism. Both the Soviet Union and the United States are good examples of countries in which federalism exists in theory, but it does not work the same way in both countries.

Soviet Federalism. On paper, the Soviet Union is a highly decentralized federation: the sixteen constituent republics have the right to conduct their own foreign policy, and all are free to secede at will. The central government is given control over national defense, foreign trade, and economic planning and development, while all other functions are left to the republics.

Anyone who has read the Soviet Constitution might be convinced that Russia has a weak central government and strong regional governments.

In fact, the opposite is true. The Presidium of the Supreme Soviet (Russia's highest de facto government body) can veto any policy or law adopted by the ministers of any republic. Therefore, no republic can successfully oppose Kremlin policy. Also, none of the republics has an independent source of tax revenue, and they may not appropriate or spend money without approval from the central government. Thus, in spite of what the constitution says, the central government has almost complete control over the republics.

Marble Cake Federalism in the United States. In the United States, also, federal theory and practice differ. It is often unclear where federal responsibilities end and state responsibilities begin. Morton Grodzins has pointed out that the three levels of administration (national, state, and local) resemble a marble cake, with each layer rising and falling sharply and intermingling with the others.[15]

Grodzins cites the case of a sanitarian (public health officer) in a rural county of a southern border state to illustrate the complexities of American federalism. The sanitarian is hired by the state after being tested according to federal merit standards, and his salary is paid jointly by the state and federal governments. But it is the county that gives him his office and pays many of his expenses. His employers are not limited to the federal, state, and county governments, either. The chief city of the county also contributes to his salary and expenses, as well as approving him as an inspector. Thus, his title, office, salary, and expenses come from four separate governments. To which does he owe primary allegiance? The answer is all four. When inspecting food and drugs that will cross state lines, he is a federal officer. When inspecting milk and foods for local use, he is a state officer. When inspecting local butcher shops for cleanliness, he is a city officer. When inspecting the city's water supply, he is a state and county officer.

Defining what responsibilities are those of the central government, and which jobs should be handled at the state level, is one difficulty the federal system fosters. But this is only one of a few serious problems inherent in federalism.

Problems of the Federal System

Federalism provides the states with the advantages of increased military security and economic benefits, along with some regional and ethnic autonomy. However, these advantages are accompanied by some difficulties. Many federal countries suffer from the balkanization, or extreme fragmentation, of local government; from lopsided representation of state units in the national legislature; and from unequal distribution of costs and services.

---

[15] The discussion follows Grodzins, "The Federal System," in *American Federalism in Perspective*, ed. Wildavsky, pp. 257–58.

In some cases, this latter problem has brought on serious fiscal crises, which have become especially severe in the United States in recent years. The following sections focus on how the United States, the federal system we know best, is affected by these problems and attempts to deal with them.

The Balkanization of Government

There are currently approximately eighty-one thousand local governments in the United States, plus fifty state governments and the national government.[16] These governments often get in each other's way (as we saw in the example at the beginning of this chapter), and the taxpayer is frequently a prime victim.

The people of Fridley, Minnesota (estimated pop. 15,173) are taxed by eleven different governmental units: the town of Fridley, the North Suburban Sanitary Sewer District, the Minneapolis-St. Paul Sanitary District, the North Suburban Hospital District, the Soil Conservation District, Anoka County, the Minneapolis-St. Paul Airports Commission, the Metropolitan Mosquito Control District, an independent school district, the state of Minnesota, and the United States government (see Figure 17-2).[17] But the balkanization of Fridley is inconsequential compared to that of the San Francisco Bay area, which has 850 separate governmental units, and greater Chicago, with 1,113 governmental units. Even the little county of Blue Earth, Minnesota (estimated pop. 44,000) is subject to 155 local units of government, 105 state agencies, and 38 federal agencies. All can tax, regulate, or supervise Blue Earth.

With so many governments, problems can result. A recent example comes from Santa Fe, New Mexico.[18] A commercial land developer, the Sangre de Cristo Development Corporation, leased fifty-four hundred acres from the Tesuque Indians, planning to use it for a golf-resort community for fifteen thousand people. Under New Mexico state law, land cannot be divided for commercial gain inside a county, or within five miles of a city, without local consent. Yet the developers started to sell the land without local approval; they ignored the state laws, neglecting to apply for building permits or to pay property or sales taxes. How was the Sangre de Cristo Corporation able to do this? They claimed that they were immune from local and state laws on the grounds that Indian land is under federal, not state, jurisdiction. This loophole prevented the state from taking immediate action to end the land sales. Instead, it had to begin a long and bizarre

16 See Robert S. Babcock, *State and Local Government and Politics*, 2nd ed. (New York: Random House, 1962) ; George S. Blair, *American Local Government* (New York: Harper & Row, 1964) ; and Robert C. Wood, *1400 Governments* (Cambridge, Mass.: Harvard University Press, 1961).
17 Henry S. Reuss, *Revenue-Sharing: Crutch or Catalyst for State and Local Governments?* (New York: Praeger Publishers, 1970), pp. 39–41.
18 *The Christian Science Monitor*, October 27, 1972, pp. 1, 7.

Figure 17-2
Layers of Government, Fridley, Minnesota *

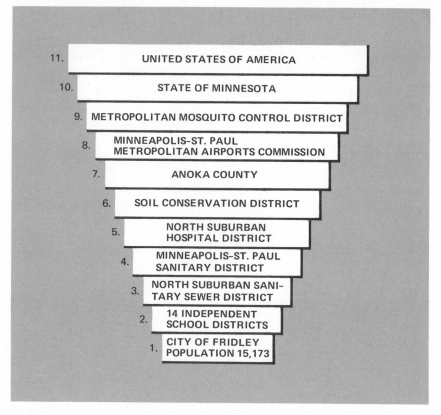

11. UNITED STATES OF AMERICA

10. STATE OF MINNESOTA

9. METROPOLITAN MOSQUITO CONTROL DISTRICT

8. MINNEAPOLIS–ST. PAUL
METROPOLITAN AIRPORTS COMMISSION

7. ANOKA COUNTY

6. SOIL CONSERVATION DISTRICT

5. NORTH SUBURBAN
HOSPITAL DISTRICT

4. MINNEAPOLIS–ST. PAUL
SANITARY DISTRICT

3. NORTH SUBURBAN SANI-
TARY SEWER DISTRICT

2. 14 INDEPENDENT
SCHOOL DISTRICTS

1. CITY OF FRIDLEY
POPULATION 15,173

* Believe it or not: A citizen of Fridley, Minnesota, is expected to exercise an informed control, through the electoral franchise, over 11 separate superimposed governments, and is taxed for their support.
Source: Henry S. Reuss, Revenue-Sharing: Crutch or Catalyst for State and Local Governments? *(New York: Praeger Publishers, 1970), p. 40.*

court battle to establish state and local jurisdiction over the land. Meanwhile, the company went on building and selling lots, and the city and county refused to provide services to the area.

Balkanization has also led to a crisis in our cities. The past decade has seen a migration of the middle classes from the central cities to the suburbs in all parts of the country. In New York City, the middle classes have moved to New Jersey, Long Island, and Westchester County, and they have been replaced in the cities by poor blacks from the rural South and newly arrived Puerto Ricans. The influx of low-income groups has increased demands on the city for welfare aid and remedial education, bringing new financial burdens to New York City just as its tax base is shrinking. If the entire metropolitan area had a single government, then the affluent suburbs (many of whose residents earn their livings in the city) could be taxed more fairly, and the financial plight of New York would be eased. But suburban areas, which would stand to lose by such an arrangement, are powerful enough in most state legislatures to block such changes. The Commission on the Cities in the Seventies, convened by the National Urban Coalition, saw metropolitan governments as a possible answer to urban problems.[19] But the recommendations of the commission, like those of the Kerner Commission [20] before it, have had little effect.

Unequal Representation

Another problem of federalism is that units of local government that are equal in size may not always receive equal treatment from the national government. In America, this inequality results from the overrepresentation of small, rural areas, which leads to the shortchanging of populous urban areas. In the Senate, Alaska, with 245,000 people, and Wyoming, with 330,000, have the same votes as New York and California, whose combined population is close to 35,000,000.

This inequality has a direct effect on the financial difficulties of urban areas, for they often lack the political muscle to win the federal aid that they rightly deserve. By contrast, the farm bloc has become the recipient of lavish federal subsidies, because of its lopsided representation. In 1967 New Yorkers each paid an average of $433 in federal income tax and received just $120 per person in federal grants the following year; meanwhile, North Dakotans paid an average of $177 each and received $357 per person in aid.[21]

There are other beneficiaries of this unequal representation. William Riker has argued that southern white segregationists have been overrepresented in the Senate; their relative strength has allowed racism to flourish.[22] Whites in both the North and the South have been able to use the federal system (with its many checks and balances and centers of power) to frustrate national efforts to end school segregation.

The Fiscal Crisis

The balkanization of local jurisdictions and the unequal representation of urban and rural states in the Senate contribute to the most pressing problem of American federalism—the financial crisis of the cities.[23] According

[19] Senator Fred Harris and Mayor John Lindsay, Co-Chairmen, *The State of the Cities: Report of the Commission on the Cities in the Seventies* (New York: Praeger Publishers, 1972), pp. 100–102.
[20] Established by President Lyndon B. Johnson in 1967 to study conditions in cities that might have led to the outbreaks of violence in the ghettoes.
[21] Harris and Lindsay, *The State of the Cities*, p. 105.
[22] Riker, *Federalism*, pp. 152–55.
[23] See also Chapter 21 of this book.

to the National League of Cities, in 1966 American cities faced expenditures of $61 billion.[24] They raised $40.2 billion in local revenues, and got $16.3 billion in federal and state aid, leaving a deficit of $4.5 billion. Six years later, expenditures jumped to $117 billion, and the deficit rose to $34.5 billion. By 1975 it is expected to reach the $50 billion mark.

Obviously, deficit spending like this cannot go on forever. Urban governments will soon be unable to borrow money, and high tax rates will drive more and more businesses and middle-class citizens to the suburbs. Their departure will mean even less money from property and income taxes, thus worsening the problem. Many suggestions have been made to deal with this crisis. (We will examine a few later in this chapter.) New York City legalized off-track betting to create a new source of tax money and quickly made millions—but not enough to end its troubles.

The fiscal crisis is especially damaging in the area of education.[25] Education is more expensive in the cities than anywhere else. Many children need

---

[24] Reuss, Revenue-Sharing, p. 30.
[25] The discussion follows Harris and Lindsay, *The State of the Cities,* pp. 50–55.

remedial programs, and well-organized teachers' and maintenance unions demand high salary scales and good benefits. Administrative costs are also high. Since 40 percent of the money to run schools is raised locally, usually through property taxes, poor cities tend to have little funding for education. In recent years, citizens in some places have chosen not to support public education, rebelling against ever-rising costs. Voters in Houston, Los Angeles, Philadelphia, and Youngstown, Ohio, have rejected important school bond issues. Youngstown was forced to close its schools for five weeks in 1969 as a result.

To make matters even worse, federal aid to education has not kept up with rising expenses. In 1967–1968 Washington provided 8 percent of local school revenues. This share fell to 6.9 percent by 1970–1971. Especially damaging were cuts in Title I money under the Elementary and Secondary Education Act (ESEA). (Title I gave federal aid to poor children.) But in only four years, funds per pupil under Title I in New York State, for example, dropped from $366 to $200, at a time when costs for education were escalating sharply.

Under federalism, rich communities can collect substantial property taxes and spend great sums on their schools, while low-income areas cannot do the same. In 1968–1969, Scarsdale, New York, spent $1,626 per pupil, and Beverly Hills, California, spent $1,131. But Boston could afford only $655 per child, and Detroit only $575 (see Table 17-1). The California State Supreme Court directly attacked this inequality in 1971 in the case of *Serrano* v. *Priest*. It held that the present method of financing education discriminates against poor communities. Possibly such court action will lead to a more equitable system in the future. At present, the cities face a difficult task in paying for the education of their children; and this is but *one* aspect of the financial plight of urban areas.

Table 17-1
Approximate per Pupil Expenditures for 1968–69

New York City	$1,031
Scarsdale, N.Y.	1,626
Los Angeles, Calif.	636
Beverly Hills, Calif.	1,131
Cleveland, Ohio	630
Shaker Heights, Ohio	968
Newark, N.J.	637
Tenafly, N.J.	922
Detroit, Mich.	575
Grosse Pointe, Mich.	875
Boston, Mass.	655
Newton, Mass.	842

Source: Department of Health, Education, and Welfare, *Urban School Crisis* (Washington, D.C.: Government Printing Office, 1970).

Possible Solutions to Federal Problems

In 1971 the City of New York expected a deficit of $800 to $900 million. Taxes were already high, and further increases might drive more people away from the city. In desperation, New Yorkers remembered 1969 mayoral candidate Norman Mailer's proposal to make New York City a separate state. The idea had been discussed in the city for a century, but in 1971 the Committee to Make New York City a State, led by Congresswoman Bella Abzug, was created. The committee was supported by more than a hundred congressmen, state legislators, and city councilmen, but it made an unsuccessful attempt to place a referendum for statehood on the November ballot.

The movement to create a fifty-first state was one of the more drastic solutions proposed to deal with the crises of an American city. Other possibilities for relieving the pressures on urban governments include federal grant-in-aid programs; revenue-sharing measures; plans to consolidate or coordinate local functions; and, on the other hand, efforts toward decentralization of city services and establishment of community control over local institutions.

Grants-in-Aid

There are approximately sixteen hundred programs of federal grants to state and local governments, ranging from flood control and water purification to school lunches and building construction (see Figure 17-3). These grants have become vital to the financial stability of many localities.

Generally, grant-in-aid programs require state and local governments to match (sometimes dollar for dollar) the money paid by the federal government. Thus, if a state wants $100 million from Washington for mass transit, it must put up $100 million itself. Ironically, poor cities and states often must bypass grant-in-aid programs because they cannot afford the matching funds. To cite one example, in 1967 Congress proposed the Rat Extermination Act to help health departments wipe out rats in urban ghettos.[26] One official complained that his city could not join the program because it would have to cut back drastically on other activities—such as mosquito, cockroach, and rabid-dog controls—in order to match the federal funding. Congress changed the bill to make rat extermination part of a larger effort at pest control.

At present, such federal grants account for 20 percent of the revenue of state and local governments.[27] The aid has generally gone for highways, welfare, and education; in fact, these three activities involved more than 80 percent of all federal aid in the early 1960s. Unfortunately, these grants-

[26] This discussion follows Reuss, *Revenue-Sharing*, p. 107.
[27] Frederick C. Mosher and Orville F. Poland, *The Costs of American Governments: Facts, Trends, Myths* (New York: Dodd, Mead, 1964), p. 53.

**Figure 17-3
Federal Aid to
State and Local
Governments**

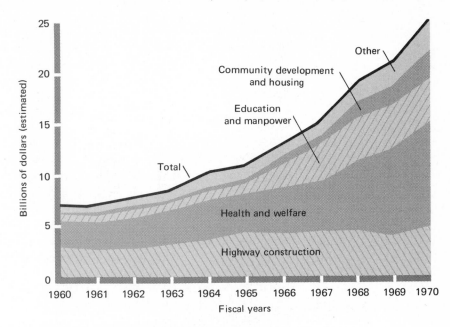

Source: Henry R. Reuss, Revenue-Sharing: Crutch or Catalyst for State and Local Governments? (New York: Praeger Publishers, 1970), p. 104.

in-aid cannot wipe out local deficits. Many cities and towns cannot use the programs because of matching requirements and the intricacies of applying for grants. In recent years, too, federal aid money has become much more scarce. In 1972 the Congress, with President Nixon's support, set up a $2.5 billion dollar ceiling on all social service grants.[28] Such grants had previously helped cities to provide for the needy, the aged, dependent children, narcotics addicts, and the mentally retarded.

Local governments have been hard pressed to make up for the loss of this money. Social service projects in the various states have become competitors as a result. If federal aid goes to narcotics addiction treatment centers in Philadelphia and Atlanta, there will be that much less available for programs in Cleveland and Denver, or for day care centers and other social services in any of these cities. What alternatives were left to local governments at a time when federal grants were being cut back drastically? One program designed to meet this crisis was revenue sharing.

Revenue Sharing

In revenue sharing, national revenues are directly distributed to local communities, with the amount that each locality receives based on its need

28 *The New York Times,* January 31, 1973, p. 51.

and its population. This idea originated in Europe, but spread to the United States in the late 1960s. In August, 1969, the National Governors' Conference called for revenue sharing as a means of taking advantage of the federal government's superior claim on tax dollars. Their plea was echoed by the U.S. Conference of Mayors, the Urban Coalition, Urban America, the National League of Cities, and the National Association of Counties. Since then, revenue sharing has been one of the most hotly debated political issues in the country.

President Nixon's revenue-sharing proposals were sent to Congress early in 1969, and again in his 1971 State of the Union Message.[29] He asked for a general revenue-sharing bill of $5 billion and a special revenue-sharing bill of $11 billion. The latter was earmarked for law enforcement, manpower training, community development, transportation, and education. After intense congressional debate, a general revenue-sharing bill was passed just before Congress recessed for the 1972 elections.[30] The bill set up a $30-billion trust fund to be distributed to local communities over a five-year period, according to a complex distribution formula. Poor central city and rural areas would be favored over more affluent suburbs in the allocation of the money.

But revenue sharing did not work out as expected. In early 1973 President Nixon proposed spending $6.9 billion on four types of special revenue sharing: urban development, education, manpower training, and law enforcement.[31] This was to replace what he called "seventy outmoded, narrower categorical grant programs." The Administration had accepted the concept of revenue sharing, but was using it as a replacement for a vast variety of federal aid programs. The revenue to be "shared" under the Administration's proposals would not come close to equalling the revenue that cities and towns would lose through the termination of the grant-in-aid programs. This redistribution could only deepen the crisis of local financing.

Consolidation of Functions

Some citizens concerned with city planning believe that reorganization may help to solve certain municipal problems. One way to reorganize is to assign some tasks to a specially created state authority. Groups like the Committee for Economic Development maintain that local governments should actually be combined (for example, in city-county units that would take over some of the functions of separate municipalities). Reducing the number of government units, theoretically, would mean that services could be provided more efficiently, without so much waste in effort and money.

[29] *Congressional Quarterly*, May 6, 1972, pp. 1000–1003.
[30] *Congressional Quarterly*, October 14, 1972, pp. 2701–5.
[31] *The New York Times*, January 31, 1973, pp. 51, 53.

In addition, the poor central cities could add wealthier suburbs, gaining a stronger tax base. There may be other motives for consolidation, however. In 1969 Richmond annexed forty-four thousand persons in surrounding areas. Since these people were mostly white, and Richmond had been 55 percent black, some argued that the main reason for the move was to reduce black voting power.[32]

The metropolitan, or regional, government has not really caught on in the United States. Our local governments resist giving up any function to a state authority or regional government. But Toronto, Canada, recently gathered thirteen surrounding municipalities into five boroughs and one city. The new metropolitan government serves over two million people—10 percent of Canada's population. Among other centralized services, one metropolitan police force has replaced the thirteen local ones (see Figure 17-4).[33] However, some feel that the answer for the United States is less, not more, consolidation.

Decentralization and Community Control

Although the financial crisis of American cities had become quite serious by the early 1970s, this was by no means the only problem resulting from federalism. Government had become more remote from the people, even at the local level. City administrations featured huge bureaucracies staffed with political appointees and entrenched civil servants. Citizens in poor urban areas, especially those from racial minorities, felt alienated from their leaders, and often with good reason.

To close the gap between the people and their government, many cities began to decentralize government services. In some cases, this meant only the establishment of local offices of city departments in various neighborhoods around the city, such as Mayor Lindsay's creation of "little City Halls" in New York. But there were also efforts to give neighborhood residents a more direct voice in local institutions by transferring some power away from central bureaucracies.

Attempts at decentralization were especially popular in urban school systems. Many administrators realized that ghetto children would learn more if schools were not seen as enemy institutions. They believed that by increasing parent involvement in the schools, they could create a partnership with community people and give children a better education.

While decentralization experiments were beginning, many inner city minority-group members—especially blacks, Puerto Ricans, and Chicanos —were feeling frustrated by the continuance of segregation in urban schools.

[32] Joseph F. Zimmerman, "Metropolitan Reform in the U.S.: An Overview," *Public Administration Review*, September–October 1970, pp. 531–43.
[33] *Reshaping Government in Urban Areas* (New York: Committee for Economic Development, 1970), p. 83.

Figure 17-4
Distribution of
Responsibility in
Metropolitan
Toronto

Others began to question the value of integration; they turned away from the goal of integration and instead demanded community control of the schools in their neighborhoods. They reasoned that since white parents controlled white schools, nonwhite parents should have the same right.

The most publicized experiment in community control took place in three districts in New York City: Ocean Hill-Brownsville in Brooklyn, the Two

Finance and Taxation		Water Supply		Health	
Assessment of property	M	Purification, pumping, and		Public health services	A
Courts of revision	MA	trunk distribution system	M	Chronic and convalescent	
Taxation of property	A	Local distribution	A	hospital	M
Debenture borrowing	M	Collection of water bills	A	Hospital grants	MA
Local improvement		**Sewage Disposal**		Ambulance services	M
charges	A	Sanitary trunk system		**Police and**	
Planning		and disposal plants	M	**Fire Protection**	
Official plans	MA	Connecting systems	A	Police	M
Subdivision approval	MA	Storm drainage	MA	Fire	A
Zoning	A	**Garbage Collection**		**Administration**	
Recreation/		**and Disposal**		**of Justice**	
Community Services		Collection	A	Magistrates' courts	M
Regional parks	M	Disposal sites	M	Court house and jail	M
Local parks	A	**Air Pollution**		Juvenile and family court	M
Recreation programs	A	Air pollution control	M	Coroner's office	M
Community centers/		**Public Education**		Registry and land	
arenas	A	Operation of school		titles offices	M
Municipal golf courses	M	system	A	**Licensing and**	
Municipal zoo	M	School sites, attendance		**Inspection**	
Regional libraries	M	areas, building programs	M	Business licensing	M
Local libraries	MA	Operating and capital		Dog licensing and pound	A
Grants to cultural societies	MA	costs	M	Marriage licenses	A
Road Construction/		**Housing**		Buildings by-laws	A
Maintenance		Low rental family		**Civil Defense**	
Expressways	M	housing	M	Emergency measures	M
Arterial roads	M	Elderly person housing	M	**Other Municipal**	
Local roads	A	Moderate rental family		**Services**	
Bridges and grade separations	MA	housing	A	Collection of fines	MA
Snow removal	MA	**Welfare**		Collection of vital	
Street cleaning	MA	Welfare assistance	M	statistics	A
Sidewalks	A	Hospitalization of indigents	M	Distribution of	
Traffic Control		Assistance to children's		hydro power	A
Traffic regulations	MA	aid societies	M	Harbor	A
Crosswalks	MA	Homes for the aged	M	Island airport	A
Traffic lights	M			Municipal parking lots	A
Street lighting	A			Preparation of voters'	
Pavement markings	MA			lists and administration	
Public Transit				of civic elections	A
Toronto Transit Comm.	M			Redevelopment	MA

M—Municipality of Metropolitan Toronto; A—Area Municipalities.
Source: *Reshaping Government in Urban Areas* (New York: Committee for Economic Development, 1970), p. 83.

Bridges area of lower Manhattan, and the P.S. 201 district in Harlem. All had an overwhelming majority of nonwhite students. Community governing boards, elected in local contests, were given a certain amount of control over schools in the districts. From the beginning, the United Federation of Teachers (UFT), led by Albert Shanker, opposed the experiment, fearing that it would threaten the teachers' tenure rights. When the Ocean Hill-Brownsville governing board and its district superintendent, Rhody McCoy, tried to transfer a few union teachers out of the district, controversy erupted. The UFT called a citywide teachers' strike, and racial and religious tensions in New York were badly inflamed. Eventually, the union's influence in the state legislature prevailed, and the movement for community control suffered a decisive setback.

Berkeley, California, a famous center of student activism throughout the 1960s, became the focus of another campaign for community control—this one for control of the police, in 1972. A referendum was placed on the ballot to divide the town into three police areas: one for the black community, one for the area where many white college students and "street people" lived, and one for the part of town dominated by white middle-class homeowners. Each area was to have control over its own police. After much campaigning, controversy, and nationwide publicity, the referendum was soundly defeated.

Despite these setbacks, the movement for decentralization and community control will probably continue through the 1970s. In many cities, neighborhood residents have united to fight urban renewal plans that might destroy the character of their communities. And alienation from vast governmental agencies is still widespread, especially among racial minorities. Many people can be expected to continue fighting for local control.

A Look at the Future

Both unitary and federal governments have been criticized often in recent years. Federal states have been condemned for their bureaucratic mazes and their inability to create effective national policies. Unitary governments have been called too centralized and too removed from local problems.

The future may see a combining of the features of each system. National governments could become financially responsible for all administrative functions, while local units may become more involved than ever in putting national policies into practice. Urban areas in America may experiment with metropolitan regional governments that will include city and suburban areas. At the same time, local authority may become more dispersed, with neighborhoods controlling their own schools, police, health services, and zoning codes.

What lies ahead is unclear, in the United States and elsewhere. But we do know that the traditional ways of dividing governmental power are having trouble meeting many of the challenges of our time. In a rapidly changing technological world, we may expect new methods of governing to fit the demands of the future.

Suggested Readings

Advisory Commission on Intergovernmental Relations. *Metropolitan America: Challenges to Federalism.* Washington, D.C.: U.S. Government Printing Office, 1966. An examination of the impact of metropolitan sprawl across traditional state lines.

Barghoorn, Frederick C. *Soviet Russian Nationalism.* New York: Oxford University Press, 1956. A study of the relationship between the Soviet republics and their national governments.

Earle, Valerie, ed. *Federalism: Infinite Variety in Theory and Practice.* Itasca, Ill.: Peacock Publishers, 1968. Studies of federalism in a variety of nations.

Elazar, Daniel J., ed. *American Federalism: A View from the States.* Essays on the development of the federal system and on the current controversies within the American federal system.

Macmahon, Arthur W., ed. *Federalism: Mature and Emergent.* New York: Macmillan, 1955. An excellent collection of essays, with Macmahon's study as a good introduction to the subject.

Riker, William H. *Federalism: Origin, Operation, Significance.* Boston: Little, Brown, 1964. A provocative essay on the origin and consequences of federalism.

Wheare, K. C. *Federal Government.* 4th ed. New York: Oxford University Press, 1964. A comparative study of federalism in Australia, Canada, Switzerland, and the United States.

FIVE

The Policies of Government

International relations

CHAPTER 18

Introduction

As nations try to apply their influence beyond their borders, as they pursue power and peace, as they attempt to ensure their survival, they often come in conflict with the goals and pursuits of other nations. American policy in Southeast Asia has collided with the interests of the People's Republic of China. Russian interests in Cuba were seen as a threat to the security of the United States. Israel and the Arab states are in continuing dispute over territorial objectives.

The pursuit of goals by nations—especially as they affect the goals and interests of other nations—creates the business of international relations. The interactions and transactions which result from conflict or compatibility of national goals and which are conducted or protected by governments constitute the business of international politics.

International Politics

The key words in the definition of international politics are "conducted or protected by governments." Many major events and transactions that cross national boundaries are conducted not by governments, but by corporations, private interest groups, and nongovernmental organizations. These interactions and transactions are a part of the international system, but without government, they are not a part of the international political system.[1]

For example, if the United States and France enter into a formal treaty commitment, then all conduct related to that treaty is immediately part of international politics. In contrast, if an American corporation purchases a subsidiary in France, the dealings of that enterprise are part of the international system, but they may not become part of the international *political* system until the French government places restrictions on operations and the corporate management seeks the assistance of the United States government in resolving the problem.

International and Domestic Politics: How Do They Differ?

It is tempting to make the analogy that international politics is simply domestic politics on a larger scale. We can look at the various alliances, systems, and subsystems on the international level and liken them to the regions, states, counties, and cities within a given nation. We might view international regulations and organizations as analogous to domestic regulations and agencies and departments. We can examine international and domestic politics, level by level, finding parallels at every step, until we reach the ultimate level—the question of sovereignty.

Within any nation there exists a final authority—an ultimate seat of power and decision making. (In Chapter 3 we defined a nation, or nation-state, as "any sizeable population with a distinct cultural identity that rules itself within formal territorial boundaries by an autonomous national government.") *Among* nations, however, there invariably exists a conflict of authority, and it is this conflict that creates international tension. As Hobbes maintained, "in all times, kings, and persons of sovereign authority, because of their independency, are in continual jealousies, and in the state and posture of gladiators, having their weapons pointing, and their eyes fixed on one another. . . ."[2]

[1] See Herbert J. Spiro, *World Politics: The Global System* (Homewood, Ill.: The Dorsey Press, 1966), p. 53.
[2] Thomas Hobbes, *Leviathan* (London: Andrew Crooke, 1651), Part 1, Chapter 13.

Sovereignty. Most nations have traditionally recognized that a nation's territorial limit extends three miles offshore into the coastal waters. Iceland, however, who depends for survival on her fishing industry, has claimed jurisdiction within a fifty-mile limit. The British, who have fished the waters off Iceland for over three hundred years, ignored Iceland's unilateral decision. In the spring of 1973 an Icelandic gunboat opened fire on a British fishing trawler which was casting its nets within fifty miles of Iceland's coast. A few days later, as the Icelandic lighthouse repair ship *Arvakur* attempted to cut the wires tying a fishing net to a British trawler, she was rammed repeatedly by a British tugboat and several trawlers.

Struggling to maintain what they believe to be their rights, and struggling for economic survival, Britain and Iceland have acted out that concept that marks the difference between international and domestic politics—the concept of national sovereignty.

Viewed in terms of the British-Iceland conflict, then, sovereignty becomes more than mere political rhetoric. It can be seen as more than just the musings of political philosophers such as Hobbes; it is more than an esoteric property that distinguishes the state from all other forms of political and social organization. It is, rather, the special characteristic of statehood which provides that the nation-state is subject to no higher authority than its own will. For practical purposes, therefore, we can define sovereignty as that condition in which there is no higher capacity for decision making.

Sovereign Equality. Hobbes, like other investigators of war-and-peace issues, suggested that if a state claims the right of sovereignty it must then grant that right to other nations. Even the United Nations, according to its Purposes and Principles, "is based on the principle of the sovereign equality of all its Members." [3] The presumption is that all states are equally capable of making independent decisions and that there is no higher authority for doing so. In reality, however, it is apparent that not all states are equally capable of executing decisions or of preventing the making of decisions that may affect their vital interests. It is also evident that some nations are less able to resist external influence upon their decision-making processes than are others. The point is, of course, that while sovereign equality may be acceptable as a doctrine, its implementation is dependent upon power. One nation may remain on equal footing with another only so long as it has the power to resist the impact and influence of that other nation. In true Orwellian fashion, all states are equal, but some are more equal than others.

Absolute Sovereignty. Governments tend to claim not only that they are sovereign, and that they are equally sovereign, but that they are absolutely sovereign as well. Absolute sovereignty—whether defined as the absolute right of a state to do what it wants within its own territory without inter-

---

[3] United Nations Charter, Chapter 1, Article 2, paragraph 1.

ference, or whether defined as the unlimited right of a nation to reach as far as necessary beyond its borders to achieve its aims—is another notion that is tied to power. Any state may claim absolute sovereignty; but the success of its policies depends largely upon its power.

Politics and Power in the Modern World

If the first building block of international politics is the doctrine of sovereignty, then the second must be the possession and use of power, for, as we discussed above, the ability of a nation to uphold its sovereign decisions and to extend its influence depends on that nation's power. Thus, we can define power in international relations to be the ability of a nation to use all of its tangible and intangible resources and assets, both internal and external, in such a manner as to influence the behavior of other nations in the determination of outcomes.[4]

In this definition, power should *not* be taken to mean force. The use of force is sporadic and relatively infrequent, while the application of power is virtually continuous in all social and political relations. Since our definition of power involves resources and capabilities as well as methods of application, we will examine the sources of power before we go on to an exploration of the reasons for and ways of using power.

Source of Power

Power, like sovereignty, must be more than mere rhetoric or attitude. It depends upon the capabilities that one nation, or group of nations, is able to bring to bear upon another. For example, a nation cannot threaten another with nuclear attack unless it (or one of its very close allies) has nuclear arms. Nor will a nation threaten economic ruin unless it commands sufficient economic power over another nation. The United States may coerce a Latin American country by a threat to reduce coffee imports, but the United States would not find such a threat very effective against the Soviet Union.

Power, then, depends upon accessibility (resources must be available for enacting the threat) and utility (the threat must be useful in affecting the behavior of another nation). In addition, power rests on credibility; if a threat is out of proportion to the value of the outcome, or if it is out of proportion to the resources of the nation making the threat, then it will not be believable.

---

[4] John G. Stoessinger, *The Might of Nations*, 3rd ed. (New York: Random House, 1969), p. 27.

What are the specific factors that make some nations more powerful than others? What are the tangible and intangible assets on which nations depend for influencing international events? The most basic—and most obvious—resources have to do with the physical properties of a country (its location, its size, its mineral deposits), and these are the determinants of power that we will examine first.

Geography. Size, terrain, climate, and natural boundaries are all important influences upon the volume and strength of a country's resources. Great Britain, for example, has frequently been able to repel invasions because of her position as an island. Similarly, a nation with many natural harbors stands a better chance of becoming an important commercial power than one with no coastline or major rivers to the sea.

Natural Resources. Even territorially large nations have not found themselves self-sufficient in the natural resources necessary for growth. Because mineral deposits are irreplaceable, exploitation leads to impoverishment and eventually to the necessity to seek external supplies. Thus, the U.S. petroleum industry has sought sources in Latin America and in the Middle East, despite its own supply.

Food, though cultivated, is also a natural resource that some countries find in short supply. The Soviet Union has had difficulty maintaining stores of food large enough for the population of that industrialized state.

As modern technology continues to require increasing amounts of materials such as manganese, tungsten, and uranium, which are found in only a few deposits, the industrial nations compete more feverishly for supplies.

The importance of natural resources is obvious: they provide the raw materials and the fuel for industrialization. Without natural resources and industry, a nation is unable to provide an adequate standard of living for its people and is unable to engage in trade which will bring it the commodities it does not otherwise have or produce. Without natural resources, a nation cannot prosper or defend itself.

Population. Although geography may determine the wealth in natural resources, and natural resources the industrial potential of the nation, all this is useless without a population capable of utilizing materials with maximum effectiveness. Just as there is no ideal size of territory, neither is there an ideal size of population. Underpopulation may result in the inability to exploit natural riches and to industrialize, thereby diminishing a nation's strength and influence. Some nations (such as Australia) have undertaken incentive programs to increase immigration. In nations such as India, where the problem is one of overpopulation, no solutions yet have been found to ease the burden.

A nation's power is determined not only by the size of its population, but also by its population distribution. Industrialization generally involves urbanization and growth, which in turn create increased demands for food and services. As cities develop and grow, the agrarian sector continues to be essential. As people are lured by the wages and the social and cultural attractions of the city, the danger of an imbalance to the economy becomes more apparent.

The ability of a nation to utilize its resources is also dependent in part upon the age distribution of its population. If a nation's power potential is to be realized, its population must include a large sector of people within the "productive limits." Labor laws and retirement standards in the United States, for example, establish that the normal productive life of employed persons is between sixteen and sixty-five years. Since the portions of the population that fall outside this range continue to absorb the resources of the nation, the state that is able to compete with others in external events is one that has the ability, through favorable age distribution, to maintain a constantly high level of production.

Government and Economics. Two important determinants of power are governmental efficiency and economic modernization. Only through efficient communication among political and industrial sectors is adequate coordination of natural resources possible. A government must be able to keep abreast of developments in all its geographic areas in order for its assessment of capabilities to be continuously up to date.

As mentioned before, economic strength is a potent determinant of power. The strength of a nation's economy affects its share of world trade, its capacity to offer rewards and enforce punishments in diplomacy, its ability to mount a technologically sophisticated defense, and its ability to make an impact upon prices and currency exchange.

Military Capability. There is probably no better measure of a nation's power potential than its military capability, particularly in a time of crisis. A situation that demands the use of military power is one that tests all of the human and material resources of a nation and measures its technology relative to that of other states.

Psychological Sources of Power. Whatever the extent of a nation's natural resources, the size and distribution of its population, the state of its economy, or the readiness of its military, its ultimate power in international affairs will depend, to a great extent, on its willingness to exert its influence. This willingness has to do, in part, with the self-image of a nation, and self-image is directly related to a nation's goals. If we know how a nation views itself, if we know what that nation values most highly, then we can begin to determine at what point and for which reasons a nation will be willing to wield its power. In short, we can begin to understand those factors that cause conflict among nations.

Conflict: Its Causes and Effects

As nations pursue their goals, they are bound to encounter other nations seeking objectives in the same places. It is likely that two nations bent on world power will, at some stage, come into conflict (though not necessarily armed conflict). But what of nations that hold peace to be their first aim? The United States, as self-proclaimed peacekeeper of the world, has come into conflict with China in Southeast Asia and with the Soviet Union in the Middle East and Cuba. And what of nations whose goals would seem to be compatible? The Soviet Union and the People's Republic of China are dedicated to extending a political system that they both hold to be beneficial to the peoples of the world; yet these nations have taken what can be described as, at best, an uneasy attitude toward each other.

In examining the goals of nations, we must keep in mind that what a nation professes to want is not always the same thing that a nation goes after; what a nation wants to do is not always what it is capable of doing; what a nation aims for is not necessarily what it eventually reaches.[5]

Goals as Cause. Organski divides national goals into four broad categories: power, wealth, cultural welfare, and peace. While no nation can be said to espouse only one of these goals to the exclusion of the others, most nations can be characterized on the basis of what they demonstrate to be their most important aim. National goals change with the times (wartime versus peacetime) and vary among types of government. In general, autocratic governments are more likely to be able to sustain and carry out unified, long-range objectives.

Some theorists maintain that there is only one overall national goal: power. As we have seen, power is essential to the sovereignty of nations. Because of this, perhaps all nations do have this goal to the extent of desiring to preserve their independence. But what of countries such as Sweden and Switzerland? For them, power can only be considered a means to an end: they must remain socially and economically powerful enough to protect their neutral stance *outside* the international power structure.

For the most part, nations do not compete internationally in order to acquire power; rather, they compete through the use of established power in order to attain or maintain influence over events and their outcomes. Power, then, is a tool as well as a goal.

Wealth, or the desire for economic prosperity, is a goal that is closely tied to power. If we look on wealth as the goal that motivates colonialism, industrialization, and control of trade, then the relationship to power is clear. If we accept economic strength as an important source of power, then the relationship is clearer still. Wealth, as a goal, however, can be pursued

---

[5] This discussion is based on A. F. K. Organski, *World Politics* (New York: Alfred A. Knopf, 1958).

as a domestic objective in which governments are primarily interested in raising the standard of living of their people.

The desire of a nation to preserve its culture sometimes comes into conflict with the goals of wealth and power. For example, Australia set a policy of denying entry to Asian immigrants at a time when it needed to increase its population for industrial purposes. At other times, the preservation of culture comes into conflict with the preservation of a particular political system, as when the Soviet Union expresses "official displeasure" toward the works of artists and writers which are deemed critical of the state. On occasion, acts and policies that might arouse public displeasure are excused by governments as being in the interests of national culture (as in Nazi Germany, for example).

The threat of nuclear warfare has made peace a more important goal than ever before. For nations in a position of power, peace is in harmony with their goals of remaining wealthy and powerful. For nations that are struggling for a position of power or for independence, peace may be a mixed blessing.

Image as Cause. Just as a nation's goals and related self-image may be a cause of conflict, so, too, the way a nation is viewed by others can provide a basis for fear or suspicion on an international level. Table 18-1 compares self-images with images held of other nations.

Often, two opposing nations hold similar images of each other. In 1968, for example, it was found that Americans and Russians viewed each other in the same way; they both saw the citizens of the other country as aggressive.[6]

Conflict Management. Conflict, according to Organski, can be handled on three levels: diplomacy, power struggle, and war.[7]

Diplomacy, as an art and as a way of dealing with conflicting goals, has long been practiced, especially by European nations. The arrangement of marriages among royal families was a sound diplomatic tradition. Alliances were formed, kingdoms rose and fell, and wars were fought or avoided on the basis of such marriages and all that they implied. Today, even though most monarchies have faded or have become impotent, diplomacy, as an art form or ritual and as a very real method for dealing with conflict, is vitally important in the international political system.

The relationship of the United States to China can be documented through a series of diplomatic encounters and attempts at encounter. Although the antagonisms, the conflicts in goals, and the potential for war between these countries are great, the two nations have relied, for thirty years, on diplomacy to resolve their problems:

---

[6] Richard H. Willis, "Ethnic and Natural Images: Peoples vs. Nations," *Public Opinion Quarterly* 32 (1968) : 186–201.
[7] Organski, *World Politics.*

In January 1945, Mao Tse-tung and Chou En-lai offered to come to Washington to negotiate with President Roosevelt. Their message never reached the American president.

Between 1945 and 1949, the United States tried unsuccessfully to mediate between Chiang Kai-shek and the Chinese Communists. The United States then backed Chiang and he set up a government in Taiwan after he was forced to retreat from the mainland. The People's Republic of China was proclaimed by the Communists in 1949.

In 1950 Truman sent the Seventh Fleet into the Taiwan Straits to deter a Communist invasion, and the United States made clear its intent to refuse recognition of mainland China or to permit the seating of Peking's representatives at the United Nations.

From 1950 to 1953, the United States forces fought mainland Chinese troops in Korea.

In 1954 the United States signed the Mutual Defense Treaty with Nationalist China.

In 1958 mainland China stepped up its shelling of the islands of Quemoy and Matsu as a test of the Mutual Defense Treaty.

In 1966 the United States modified its mainland Chinese position of containment and isolation to a position of "containment but not isolation."

In 1967 President Johnson used informal contacts in Warsaw to inform the Chinese that the U.S. was not planning a war with them.

At the end of 1969, the United States began to relax trade and travel restrictions on China.

In April 1971, the Chinese invited an American table-tennis team, with accompanying journalists, to tour China.

In the late summer of 1971, Henry Kissinger traveled to China and President Nixon announced that he would visit Peking on the invitation of Chou.

In February 1972, President Nixon visited the People's Republic of China, and a joint communique was released by the two governments stating their intent to pursue a spirit of cooperation.

When diplomacy fails, or is discarded, nations in conflict often become locked in a power struggle. The Soviet Union and China, Israel and the Arab States, the United States and the Communist nations—the struggles may go on for decades, changing in intensity but not in intent. Falling between diplomacy and outright war, a power struggle is often maintained on several levels: recognition (a byproduct of diplomacy, discussed later in this chapter) can be denied, trade can be stopped, sides can be taken, aid can be requested or given, incidents can be provoked, and small battles can be fought. At times, a power struggle can be alleviated through diplomacy (as

Table 18-1
National and Foreign-Image Profiles

Country in Which Survey Was Made	Australia			Britain					Germany						France		
People Described — Adjective	U.S.	Russ.	Self	U.S.	Russ.	Self	Fr.	Chin.	U.S.	Russ.	Self	Brit.	Fr.	Chin.	U.S.	Russ.	Self
Hardworking	33%	52%	43%	32%	53%	57%	24%	40%	19%	12%	90%	13%	4%	18%	37%	51%	46%
Intelligent	46	16	53	38	12	52	32	17	34	4	64	34	22	6	37	15	79
Practical	49	19	49	38	21	47	20	11	45	8	53	20	5	3	81	11	17
Conceited	42	14	17	52	13	11	29	2	15	3	15	23	20	—	24	14	30
Generous	40	4	63	52	3	48	14	7	46	2	11	14	5	1	34	7	62
Cruel	2	37	—	3	39	1	5	18	2	48	1	3	10	6	4	41	—
Backward	3	28	9	4	36	6	9	37	1	41	2	3	10	12	2	56	4
Brave	21	26	57	19	31	59	14	21	6	11	63	8	7	6	26	42	56
Self-controlled	18	15	26	10	9	44	3	15	11	3	12	24	5	5	34	9	12
Domineering	23	57	4	37	42	6	11	2	10	12	10	21	12	1	46	49	4
Progressive	77	25	39	58	21	31	14	8	58	2	39	17	7	1	75	19	34
Peace-loving	42	7	71	39	6	77	21	22	23	5	37	15	12	5	26	10	69
Impossible to characterize	a	a	a	8	18	5	30	32	17	34	5	34	49	71	4	12	3
Average no.: Positive adj.	3.3	1.6	4.0	3.0	1.6	4.1	1.4	1.4	2.4	.5	3.7	1.4	.6	.4	3.5	1.6	3.7
Neg. adj.	.7	1.3	.3	1.0	1.3	.2	.5	.6	.3	1.0	.3	.5	.5	.2	.8	1.6	.4

[a] Not tabulated.

Country in Which Survey Was Made	Italy			Netherlands						Norway			United States		
People Described (Adjective)	U.S.	Russ.	Self	U.S.	Russ.	Self	Brit.	Fr.	Chin.	U.S.	Russ.	Self	Russ.	Brit.	Self
Hardworking	39%	22%	67%	49%	36%	62%	23%	6%	12%	56%	36%	43%	49%	43%	68%
Intelligent	34	13	80	33	8	49	22	8	7	31	6	32	12	49	72
Practical	59	5	24	61	6	36	24	5	3	54	9	22	13	32	53
Conceited	22	12	24	15	10	14	24	10	2	11	7	19	28	38	22
Generous	60	5	41	40	3	23	7	16	2	39	5	31	3	13	76
Cruel	3	55	3	2	53	—	3	2	12	1	19	1	50	3	2
Backward	2	58	7	1	43	1	2	8	20	1	25	7	40	11	2
Brave	18	22	45	25	21	37	20	20	9	16	20	42	28	43	66
Self-controlled	16	4	5	16	3	36	34	3	9	15	5	21	14	35	37
Domineering	11	45	8	16	50	5	21	5	2	10	51	3	49	33	9
Progressive	32	13	17	57	15	43	17	10	4	42	7	27	15	25	70
Peace-loving	29	6	27	40	6	68	26	15	9	35	7	69	7	42	82
Impossible to characterize	9	20	7	10	13	8	22	46	54	13	31	8	17	15	3
Average no.: Positive adj.	2.9	.9	3.1	3.2	1.0	3.6	1.7	.8	.5	2.9	.9	2.9	1.4	2.8	5.2
Neg. adj.	.4	1.7	.4	.3	1.6	.2	.5	.3	.4	.2	.8	.3	1.7	.9	.4

Source: William Buchanan and Hadley Cantril, How Nations See Each Other (Urbana, Ill.: University of Illinois Press, 1953), pp. 46–47.

in the case of the United States and China), and at other times a power struggle can erupt into full-scale war.

Appalled at its effects, historians, political scientists, and other researchers have long sought to explain the causes of war. What is the trigger mechanism for war? Is there a recognizable point at which nations arrive at the brink of war? If so, is there some way to prevent the "inevitability" of its occurrence?

Inis Claude proposes that war is a result of several factors:

1. national "temper tantrums"

2. ignorance or misunderstanding of the facts involved in a crisis

3. national pride

4. lack of imagination of leaders

5. selfishness and cynicism of leaders

6. lack of proper machinery for settlements short of war.[8]

To examine the causes of war is to study the methods for keeping peace. In the following section we will investigate some of the ways in which nations have been able to maintain peace—or at least an absence of war—while pursuing their goals.

Keeping Peace and Achieving Goals

The international system that we know today is the consequence of a lengthy historical process that reflects changes in diplomatic conditions and international power distributions. As the power structure has changed, nations have developed a variety of strategies for maintaining their influence. They have also developed a system of international law and a structure of international organization in the hope of containing the power drive within the bounds of peace.

Balance of Power

In general, the expression "balance of power" is used to describe any power distribution. More specifically, it refers to an equilibrium in which individual nations or groups of nations check each other's power. In other

---

[8] Inis L. Claude, Jr., *Swords into Plowshares* (New York: Random House, 1956).

words, when there is a balance of power, no one state or alliance is strong enough to impose its will upon the rest.[9]

Whether or not a true balance of power has ever existed has been the subject of much debate. Organski sees international conflicts today as being governed by the principle of power transition rather than power balance. Newly arrived powers challenge the old powers for a redistribution of colonies, markets, and industry, and these challengers may draw to their side some lesser nations which feel exploited by the old powers.[10] In this century, the United States and Russia have replaced England, France, and Germany as the leading powers, and in the next century, China and Japan might very well replace the United States and the Soviet Union.

Bipolarity and Multipolarity. The diplomatic, political, and military conditions that emerged after World War II were so profound as to bring entirely new characteristics to the international system. The process of reducing the number of great powers, already begun by World War I, reached its conclusion with the emergence of two giants: the United States and the Soviet Union.

This bipolarity resulted from several conditions. First, the European nations that were involved in the world wars were temporarily diminished in power. Second, traditional methods of diplomacy had failed, and new ones had yet to be found. The failure of diplomacy was largely a result of the third characteristic of the age—namely, ideological conflict, or the tendency for nations to adopt either of only two sets of governmental principles: democracy-capitalism or communism-socialism. The combined effect of these factors was the establishment of a power distribution known as tight bipolarity. This is defined as an international system in which all, or virtually all power is clustered around two major poles.

The word *tight* is used simply to describe the quality of cohesion in a bipolar system. It indicates that, for military and ideological purposes, the tendency of second- and third-ranking states is to cling very tightly, in extreme dependence, to the major powers.

International political patterns underwent major changes from 1955 to 1965. In the Soviet sphere of influence, there was a growing tendency toward polycentrism in Eastern Europe in which the decision making in Moscow gave way to demands on the part of her satellites. At the same time, the People's Republic of China and the Soviet Union had a growing disaffection for one another. The Western counterpart of these strains was located principally in Western Europe, where postwar recovery began to break American

[9] Inis Claude, Jr., sees the balance of power as a function of the never-ending struggle for power and dominance in international relations. Claude, *Power and International Relations* (New York: Random House, 1962).

[10] Organski, *World Politics*, especially the chapter entitled "Goals and Patterns of Conflict."

control over economic and political decision making. Thus, while it could not yet be said that bipolarity had broken down, the tightness of the configuration began to give way, resulting in loose bipolarity.

Today there is a growing tendency to identify the international power distribution as one of multipolarity, based on the argument that China has now achieved the status of a distinct pole, that the uncommitted countries comprise a separate pole, and that Western Europe and Japan have virtually terminated their dependence upon the United States. It is clear, however, that neither China, Europe, Japan, nor the Third World (uncommitted countries) will, in the near future, be able to make entirely independent military, diplomatic, or political decisions. Ideology, alone, binds some of these countries to one of the giants, and lack of significant nuclear strength makes dependence even more necessary. At present, the international system appears to be in transition from loose bipolarity to multipolarity.

Collective Security. In international relations, the concept of collective security embodies the principle that everyone is his brother's keeper.[11] The primary motive behind efforts at international organization in our century, collective security means that aggressive and unlawful force by any nation against another will be met by the combined force of all nations. As originally conceived by President Wilson, collective security would not be an alliance system; rather, it would be a global substitute for alliances and other attempts at achieving a balance of power.

Although collective security has not been realized within the world community, the desire for it has not been abandoned. To date, however, its support has come more in the form of words than in the shape of deeds.

Strategies for Power and Peace

Unable to implement collective security, nations resort to a variety of strategies in order to preserve their sovereignty, pursue their goals, and extend their power and influence. While working together toward a system of world government, nations also work alone to promote their interests. They wield power and test the power of other states through such strategies as brinkmanship, conciliation, deterrence, and recognition. They woo with aid and pressure with boycott. They arrive at mutual satisfaction through negotiation and treaty, and through controlled conflict.

Brinkmanship. The strategy of brinkmanship is based on a nation's show of readiness to risk war. This is a highly coercive technique which requires a credible threat and show of force. For example, in 1938 Hitler was more ready to risk war than was the rest of Europe, thus giving him a bargaining

[11] This discussion is based on Claude, *Swords into Plowshares.*

advantage over Prime Minister Chamberlain, who was interested in avoiding a conflict.

The threat of nuclear warfare lends new proportions to the concept of brinkmanship. On the one hand, the possession of nuclear power may enlarge the strategic options of a state which knows that another state is not capable of nuclear retaliation. In a bilateral nuclear situation, however, the possibility of nuclear retaliation makes the brink so sensitive that the benefits of nuclear power are diminished. In this situation, the most productive step is often withdrawal from the brink rather than further escalation.

In situations where the risks of brinkmanship are great, governments have sought to develop ways of assessing the dangers of various actions. Game theory, a branch of applied mathematics, is one approach that provides a decisional model for determining the most advantageous policies in conflict situations.[12] According to game theory, parlor games (such as bridge or poker) have certain features in common with social and political conflict situations: the existence of opposing interests; the lack of complete information by the participants, as in poker; the interplay of rational decisions, as in chess; and chance factors. In game theory, the strategy is to seek the most favorable result: try to win, but if a win is impossible, then try to give up as little as possible; the "game plan" should include a guarantee of a certain minimum outcome, regardless of what the opponent decides or what chance introduces.

If U.S. decision makers were to use game theory to decide how to respond to a Soviet threat to back the Arab nations in a total war against Israel, they would have to ask themselves several questions before constructing a game plan: (1) What strategies are available to the United States? (2) What strategies are available to the Soviets? (3) What would be the outcome of the possible pairings of strategies? (In other words, if the Soviet Union does this, and the United States does that, then what would result? (4) What value does the United States place on the various outcomes? (5) What value is the Soviet Union thought to place on these outcomes? Only after answering these questions, could the United States begin to map out its strategy—whether to go for a win, and how to go for it; whether to go for the smallest possible loss; or whether to withdraw from the conflict.

Conciliation and Deterrence. Deterrence is a strategy used by states to make it clear to other states that the costs of aggression will be unacceptable. Conciliation describes a condition of mutual agreement to settle differences.

Although World War II did not necessarily *result* from a policy of conciliation, it did *follow* such a policy. However, even with the advantage of hindsight, political scientists cannot agree that a policy of deterrence

[12] This discussion is based on Richard C. Snyder, "Game Theory and the Analysis of Political Behavior," in *International Politics and Foreign Policy,* ed. James N. Rosenau (New York: The Free Press, 1961); and Thomas C. Schelling, *The Strategy of Conflict* (Cambridge, Mass.: Harvard University Press, 1960).

would have prevented war. Deterrence may stave off war, but it may also close the door to a settlement which would abolish the need for deterrence. By the same token, conciliation may also stave off war, but it can lead to disaster if the motives of the antagonist are misjudged.

Recognition. Recognition as an international political strategy can take four forms. Most common is recognition of the formation of a new state, such as the numerous recognitions of Bangladesh. Second most common is recognition of the establishment of a new political regime, as in the initial U.S. recognition of Castro's Cuba in 1959. Third, governments may often recognize one another as economic partners without establishing formal diplomatic relations, as is the case with the growing Sino-American trade relationship. A fourth situation, although rare, occurs in time of war when belligerent nations recognize the commercial rights of neutral nations.

Foreign Aid. Although foreign aid can serve a very humane purpose, it can and does also serve as a tool by which the donor nation extends its power and influence to recipient nations.[13] Like any instrument of policy, it has its limits; it does not always produce the desired results in terms of the recipients' long-range political evolution. Neither, however, is it always successful from the donor's point of view.

Roughly half of United States economic assistance is administered through the Agency for International Development (AID). The remainder is channeled through a multitude of non-AID programs, including the Food for Peace program, Peace Corps programs, long-term loans from the Export-Import Bank, and various United Nations agencies.

Figure 18-1 shows the allocation of United States Overseas Loans and Grants from 1949 to 1966. The countries that received aid in any given period are the ones in which the American government wished to wield influence at the time. Table 18-2 provides a look at U.S. foreign aid in 1970. The amounts of money spent provide ample testimony to the importance a major power places on the political efficacy of foreign aid.

Pressures and Boycotts. Although relatively new as instruments of power in international politics, pressures and boycotts have sometimes been found effective as strategies for influence.

In the 1970s, the multilevel boycott of South Africa for her aparthied policy has received a great deal of attention from the press. In sports, she has been excluded from participating in international cricket, rugby, tennis, soccer, and Olympic Games. Economically, she has been threatened by foreign corporations who do business in the country. Socially, she has been under pressure from her neighboring states to change her internal policies.

The proof of the effectiveness of pressure and boycott can be seen in the

---

[13] This discussion is based on Joan M. Nelson, *Aid, Influence, and Foreign Policy* (New York: Macmillan, 1968).

Figure 18-1
Changing Geographic Allocation of U.S. Economic Aid, 1949–1966 (A.I.D. and Predecessor Agencies)

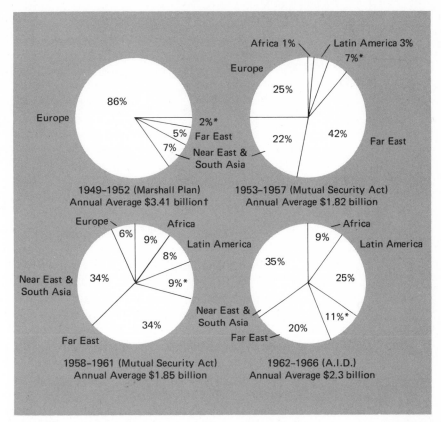

1949–1952 (Marshall Plan)
Annual Average $3.41 billion†

1953–1957 (Mutual Security Act)
Annual Average $1.82 billion

1958–1961 (Mutual Security Act)
Annual Average $1.85 billion

1962–1966 (A.I.D.)
Annual Average $2.3 billion

* Contributions to international organizations; administrative and other nonregional expenses.
† Period covers four-and-a-quarter years, from April 1948 through fiscal year 1952.
Source: A.I.D., U.S. Overseas Loans and Grants, 1945–1965, and Operations Report, FY 1966.

results. Sports-loving South Africans have begun to allow blacks from their country to take part in sports events, and they have permitted mixed teams from other countries to play in South Africa.[14] Foreign corporations, such as General Motors and Polaroid, with plants operating in South Africa, have been pushed to improve working conditions for black employees. The presence in South Africa of black diplomats important to the nation's foreign policy has forced South Africa to open formerly all-white hospitals and suburban homes to them.

The success in the South African example is offset, however, by the ineffectiveness of the global boycott against Southern Rhodesia. Despite a United Nations Security Council decision in 1967 to impose an economic embargo on the Smith regime, many nations have found escapes from the

[14] Anthony Lewis, "When Pressure Works," *The New York Times*, May 12, 1971.

Table 18-2

U.S. Foreign Aid, Calendar Year 1970 (in millions)

Region	Net Grants
Military grants	$ 679
Western Europe	3
Eastern Europe	9
Near East and South Asia	228
East Asia and Pacific	686
Africa	162
Western Hemisphere	200
Other and unspecified	449
TOTAL	$2,418

Source: Office of Business Economics, U.S. Department of Commerce.

obligation. The United States, for example, continues to import chromium despite U.S. participation in the decision to sanction. Due to this and other failures of implementation by other governments, the boycott has not had a substantial effect on Rhodesia's economy.

Negotiations, Agreements, and Treaties. Although negotiations have long been an important means for settling international disputes, the process has gained long-lasting public attention in recent years because of the lengthy Vietnam "peace talks." Arthur Lall defines negotiation as "the process of consideration of an international dispute or situation by peaceful means, other than judicial or arbitral processes, with a view to promoting or reaching among the parties concerned or interested some understanding, amelioration, adjustment, or settlement of the dispute or situation." [15]

Negotiations can be inhibited by several factors: disparities in power levels (as between the United States and Cuba), prior international commitments (the U.S. commitment to South Vietnam), or self-image (an emerging nation that takes a rigid negotiating posture). A country that has suffered a reduction in power is generally more willing to negotiate than is a nation on top or on its way to the top. [16]

International agreements are arrangements or understandings between or among nations. Treaties are formal agreements. They are made possible as a form of international strategy by the existence of common problems, and they offer a means by which nations can achieve some part of a common goal together.

Arms control is one problem that nations have attempted to solve through agreement and treaty. Pollution of the environment and skyjacking are two other areas in which international agreement is beginning to be reached.

[15] Arthur Lall, *Modern International Negotiation: Principles and Practice* (New York: Columbia University Press, 1966).
[16] *Ibid.*

International Organizations

Taken in the broadest sense, international organization encompasses all forms of institutionalized multinational diplomacy. The problem is, then, to separate from the broad concept the particular forms of multinational institutions so that we have some basis for distinguishing among institutions such as NATO, the Common Market, and the International Court of Justice. Although there are several bases, and sub-bases, on which organizations may be characterized, we will examine them here in three divisions: the security organizations, other functional organizations, and the legal organization. Because the United Nations, by design and by action, cuts across these categories, this organization will be discussed separately.

Security Organizations. An organization dedicated to the security of its members is created or necessitated by hostile external competition or confrontation. Among these organizations, the most typical take the shape of institutionalized alliances (NATO, SEATO, the Warsaw Pact), an alliance by pledge without formal structure (the Japanese-American Treaty of Mutual Assistance), or a tacit agreement based on the identification of mutually shared objectives (U.S. aid to Israel, Soviet assistance to the Arab states).

In general terms, the politics of security is the politics of power coalition —a concept that is virtually as old as human relations. In modern international relations it dates back to the origins of the system of multiple national units of the period from 1815 to 1914. From the end of the Napoleonic Wars to the beginning of World War I, the international system was a confusion of shifting alliances as nations switched their positions i.. the hope of safeguarding peace by offsetting power potential.

Despite the attempts by the League of Nations and the United Nations to organize for collective security, alliances are once again a visible feature of international politics. Since World War II, nations have chosen to align themselves not only on political issues but into military blocs as well. The alliances with which we are so familiar today, such as NATO, SEATO, and the Warsaw Pact, exist expressly because their members have perceived the existence of military threat. Alliances, therefore, might more correctly be considered instruments not of collective security, but of collective self-defense (or "selective security") among friends.

The Warsaw Pact, signed on May 14, 1955, states as its purpose that it will "provide for consultation on common interests and for mutual assistance in case of military attack." The North Atlantic Treaty, signed in April 1949, binds its members to an agreement "that they would separately and jointly, by means of continuous and effective self-help and mutual aid, maintain and develop their individual and collective capacity to resist armed attack." The Treaty goes on to an agreement that "an armed attack against one or more of them in Europe or North America shall be considered an attack against them all. . . ."

Statesmen and analysts have by now generally accepted collective security as either an idea before its proper time, or an idea which, in current circumstances, is sadly outdated. Accordingly, they have turned the attention of the U.N. to a new mechanism—peace-keeping. Designed in 1956 by Dag Hammarskjold for maintaining peace in the Middle East, and used twice subsequently in the Congo and in Cyprus, peace-keeping involves the deployment of a lightly armed international force to a position between combatants in order to prevent further armed clashes. This method is intended to achieve peace in the short run by physical interposition, and in the long run by securing time for productive diplomacy. It is apparent, however, that this mechanism has no useful application in disputes that directly involve the major powers.

Functional Organizations. Since security organizations exist for a single purpose, they are considered by many to be functional organizations. However, in its traditional form, functionalism focuses on those aspects of human need and desire outside the realm of the political.[17] Therefore, a functional organization would not concern itself with Soviet-American power politics on the Indian subcontinent but would concentrate instead on concrete organizational tasks, such as how to increase the food supply, how to implement birth control, or how to raise the literacy rate. The functional approach to international relations "should help shift the emphasis from political issues which divide to those social issues in which the interest of the peoples is plainly akin and collective; to shift the emphasis from power to problem and purpose."[18] However, even functional efforts are often undermined when nations attempt to politicize the function. For example, the 1972 U.N. Conference on the Human Environment in Stockholm was marred by the politicization of such issues as membership, American use of defoliants in Southeast Asia, and disassembling of nuclear stockpiles.

While the European Common Market and the Soviet bloc Council for Mutual Economic Assistance (CMEA) have obvious political implications, their stated purposes are functional. The Common Market has as its goal the promotion of close economic cooperation among its members. CMEA was organized "to promote the coordinated development of the national economies and the acceleration of economic and technological progress in the member states."

The most clear-cut examples of functionalism can be found in structures such as the International Labor Organization, the Food and Agriculture Organization of the U.N., and UNICEF. Functionalists predict that as organizations such as these succeed in their respective tasks, the "international order" will inevitably be strengthened at the expense of nationalism and power politics.

[17] Ernst B. Haas, *Beyond the Nation-State: Functionalism and International Organization* (Stanford, Calif.: Stanford University Press, 1964).
[18] David Mitrany, quoted in Haas, *Beyond the Nation-State*, p. 7.

Legal Organization. The law of nations emerged in the Renaissance and Reformation along with the modern European state system and the doctrine of sovereignty.[19] Law was able to arise among the states of Europe because of their common cultural background. Shared values led to a sense of shared responsibility for conduct and social concern.

International law is based not only on the principles of sovereignty and shared responsibility, but also on the doctrine of fundamental rights and the consent of regulation. The sources of today's international law are treaties, international custom, the general principles of law recognized by civilized nations, and judicial precedent.

The International Court of Justice (ICJ), often called the World Court, was established in 1945 and is seated in The Hague. Created by United Nations Charter, the ICJ consists of fifteen judges elected for renewable nine-year terms by separate majority votes of the U.N. General Assembly and Security Council. Although the court's membership is equal to that of the United Nations, it has no jurisdiction in disputes among these nations unless the governments themselves consent, either in advance or at the time of conflict.

The limitations of the court are apparent in the matter of the Icelandic-British fishing dispute. West Germany joined the dispute on the side of the British, and the two nations took the problem to the International Court of Justice. But Iceland denied the court's jurisdiction and declined to defend her actions before the court on the ground that defense of the territorial sea is a matter exclusively for domestic jurisdiction.

The United Nations. The primary global, multipurpose organization of our age is the United Nations.[20] It is capable of discussing, within limits, virtually any issue that its members wish to have discussed. It serves two fundamental purposes simultaneously: it is another of several vehicles for the implementation of members' respective foreign policies, and it is a collective institution capable of undertaking independent action.

The statesmen who assembled at San Francisco in 1945 at the United Nations Conference on International Organization did so with the hope that succeeding generations might be saved "from the scourge of war." Their fundamental intent was to improve international responsibility and to spread out decision making in order to diffuse the potentially catastrophic consequences of sovereignty. Collective security—the hope that the all-against-one concept might deter international aggression—was revived as the basic method of organizing force against potential war. Yet those who drafted the United Nations Charter provided that "nothing in the present Charter

---

[19] This discussion is based on J. L. Brierly, *The Law of Nations*, 6th ed. (New York: Oxford University Press, 1963).

[20] The term *global organization* is used here to distinguish the United Nations from other types of organization, such as regional (the Organization of American States) and ethnic or cultural (the British Commonwealth).

"Tell you what I'll do. You back me on the Trusteeship issue and my wife will lend your wife our Mrs. Twickins for two afternoons a week."

shall impair the inherent right of individual or collective self-defense if an armed attack occurs against a Member of the United Nations. . . ."[21] Chapter 8, which follows immediately, establishes the framework with which "Regional Arrangements" may be organized for defensive purposes. Under these provisions, the United Nations permits members to circumvent the principle of collective security and to revert to the mechanism of the interstate alliance.

Dag Hammarskjold, the U.N. Secretary-General from 1953 until 1960, argued that, despite its apparent weaknesses and contradictions, the U.N. could be thought of as "a dynamic instrument of government. . . ."[22] Although Hammarskjold did not pretend that the U.N. has supranational capability, he nevertheless maintained that the organization's capacity as an international force is not limited to the absolute agreement of the member states. In essence he believed that the United Nations is the sum of its members plus one—the additional one being the organization itself.

Unfortunately, the two occasions upon which the U.N. attempted to be most innovative in terms of collective decision making led to controversies of major proportions. One occasion was the creation of the United Nations Emergency Force for the Middle East in 1956 by the General Assembly, which touched off a diplomatic battle regarding the authority of the General Assembly to intervene in matters relating to the maintenance of international

[21] United Nations Charter, Chapter 7, Article 51.
[22] Dag Hammarskjold, "Two Differing Concepts of United Nations Assayed," *UN Review* 12–17 (1961): 12.

peace and security. The other incident was the Secretary-General's handling of his instructions from the Security Council relating to the U.N. operation in the Congo in 1960. In the latter instance, the Soviet Union charged that the Secretary-General acted in a pro-Western manner, and this charge precipitated a life-or-death crisis for the United Nations.

In nonsecurity matters, the history of United Nations innovation is much brighter. By its functional activities, the U.N. has contributed to the resolution, or easing, of many of the problems which lie behind international conflict. International economic development, elimination of colonialism, peaceful uses of atomic energy, protection of human rights, concern for the environment—these and scores of other issues have shaped the U.N.'s role in the modernization of international relations.

Conclusion

What of the future? Will the nations of the world—each struggling to maintain its sovereignty, each seeking to realize its goals—cooperate with others to achieve peace and security? Will concern for national security give way to action for international good? Can functionalism reduce the quest for power? Can international law prevail over national or regional outrage?

International institutions, while not flawless mechanisms for the transformation of the international system, are more than simply the vehicles of the foreign policies of their most powerful members. Together, modern international organizations have contributed to the peaceful transformation of the international system, not so much by compelling the uncooperative as by dealing collectively with some of the causes of war: poverty, starvation, disease, inadequate communication, and so on. The questions asked here cannot be answered in the affirmative on the basis of our current record. However, we need not look upon our attempts as just the misguided notions of naive internationalists who would rewrite the conditions of world order in the manner of a fairy tale. Perhaps Dag Hammarskjold most adequately summarized the past and the future of international relations when he wrote in 1956:

To rejoice at a success is not the same as taking credit for it. To deny oneself the first is to become a hypocrite and a denier of life; to permit oneself the second is a childish indulgence which will prevent one from ever growing up.[23]

---

[23] Dag Hammarskjold, *Markings* (New York: Alfred A. Knopf, 1970), p. 128.

Suggested Readings

Beloff, Max. *Foreign Policy and the Democratic Process*. Baltimore: Johns Hopkins University Press, 1955. An examination of the problems of foreign policy making in a democratic nation.

Claude, Inis, Jr. *Power and International Relations*. New York: Random House, 1962. A discussion of the subject from a balance-of-power perspective.

Dahl, Robert A. *Congress and Foreign Policy*. New York: Harcourt Brace Jovanovich, 1950. An examination of congressional and executive relations in U.S. foreign policy making.

Fulbright, J. W. *The Arrogance of Power*. New York: Random House, 1966. The chairman of the Senate Foreign Relations Committee questions the role of the United States in world politics.

Hilsman, Roger. *To Move a Nation: The Politics of Foreign Policy in the Administration of John F. Kennedy*. Garden City, N.Y.: Doubleday, 1967. A detailed review of foreign policy making under the Kennedy Administration.

Mills, C. Wright. *The Making of World War III*. New York: Simon and Schuster, 1958. One of America's leading social critics argues that capitalism is a basic cause of war.

Morgenthau, Hans J. *Politics among Nations*. 4th ed. New York: Alfred A. Knopf, 1967. A leading text on realism and power as the basis of conducting foreign policy making.

Riker, William H. *The Theory of Political Coalitions*. New Haven, Conn.: Yale University Press, 1962. An argument against balance-of-power theories.

Schelling, Thomas C. *The Strategy of Conflict*. Cambridge, Mass.: Harvard University Press, 1960. A brilliant reexamination of the many facets of international political strategy.

Stoessinger, John G., *The Might of Nations: World Politics in Our Time*. 3rd ed. New York: Random House, 1969. A basic text on international relations.

Minority rights
and government policy
CHAPTER 19

The delegates who attended the 1972 Democratic National Convention were different from the delegates to any other political convention. Between 1968 and 1972, the Democrats had instituted a number of reforms that radically changed the delegate makeup of the convention. According to the new rules, each state delegation had to include blacks, Spanish-speaking Americans, women, and youth in proportion to their representation in the party in that state. The view from the television booths overlooking the convention floor was unlike anything ever seen in previous conventions.

Ten or fifteen years ago, choosing delegates in part *because* they were black or female would have been unthinkable. At that point the aim of civil rights groups was to make the American political system and the American public color-blind. In many circles it was considered bad taste to acknowledge that the person one was talking to was black or Puerto Rican or Polish; race and ethnic background were to be ignored. The quota system in the Democratic party reforms is evidence that attitudes about minorities in this country have changed. In part, this chapter is addressed to these changes.

The "minority problem" is not unique to the United States. Large numbers of Indians, Pakistanis, West Indians, Algerians, and Italians have migrated to Great Britain, France, and Germany in search of jobs. Willing to work for the lowest wages, these immigrant groups are perceived as economic threats by the working classes of their host countries, creating the kind of hostility that makes for a minority problem. In 1972, Uganda began to deport the Asians and Indians who have long dominated the shopkeeping levels of their societies. Pakistan was split apart in 1972 by a civil war that was, in large part, a result of ethnic differences. Russian Jews cannot practice their religion or freely leave Russia for Israel. Racism is institutionalized in South Africa, where the system of apartheid permits 3.8 million whites to exclude 18 million nonwhites from the political system solely on the basis of color. Tribal differences among black Africans have led to civil war and near-genocide in the Congo, Nigeria, and Burundi. In short, the minority problem is worldwide.

What do these different peoples in different circumstances share? What do the Catholics of Northern Ireland, the blacks of South Africa, and American women have in common?

Minority Groups and Civil Rights

Minority Groups: A Definition

The Catholics of Northern Ireland are a numerical minority. They live apart from the Protestant majority through choice, custom, poverty, and unofficial discrimination. No law states that Catholics are to be treated any differently from Protestants. As citizens of the United Kingdom, Catholics are entitled to vote; but because of their small number, they are outvoted in most elections. Economic as well as political power rests in the hands of the Protestant upper class. This means that when a Catholic applies for a job, he applies to a Protestant; when he has no job and applies for welfare, he applies to a Protestant; when he appeals to a policeman, he appeals to a Protestant. This situation is particularly tense because Northern Ireland is politically, but not geographically, separated from the Republic of Ireland, a Catholic country whose church plays a significant role in politics.

The blacks of South Africa are not a numerical minority—they outnumber whites by nearly five to one. But blacks are excluded from the political system—and from the society—by law. No black is allowed to live in a white district, or even to enter a white district after dark without a pass. If a black moves near a white, urban area to work he may not bring his family with him—although, for the purpose of conception, a wife is allowed to visit her husband for a period of no longer than two weeks. Blacks do not have the vote in South Africa; they are not allowed to use white facilities; and they may be imprisoned without trial at any time, at the discretion of local officials.

American women are not a numerical minority, nor are they segregated from the general population. In fact, the question of whether women in this country constitute a minority is debatable. They have the legal right to vote, to hold political office, to run corporations, and so on. By law, they are full citizens. But by custom, few women seek positions of power. Those who do often find the "male establishment" quite resistant.

What do these different groups of people have in common? First, their position in society—their status—is determined by accidents of birth: religion (being born in a particular religious community), color, and sex. These accidents, rather than individual ability or achievement, govern their opportunities in life.

Second, they cannot change their status—they cannot change the fact that they were born Catholic, or black, or female. This distinction is important. If a person decides to live outside the mainstream of his society—if, for example, a young American decides to join the Krishna people and adopt Indian dress and life-style—he may find his choice provokes discrimination. But he can always go back to the mainstream if he so desires; he is not locked into a minority status.[1] The same is true for ideological minorities. People join SDS or the John Birch Society by choice; they are not born to that particular ideology. They can leave the group at any time, and there is always a chance that they will become a majority in a future election. In contrast, minority status is hereditary and permanent.

Of course, not all minorities are subject to discrimination. As noted earlier, a white minority dominates South Africa. In Burundi, six hundred thousand Watusi control over three million Bahutu. In many counties in Mississippi blacks form an overwhelming majority, but for years there was not a single black official in that state. What the Catholics of Northern Ireland, the blacks of South Africa, the women of America, the Bahutu, and Mississippi blacks have in common, then, is a lack of political power—based on inherited factors they cannot change. Thus, in 1950 the U.N. Secretary General suggested that a minority be defined as a "more or less distinct group, living within a State, which is dominated by other groups."[2]

Race. The most common criterion for minority status—and the most familiar to Americans—is race. As any anthropologist will point out, the concept of biological racial differences is completely artificial. Sociologists Norman

---

[1] Of course, a person can change his religion, but in most societies that consider religious and ethnic background a criterion for status, converts are not considered equal to those born into the religion.
[2] United Nations, Secretariat, *Definition and Classification of Minorities* (E/C 4/Sub 2/85), 1950, p. 26.

"I've had a few feelers from Washington. They want to give the country back to us."

Reprinted by permission of William Von Riegen.

R. Yetman and C. Hayle Steele demonstrated the arbitrary nature of racial categories by comparing their application in different cultures.[3] In the United States, a person with black or Indian "blood"—that is, a person with black or Indian ancestry—is considered to belong to that respective race. But in most of Latin America, the term *Indian* is reserved for people who live according to old ways: a person of Indian ancestry who is modern in life-style is a Costa Rican or a Mexican, for example, not an Indian. The same is true of North American Indians, who consider a person "full-blooded" if he adheres to traditions. When Panamanians, who are dark skinned, use the word *Negro*, they are referring to the English-speaking, Protestant Jamaicans. In Peru, someone who is upper-class is called white, whatever his color. Hitler considered Gypsies as unworthy of German citizenship as the Jews, although Gypsies are "pure Aryans." The Japanese believe members of the Buraku caste are racially inferior, although there are no visible differences between them and the other Japanese people.

But however absurd, ideas about race have played a significant role in the history of this and other countries. It is difficult to say just how these ideas got started. Winthrop A. Jordan suggests that the belief that blacks

[3] Norman R. Yetman and C. Hayle Steele, Introduction to *Majority and Minority: The Dynamics of Racial and Ethnic Relations* (Boston: Allyn and Bacon, 1971).

are biologically inferior fulfilled a specific need in the United States. This country was founded on the principle that all men are created equal and have certain rights, but in order to justify slavery, many Americans had to believe that Negroes were less than men.[4] Arguments to support this belief ranged from the idea that Africans were not as highly evolved as Europeans to claims that slaveowners were being kind by introducing the African pagan to white, Christian ways.

Human Rights

One of the legacies of World War I and World War II was the principle of self-determination: all people have the right to decide for themselves how they will be governed and by whom.[5] Hitler had shown the world that it is risky to look the other way when a powerful nation threatens aggression against its neighbors. In addition, political leaders in colonies around the world had gained considerable public sympathy for their right to self-government.[6] By the late 1940s, the consensus among governments was that self-determination was not only morally right, it was also a road to world peace.

But while most governments in this period subscribed to the principle of self-determination for colonies, few wanted to apply the same principle to minority groups within their own borders. Only a few modern countries are nations in the sense of being one people with one culture, one language, and one set of beliefs and values. Many national boundaries were drawn in treaty rooms or by colonial administrations. In some cases a specific people was split apart—the Somalis in East Africa, for example, now occupy Somalia, parts of Ethiopia, Kenya, and the French territory of Afars and Issas; in others, traditional enemies were welded into a single state—as was the case with the Pakistanis and Bengalis. In addition, it is easier to travel from country to country today than it was in the past. Industrialization has proceeded unevenly, creating more jobs in some countries than in others, and attracting people from less-developed to more-developed nations. In short, most modern nations are heterogeneous.[7]

---

[4] Winthrop A. Jordan, *White over Black: American Attitudes towards the Negro, 1550–1812* (Chapel Hill: University of North Carolina Press, 1968), pp. 44–63. See also Charles E. Silberman, *Crisis in Black and White* (New York: Random House, 1964); and Alvin Rabushka and Kenneth A. Shepsle, *Politics in Plural Societies: A Theory of Democratic Instability* (Columbus, Ohio: Charles E. Merrill Books, 1972). The latter work presents the thesis that discord in plural societies is built into the system and will manifest itself in violent conflict, if no external threat is present to hold the society together.

[5] See the discussion in Chapter 4.

[6] Vernon Van Dyke, *International Politics*, Part 2 (New York: Appleton-Century-Crofts, 1972). For a more detailed discussion, see his *Human Rights, the United States, and the World Community* (New York: Oxford University Press, 1970), Chapter 5.

[7] The uniting of diverse people in the United States is compared to the same process in other countries in Seymour Martin Lipset, *The First New Nation: The United States in Historical and Comparative Perspective* (Garden City, N.Y.: Doubleday, 1967), Chapter 2, "Formulating a National Identity," pp. 69–111.

Still world leaders felt that an international agreement on basic civil rights would be a step toward world peace. The result was the *Universal Declaration of Human Rights*, adopted by the U.N. General Assembly in 1948. This document states that all people have certain inalienable civil rights, which include the right to life, liberty, equality, and participation in government.[8]

It is important to note that this declaration states that all people have certain rights and freedoms—as *individuals*. There is no mention of the rights of minority *groups*. This distinction is subtle. It means, for example, that an Italian child living in Germany, where his father found work, is entitled to receive the same education as a German child, but he is not entitled to special classes in the German language or to classes in Italian. Germany may choose to help the Italian child—and in fact does provide special cultural services for resident aliens. But this is a matter of domestic, not international, policy.

Minority Rights

Ideally, universal application of the human rights outlined by the United Nations would eliminate the "minority problem" altogether. The Catholics of Northern Ireland, the Bantus of South Africa, and American blacks would achieve full equality. But the ideal and the reality are two different things. First, many people identify strongly with the ethnic and racial groups to which they belong. Its successes are their successes; its friends and enemies, their friends and enemies. As Jerome D. Frank notes, many people "would rather die than be absorbed into an alien group."[9] Increasingly, ethnic minorities in America and elsewhere are seeking complete cultural autonomy, and a degree of political autonomy in forms like community control.

Second, life, liberty, equality, and the right to participate in government today may mean little if an individual belongs to a group that has been discriminated against for generations. According to this view, equality cannot be achieved unless the group is granted temporary special privileges and thus enabled to improve its status.[10] Are cultural autonomy or reverse discrimination viable solutions? Let us take a look at a few case studies of minority groups to see how successful the traditional solutions have been.

---

[8] In *International Politics* Vernon Van Dyke points out that the specific freedoms inherent in these rights may be interpreted differently. The United States considers an uncensored press a free press; the USSR feels censorship protects the people from capitalist domination of the press, which they claim occurs in the United States.

[9] Jerome D. Frank, *Sanity and Survival* (New York: Vintage Books, 1968), p. 104.

[10] Ivo D. Duchacek, *Comparative Federalism: The Territorial Dimension of Politics* (New York: Holt, Rinehart and Winston, 1970), p. 97.

The Black Experience in America [11]

Many of the first immigrants to America in the seventeenth century came as indentured servants. Contracts with the people who had paid their passage required them to work as laborers and servants for a specific number of years. Some had accepted these contracts because of poverty or religious persecution in their homelands; others chose servitude over jail terms; still others had been kidnapped. The first Africans to come here fell in the latter category. Although some worked in towns and on farms in the North, most were taken to the South where the need for labor was greatest.

In the mid-1600s, the Virginia House of Burgesses declared that African laborers could not be indentured, thus freeing their bosses to hold them in perpetual servitude. Gradually, colonial courts established a system of codes governing master-slave relations. Blacks and their children were considered private property; helping a slave to escape was thievery. Blacks in most southern states could not own property or sign contracts (such as a marriage contract). For purposes of taxation and census, slaves were considered three-fifths of a person.

Although slaveowners tried to create the impression that African immigrants accepted this role docilely, attempts to escape and rebellions were frequent. Abolitionists in the North and West pressed for change, and some southerners freed slaves after a time. But for the most part, the courts upheld the landowner's rights over his slaves. In fact, Article I, Section 9 of the Constitution, signed in 1787, states that Congress shall *not* prohibit the slave trade before 1808.

The Civil War and the Postwar Period

In 1863—two years after the Civil War began—President Lincoln issued the Emancipation Proclamation, which freed the slaves in Confederate-held territory. In the next seven years, the three major civil rights amendments were added to the Constitution.[12] During Reconstruction, the South was occupied by northern soldiers and bureaucrats who controlled local government. The Freedman's Bureau was established; Congress passed a bill prohibiting segregation in transportation, schools, and public accommoda-

[11] For classic discussions of the black experience in America, see Silberman, *Crisis in Black and White*; and Gunnar Myrdal, *American Dilemma*, rev. ed. (New York: Harper & Row, 1962).

[12] These amendments, although they were a vast improvement over the previous situation, do not give quite as much protection as is sometimes assumed. The Thirteenth Amendment prohibits slavery and involuntary servitude (except as punishment when a person has been convicted of crime). The Fourteenth Amendment states that all persons born or naturalized in the U.S. are citizens, and that no state can make laws that infringe on their rights as United States citizens. The Fifteenth Amendment says that neither federal, state, nor local government can deny a person the right to vote because of "race, color, or previous condition of servitude."

tions (1875); Mississippi sent a black senator to Washington. But this was the exception: most ex-slaves became sharecroppers—an arrangement one author called a mere "permutation of slavery."[13]

In 1877 federal troops were withdrawn and the control of local government returned to southern officials—mostly landowners who called themselves "Redeemers." Much of the intent of the Civil War abolitionists began to erode. The Supreme Court declared the 1875 Civil Rights Act unconstitutional: the Fourteenth Amendment, it argued, prohibits *states* from discriminating against people because of race, but it does not prohibit individuals from doing the same. Social and economic conditions in the South worsened steadily over the next ten to fifteen years. Small farmers, black and white, were extremely poor; and there was evidence of widespread corruption in the Redeemer administrations. To divert public attention and to stop a growing biracial, Populist movement, Redeemers began to blame a variety of ills on blacks. Desperate politicians pointed out that white small farmers might be hungry, but at least they weren't black. In the 1890s, southern states enacted a wide range of "Jim Crow" laws to exclude blacks from white facilities and white society.[14] In many states, for example, interracial marriage was forbidden. Blacks could not ride on white trains, eat at white restaurants, use white bathrooms. These laws were based on the 1896 Supreme Court decision in the case of *Plessy* v. *Fergusen*, which established the separate-but-equal doctrine. According to this doctrine, all citizens have certain rights, but the Constitution does not say they must exercise those rights in the same schools, trains, and restaurants. The facilities could still be segregated by race, as long as each race had equal facilities.

Of course, blacks were a majority in many parts of the South. In theory, they could have elected representatives to vote down these laws; in reality, few blacks had the vote.[15] Local officials circumvented the Fourteenth Amendment by enacting poll taxes, which blacks couldn't pay, and literacy and property qualifications, which blacks couldn't meet. To protect whites who had neither money, education, nor property, some states added "grandfather clauses" to their voting regulations: if a man's grandfather had voted prior to 1860, he needn't meet the other voting qualifications. In 1860, blacks were still in slavery.

Black Consciousness in the Twenties

The first opportunity for significant numbers of blacks to escape this situation came during World War I. War-related industries needed labor,

[13] Badi G. Foster, "Government and Afro-Americans," in *The Performance of American Government: Checks and Minuses*, ed. Gerald M. Pomper (New York: The Free Press, 1972), p. 327.

[14] For a detailed discussion of the rise of Jim Crow laws, see C. Vann Woodward, *The Strange Career of Jim Crow*, 2nd ed. (New York: Oxford University Press, 1966).

[15] See V. O. Key, Jr., *Southern Politics, In State and Nation* (New York: Vintage Books, 1949), Part 5, "Restrictions on Voting."

and so blacks began to move to large urban centers in the North and Mid-west. Socioeconomic conditions for these city-dwellers improved markedly over the next four decades: social welfare agencies established under the New Deal helped blacks as well as whites; Roosevelt established a Fair Employment Commission, under pressure from A. Philip Randolph, a black union leader; World War II renewed the need for labor and for soldiers.

Several civil rights groups were founded during this period, most notably the National Association for the Advancement of Colored People, which was established in 1909. Recognizing that blacks could not rally enough votes to wield political power, the NAACP focused on the courts. Here it worked to establish guarantees for individual rights. Success, the NAACP felt, depended on a coalition of blacks and white liberals; separatist movements, strikes, and the like would only hurt the cause.

Not all blacks agreed with the NAACP position. In the twenties Marcus Garvey mobilized large sectors of the black community (particularly in northern urban centers) behind The United Negro Improvement Association.[16] A separatist, Garvey emphasized the distinct history and culture of black people around the world and the superiority of the black race. His goal was to found an empire in Africa, so that American blacks could return home. In the thirties, W. E. B. Du Bois, one of the founders of the NAACP, left that organization because he had come to disagree with its emphasis on integration. "The only thing that we not only can, but must, do," he argued, "is voluntarily and insistently organize our economic and social power, no matter how much segregation it involves." [17]

The Early Civil Rights Movement

By 1950 most of the members of immigrant groups who had shared urban ghettos and unskilled jobs with blacks in previous years had worked their way into the middle class. To them, America was indeed the land of opportunity. Most citizens assumed that in time blacks would follow the same pattern.[18] Racism was generally considered a southern phenomenon (an illusion that was shattered when riots broke out in the mid-sixties in several northern cities).

Then, in 1954, Oliver Brown—a black man—won his suit against the Board of Education of Topeka, Kansas. Brown wanted his daughter to be

[16] A very readable essay on the role of Harlem as a center for the black renaissance of the nineteen-twenties, and the parts played in that movement by Marcus Garvey and A. Philip Randolph is Jervis Anderson's "Early Voice: From Florida to Harlem," *The New Yorker*, December 2, 1972, pp. 60-120.

[17] Quoted in Charles V. Hamilton, "The Nationalist vs. the Integrationist," *The New York Times Magazine*, October 1, 1972, p. 40.

[18] For a discussion of why blacks did not follow other minorities out of the slums, see Karl E. and Alma F. Tacuber, "The Negro as an Immigrant Group," *The American Journal of Sociology*, January 1964, pp. 374-82.

able to attend the local school; NAACP lawyers argued his case to the Supreme Court. In the 1954 *Brown* v. *Board of Education* decision, the Court specifically overturned the separate-but-equal doctrine in the field of public education established fifty-eight years earlier. Chief Justice Warren argued that education is "the most important function of state and local government," and that segregated schools generate a sense of inferiority in black children that "may affect their hearts and minds in a way unlikely ever to be undone."

A year later, Mrs. Rosa Parks of Montgomery, Alabama, refused to give her seat on a public bus to a white man, defying Jim Crow laws in Montgomery and throughout the South, which required blacks to sit in the back of the bus and to give up their seats to any white person. The black community of that city rallied behind the young Reverend Martin Luther King, and for over a year boycotted the public transportation system. The blacks of Montgomery chose to walk or use motor pools rather than ride the segregated buses.

These two events had enormous impact for several reasons. First, southern political leaders openly defied the Court ruling on school desegregation. When Governor Faubus of Arkansas blocked the door of a school in Little Rock, President Eisenhower, who firmly believed that the chief executive should not become involved in regional issues and that the government cannot force people to change, had no other choice but to send federal troops there. The majority of the northern public was outraged by some southerners' attitudes toward the Court and the law, and by the way certain southern police reacted to black protesters, despite the widespread (though less formal) practice of segregation in the North.[19]

Blacks in Montgomery found that together they *could* influence public policy: the city needed their combined bus fares. Further, in organizing this boycott, blacks developed a tactic for combatting the superior strength of local officials: nonviolent demonstration, based on Gandhi's principles of passive resistance. This tactic, combined with litigation, proved to be successful. On November 13, 1956, in consequence of a suit brought by the NAACP, the U.S. Supreme Court upheld the judgment of a lower federal court that it was unconstitutional for a state to require racial segregation on public buses. Blacks also discovered at this time an indirect source of national political power. A president cannot be elected in this country without winning the big industrial states in the North. Many of the big cities in these states had a substantial black population, and many northern voters were sympathetic toward southern blacks and would therefore vote for candidates who were sympathetic to them too.

In 1957 Congress passed the first civil rights legislation since Reconstruction.[20] In brief, the Voting Rights Act restated the rights guaranteed in the Thirteenth, Fourteenth, and Fifteenth Amendments, and authorized the Justice Department to back up these rights with civil suits. At this point, progress for black Americans seemed assured. Why then did the race issue "blow up" in the sixties?

The Sixties

The Civil Rights Act of 1957 had little effect. It had been weakened considerably in House and Senate committees, and so gave the Justice Department little ammunition to fight racial discrimination with. For example, local voting registrars were not required to show their files to federal officials. This made it extremely difficult for the government to build a case against them for preventing blacks from voting. In addition, procedures for filing suit were discouragingly complicated, especially to blacks who feared reprisals for daring to inquire about the law. Finally, local FBI agents, who might have initiated investigations on their own, depended on cooperation from local officials; they were reluctant to alienate these officials by looking into voting rights.[21] In summary, the law was not terribly effective: not one

[19] E. E. Schattschneider in *The Semisovereign People* (New York: Holt, Rinehart and Winston, 1960), p. 16, wrote: "Competitiveness is the mechanism for the expansion of the scope of conflict. It's the *loser* who calls in outside help." Thus, the appeal of southern blacks to the rest of the country came out of their losing position.

[20] For a discussion of the politics behind this bill, see J. W. Anderson, *Eisenhower, Brownell, and the Congress* (Tuscaloosa, Ala.: University of Alabama Press, 1964).

[21] Allan Lichtman, "The Justice Department's Lack of Vigor," in *Politics American Style*, ed. Terrence P. Goggin and John M. Seidl (Englewood Cliffs, N.J.: Prentice-Hall, 1972).

**Figure 19-1
Percent of
Americans below
the Poverty Line,
by Race, 1959–
1970**

	1959	60	61	62	63	64	65	66	67[r1]	68[r]	69[r]	70[r]
Black and other	56.2	55.9	56.1	55.8	51.0	49.6	47.1	41.7	37.2	33.5	31.1	32.1
White	18.1	17.8	17.4	16.4	15.3	14.9	13.3	12.2	11.0	10.0	9.5	9.9

[r]Based on revised methodology for processing income data; see Series P-60, No. 76, for explanation.

[1]Due to coding errors, data for 1967 are not strictly comparable with those shown for 1966 and 1968 through 1970. It is estimated that this error may have overstated the number of poor families in 1967 by about 175,000 and the number of poor persons by approximately 450,000.

Source: Current Population Reports: Consumer Income, U.S. Department of Commerce/ Bureau of the Census (Government Printing Office Series P-60, no. 77, May 7, 1971), p. 3.

suit was filed in Mississippi during the entire Eisenhower administration.

Second, although socioeconomic conditions for blacks had improved steadily over the first part of the century, blacks had not kept pace with other Americans. Sociologist Rashi Fein estimates that in 1960 blacks were approximately twenty years behind whites in health, education, employment, and income. In that year the infant mortality rate for blacks was double that for whites; life expectancy for a black man was six years less than for a white man. Fewer blacks than whites had completed high school, and those who had, were generally paid less than whites with an equal education. Fein estimates the median income of blacks in 1964 as 56 percent that of whites. The unemployment rate for blacks was double that for whites, and many more blacks were underemployed—that is working part time or for part of the year (see Figure 19-1).[22]

Apathy in enforcing the law and poor socioeconomic conditions partially explain the unrest of the sixties. But perhaps the best explanation is the story of one black man's childhood.

I remember being suddenly snatched awake into a frightening confusion of pistol shots and shouting and smoke and flames. My father, a follower of Marcus Garvey, had shot at the two white men who had set the fire and were running away. Our home was burning down around us. We were lunging and bumping and tumbling all over each other trying to escape. My mother, with the baby in her arms, just made it into the yard before the house crashed in. . . . The white police and firemen came and stood around watching as the house burned down to the ground. . . .

One night two years later, I remember waking up to the sound of my mother screaming again. When I scrambled out, I saw the police in the

---

[22] Rashi Fein, "An Economic and Social Profile of the Negro American," *Daedalus*, Fall 1965, pp. 815–46.

livingroom; they were trying to calm her down. She had snatched on her clothes to go with them. . . .

My mother was taken by the police to the hospital. . . . My father's skull, on one side, was crushed in, I was told later. Negroes in the town have always whispered that he was attacked, and then laid across some tracks for a street-car to run over him. . . .

We children adjusted more easily than our mother did. We couldn't see, as she clearly did, the trials that lay ahead. As the visitors tapered off, she became very concerned about the collecting the two insurance policies. . . . The company that had issued the bigger policy was balking at paying off. They were claiming that my father had committed suicide. . . .

When the state Welfare people began coming to our house, we would come from school sometimes and find them talking with our mother, asking a thousand questions. They acted and looked at her, and at us, and around in our house, in a way that had about it the feeling—at least for me—that we were not people. In their eyesight we were just things, *that was all. . . . We began to go swiftly down hill. . . .*

Sometimes, instead of going home from school, I walked the two miles up the road to town. I began drifting from store to store, hanging around outside where things like apples were displayed, . . . and I would watch my chance and steal me a treat. . . .

Meanwhile, the state Welfare people kept after my mother. By now, she didn't make it any secret that she hated them, and didn't want them in her house. But they exerted their right to come, and I have many, many times reflected upon how, talking to us children, they began to plant the seeds of division in our minds. . .

As my mother talked to herself more and more, she gradually became less and less responsive to us. And less responsible. The house became less tidy. We began to be more unkempt. . . . We children watched our anchor giving way. . . . Soon the state people were making plans to take over all my mother's children. She talked to herself nearly all the time now, and there was a crowd of new white people entering the picture—always asking questions. . . . Eventually my mother suffered a complete breakdown, and the court orders were finally signed. They took her to the State Mental Hospital where she remained for 26 years. . . .[23]

This story took place, not in the South, but in Michigan. It comes from Malcolm X's account of his childhood.

The sixties began with a lunch-counter sit-in in Greensboro, North Carolina. On February 1, 1960, four students from the Negro Agricultural and Technical College of Greensboro, North Carolina, made several small purchases from a local variety store, then they sat down at the lunch counter to order coffee. But the lunch counter only served whites, and they were turned away. They refused to leave the store, however, occupying their seats until closing time. This act was the beginning of the sit-in movement. In the spring and summer of 1960 this movement spread to other parts of the

[23] Malcolm X, with the assistance of Alex Haley, *The Autobiography of Malcolm X* (New York: Grove Press, 1964), pp. 1–22.

South, as thousands of black and white protesters staged sit-ins at all-white establishments, such as libraries and hotels.

Two years later, in September 1962, James Meredith enrolled in the University of Mississippi with the assistance of fifteen thousand federal soldiers, and six hundred U.S. marshals. President Kennedy, like President Eisenhower in the Little Rock incident, had no other choice but to send federal troops to Mississippi to protect Meredith's civil rights, for he was faced with the state of Mississipi's efforts to defy a court order and block Meredith's enrollment.

In 1963, the centennial year of the Emancipation Proclamation, the civil rights movement came together with its fullest impact. On August 28, Martin Luther King, Jr., led 250,000 demonstrators in the March on Washington. This march, which was the largest single protest demonstration in U.S. history, brought together major black and white organizations in an attempt to dramatize to the nation and to the world the urgency of solving the problems of black people in the United States. The march also provided the most significant endorsement of the nonviolent direct action protest. But in 1963 the nation also saw Birmingham, Alabama, police turn fire hoses and dogs on unarmed black demonstrators; and in the same city, four young girls were killed in a fire bombing of a church.

In 1964, the mood of the country was mirrored in President Johnson's landslide victory over Barry Goldwater. Along with Johnson's election came a liberal congressional majority that was strong enough to overcome opposition to Johnson's civil rights legislation and pass two bills. The Civil Rights Act of 1964 prohibits discrimination in publc accommodations— restaurants, gas stations, hotels, and so on. It also prohibits discrimination in employment and in unions; and federal aid to any program that discriminates will be suspended. The Voting Rights Act of 1965 was a considerable improvement over its 1957 predecessor. It empowered the Justice Department to suspend literacy qualifications in counties with less than 50 percent voter registration, and to send in federal registrars when it suspects discrimination or intimidation. Preventing a qualified person from voting was made a federal crime.[24]

The Radicalization of the Civil Rights Movement. By the time these laws were passed, however, racial problems were breaking out in other areas, and the civil rights movement had begun to change, reflecting the impatience of blacks who still had not achieved equality. The riot in Watts, a black

[24] For more information on the voting behavior of blacks, see William R. Keech, *The Impact of Negro Voting: The Role of the Vote in the Quest for Equality* (Chicago: Rand McNally, 1968) ; and the Report of the United States Commission on Civil Rights, *Political Participation: A Study of the Participation by Negroes in the Electoral and Political Processes of 10 Southern States since the Voting Rights Act of 1965* (Washington, D.C.: U.S. Government Printing Office, 1968).

section of Los Angeles, took place in the summer of 1965. Traced to a white policemen's arrest and alleged mistreatment of a black youth, the riot, which lasted six days, took its toll in looting, burning, and sniping. Before the national guardsmen and state police could control the rioting, thirty-five were dead and nearly nine hundred were injured.

In 1966 the Black Panther Party was formed. The original movement was founded on the idea that American society is corrupt and, at best, callously indifferent to ghetto blacks. The Panthers regarded established channels of authority as oppressors of blacks and, when necessary, they advocated the use of violence to defend themselves against the white power structure.

The same year, the Student Nonviolent Coordinating Committee (SNCC) expelled its white members. And Stokely Carmichael, one of SNCC's leaders, became a spokesman for black power. In the early 1960s both SNCC and Carmichael belonged to the integration-oriented civil rights movement. At that time, SNCC membership was made up of both white and black college students whose aims were to register black voters in the South, establish health clinics and cooperatives, and teach rural blacks to read and write. But after the 1964 Democratic Convention failed to seat the SNCC-founded Mississippi Freedom Democratic Party in place of the regular Mississippi delegation, SNCC and Carmichael began to change their orientations. From a goal of integration, SNCC shifted to one of black liberation. And Carmichael became even more radicalized: he believed that American society would only take action when threatened with violence. In 1968 he broke with SNCC and moved to the more radical Black Panthers.

In the summer of 1967 riots broke out in Newark and Detroit, leaving many dead and vast areas burned to the ground. In the *Report of the National Advisory Commission on Civil Disorders* (1968), the Kerner Commission, appointed by President Johnson, blamed those disorders on racial divisions throughout American society, and warned that "our nation is moving toward two societies, one black, one white—separate and unequal." In the same year Congress passed another Civil Rights Act prohibiting discrimination in housing. In 1968 Martin Luther King, Jr., was assassinated and riots erupted in major cities around the country.

Why did the ghettoes explode *after* Congress had passed three strong civil rights bills? Why did the civil rights movement turn into cries for black power and (with the Panthers) revolution? One possible explanation is the role played by the media. The attention given these bills in both newspapers and television led many Americans—blacks and white—to expect immediate progress.[25] But it takes time to enforce laws—sometimes years. In addition,

[25] Edward Banfield, in *The Unheavenly City: The Nature and Future of Our Urban Crisis* (Boston: Little, Brown, 1968), especially pages 3–22, argues that the rising expectations of blacks, which cannot possibly be met, are at the root of the current crisis in race relations.

it is difficult to legislate against de facto, or unofficial, segregation, such as exists in the North. Unemployment, closed unions, poor housing, and run-down schools have much the same effect as Jim Crow laws.

But perhaps more important, the black community—particularly in big cities—has become increasingly politicized over the last decade. TV coverage of demonstrations in the South and riots in the North showed blacks in iso-lated communities that they had "brothers" all over the country—in Cali-fornia, Michigan, New Jersey, Washington, D.C. (For a more detailed dis-cussion of the effect of the media on black consciousness, see Chapter 9.) The war in Vietnam also played a role. Malcolm X reasoned that if the government sanctioned violence in Vietnam, it could not censure the violence of blacks who sought to defend their own people and communities in this country against white oppression.[26] The independence movement in Africa in the 1950s also affected black Americans. Many blacks began to look to Africa for their cultural roots, and to see themselves as a colonized people. As a result of these factors a number of distinct ideologies developed in black America in the sixties.[27]

Afro-American Ideologies [28]

The civil rights movement of the late fifties and early sixties was based on the belief that the American system is right in principle, but not in practice. With nonviolent demonstrations, Reverend King and others hoped "to awaken a sense of moral shame in the opponent," to show northern liberals how blacks were treated in the South, and to prevail upon the federal government to intervene. Demonstrations were directed against specific dis-criminatory laws and practices, primarily in the South. The ultimate goal of the movement was integration: full participation in society and government for black Americans. Toward this end, civil rights leaders in the early sixties actively sought white participation. Only a coalition of blacks and whites, they argued, could end segregation; ultimately, all races would live together without distinctions. The emphasis was on morality, on traditional democratic values, and on achieving American ideals. Reverend King felt that the civil rights movement could do more for the country than eliminate racial in-

[26] Malcolm X, *The Autobiography of Malcolm X*, p. 8.
[27] One of the most significant discussions of the black power movement in America can be found in Charles V. Hamilton and Stokely Carmichael, *Black Power: The Politics of Liberation in America* (New York: Vintage Books, 1967). The authors view black power as an alternative to violence. For, under this doctrine, blacks are involved in determining how they will live. They cannot remain pawns of the white establishment. Rather, they must receive an equitable distribution of goods and services, and decision-making power.
[28] This section is based on Kenneth M. Dolbeare and Patricia Dolbeare, *American Ide-ologies: The Competing Political Beliefs of the 1970s* (Chicago: Markham, 1971), Chapter 5; and Jerome H. Skolnick, "Black Militancy," in *The Politics of Protest: Violent Aspects of Protest and Confrontation*, A Staff Report to the National Commission on the Causes and Prevention of Violence, 1969, pp. 97–135.

justice. If successful, "it will have enlarged the concept of brotherhood to a vision of total interrelatedness." [29]

Black Separatists. But not all blacks seek integration into American society, as noted above. Perhaps the strongest separatist group in the early sixties and today is the Black Muslim movement founded by Elijah Muhammad. The Muslims are a religious community, distinguished from their neighbors by their beliefs, dress, customs, and names. Muslims also reject the "slave names" given their great-grandfathers by white masters. According to the teaching of Elijah Muhammad, the world is divided into the Black Nation—including black and brown people around the world—and the white race. The white race is inherently evil, as evidenced by the centuries in which they have enslaved nonwhites. In the present, Black Muslims seek separate communities and eventually a separate state. They believe Allah will someday return to earth to destroy whites and unenlightened nonwhites in the Apocalypse.

Because the Black Muslim movement is a religious sect, and because Muslims do not seek entry into American politics and society, they do not often "make the news." However, their ideas, communicated primarily through Malcolm X, have had a strong impact on the thinking of many black leaders. Malcolm X broke with Elijah Muhammad in 1964 to form the Organization of Afro-American Unity—at least partly because he rejected the passivity of waiting for the Apocalypse. He was assassinated shortly thereafter, but his ideas have found voice in the black power movement.

Black Power. Like the Muslims, black power advocates reject the civil rights movement's goal of complete integration and emphasize instead the distinctiveness of Afro-American culture and history. However, Stokely Carmichael [30] and others interpert race relations politically and economically —not in religious terms. (In this they differ, too, from the civil rights leaders who saw racial problems in moral terms.) Black power advocates like Carmichael believe that blacks in this country have been exploited for generations. Without black labor, America never would have become the rich, powerful nation it is today for whites.

In the struggle against economic and political oppression, black power spokesmen identify with nonwhite, colonized people the world over. They point out that from an international perspective, nonwhites are *not* a minority, and see Afro-Americans as part of the Third World.

In terms of goals, black power seeks cultural autonomy and community control—that is, control of local schools, local police, and the agencies that deal with the black community. They seek this, first, because they do not believe white Americans will willingly give up their power over blacks, and

---

[29] See Martin Luther King, Jr., *Why We Can't Wait* (New York: New American Library, 1964), p. 152.
[30] See Hamilton and Carmichael, *Black Power: The Politics of Liberation in America.*

second, because they reject certain values implicit in American society. Specifically, many black power advocates reject materialism—the value of property over life that allows a policeman to shoot someone for suspected thievery—and competitiveness. Eldridge Cleaver used Darwinian terms to state this position. He saw the weak in society as the natural prey of the strong and cited as examples the "rat-race political system of competing parties, . . . our dog-eat-dog economic system of profit and loss, and . . . our adversary system of justice wherein the truth is always secondary to the skills and connections of the advocate." [31] African societies, black nationalists argue, are based on cooperation. Individual success is less important than the survival of the group; no person goes hungry or homeless. But other black leaders, like Floyd B. McKissick and Roy Innis, feel that material gains in the black community can only help the black power struggle. McKissick believes that the political power of ghetto blacks can be improved if their economic position is improved. And in order to promote this same goal, Innis founded the Harlem Commonwealth Council, which encourages black-owned businesses and black-directed economic institutions in Harlem.

The Black Panther Party. The Black Panther Party, founded in Oakland, California, by Huey P. Newton and Bobby Seale, accepts some, and rejects other of the black power positions. Marxist in ideology, the Panthers consider the American government exploitative—the machine of a capitalist ruling class. But while they see blacks as the most severely oppressed group in this country, they do not consider blacks the only victims of the system. Unlike the black power leaders, the Panthers have formed alliances with white radicals. In 1968, for example, Panther Eldridge Cleaver ran as the presidential candidate for the Peace and Freedom Party.[32]

As Marxists, the Panthers believe they must defend themselves when necessary, against the white power structure. They train in guerrilla tactics, pointing to Vietnam as an example of a smaller power fighting a stronger one. However, revolution is an ultimate, not immediate goal. One of the Panthers' first acts after the party was founded was to form armed patrols to follow the police around the black community in Oakland. This, they felt, was the only way to prevent police brutality. Black Panthers see self-defense as a right, and even a moral obligation. It would be a mistake, however, to look at the Panthers only in terms of their revolutionary stand. The Panthers have approached the problems of the black community in increasingly nonviolent ways in recent years. They have set up health clinics and a free breakfast program that feeds thousands of hungry black children each month. Their program of nonviolent self-help as an alternative to

[31] Eldridge Cleaver, *Soul On Ice* (New York: Dell, 1968), p. 84.
[32] Cleaver has since been expelled from the Panthers because of disagreements with Newton and other Panther leaders.

radical revolution has progressed so far that in 1973, Panther leader Bobby Seale ran for mayor in Oakland, California,

Perhaps the most important difference between the Panthers and other black liberation movements is that they are based in the ghetto. The leaders of the earlier civil rights movement were largely middle-class and highly educated. Pacifists, they believed Americans would change once they recognized the immorality of racism. In contrast, the Panthers interpret the black situation in terms of economics and power, not morals. They appeal to the sense of impotence, alienation, and impatience—to the anger—in the ghetto. During the riots of the sixties, the Panthers generally had more influence on the streets than the civil rights leaders.

In an analysis of attitudes among black leaders in mid-1972, Charles V. Hamilton describes two camps. Integrationists—such as Roy Wilkins, executive director of the NAACP—favor busing to end de facto segregation in schools and scatter-site housing [33] to disperse ghetto neighborhoods. Both programs, they argue, would help reduce economic and cultural differences between blacks and whites. Nationalists—such as Roy Innis, national director of CORE—argue that the black community must stay together geographically if it is to gain control of local institutions such as schools, the police, and health facilities. In addition, they feel that integrated schools perpetuate feelings of inferiority in black children. Hamilton points out that control of local institutions is a source of economic power—power to hire, to purchase supplies, to award building contracts. According to the nationalist view, then, community control—not dispersal and integration— is the route to self-sufficiency.[34]

Minorities in Other Countries

How do other governments deal with the question of minority rights? Most, according to Vernon Van Dyke, deny that a minority problem exists. For example, in Latin American countries that include a wide range of racial and ethnic groups, the term *minority* is reserved for groups of people involuntarily transferred "en bloc" from one nation to another.[35] In contrast, some countries have acknowledged minority problems and instituted quota systems to guarantee minorities representation in government.

The nation of India includes a number of different racial and religious groups. The Muslims, who ruled India under the Mongol Empire, are greatly outnumbered by the Hindus; the Hindus themselves are divided into strictly defined castes and sects. In 1909 the British decided that the best way to

[33] That is, building small, low-income housing-projects in middle-class and suburban neighborhoods.
[34] Hamilton and Carmichael, *Black Power: The Politics of Liberation in America.*
[35] Van Dyke, *International Politics*, p. 65.

deal with these traditional divisions was to give each religious or racial community a proportion of the seats in the provincial and Central councils. A Hindu voted for Hindu representatives; a Muslim, for Muslims. This policy, in modified form, was carried over into the constitution of modern India, so that even the poorer, underdeveloped castes are assured representation. If the prime minister decides Untouchables or Anglo-Indians are underrepresented, he (or she) can nominate new members of Parliament. The same is true in Indonesia. And legislative seats in Lebanon are divided proportionally among fourteen religious groups; the president is a Maronite Christian, the prime minister a Sunli Muslim, the minister of foreign affairs a Greek Orthodox.

In Cyprus, an island where Greeks outnumber Turks seven to three, a similar system failed. The 1959 constitution provided for a Greek president and a Turkish vice president—each with veto powers—and proportionate representation in Parliament, the cabinet, the army, and the police force. When the president proposed reforms that threatened the Turkish community in 1963, fighting broke out, and a U.N. peace-keeping force was called in.[36] The conflict has continued, in largely muted form, until the present time.

Minority Rights in Great Britain

Great Britain, like the United States, has been unwilling or unable to successfully integrate nonwhites into society. Until the 1950s, Britain had a long history of mistreating newcomers.[37] Irish and Jewish immigrants in the nineteenth and twentieth centuries had met with substantial hostility and discrimination. The public response was no different when nonwhites from the West Indies, Pakistan, and India began arriving in the 1950s and early 1960s. A 1956 survey showed that 98.5 percent of white Britons did not wish to have nonwhites as lodgers, and only seventeen percent thought whites and nonwhites were of equal intelligence.[38]

By the end of the 1950s, nonwhite immigration was rising sharply, and so was the public clamor for strict controls. In 1962 the Conservative party yielded to this outcry by passing the Commonwealth Immigrants Act. Henceforth, only blacks with job vouchers (largely skilled professionals) and their relatives would be allowed to enter Britain. This leveled off immigration at about fifty thousand nonwhites per year, but the public was still not satisfied.

In the mid-1960s the rise of antiblack feelings among white workers led the Labour party to drop its opposition to immigration controls. In 1965

[36] Duchacek, *Comparative Federalism*, pp. 101–8.
[37] The discussion on immigration follows two important works on race in Britain: Paul Foot, *Immigration and Race in British Politics* (Harmondsworth, Middlesex: Penguin Books, 1965); and E. J. B. Rose et al., *Colour and Citizenship: A Report on British Race Relations* (London: Oxford University Press, 1969).
[38] Foot, *Immigration and Race in British Politics*, p. 128.

Harold Wilson's Labour government issued a White Paper creating a ceiling for immigrants with job vouchers of eighty-five hundred per year. Then, three years later, the Labour party passed the Kenya Asians Act, restricting the entry rights of those citizens despite their British passports. Many Britons were outraged by this act; the Labour government, they felt, believed only in the equality of white British citizens. There was little doubt that the only reason for the new regulations was color. At the same time that immigration from nonwhite Commonwealth nations was being severely curtailed, there was an increase in the entry of people from the white Commonwealth nations (Australia, Canada, and New Zealand), Ireland, and Western Europe.

Despite continuing efforts to curb black immigration, by the early 1970s some 1.5 million nonwhites were living in Britain—about 2.5 percent of the population.[39] The nonwhites tended to concentrate in urban areas, where employment opportunities were greatest: almost half lived in London, and another 14 percent resided in the West Midlands.

Although many nonwhites had been skilled professionals in their home countries, in Britain their status was uniformly low. In fact, only 7 percent of former white-collar workers held similar positions in Britain; over 90 percent of the immigrants occupied manual jobs. As a result, they could hardly afford decent housing; immigrant households in London had 29 percent less space than those of whites. Nonwhites were relegated to the lowest paying, lowest status work and the most crowded and deteriorated housing.[40]

Many began to see a pattern of racial discrimination. Such charges were substantiated by a 1966 survey conducted for the government by Political and Economic Planning (PEP).[41] After extensive interviewing, PEP reported that over 80 percent of Britain's blacks believed that a color bar existed. And the PEP situation tests of discrimination indicated that, if anything, blacks underestimated the amount of racial prejudice that they faced. PEP sent English, Hungarian, and West Indian testers with similar qualifications to apply for jobs and housing. While the British tester was offered thirty of forty jobs advertised, the West Indian was offered only three. In housing, the West Indian was discriminated against by two-thirds to three-quarters of all rental agents and accommodation bureaus.

After this report became public, pressure mounted on the Labour government to take stronger action against racial discrimination. It passed the 1968 Race Relations Act, which improved upon its 1965 predecessor by widening the jurisdiction of the Government's Race Relations Board, so that the Board could deal with complaints in the areas of employment and housing. Nevertheless, civil rights activists were disappointed by the weak enforcement procedures contained in the Act. It was also clear that the gov-

[39] British Information Services, *Race Relations in Britain* (London: Central Office of Information, 1972), pp. 1–3.
[40] Rose et al., *Colour and Citizenship*, pp. 121–80.
[41] This discussion is based on W. W. Daniel, *Racial Discrimination in England* (Harmondsworth, Middlesex: Penguin Books, 1968).

ernment agencies charged with the task of promoting the integration of non-whites into Britain—the National Committee for Commonwealth Immigrants and its successor, the Community Relations Commission—were stymied by their liason role between the white establishment and angry nonwhites. Labour's efforts seemed token at a time when the racial situation was becoming more tense each year. And the worst was yet to come.

In April 1968, John Enoch Powell, Conservative member of Parliament, former cabinet minister, and noted classical scholar, delivered a tirade against nonwhite immigrants that electrified the nation and polarized the racial climate as never before. Entire areas of Britain, he claimed, would become black unless further immigration controls were adopted and repatriation of nonwhites already in Britain was begun.[42] He charged that many whites now felt that they were "strangers in their own land." "As I look ahead, . . . I am filled with foreboding. Like the Roman, I seem to see the River Tiber foaming with blood."

Reaction to Powell's unprecedented speech was immediate and explosive. An angry Conservative party leader Edward Heath dismissed Powell from the party's Shadow Cabinet. There was intense criticism of the speech from Labour politicians and intellectuals. But much of the white public had found its champion: polls showed 75 to 90 percent of the people behind Enoch Powell—and 41 percent thought he would make a better prime minister than Heath.

Spontaneous demonstrations in support of Powell erupted around the nation. The respected member of Parliament had legitimized racial prejudice; many whites were now able to vent their feelings more freely than ever. In December 1968, the Archbishop of Canterbury, Britain's top clergyman, was shouted down in a church in Basildon and called a traitor because of his sympathy for nonwhite immigrants.

Powell had warned of racial bloodshed, and, not suprisingly, his prophecy was soon realized. Racial violence broke out in urban centers soon after the speech. In one London district alone, there were thirteen attacks on Pakistanis within two months after Powell's tirade. Finally, in July 1969, serious violence erupted. After the stabbing of a white man in Leeds, one thousand white rioters rampaged and terrorized nonwhite neighborhoods.

The increase of such racial attacks against nonwhites helped to nurture the rapid growth of a black power movement in Britain. Multiracial civil rights groups such as the Campaign Against Racial Discrimination (CARD) fell under the control of young and militant black power advocates. In December 1968, over eight hundred persons attended the nation's first black power conference, where many local Indian, Pakistani, and West Indian organizations were represented. In early 1969 the Black People's Alliance

---

[42] The discussion of Powell's speech and public reaction follows *The New York Times Magazine*, December 15, 1968, pp. 35, 147; and James Kenney, "The Writing on the Wall," *America*, September 21, 1968, p. 209.

organized a march of five thousand people in London that led to bitter confrontations with the police.

While blacks were moving toward a more strident black power position, Enoch Powell continued to set the tone for discussion on the race question. He seemed to pull the political spectrum along with him; Heath and Wilson often condemned Powell, but usually seemed to move toward his proposals a few months later. By late 1968 Powell was demanding a Ministry of Repatriation and a total halt to all black immigration. As leader of the Conservative party in Parliament, Heath denounced Powell, but only a few months later Heath asked for immediate legislation to give the government complete control over immigration, with total power to determine how many nonwhites, if any, would be allowed to enter Britain. One of the factors in the Conservative party's surprise victory over Labour in the 1970 election was the votes the Conservatives received from Powell's supporters, even though they never asked directly for this support.

The same trends continued into the 1970s. London witnessed a wave of terror against Pakistanis in the East End and further clashes between police and black power demonstrators. Powell did not cease in his efforts to force repatriation of blacks, and seemed to enjoy more public support each year. Meanwhile, unemployment and truancy among West Indian youths were reported to be nearly twice as great as among white youth.[43] All indicators suggested that the racial tension, polarization, and violence of the 1960s might even worsen in the 1970s.

Thus, Britain has witnessed the development of a most serious race problem in the past two decades. The pattern has been disturbingly similar to that of the United States: concentration of blacks in urban ghettoes; discrimination against them in employment and housing; inadequate governmental efforts to fight racism and aid black integration into society; increasingly open expression of racial prejudice by whites; a turn toward the provocative politics of black power in nonwhite communities; the rise of an important political spokesman to express the discontent of working-class and lower-middle-class whites; perceptible and steady movement by both major parties to the right on the race question; and a cycle of growing polarization leading to racial violence. It is evident that the racial problems of the United States are by no means unique.

Minorities in the USSR

The situation in the USSR is also complex.[44] The Soviet Union today includes some 109 distinct ethnic groups. This diversity is the result of three

[43] Colin McGlashen, "The Making of a Mugger," *New Statesman* 84 (October 13, 1972): 496–97.
[44] This section is based on Stanley Rothman, *European Society and Politics* (New York: Bobbs-Merrill, 1970), pp. 217–24.

centuries of expansion by the Great Russians, who come from the Moscow area. The Great Russians, who are today 55 percent of the population, still dominate Soviet government (see Table 19-1). Among the large minorities are the Ukrainians, the Byelorussians, the Uzbeks, and Tartars. Each of these groups has roots in a particular area; each speaks a different language. The Great Russians (in the past) belonged to the Orthodox Church; the Uzbeks and Tartars are Muslims; large numbers of Ukrainians are Catholic. In addition, the Ukrainians are closer to the West than any other Soviet people and traditionally consider themselves superior to their eastern neighbors.

Until the late nineteenth century, Russian tsars allowed these territories considerable autonomy. However, in 1881 Alexander III replaced this policy with one of forced assimilation. Local cultural activities were prohibited, traditional leaders were killed; and the Russian language was forced on all peoples. This policy was militantly enforced for the remainder of the Romanoff period.

In the early days of the Russian Revolution, Lenin argued for a return to national or ethnic autonomy. He did so to gain support for the unstable Communist government, for both the Russian majority groups and the Western powers were threatening the newly formed government. Minorities, Lenin stated, should be allowed to speak their own languages, run their own schools, and even to secede if they wanted. The Soviet Union would be a federation of relatively independent republics.

In 1933, Stalin overruled this position. He reasoned as follows. The leadership of most Soviet minorities was in the hands of the bourgeois elite. The Socialist Democrats, who were later called the Communists, had a moral obligation to intervene on behalf of the working people when these leaders sought to take control. Further, he argued that ethnic loyalties were part of the old order; in the new socialist state all workers would be united.

Table 19-1
Ethnic Composition of the Soviet Population and Government

Nationality	Percentage of Population 1959	Membership in Central Committee 1961	1966	Membership in Presidium 1961	1966	Membership on Council of Ministers 1962	1966
Great Russians	54.65	58.29%	57.95%	61.90%	58.33%	66.07%	72.46%
Ukrainians	17.84	20.00	18.46	14.29	16.67	17.86	20.29
Byelorussians	3.79	3.43	5.13	4.76	8.33	0	1.45
Armenians	1.33	1.71	1.54	4.76	0	1.79	1.45
Jews	1.09	0.57	0.51	0	0	1.79	1.45
Tartars	2.38	0.57	0.51	0	0	0	1.45
Komis	0.21	0	0	0	0	1.79	1.45
Others	18.71	15.43	15.90	14.29	16.67	10.70	0

Source: Table 6.7 in Stanley Rothman, European Society and Politics (New York: Bobbs-Merrill, 1970), p. 221.

However, Communist leaders did believe in self-determination, and during the twenties they had encouraged local leadership in the party and government. (Great Russian and Jewish officials had sometimes been removed to make room for natives.) For at least ten years, local leaders were helped and encouraged—until they began to seem too independent. At that point Soviet authorities would step in, jail or exile local spokesmen, and start the cycle again by seeking new indigenous officials.

In the thirties, however, the Soviet government began to turn its attention to economic matters—specifically, collectivization and industrialization. Large numbers of Great Russians were sent to distant territories to speed the collectivization process and to serve as technical advisors in industrial projects. This migration was accompanied by a new wave of purges, this time directed at the more traditional members of local communities who resisted change. Ukrainian peasants and the nomadic people in the East suffered most from these purges. But gradually industrialization and the presence of the Great Russians, who served as representatives of the central government, encouraged interdependence among Russian peoples and wider loyalty to the state.

This is not to say that the Soviet Union solved its minority problem. The same group of the population who once comprised the Great Russians continues to dominate politics, and minorities on the fringes of Soviet society continue to rebel. Soviet Jews, for example, find they are sometimes excluded from universities, professional jobs, and government positions. Some have tried to move to Israel, and some have succeeded. However the Soviet government imposes a high tax on emigrants—sometimes equal to a year's salary. In the early 1970s, American Jews—particularly the Jewish Defense League—brought this policy to the attention of the world press and petitioned for the United Nations to intervene. Senator Henry Jackson introduced legislation in 1973 that would require the Soviet Union to ease restrictions on Jewish emigration, in order to be granted "most-favored-nation" status in trade relations with the United States.

Conclusion: A Solution to the Minority Problem?

The problem of preserving minority rights is not easily solved. No matter what local law has dictated, it has been impossible for any country to protect *all* the rights of minority group members. This has been the rule rather than the exception in countries throughout the world, and we can look to South Africa, Northern Ireland, India, Great Britain, the USSR, and the United States for evidence.

What directions can minority groups take to ease the burden of discrimination? They could aim at cultural autonomy—setting up a separate state for all the blacks in the United States, or separating French Canada from

British Canada. Or they could rely on the quota system to provide them with equal representation within their societies. Both these alternatives present problems when carried to their logical ends. If black Americans form a separate state, then what about Chicanos, Puerto Ricans, Jews, Irish-Americans, Italian-Americans, and so on? The population of the United States could be fragmented into hundreds of minority groups, each with its own interests to protect and goals to attain. The quota system, as proven by the 1972 Democratic National Convention, can be a viable means of ensuring fair representation. But even this system is imperfect since it is actually another form of discrimination—in this case, against the majority. But, more importantly, the quota system cannot ensure equal treatment in the day-to-day problems of minority group members, such as finding housing or getting jobs.

Can—and should—the international community intervene in situations where a people's civil and human rights are being violated? The U.N. is firmly committed to the protection of human rights; but it is equally committed to the sovereign right of nations to govern their internal affairs. Every year African nations propose sanctions against the Union of South Africa; every year these sanctions are voted down.[45]

The policies of national governments, the interaction of interest groups, and the role of the international community all play a part in the dynamics of the minority and majority in the political process. In many cases, government policies are unable to satisfy the needs of all political actors. The breakdown of the political system, which can occur when groups feel they must take radical action to better their social and political position, is the subject of Chapter 20, "The Politics of Violence."

---

[45] See the discussion in Colin Legum, "Color and Power in the South African Situation," *Daedalus* 96, no. 2 (Spring 1967): 483–95. Legum argues that blacks and whites in South Africa are on a "collison course"; only the application of external pressure from the international community and violence from within South Africa will succeed in bringing about change.

Suggested Readings

Carmichael, Stokely, and Hamilton, Charles V. *Black Power: The Politics of Liberation in America*. New York: Vintage Books, 1967. An argument advocating the need for black power, with suggestions on how it is to be attained.

Carter, Gwendolen M. *The Politics of Inequality*. 2nd ed. New York: Praeger Publishers, 1959. An examination of racial separatism in South Africa.

Franklin, John Hope. *From Slavery to Freedom*. New York: Alfred A. Knopf, 1967. A historical study of blacks in America.

Jordan, Winthrop A. *White over Black: American Attitudes towards the Negro, 1550–1812*. Chapel Hill: University of North Carolina Press, 1968. An examination of past attitudes toward blacks compared with those of today.

Myrdal, Gunnar. *An American Dilemma: The Negro Problem and Modern Democracy.* Rev. ed. New York: Harper & Row, 1962. A classic study of race relations in the United States, with emphasis on the gap between American rhetoric of equality and black inequality.

Report of the National Advisory Commission on Civil Disorders. New York: Bantam Books, 1968. An examination of the causes and consequences of the black protest movement in America.

Report of the U.S. Commission on Civil Rights. *Political Participation: A Study of Participation by Negroes in the Electoral and Political Processes Since the Voting Rights Act of 1967.* Washington, D.C.: U.S. Government Printing Office, 1965. An examination of the impact of the Voting Rights Act of 1965.

Silberman, Charles E. *Crisis in Black and White.* New York: Random House, 1964. Contemporary racial problems are reviewed from a historical perspective.

Skolnick, Jerome H. *The Politics of Protest.* Washington, D.C.: U.S. Government Printing Office, 1969. An analysis of protest, confrontation, and violence as perpetrated by government and nongovernment groups.

Watters, Pat, and Cleghorn, Reese. *Climbing Jacob's Ladder: The Arrival of Negroes in Southern Politics.* New York: Harcourt Brace Jovanovich, 1967. A study of the civil rights movement of the fifties and early sixties.

The politics
of violence
CHAPTER 20

Before November 22, 1963, many Americans complacently assumed that assassinations, riots, and student uprisings couldn't happen in modern America. Presidents could be shot or deposed by military coups in Latin America and Indochina; starving peasants might riot in New Delhi; police could trade shots with students in Mexico and Japan—but it was unthinkable that similar acts could take place in Los Angeles or Dallas or anywhere in the "civilized," twentieth-century United States. And then, in the 1960s, such acts did happen here.

Since 1963, the United States has frequently been the scene of politically based acts of violence. During the five years from 1963 to 1968, for example, over two million Americans engaged in political strife—principally in civil rights demonstrations and anti-Vietnam War rallies. During these same five

"I prefer a small screen . . . the violence isn't so frightening!"

Reprinted by permission of Joseph Serrano.

years, over nine thousand people were injured in political violence; two hundred died as a result of the violence; and more than seventy thousand persons were arrested for strife-related activities.[1]

The assassination of President Kennedy marked the beginning of a decade of political violence in America. But violent upheavals have occurred in many other nations. During the same decade, millions of people died in civil wars and tribal rivalries in the Congo, Nigeria, Pakistan, Burundi, and Indonesia. In 1968 the Soviet Union sent tanks into Czechoslovakia to prevent the more liberal Alexander Dubcek from "Westernizing" the nation too far. The government of Greece was overthrown by a military coup in 1967. Intermittent troubles between Protestants and Catholics started in Northern Ireland in 1966 and became more violent in 1969; finally Britain sent troops to Belfast to prevent an out-and-out civil war (although their presence there today often seems to intensify the conflict). Left-wing terrorists in Latin America murdered foreign businessmen and diplomats, or kidnapped them for high ransom, to finance and publicize their causes. Arab guerrillas

[1] Ted Robert Gurr, "A Comparative Study of Civil Strife," in *Violence in America: Historical and Comparative Perspectives* ed. Hugh Davis Graham and Ted Robert Gurr (New York: New American Library, 1969), p. 546.

hijacked commercial airplanes and kidnapped members of the 1972 Israeli Olympic team at Munich, Germany, as ransom for political prisoners. There was racial unrest in Britain, and students rioted in Germany, France, and Japan. Hardly a day passed without some new incident of violence in the headlines.

Violence has existed as a way of political life in many areas of the world, particularly in many Latin American countries, in Indonesia, in the Middle East, and in many African states. But what is particularly disturbing is the pervasiveness of disorders in other nations popularly noted for their domestic tranquility. While in most societies peaceful evolution and peaceful demonstrations outnumber violent disturbances, the evidence is abundantly clear that in the majority of those same societies there also exists a considerable amount of violent protest, turmoil, or other manifestations of civil strife. In many of these countries, the citizens have available to them traditional legitimate means by which to express their wishes to those in authority and to influence the direction of public policy. But increasingly, the public has been speaking and making known its will through political violence. Why has it become necessary for the public to speak so loudly?

Political Violence: Some Definitions

Broadly defined, political violence is any extralegal act or threat of injury to persons, damage to property, or disruption, whose purpose, targets, or effects are political.[2] A soldier who shoots a revolutionary trying to overthrow a legitimate government and a policeman following orders to use his nightstick to break up a demonstration are not engaging in political violence. Except in cases of subjective brutality, they are acting within the law, as agents of their government. But the revolutionary who shoots back at the soldier and the rioter who hurls bricks at the police *are* engaging in political violence. Both revolutionary and rioter are using force without legal sanction in the hope of changing—or at least damaging—political and economic institutions of society.

Clearly, a revolution in which one ruling group in a country is supplanted by another group is a political act; but is a spontaneous outbreak on ghetto streets political? It is, in the sense that the rioters are attacking symbols of authority (police) and symbols of the economic and social system (stores). Both the revolution and the spontaneous outbreak are challenging the exercise of power in particular segments of the political system.

[2] See Harry Eckstein, "On the Etiology of Internal Wars," in *Anger, Violence, and Politics: Theories and Research*, ed. Ivo K. Feierabend, Rosalind L. Feierabend, and Ted Robert Gurr (Englewood Cliffs, N.J.: Prentice-Hall, 1972), pp. 9–30; and H. L. Nieburg, *Political Violence* (New York: St. Martin's Press, 1969), pp. 133–63.

"Good night, Ed—
get home safe!"

Reprinted by permission
of *The American Legion
Magazine.*

Violence as Protest

Whether it is expressed in the desperate act of a single individual, in the contagious rage of a crowd, or in an organized rebellion, political violence is always an act of protest against existing authority. In a sense, disruption and violence are the last resources of the powerless groups in a society. In conventional politics, individuals and groups bargain with one another for economic and political advantages. For example, the federal government can demand that construction unions admit blacks because the government funds numerous building contracts. Truck drivers can demand higher wages because businessmen cannot carry on without their services. Confrontations between the government and private organizations, and between industry and labor, are frequent, but they are relatively even fights, in the sense that both contending parties need each other. But what of the groups that do not wield political power? How can they make known their grievances?

In theory, at least, citizens have three methods through which they are able to influence the direction of public policy and make known their wishes: by expressing their collective public opinion; by working through political parties for the attainment of some particular goal; or by forming interest groups to achieve their political ends. (We say "in theory" because there is never any automatic guarantee that the existence of political parties or interest groups, or the expression of public opinion will automatically affect governmental decision making.) But if a group has been unable to make itself heard through conventional channels, what are its options?

First, its members can resign themselves to existing circumstances and take no political action. Second, they can try to take political action without upsetting the existing political system.[3] They can protest peacefully, as U.S. blacks did in the late 1950s. However, a nonviolent protest can only be successful if the movement wins the support of third parties or a wider public who are in a position to influence those in authority. The members of the protesting group must be dedicated, and the leader has a delicate task of public relations. He must organize his constituents and hold their interest without being able to offer them immediate tangible rewards. He must attract the media, for the success of protest activity is directly related to the amount of favorable publicity it receives. But a moderate leader may lose both his constituents and the media by not being able to offer progress to one and exciting news stories to the other; and a militant leader, while giving journalists a good story, may offend third parties and officials. The official groups which the protest is aimed against may undercut the movement by offering symbolic rewards, such as setting up a study commission or establishing a single job training program—which does not in fact make a dent in massive ghetto unemployment. The officials may postpone taking action too, in the hope that the protesters will run out of energy, and the intensity of the protest may not be sustained or will lose its newsworthiness.

A third alternative for politically weak groups is to use violence or the threat of violence as a negative inducement to bring about change in society. Burning buildings, overturning automobiles and buses, erecting barricades, and indulging in guerrilla warfare may accomplish what peaceful marches, sit-ins, and demonstrations have not accomplished, for such actions provoke immediate reaction. The transition from apathy and peaceful protest to violence may be the result of frustration with the system, and it may not be conscious. To the extent that political violence is spontaneous and irrational, according to H. L. Nieburg, it can be looked upon as a symptom of a breakdown in the political system—"as society's early warning system, revealing deep-rooted political conflicts which are gathering strength beneath the surface of social relations."[4]

Forms of Political Violence

Three types of political violence have been distinguished by Ted Gurr, depending upon which classes of the population are involved and how spontaneous or how well planned the violent action is.[5] They are turmoil, internal war, and conspiracy.

[3] Michael Lipsky's "Protest as a Political Resource," *American Political Science Review* 64, no. 4 (December 1968): 1144–58, is an interesting discussion of the difficulty of organizing and leading a nonviolent, minority movement.
[4] Nieburg, *Political Violence*, p. 9.
[5] Ted Robert Gurr, *Why Men Rebel* (Princeton, N.J.: Princeton University Press, 1970), p. 11.

Turmoil refers to the largely spontaneous, random violence of riots, mass demonstrations, strikes, and political clashes. In this category would be confrontations between blacks and white policemen such as occurred in Watts, Newark, Detroit, and other cities in the United States, and outbursts between students and university administrators which occur periodically in scores of European and American cities. This form of violence is disorganized, fairly short-lived, and lacks direction. Its only goal may be to inflict damage on people and institutions that symbolize power and oppression; it rarely has a specific, long-range objective in mind. Turmoil breaks out when numbers of people are discontented and feel deprived in some fashion, but their discontent is not guided in specific channels by firm leadership.

Internal war is a far different kind of political strife. It consists of an organized, intense attack upon authority, and it develops when not only the masses but also numbers of skilled and educated people in a nation feel deprived of their rightful rewards and their place in government. To be successful, an internal war must have both the widespread support of the people and leadership by members of the elite. It may take various forms: a large-scale revolution, guerrilla warfare, civil war. Internal war is fought to change a constitution, to overthrow an existing regime, to secede, or to change government policies; its goals are tangible and specific.[6] The strife between East and West Pakistan, which led to the formation of the new nation of Bangladesh in 1971, is a recent example of internal war.

Conspiracy refers to small-scale but highly organized violence, such as coups d'état, barracks revolts, palace revolutions, and mutinies, usually involving a few members of the elite. A conspiracy occurs when members of the elite have a strong grievance against the conduct of government by the persons in power, but the public is either unaware of what is going on or apathetic. In July 1971, a conspiracy organized by military officers attempted to overthrow the government of King Hassan of Morocco, but the coup was unsuccessful and several of the plotters were executed. Little more than a year later, another attempt was made on the king's life when Moroccan air force planes fired upon his jetliner; but again the King escaped unharmed. The conspiracy was organized by high government officials and military officers, and had no widespread support among the people of Morocco.

In this chapter, we will be concerned primarily with turmoil and internal war, which are the types of violence indicating that large numbers of people are disturbed with their political system. What malfunctions in the system cause political unrest?

---

[6] Eckstein, "On the Etiology of Internal Wars," in *Anger, Violence, and Politics*, ed. Feierabend et al.

What Causes Political Violence?

Why did black ghettoes in America explode in the mid-sixties? Why did the Ibos suddenly take up arms against the federal government of Nigeria, after living side-by-side with the Yoruba and Hausa tribes for generations? Why, at Tel Aviv airport, did Japanese terrorists working for Arab guerrilla organizations machine-gun tourists who had no direct influence on the Israeli government? [7]

Precipitating Incidents, Economics, and "Riffraff" Theories

It is tempting to explain acts of political violence in terms of specific precipitating incidents. It is convenient to say that black Americans rioted in 1968 because Martin Luther King, Jr., was shot by a white man; that Ibos rebelled because Muslims in Northern Nigeria had attacked and killed hundreds of Ibo shopkeepers and clerks. But similar incidents have occurred elsewhere in the world with different results. The people of India did not riot when Gandhi was assassinated, although he undoubtedly meant as much to his followers as King did to his. A precipitating incident may act like "the flintwheel of a cigarette lighter"; [8] it may be the spark that sets off the conflagration. But to ascribe all political violence to isolated incidents does not explain why one particular set of circumstances is inflammable while another is not, why black Americans rioted but Indians did not. The short-run precipitants cannot adequately explain why political violence occurs.

Some political thinkers have attributed political unrest and violence to economic oppression. For example, Marx believed that the suppression and degradation of the workers under capitalism would lead inevitably to revolution. But economics *alone* does not explain political violence. If it did, to paraphrase Trotsky, the masses would always be in revolt. Surveying history, James Davies contradicts this economic explanation and observes that revolutions do not occur in "generally impoverished societies." The very poor tend to develop an attitude of fatalism, a belief that life is hard and simply must be endured. Moreover, their energy is absorbed in the difficult task of staying alive from day to day, and their horizons are limited to their own family or their own little community.[9]

[7] For an excellent selection of readings on the causes of political violence, see Feierabend et al., eds., *Anger, Violence, and Politics*, Parts 1 and 2.

[8] Eckstein, "On the Etiology of Internal Wars," in *Anger, Violence, and Politics*, ed. Feierabend et al., p. 13.

[9] James C. Davies, "Toward a Theory of Revolution," pp. 68–69 in *Anger, Violence, and Politics*, ed. Feierabend et al. Davies cites a study conducted at the University of Minnesota during World War II, where volunteers went on a starvation diet. Very quicky they became totally preoccupied with fantasies of food. See J. Bresek, "Semi-starvation and Nutritional Rehabilitation," *Journal of Clinical Nutrition* 1 (January 1953): 107–38.

Still another attempt to explain political violence is the "riffraff theory," which suggests that rioters and terrorists are only the uneducated, the unemployed, and the emotionally unstable elements of society. Alienated by repeated personal failure, such people presumably have no respect for law and order, persons, and property, and are extremely susceptible to "mob hysteria." However, studies have disproved the riffraff theory. The Kerner Commission, appointed by President Johnson in July 1967, found that the "typical rioter" in Watts was not a migrant but a lifelong resident of that city, was better educated than nonrioting ghetto residents, was employed but working at a low status job, was informed about politics, and was proud of his race.[10] In the United States, civil rights marches and peace demonstrations in the 1960s and early 1970s included persons from all walks of life and professions: clergymen, students, businessmen, professional people. And the same cross-class participation in civil disturbances is found in other nations. A study by the National Commission on the Causes and Prevention of Violence, which surveyed participation in violence in 114 nations, found that during the years 1961–1965, members of the working classes took part in 73 percent of the turmoil events in all the nations, and members of the middle classes took part in 61 percent of these events. In more advanced English-speaking and European nations, 70 percent of the middle classes participated in demonstrations. Furthermore, during the same period, in fifty-four internal wars for which information is available, all three classes of society—workers, middle classes, and elite—took part. The Commissions' findings are shown in Table 20-1. Surely these figures should put to rest the riffraff theory.

Since poverty and riffraff elements are found to some degree in almost all societies, but they are not the primary causes of turmoil or internal war, what are the causes? In their continuing effort to explain violence, political scientists have begun to look deeper for preconditions—for the changes that make poverty or political repression suddenly unbearable and give "agitators" an audience. Both social and psychological theories have been advanced in recent years.

Social Factors

Many political theorists today emphasize the roles of economic change, of class structure, and of the political system in the outbreak of violence in a nation. The three authors whose views are presented in this section argue that it is erratic activity or inconsistency in economic, class, and political situations which forms a key factor in riots, mass demonstrations, and revolutions.

[10] *Report of the National Advisory Commission on Civil Disorders* (New York: Bantam Books, 1968), pp. 128–35. See also Nathan S. Caplan and Jeffers M. Paige, "A Study of Ghetto Rioters," *Scientific American* 269 (1968): 15–21.

Table 20-1
**Specific Socioeco-
nomic Classes
That Participated
in Civil Strife,
1961–1965, by
Type of Strife**

Type of Socioeconomic Class	Percentages of Events in Which Specified Classes Are Reported to Have Participated [a]		
	Turmoil		Internal War
	All Nations [b]	European Nations [c]	All Nations [b, c]
Working classes:			
Peasants, farmers	18	17	93
Urban workers, unemployed	40	41	36
Any working-class groups [d]	73	67	100
Middle classes:			
Students	45	54	27
Petite bourgeoisie	8	11	24
Professionals	11	12	33
Any middle-class groups [d]	61	70	63
Regime classes:			
Military, police	1	2	31
Civil servants	3	5	23
Political elite	3	7	31
Any regime groups	7	13	48
Percentage of events in which two or more of the three general classes participated	39	47	76

[a] Percentages for specific classes are based on events for which specific information on participation is reported. Percentages for the three general types of classes are based on events for which either specific or general information is reported. A class is said to have participated if it apparently made up more than a tenth of the rank and file or more than a third of the leadership of an event.

[b] Data for events in 114 nations and colonies.

[c] Data for events in twenty-seven Eastern and Western European nations plus developed English-speaking countries elsewhere, including the United States. Only two internal wars occurred in these countries, too few to justify inclusion of separate group-participation data.

[d] These percentages include a large number of events for which general but not specific class participation is known, hence they are not directly comparable with the percentages shown for specific class participation.

Source: Ted Robert Gurr, "A Comparative Study of Civil Strife," in Violence in America: Historical and Comparative Perspectives, *ed. Hugh Davis Graham and Ted Robert Gurr (New York: New American Library, 1969), p. 555.*

A Sharp Reversal in Economic and Social Development. James Davies analyzed several revolutions and came to the conclusion that violent disturbances within a country are linked to the consequences of "a prolonged period of objective economic and social development . . . followed by a short period of sharp reversal." [11] So long as a population experiences chronic poverty and unrelieved repression, it is apathetic and resigned—unable to take political action. However, believes Davies, once people have reason to hope that their lives will improve—once the burden of oppression has begun to lift—they develop a new set of expectations and look for continued improvement. If their expectations of a better life continue to grow steadily, but the actual satisfaction of these needs is suddenly threatened or is blocked, the resulting anxiety and frustration eventually lead the people to rebel. This situation is shown graphically in Figure 20-1, with the attitude of frustration represented in what Davies terms a J-curve. The heavy broken line in the figure represents the people's expectation of continued greater opportunity to satisfy their basic wants, and the solid line curving in the pattern of a tilted letter *J* represents the actual satisfaction of those wants. The solid line rises steadily for a time, paralleling the broken line; but then some events occur which interrupt its progress, and a steadily widening gap appears between what the people have come to expect and what they actually get. A temporary setback is not sufficient to set off a rebellion; a disastrous harvest in one growing season, for example, which diminishes the food supply of a nation, may be followed by a year of abundance. But when the gap reaches intolerable proportions—when the people fear that the gains that they have achieved will be taken from them, and their mood becomes sufficiently resentful—they rebel. It is this state of mind, the mood of frustration and despair, which ultimately triggers the revolution.

Davies has shown that linked J-curves ultimately plotted the pattern of the Russian Revolution in 1917. Following the emancipation of the serfs in 1861, the Russian masses experienced the first glimmerings of improvement in their lot. A momentary halt to their upward progress occurred at the time of the assassination of Alexander II in 1881, but then their expectations rose again as they moved from the land to the cities and tasted the first benefits of the Industrial Revolution. In 1904–1905, however, the defeat of the army in the Russo-Japanese War and the reintroduction of oppression and terror under Nicholas II initiated the downward trend of the J-curve. This down-trend continued until the combination of cumulative civilian distress during the first years of World War I and the military defeat against the Germans left the people with hopeless feelings about the future, and precipitated the revolution.[12]

Davies does not claim that all rebellions follow the patterns of the J-curve. Many frustrating situations fall short of producing profound revolutions.

[11] Davies, "Toward a Theory of Revolution," in *Anger, Violence, and Politics*, ed. Feierabend et al., p. 68.
[12] *Ibid.*, pp. 73–77. Davies also charts the rise and fall of expectations in the Dorr's Rebellion in America in 1842 and in the Egyptian Revolution of 1952.

Figure 20-1
The J-Curve of Frustration

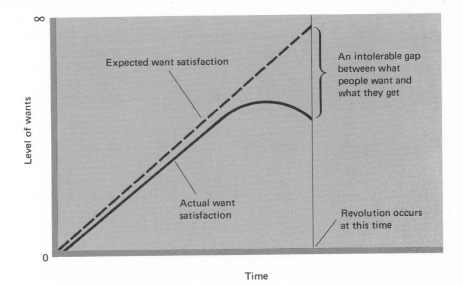

Source: Adapted from James C. Davies, "Toward a Theory of Revolution," in Anger, Violence, and Politics: Theories and Research, ed. Ivo K. Feierabend, Rosalind L. Feierabend, and Ted Robert Gurr (Englewood Cliffs, N.J.: Prentice-Hall, 1972), p. 69.

But a pattern similar to the J-curve can be seen leading up to the riots in the United States in the 1960s. The seeming judicial and legislative victories of the civil rights movement in the fifties and early sixties, and the well-publicized struggle for equal rights in the South, aroused expectations and hopes among blacks all over the nation. When these hopes were not fulfilled, the mood of frustration led to large-scale violence in the cities in the North.

An Ambiguous Class Structure. Johan Galtung suggests that the ambiguity in a society's class structure may also spark violent behavior.[13] Social stratification is apparently a universal phenomenon. In contemporary societies, individuals may be ranked according to a number of criteria—wealth, education, race, sex, family, and so on. Galtung refers to those individuals who rank highest in any specific criterion as the "topdogs," and those who rank lowest as the "underdogs." A person who ranks high in all criteria is a "complete topdog," and someone ranking low on all issues is a "complete underdog." But invariably, many individuals are caught between the two extremes. A poor white person in the United States, for instance, or in Rhodesia or the Union of South Africa, would be a racial topdog though an economic underdog. The nouveau riche in any society are economic topdogs but cultural underdogs. This condition of "rank disequilibrium," according to Galtung, is one source of political unrest, for people who have one foot in the middle or upper classes resent the barriers that prevent them from

[13] Johan Galtung, "A structural theory of aggression," in *Anger, Violence, and Politics*, ed. Feierabend et al., pp. 85–97.

attaining full middle- or upper-class status. Leaders of the civil rights movement in the United States, for example, were usually topdogs by every criterion except race. Many black rioters interviewed by the Kerner Commission felt that their race kept them from achieving the life-style they deserved.

Rank disequilibrium is particularly common in underdeveloped nations. As these countries strive to modernize, traditional class systems based on family and tribal memberships may be upset. For a time, large numbers of people may be caught in the no-man's-land between social classes. Many African nations, for example, send hundreds of their young people abroad for higher education and technical training. When these men and women return home, they often find that there are only a few available jobs in which they may use their newly acquired skills. Their education entitles them to topdog status, but economically and politically they remain underdogs because of limited job opportunities. The civil war in Nigeria was in part the result of just such a class struggle. When the country was still part of the British colonial system, the Ibo tribe had acquired more education and more experience in business and in government bureaucracies than had other Nigerian tribes. When Nigeria won its independence, the Muslim leaders of the nation feared that the Ibos would usurp their dominant role in the northern part of the country. The Ibos in turn resented being held back from positions that their education and experience qualified them for. When a number of disequilibrated people unite under a common ideology or a common leader (or, as in the case of the Ibos, against a common enemy), revolution is likely to occur, says Galtung.

Ambiguous Patterns of Authority. Adopting still a different viewpoint, Harry Eckstein has focused on the role of the ruling elite, rather than on changes in the economic or social status of the masses, to explain the causes of political violence.[14] He argues that a government will tend to be unstable if its pattern of authority is very different from the authority patterns of the society it is a part of. For instance, if the authority patterns of the families, schools, and employers in a nation are democratic, then the citizens of that nation will not easily submit to a totalitarian form of authority in government. Similarly, if a government tends to change very abruptly its methods of exercising its authority, so that its citizens do not know what is expected of them and lack clear guidelines for their behavior, then the citizens may rebel to escape their feeling of insecurity. It is relatively easy for a government to control turmoil or rebellion—through the application of sheer force, by granting concessions to pacify the people, or through diversions such as external war. However, if force is applied indiscriminately or inconsistently, it may serve only to recruit new members for the rebels. The struggle between Catholics and Protestants in Northern Ireland, for example, became more intense when the British instituted a policy of intern-

---

[14] Eckstein, "A Theory of Stable Democracy," in *Anger, Violence, and Politics*, ed. Feierabend et al., pp. 98–106.

ment without trial. Similarly, concessions and diversions may backfire. Israel has argued that concessions to political activists such as Arab skyjackers only encourage further terrorism. A diversion such as external war, as Russia found out during World War I, may lead to more intense political violence at home; the defeats suffered by the Russian army at the hands of the Germans were a key factor in the early stages of the Russian Revolution of 1917.

Eckstein argues that turmoil and revolution are most likely to occur in a nation when those in power have lost their own sense of destiny, their ability to govern effectively, and their legitimacy in the eyes of the people. This weakening of the government allows distinct, often contradictory, codes of behavior to develop. These conflicting standards and expectations, particularly with regard to authority, then breed turmoil. The Kerner Commission Report suggests that the United States was experiencing just such a crisis of authority in the years leading up to the black ghetto riots. All national leaders had condemned violence. Yet police stood by as whites attacked nonviolent black demonstrators in the South, and local and state officials in some states openly defied the law and the authority of the federal government by resisting desegregation orders. According to Eckstein, such ambiguity in patterns of authority is a key precondition for political violence.

Psychological Factors

The question of why people react violently to economic, social, and political situations is as complex as the question of what produces an inflammatory social environment. In most of the examples we have cited so far, the rioters and rebels were outnumbered by the forces of those in authority. Why, with the odds against them, did people risk their lives to break store windows in Detroit, or to stop a Protestant parade in Belfast? Various theories have been proposed to answer this question.

Frustration-Aggression Theory. Ted Gurr sees political violence as an expression of the intense frustration felt by a number of individuals within a society. Frustration can occur either when people fear that they cannot attain something to which they believe they are entitled, or when they feel that they are about to lose something which they had already achieved and enjoyed, such as the right to vote, membership in a political party, or a decent living wage. And Gurr sees this condition of "relative deprivation"—the discrepancy between what individuals think they should have and what their environment can provide them—as an essential precondition for violence. Usually it is only when they have exhausted all acceptable routes to their goal that people become violent. Demonstrations and riots may be productive, removing the barriers between people and their goal, or they may be counterproductive, inviting repression. But in either case, the violence provides release from intolerable frustration. Aggression, writes Gurr, is "an innate response activated by frustration." [15]

Ivo and Rosalind Feierabend offer a similar analytical interpretation of the causes of violence in the concept of "systemic frustration," which they relate to two basic psychological-political conditions. [16] The first of these is "want formation," or the level of goods and services that individuals within societies believe is due them. The second related condition is "want satisfaction," or the degree to which individuals perceive that their wants are achieved. When, for example, individuals' want formation is high and their want satisfaction is low, they experience frustration. When this frustration takes on broader systemic characteristics—that is, when it is experienced collectively, by many individuals and groups within the society—then it is referred to as "systemic frustration."

If most individuals' expectations within a given political system are low and the satisfactions received are low, then low levels of systemic frustration will probably be realized. Apparently, this is the case in many traditional societies, such as Afghanistan and Ethiopia, which are not yet caught up in the modernizing web. These nations are politically quite stable. In transitional societies, which are attempting to modernize, wants formation tends to be rather high, while because of the difficulties inherent in developing a technological system, want satisfactions remain unachieved. Accordingly, systemic frustration is high, and these societies tend to be politically unstable. In nations which have modernized and have attained high development in education, science, and technology, people's wants and expectations are high, but society is capable of satisfying those wants. Therefore, systemic frustration is low, and these countries are politically stable.

To help prove and validate this relationship between systemic frustration and political stability, the Feierabends classified nations according to the degree of systemic frustration that could be measured within them and cross-related these data to the degree of stability or instability observed in those nations. They used eight indices to measure systemic frustration: (1) the degree of literacy in a nation, (2) degree of urbanization, (3) number of newspapers, (4) number of telephones, (5) calorie intake per capita, (6) ratio of physicians to population, (7) number of radios, and (8) the gross national product. These eight indicators were considered to be adequate guides to measure the socioeconomic status of a nation, and to determine either (a) the amount of satisfaction expected by individuals living under the system (their "want formation"), such as adequate educational opportunities and urbanization, or (b) the degree of satisfaction provided by the political system ("want satisfaction"), such as medical care, good nutritional

[15] Ted Robert Gurr, "Psychological Factors in Civil Violence," in *Anger, Violence, and Politics*, ed. Feierabend et al., pp. 31–57; 33.
[16] Ivo K. and Rosalind L. Feierabend, "Systemic Conditions of Political Aggression; An Application of Frustration-Aggression Theory," pp. 136–83 in *Anger, Violence, and Politics*, ed. Feierabend et al.

standards, extensive communication facilities, or other amenities furthered by a high gross national product. The Feierabends' findings corroborated their theory that the higher the rating of systemic frustration, the greater the political instability of a nation; and conversely, the lower the systemic frustration of its citizens, the greater the political stability. From their measurements with the eight indicators, the Feierabends gave this description of a modern nation which would tend to be politically stable:

It is a society which is 90 percent or more literate; with 65 or more radios and 120 or more newspapers per 1,000 population; with 2 percent or more of the population having telephones; with 2,525 or more calories per day per person; with not more than 1,900 persons per physician; with a GNP of $300 or more per person per year; and with 45 percent or more of the population living in urban centers.[17]

Alienation. David Schwartz suggests that alienation is another key psychological precondition for political violence.[18] In the ordinary process of growing up, he points out, people are socialized. They develop certain expectations with regard to government, informal organizations, and social institutions such as the family. For example, they learn to obey traffic signals so that transportation may proceed in an orderly manner, to pay for the items in a store so that commerce may be conducted equitably and rationally, to protect younger brothers and sisters so that they may remain safe from harm. And they expect certain things in return. They expect the law to protect them, stores to be open at regular hours, younger siblings to respect them. However, if a person begins to feel that the social and political system in which he lives threatens him, or that it no longer protects him or fulfills his needs, he may become alienated from the system.

Schwartz describes several stages in the transition from feelings of alienation to open expression of violence. At first, the person believes that he does not fit into the system, yet feels that he is powerless to change the system itself. He may attempt to withdraw, isolating himself from the community and concentrating on personal goals. Gradually, however, he will start looking for new institutions to replace those he no longer believes in. If he does not find them, he begins to feel increasingly threatened and angry, and very likely, he will direct his anger against symbols of government authority. At this point, writes Schwartz, he is psychologically ready to participate in political violence.

The Kerner Commission implies that alienation is practically inevitable in the black ghetto, where unemployment, broken families, exploitative relationships, and high crime rates create a constant state of insecurity and tension.[19]

[17] *Ibid.*, p. 145.
[18] David Schwartz, "Political Alienation: The Psychology of Revolution's First Stage," in *Anger, Violence, and Politics*, ed. Feierabend et al., pp. 58–66. For more on alienation and revolts, see Richard Schacht, *Alienation* (Garden City, N. Y.: Doubleday, 1971).
[19] *Report of the National Advisory Commission on Civil Disorders*, p. 205.

Adding to their hostility is the blacks' view of the police as agents of white oppression, not as protectors. Ghetto residents thus lack social and political institutions they can trust. This lack, according to C. Richard Hofstetter, explains the riots that followed Martin Luther King's death.[20] Dr. King was one of the only links between the black community and the American political system; with his death, many blacks felt completely estranged from the governmental system.

Thus, political scientists have identified several long-term preconditions which seem to lead to political violence: a period of rising hopes followed by a sharp setback (the J-curve); rank disequilibrium, in which individuals are caught between social classes and resent their unsettled position; a breakdown in the legitimacy of leaders which promotes conflicting patterns of authority; general frustration caused by a feeling of relative deprivation; and political alienation. These preconditions tend to combine in specific incidents of violence. Relative deprivation may set the stage for a J-curve; the J-curve, rank disequilibrium, and a breakdown in government's legitimacy may all lead to frustration and political alienation.

At the beginning of this chapter we suggested that all political violence is an expression of protest against existing authority, and an attempt to change the political system. Was the violence of the sixties in America successful in this respect? Did the sixties represent an unprecedented breakdown of authority for America? We turn now to a brief history of political violence in the United States.

Political Violence in America

The "long, hot summers" of 1967 and 1968 did have an effect on government policy in the United States. While complete equality of all citizens is still a long way off, local officials in many communities have actively recruited leaders of minority groups for social and economic programs, and local party organizations have supported candidates having nonwhite racial origins. New York City has decentralized its school system so that local communities have some control of their schools, and hence have a greater interest in them and a greater feeling of involvement. Police are being trained in nonviolent techniques for controlling angry crowds. However, many white Americans still resent the government's concern for ghetto blacks, Puerto Ricans, or Mexicans. They argue that in the long history of our

---

20 C. Richard Hofstetter, "The Impact of Martin Luther King's Death on Affect for the Political System," in *Political Behavior in the United States: Readings in American Government*, ed. Fred W. Grupp, Jr. and Marvin Maurer (New York: Appleton-Century-Crofts, 1972), pp. 178–92. According to Hofstetter's theory, riots did not break out when Kennedy was shot, because Kennedy supporters had other links to the political system. Hofstetter also notes that the riots in black communities served as a model for violence in other areas.

"melting pot," other minorities have been able to win entry into American society on their own, without recourse to demonstrations and violence. Why should blacks, for example, be rewarded for their disruptive behavior?

In answer, Richard Rubenstein counters that the idea that Americans have always lived peacefully with one another, except during the Civil War, is a myth. Every immigrant group—from early Anglo-Saxon settlers to the later-arriving Irish, Italians, Chinese, and Jews—has had to struggle against discrimination and fight for acceptance. Battles between labor and management have peppered the history of America for over fifty years; and farmers' rebellions, range wars, vigilante groups, family feuds, and organized crime have all contributed to the violent picture. The history of the American Revolution and the Civil War is well known, but Rubenstein identifies five other areas of major internal revolts in American history.[21]

The Farmers' Revolts

In the mid-eighteenth century, most of the land along the Appalachian frontier of the American colonies was owned by absentee landlords and worked by small tenant farmers. This arrangement worked satisfactorily until the British authorities began raising taxes in the 1760s. The landowners tried to pass the tax burden along to their tenants, but the small farmers could not afford higher rents. Threatened with terms in debtors' prison or sentences of forced labor for failure to pay the new taxes, the frustrated farmers rebelled. One thousand of them marched on Philadelphia in 1764, demanding tax reforms. In North Carolina, vigilante groups known as the Regulators took the law into their own hands, drove out tax collectors and judges who might foreclose mortgages, and assumed de facto control of several counties for a period of three years.

In 1786, a mob of farmers under the leadership of Captain Daniel Shays fought to obtain a voice in the Massachusetts legislature to protest unjust taxes levied upon them, but opposing merchants and landowners hired an army of their own and defeated Shays's forces. In Pennsylvania, in the 1790s, farmers rebelled when the government imposed a tax on whiskey— their major source of income. This "Whiskey Rebellion" collapsed only after President Washington ordered twelve thousand men into the western counties of the state.

Each of these revolts was a protest against external domination by absentee landlords and absentee government. The farmers' way of life and livelihood were threatened by distant forces over which they had no control.[22]

---

21 Richard E. Rubenstein, *Rebels in Eden* (Boston: Little, Brown, 1970). The next four sections rely heavily on his chapters 2–4.

22 In this, the farmers' revolts were similar to the ghetto riots of the 1960s, which were directed against absentee businessmen, absentee landlords, and the agents of absentee government (the police), who controlled the rioters' homes and the sources of their livelihoods.

The Postwar Southern Revolt

After the Civil War, the South was an occupied territory. Radical Republicans who had little sympathy for the southern way of life controlled local politics, and their policies were backed by federal troops. The Republicans encouraged blacks to vote and to run for political office, and many did so. To most white southerners, the Reconstruction administrations were an alien and hostile force seeking to destroy the traditional southern social order. In addition, the South was extremely poor after the war. Housing, small industry, and farms had been destroyed in the fighting, and southerners tended to blame their impoverished circumstances on the occupying Republican government.

Although defeated in battle, southerners were not willing to accept alien occupation calmly. Within a few year, organizations such as the Ku Klux Klan, which had originally been fraternal and social, became the base for a second revolt. Working at night and in disguise, the Klan terrorized those blacks who were taking advantage of the benefits offered under Reconstruction and the "carpetbaggers" who supported them. Houses were burned; men were tarred and feathered and sometimes lynched. Although the Klan's actual membership may have been small, support for its vigilante activities was widespread. Rubenstein sees a similarity between the activities of the Klan and events of recent history:

The conflict was waged according to principles of guerrilla warfare which have sinced been codified by Mao Tse-tung, Ho Chi Minh and others—use of a sympathetic civilian population to shelter the insurgents, avoidance of open battle, politicization of the rebel arm, and so on.[23]

In the postwar struggle for political dominance, the southerners won; they regained control of local government and put blacks back "in their place." By the time Congress investigated and condemned the Klan in 1870–1871, most blacks and liberal whites were too intimidated to struggle against the white supremacy doctrine. Local government officials openly supported the Klan and other vigilantes or at least pretended not to be aware of their activities. Federal troops and Reconstruction officials withdrew, and the southern whites were once again in control of southern society.

Labor-Management Antagonism

The struggle between labor and management in the United States lasted more than fifty years—from the end of the Civil War to the passage of the Wagner Act, which granted government protection to unions in 1935. Al-

---

[23] Rubenstein, *Rebels in Eden*, p. 28.

though rarely labeled a "war" or "rebellion" in the history books, the birth of the labor movement constituted one of the bloodiest chapters in American history.

In most instances, violence broke out among the workers when industrialists threatened to lower wages, either because the economy was not flourishing or because newer immigrants were willing to work for less money. When workers began to organize strikes, management fought back by importing new workers ("scabs") to replace the strikers, hiring private armies (which were sometimes recruited from organized crime), and occasionally appealing to the government to bring in troops. Workers were locked out and forced away from company gates. The bloodiest confrontations took place in the isolated mining and timber towns of Pennsylvania, Kentucky, and the West. In the 1870s, Irish miners known as the Mollys used sabotage and assassination to gain control of mining towns in western Pennsylvania; railroad workers rioted and destroyed parts of Baltimore and Pittsburgh; labor terrorists bombed Haymarket Square in Chicago in 1886 and The *Los Angeles Times* building in 1910. Reactions of management were just as brutal. In Idaho, striking miners were herded into bullpens; in Colorado, miners' wives and children were murdered by management gunmen in the "tent massacre." Federal troops were called in to put down rail and steel strikes in 1910. Just before the Wagner Act was passed, ten striking steel workers were gunned down in Chicago. The most violent episodes in the labor-management conflict took place before industries were unionized or when unions still were comparatively weak and workers were defenseless against management.

Urban Riots

America's cities, too—particularly those along the coasts—have a long history of political violence. From 1840 on, successive waves of immigrants battled one another for territory and opportunities. Each ethnic group—the Irish, the Italians, the Jews, to name a few—wanted a neighborhood of its own so that it could have a voice in the local political machinery and at the same time maintain its cultural traditions. Once the immigrants had established themselves, they expected to keep their hard-earned niche, and violence broke out whenever a newly arrived group threatened to displace a relatively settled community.

City-dwellers rioted against the influx of the Irish on the East Coast in the 1840s, and against the Chinese and Japanese on the West Coast in the 1860s and 1870s. Italians were lynched in New Orleans, and Jews were threatened and attacked in New York. Ethnic gang wars and riots were common throughout the last half of the nineteenth century. In 1863, in one of the worst riots in American history, the Irish in New York attacked draft offices recruiting soldiers for service in the Civil War, killed police and firemen, looted stores, and lynched blacks who threatened their waterfront jobs. As Rubenstein writes,

. . . in America, freedom, prosperity and social status are not handed over politely to newcomers, nor are they simply earned by individual effort. They are fought for and taken, often by methods every bit as violent and dirty as those used by the power structure to keep newcomers "in their place." [24]

The urban clashes finally subsided as immigrant groups gained control of segments of the local government and local economy.

Racial Violence

Prior to World War I, racial violence in the United States was largely confined to the South and was carried out by terrorist organizations such as the Ku Klux Klan, with blacks only occasionally fighting back. (Blacks' resistance in the New York draft riot of 1863 was an exception.) However, war-related jobs brought large numbers of blacks to the large cities in the North, and like other immigrants, they had to fight for a place to live and the right to work.

The Chicago riot of 1919 and others that followed until World War II were territorial or communal—they were direct confrontations between groups of whites and blacks over some contested area.[25] The northern cities were crowded, and whites resented the black immigrants. Usually violence erupted after a series of minor incidents in disputed territory that was neither wholly white nor wholly black. Within a few hours of some isolated dispute, gangs of whites would begin invading the fringes of black neighborhoods, looking for fights. Usually the police stood by and looked on, without taking any action; sometimes they actively supported the whites. Although blacks fought back to defend themselves, they did not take the offensive by counterattacking white neighborhoods.

However, the riot which took place in the Harlem area of New York City in 1943 was different for several reasons. It took place in the heart of a black community, not on its fringes. The violence was directed at property and particularly at retail stores, most of which were owned by white proprietors. And the wrath of the rioters was vented not against white civilians, but against the police who protected that property and tried to stop looting. As has become the pattern in "modern" riots, the Harlem riot was set off by unpopular police actions. A crowd gathered and responded by throwing rocks and bottles at the police. Eventually store windows were broken and the riot entered the looting phase. When the police took decisive countermeasures, rioters turned to arson, fire bombing, and occasional sniping.

[24] *Ibid.*, p. 15.
[25] This section is based on Morris Janowitz, *Political Conflict: Essays in Political Sociology* (Chicago: Quadrangle Books, 1970), pp. 171–203.

Morris Janowitz labels these disorders "commodity riots," to distinguish them from the earlier racial and ethnic communal riots—for in Harlem the rioters attacked stores and police, not civilians, and they fought for goods, not territory.

Although he considers commodity riots an expression of economic rather than political frustration, Janowitz notes that the riots in Harlem, and more recently in Watts, Detroit, and Newark, had political overtones in the sense that they represented a group consciousness. A much greater percentage of the black population participated in these riots than had joined the earlier communal struggles.

From an historical perspective, then, the civil violence of the sixties did not represent a radical break from "normalcy" in the United States. Riots, confrontations, armed vigilantes, and marches are by no means new to the United States. The black liberation movement, the growing nationalism of other American minorities, the radical student movements, the confrontations between citizen groups and police and politicians in the sixties, all can be seen as part of a continuing pattern. The rebels of the sixties may have developed new styles of protest, but their presence is consistent with the American past.

However, a point worth noting is that, with few exceptions, the civil violence throughout American history has been directed toward specific, limited objectives—not toward a total change in the nation's political and social system. As Ted Gurr has remarked,

Civil-rights demonstrators have asked for integration and remedial governmental action on Negro problems; they have not agitated for class or racial warfare. Peace marchers vehemently oppose American foreign policy and some of the men who conduct it; none of them have attempted to overthrow the political system. Black militants talk of revolutionary warfare; such sentiments are rarely voiced by those who participate in ghetto riots. By the testimony of most of their words and actions, they have been retaliating against the accumulated burden of specific grievances: inconsistent and coercive police control, economic privation, and social degradation.[26]

Even the Ku Klux Klan and other vigilante groups were not opposing the political system; rather, they saw themselves as protecting the system against attack by blacks, criminal elements, and other presumed enemies.

Political Violence in the Modern World

Is the United States an unusually violent society? Not really, for as we mentioned at the beginning of this chapter, internal revolts, guerrilla wars, and

[26] Gurr, "A Comparative Study of Civil Strife," in *Violence in America*, ed. Graham and Gurr, pp. 558–59.

terrorism have occurred in nations all over the world in the last decade, for varying reasons and with varied results. While civil rights demonstrations and ghetto riots have taken place in the United States, minority groups in other nations have been striving either for more active assimilation into national life or for greater political autonomy. Racial tension has flared between the nonwhite Commonwealth immigrants and the whites in Great Britain. In March 1968, Parliament passed a law designed to discourage Asians living in East Africa and holding British passports from emigrating to the British Isles. Religious tension has erupted between the Arabs and Jews in Israel. Beginning in 1971, the Philippine Republic experienced such civil, political, and religious unrest that in September 1972 President Marcos declared a state of martial law. From the Mediterranean Coast to the Cape of Good Hope, African nations have been beset with assassinations and attempted or successful coups ever since the former British, French, and Belgian colonies began to achieve independent status.

Can any general conclusions be drawn about the factors affecting civil disorder within the political systems in all corners of the globe? For one, the feeling of actual deprivation—or perceived deprivation of any kind—is perhaps the greatest contributor to civil disorder throughout the world. Whether it be expressed in the riots of Senegalese students, who seized Dakar University in 1968 in protest against a cut in their educational stipends, or in the uprising of Polish workers in Gdansk in 1970 over the high prices of meat, clothing, and other necessities, the basic cause of political violence is the belief of the rioters that they are being deprived of something that they are entitled to.

However, while one factor is predominant, usually civil violence has more than one contributing element. The most recent episode of Northern Ireland's long-standing struggle began as a nonviolent civil rights movement, with a frustrated Roman Catholic minority, which felt itself deprived of adequate job opportunities and other rights, seeking a role in a Protestant-dominated political system. Protestants reacted strongly against this movement, primarily because they feared the possibility of reunification with the neighboring Catholic Republic of Ireland—a move they have tried to block for over fifty years. The violence became so intense that the British sent in troops to maintain order until a peaceful solution could be reached; ultimately, they decided to imprison suspected terrorists without assessing charges, without trial, and without imposing fixed sentences. This policy turned previously moderate Catholics against the British troops they had once considered their protectors, and alienated them from a seemingly unsympathetic British government. The Catholics' feelings of deprivation and frustration were coupled with alienation from the existing authorities.

The civil war in Pakistan was an example of feelings of deprivation joined with thwarted expectations, in the classic form of a J-curve. In the general elections in 1970, the Bengalis of more populous but very poor East Pakistan won a majority of seats in the National Assembly and expected that their leader, Sheikh Mujibur Rahman, would become Prime Minister. However, the more prosperous West Pakistanis threatened to boycott the Assembly, and it never convened. The Bengalis, frustrated in their chance to obtain a leading role in the government, called a general strike and threatened to stop paying taxes. The West Pakistanis moved in to quell the strike and the civil war began, ending in the establishment of the independent Bengali state of Bangladesh.

The civil wars in Africa in recent years were even more complex. Many modern African nations include tribes traditionally hostile to each other, so in part the wars in the Congo, Nigeria, and Burundi were tribal or ethnic. But other factors were involved. Many Africans expected independence to bring concrete economic and social improvements, but their governments were unable to meet these expectations. Conflicts between traditional patterns of tribal authority and the new governments were frequent. Finally, the first steps toward mass education and modernization left many people uncertain and dissatisfied with their status in the new countries.

Another general conclusion is that modern technology has proved to be a mixed blessing for advanced nations. It is true that, thanks to their ability to mass-produce consumer goods, these countries are able to satisfy the material wants of their citizens. But they are not immune from civil disorders, partly because they have major communications networks that can propel local issues into broadly national issues overnight. Reports of riots can be circulated almost immediately, and the media and TV cameras may play up violence to appear more extensive than it actually is.

The other side of the communications issue is, of course, that in backward countries without good communications facilities, an uprising may be localized more easily. However, rebels may conduct guerrilla warfare more successfully in the less developed and more rural nations. One of the longest guerrilla operations in recent history has been going on in Portuguese West Africa, where the Angolan Liberation Army has been fighting for independence from Portugal for more than a decade. The rebels are able to retreat into the wilderness and take refuge in the territory of sympathetic neighboring states.

Can the world's political systems ever find a way to avoid political strife? Rather obviously, it will be difficult to achieve total tranquility within the world's present political communities. The elements that contribute to civil strife are far too numerous and too complicated for any simple solution to be drawn out of a hat. But based upon what we know, as learned through systematic research and from first-hand observation, the answer does not lie in simplistic police-state practices of governing by sheer force, but in making the political processes work for all the diversified segments within the political community. This is far easier to say than to achieve, because many of the world's political communities are almost irreconcilably divided by severe cleavages, with little prospect for calm compromise. Greek and Turkish factions have been at odds on the island of Cyprus since 1955.

There are periodic flare-ups of chronic separatist groups such as the Catalonians and the Basques in Spain, the German-speaking communities in the Tyrol of northern Italy, and the Ukrainians in the USSR. There have been conflicts between the Flemish and the Walloons in Belgium, and in Canada, the sharp division between French- and English-speaking Canadians has led to a separatist govement in the Province of Quebec.

Almost any modern government is so complex and has such comparatively limited resources at its command that, unfortunately, there will always be those groups in the society who feel relatively deprived by the existing political system. The old saying that "you can't please all of the people all of the time" is only too true. If these groups lose faith that the system will distribute societal goods equitably among all citizens, then with sufficient motivation, their resentment will probably express itself in one of the three varieties of civil strife. Until governments are able to successfully satisfy the needs of the various sectors of society, turmoil will probably continue to manifest itself—and at some cost in human life.

If we return to our original question, then—why political violence?—we are forced to answer that the fault lies at the heart of political organization itself: no state can represent a total consensus of opinions; no political decision can possibly satisfy all sectors within a political society. And, unfortunately, when there are many possible solutions to a particular political or social problem, it is difficult to prove that one political decision is more right or better than a series of others; the proof of the effectiveness or ineffectiveness of a political decision is usually discovered only by living with it.

While agreement among all parties within a political system is almost impossible to achieve, there are alternatives to chaos. We could hope that intelligent public opinion will be strong enough to have some impact; that political parties will speak for all the various interests of the system and translate those interests into official policies; and that interest groups operating under some self-imposed standards of political decency will continue to influence government. Even when these alternative processes appear to work, however, we still cannot guarantee that the society will maintain its stability. On the other hand, we should not be so blind as to argue that political stability above all else is the most important political value. Quite clearly, when governments fail to recognize that they are agents of the people, then the people have a right to speak, and speak loudly, if need be.

Suggested Readings

Bondurant, Joan V. *Conquest of Violence: The Gandhian Philosophy of Conflict.* Princeton, N.J.: Princeton University Press, 1958. An argument for nonviolence, with reference to employable tactics.

Feierabend, Ivo K., Feierabend, Rosalind L., and Gurr, Ted Robert, eds. *Anger, Violence, and Politics: Theories and Research*. Englewood Cliffs, N.J.: Prentice-Hall, 1972. The best collection of papers available on this subject.

Gaham, Hugh Davis, and Gurr, Ted, eds. *Violence in America*. New York: The New American Library, 1969. A collection of up-to-date studies of violent conflict in America.

Gurr, Ted. *Why Men Rebel*. Princeton, N.J.: Princeton University Press, 1970. A theoretical analysis of the causes and types of violent behavior.

Leites, Nathan, and Wolf, Charles, Jr. *Rebellion and Authority*. Chicago: Markham, 1970. An in-depth comparative analysis of rebellions.

Luttwak, Edward. *Coup d'Etat*. New York: Alfred A. Knopf, 1968. A fascinating study of how a coup d'etat is organized.

Nieburg, H. L. *Political Violence: The Behavioral Process*. New York: St. Martin's Press, 1969. An examination of the causes and consequences of violence in America.

Rubenstein, Richard E. *Rebels in Eden*. Boston: Little, Brown, 1970. A historical view of violence in the United States.

The cities: Government's role in an age of technology

CHAPTER 21

In *Notes on Virginia* (1781), Thomas Jefferson expressed his hope that America would remain a nation of small farmers:

While we have land to labor then, let us never wish to see our citizens occupied at a workbench. Let our workshops remain in Europe. It is better to carry provisions and materials to workmen there, than to bring them to the provisions and materials, and with them their manners and principles. The loss by transportation of commodities across the Atlantic will be made up in the happiness and permanence of government. The mobs of great cities add just so much to the support of pure government, as sores do to the strength of the human body.[1]

[1] Quoted in Max Beloff, *Thomas Jefferson and American Democracy*, (New York: Crowell-Collier, 1962), p. 82.

Jefferson did not want the unwholesome spectacles of London and Paris—the dirty, crowded streets; the unruly mobs; the evil ways—to be repeated in the new world. In time, however, he and others realized that the United States required some industry and urbanization if it was to achieve economic independence from Europe. But Jefferson never considered cities anything more than a necessary evil.

The proportion of Americans living in or around cities has increased steadily since Jefferson's day: from 10 percent in 1790 to over 70 percent in 1970.[2] But some skeptical Americans still share Jefferson's attitudes toward cities. They view New York, Chicago, Los Angeles, and other urban centers as islands of disorder and decay: to paraphrase Jefferson, as sores on the face of affluent America. In spite of our apparent sophistication, an undercurrent in the national subconscious still links cities with liberal permissiveness, radicalism, intellectual elitism, as well as pollution, crime, and drug addiction. Cities are considered somehow *un*-American. To a degree, of course, these associations are true. Traditionally, American cities have housed the unassimilated. The foreign-born and the outcasts—from the Irish in the days before the Civil War to the Germans, Jews, Italians, Poles, Greeks, blacks, and Puerto Ricans—tended to settle in urban neighborhoods. For most of these people, however, the city has been only a temporary home. As soon as they could, they have moved to the suburbs.

But in the last ten to twenty years, the population of cities has been rising.[3] This is so even though many middle-class people have deserted the city, taking their tax dollars, their votes, and their skills with them. People in search of economic and social opportunity come to cities, and in large measure account for the population increase. But it is clear that cities cannot survive without a middle class and without the private businesses that come with it. The dilemma of the cities cannot be overemphasized. We must ask ourselves whether the cities can indeed survive.

Today as in the past, cities are the centers of the arts, educational and social experiments, science, fashion and style. They also have a great many social problems: broken homes, substandard housing, welfare, crime, and drug addiction. Extremes of wealth and poverty are more apparent in cities than in small towns; the problems of pollution and public transportation more urgent; strikes and demonstrations more visible. In addition, city governments have developed haphazardly. Outdated boundaries and ambiguous lines of authority—as well as the legacy of antiurbanism—complicate already difficult problems.

Prescriptions for city ills vary widely. The one point that many urban-

[2] Senator Fred R. Harris and Mayor John V. Lindsay, Co-chairmen, *The State of the Cities. Report of the Commission on the Cities in the Seventies* (New York: The National Urban Coalition and Praeger Publishers, 1972), p. 71.

[3] U.S. Department of Housing and Urban Development, "The Problems Associated with Rapid Urban Growth," in *HUD International Series*, Supplement no. 5 (January 20, 1972), p. 4.

ologists agree on is that "Business as usual is a terminal illness for cities." [4]
Change—social, economic, and political—seems inevitable. In this sense, the
city is a laboratory for the future.

The Growing City and Its Problems

One of the most serious problems that municipal governments face is the
enormous growth of the urban population. During the last several decades,
the population in urban areas around the world has increased at an astounding rate. The New York metropolitan area, for example, had a population
of approximately twelve million in 1950; by 1970, the population had increased to over sixteen million. During the same twenty-year period, the
population of Tokyo nearly doubled. Even a proportionately small growth
in population puts an enormous strain on city government: London's population during this period grew only slightly, by comparison, but this growth
meant that the municipal government had to meet the needs of more than
one million more people (see Table 21–1).

The increased urban population has changed the demographic makeup of
many countries, for the population of these countries is no longer spread
over large geographic areas. Rather, major centers of population have
formed in cities (see Table 21–2).[5] The rate of this change has been very
rapid. In 1920 approximately 20 percent of Japan's population lived in
urban areas; today the figure has skyrocketed to 85 percent. This kind of
rapid growth, which often occurs within the span of a few years, challenges
the capacity of the political system to respond quickly and equitably.

The Increasing Demand for City Services

City governments are reeling under the burden of the population explosion,
for they cannot meet the present and future requirements of their inhabitants.
City services must be expanded to meet the needs of the rising populations,
but often population increases are so rapid and so great that the city cannot
hope to keep up with them. It is very difficult, for example, for a city whose
population increased by 10 percent within a span of five short years to
provide a 10 percent increase in governmental services, for in many large
cities, this kind of increase means the addition of hundreds of thousands of

[4] Harris and Lindsay, *State of the Cities*, p. 110.
[5] The high growth rate of central cities appears to be related to the process of industrialization. The highest degree of urbanization (movement of the population to the
central city) occurs in countries making the most rapid strides toward industrialization;
people swarm to the cities for economic and social opportunity. When the rate of industrialization declines, so does the rate of urban growth.

Table 21-1
The 20 Largest Cities in the Organization for Economic Cooperation and Development (OECD) Countries and How They Have Grown

Rank in 1970	Urban Agglomeration	Population in Thousands			Rank in 1950
		1950	1960	1970	
1	New York	12,331	14,114	16,077	1
2	Tokyo	6,277	9,684	12,199	3
3	London	10,393	10,953	11,544	2
4	Los Angeles	4,009	6,489	9,473	7
5	Paris	5,998	7,287	8,714	4
6	Chicago	4,935	5,959	6,983	5
7	Essen-Dortmund-Duisburg	4,597	5,587	6,789	6
8	San Francisco-Oakland	2,028	2,431	4,490	14
9	Detroit	2,667	3,538	4,447	9
10	Philadelphia	2,930	3,635	4,355	8
11	Osaka	1,956	3,012	3,307	15
12	Madrid	1,618	2,260	2,990	22
13	Birmington	2,583	2,775	2,981	10
14	Rome	1,605	2,020	2,920	23
15	Sydney	1,702	2,134	2,720	20
16	Washington, D.C.	1,291	1,808	2,666	31
17–18	Boston	2,239	2,413	2,600	12
17–18	Istanbul	983	1,467	2,600	46
19	Manchester	2,509	2,525	2,541	11
20	Toronto	1,075	1,720	2,511	41

Source: U.S. Department of Housing and Urban Development, "The Problems Associated With Rapid Urban Growth," in HUD International Series, Supplement no. 5 (January 20, 1972), p. 4.

people to the population. The demand for services, including public housing, schools, transportation, and so on, empties the city's pocket book and planning capacity. And the same number of demands is placed on the private sector of the community. Job opportunities, for example, must be available to meet the needs of the increased population.

As the public and private sectors of the city try to meet the demand for increased services, they are often paralyzed by the number of people they must serve. For example, there seems to be no way for New York City to prevent rush-hour crushes on the subways and roads, for the city's transportation network is saturated—just too many people use it. And the services that are available become increasingly expensive. When this happens, many people who are financially able leave the city for the less highly populated, less expensive suburbs. The central city is left in a condition of fiscal and social chaos; city services are supported by those who really cannot handle the tax burden. To these people, the city has become a social and economic

Table 21-2
The Urban Population of Countries

	1950	1960	1970	Annual Growth Rate %	
	%	%	%	1950–60	1960–70
Australia	72.1	81.0	88.5	3.5	2.7
Japan	37.4	63.5	84.4	6.6	3.7
Germany	72.5	77.6	82.4	1.6	1.7
Denmark	67.3	74.1	80.1	1.7	1.6
United Kingdom	78.5	79.3	80.1	0.5	0.7
United States	64.0	69.9	75.2	2.7	2.1
Canada	61.7	68.5	74.7	3.8	2.8
Netherlands	70.5	67.5	72.2	0.8	2.0
Iceland	61.0	66.5	71.7	3.0	2.7
Belgium	63.4	66.2	71.2	1.0	1.1
France	54.1	61.3	70.2	2.2	2.2
Finland	41.5	55.9	68.4	4.0	2.7
Sweden	55.4	61.0	66.1	1.6	1.6
Luxembourg	58.8	62.6	65.6	1.2	1.4
Greece	51.0	57.0	62.6	2.1	1.6
Switzerland	48.2	54.2	59.8	2.6	2.5
Spain	48.7	53.9	59.1	1.9	1.7
Norway	42.2	48.7	54.9	2.4	2.0
Italy	44.0	47.8	51.5	1.4	1.5
Austria	49.0	50.0	51.0	0.4	0.8
Ireland	40.6	45.7	50.7	0.7	1.4
Yugoslavia [1]	17.2	27.2	38.7	5.9	4.8
Portugal	31.2	33.9	36.5	1.3	1.7
Turkey	22.1	26.6	31.2	4.8	4.2
AVERAGE	52.2	58.3	64.4	3.28	2.27

[1] Special status within OECD.
Source: U.S. Department of Housing and Urban Development, "The Problems Associated with Rapid Urban Growth," in HUD International Series, Supplement no. 5, p. 3.

trap. Having once fled rural areas for the prosperity and promise of the central city, the poor only find an intolerable way of life.

The Individual's Decreasing Voice in City Government

In a growing urban area, individuals find that they have a steadily decreasing voice in formulating governmental policies. Where the small-town inhabitant could stand up and voice his opinion about proposed governmental programs at the town meeting, the city-dweller finds his voice muted among the voices of millions of others. His attempts to influence city policy are frustrated at every turn, and he often loses his desire to participate in government at all. However, apathy is only one symptom of this frustration. Within the last decade, a more visible symptom has erupted in U.S. cities —the urban riot. When the rioters in Watts and Harlem, for example, used violence and physical strength against the political system, they were also expressing their powerlessness: they had no control over the programs that determined their social and economic conditions and no meaningful link with city government.

Many city governments have been trying to deal with this problem by bringing government closer to the people. In New York City, for example, the school system has been decentralized so that each community controls school policy and the education of its children. Many cities have also set up "little city halls," in an attempt to bring big city government closer to the people. While a central city government could easily overlook local community needs, little city halls are designed to be more responsive to community problems and to add to the accountability of city government.

Overlapping Jurisdictions

As the urban population expands, it moves outward from the core city to suburban areas. This creates a vast population network, encompassing many governmental jurisdictions. Prior to 1960, the bulk of the U.S. population lived in cities. Between 1960 and the early 1970s, however, the population center shifted from the central cities to the surrounding suburbs.

While this population movement in itself is not undesirable, its consequences for rational governmental planning are quite serious. As the metropolitan population spills over into surrounding governmental jurisdictions, the ability of one governmental unit to plan and provide programs becomes questionable. While a city government may attempt to come to grips with problems within its jurisdiction, it has no control over the policy planning of the surrounding governmental units. It is essential to attain uniform, metropolitan-wide policies because the problems of cities and their surrounding areas are integrally tied together. It does little good, for instance, for Chicago's city government to place strict controls on air pollution if industrial centers a few miles away in Indiana spew forth their soot into the air currents that reach the central city. Similarly, improving a city's mass transportation system is meaningless unless the surrounding areas have also improved their mass transit links to the city. This problem becomes enormous when we realize, for example, that the New York metropolitan area is made up of nearly fourteen hundred overlapping governmental units. These include the central city government, suburban and county governments, and smaller governmental units like school districts.[6] The National Urban Coalition's Commission on the Cities in the Seventies estimates that the average metropolitan area, which consists of a city and its suburbs, includes ninety-one

[6] The problem of overlapping jurisdiction in New York City is discussed in Robert C. Wood, *1400 Governments* (Cambridge, Mass.: Harvard University Press, 1961).

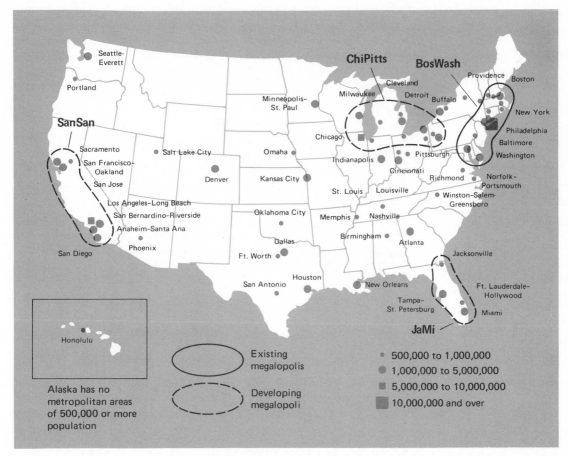

**Figure 21-1
Populations of the
Largest Metro-
politan Regions**

Some unbanologists predict that the major cities along the coasts and the Great Lakes will grow together, forming continuous urban strips—what Jean Coleman named "megalopoli."

distinct political units run by 350 elected, and hundreds of nonelected officials (see Figure 21–1).[7]

Economic and social factors are forcing suburban areas to cooperate with the central cities, for the suburbs are no longer the haven of the rich. They are facing increased demands for low-income housing, expanded educational facilities, mass transit, and so on. The only way to meet this critical metropolitan challenge is to integrate policy planning among the numerous governmental jurisdictions.

New Forms of Urban Government

The need to restructure metropolitan area governments to provide for more rational problem solving is urgent. New forms of government that

[7] Harris and Lindsay, *The State of the Cities*, p. 100.

reach far beyond the geographic limits of the central city itself are essential if spreading urban problems are to be resolved. A kind of *metropolitan federation,* in which the central city and the surrounding communities work together under the umbrella of one governmental unit, is needed. This concept has been tried in several metropolitan areas. In Toronto, Canada, for example, an area-wide governmental body, which is made up of the central city and surrounding communities, deals with metropolitan problems, deferring to the local communities when a problem has a purely local nature. This kind of area-wide council is also seen in London, England, and Miami, Florida.

Unfortunately, these reforms are not easily made. Asking local community governments to relinquish their powers to an area-wide council is, in a sense, questioning their reason for being. Entrenched local bureaucracies and political organizations feel the threat of elimination if they transfer their powers and functions to a metropolitan federation. This appears to be the major political battle ground in the urban crisis. And the major issue centers around the conflict between local autonomy and the need for area-wide governmental problem solving.

An Alternate Approach: The New City

Urban problems can be solved by working within the structure of existing cities or by creating a totally different urban structure in a "new city." Advocates of the new-city movement point to the fact that the money that has been spent on existing cities has brought few permanent changes. Because of this lack of success, many governments have complemented their programs of urban redevelopment with programs designed to create new cities. Great Britain has led the nations of the world in the new-city movement; since 1946, the British government has endorsed their planning and construction. In the United States, new cities have recently been created in Reston, Virginia, and Columbia, Maryland. This trend has rapidly increased since the federal government passed legislation in 1968 encouraging the development of new cities. Although new cities do not provide the answer to existing urban ills, they do provide a meaningful testing ground for alternate urban life-styles.

The City in the American Political System

The United States Constitution does not mention cities. Amendment 10 states that all powers not delegated to the federal government are "reserved to the States respectively, or to the people." Cities are established by state legislatures in charters that specify the form a city government will take and its powers. In effect, cities are administrative agencies of states. Depending on the charter, a state may refuse a city the right to levy taxes, make certain expenditures mandatory, or disband its government altogether. The Supreme Court ruled in 1923 that cities "have not the inherent right of self-government which is beyond the legislative control of the state" (*Trenton* v. *New Jersey*).

Little and Diffuse Authority

While European city governments may do anything that is not expressly prohibited by law, the reverse is true for American city governments. As Edward Banfield and James Wilson write, "a city cannot operate a peanut stand at the city zoo without first getting the state legislature to pass an enabling act, unless perchance, the city's charter or some previously enacted law unmistakably covers the sale of peanuts." [8] Thus, cities are dependent on state legislatures, which more often than not are dominated by noncity representatives who have little sympathy for city problems.[9]

In addition, cities share local authority with a variety of special districts, such as school, fire, and sanitation districts; and with public authorities, such as port authorities, park departments, and water and power commissions. Some of these agencies have the power to issue ordinances (no bicycles in the park), levy taxes (fees for a public beach), and issue bonds. The mayor may appoint the water and parks commissioners, but he has little control over them once they are in office. The agencies are independent.

An example of such an agency is the Port of New York Authority, established as a public corporation in 1921. The Port Authority controls transportation facilities, including airports, bus terminals, bridges, tunnels, and piers in the New York-New Jersey metropolitan area. It is governed by a board of twelve directors appointed by the governors of the two states for overlapping terms. These officials are free to invest the money collected from tolls and bonds as they see fit, without consulting local officials or local citizens and may thus have a great effect on the urban area. In the early seventies, the Port Authority constructed the two huge towers of the World Trade Center in lower Manhattan. Although this project may help to increase revenues for the City of New York, it also adds heavily to the burden on subways and sewers, for which the Port Authority has no responsibility.

Partly as a result of these independent agencies, city government is highly decentralized. In New York, for example, the mayor controls the city bureaucracy and is relatively free from interference by the city council. However,

[8] Edward C. Banfield and James Q. Wilson, *City Politics*, (New York: Vintage Books, 1966), p. 65. The following discussion is based on Part 2 of this book, "The Structure of City Politics."

[9] Before apportionment reforms in the sixties, Los Angeles (pop. 5,000,000) had the same number of state representatives as Alpine County (pop. a few thousand). Miami (pop. 495,000) sent three representatives to the Florida State assembly; Glade County (pop. 2,199) sent one. *Ibid.*, p. 70.

this authority is checked by the Board of Estimate, which includes the controller, the president of the city council, and five borough presidents—all of whom are elected independently of the mayor. The Board of Estimate has the final say on the city's budget. In Los Angeles, which has been called "twenty-seven suburbs in search of a city," municipal authority is divided among the mayor, the city attorney, and the controller. These executives have neither official nor political control over the fifteen city councilmen, who are elected at different times from different districts. Nineteen of Los Angeles' twenty-eight departments are virtually beyond the control of the mayor, the council, and the voters. In addition, the voters of Los Angeles themselves have changed zoning laws, awarded higher pensions to firemen and policemen, decided to build a stadium for the Dodgers, and rejected public housing in referendums.

Thus, city officials' hands are tied in a number of ways. Coordinated, long-range planning is practically impossible in major metropolitan areas. The result is that "many things are not done because it is impossible to secure the collaboration of all those whose collaboration is needed [state legislators, other city officials with special interests, independent department heads, voters]. . . . Measures are frequently compromised so as to 'give something to everybody' in order to get them accepted." [10]

Because cities are subunits of states, without legal status in the U.S. Constitution, their relationship to the federal government is not clearly defined. There is no congressional committee or subcommittee on urban affairs. Until 1965, when the Department of Housing and Urban Development (HUD) was established, there was no cabinet-level agency to deal with urban problems. If a city wants to upgrade a particular neighborhood with new housing, special educational programs such as Head Start, increased health facilities, and improved transportation, it must apply to at least three federal agencies—the Department of Housing and Urban Development (HUD); the Department of Health, Education and Welfare (HEW); and the Department of Transportation. "Programs are defined functionally, such as housing or highways, rather than as general aid to cities, and most of the money is offered across the board rather than just to the very large cities, or to those with the most severe problems." [11] The mayor of Newark, a devastated city, competes with the mayor of Atlanta, a prospering city, on an equal basis. Even the very process of applying for federal funds is time-consuming and expensive.

The American City As It Reflects the Problems of the Nation

Novelist Norman Mailer, who campaigned for the Democratic nomination for mayor of New York in 1969, described that city's problems as follows:

[10] Banfield and Wilson, *City Politics*, p. 111.
[11] Robert Salisbury, *Governing America* (New York: Appleton-Century-Crofts, 1973), p. 76.

How is one to speak of the illness of a city? A clear day can come, a morning in early May like the pride of June. . . . Everyone speaks of the delight of the day on the way to work. . . .

Yet by afternoon the city is incarcerated once more. Haze covers the sky; a grim, formless glare blazes back from the horizon. The city has become unbalanced again. By the time work is done, New Yorkers push through the acrid lung-rotting air and work their way home, avoiding each other's eyes in the subway. Later, near midnight, thinking of a walk to buy The Times, *they hesitate—in the darkness a familiar sense of dread returns, the streets are not quite safe, the sense of waiting for some apocalyptic fire, some night of long knives hangs over the city. . . .*

Midtown Manhattan is next to impenetrable by vehicle from midday to evening—the average rate of advance is, in fact, 6 miles an hour, about the speed of a horse at walk. . . . Tempers blow with lost schedules, work suffers everywhere. . . .

Beneath that mood of pestilential clangor, something worse is ticking away —our deeper sense of a congealed and continuing human horror. If there are eight million people in New York, one million are on welfare. . . . Not a tenth of those welfare cases will ever be available for work; they are women and children first, then too old, too sick, too addicted, too illiterate, too ignorant of English. . . . Poverty lies upon the city like a layer of smog. . . .

Our parks deteriorate, and after duty our police go home to suburbs beyond the city—they come back to govern us from without. And municipal employees drift in the endless administrative bogs of Wagnerian systems of apathy and attrition. Work gets done at the rate of work accomplished by a draft army in peacetime at a sullen out-of-the-way post. The Poverty Program staggers from the brilliance of its embezzlements. . . .

Our first problem is that no one alive in New York can answer with honesty the question: Can New York be saved? [12]

Some of the most serious domestic problems facing the United States—pollution, crime, violence, traffic, poverty, apathy, corruption—seem to converge on the cities. Have "events conspired against them"? Possibly.

Money

In November 1970, the financial situation in cities across the country was so bad that many were cutting personnel and services. In Cleveland, Mayor Carl Stokes cut the city budget by 20 percent; laid off 15 percent of the city's employees; closed the police academy, dismissing that year's class; and halted all demolition of abandoned buildings. (Cleveland did not have the money to tear down old buildings, much less to build new ones!) [13] In the same year, the U.S. Conference of Mayors, meeting in Denver, Colorado,

---

[12] Norman Mailer, "Why Are We in New York?" *The New York Times Magazine*, May 18, 1969, pp. 30–31; 96, 108.

[13] Harris and Lindsay, *The State of the Cities*, p. 103.

passed a resolution calling for a cutback in funds for the space program, the military, highways, and agriculture, and increased federal aid to cities. Eighty percent of the nation's taxable wealth is concentrated in cities. Why, then, is urban America on the verge of bankruptcy?

The Problem. First, most of a city's tax dollars go to the federal and state governments. Some of this money is returned, but not in proportion to city population or problems. According to one estimate, New York City pays $14 billion to the federal government in income and corporate taxes. Only $3 billion is returned, which means New York must raise an additional $4.5 billion locally to meet its $7.5 billion budget. As Mailer wrote, "In relation to the Federal Government, the city is like a sharecropper who lives forever in debt at the company store." [14]

Second, because there are more people in cities than elsewhere, the city must provide more services: more education, more transportation, more police, garbage collection and so on—what Lamb calls the "housekeeping chores." [15] The city provides these services not only to its residents but also to those who commute to the city from the suburbs for work or for entertainment. Usually services are funded with local taxes, which suburbanites do not pay. In addition, the city must compete with private companies and "more desirable" residential communities for personnel. The cost of recruiting, training, and paying a policeman, for example, has risen sharply in the last decade.

Third, the cities' tax base has declined in recent years as the middle and upper classes and, perhaps more importantly, businesses have moved to the suburbs. In the past, manufacturers had to locate in cities to be near the ports and railroads that brought them raw materials. Today, with the expanded interstate highway system, trucks are replacing ships and trains as major carriers, making out-of-town locations more economical. In addition, manufacturing techniques have changed. Many companies need a huge amount of space for assembly-line production, and city real estate is too expensive for them. At the same time, consumer industries, which need buyers more than space, have followed their customers to the suburbs. Added to this is the fact that cities rely on real-estate and sales taxes as their major source of revenue. This tax bite discourages investors from establishing businesses in cities.

The decline in industry in central cities means a decline in jobs, especially for unskilled and semiskilled labor. A worker earning a minimal salary cannot afford to commute to the suburbs by car or by train; nor is he able to find inexpensive housing near suburban jobs. As a result, unemployment rates are much higher in central cities than elsewhere. The Commission on the Cities in the Seventies estimated that the unemployment rate for whites in the United States as a whole in 1970–1971 was approximately 6.6 per-

---

14 Mailer, "Why Are We in New York?"
15 Karl A. Lamb, *The People, Maybe: Seeking Democracy in America* (Belmont, Calif.: Duxbury Press, 1970).

cent; for blacks 10.3 percent. However, the unemployment rate for blacks living in the inner city was 14 percent, and the rate for young urban blacks was 34.5 percent. This means that cities are called upon to provide more social services—welfare, medical care, subsidized housing, job training— than suburban or rural communities. In a very real sense, the nation's major metropolitan areas have become the "two societies" prophesied in the Kerner Commission Report—a poor, black inner city, surrounded by affluent, white suburbs.

Proposed Solutions. Rising costs and a declining tax base place cities in a double bind: if they raise taxes to provide needed services; they risk losing more businesses and middle- and upper-class residents; if they do not, and the cities deteriorate, they risk the population loss nonetheless. If cities and their suburbs were joined in single political units, the cost of housekeeping and social services would be spread across a larger, more affluent tax base. The flight to the suburbs to avoid these costs—by companies and individuals —might be stopped. Suburbanites could be taxed for the city services they use. Urbanologists realize, however, that it is unrealistic to expect the suburbs to willingly accept unification with the cities. Most big-city mayors, therefore, look to the federal government for aid.[16]

Welfare

The Problem. In 1970 some 25.7 million Americans were living below the poverty level, which, according to the Social Security Administration, was $3,968 for an urban family of four.[17] Of that number, 12.7 million were receiving some form of public assistance—because they were blind or disabled, unemployed or unemployable, or too old or too young to work. The Commission on the Cities in the Seventies estimated that only 5 percent of these welfare recipients were potentially employable (or 12 percent if women with small children are included).

Public assistance is administered through four programs: Old Age Assistance, Aid to the Blind, Aid to Permanently and Totally Disabled, and Aid to Families with Dependent Children (see Table 21–3). Aid to Families with Dependent Children covers unemployed but able adults and children. The number of people receiving benefits under AFDC rose 38 percent between 1950 and 1960, and another 38 percent between 1960 and 1969 (while the population rose only 18 and 12 percent respectively). The cost of welfare rose 239 percent between 1960 and 1969 alone. In 1972, the total AFDC budget was

[16] In 1970, for example, the white suburban community of Glen Park tried to "disannex" itself from predominantly black Gary, Indiana. See Lamb, *The People, Maybe,* p. 393. For our discussion of the federal government's role in solving the fiscal crises of the cities, see Chapter 17, "Unitary and Federal Models of Government."

[17] Unless otherwise noted, data are from Harris and Lindsay, *The State of the Cities,* pp. 37–44.

Table 21-3
**Public Assistance
in the United
States in 1970**

Program	Number of Recipients
Old Age Assistance	2,081,000
Aid to the Blind	81,000
Aid to Permanently and Totally Disabled	933,000
Aid to Families with Dependent Children:	
Children	7,032,000
Adults	2,625,000 *
TOTAL	12,752,000

* 857,692 of these are women with small children; 133,320 are unemployed men seeking work.
Source: Harold Wolman, unpublished background paper for Counterbudget (New York: Praeger Publishers, 1971), in Harris and Lindsay, The State of the Cities, p. 40.

$6.8 billion, $3.8 billion of which was paid with federal funds; the remainder comes from state and local taxes. The federal government sets guidelines for welfare, but state governments determine actual payments. The benefits for a family of four in 1970 ranged from $2,000 to $4,000.[18]

We seldom hear anyone objecting to public assistance for the blind, the disabled, the elderly, or for the children; welfare for able-bodied adults, however, is another story. Many critics on the right and left feel that AFDC encourages unemployment and perpetuates the "cycle of poverty." Why? If a person on welfare finds a full- or part-time job, he immediately loses all of his benefits. However, if he works forty hours a week, fifty-two weeks a year for the federal minimum wage of $1.60 an hour, he earns only $3,328, which is below the federal poverty level. In addition, AFDC is aimed primarily at fatherless families. If a man earns $3,000 to $4,000 a year, his family cannot receive any assistance; if he leaves his family, it becomes eligible for benefits that sometimes exceed his salary. AFDC is thus accused of discouraging people from looking for work and encouraging families to break up.

Proposed Solutions. Many attempts have been made to break this cycle, but solutions are not as easy as criticisms. President Nixon introduced a "workfare" proposal to Congress in 1971. Under this bill, a family of four would have received a guaranteed annual income of $2,400—whether or not the adults in the family worked. Families earning up to $4,320 would be eligible for some benefits, and all employable adults would be required to work. In addition, payments would be standardized across the country.[19]

18 Walter E. Volkomer, *American Government* (New York: Appleton-Century-Crofts, 1972) p. 799.
19 John A. Hamilton, "Welfare: It May Soon be Known as Workfare," *The New York Times*, June 27, 1972, Section 4, p. 4.

In spite of its advantages, the bill was defeated in the Senate in the spring of 1972, for several reasons. Conservatives objected to the principle of a guaranteed annual income. Liberals argued that the annual income of $2,400 was far too low, and that the bill had no provision for creating jobs, or job skills, where none existed. Undoubtedly, modified proposals will be submitted to Congress in future sessions, for no one is satisfied with the public assistance programs as they now stand.

Housing

The Problem. The effects of urban poverty are most visible in the blocks of run-down tenements, rooming houses, "welfare hotels," and abandoned buildings—the ghettoes which so much has been written about since the riots of the sixties. Anthony Downs defines a ghetto as an area where people are forced to live because of ethnic, racial, and economic segregation.[20] They cannot afford housing elsewhere, or if they can afford it, they cannot find it.[21] Jane Jacobs, distinguishing between poor but liveable neighborhoods and slums, writes that "the key link in a perpetual slum is that too many people move out of it too fast—and in the meantime, dream of getting out," instead of devoting more efforts to making it liveable.[22]

The number of substandard housing units in this country has decreased markedly in the past two decades (see Table 21–4). Recent surveys indicate, however, that a substantial number of urban Americans are still living in relatively primitive conditions. Of families on welfare in 1971, 11 percent had no private kitchen, and over 22 percent had no hot or cold running water, no private flush toilet, and no private bath or shower, despite strict housing codes in virtually every city.[23] How are slums created? Some urbanologists blame the deterioration of city neighborhoods in part on the federal government's lack of foresight. Programs designed to enable every American to have "a decent home and a suitable living environment" (to quote the 1948 Housing Act) had quite the opposite effect for some Americans.

The federal government first entered the housing field in the 1930s with the creation of the Federal Housing Administration and the passage of several bills designed to promote individual home ownership. The U.S. government added to the supply of money for home loans, insured mortgages issued by private banks, and made local property taxes and interest on mortgages tax deductible. The Commission on the Cities in the Seventies estimated that

[20] Anthony Downs, *Urban Problems and Prospects* (Chicago: Markham, 1970) p. 27.
[21] For a discussion of racial segregation in the North and the profit to be had in "block busting" and ghetto making, see Jack Rothman, "The Ghetto Makers," *The Nation* 193 (October 7, 1961): 222–25.
[22] Jane Jacobs, *The Death and Life of Great American Cities* (New York: Vintage Books, 1961), p. 271.
[23] Harris and Lindsay, *The State of the Cities*, p. 43.

Table 21-4
Comparison of Standard and Substandard Housing in the United States, 1950– 1970 *

Years	All Units (millions)	Substandard Units (millions)	Percent Substandard
1950	46.1	17.0	36.9
1960	58.5	11.4	19.5
1970	69.5 (est).	6.9	9.9

* These data reflect the demolition of 10.1 million units, the building of 30 million units, for a net increase of 80.7 percent (while the population increased 35 percent). They do not include 3.9 million overcrowded units.
Source: Anthony Downs, Urban Problems and Prospects, (Chicago: Markham, 1970), p. 117.

tax deductions to homeowners in 1969 amounted to $4.5 billion.[24] In effect, the government subsidizes middle-income housing.

These incentives contributed heavily to the middle-class exodus to the suburbs, where land is less expensive than in the city. Indirectly, they also contributed to the exclusiveness of these suburbs. New communities need roads, sewers, police, schools, and other services and conveniences. To ensure a sound tax base, suburban communities often enact zoning regulations that prohibit inexpensive or high-density housing—regulations that keep the working poor crowded in the inner city.

The federal government has subsidized low-income, inner city housing in an attempt to make cities more liveable, but has met with limited success. The Housing Acts of 1937, 1949, and 1954 provided federal funds to local governments in the form of loans and subsidies for low-rent housing. The Department of Housing and Urban Development (HUD) was created in 1965 in large part because these programs backfired. The huge low-income housing projects of the forties and fifties gave poor families more toilets and more windows, but they also destroyed communities. To make room for the projects, hundreds of families were displaced, and with them went the people and places that were the essence of the community—friendly shopkeepers, store-front social clubs, familiar corners, and police who knew residents by name.[25] For the most part, these projects created high-density neighborhoods where people were strangers within the same building. In addition, some cities intepreted urban renewal to mean "slum clearance." When low-rent districts were torn down, they were replaced by expensive housing former residents could not afford.

Proposed Solutions. HUD's Model Cities Program attempts to create better communities—not just buildings. Funds for housing are supplemented

24 Harris and Lindsay, *The State of the Cities*, p. 39.
25 For a study of the effect of low-income projects on an East Harlem neighborhood, see Ellen Lurie "Community Action in East Harlem," in Leonard J. Duhl, *The Urban Condition* (New York: Basic Books, 1963).

with grants to state and local health, welfare, education, and recreation agencies; grants to private social agencies and community projects; and loans to local small businessmen. The program coordinates its plans with an eye to using money and people to their greatest advantage, and attempts to upgrade neighborhoods on all levels. To date, the Model Cities Program is still experimental; only a few cities are participating.

Another much-discussed solution to the housing problem is the elimination of the ghetto—either by building relatively small low-income units in middle-class, suburban areas (scatter-site housing) or by providing poor families with rent subsidies so they can find homes on their own.[26] Both programs have been tried on a limited basis. As noted above, however, suburban towns often zone out low-cost housing. Unless the courts decide that economic discrimination is equivalent to racial discrimination, large-scale dispersal seems unlikely. In addition, some black leaders feel it is in their people's best interest to remain in inner cities, for, very shortly, blacks will be a majority in several big cities, which could give the black community control of local government and the federal funds for upgrading ghetto neighborhoods.

The issue of community control of urban renewal is hotly debated. Some favor long-range, city-wide planning; other urbanologists argue that neighborhood direction of urban renewal would be more effective than existing programs.[27]

Crime

The Problem. Crime rates have risen dramatically in recent years. The FBI Crime Index reported an overall increase of 16 percent in 1967, 11 percent in 1968, and another 11 percent in 1969. In the first six months of 1971 alone, total crime rose 7 percent, and violent crime rose 11 percent. Between 1960 and 1969, arrests on narcotics charges rose 492 percent for adults, and even more notably, 2,453 percent for juveniles. One hundred policemen were killed on duty in 1970—an increase of 257 percent since 1960. Most serious crimes are committed by young men. Usually the offender and victim are of the same race, with nonwhites far more likely to be victims of crime than whites. A third of all robberies and a fifth of all rapes take place in cities with a population of one million or more. However, in the early seventies, the crime rate was rising faster in the suburbs than in inner cities.[28]

No doubt poverty, unemployment, and bad housing contribute to the crime

[26] "Housing: Try Horse Sense," *Newsweek* 80, no. 5 (July 31, 1972), p. 71.
[27] See especially Jane Jacobs, *The Death and Life of Great American Cities*.
[28] FBI Uniform Crime Report for 1967, 1968, 1969; Harris and Lindsay, *The State of the Cities*, pp. 76–80. These data are somewhat controversial. Critics of the FBI Report argue that the increase in crime rates is largely due to improved methods of recording crime. They point out that some cities keep more accurate records than others; that more juveniles than adults are arrested *for minor offenses—inflating the juvenile crime rate.*

rate, but it is difficult to make reliable correlations between living conditions and arrests. Marvin Wolfgang suggests that the *combination* of poverty and big-city anonymity creates a "criminogenic" atmosphere. In a small town, a robber or auto thief probably knows the victim and the police by name or at least on sight; and community sanctions against antisocial behavior are strong. In cities these restraints are missing. Crime is depersonalized: [29] the victim and the culprit are strangers. In addition, the opportunities and incentives for theft are greater in cities. Poverty, lack of legitimate social and economic opportunities, ready access to weapons, and the fact that aggressive responses are expected—or at least tolerated—on ghetto streets also contribute to high city crime rates.[30]

Another very important factor in the rising crime rate is drug addiction. No one knows exactly how many people in this country are addicted to heroin—estimates range from 150,000 to 250,000. Each of these addicts spends from $10 to $100 a day to support his habit. The Commission on the Cities calculates that if every addict steals $20 a day to buy drugs, the total cost per day is $4 million; on a yearly basis, this figure skyrockets to $1.5 billion. Although data relating crime to addiction are scant, some criminologists guess addicts are responsible for 85 percent of all serious crimes against property.[31] The cost—in lives and property—falls mainly on cities. Nearly half the nation's addicts live in New York City.

Proposed Solutions. Programs to stop the rise of crime vary from one city to another. Some are aiming for better police-civilian relations to encourage people to report crime and help police locate offenders. Some have reassigned police to high crime districts at peak times, especially late in the evening. Major cities now sponsor a variety of treatment centers for addicts, ranging from programs modeled after Alcoholics Anonymous to methadone clinics.[32] Many political officials are campaigning for tighter national laws against hand-guns. Because few cities can afford to increase their police forces, the emphasis in all these programs is on increased effectiveness and efficiency.

Transportation

In the mid-fifties, the federal government established a trust fund to finance a massive interstate highway system linking America's major cities. The fund

[29] Murder is an exception: most murders are committed by members of the family.
[30] Marvin E. Wolfgang, "Urban Crime," in *The Metropolitan Enigma*, ed. James Q. Wilson (Garden City, N.Y.: Doubleday, 1970), pp. 196–98. See also Ramsey Clark, *Crime in America: Its Nature, Causes, Control and Correction* (New York: Simon & Schuster, 1970).
[31] Harris and Lindsay, *The State of the Cities*, pp. 86–92.
[32] Methadone was designed to stop an addict's craving but block any "high," and has been made available through treatment programs in many cities. There is considerable evidence, however, that methadone is leaking onto the black market, thus compounding the problem of addiction and crime.

is drawn primarily from taxes on gasoline, so that the people who use highways are the ones to pay for them. It provides 90 percent of construction costs, leaving states to raise the remaining 10 percent—usually by collecting tolls. The interstate highway system now runs some fifty-one thousand miles and the cost of construction was $70 billion.[33]

The Problem. When the highway trust fund was created, few officials foresaw the effect the highway system would have on cities. Highways made it possible for people who work in the city to buy homes in the suburbs. The suburbs spread, and in time, owning one or two cars was practically mandatory for suburban residents. Highways also enabled manufacturers to leave downtown sites for suburban locations, indirectly creating high rates of unemployment in central cities. As Daniel P. Moynihan said, the interstate system "had more influence on the shape and development of American cities and employment than any initiative of the middle third of the twentieth century." [34]

In addition, the trust fund encouraged states to solve their transportation problems with roads. Alternative modes of transportation were neglected because the federal government does not pay 90 percent of the cost of buses, subways, or trains; nor does it pay for widening old city streets, traffic control, or parking lots. The effect of the interstate highway system, then, is to bring cars to the city; from that point on, they are on the city's hands. The cost to cities in street repairs, and property damage from pollution—not to mention work hours and tempers lost in traffic jams—is enormous. In a special address to Congress in March 1971, President Nixon called for a more balanced transportation program, noting that "Approximately 94 percent of all travel in urbanized areas is by automobile; yet, about 25 percent of our people—especially the old, the very young, the poor, and the handicapped—don't drive a car."

Most mass transit systems are run by public corporations created in the early part of the century. They depend on fares and on small state and local subsidies for funds. These corporations are in financial trouble today because the number of riders has declined, while the costs of equipment and personnel has skyrocketed. If transportation authorities raise fares, they are likely to lose still more riders. However, state legislators seem reluctant to help them out. As Banfield comments, nobody likes public transportation—not even the people who depend on it.[35] The Department of Transportation and HUD provide some assistance, but most of this money goes for repairs, not for expansion and improvements.

To complicate matters, in the last few years even highways have come

---

[33] Harris and Lindsay, *The State of the Cities*, p. 65.
[34] Quoted by Juan Cameron, *Fortune* 84, no. 1 (July 1971), p. 78.
[35] See Edward C. Banfield, *Political Influence* (New York: The Free Press, 1961), pp. 91–125, for a discussion of the politics surrounding subsidies for the Chicago Transit Authority.

under attack. Metropolitan residents complain of air and noise pollution, the danger to children, and the disruption of neighborhoods. (Highways are often run through residential districts rather than through commercial districts, where real estate is more expensive.) In at least fifteen cities, angry citizens and local officials have stopped highway construction.[36] For example, in Seattle, residents blocked plans for new highways—and at the same time, voted against a bond issue to finance improved public transportation.

Proposed Solutions.   In 1964 Congress passed the Uran Mass Transportation Act, which provides funds for demonstration projects.[37] The purpose of this program is to study urban transportation, try new solutions, and encourage private investment in transportation technology. Five cities (Atlanta, Dallas, Denver, Pittsburgh, and Seattle) are participating. In the meantime, New York City has broken ground for a new subway line, and San Francisco opened a monorail public transportations system (Bay Area Rapid Transit, or BART), which will link it with neighboring Oakland. If this is successful, a similar project will be started in Los Angeles, where public transportation is virtually nonexistent. Other cities have tried banning cars from certain areas for short periods. New York established bus lanes on some of the highways leading into the city, in the hope of making drivers stalled in bumper-to-bumper traffic realize that bus passengers have the advantage. A large part of the transportation problem seems to be coaxing people out of comfortable private cars and into mass transit vehicles.

Pollution

The Problem.   Cars are responsible for 91 percent of the air pollution in Los Angeles—a city that has forbidden its school children to run, skip, or jump on thirty-four different days because the pollution was so bad.[38] Breathing New York City air for a single day is estimated by some to be the equivalent of smoking two packs of cigarettes, and the damage to property from air pollution in New York is estimated at $13 billion per year. Industrial wastes and sewage have made the waterways around cities unsafe. According to many ecologists, Lake Erie is dead; the Hudson, the Charles, the Potomac, and other rivers are dying. Every day, New York City hauls eight hundred tons of garbage out to sea, burns seven thousand tons in city incinerators, and carts the remains to landfill sites on Staten Island and in New Jersey.[39] New York City spends thirty cents to pick up a single dis-

[36] Cameron, *Fortune*.
[37] C. H. Broley, "The Center City Transportation Project," in *Industrial Approaches to Urban Problems*, ed. Jordan D. Lewis and Lynn Lewis (New York: Praeger Publishers, 1972), pp. 95–107.
[38] Harris and Lindsay, *The State of the Cities*, pp. 64, 67.
[39] Roger Revelle, "Pollution and Cities," in Wilson, *The Metropolitan Enigma*, p. 130.

"How was it in the city?"

carded bottle, an enormous cost when we consider that the average American throws out four pounds of trash a day.[40] Many ecologists believe that if methods of controlling air and water pollution and techniques for disposing of solid waste are not improved, our major cities will be unliveable by the year 2000.

Until quite recently, pollution was not an "issue." [41] Few citizens and few public officials realized the long-term effects of DDT or phosphates. Responsibility for the environment was divided among a number of federal agencies, each of which had its own regulations and its own procedures. In the early sixties, residents of Santa Barbara, California, who wanted to stop Union Oil from drilling offshore could not determine whether the Department of the Interior, the U.S. Geological Survey, the Army Corps of Engineers, or the Bureau of the Budget was in charge. Santa Barbara was unable to prosecute its case: over three million gallons of oil spilled into the ocean in May 1969.[42]

Proposed Solutions. However, there is some evidence that this situation has begun to improve and will continue to do so. Public pressure, organized

[40] Harris and Lindsay, *The State of the Cities*, p. 68.
[41] See Charles O. Jones, "From Gold to Garbage: A Bibliographical Essay on Politics and the Environment," *American Political Science Review*, 66, no. 2 (June 1972): 588–95.
[42] Malcolm F. Baldwin traces the story in *Law and the Environment* (New York: Walker, 1970). For further discussion of politics and the environment, see Richard A. Cooley and Geoffrey Wandesforde-Smith, *Congress and the Environment* (Seattle: University of Washington Press, 1970).

into a number of environmental protection groups, spurred Congress to reject plans for supersonic jets, delayed the start of a trans-Alaskan oil pipeline, and halted construction of more than a dozen nuclear power plants. In 1971 private industry spent over $3 billion on pollution controls. In that same year, the Nixon administration set up the Environmental Protection Agency (EPA), a "super-agency" with departments from five other federal agencies. Among other acts, the EPA has revived an 1899 law requiring a federal permit to discharge wastes into navigable waters and has placed an embargo on certain 1973-model Fords, pending investigation of pollution control devices. Perhaps more important, the salmon have returned to at least one formerly uninhabitable river, indicating that at least some of the effects of pollution can be reversed. More recently, the EPA has suggested guidelines for selected U.S. cities to limit automobile use and to ban automobile traffic during certain hours.

But cleaning up the environment is not a simple matter of creating an agency, establishing standards, and enforcing them. Pollution controls cost money—and sometimes jobs. Already mills have closed in New Hampshire and Washington state because they couldn't afford to clean up, and thousands were left unemployed. In addition, pollution control devices sometimes require huge amounts of electricity, generated with the earth's limited supply of fossil-fuels. A new, nonpolluting papermill in Willamette, Oregon, for example, uses $20,000-worth of electricity a month. (One businessman commented that "Ruckelshaus [former head of the EPA] is the best friend America's economy has had since Karl Marx.") [43]

Of course, carbon monoxide, DDT, and atomic fallout do not recognize city, state, or national boundaries: pollution is a *global problem*. The United Nations Conference on the Human Environment, held in Stockholm in June 1972, was a first step toward establishing channels for international cooperation.[44] All of this activity indicates that pollution control is one area in which cities can legitimately *expect* state and federal assistance. The only question is whether that aid is too late.

Civil Servants and City Politics

Congress, state legislatures, and city councils can enact welfare reform, housing and transportation programs, and strong antipollution laws. Whether or not they are implemented depends in large measure on individual bureau-

---

[43] "Cleanup, How the U.S. Is Doing the Job," "The Old Millstream Cost 275 Jobs," *Newsweek* 74, no. 24 (June 12, 1972) : 38, 46, 47.
[44] Among issues discussed at this conference were the developed nations' responsibility for existing pollution, the need for development in the third world (which cannot afford to stop using DDT if it means a bad crop), and the pollution from war. *Newsweek (Ibid.,* p. 43) estimates that herbicides sprayed on Viet Nam completely stripped some 5.5 million acres of foliage, and that bombs have created close to twenty-six million craters, twenty-five feet deep and forty feet in diameter.

crats, policemen, social workers, and so on. New York City employs 371,000 people; salaries account for over half of the city's budget.[45] For this reason alone, unionization of city employees has had a significant impact on city government and city politics.

In the early sixties, city workers accounted for only 5 percent of union membership. Few cities recognized municipal unions, and some states had laws against strikes by public employees. By 1970 fifteen states had recognized employee organizations; membership in the American Federation of State, County, and Municipal Employees (to name one) had risen from 180,000 in 1960 to 425,000; the number of man-hours lost in strikes had increased thirty times over, from 58,000 in 1960 to 2,026,000. Often the strikes involved essential services. During the first six months of 1970, for example, there were strikes by prison guards (New Jersey), sanitation men (in five cities) teachers (in seven cities), bus drivers (in three cities), hospital employees (in two cities), policemen (in three cities), and firemen (in two cities). Municipal unions today are more numerous and more militant than ever before.

Unions have a direct impact on city politics. Elected officials will go to great lengths to avoid unpopular strikes. Closed schools and uncollected garbage antagonize voters, and unions themselves represent large blocs of voters. If a mayor is rigid and uncooperative in negotiations with the police or taxi drivers, he may loose their voters as well as the votes of people inconvenienced by a strike. In addition, unions can use their numerical strength and financial resources to lobby and campaign. In 1966, for example, New York's Patrolmen's Benevolent Association spent over $500,000 on ads opposing the creation of a Civilian Review Board. The board was defeated in a city-wide referendum.

Municipal unions also influence policy decisions. When a mayor agrees to a union's wage demands, he must either raise taxes (an unpopular move) or cut the budget in other areas, perhaps reducing essential services. In addition, unions sometimes bargain for a role in policy decisions. In New York, striking welfare workers won their demand for reduced caseloads on the grounds that they could improve services to clients. In Michigan, teachers bargained over such issues as class size, student discipline, and teaching loads. Nonprofessional unions play a major role in determining how many men are required to do a specific job and which men will do which jobs. In at least nineteen cities, union contracts limit the city's right to subcontract work to private companies.

Looking to the future, most observers feel that as municipal unions finish their initial tasks of organizing employees, winning basic wage demands, and acquiring legitimacy as bargaining agents, they can be expected to exercise increasing political muscle in big cities.

---

[45] This section is based on Robert H. Connery and William V. Farr, eds., *Unionization of Municipal Employees*, Proceedings of The Academy of Political Science, vol. 30, no. 2, 1971.

In summary, American cities seem ill prepared for the problems they face in the seventies. Authority to govern cities is fragmented in a way that makes it difficult for officials to formulate and carry out sound policies; outdated boundaries isolate cities from their affluent suburbs. In part, cities are the victims of social forces (for example, the industrialization that attracted farmers from Europe and this country to American cities and then replaced them with new machines); in part, they are the victims of neglect. Federal policies in housing and transportation have encouraged the growth of the suburbs at the expense of the cities. The social costs of these policies however, in unemployment and crime, fall mainly on the cities, which clearly have neither the power nor the funds to solve them alone.

The City in Japan

One hundred years ago, Japan was a feudal, agricultural, and, by European standards, backward nation—hardly a likely candidate for an industrial revolution. But unlike many of its Asian neighbors, Japan had two important natural resources: coal—a source of energy, and silk—an export crop to provide the cash for industrialization. Japan also had a strong incentive to industrialize. A mountainous island nation, Japan, like England, cannot produce enough food for its population. It must either expand its territorial possessions or produce exports to pay for imported food. In the early part of this century, Japan tried the former course; after World War II, it chose the latter.

Today Japan is one of the most industrialized nations in the world, with a Gross National Product exceeded only by those of the United States and the Soviet Union. It is also one of the most densely populated countries. Most of Japan's industry and most of its people are concentrated on a narrow plain —which occupies 1.2 percent of the available land—between the mountains and the sea, and near the coal deposits, ports, and rail lines. Seventy percent of Japan's population lives in cities; 58 percent of that number live in Tokyo, Osaka, and Nagoya.[46] With a population of over twelve million in 1970, the capital city of Tokyo was the second largest city in the world, after New York.

Like American city governments, the Tokyo Municipal Government has developed piecemeal. The national government holds ultimate authority in most matters. It controls housing, transportation, and social services, sometimes awarding new enterprises to public authorities rather than to the city government. Authority is fragmented: administrative responsibilities are shared with special wards, cities, towns, and villages within Tokyo's bound-

[46] Japan Trade Center Information Service, "Land and People of Japan," 1972.

aries. As in American cities, commuters who work in Tokyo but live outside the city do not pay city taxes. Tokyo depends on the national government much as New York City depends on Albany and Washington. This relationship is particularly tense because Tokyo houses the national government, and because it once fought for autonomy and lost.[47]

Unemployment and Social Services

Unemployment is not as severe a problem in Japan as it is in the United States or in European countries. In 1970 the overall jobless rate was 1.2 percent,[48] compared to 6.6 percent in the United States. In part, this is because Japan's economy has expanded so rapidly. Labor shortages are a bigger problem than unemployment, partially because the Japanese work for much lower salaries than do workers in any other major industrial nation. Why? Edwin O. Reischauer suggests that for centuries the Japanese have looked down on the ostentatious display of wealth.[49] They tend to prefer job security to high salaries, and Japanese industries provide a high degree of security. Many of Japan's workers are "permanent employees"—they cannot be laid off, and they receive a guaranteed income until retirement. Salaries increase with seniority, so that it is to the worker's advantage to remain with one company. The company provides a variety of social services, from health insurance and sick-pay to child-care centers, as well as recreational services, including country outings and reduced rates at restaurants and hotels for personal entertaining.[50]

But not all workers are permanent employees, and the national government provides Social Secuirty, health and job insurance, and Welfare. These services are funded with local and national taxes and with Social Security salary deductions, as in the United States. In 1970 Japan spent 6.5 percent of its national income on social services—an increase of 19 percent over 1951. Despite this increase, however, it spent far less than most industrial nations. In 1963 the Social Security expense per capita in the United States was $197; in Sweden $281; in Japan $32. The payments to the elderly or disabled are barely adequate. In addition, most Japanese consider public assistance a last resort, and fear they will be personally obligated to the official who arranges their payments.[51]

[47] William A. Robson, *Report on Tokyo Metropolitan Government*, December 1967.
[48] *Nippon, A Charted History of Japan*, ed. Tsuneta Yano Memorial Society (Tokyo: Kokusei-sha, 1971), p. 45.
[49] These attitudes are discussed in Edwin O. Reischauer, *The United States and Japan*, 3rd ed. (New York: Viking Press, 1965), pp. 151–71.
[50] For a discussion of the relationship between the company and white-collar workers in Japan see Ezra F. Vogel, *Japan's New Middle Class* (Berkeley: University of California Press, 1963), Chapter 2.
[51] *Nippon, A Charted History of Japan*, Chapter 36.

Housing

The housing shortage in Tokyo is acute, despite the fact that the Japanese generally require less space for living than the average Western family. In proportion to the average worker's salary, housing in Tokyo and other large cities is prohibitively expensive. According to a White Paper issued by the Tokyo Municipal Government in 1971, after a series of fatal accidents attributed to overcrowding, the city needs six hundred thousand new units to house its current population adequately. Of existing units, approximately 30 percent are substandard. The report cites in particular some eight hundred thousand wooden apartment buildings where families of five and six often occupy a single, 9.9 square meter room. The Municipal Government is building low-rent housing projects, but not fast enough. (The population of Tokyo has tripled since 1945.) These problems are aggravated "by numerous environmental problems such as the threat of floods and landslides, noise and soot, the obstruction of sunshine and proper ventilation, intrusion of automobiles into back alleys that deprive people of their indispensable living space, and the inconvenient commuting situation." [52] It is not uncommon for a person living outside Tokyo, where housing is less expensive, to commute an hour and a half to his job. Japan, like America, is becoming a nation of commuters.

Transportation

Japan boasts one of the most efficient and modern rail systems in the world. The New Tokaido Line, which opened in 1964, offers high-speed, luxury trains traveling at an average speed of one hundred miles per hour, linking Tokyo and Osaka in a little over three hours. Japanese railways carry more passengers than any other railway in the world. One reason is that the roads in Japan are not very good, as compared to those in other industrialized nations; until quite recently, there were few expressways. However, this seems to be changing. The number of cars in Japan rose from 600,000 in 1960 to 2.4 million in 1970. An old city, Tokyo is not designed for cars. Many streets do not have sidewalks; accidents and traffic jams are frequent. At times the pollution from cars is so bad that traffic police have to leave their posts to breathe oxygen every hour or two. In 1972 the Tokyo Municipal Government planned a series of measures to restrict the number of cars entering the city, but under pressure from business decided to implement them on a voluntary basis.[53]

[52] "White Paper Announced on Tokyo's Housing Problems," *Tokyo Municipal News*, 21, no. 4 (May–June 1971): 6.
[53] See Donald Kirk, "Pollution of Fuji-san," *The New York Times Magazine*, March 26, 1972, pp. 33, 65 ff.; "Don't Underestimate Nippon," *Nation*, June 17, 1968, p. 780; "Japan's Troubled Railroads," *Business Week*, April 24, 1971, pp. 38, 40.

Pollution

Cars are not the only source of pollution in Japan. The entire coastal plain suffers from industrial fallout.

Today, whizzing by the sea at 150 miles an hour in a "bullet" train, one marvels at the snow-swept cone of Fuji-san rising majestically from a plain covered with twisting power lines, jutting smokestacks, sprawling factories and feeder roads, shining wonders of the past decade of Japan's neoindustrial revolution.[54]

"Itai-itai" or "scratching disease" from cadmium poisoning is common in all industrial areas. Mercury poisoning, which claimed over 150 victims in the early fifties, is now appearing in children of mothers who had shown no symptoms. Over 6,000 people reported to clinics with sore eyes, headaches, and arm and leg numbness as a result of smog on July 18, 1970; 43 students from one high school alone were hospitalized. The Japanese have begun to refer to pollution as "kogai" or "public hazard." In 1971 the government appointed a cabinet-level official for environmental problems, but to date little has been done to control industry. Responsibility for enforcing anti-pollution law falls to forty-six local prefectures whose rules vary widely. In addition, the national government is reluctant to pass laws that would raise the price of export products. The situation is similar to that in the United States. In fact, when consumer advocate Ralph Nader visited Japan, at the invitation of consumer and environmentalist groups, the auto companies refused to let him visit their plants. They had been warned about him, the story goes, by General Motors.[55]

Although there are some differences between America's cities and Japan's —Japan has less unemployment, more difficulties with housing and pollution —their problems are remarkably similar. The urban crisis, it seems, is world-wide.

The Future of the City

Are cities dying? Many observers feel they are. Can they be saved? Not without change—change in national priorities, change in political structures, and perhaps change in attitudes toward cities as well.

---

[54] Kirk, "Pollution of Fuji-san." p. 33.
[55] *Ibid.*, pp. 33, 68.

Proposed Solutions

Federal Funds. First and foremost, the cities need money—money to maintain services at their current level, money to rebuild. There is nothing radical in the idea of federal subsidies for cities. The government subsidizes farmers, with payments for unused fields; and industry, with tax breaks, military contracts, and (indirectly) with protective tariffs. It subsidized the growth of the suburbs with home loans and the Interstate Highway System. Some suggest channeling more of this money into feeding the urban poor; into new technology for mass transit and low cost, prefabricated housing; into loans to city landlords and neighborhood improvement associations. As the Commission on the Cities in the Seventies writes, "If this country could afford to spend $17 billion on a Marshall Plan for the cities and states of Europe, $18 billion to defend South Korea, and as yet uncounted billions to 'save' Vietnam, then it can surely afford the money it takes to solve the problems of the cities." [56]

Governmental Solutions: Centralization, Consolidation, and the "Fifty-first State." One difficulty with subsidies is making sure they reach the people who need them. The political structure in major metropolitan regions has developed piecemeal. Boundaries are outdated; various state and local agencies compete for power, money, and personnel; in a sense, there is too much government and too little authority. For this reason, many urbanologists argue for centralization—for joining city and suburbs into single political units. In a few cases (notably, Los Angeles and Oklahoma City), cities have annexed neighboring areas. However, in most states, annexation is decided in referendums—and suburban communities do not want to be joined to cities.

Another possible solution is limited consolidation. Under the Lakewood Plan in Los Angeles County, for example, local governments buy police protection, tax and health services, and traffic control maintenance from the county. Dade County, Florida, which includes the city of Miami, has established a single authority—the Metro—to control zoning, urban renewal, and transportation (highway construction and public buses) for the entire county. According to residents, who have voted down Metro opponents in several referendums, this program has been successful. [57]

Others have recommended breaking the ties between city and state government. In 1959, the New York City Council appointed a committee to study the possibility and legality of the city seceding and becoming an independent state. [58] In 1969 Norman Mailer, candidate for the Democratic mayoral nomination, campaigned for a fifty-first state. Mayor Lindsay, in a speech to

[56] Harris and Lindsay, *The State of the Cities*, pp. 103–4.
[57] Volkomer, *American Government*, pp. 173–74.
[58] Banfield and Wilson, *City Politics*, p. 68.

NATO's Conference on Cities in 1970, suggested that America's big cities be given a special status under the Constitution—federal charters that would enable them to deal directly with the federal government on matters of trade, finance, and social welfare. This, he argued, "would formalize the federal responsibility for the national scope of urban development."[59]

However, not all urbanologists favor centralization. Many feel impersonality is the city's greatest problem, and that aid to cities will only be effective if it is administered on a neighborhood-by-neighborhood basis through community organizations. Proponents of self-determination for communities point to instances of spontaneous local action. Block associations in many cities have hired guards, planted trees, repainted building fronts, cleared vacant lots, and organized shopping cooperatives. In other neighborhoods, youth gangs have rid their "territory" of dope pushers. The Black Panthers in Oakland, Chicago, and New York organized street patrols, gave classes in self-defense, and ran a breakfast program for community children. The Guadalupe Organization in a Chicano community outside Phoenix has channeled federal funds, gifts, and volunteer services back into the community. Trainees in the building trades, for example, learn while rebuilding community homes and the local church—an old Yaqui temple.[60] Decentralists argue that cities should be run as loose federations, with the city government dispensing funds to neighborhoods who would decide for themselves how the funds should be spent.

Conclusion: As the Cities Go, So Goes Society

Cities are in a sense miniature models of the larger society, for within their narrow geographic and political bounds are the problems that face the nations of the modern world. Can municipal governments ever hope to meet and overcome these problems? This only seems possible if the general society is working toward the same goals. Cities can really do no more than reflect the efforts of the nations they are part of. They will never be able to take the lead in solving such problems as pollution, poverty, and inadequate housing and health care, because these problems are already on the verge of defeating the cities. This effort must be initiated at the national level, where the resources are more plentiful. At this point, cities are fighting just to survive; they have the strength to do little more.

While the future of big cities is uncertain, the search for remedies for financial, political, and social problems will undoubtedly influence the shape of society in the years ahead. The battle for a decent living environment for all, for total employment, for healthy air and a drug-free population is being fought on urban ground.

---

[59] Harris and Lindsay, *The State of the Cities*, p. 102.
[60] *Ibid.*, pp. 13–14.

Suggested Readings

Altshuler, Alan A. *Community Control: The Black Demand for Participation in Large American Cities*. New York: Pegasus, 1970. An examination of decentralization as an alternative to the present dominance of major city governments.

Banfield, Edward C. *The Unheavenly City: The Nature and the Future of Our Urban Crisis*. Boston: Little, Brown, 1970. An argument for allowing central cities in the United States to operate more independently.

Bish, Robert L. *The Public Economy of Metropolitan Areas*. Chicago: Markham, 1971. A theoretical argument, with empirical examples, that concerns the public economy of metropolitan areas.

Bollens, J. C., and Schmandt, H. J. *Metropolis: Its People, Politics, and Economic Life*. New York: Harper & Row, 1965. A comprehensive examination of metropolitan government.

Downs, Anthony. *Urban Problems and Prospects*. Chicago: Markham, 1970. An excellent collection of essays on the state of the city.

Gottman, Jean. *Megalopolis*. Santa Barbara, Calif.: Twentieth Century Fund, 1961. One of the first analyses of the megalopolis.

Mumford, Lewis. *The City in History: It Origins, Its Transformations, and Its Prospects*. New York: Harcourt, Brace & World, 1961. An examination of the past and future of cities around the world.

Robson, William A., ed. *Great Cities of the World: Their Government, Politics and Planning*. New York: Crowell-Collier and Macmillan, 1954. A collection of essays on cities in different nations.

Sayre, Wallace S., and Kaufman, Herbert. *Governing New York City*. New York: W. W. Norton, 1965. A brief study of New York City politics and government.

Wilson, James Q., ed. *The Metropolitan Enigma: Inquiries into the Nature and Domain of America's Urban Crisis*. Cambridge, Mass.: Harvard University Press, 1968. A collection of studies on all aspects of the urban crisis.

Wood, Robert C. *Suburbia: Its People and Their Politics*. Boston: Houghton Mifflin, 1959. A study of suburban politics.

Glossary

Abortion Law Reform Association (ALRA). In Great Britain, a pressure group that conducted a thirty-year fight for liberalization of abortion laws, finally winning victory with the Abortion Act of 1967.

absolute equality. 1. The doctrine that each nation-state has the right to do whatever it wants within its own territory without interference. 2. The doctrine that each nation-state has the right to do whatever it wants beyond is borders, subject only to limitations as to its capabilities relative to those of other nation-states.

administocracy. A privileged clique of government administrators who are not directly accountable to the public but who nevertheless possess broad policy-making powers.

administration. In a government, the organizational process of implementing the laws enacted by the legislature and the policies promulgated by the executive.

administrative law. The body of regulatory orders or directives, issued by appropriate government agencies, that are essentially interpretations or applications of statutory laws enacted by legislative bodies.

Administrative Procedure Act (1946). An act of the U.S. Congress which requires that proper judicial standards be applied to all administrative hearings, tribunals, or similar proceedings.

Agency for International Development (AID). An agency within the U.S. State Department that administers approximately half of all U.S. nonmilitary assistance to underdeveloped and developing nations.

Aid to Families with Dependent Children (AFDC). The largest of the four basic programs through which federal public assistance (welfare) is administered. It covers unemployed but able-bodied adults (especially mothers) and their children.

all-or-none principle. The tendency of people who use one communications medium heavily to also use the others heavily.

American Medical Association (AMA). In the United States, a powerful pressure group that represents a large percentage of licensed physicians.

American Political Science Association (APSA). The major professional organization of academic political scientists in the United States. It was founded in 1903 and currently has a membership of over 16,000.

anarchism. A political ideology that advocates the abolition of all government.

apathy. In a political system, the state of mind that leads to indifference.

appellate court. A court that hears appeals from lower courts.

apportionment. The process by which legislatures establish the representation of legislative districts according to population.

area sampling. A method of sampling by which interviewers zero in on geographic districts selected for their representative features and choose their respondents at random within each district.

aristocracy. A system of government in which an elite class rules. Aristotle defined aristocracy as a form of government in which an elite benevolently rules in the best interest of the people.

Aristotle (384–322 B.C.). A Greek philosopher whose work *Politics* was the first systematic study of government and politics.

authoritarianism. A system of governmnet in which a particular individual or group controls the political life of society, while the nonpolitical aspects of society are generally left in private hands.

authority. 1. The legal or moral right of one person or institution to regulate the actions of another person or the public at large. 2. A form of power based on recognition of this right.

autonomy. Control by a governmental unit of its own political, economic, and military affairs; national independence.

balance of power A condition and maintenance of an equilibrium in which the ambitions of individual nations or alliances are held in check by the lack of a dominating strength capable of imposing its will on the others.

Bay Area Rapid Transit (BART). An experimental monorail system linking San Francisco and Oakland, California; it is the most modern mass transportation system in the United States.

behaviorism. The major school of political science in the United States since World War II, focusing on actual human behavior rather than institutional mechanisms; it uses a rigorous empirical methodology borrowed from the natural sciences.

bicameralism. A term used to describe a system in which there is a two-house legislature—an upper house and a lower house.

Bill of Rights. The first ten amendments of the U.S. Constitution, which protects many of the basic rights and liberties of the American people.

bipolarity. An international system characterized by the dominance and rivalry of two giant powers.

black nationalism. In the black liberation movement, any of several strategies that emphasize the necessity of black communities to stay together geographically and to win control of and upgrade their local institutions.

black power. In the black liberation movement, a nationalist strategy—sometimes linked to terrorist tactics or to encouragement of black capitalism—that urges the achievement of local control of ghettoes (rather than integration) and the vigorous use of combined political and economic bargaining power to extract concessions from the majority.

boycott. A collective abstention, as a means of protest, from buying a product, patronizing an establishment, or participating in an institution or public event.

brinkmanship. The practice of boldly threatening war (especially nuclear war) in order to gain a bargaining advantage.

British Broadcasting Corporation (BBC). A public corporation, created in 1927, that operates Great Britain's government radio and television networks and is supported by license fees and foreign program sales rather than by commercial advertising.

broker (consensus) party. A type of political party that draws its leadership and support from several different groups, playing down their ideological differences and exhibiting great flexibility on issues.

Brown v. Board of Education (1954). A U.S. Supreme Court case that declared unconstitutional the separate-but-equal doctrine as previously applied to public schools.

Bundesrat. The upper house of the West German parliament.

Bundestag. The lower house of the West German parliament.

bureau. In the U.S. government, the chief subdivision within a department.

bureaucracy. A large-scale organization of appointed officials—with a hierarchy of authority and fixed rules and procedures—that operates in a uniform and predictable manner in its application of broad policies to particular siutations.

Burkean representation. A legislative practice based on a belief that the lawmaker should primarily represent the national interest, the good of mankind, or a particular set of moral or ideological principles, rather than a particular group or region.

cabinet department. In the U.S. government, any one of the eleven major departments in the executive branch that are charged with carrying out legislative and executive policies. Each department is headed by a secretary who is appointed by the president (with the consent of the Senate) and who serves at his pleasure.

cabinet government. A plural executive, responsible to the legislature, with decision-making powers formally shared by the prime minister, the ministry, and the cabinet, with the prime minister empowered to dismiss cabinet ministers who oppose him.

cadre. The nucleus of activists within a political party.

cadre party. A highly centralized type of party that only recruits from the politically active elite.

candidate orientation. A voter's attitudes about a particular candidate, apart from his feelings about issues or his regular party affiliation.

canon law. The body of official laws governing practical matters, as well as matters of faith, within the Roman Catholic church.

capitalism. An economic system generally characterized by private rather than state ownership of most of the means of production, distribution, and regulation of production by competition in a relatively free marketplace.

captive executive. An official head of government who is actually controlled by a higher power, such as a military general staff, a totalitarian party, or a foreign occupation force.

case law. Law that is based on individual legal decisions rather than on a comprehensive code of statutes.

case study. An in-depth study of a single event or institution that allows tentative generalizations to be formed about similar events or institutions.

Caucus for a New Political Science. A movement, formed within the American Political Science Association in 1967, whose aim is to redirect the resources of the profession into radical social criticism and activism.

caudillo. In Latin America, a charismatic military leader who is frequently responsible for coups d'état against incumbent governments.

cell. The basic unit of a Communist party.

Central Committee of the Communist Party of the Soviet Union (CPSU). The highest official tribunal within the Soviet Communist party.

chinjōdan. In Japan, a petition group sent to Tokyo by a rural community to plead its case before government officials and politicians.

civil law. The body of law that provides redress for private individuals or corporations that feel that injuries have been done to them. Because the injuries involved are held not to endanger the peace or welfare of the community, the individuals or corporations, not the state, are responsible for prosecution.

Civil Rights Act of 1964. An act of the U.S. Congress that prohibits discrimination in public accommodations, employment, and trade unions, and provides for suspension of federal aid to any program guilty of discrimination.

civil rights movement. In the U.S. South, the nonviolent protest movement (1954–1964), which was based on an alliance of blacks with white liberals and motivated by morality rather than ideology, and which aimed at desegregation through dramatic appeals to the nation's conscience and resulting federal intervention.

civil servant. Any person who works for a government in a nonmilitary capacity.

Civil Service Commission. In the U.S. federal government, the agency, headed by a bipartisan group of three members, that oversees our civil service system.

classical democracy. 1. A hypothetical form of democracy in which all political decisions would be made directly by the masses rather than by elected representatives. 2. The form of government in ancient Athens, said to have been closest to the ideal of mass participation.

class voting. The tendency of voters in democratic countries to vote for the party that is historically identified with their social class, such as the Laborite sway of blue-collar workers in Great Britain.

coalition. The joint forces of two or more persons or organizations who share a complementary goal.

Code Napoleon (1804). The first modern codification of European law (essentially, a reinterpretation of Roman law), which rejected feudal and religious influences, provided the legal framework for the industrial revolution, and is used in some form in most of today's world.

Code of Justinian (Corpus Juris Civilis). The definitive code of Roman Law, developed in Constantinople (c. A.D. 533) under Emperor Justinian and generally regarded as the foundation of most modern European legal systems.

codified law. The body of written laws, as opposed to unwritten mores, traditions, and beliefs.

coercion. A form of power by which a person or institution forces people to do their will.

cognitive dissonance. A tension-producing condition in which one's interpretations do not correspond to the actual facts of an event.

collective goods. Any services or benefits that are available to the general public rather than reserved exclusively for those who invested money or effort in obtaining them.

collective security. The principle or practice by which aggression of any nation against another is met by the combined deterrent force of all nations.

collectivism. A system of values that stresses the needs of the tribe, clan, village—and ultimately the state—over those of the individual.

committee system. In a legislature, a division of labor by which the legislators are assigned to various committees to screen the thousands of bills introduced at each session, to pick out those few that merit serious consideration, and to work out an agreement on their precise wording and scope.

commodity riot. In the United States, the most common type of civil disturbance, directed at property, particularly retail stores, and at the police.

common law. A body of law derived from judicial decisions that supplements statutory law.

Commonwealth Immigrants Act. In the United Kingdom, an act of Parliament passed under Conservative party sponsorship, which established controls on the immigration of nonwhites from the West Indies, Pakistan, and India.

communications channel. The medium through which a message is transmitted, such as a television program or newspaper editorial.

communism (or Marxism-Leninism). The major leftist political ideology in today's world, based on the teachings of Karl Marx and V. I. Lenin. It promises the realization of a classless, stateless, ideal society usually through violent revolution, with the overthrow of existing social and political structures and the establishment of a temporary totalitarian dictatorship.

community control. In urban politics, the demand of citizen groups within local communities for participation in the policy making and administration of the institutions that serve their communities, such as schools and hospitals.

comparative government. The branch of political science concerned with identifying the similarities and differences between national political systems.

comparative study. In political science, a study that compares, without control of variables, several similar institutions, events, or systems. The object is to detect, but not to prove, important influences, relationships, and similarities.

conciliation. In international relations, any policy aimed at settling a tense conflict situation through unilateral or mutual concessions.

confederation. A system of government in which authority is divided between a central government and local governments, with the latter often having retained sovereignty and power to veto actions of the central government.

conference committee. In the U.S. Congress, a committee formed of members from both the House and Senate to work out a compromise when different versions of a bill have been passed in each house.

conservatism. Generally a trend in democratic ideology that emphasizes the importance of national traditions, social stability, and the responsibility of each individual for his or her success or failure in the world.

constituent republic. In the Soviet Union, any one of the sixteen Soviet republics that have the constitutional, but not actual, right to conduct their own foreign policies and to secede. Each constituent republic represents a definite nationality.

constitution. 1. The system of rules and customs by which a government conducts its affairs. 2. A document prescribing such a system.

constitutional government. Government in which authority is distributed and limited by written or unwritten laws that are to be obeyed by all officeholders.

constitutional law. The body of law consisting of judicial decisions interpreting a nation's constitution.

co-option. The practice of controlling or attempting to control a protest movement by offering its leaders elite status and privileges and by making symbolic concessions to the members of the movement.

correspondence theory. The theory that the representative of a given district should reflect the dominant ethnic, religious, or social characteristics of his district; in the legislative body as a whole, each ethnic, religious, or social group or class should be represented in proportion to its size in the total electorate.

Council for Mutual Economic Assistance (CMEA). An economic alliance of the USSR and Eastern European states aimed at coordinating the planning of their national economies and accelerating their technological development.

Council of State. The most important of the three *grands corps* (elite departments) of the French governmental bureaucracy. It acts as the final court of appeals for the nation's lower-level administrative courts.

criminogenic environment. A crime-breeding environment, as is produced in some urban neighborhoods by the combined effects of big-city anonymity and poverty.

cultural autonomy. A political condition in which a minority group or people within a larger nation or empire uses its own language in local governmental affairs, maintains its own national traditions in the arts and religion, and runs its own schools.

decentralization. In city government, the policy of transferring power away from the central administration and bringing it down to the neighborhood level, often by establishing channels for community participation.

decline-of-ideology thesis. The thesis that traditional class ideologies have lost their relevance in the affluent societies of contemporary Western Europe and North America and can be expected to wither away. It was written about in the 1950s and early 1960s by Seymour Lipset, Daniel Bell, and other prominent social scientists, but was called into serious question by the turbulent politics of the late 1960s and early 1970s.

deficit spending. The fiscal practice by which a government spends more than it takes in, year after year, by constantly enlarging and refinancing the public debt.

demands. In a political system, the direct and indirect messages by which the people express their desire for reforms or for new initiatives on the part of government.

democracy. The traditional ideology of democratic governments and parties, based on the principles of representative government, universal popular suffrage, constitutionalism, and respect for both the majority's right to govern and the individual's basic rights.

democratic centralism. The theory of organization by which Communist parties and governments operate, based on the principle of strict adherence by the minority to the decisions of the majority or to the leading bodies chosen by the majority.

democratic elections. An electoral system whose rarely realized ideals are: clear policy alternatives offered by competing candidates, voters deeply concerned with policy questions, accurately reflected majority preferences in election results, and elected officials bound by their campaign promises.

democratic socialism. The ideology, popular in many Western European countries, based on both economic and political concerns, which advocates comprehensive social welfare programs, nationalization of major industries, and the eventual achievement of economic equality through the extension, rather than the overthrow, of political democracy.

Department of Housing and Urban Development (HUD). A cabinet-level agency established in the U.S. federal government in 1965 to coordinate federal urban programs.

deterrence. In international relations, any policy aimed at the prevention of war by mobilizing sufficient military strength to inflict extensive damage on a potential aggressor.

deviating election. An election in which one party draws enough support from members of the opposing party—such as through a special issue or a charismatic candidate—to attain victory without eroding the losing party's long-range electoral base.

devotee party. A type of party built around a single charismatic leader, such as the Nazis under Hitler.

dictatorship of the proletariat. In Communist (Marxist-Leninist) theory, a revolutionary state dominated by the proletariat (working class) and using its coercive instruments of government (army, police, courts) to deny political rights to individuals and groups regarded as counterrevolutionary.

diplomacy. The art or method of intergovernmental communication and negotiation by which decisions are made, conflicts are resolved or sharpened, and alliances are formed.

direct democracy. A political system that allows all citizens to participate personally in the decision-making process.

discretionary implementation. The practice or prerogative of exercising flexibility or independent judgment in the implementation of public policy.

distortion. In a communications system, the deliberate or accidental changes in the content of a message during transmission or reception.

divine right. The theory that the authority of rulers comes from God rather than from the governed.

dominant party system. A political system in which a single powerful party wins every election, year after year, yet allows opposition parties to function freely.

Economic Opportunity Act of 1964. An important act of the U.S. Congress, resulting from former President Lyndon Johnson's "war on poverty," that was intended to cure social ills in urban and rural poverty areas through an influx of federal aid and encouragement of community self-help projects.

economics. The production and distribution of goods and services for society, authoritative only insofar as it is enforced by the state.

elastic clause. The last clause in Article I, Section 8 of the U.S. Constitution that grants Congress the power to enact all legislation necessary and proper to carry out the explicit powers of Congress.

electoral college. The body of electors, representing each state and the District of Columbia, that directly elects the president and vice president of the United States.

elite. A small group of people or a social class within a larger group, that makes decisions (or controls others who do) as to "who gets what, when, and how."

elitism. Any of several social or political theories that assert the dominance of single or plural elites in society's decision-making processes.

English common law. The body of judicial case law which originated in medieval England and which relies heavily today on precedent and occupies a central position in the British legal system.

Environmental Protection Agency (EPA). A "superagency" established in 1971 by the Nixon administration to coordinate all federal efforts in the fight against pollution.

equal time requirement. A provision of the 1934 Federal Communications Act that requires a broadcasting station that gives or sells air time to a political party or candidate to also give or agree to sell equal time to all other legally qualified parties or candidates.

equity (or chancery) law. The body of preventive law, originally developed in England, of which a single feature, the injunctive process, is used widely today.

European Common Market. An economic bloc established in 1958 by Belgium, France, Italy, Luxembourg, the Netherlands, and West Germany and joined in 1973 by Great Britain, Denmark, and Ireland with the aim of promoting economic integration among its members.

experimental research. In political science, the method of inquiry that attempts, through the control of variables, to imitate the rigorous empirical approach used in the natural sciences.

fascism. A right-wing totalitarian political system, such as that of Italy under Mussolini, in which all sources of power are used to strengthen the existing social order and to glorify the state.

federal agency. In the U.S. government, an office or establishment—usually performing a single, highly complex function—that is within the executive branch and generally independent of the cabinet departments.

Federal Communications Commission (FCC). The U.S. government regulatory agency, created in 1934, that oversees all forms of broadcasting systems.

federal corporation. In the U.S. government, a public enterprise, such as the U.S. Post Office, that combines the funcions of a government agency with those of a private business and serves a vital but unprofitable need that the private sector cannot meet.

federal court system. In the United States, the basic federal courts, which include the Supreme Court, eleven circuit courts of appeals, and ninety-three federal district courts.

federal district court. The basic unit in the U.S. federal court system, having jurisdiction over all violations of federal law, both civil and criminal. There are ninety-three federal districts.

federalism. A system of government in which power is divided between the national government and the state, provincial, or local government, each having final authority in its own sphere of influence.

feedback. In a political system, the reaction of the people, political institutions, or other political groupings to government outputs.

felony. In criminal law, a major offense, such as robbery or murder, usually punished by a heavy fine, imprisonment, or both.

field research method. In political science, the testing of hypotheses by comparing two or more real-life communities or situations that are "matched" in all important variables except the one under study.

forced assimilation. A governmental policy whereby a nation or empire forces a minority group or a subject people, through violence or the threat of violence, to abandon their language and traditional culture in favor of the language and culture of the majority or dominant people.

formalistic impersonality. The tendency of bureaucrats to carry out the goals of the government in power with strict impartiality, regardless of personal feelings.

free elections. Elections that provide voters with a meaningful choice by including, as minimum conditions, two or more competing parties or factions, freedom of candidates and the public to debate fundamental issues, and a secret ballot.

free-rider syndrome. The willingness of the public to accept collective goods without paying for them or working to extend them.

functional organization. In international relations, an organization that focuses on the concrete economic and social needs of the world rather than on political power struggles.

functional representation. A system of representation based on the major social or economic interests rather than on territorial units.

game theory. The branch of applied mathematics that analyzes social and political conflict situations in terms of their similarity to parlor games. The object is to guarantee a maximum gain or minimum loss for a particular player.

gerrymandering. In legislatures, the practice of redrawing boundaries in order to give special advantage to the candidates of the majority party, faction, or coalition.

ghetto. An area within a city in which a minority group is forced to live because of de facto racial and economic segregation.

grant-in-aid program. In the United States, a type of federal aid program that requires state and local governments to match (sometimes dollar for dollar) the money paid by the federal government.

Great Russians. In the Soviet Union, the largest ethnic group (55 percent of the population), which dominates the government and Communist party. The

Great Russians originally came from the Moscow area and were Orthodox Christians; they have now spread throughout Soviet territory, including Siberia and the minority republics.

group salience. The degree to which a group member sees his affiliation to the group as important.

historical analysis. In political science, a method, which flourished in the nineteenth century, that attempts to draw purely tentative generalizations through the study of past political events, using such primary sources as newspapers, public records, and personal accounts.

home rule. Self-government by a racial, ethnic, or religious minority within a larger national community; also, self-government by a dependent nation within an empire.

House of Commons. In Great Britain, the lower house of Parliament; nevertheless, the house with the greater responsibility for policy development.

House of Lords. In Great Britain, the upper house of Parliament.

idealization syndrome. The tendency of young children to attribute only positive characteristics to the government and the people who run it. This syndrome often includes an intense, naive attachment to national symbols and heroes.

ideology. A system of abstract beliefs providing the basis of action for a political party, government, or mass movement.

impeachment. A bill of indictment against a high official. In the U.S. House of Representatives, a majority vote can impeach a federal official for "high crimes or misdemeanors," and can obligate the Senate to remove him from office (by a two-thirds vote) or to acquit him.

independent regulatory agency. In the U.S. government, a quasi-judicial commission or authority, such as the Federal Communications Commission, which is charged with the economic regulation of private businesses that directly affect the public welfare.

individualism. A theory, common to many industrialized Western democracies, that favors the political and economic independence of individuals and stresses individual initiative.

indoctrination. The process of formally instructing a person in an official creed or doctrine.

initiative. A petition mechanism by which voters may bypass legislators and directly place proposed laws or constitutional amendments on the ballot.

injunction. A court order enjoining an individual or group from doing something that the individual or group have not yet done.

inputs. In a political system, the demands and supports that influence the governmental process.

institutionalism. The major school of political science in the United States until World War II, focusing on formal and informal political institutions and relying on observation and description rather than on experimental research.

integration. In the black liberation movement, the traditional strategy of achieving equality through dispersing the black minority within the white community.

interest group. A group that attempts to promote the needs of its leaders and members by placing pressure on the policy-making institutions of society, but not by running candidates for public office or by regarding itself as accountable to the public at large, as does a political party.

internalized motivation. A motivation for voting that stems from a belief (learned through the family, school, or other agency of socialization) that voting is an important civic responsibility.

internal war. The large-scale, highly organized forms of violence—such as revolutions, guerrilla wars, and mutinies—which involve both the masses and the elite.

International Court of Justice (ICJ) (or World Court). The constitutional court of the U.N. and the highest tribunal of international justice, seated at the Hague. Its jurisdiction includes all disputes—which the involved states can submit to voluntarily or through prior acceptance of the court's compulsory jurisdiction—and constitutional questions on which the U.N. can request advisory opinions.

international law. A body of law—consisting of international treaties, conventions, and established customs recognized by most nations—based on voluntary compliance and reciprocal benefit, threat, coercion, or deprivation.

International Political Science Association (IPSA). An international body of scholars, established in 1948 under the auspices of UNESCO, with which the national political science associations of thirty-three nations are affiliated.

international politics. The sum total of interactions that take place between states in their pursuance of national goals, with their governments playing a direct or indirect, open or covert, pacific or bellicose role.

international relations. The competition and cooperation that take place among nations and states as they pursue their respective goals.

internment. Generally, a policy of imprisoning or detaining groups of individuals within the political system who are suspected of antisystem sentiments or behavior. An example of this is the policy of the British army in Northern Ireland in the early 1970s of arbitrarily imprisoning suspected terrorists (chiefly Catholics, not Protestants) without assessing charges, without trial, and without imposing fixed sentences. This policy alienated moderate Catholics and strengthened popular sympathy for the extremist Irish Republican Army (IRA).

Interstate Highway System. The federal superhighway system, authorized by Congress in 1944 and begun under trust-fund financing in 1956. By the time its construction is completed in the late 1970s, it will carry more than 20 percent of all highway traffic in the United States.

issue orientation. A voter's attitudes toward a particular issue, apart from his feelings about candidates or his regular party affiliation.

J-curve. The graphic representation of a sudden decline, after a prolonged period of social and economic progress, in a society's ability to fulfill the awakened aspirations of its members.

Jim Crow laws. A wide range of laws enacted chiefly during the 1890s in the U.S. South to exclude blacks from white facilities and from white society in general.

joint committee. A committee formed of members from both the U.S. House of Representatives and the Senate to study legislation currently under consideration in both houses.

judicial activist. A judge who advocates extensive use of the power of judicial review.

judicial quietist. A judge who advocates only the most cautious use of the power of judicial review.

judicial restraint. The general doctrine among jurists that is based on the presumption that acts of the legislature are constitutional and should be declared unconstitutional only under exceptional circumstances.

judicial review. The process by which courts rule on the constitutionality of governmental actions.

Kenya Asians Act. In the United Kingdom, an act of Parliament—passed under the sponsorship of the Labor party in 1968—which restricted the entry rights of Pakistanis and Indians from Kenya, despite their British passports.

Ku Klux Klan. Begun in the Reconstruction South, originally a secret fraternity of white ex-Confederates who assumed vigilante functions against the carpetbaggers and blacks who supported Reconstruction. Various branches of the Klan still exist in the United States and are not confined to the South.

laboratory research method. In political science, the testing of hypotheses through artificial, small-scale social situations in which all relevant variables are carefully controlled by the researcher.

laissez-faire ("let alone"). The doctrine of government noninterference in the economy.

Lakewood Plan. A metropolitan limited consolidation scheme under which local governments within Los Angeles County, California, buy police protection, tax and health services, and traffic control maintenance from the county government, thereby limiting the number of governmental units providing services within the metropolitan region.

Länder. Any one of the ten states into which the German Federal Republic (West Germany) is divided.

landtag. In West Germany, a state legislature.

lateral entrance. The administrative policy—designed to spark creative thinking and innovation—of bringing in knowledgeable outsiders to all levels of bureaucracy, rather than always filling vacant spots from within.

law. 1. The principles and regulations established by a government, applied to a people, and enforced by a judicial decision. 2. The basic religious or moral precepts of a people, believed to have their source in divine revelation or natural reason.

left-right continuum. The conventional scale, or spectrum, of parties and ideologies by which radicals and revolutionaries are placed on the left, moderates in the center, and conservatives and reactionaries on the right.

legal realism. The doctrine that states that judges, in the course of making decisions, inevitably make policy to a certain extent, that they should not shy away from doing so, and that the law must keep pace with the changing needs of society.

legitimacy. The ability of a governmental system to sustain the faith and trust of the people.

liberalism. Generally a trend within democratic ideology that emphasizes the importance of civil liberties and of vigorous governmental action to guarantee the economic and social welfare of the individual.

liberties. The juridicial expression of rights, as in a constitution.

limited democracy. A political system in which the rights and liberties of the citizens are limited by such special factors as a gross imbalance of strength in politics and frequent government intervention in public affairs.

lobbying. The practice of trying to influence legislators in favor of some special interest, by personal persuasion, public testimony, or the dissemination of published materials.

low-profile publicity. A type of publicity that promotes a group's objectives indirectly, by promoting certain ideas the group favors but not linking those ideas to the group's name.

McCarran Act of 1950 (Internal Security Act). An act of the U.S. Congress aimed at countering cold war subversion. It barred Communists from working for the federal government or in defense-related industries, established a Subversive Activities Control Board, and required organizations thought to be Communist influenced to register with the Attorney General. The U.S. Supreme Court has since declared most of these provisions unconstitutional.

Machiavelli, Niccolo (1469–1527). An Italian Renaissance statesman and political thinker who believed in studying men and governments as they are—not as they should be.

Madisonian democracy. The theory of government, advocated by James Madison (1751–1836) and other Founding Fathers, that emphasized the need for checks and balances, federalism, and popular suffrage as safeguards against minority or majority tyranny.

maintaining election. An election in which no issues or candidate preferences are sufficiently significant to cause a major deviation from the normal vote.

majority leader. In each house of the U.S. Congress, the leader and chief spokesman of the majority party, elected by party caucus.

manipulation. A form of power by which one or more persons trick others into doing their will.

Marbury v. Madison (1803). The first U.S. Supreme Court decision in which an act of Congress was declared to be partially unconstitutional.

mass media. Public communications channels, such as newspapers and television, which transcend the limits of person-to-person contact and are able to reach large, widely scattered audiences rapidly.

mass party. A type of party that has open membership, attempts to expand its ranks by recruiting across social-class lines, and seeks the largest membership possible.

mass transit system. Any system of public transportation designed to carry large numbers of people from point to point within a metropolitan area.

Max Weber (1864–1920). The German sociologist who made the first systematic analysis of bureaucracy and bureaucrats.

media candidate. A candidate for public office whose campaign emphasizes his personal charisma, as projected by the mass media, rather than his ideas or platform.

megalopolis. A region embracing two or more metropolitan areas that are so closely situated as to be regarded as a single urban complex, such as the continuous urban strip on the northeastern coast of the United States from Boston to Washington, D.C.

merit system. In a bureaucracy, the system of hiring and promoting staff members strictly on the basis of merit as determined by examinations or by objective assessments of on-the-job performance.

message. In a communications system, a body of information or set of demands that is expressed through symbols with the intention of affecting the thoughts or actions of a receiver, or audience.

metropolitan area. A large city and its satellite industrial cities and suburbs.

metropolitan federation. A form of urban government in which a central city and its surrounding communities work together under a regional government and in which responsibilities are divided between the regional government and the participating communities.

metropolitan government. A type of local government embracing an entire urban area, such as a central city together with its surrounding suburbs or satellite cities.

minority group. A distinct group—especially an ethnic, religious, or racial group—which is within a given nation or community and dominated by a larger group.

minority leader. In each house of the U.S. Congress, the leader and chief spokesman of the minority party, elected by party caucus.

Miranda v. Arizona (1966). A U.S. Supreme Court case which helped to establish that a criminal suspect, as soon as detained, must be informed of his rights to remain silent and to have a lawyer present during police questioning.

misdemeanor. In criminal law, a minor offense, such as public drunkenness and prostitution, normally punished by a fine.

Model Cities Program. An experimental federal program, administered by HUD, which supplements housing grants with community improvement grants.

modernizing nationalism. The dominant ideology of most underdeveloped or developing nations in Asia, Africa, or Latin America, based on a belief that the elemental needs of the nation (unity, industrialism, independence from the former colonial powers) must take primacy over the rights of the individual.

Molly Maguires. In the early 1870s, a secret organization of Irish miners in the Pennsylvania coal districts who allegedly used sabotage and terrorism in their campaign against the mine owners.

muckraking. Journalism that boldly exposes social and political abuses in order to bring about reform.

multiparty system. A political system in which popular support is divided among several parties, any one of which can only hold power by forming a coalition with one or more other parties.

multipolarity. An international system based on the dominance and rivalry of three or more giant powers.

nation (or nation-state). Any sizeable population possessing a distinct cultural identity and ruling itself within formal territorial boundaries.

nationalism. The love of one's homeland, national culture, and historical heritage, and a strong devotion to the political independence of one's nation.

national socialism or Nazism. The official ideology in Hitler's Germany, a specific brand of fascism that included a theory of Aryan racial supremacy, anti-Semitism, unquestioning trust in the leadership as the embodiment of the national will, and the demagogic use of pseudoleftist rhetoric.

natural rights. A term used to describe the belief that each individual possesses certain political and moral rights.

negotiations. The bargaining process by which bilateral and/or multilateral international decisions are made.

New Left. An amorphous radical movement in the United States that developed during the 1960s, consisting mainly of young people who rejected the style and dogmas of all political establishments and favored moral protest, small group initiatives, and "participatory democracy."

new politics, the. A grassroots electoral movement that aims at creating a new style in American politics (issues instead of personalities, amateurs instead of regulars, and moral integrity instead of the "politics of compromise") in order to make government more responsive to the needs of the youth, minority groups, and other traditionally powerless groups.

nomination. The process by which political parties and the general electorate choose whom to put on the ballot as party candidates.

nondecision. In the pluralist theory, the failure of an individual to take a position or to act on an issue because of such factors as fear, ignorance, or political opportunism.

normal vote. The percentage by which the vote would be divided if every voter voted for the party he is most sympathetic with.

normative statement. A statement—which cannot be proven true or false through empirical observation—involving a subjective assessment that something is good or bad in and of itself.

North Atlantic Treaty Organization (NATO). The major Western defense alliance, created by treaty in 1949.

objective statement. A statement—which can be proven true or false through empirical observation—describing the way things are, without the intrusion of value judgments.

off-year election. In the United States, any election held during a nonpresidential election year.

oligarchy. A system of government in which an elite group rules. Aristotle defined oligarchy as a form of government in which an elite selfishly rules in its own interest.

ombudsman. In Sweden (and, similarly, in Denmark, Norway, Finland, and New Zealand), a parliamentary commissioner who has broad powers to investigate and act on citizens' complaints of discrimination, arbitrary behavior, or negligence on the part of the government bureaucracy.

one-party system. A political system in which a single party controls every level of government and is the only party legally allowed.

opinion curve. A representation, by a curved line on a chart, of the statistical distribution of sampled opinions along a range from one extreme position to the opposite extreme.

outputs. In a political system, government allocation of values and rewards for society in response to the demands and supports of the participants in the political process.

overload. In a communications system, a condition in which the channels or receivers become saturated with messages and cannot properly transmit or evaluate them.

parliamentary democracy.   A political system in which the head of government is directly responsible to the parliamentary majority. He and his cabinet members must be members of Parliament, and if their legislative program fails to pass, they must resign, call for new elections, or both.

participant political culture.   A political culture in which ordinary citizens are actively involved in political and civic affairs.

party identification.   A sense of loyalty to a particular political party and a tendency to vote for its candidates.

passive consent.   An unquestioning acceptance or approval of the status quo expressed by failing to vote or to otherwise act against it.

people's democracy.   A term used by several Communist countries to describe their systems of government, which they regarded as democratic because of their so-called classless society.

persuasion.   A form of power by which one or more persons rationally convinces others to do their will.

picketing.   The practice of maintaining a line or procession of protestors, usually with placards, outside the establishment that is the object of the discontent in an attempt to express demands or grievances and, in the case of a strike or boycott, to discourage entry by nonstriking workers or customers.

Planning, Programming, Budget System (PPBS).   The quantitative data system—introduced by former Secretary of Defense Robert S. McNamara in the early 1960s—designed to enable executive agencies to identify and assess clearly their major goals and to relate these to budgetary needs.

plebiscite.   A direct popular vote on a constitutional amendment or on any other public issue.

Plessy v. Ferguson (1896).   A U.S. Supreme Court case that established the separate-but-equal doctrine.

plural executive.   An executive system that contains several officers elected independently of the chief executive and exercising important executive powers in their own right.

pluralism (or plural elitism).   The theory that America is ruled by a number of specialized, competing elites whose membership varies with the times and with the issues.

pluralist democracy.   A form of democracy in which the competition of interest groups creates a balance of influence preventing the dominance of any single group.

policy impact studies.   An offshoot of structural functionalism that focuses on the content of policy and its actual impact on society as a whole.

Politburo of the CPSU.   The relatively small body of the CPSU which dominates the Central Committee and the Secretariat of the Soviet Communist party, and which also has a large number of members serving on the Soviet government's Council of Ministers.

political alienation.   A state of mind in which a person feels that the social and political system in which he lives threatens him, or that it no longer protects him or fulfills his needs. This estrangement may progress through several stages from withdrawal or isolation to verbal protest to possible violent protest.

political culture.   The system of beliefs, values, and symbols that determines how a people interpret the proper role of their government.

political party. An organization formed by citizens who generally share some common values and goals, and who all share the ambition of attaining direct representation in, or control over, the policy-making institutions of government.

political socialization. The process of education and conditioning through which the individual absorbs the political culture of his society, adopts his basic political perceptions, learns his rights and duties in relation to government, and gains a picture of the structure and mechanisms of the political system.

political subculture. The culture of a specialized societal group, whose differences from the dominant political culture affect the way in which it views both particular issues and the overall role of government.

political system. A set of human interactions, within a given social environment, that serves the function of authoritative decision making for society: receiving inputs, producing outputs, and reacting to feedback.

political theory. The branch of political science concerning the definition of basic terms and concepts and examining the general nature, functions, and purposes of political processes, communities, and institutions.

political violence. Any extralegal act or threat of injury to persons, damage to property, or disruption whose purpose is to protest or influence the policies of government.

polity (constitutional democracy). In the philosophy of Aristotle, a system of government in which all citizens have a voice in selecting leaders and framing laws but are subject to the restraints of formal constitutional procedures.

poll. An effort to measure public opinion on a particular question or set of questions by obtaining a limited sample of individual opinions from which certain conclusions are drawn.

polycentrism. A condition marked by many centers of Communist ideology rather than a single one, such as Moscow.

populism. In the United States, a trend within democratic ideology that stresses the government's role as the defender of small business and the common man against large concentrations of wealth.

populist democracy. A democracy in which the common man determines policy by exerting pressure on his elected representatives.

Port of New York Authority. An independent local public authority, established as a public corporation in 1921, that controls airports, bus terminals, bridges, tunnels, piers, and other transportation facilities in the New York-New Jersey metropolitan area. Its board of directors is appointed by the governors of the two states.

positional method. According to the sociology of C. Wright Mills, the determination of an individual's elite status (i.e., his ability to exert power) by the social and professional positions he occupies.

power. The ability of a nation to influence or control the behavior of other nations by using all its tangible and intangible resources and assets.

power elite. According to C. Wright Mills, a small group of interchangeable persons said to dominate executive positions in the U.S. government, armed forces, corporations, and banks.

power struggle. Political conflict that falls between diplomacy and war and involves the exertion of such pressures as denial of recognition, trade embargoes, arms races, wars by proxy, and espionage and subversion. Such struggles may go on for decades—as has the cold war between the United States and the Soviet Union—changing in intensity but not in intent.

presidential system. A political system in which the head of government is elected by the people, rather than by the legislature, and serves for a fixed term.

president's rule. In India, the direct rule of a member state by the national government during a formally declared emergency in which the constitution is suspended.

pressure system. In a modern society, the network of organized special-interest groups that devote their time, effort, and resources to influencing government policy.

primary election. The mechanism of nominating party candidates by the direct vote of registered party members (closed primary) or of unrestricted registered voters (open primary).

primary group. Any small group (such as a family, office clique, or teenage gang) in which personal ties are of fundamental importance.

program. A specific measure aimed at influencing the direction of government activity and public life.

propaganda. The subjective manipulation of information in order to support particular concepts.

proportional representation. A multimeter electoral system in which each party wins legislative seats in proportion to its total popular vote.

protest. The expression of dissatisfaction with policies or conditions through dramatic public demonstration rather than through such institutionalized channels as lobbying and electioneering.

proxy representation. A legislative practice based on the belief that the lawmaker should only represent the immediate wishes of his own constituency and should reflect no free will of his own.

public interest. The hypothetical interests of society as a whole, as distinct from the interests of any single pressure group or individual.

public opinion. The sum total of the many and ever-shifting attitudes that people hold regarding issues, personalities, and events of the day.

public policy. Any authoritative action of government.

quantitative data system. A sophisticated system of quantitative measurement and empirical analysis, used in determining the objectives, costs, and benefits of a government program.

quota method. A method of sampling by which the interviewer chooses among respondents to maintain representative ratios of income, age, sex, religion, and party preference.

quota system. A method of ensuring fair treatment or representation whereby minorities are guaranteed a certain fixed, or minimum, number of jobs, delegates, and similar considerations.

Radical Right. The extremist wing of American conservatism that believes the United States to be in mortal danger from a domestic and foreign Communist conspiracy, often advocating authoritarian rule and moral and religious traditionalism as means of defense. This movement includes such groups as the John Birch Society, the Christian Anti-Communist Crusade, and the Minutemen.

random sample. A sample whose representativeness is assumed by choosing the individual respondents at random from a list that includes every individual in the population being studied.

rank disequilibrium. The social condition in which a segment or class of the population is privileged in one respect but oppressed in another, such as the middle-class blacks in the United States, whose income and education entitle them to "topdog" status but who remain racial and political "underdogs."

realigning election. An election in which large numbers of voters permanently change their allegiance from one party to another.

receiver. The audience that a particular message is directed to.

recognition. In international relations, the formal act by which a nation acknowledges as its sovereign equal a new state or new political regime.

referendum. A direct popular vote on a proposal placed on the ballot by a legislature or by a constitutional convention.

Regulators, the. In prerevolutionary North Carolina, backwoods farmers who banded together in vigilante groups against the colonial tax collectors and judges to prevent foreclosure of mortgages. This group assumed de facto control of several counties until its defeat by the colonial militia in 1771.

relative deprivation. According to the frustration-aggression theory of Ted Robert Gurr, the discrepancy between what individuals think they should have and what their environment can actually provide them with.

repatriation. In the United Kingdom, a policy, proposed by John Enoch Powell and others, of forcing nonwhite immigrants to return to their countries of origin.

representation. A relationship between legislators and the public whereby the former are regarded as acting in the name of or with the mandate of the latter, especially as a result of elections.

representative democracy. A political system that allows all voters to participate indirectly in the decision-making process through their elected representatives.

representative sample. A sample selected in such a manner as to represent proportionally all population characteristics likely to influence public opinion.

reputational method. According to Floyd Hunter, the determination of an individual's elite status by the public's opinion of his status.

residency laws. In the United States, legal restrictions on voting rights, which prevent a citizen from voting in his state of residence unless he has lived in that state for a certain period of time and has registered well before election day.

revenue sharing. A proposed federal aid policy whereby some national revenues are directly distributed to local communities on the basis of population and need.

reverse discrimination. A policy whereby a minority group is temporarily granted special privileges in order to help it overcome generations of discrimination and to gain equality with the majority population, especially in terms of socioeconomic status.

riffraff theory. The theory, largely discredited by social scientists, that riots and terrorism are chiefly the work of the uneducated, unemployed, and emotionally unstable, who are said to have no respect for social values and to be extremely susceptible to mob hysteria.

sample. A part of a given population whose opinions are studied to gain information about the whole.

scatter-site housing. Small-scale housing projects built for low-income families at scattered locations in middle-class suburban areas.

science. 1. The accumulated body of objectively verifiable knowledge concerning man, nature, and society. 2. The sequence of interrelated thoughts and actions by which such knowledge is gained.

scientific method. A three-step method involving the identification of a problem, the formulation of a hypothesis, and the systematic observation of events (usually in a controlled experiment) to confirm or disprove the hypothesis.

scientific polling. A technique of polling, developed in the United States in the 1930s, based on the use of representative samples.

secession. The formal act by which a state or local government withdraws from a larger political community (especially from a federation).

Secretariat of the CPSU. The administrative body of the Soviet Communist party.

sedition. Any criticism of the government or of government officials intended to produce discontent or rebellion among the populace.

Sedition Act of 1798. An act of the U.S. Congress aimed at suppressing the activities of the Jacobins (American defenders of the French Revolution) during an undeclared naval war between the United States and France.

Sedition Act of 1918. An amendment to the Espionage Act of 1917, aimed at suppressing the activities of socialists and pacifists opposed to American involvement in World War I.

seditions conspiracy. The small-scale but highly organized violence of such uprisings as a coup d'état, barracks revolt, and palace revolutions, usually involving a few members of the elite.

selective attention. The tendency of a receiver to be distracted from a message by other matters, or to take in only the part of a message he is interested in.

selective perception. In communications theory, the tendency of a receiver to take in only the parts of a message that fit his preconceived ideas or prejudices.

self-determination. The freedom of a people to decide for themselves how they will be governed and by whom.

self-fulfilling prophecy. In the social sciences, a prediction that influences human behavior in such a way as to help bring about the very event predicted.

seniority system. The practice, in the U.S. Congress, of awarding committee assignments and chairmanships on the basis of a legislator's length of service.

separate-but-equal doctrine. An interpretation of the Fourteenth Amendment's equal-protection clause, which holds that races can be segregated by state law in such places as restaurants and schools, as long as the facilities for each race are equal.

separation of powers. The division of a single government into three distinct branches—executive, legislative, and judicial—with each branch possessing sufficient authority to partially check the authority of the others.

separatism. In the black liberation movement, a nationalist strategy that urges a separate Afro-American state, either somewhere within the continental United States or in Africa.

Serrano v. Priest (1971). A California State Supreme Court case in which the judges ruled that the prevailing method of financing public education in California discriminated against low-income communities.

single elitism. The theory that America is ruled by a single, relatively closed upper-class elite, which responds to public pressure only when its position is threatened.

Smith Act of 1940. An act of Congress that made it a crime to advocate the violent overthrow of the U.S. government, to distribute literature urging such an overthrow, or to knowingly join any organization or group that advocated such an overthrow.

socialism. An economic system in which the government, rather than private individuals, owns and operates the major means of production and distribution of goods and services.

socialization. The process of education and conditioning through which the individual learns the behavioral norms of his society.

sovereign equality. The doctrine that each nation-state has the right to sovereignty (i.e., the right to recognize its own will as the highest authority for its actions) and should recognize that right in its neighbors.

sovereignty. The doctrine, fundamental to statehood, by which a nation recognizes no authority higher than its own.

soviet. In the Soviet Union, the basic legislative unit that controls each unit of government at the local level and whose members are elected by the people.

Speaker of the House. In the United States, the presiding officer of the House of Representatives.

special committee. A temporary committee created to deal with a specific issue. *standing committee.* A permanent legislative committee.

stare decisis ("let the decision stand"). Legal precedent, or the precedent of decisions by previous judges.

statutory law. The body of laws established by legislative acts, or statutes.

straw poll. A poll conducted without strict regard for the representativeness of the sample, as in the questioning of passers-by on a streets or the mailing of questionnaires to magazine subscribers.

strike. A cessation of work by employees, whose aim is to cut-off the profits of their employer in order to force him to concede to such demands as higher wages and improved working conditions.

structural functionalism. An outgrowth of behaviorism that borrows concepts from biology to facilitate the study of the interdependency of parts in a political system and to draw distinctions between political systems in various stages of development.

subsystem autonomy. The freedom of private and semi-private institutions, such as churches, unions, and colleges, to run their own internal affairs without governmental interference.

suburb. 1. A residential area contiguous to a city. 2. Any part of a metropolitan area outside of the central city.

supports. In a political system, the people's passive recognition of the legitimacy of their government and their active participation in its processes.

Survey Research Center (SRC). The major center in the United States for voting-behavior analysis, located at the University of Michigan.

symbolic elections. Elections that exert little influence on the political decision-making process but enhance social stability by making the public believe it is participating.

system. A collection of individual parts that work together toward a common end.

systemic frustration. According to the frustration-aggression theory of Ivo and Rosalind Feierabend, the frustration experienced collectively by many individuals or groups within a given society as a result of high want formation and low want satisfaction.

"televisation." The process by which television has become the dominant mass medium in the United States and Western Europe, remolding the forms of democratic political life.

territorial (communal) riot. In the United States, a type of riot that was common in northern cities during the period between the two world wars, in which a direct confrontation took place between groups of whites and blacks over some contested neighborhood. Usually the fighting occurred on the fringes of the black neighborhood, with whites as the invaders.

ticket splitting. The practice of dividing one's vote between candidates of more than one party.

tight bipolarity. In international politics, the tendency of the world's middle-level powers to cling dependently to one of the giant powers.

totalitarianism. A political system in which a highly ideological party holds exclusive political, economic, military, and judicial power, which is used in an attempt to control all aspects of human life in the society.

Trenton v. New Jersey (1923). A U.S. Supreme Court case which established that cities, as "legal creatures" of the state, do not have an inherent right to self-government beyond the legislative control of their state governments.

two-party system. A political system in which two major parties vie for power, while other parties have only minor political strength.

unicameralism. The vesting of all legislative responsibilities in a single house.

Union of Central African States. A loose federation formed in 1968 by Chad, the Central African Republic, and the Congo-Brazzaville to provide a united market and production area.

union shop (or closed shop). A business establishment in which the employees are required to belong to the union.

unitary state. A system of government in which the central government constitutionally possesses total political authority and can override the decisions of the local governments.

United Nations (UN). The major global international organization today, established in 1945, whose 133 member nations have headquarters in New York City and whose goals are international peace and cooperation.

U.S. Circuit Court of Appeals. In the U.S. federal court system, any one of eleven circuit courts that have appellate jurisdiction over the varying number of federal district courts within their respective circuits.

U.S. Supreme Court. The highest court in the U.S. federal court system, consisting of nine justices, which is empowered to hear appeals from all lower federal courts and all state supreme courts, if a substantial federal question is involved. In almost all instances, the U.S. Supreme Court decides which cases it will hear.

Universal Declaration of Human Rights. A document, adopted by the United Nations General Assembly in 1948, that symbolically affirms the basic moral, political, juridicial, and socioeconomic rights of all peoples.

Urban Mass Transportation Act of 1964. A federal act that provides funds for studying urban transportation, trying new solutions, and encouraging private investment in transportation technology. It has led to the establishment of "demonstration projects" in five U.S. cities.

urban renewal. In an inner city, the planned, governmental-sponsored demolition of slums, abandoned factories and warehouses, and other deteriorated areas, with the aim of building new housing or new business or civic districts.

values. The costs and services regulated by government, including tangibles (money, taxes, property) and abstract, or symbolic, goods (ideals, ethical standards, freedom).

vote power. The strength of a voting bloc as measured by its size, rate of turnout on election day, and loyalty to a given party.

voting bloc. Any group of people with similar political interests who are likely to vote in the same way.

Voting Rights Act of 1965. An act of the U.S. Congress primarily intended to guarantee the voting rights of Southern blacks. It empowers the Justice Department to suspend literacy qualifications in counties with less than 50 percent voter registration and to send in federal registrars when discrimination is suspected. It also makes the prevention of qualified persons from voting a federal crime.

want formation. The level of goods and services that individuals within a given society believe is due them.

want satisfaction. The degree to which individuals within a given society perceive that their wants have been satisfied.

war. The form of political conflict by which a nation or civil faction uses organized military force in a series of violent encounters to compel an adversary nation or faction to do its will.

Warren Court (1953–1969). A term used to describe the U.S. Supreme Court under Chief Justice Earl Warren, which dealt with many important issues concerning civil and criminal rights and legislative reapportionment.

Warsaw Treaty Organization (Warsaw Pact). A twenty-year mutual defense alliance, created by treaty in 1955, between the USSR and the Eastern European states, excluding Yugoslavia.

watchdog. A lobbyist whose special task is to keep his group informed about the latest legislative developments.

welfare state. A system in which the government regulates some aspects of the economic and social orders but leaves the ownership of most means of production and distribution of goods and services in private hands.

whip. In each house of the U.S. Congress, the second most important leader in the majority and minority parties, who serves as the liaison between the party leadership and the ranks, informs the members of how the leaders would like them to vote, and assesses projected vote totals.

Whitaker and Baxter. A California advertising firm that pioneered in political public relations, especially in the "packaging" of candidates.

workfare. A welfare reform scheme, based on the idea of a guaranteed annual income, drafted by the first Nixon Administration in 1971 but never enacted into law by Congress.

yellow press. The mass circulation of daily newspapers that arose in the United States in the mid-1890s, emphasizing sensationalism and human interest and reaching a vastly wider market than the elite-oriented newspapers of previous generations.

youth vote. In Britain and the United States, the voting bloc of recently enfranchised eighteen- to twenty-year-old citizens.

(Acknowledgments continued from page iv)

Part Four, pp. 382–83 Preparation of Federal Income Tax Forms, Andover, Mass. (United Press International Photo); Ivory Coast, Judge at Abidjan Courthouse (Photographed by Marc and Evelyn Bernheim, Rapho Guillumette Pictures); Kosygin Speaking to Session (Tass from Sovfoto); Off-Track Betting Office (Photographed by Joel Gordon).

Part Five, pp. 508–9 Black Militants, Close-Up (Courtesy Pierre Orin); Turkey, Past and Present (Photographed by H. Cartier-Bresson, Magnum Photos, Inc.); Police Barrier and Demonstrators (Courtesy Pierre Orin); Park and Steelworks in Dortmund, West Germany (Photographed by L. Freed, Magnum Photos, Inc.); Ivory Coast Car Assembly (Photographed by Marc and Evelyn Bernheim, Rapho Guillumette Pictures).

Cover Courtesy of Magnum Photos, Inc., and Tass from Sovfoto.

Tables, Figures, and Text Excerpts

Table 3–1 From *Comparative Politics: A Developmental Approach*, Gabriel A. Almond and G. Bingham Powell, p. 217. Copyright © 1966 by Little, Brown and Company (Inc.). Reprinted by permission.

Table 5–2 Printed from "Some Conditions of Democracy" by Deane E. Neubauer. Printed in *American Political Science Review*, 61. (December 1967), p. 1005.

Table 6–1 Source: Metropolitan Applied Research Center, Inc., and Joint Center for Political Studies; printed in Congressional Quarterly Weekly Report (1971), p. 27.

Table 8–1 *The Civic Culture: Political Attitudes and Democracy in Five Nations*, by Gabriel A. Almond and Sidney Verba (copyright © 1963 by Princeton University Press): Table, "Per Cent Who Say The Ordinary Man Should Be Active In His Local Community," p. 176. Reprinted by permission of Princeton University Press.

Figure 8–1 From Edward S. Greenberg, *Black Children and the Political System*, Public Opinion Quarterly, 34, Fall 1970, p. 339.

Table 8–2, poll From Hazel Erskine, "The Polls: Freedom of Speech," in *Public Opinion Quarterly*, Volume 34 (Fall 1970), pp. 495–96. Poll taken in May of 1969 by American Institute of Public Opinion (Gallup Poll).

Table 8–3, poll Harris Survey. © Washington Post Co., June 10, 1967.

Table 9–2 and Table 9–3 The Roper Organization, Inc., "An Extended View of Public Attitudes Toward Television and Other Mass Media, 1959–1971" (New York: Television Information Office, June, 1971) pp. 3, 2.

Table 10–2 From *Congressional Quarterly Weekly*, Vol. 29, 32, August 6, 1971, p. 2.

Table 10–3 Lester W. Milbrath, *The Washington Lobbyists*, © 1963 by Rand McNally and Company, Chicago, pp. 213, 240, 257. Reprinted by permission of Rand McNally College Publishing Company.

Figure 11–1 From *Major Foreign Powers*, 6th Edition, by Gwendolen M. Carter and John H. Herz, copyright © 1972 by Harcourt Brace Jovanovich, Inc. and reproduced with their permission.

Table 11–1 From "A Note on the Fractionalization of Some European Party Systems," by Douglas Rae is reprinted from *Comparative Political Studies*, Vol. 1, No. 3 (Oct. 1968) p. 417 by permission of the Publisher, Sage Publications, Inc.

Table 11–2 From Herbert McClosky, Paul J. Hoffman, and Rosemary O'Hara, "Issue Conflict and Consensus," *American Political Science Review*, 54 (June, 1960) p. 411.

Table 11–3 From *Communist Party Membership in the U.S.S.R.*, 1917–1967, by T. H. Rigby (copyright © 1968 by Princeton University Press). Reprinted by permission of Princeton University Press.

Table 11–4 Reprinted by permission of the publisher, from *Financing the 1968 Election* by Herbert E. Alexander (Lexington, Mass.: Lexington Books, D.C. Heath and Company, 1971), p. 82.

Figure 12–1 Reprinted with permission of Macmillan Publishing Co., Inc. from *Political Life* by Robert Lane. © The Free Press of Glencoe, a Division of Macmillan Publishing Co., Inc. 1962.

Table 12–1 and Table 12–2 Tables reprinted from *Critical Elections and the Mainsprings of American Politics*, by Walter Dean Burnham, 1970, with the permission of the publisher, W. W. Norton and Company, Inc.

Table 13–1 From *Congressional Quarterly Weekly Report*, 30, no. 28, (July 8, 1972), p. 3.

Table 13–2 Reprinted by permission from Austin Ranney, "Candidate Selection and Party Cohesion in Britain and the United States," in William J. Crotty, ed., *Approaches to the Study of Party Organization* (Boston: Allyn and Bacon, 1968), p. 144.

Figure 14–1 Reprinted from "The Growth of the Seniority System in the U.S. House of Representatives" by Nelson W. Polsby, Miriam Gallaher and Berry Spencer Rindquist. Printed in *American Political Science Review*, LXII, No. 3 (September 1969), p. 793.

Table 14–1 Compiled from data in Gerhard Loewenberg, *The Remaking of the German Party System*, Polity, II (1968), p. 513.

Excerpt, pp. 426–27 From Chapter 5, "The Study of Formal Organization," by Peter M. Blau, in *American Sociology: Perspectives, Problems, Methods*, edited by Talcott Parsons, © 1968 by Basic Books, Inc., Publishers, New York.

Figure 17–1 From *Comparative Federalism: The Territorial Dimension of Politics* by Ivo D. Duchacek. Copyright © 1970 by Holt, Rinehart & Winston, Inc. Reprinted by permission of Holt, Rinehart & Winston, Inc.

Figure 17–2 and Figure 17–3 From *Revenue-Sharing: Crutch or Catalyst for State and Local Governments?* by Henry S. Reuss. © 1970 Praeger Publishers, Inc., New York. Excerpted and reprinted by permission.

Figure 17–4 From *Reshaping Government in Metropolitan Areas* (New York: Committee for Economic Development, 1970), p. 83.

Table 18–1 From William Buchanan and Hadley Cantril, *How Nations See Each Other*, (Urbana: University of Illinois Press, 1953) pp. 46–47.

Excerpt, pp. 548–49 Excerpted from *The Autobiography of Malcolm X*, by Malcolm X with the assistance of Alex Haley. Reprinted by permission of Grove Press, Inc., copyright © 1964 by Alex Haley and Malcolm X, © 1965 by Alex Haley and Betty Shabazz.

Table 19–1 From "The Rulers and Rules" by Yaroslav Bilinsky, *Problems of Communism*, Sept.–Oct. 1967, pp. 23–25. Published by United States Information Agency.

Table 20–1 From Hugh Davis Graham and Ted Robert Gurr, "A Comparative Study of Civil Strife," *Violence in America: Historical and Comparative Perspectives*, A Report to the National Commission on the Causes and Prevention of Violence, June 1969 (New York: New American Library, 1969).

Table 21–1 and Table 21–2 U.S. Department of Housing and Urban Development, "The Problems Associated with Rapid Urban Growth," in *HUD International Series*, Supplement 5 (Jan. 20, 1972), pp. 4, 3.

Figure 21–1 Reprinted with permission of Macmillan Publishing Co., from *Sick Cities* by Mitchell Gordon © Mitchell Gordon 1963.

Table 21–3 From Harold Wolman, unpublished background paper for *Counterbudget* (New York: Praeger 1971), in Fred R. Harris and John V. Lindsay, *The State of Cities: Report of the Commission on Cities in the 70's* (New York: Praeger, 1972) p. 40 © 1972 by the National Urban Coalition. Reprinted by permisson of Praeger Publishers, Inc., New York.

Table 21–4 From "Moving Toward Realistic Housing Goals" by Anthony Downs, in *Agenda for the Nation*, ed. by Kermit Gordon (© 1968 by the Brookings Institution, Washington, D.C.). Source of table: "Urban Needs and Economic Factors in Housing Policy" by Frank S. Kristof, prepared for the National Commission on Urban Problems.

Index